FROM A YANKEE TO A REBEL DIARY:
THE COLLECTIVE CIVIL WAR DIARIES OF PRIVATE GEORGE WASHINGTON HALL, 14TH GEORGIA INFANTRY, AND PRIVATE JACOB L. ELSESSER, 9TH PENNSYLVANIA RESERVES

Mary T. Hall

Lot's Wife Publishing
Staunton, VA

2025

Copyright 2025 © Mary T. Hall. All rights reserved. No part of this book may be reproduced in any form or by any electronic or mechanical means, or the facilitation thereof, including information storage and retrieval systems, without permission and writing from the author, except by a reviewer, who may quote brief passages in a review. Any members of educational institutions wishing to photocopy part or all of the work for classroom use, or publishers who would like to obtain permission to include the work in an anthology, should send their inquiries to the author.

Cover design and interior layout by Jennifer Wood Lee.

Cover photos: George Washington Hall (L), Leta McGregor Thayer (C), Jacob L. Elsesser (R)

Library of Congress Control Number: 2025920753
ISBN: 978-1-934368-81-7

Published by
Lot's Wife Publishing
P.O. Box 1844
Staunton, VA 24402

For Leta and my parents,
Colonel Robert E. and Maude (Theresa) Warden Hall.

Mission accomplished.

TABLE OF CONTENTS

Foreword vii

Preface xi

1. "I left my home and my Dear Mother"
   Georgia: 1861 1

2. "I came as near dying as any body ever did to live"
   Western Virginia: 1861 9

3. "My feet was so sore that I could scarcely put them to the ground"
   Northern Virginia to the Peninsula: January – late May 1862 29

4. "It seemed like ten thousand bullets passed over our heads"
   Seven Pines /Fair Oaks: May 31 – June 26, 1862 50

5. "I will turn it from a Yankee to a Rebel diary"
   Seven Days: June – July 1862 69

6. "I taken the small pox"
   Central Virginia and the Shenandoah Valley:
   August 1862 – March 1863 103

7. "For all who knew him esteemed and respected him highly"
   Virginia and Maryland: March – June 1863 151

8. "It seemed that it was impossible for a living creature to have escaped"
   Gettysburg: June 5 – July 24, 1863 188

9. "It was the most solumn scene I ever saw"
   Virginia: July 25 – December 31, 1863 223

10. "Today I draw my furlough"
    Virginia and Florida: January 1 – April 1864 255

11. "So ends the most eventful day of my life"
    Virginia: May 1 – May 12, 1864 281

12. "I sigh and pray for Dixie"
    Fort Delaware: May 13, 1864 – December 1864 304

13. "It was a joyful time for us to be set at Liberty once more & breath[e] the air of freedom"
    Fort Delaware and Home: January 1 – March 28, 1865 351

14. The diaries of Private Jacob L. Elsesser 360

15. After the War: Two Men Serving the Better Good 414

Appendix A. "It seemed one way I could contribute something to the history of our country" – the story behind the Thayer Manuscript 424

Appendix B. Poems and Songs 432

Appendix C. Hall's Daily Log: April 1862 – May 1863 450

Appendix D. Hall's Weather Log: April 1862 – May 1863 454

Appendix E. Elsesser's Diary of Co. B 9th Regt. P.R.C. 460

Bibliography 480

Acknowledgments 494

Author's Biography 498

Index 500

FOREWORD

Rarely does a diary convey more than one voice and one world view. Diaries tend to be a dialogue between the diarist and themselves. They are not intended to be shared with others. They are sometimes only brief notations, terse reminders to the writer in their own brand of shorthand. Generally, diaries are not a full story, but glimpses to jog memories—from the mundane to the terrifying. They are the seeds of thought to provoke a more fulsome conversation sometime in the future. It is truly unique when a diary boasts two voices—the thoughts and impressions of two individuals in a shared space, perhaps even a shared experience. Often in war, that usually involves the demise of one and the practical adaption of the other. A Virginia soldier once wrote that his tentmate was killed in battle and that night he wore the dead man's clothes. It would stand to reason that men with a manic penchant for pen and paper to chronicle their actions would readily coopt a partially filled journal to jot their own impressions where another person's chapter had clearly ended. In most instances, the second diarist was in the same unit or someone on the same side to avail themselves of the empty pages.

It is even more improbable when two voices come together from opposite sides. In the white-heat chaos of combat, soldiers rarely stop to go through the private possessions of their enemies. Soldiers often destroyed their own personal correspondence before going into battle, afraid their letters would fall into coarse and unsympathetic hands. A journal in many ways was a key—a Rosetta Stone—to unlocking the writer's deeper thoughts and impressions of great events. They were kept close and guarded. Some soldiers had no compunction about rooting through the clothes and effects of the dead, but most shied away from such acts unless driven by necessity. In cases of want, diaries were rarely heeded. Those that were often drew wry comments around the campfire. Only a very select few diaries became the prized possessions of the gatherers. One can only imagine the thoughts of the reader who inherited the legacy of the previous owner's observations and dreams.

I have only seen two such diaries shared between enemies—the one George Washington Hall found lost or discarded by Jacob L. Elsesser; the other one was taken by a Federal soldier, Joseph Myers, from a dead Confederate, Corporal Thomas J. Lutman, during the Chancellorsville Campaign of 1863. In the case of Hall, the writer merely continued on with his own narrative. With Joseph Myers, he only added one piece to the diary to chronicle the circumstances surrounding the death of the original diarist. Myers, a member of the 23rd Pennsylvania in the Federal Sixth Corps, helped overrun Marye's Heights in the Second Battle of Fredericksburg on May 3, 1863. The Union attackers captured several cannon from the highly vaunted Washington Artillery of New Orleans. The Federal took Lutman's diary and added a lengthy postscript, observing, "The owner of this Diary, T. J. Lutman, a corporal was in the act of firing his gun when he was ordered to desist—the stars and stripes having already been planted on the work by a member of the Maine 6th, but persisting he fired the gun and had his brains blown out as a consequence of his willfulness." Myers essentially saved Lutman's diary as a eulogistic relic of the battlefield.

In the case of George Washington Hall, of the 14th Georgia Infantry, he never met his adversary or knew his story. He found Jacob L. Elsesser's diary left near the battlefield of Mechanicsville, or Beaver Dam Creek. Elsesser's unit, the 9th Pennsylvania Reserves, defended the position in the opening battle of Robert E. Lee's offensive that came to be known as the Seven Days' Battles around Richmond. Hall pursued the Federals for a week of endless fighting and marching. Union Major General (Maj. Gen.) George B. McClellan burned and abandoned tons of supplies in his haste to shift his army to a secure base at Harrison's Landing on the James River. Confederates profited from the largesse of good things McClellan's army abandoned. Lee's soldiers enjoyed everything from exotic canned delicacies to new underwear—and most coveted of all: writing paper. Soldiers snatched up unused stationery and delighted in corresponding with family and friends on captured Union letterheads. George W. Hall likely had ample opportunity to find a new uncracked diary—but he carried Jacob Elsesser's book. It was a souvenir of his regiment's first major battle under Robert E. Lee—and Hall's first taste of battlefield victory. In some way, Elsesser's diary became the fruit of that victory in a very real and personal sense for George Hall. Hall not only preserved the diary, he preserved Jacob Elsesser's words and thoughts. He became the keeper of his adversary's ideas, dreams, and memory. On top of that, Hall added his own thoughts, hopes, fears, and aspirations—adding to the narrative and ultimately, blending their story.

It is truly exceptional under just about any circumstance for two enemies to share a diary, but to have two soldiers from marquee units is something uniquely special. Jacob Elsesser served in the 9th Pennsylvania Reserves, a high caliber regiment that saw an incredible amount of action during the Civil War. Their colonel was the controversial Conrad Feger Jackson, the son of a military-minded father and a member of the Society of Friends, who banished ("shunned") him from their sect. The 9th Reserves fought on the Peninsula, Second Manassas, Antietam, and Fredericksburg (where C. Feger Jackson was killed)—often being among the first troops thrust into battle. By the end of 1862, the unit's historian admitted their ranks were "shattered." They were relegated to the Washington defenses only to be returned to the Army of the Potomac for the Battle of Gettysburg. They remained with the army until they were relieved and sent home the day before the bloody Overland Campaign of 1864 commenced. Their term of enlistment expired and they were the first of the Pennsylvania Reserve units to be sent home, Jacob Elsesser with them.

George Washington Hall served with the 14th Georgia. This regiment joined one of the best-known divisions in Robert E. Lee's Army of Northern Virginia. They served in Maj. Gen. Ambrose Powell Hill's "Light Division," and saw heavy action on many of the same battlefields as the Pennsylvania Reserves. A. P. Hill's Confederates became the offensive sledgehammer for assaults at Mechanicsville (Beaver Dam Creek), Gaines's Mill, and Glendale. They turned retreat into victory at Cedar Mountain. They secured the surrender of the Federal garrison at Harpers Ferry and saved the day for Lee's army at Antietam. They bore the brunt of the Federal breakthrough at Fredericksburg—a breakthrough spearheaded by the Pennsylvania Reserves. The 14th Georgia fought in "Stonewall" Jackson's flank attack at Chancellorsville and battled through Gettysburg and the maw of the Overland Campaign of 1864, where many including Hall were lost to the regiment. The shadow of the 14th Georgia continued to battle through the siege of Petersburg and surrendered at Appomattox Court House in April 1865.

Mary T. Hall is ideally suited to edit the shared diary of George Washington Hall and Jacob L. Elsesser. Mary Hall is an academic professor with a professional approach to contextualizing the individuals and their actions through the Civil War and beyond. Mary is also a direct descendant of George Washington Hall and is able to take calculating words, facts, and figures, and return them to the realm of flesh-and-blood humanity. Mary Hall pursued sources and leads relentlessly and it was my great privilege and pleasure to share and learn with her about two men who never knew each other but shared a common bond of the written word. This book, *From a Yankee to a Rebel Diary*, will be a valuable addition to anyone's library.

Francis Augustín O'Reilly
Author of *The Fredericksburg Campaign: Winter War on the Rappahannock*
(Baton Rouge: Louisiana State University Press, 2002).

PREFACE

On the morning of June 27, 1862, a young private in the 14th Georgia Infantry Regiment marched with his regiment through a smoke-filled campsite freshly abandoned by Union troops after the battle at Beaver Dam Creek near Mechanicsville, Virginia. Those Union troops, members of Major General (Maj. Gen.) Fitz John Porter's V Corps in Maj. Gen. George B. McClellan's Army of the Potomac, had withstood Maj. Gen. A. P. Hill's bloody frontal assault across Beaver Dam Creek the previous afternoon, aided in no small part by their well-fortified position on high ground behind the creek. Before dawn on June 27, the Union troops, with the 9th Pennsylvania Reserve Regiment serving as the rear guard, raced a few miles southeast to assume another strongly-fortified position, also on a ridge behind a creek, for a battle on an even grander scale, at Gaines's Mill. In their haste, the Union soldiers abandoned or tried to burn weapons, food, haversacks, shoes, clothing, and other stores, much of which the Confederate troops were able to salvage as they marched through the Federal camp.

Many of the young private's comrades availed themselves of highly practical items such as food, shoes, and blankets. But the only item we know with certainty that the young private from the 14th Georgia picked up was a small, commercially-published diary titled *Daily Pocket Remembrancer for 1862*. Inscribed on the flyleaf was the name "J. L. Elsesser" and "Co. B 9th Regt. PR.C."[1] The diary contained handwritten entries from January 1 through June 26, 1862. The Confederate private wrote in the space

---

1. This was Private Jacob L. Elsesser's abbreviation for his unit, Company B, 9th Regiment of Pennsylvania Reserves Corps, more commonly known as the 9th Pennsylvania Reserves.

allotted for June 27, 1862, that he was turning the small book from a "Yankee" to a "Rebel" diary. Thus did the "blue" diary of a Union private, with almost six full months of entries from 1862, become the "grey" diary of a Confederate private.

The Confederate private, George Washington Hall, was my great-grandfather, born on August 25, 1841, in Talladega County, Alabama. Nothing is known of his biological father, other than that he was likely born in Georgia. His mother, Rachel Holly, born in South Carolina in 1821, was described as a pious woman. Hall spent part of his childhood in Sumter County, Georgia, living with or near an uncle, John E. Hall, a prominent Americus, Georgia, druggist.[2]

Hall moved to nearby Worth County, Georgia, as a teenager in 1857.[3] The 1860 federal census for Worth County shows that George, then a 19-year-old farmer, resided with his mother Rachel; her then-husband Edwin N. Holly, a blacksmith; and five half-siblings.[4] The census also notes that Hall had attended school within the year. If war had not erupted, George Washington Hall would have likely quietly moved through life as a farmer in the rural southwest Georgia countryside. But just seven weeks after the attack on Fort Sumter, Hall joined the Yancey Independents, a company of Worth County volunteers that would later become Company G of the 14th Georgia Infantry Regiment.

Except for absences due to hospitalization and a month-long furlough, Hall served continuously with Company G until his capture at the Battle of Spotsylvania in May 1864. The 14th Georgia spent the bulk of the war in Virginia, commencing with a brutal fifteen weeks in western Virginia in the fall of 1861. After spending the winter near Manassas, the regiment moved in the spring of 1862 to southeast Virginia for the Peninsula Campaign, where it fought in the battles at Seven Pines/Fair Oaks,

---

2. John E. Hall served as a district delegate to the 1867-1868 Georgia constitutional convention. His son, Lyman Hall, an 1881 graduate of the U.S. Military Academy, served as second president of Georgia Tech University in Atlanta.
3. [Samuel Boykin], *History of the Baptist Denomination in Georgia with Biographical Compendium and Portrait Gallery* (Atlanta, GA: Jas. P. Harrison, 1881), 241. The biographical compendium contains Hall's biography. All page references herein are to this biographical section.
4. U.S. Census Bureau, 1860 Federal Census for Worth County, Georgia, accessed April 4, 2020, http://genealogytrails.com/geo/worth/records/1860worth.html.

Mechanicsville/Beaver Dam Creek; Gaines's Mill, and Frayser's Farm/Glendale.[5] Due to illness and hospitalization during the latter part of 1862 and early 1863, Hall missed the regiment's battles at Cedar Mountain, Second Manassas, Harper's Ferry, and Fredericksburg. He returned to his regiment shortly before its most significant battles in 1863, those at Chancellorsville and Gettysburg.

Hall spent most of the winter of 1863–1864 with the regiment in the Shenandoah Valley area of Virginia. During a 30-day furlough beginning in February 1864, he traveled to visit his family, who had moved to Liberty County, Florida, after his enlistment. While on furlough, Hall met Amanda M. E. Mobley, whom he would marry shortly after the end of the war. Returning to his regiment in Virginia in time for the beginning of Lieutenant General Ulysses S. Grant's Overland Campaign, Hall fought at both the Wilderness and at Spotsylvania Court House in May 1864. After being captured in battle at Spotsylvania on May 12, 1864, he spent nine months as a prisoner of war at the Union prison camp at Fort Delaware, Delaware. Hall was paroled for exchange in March 1865, after which point he commenced a post-release furlough. After a sixteen-day journey from Virginia, mostly by rail and on foot, he arrived home in Liberty County, Florida, on March 28, 1865. As one of his granddaughters later wrote, Hall "went in a foot-soldier and came out one, bare-footed."[6] He was still on furlough when his regiment surrendered at Appomattox on April 9, 1865.[7]

Jacob L. Elsesser, the Union private who first owned the *Daily Pocket Remembrancer*, was born in France in 1828 but immigrated to Philadelphia, Pennsylvania, with his parents when he was only a few months old. After his father died, young Jacob and his mother moved to Pittsburgh and, later, to nearby Etna, Pennsylvania. Elsesser was elected

---

5. Several major battles of the Civil War, such as several of those shown here, are referred to by dual names. Union forces usually named battles after nearby landmarks such as rivers, streams, or creeks, while Confederates generally named battles after nearby towns where they had bases. As historian James McPherson notes in his seminal history of the Civil War, *Battle Cry of Freedom*, most dual battle names had no intrinsic superiority over their alternatives; consequently, he often uses dual names interchangeably. James McPherson, *Battle Cry of Freedom* (Oxford University Press, 1988), 346n2.
6. Leta McGregor Thayer to Director of Libraries, University of Georgia, Athens, Georgia, December 18, 1969. Copy in possession of Mary T. Hall.
7. Out of the total of over 165 soldiers who served in Company G, fewer than two dozen surrendered at Appomattox. R. A. Brock, ed., *Southern Historical Society Papers: Paroles of the Army of Northern Virginia* (Richmond, VA: 1887), 15:393-396.

justice of the peace (magistrate) for Etna, but he walked away from his law books (and his boot-making business) in May 1861 to enlist in Company B of the 9th Pennsylvania Reserves, also known as the 38th Pennsylvania Volunteer Infantry Regiment.

Hall was an unmarried teenage farmer with scant formal education when he enlisted in the Yancey Independents. Elsesser was a family man in his early thirties who had studied law and was serving in public office in his hometown. Seemingly, they had little in common. But both had enlisted in May 1861 and left for camp the following month. One was sworn into Federal service and one into Confederate service within five days of each other in July 1861. Although it was improbable that the two men ever fired directly at the other, they were present at engagements where they were likely no more than several hundred yards apart. Both survived the war's greatest battle as bystanders to American history's most famous infantry charge at Gettysburg on July 3, 1863. Ironically, their shared experience of campaigning for their respective armies ended the same day, May 12, 1864, when Hall was taken prisoner at Spotsylvania and when Elsesser's regiment was dissolved at the expiration of its three years of obligated service.

George Washington Hall, left, and Jacob L. Elsesser. *(Photos courtesy of Mary Jeannette Howle and Melvin Truman)*

After the war, both devoted their lives to serving others, Hall as a prominent Baptist preacher in north and central Florida and Elsesser resuming his pre-war duties as justice of the peace for his small town in western Pennsylvania.

Hall and Elsesser were only two of the tens of thousands of soldiers who chronicled their lives in diaries during the war. Hall had begun his "journaling" in April 1862, using a small pocket notebook to record a retrospective of his experiences going back to Lincoln's election and his decision to enlist. After coming into possession of Elsesser's diary, Hall initially used both his pocket notebook and the *Daily Pocket Remembrancer* until mid-1863, when he resorted to exclusive use of the *Daily Pocket Remembrancer*.

Unfortunately, Hall's pocket notebook and the *Daily Pocket Remembrancer* appear to have been discarded by accident several decades ago. However, both the Library of Congress and the Hargrett Rare Books and Manuscript Collection of the University of Georgia Libraries hold a bound, typed manuscript of the diary entries. This manuscript, titled *Diary of George W. Hall, 14th Georgia Volunteers, Confederate States of America, 1861-1865*, was typed in the late 1920s by Mary Leta McGregor Thayer, George Washington Hall's granddaughter (and my first cousin, once removed). Leta Thayer, who had a keen sense of need to preserve history, had borrowed the diaries from her uncle, Willis W. Hall, a prominent Miami educator, real estate entrepreneur, and fruit grower. As Thayer's husband, Clarence Putnam Thayer, wrote in a 1929 letter to Charles Sandrock, one of Elsesser's descendants, Leta wanted to copy the contents of the diaries "before the ink fades too much."[8] Thayer and her husband had hoped to have her manuscript published but that project never materialized during their lifetimes.

The public would have been none the wiser if Leta, then a 30-year-old daughter of the South, had elected to omit the Union soldier's entries from a manuscript dedicated to a beloved grandfather who had fought for the Confederacy. Yet she not only incorporated Jacob Elsesser's entries into her manuscript, but she also made inquiries as to his military service to the U.S. War Department, the Bureau of Pensions in the U.S. Department of the Interior, and the Adjutant General of the Commonwealth of Pennsylvania. Thayer's affidavit and memorandum regarding the preparation of the manuscript and her research inquiries are contained in Appendix A. They are a testament to the fact that, but for her initiative, the voices of these two men would have likely disappeared from history. As

Leta McGregor Thayer, who believed her transcription was one way she could "contribute something to the history of our country." (*Image courtesy of Mary Jeanette Howle*)

---

8. C. P. Thayer to C. A. Sandrock, April 20, 1929. Copy in possession of Mary T. Hall.

she later wrote to the Library of Congress, this seemed one way she could contribute to our nation's history.

Copying and organizing the contents of the pocket notebook posed major editing issues for Leta Thayer. Some pages were missing and others contained illegible writing, "much faded, written in pencil and ruined from water," as she noted. Although the entries in the *Daily Pocket Remembrancer* run in chronological order, Hall's entries in his pocket notebook do not. Leta Thayer's manuscript faithfully follows the sequence of entries as they appeared in the pocket notebook, however illogical the sequence seemed. The entries in the pocket notebook are a hodgepodge of long narratives, daily entries, patriotic songs and poems, Sunday religious reflections, company musters, thirteen months of weather observations, and thirteen months of a daily log of events. Not only are many of the entries out of chronological order but there are often multiple entries, some spanning both the pocket notebook and the *Daily Pocket Remembrancer*, for many dates in 1862 and 1863. For example, Hall discusses July 1, 1862, the date of the battle of Malvern Hill, in three locations in the pocket notebook and as a daily entry in the *Daily Pocket Remembrancer*.

Hall's use of such diverse content unquestionably makes his diaries more robust, but it denies the reader of the opportunity to follow his war from start to finish; instead, readers attempting to read Leta Thayer's manuscript straight through would find themselves bouncing back and forth among dates and campaigns, at least until mid-1863 when Hall settled into using only the *Daily Pocket Remembrancer*. My task in editing the Hall diaries was to either offer the diaries just as Thayer typed them or to reposition the entries into chronological order to assist readers. Electing humanitarianism over originality, I reorganized both Hall's and Elsesser's entries into fourteen numbered chapters running chronologically over the course of the war.[9]

Each chapter commences with my contextual commentaries, follwed by narratives or daily entries. Chapters 4 through 9 are the most challenging to read; they consist of both Hall's narrative material and daily entries (with significant duplication between the

---

9. In reorganizing the material chronologically, I have dispensed with virtually all references to the pagination used by Thayer, who had divided the diaries into five sections, each with independent page numbering. Although Hall's diary has been cited in numerous books and articles, using Thayer's pagination is of little help to those trying to locate specific passages.

two volumes) from the Peninsula Campaign in 1862 until just after Gettysburg in the summer of 1863. Chapters 10 through 13 consist solely of Hall's entries in the *Daily Pocket Remembrancer* and run from July 1863 through the end of the war.[10] Chapter 14 contains Elsesser's daily entries from January 1 through June 26, 1862, as well as a discussion of his major life events prior to the war and a broad summary of his activities in the war. Chapter 15 summarizes the lives of both men after the war. Although this book tends to be heavily weighted towards Hall's material, let there be no doubt that I salute Jacob Elsesser for his service.

My contextual commentaries are not intended as a stand-alone narrative of Civil War operations or even as regimental histories; rather, I have sought simply to provide context to both men's diary entries and experiences during the war. As context sources, I relied not only on many of the superb general histories of the war but also on specific narratives for the 14th Georgia and 9th Pennsylvania Reserves.

For the 14th Georgia, my primary sources included the contemporaneous war-time correspondence of Lieutenant Josiah B. Patterson of Company E, 14th Georgia,[11] and the post-war memoirs of Lieutenant David Champion of Hall's Company G, 14th Georgia.[12]

I have also relied heavily on James M. Folsom's *Heroes and Martyrs of Georgia: Georgia's Record in the Revolution of 1861* for its histories of the 14th Georgia and Edward L. Thomas's brigade. Published in 1864, Folsom's book only covers operations through the battle of Jericho Ford in May 1864 but provides extremely informative regimental

---

10. Some portions of the book, such as Hall's weather log and the daily log, have been relegated to appendices, too unwieldy to include in chapters but of too much potential utility to abandon altogether.
11. Patterson's correspondence provides great detail on the miseries experienced by the 14th Georgia in its first year of service. His letters may be found at "The Incomplete Correspondence of Lt. Josiah B. Patterson and the 14th Georgia Volunteer Infantry – An Outline," Atlanta Historical Society, Atlanta, GA [hereafter "Incomplete Patterson Correspondence"].
12. In a written statement on the origin of the David Champion memoirs, his great-granddaughter wrote in 1990 that her father had told her that Champion had rewritten the "diary" after the war from his notes. David Champion, *Memoirs*, United Daughters of the Confederacy, Atlanta, GA [hereafter Champion, *Memoirs*]. It is not evident when Champion wrote his memoirs but several factors suggest it was an appreciable period after the war. For example, he quotes from John Esten Cooke's 1876 book *A Life of General Robert E. Lee*. Moreover, a number of inaccuracies, beginning with errors as to his enlistment date, the regiment's commanding officer, and the regiment's location in the summer of 1861, strongly suggest a long lapse of time between those 1861 events and Champion's memorialization of them.

and brigade histories up to that point in the war.[13] The chapter on the 14th Georgia was written by Captain Thomas C. Moore, the regimental adjutant and former Assistant Commissary of Subsistence. Captain William Norwood wrote the chapter on Thomas's Brigade, in which the 14th Georgia served from mid-1862 through the end of the war. Not surprisingly, the 14th Georgia received prominent mention in James Folsom's book because his brother, Colonel (Col.) Robert W. Folsom, was the regiment's commander from 1862 until his death, at the age of 28, in May 1864 from wounds incurred during the battle of the Wilderness.

In writing my context material, I was greatly aided by the "National Archives' Compiled Service Records of Confederate Soldiers Who Served in Organizations from the State of Georgia from Georgia Units," which I accessed on Fold3, Ancestry.com's military history subsidiary. Regrettably, most of the company and regimental records for the 14th Georgia between November 1861 through May 1864 are missing. The scattered documents that do exist in the National Archives for this gap period consist mainly of miscellaneous pay vouchers, equipment authorizations (including an 1863 requisition for drums for the regiment), and death claims submitted to the Confederate government by surviving family members.

The National Archives service records for Union soldiers are not as extensive as those for Confederate soldiers; in fact, Elsesser's primary document on Fold3 are index entries related to his pension.[14] I was able to summarize Elsesser's war from start to finish by merging his 1862 entries with the contents of a separate diary that Elsesser completed at some point after May 1864. Titled *Diary of Company B*, the handwritten contents were typed into a manuscript by Elsesser's great-great-grandson, Melvin Truman, who kindly provided me a copy of his typed draft of the manuscript and a photocopy of the handwritten original. I made some additional edits to the *Company B* manuscript, which is included herein as Appendix E. This unit diary is helpful in confirming the various points in the war where Hall's and Elsesser's universes collided. As secondary

---

13. James M. Folsom, *Heroes and Martyrs of Georgia*: *Georgia's Record in the Revolution of 1861* (Macon, GA: Burke, Boykin, 1864), 145. Folsom apparently intended a second volume but none is known to exist.
14. "Organization Index to Pension Files of Veterans Who Served Between 1861 and 1900." database with images Fold3 (https://www.fold3.com/publication/57/civil-war-pensions-index).

sources, I relied extensively on J. R. Sypher's *History of the Pennsylvania Reserve Corps: A Complete Record of the Organization and of the Different Companies, Regiments, Brigades Complied from Official Reports and Other Documents, 1865*; Samuel P. Bates's *History of Pennsylvania Volunteers, 1861-5*; and Uzal W. Ent's recent *The Pennsylvania Reserves in the Civil War: A Comprehensive History*.

In addition to organizational issues, I faced another dilemma common to most editors of nineteenth-century diaries: how to preserve as much original writing as possible yet still produce a readable product. In trying to balance these two objectives, I endeavored to follow the guidance provided me by Jane Johansson, editor of Col. Albert Ellithorpe's Civil War diary, who essentially advised that the lighter the editing, the more an editor preserves the "flavor" of a diarist's voice.[15]

First, both Hall and Elsesser often failed to start sentences with a capital letter, so I changed lower case letters at the start of sentences to upper case letters without using brackets to indicate the change. As for punctuation, I added periods at the ends of sentences as needed, especially in Hall's entries.[16] I have changed commas to apostrophes where apostrophes were likely intended, such as in the word "o'clock." I have not added apostrophes to indicate possession except where their absence would materially alter the sentence. I retained the underlining shown in Thayer's manuscript. I have generally not changed verb tenses, run-on sentences, or archaic spelling (like "verry" and "waggon") and antiquated abbreviations (such as "&c" for *etc.*). I did remove or edit a few letters that were almost assuredly due to a typing error, such as a double vowel where none seemed logical. Bracketed material indicates my best guess at missing words or letters. Where I could not guess the diarist's likely intent, I left the brackets empty. Both men's writing is generally readable even without excessive editing (and Hall's writing certainly improved over the course of the war), but implementing these few changes on top of their original words hopefully makes the three diaries – Hall's pocket notebook, the dual-authored *Daily Pocket Remembrancer*, and Elsesser's *Diary of Company B* – much easier to read while still preserving the flavor of the men's voices.

---

15. Jane Johannson, ed., *Albert C. Ellithorpe, the First Indian Home Guards, and the Civil War on the Trans-Mississippi Frontier* (Louisiana State University Press, 2016).
16. For many of Hall's entries, Thayer left three or four spaces at the end of sentences that trailed off without terminal punctuation.

As Thayer noted in a 1969 memorandum, the diaries contain "the names of many individual soldiers so it is possible that those who are searching historical records will be able to make use of this information." Hall provides two rosters of his company, one in June 1862 and another a month later; however, these lists do not reflect all the men who ever served in Company G, such as those who joined after the summer of 1862. Where possible, I have attempted to identify (and index) Confederate and Union soldiers by their full names, a task complicated by multiple spellings of some names even within National Archive records. For many soldiers, I simply added their first names in brackets. I extend my apologies for any errors in how I have stated soldiers' names.

Both Hall and Elsesser wrote daily entries that consisted of only a few words summarizing the day's weather, and Hall maintained a separate weather log for thirteen months of the war. Such entries may be tedious to read, but they are hardly irrelevant. As Robert K. Krick noted, "Weather has at least some effect on everything soldiers do. Occasionally it levies more impact than do strategy or tactics or materiel."[17] Many soldiers on both sides had to adapt to conditions that they may have never experienced before and overcome illness caused by exposure to the elements and other environmental factors, such as polluted drinking water.

Like Krick, I include the weather for reference purposes, not analytical ones, but readers would do well to consider how frontal assaults by infantrymen might have been more successful if they attacked on dry ground rather than trying to slog "double quick" through mud; if rivers and streams had not been made impassable by heavy rains; and if rainfall had not rendered weapons incapable of being fired. In fact, a thunderstorm at Spotsylvania on the night of May 11-12, 1864, not only helped mask the noise of advancing Union corps movements but also wet the percussion caps on many of the weapons that Confederate troops had loaded before falling asleep.[18]

The collective entries in Hall's pocket notebook, the joint *Daily Pocket Remembrancer*, and Elsesser's *Diary of Company B* reveal the lives of two soldiers who saw war from the bottom up as privates, a rank which Hall describes as a "post of honor." As historian

---

17. Robert K. Krick, *Civil War Weather in Virginia* (University of Alabama Press, 2007), 6.
18. Williamson Murray and Wayne Wei-Siang Hsieh, *A Savage War: A Military History of the Civil War* (Princeton University Press, 2016), 382; G. Bradwell, "Spotsylvania, May 12, 13, 1864," *Confederate Veteran*, March 1920, 102.

Gordon Rhea observes, "Generals set armies in motion; privates are cogs in the wheels of military machines. But what privates do can irretrievably affect the meshing of the martial gears and determine the outcome of battles and wars."[19] In the chapters that follow, you will read the experiences of two privates in arguably the most reliable of narratives: their own words. In the words of historian Henry Steele Commager, "[I]n the American Civil War Everyman was, indeed, his own historian."[20]

---

19. Gordon C. Rhea, *Carrying the Flag: The Story of Private Charles Whilden, the Confederacy's Most Unlikely Hero* (Basic Books, 2004), 3.
20. Henry Steel Commager, *The Blue and the Gray* (Bobbs-Merrill, 1950), xix.

1

"I LEFT MY HOME AND MY DEAR MOTHER"
GEORGIA: 1861

As historian Bell Wiley wrote over sixty years ago, it was "doubtful that any people ever went to war with greater enthusiasm than did Confederates in 1861."[1] Nineteen-year-old farmer George Washington Hall embodied that enthusiasm, enlisting on May 31, 1861, in the Yancey Independents, the first company of volunteers to leave Worth County, Georgia. Hall's reason for enlisting, as set forth on the first page of his diary, was his belief that Abraham Lincoln had "Sent Hordes of Goths and Vandals" to overrun the South and take its citizens' freedom, homes, and property. Hall believed he needed to "repel the invader."

In July 1861, the Yancey Independents joined nine other companies to form the 11th Georgia Regiment of Volunteers. In the early months of the Civil War, Confederate volunteer infantry companies generally originated in small geographic areas such as a county or city. Local civic leaders recruited men to enlist in a company, which, in turn, became part of state-organized regiments. Many soldiers saw themselves as extensions of their hometowns or home counties, the populations of which provided moral support and, as in the case of Worth County, clothing and supplies, to the volunteers. This type of cohesion tied company soldiers to each other and to their home counties. Not surprisingly, the volunteers usually elected community leaders to serve as company

---

1. Bell I. Wiley, *The Road to Appomattox* (1956; repr., Louisiana State University, 1994), 43.

officers. Officers with previous military experience, such as Captain (Capt.) William A. Harris of the Yancey Independents, were especially prized.

Harris organized the Yancey Independents and served as its first captain. He had volunteered during the Mexican-American War as a private in the Macon Guards, Company C of the 1st Georgia Infantry. Although his regiment never saw combat in Texas or Mexico, Harris's one-year enlistment gained him experience in military life and combat support operations.[2] After the war, Harris followed in his father's footsteps and became an attorney, initially practicing law in Irwin County, Georgia. When Worth County was created out of Irwin and Dooly counties in 1853, Harris provided the name for the new county in honor of his brigade commander in Mexico, U.S. Army Maj. Gen. William J. Worth.[3] Harris, who relocated to Isabella, represented Worth County in the Georgia state senate prior to the Civil War and served as a county judge.[4] An 1861 letter to the *Albany Patriot* described Harris as a "gentleman well known in Georgia and in whose bosom burns as noble and gallant a spirit as patriot warrior ever felt. In personal prowess he is of the real Napoleonic stamp. . . ."[5]

Prior to organizing the Yancey Independents, Harris had already attempted to raise a local company, the Holmes Rifles, from Worth County men.[6] Terrell T. Mounger, a physician and former inferior court judge who later succeeded Harris as commander of

---

2. "Mexican War Service Record Index," database and images, Fold3 (www.fold3.com/image/307214851); General Index Card, William A. Harris; citing National Archives and Records Administration microfilm publication "Indexes to the Carded Records of Soldiers Who Served in Volunteer Organizations During the Mexican War, compiled 1899 - 1927, documenting the period 1846 – 1848," M616, Roll 0016, Record Group 94, National Archives, Washington, D.C.; Wilbur G. Kurtz, Jr., "The First Regiment of Georgia Volunteers in the Mexican War," The Georgia Historical Quarterly 27, no. 2 (December 1943): 312.
3. Lillie Martin Grubbs, *History of Worth County, Georgia, for the First Eighty Years, 1854-1934* (J. W. Burke, 1934), 3. The town of Isabella, which became the county seat, was named in honor of General Worth's wife.
4. Grubbs, author of the seminal history of Worth County's early years, identified Harris as "probably the most prominent person in the early history of the county." Grubbs, *History of Worth County*, 193.
5. "Yancey Independents," *The Albany Patriot*, June 27, 1861, https://gahistoricnewspapers.galileo.usg.edu. This letter to the editor was signed FULTON, which suggests that it was likely written by Robert H. Fulton, then a private (and later captain) in Company G.
6. Harris likely named this company in memory of Captain Isaac Holmes, his former company commander, who died from disease in Mexico in 1846. John Campbell Butler, *Historical Record of Macon and Central Georgia* (J. W. Burke, 1879), 173.

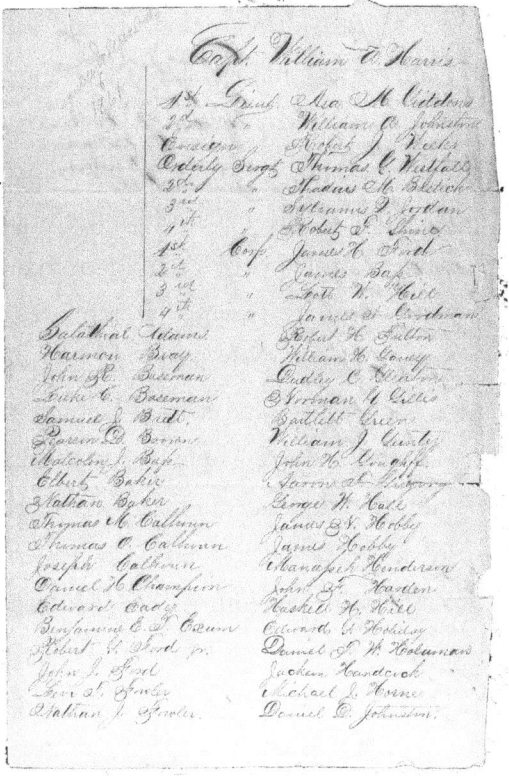

Handwritten muster of the Yancey Independents. This list was duplicated in the June 27, 1861, issue of the *Albany Patriot*.

Company G, had likewise attempted to raise a company, the Worth Guards.[7] However, both companies were disbanded in May 1861 due to the family commitments of its soldiers.[8] Harris then organized another company, the Yancey Independents, who were described as men who "were born as it were with rifles in their hands, and if sharp shooters

---

7. Grubbs, *History of Worth County*, 51. The formation of the Holmes Rifles preceded the firing on Fort Sumter in early April 1861.
8. "We learn from Capt. Wm. A. Harris, that owing to the number of married men in the ranks of the Holmes Rifles, Capt. Harris, and Worth Guards, Capt Mounger, that the two companies in Worth county, have disbanded, and a new one organised under the name of the Yancey Independents, composed of the young men of Worth county, Capt Harris commanding. He has tendered the services of his company, and is ready to march to any point at a moments notice. It is due the two former companies to say, that it was impossible for them to leave their families, they being in very moderate circumstances, and their families entirely dependent upon them." "Yancey Independents," *Milledgeville Southern Recorder*, May 21, 1861, https://access.newspaperarchive.com.

Muster-Roll of the Yancey Independents.

OFFICERS.

Captain, ... WILLIAM A. HARRIS.
1st Lieut., ... ASA M. GIDDENS.
2d Lieut., ... WILLIAM A. JOHNSTON.
Ensign, ... Robert A. Weeks.
Orderly Sergeant, ... Thomas G. Westfall.
2d   "   ...... Thadius M. Bostick.
3d   "   ...... Sylvanus Q. Jordan.
4th   "   .... Robert F. Shine.
1st Corporal, ... James H. Ford.
2d   "   .... James Bass.
3d   "   .... Lott W. Hill.
4th   "   .... James J. Goodman.

PRIVATES.

Salathial Adams,
Harmon Bray,
John R Baseman,
Luke C Baseman,
Samuel J Britt,
Pearson D Brown,
Malcolm J Bass,
Elbert Baker,
Nathan Baker,
Thomas M Calhoun,
Thomas O Calhoun,
Joseph Calhoun,
Daniel H Champion,
Edward Eady,
Benjamin E T Etum,
Robert G Ford, Jr,
John J Ford,
Levi T Fowler,
Nathan J Fowler,
Robert H Fulton,
William H Ganey,
Dudley C Gleaton,
Norman G Gillis,
Bartlett Green,
William J Gunter,
John H Goughff,
Aaron T Gregory,
George W Hall,
James N Hobby,
James Hobby,
Manasseh Henderson,
John F Harden,
Haskell H Hill,
Edward G Holiday,
Daniel T W Holaman,
Jackson Handcock,
Michael J Horne,
Daniel D Johnston,
John Jirkins,

Julius M Jones,
Albert B Kersh,
James C Lunsford,
Wm Lane,
William L Land,
Rodrick M McRaney,
George W McRaney,
Wm T Meadows,
Henry Moore,
Abel C Massey,
George W Massey,
Silas M Massey,
Robert D Massey,
Samuel S Nipper,
Joseph C Omooney,
John T Pearce,
William W Pasey,
Henry Clay Quiet,
Asa C Rodgers,
Martin J Rodgers,
John A Rhodes,
John W Rouse,
George W Spring,
Joseph L Spring,
Joseph L Sumner,
Green Shiver,
Jackson W Shiver,
John J Shiver,
John C Smith,
Rienzie Stephens,
Marion Simmons,
Andrew J Tabor,
Thomas Tipton,
Eli Vickery,
Wm W Walker,
Berrien A Williams,
Thomas L Wheelus,
Romulus Weeks.

Roster of the Yancey Independents in the June 27, 1861, issue of the *Albany Patriot*.

are wanted, there is none better."[9] A handwritten muster for the Yancey Independents from June 1861 shows that Hall was one of 88 officers and enlisted personnel.[10] The initial company officers were Capt. Harris, First Lieutenant Asa Giddens (former postmaster), Second Lieutenant William A. Johnston (schoolteacher), and Second Lieutenant (Ensign) Robert Weeks (court clerk). However, this slate of officers was short-lived: Weeks died of illness in western Virginia in September 1861; Giddens resigned his commission in early October 1861; Harris, who missed the regiment's movement to Virginia, left the company for regimental office early in 1862; and Johnston died of illness near Richmond in July 1862.[11]

---

9. "Yancey Independents," *Milledgeville Southern Recorder*, May 21, 1861, https://access.newspaperarchive.com.
The company was apparently named for William Lowndes Yancey, a native Georgia "Fire-Eater" who argued for secession. William Warren Rogers, "The Confederate Nation Reflected: Names of Georgia's Civil War Companies," *The Georgia Historical Quarterly* 93, No. 1 (Spring 2009): 84-85.
10. The full muster was also published in the *Albany Patriot* on June 27, 1861. The names shown in that article are identical to the ones on the handwritten muster.
11. Officers had the luxury of resigning their commissions, an escape route from war denied to enlisted troops.

According to Hall, the Yancey Independents encamped at Isabella (likely at "Camp Vason" at or near San Bernard, the first county seat) from June 5, 1861, until July 9, 1861, "drilling every minute of time [they] could." The citizens of Worth County rallied around the Independents. County women presented the company with a battle flag, and an Albany newspaper wrote of an incident where a thirteen-year-old boy, bereft over being too young to enlist, had donated five dollars to Harris for the company's use.[12]

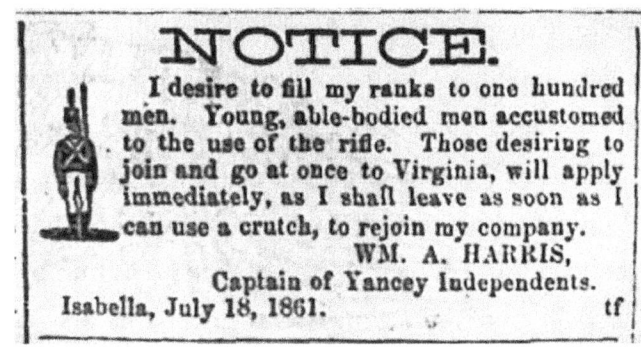

Advertisement from the *Albany Patriot*

On July 9, 1861, Governor Joseph Brown issued the Yancey Independents, as Company G of the 11th Regiment of Volunteers, orders to report to Atlanta on July 15, 1861, to serve for three years or the duration of the war.[13] Confederate service records show July 9, 1861, as the formal enlistment date for Hall and the over 90 other enlisted troops in Company G.[14] The company departed Isabella on July 13, 1861, marching west to Albany, Georgia, where they embarked by rail for Atlanta. Upon arriving in Atlanta, Hall's company encamped at Walton Springs and drew arms and equipment, including rifles, knapsacks, tents, and cooking utensils.[15]

As was typical for Confederate infantry regiments, the regimental command structure for the 11th Georgia consisted of one colonel, one lieutenant colonel, and one

---

12. "Camp Vason" *Albany Patriot*, June 13, 1861, https://gahistoricnewspapers.galileo.usg.edu.
13. "Eleventh and Twelfth Regiments," *Southern Confederacy*, July 13, 1861, https://access.newspaperarchive.com.
14. "Civil War Service Records, Confederate Records," Fold3 (www.fold3.com/image/35574189); Georgia Fourteenth Infantry, "Company Muster Roll Sept-Oct 1861," entry for "George W. Hall;" citing National Archives and Records Administration microfilm publication "Compiled Service Records of Confederate Soldiers Who Served in Organizations from the State of Georgia," M266, Roll 0285, Record Group 109, National Archives, Washington, D.C. Less than a dozen men in the company who enlisted on July 9, 1861, were present at Appomattox.
15. Letter to the Editor, Milledgeville *Southern Federal Union*, July 23, 1861, https://access.newspaperarchive.com.

major. Company G and the other nine companies in the regiment elected regimental officers on July 17, 1861.[16] As colonel, the regiment elected Arnoldus V. Brumby, a West Point graduate and Seminole War combat veteran who founded the Georgia Military Institute in Marietta, Georgia, in 1851. The regiment elected 22-year-old schoolteacher Whiteford Ramsay as lieutenant colonel and physician Felix Price as major. The command slate quickly unraveled, however: Brumby arrested Price, who faced a court-martial before the regiment ever reached its first camp in western Virginia; Ramsay resigned in early August 1861; and Brumby himself resigned in mid-November 1861.

Company G went to war without its company commander. While still in Georgia, Harris had broken his leg, which left him temporarily disabled. First Lieutenant Giddens, serving as acting company commander, was responsible for getting the Yancey Independents to Atlanta and then to Virginia once Governor Joseph Brown released the regiment for Confederate service. Harris, however, actively continued to recruit men for the company through advertisements in the *Albany Patriot* for "[y]oung able-bodied men accustomed to the use of the rifle."[17] Those interested in joining needed to apply immediately because he planned to rejoin the company as soon as he was able to use a crutch.[18]

Hall's Company G departed Atlanta on July 17, 1861, and took a rail route to Lynchburg, Virginia, via north Georgia, eastern Tennessee, and western Virginia. An article from the *Lynchburg Republican*, which was reprinted in multiple Union newspapers, reported that the "11th Georgia Regiment, under the command of Col. Brumby, were expected to arrive in Lynchburg, Saturday night last, where they are to rendezvous and be mustered into service. The whole regiment is well armed with superior rifles and muskets."[19] The company arrived at Lynchburg on July 21, 1861, the date of the Confederate victory at Manassas. Hall took his oath of allegiance to the Confederacy

---

16. "Vote for Field Officers 11th Regiment," *Milledgeville Southern Recorder*, July 23, 1861, https://gahistoricnewspapers.galileo.usg.edu.
17. William A. Harris, "Notice," *The Albany Patriot*, August 22, 1861, https://gahistoricnewspapers.galileo.usg.edu.
18. William A. Harris, "Notice," *The Albany Patriot*, August 22, 1861, https://gahistoricnewspapers.galileo.usg.edu.
19. "Troops Coming," *Baltimore Daily Exchange*, July 29, 1861, and *Philadelphia Inquirer*, July 30, 1861, https://access.newspaperarchive.com.

two days later. Upon entering Confederate service, the regiment was redesignated as the 14th Georgia Infantry Regiment, although some Georgia newspapers continued to refer to Brumby's regiment as the 11th Georgia for several more months. Indeed, the regiment was the subject of numerous articles in Georgia newspapers over the next five months, but the reports seldom contained positive news.

Pocket Notebook Narrative of April 1, 1862

Camp Bartow near Fredericksburg,
Spotsylvania Co., Virginia
April 1st, 1862[20]

The autumn of 1860 witness[ed] the election of a Black Republican for President of the United States.[21] Before that time our Country was prosperous and happy, and every where was peace and plenty, and we had the most glorious government, and the best arts and institutions on the globe, but "oh!" what a change come over us in a verry short time. Our Political horizon was darkened by a fierce cloud which was soon in our zenith; and engulfed us all in war and bloodshed. Abraham Lincoln Sent Hordes of Goths and Vandals to over run our beloved South to Subjugate us and take freedom and our homes and property from us. Our Country called for volunteers to repel the invader, and I left my home and my Dear Mother and everything that was near and [dear] to me and enlisted my services May 29th, 1861.

---

20. Hall's lengthy narrative of April 1, 1862, overlaps with another long narrative on April 20, 1862.
21. The term "Black Republican" was a pejorative in reference to Lincoln's views on the expansion of slavery in the western territories.

And on the 5th of June we went into camp life at Isabella Worth County Georgia my native State. We remained in camp at Isabella until July 9th drilling every minute of time we could, and on that day we received orders to march to the Scene of war, and on the 13th we left Isabella and a good many of our Co[mpany] (poor fellows) for the last time and on the 14th we took the cars[22] in Albany, and on the 15th arrived at Atlanta Ga where we drew knapsacks Tents cooking utensils canteens haver-sacks and our Rifles cartridge boxes &c. We left Atlanta on the 17th and proceeded on the cars through Tennessee which is a verry fertile and productive State, by the way of Dalton Ga and Cleveland Tenn Knoxville Tenn Jonesborough Tenn and Bristol Va and arrived at Lynchburg on the 21st the day that the great Battle of Manassas was fought. At Lynchburg we were mustered in the Service of the Confederate States of America, and took the oath of allegiance.

---

22. Both Hall and Elsesser refer to riding on railroads as "taking the cars." Each went to war and, years later, came home from war on journeys that included rail travel. In the interim, their respective regiments moved troops over rail lines, fought over – and along – rail lines, guarded rail lines, destroed rail lines, marched along rail lines, and were supplied by rail lines. As rail historian Edwin A. Pratt maintains, given that the area of military operations in the Civil War was equal almost to the area of Europe and that advancing armies could not always expect to simply live off the countryside, "without the help of railways [the war] could hardly have been fought at all." Edwin A. Pratt, *The Rise of Rail Power in War and Conquest, 1833-1914* (Lippincott, 1916), 11.

2

"I CAME AS NEAR DYING AS ANY BODY EVER DID TO LIVE" WESTERN VIRGINIA: 1861

Upon being inducted into Confederate service, the 14th Georgia received orders to proceed via Staunton, Virginia, to the rail station at Millboro, Virginia.[1] On July 29, 1861, the regiment rode by train to Staunton, traveling in box cars with no seats or food. Upon reaching Staunton, they learned that their orders had been modified; instead of proceeding by rail to Millboro, they marched to Monterey, Virginia, having stayed in Staunton only long enough to cook a meal. Monterey, some fifty miles northwest of Staunton, served as headquarters for the Confederate Army of the Northwest. Arriving in Monterey on August 3, 1861, the regiment was ordered by General Robert E. Lee, himself newly arrived to the Army of the Northwest, to march the following day to Huntersville, Virginia (now West Virginia). One officer in the regiment wrote home that Lee, then Jefferson Davis's principal military advisor, had complimented the 14th Georgia "highly."[2] For the next fifteen weeks, Hall's regiment participated in Lee's uninspiring Western Virginia Campaign.

The march to Huntersville was a difficult one, requiring a zigzag march over the mountainous terrain of the Alleghenies. On August 5, 1861, the regiment reached

---

1. "Send the Eleventh [Fourteenth] and Twelfth [Fifteenth] (A. V. Brumby and T. W. Thomas) Georgia Regiments to Millborough via Staunton. Orders will await them at Millborough." United States War Department, *War of the Rebellion: A Compilation of the Official Records of the Union and Confederate Armies*, 128 vols. (Washington, D.C.: Government Printing Office, 1880-1901) Ser. I, vol. 51, pt. II, p. 195. Hereafter cited as *OR*.
2. "Letter from an officer of Col. Brumby's Regiment to his father," Milledgeville *Southern Federal Union*, August 20, 1861, https://access.newspaperarchive.com.

The rail station at Staunton figured prominently in Hall's war experiences. In March 1863, he "took the cars" from Staunton to rejoin his regiment on the Rappahannock after his hospitalization. In December 1863, he rode by rail to Staunton to join Early's forces in the Shenandoah Valley. In March 1864, he marched twenty-five miles to the rail station in Staunton to commence his furlough to Florida. (Image from Staunton, Va. / drawn from nature by Ed. Beyer; W. Rau. ca. 1857, Library of Congress)

Huntersville, a town described by Capt. Harris as the "filthiest hole on God's earth."[3] Although the town itself was on the slope of a mountain, camps were set up on "bottoms," small strips of land between the mountains with little fresh air to provide relief from the heat and offering only "slow-moving, bad-looking water," according to one Tennessee regimental commander.[4] A soldier in Company K of the 14th Georgia described their living area as "a low, flat, mucky field, upon the margin of a dirty, warm stream of water" that "soon became one vast mud vat, through which we were compelled to walk day and night, exposed to heavy rains, dews, and dense fogs. From these causes, being human and subject to disease, we were taken sick by scores, with measels, mumps, typhoid fever, and pneumonia."[5] A Tennessee chaplain, describing Huntersville

---

3. William A. Harris, "War Correspondence, Sept. 22, 1861," *Albany Patriot*, Oct. 3, 1861, https://gahistoricnewspapers.galileo.usg.edu.
4. Jamie Gillum, *History of the Sixteenth Tennessee Volunteer Infantry Regiment in the American Civil War*, Vol. 1, *We Were Spoiling for a Fight, April 1861-August 1862* (CreateSpace Independent Publishing Platform, 2011), 49.
5. J. F. B., "Hardships and Sufferings of Our Troops – An Appeal to the Ladies of the South," *Savannah Republican*, November 1, 1861, https://access.newspaperarchive.com. The author, J.F.B., was likely Private John F. Broom. Typhoid fever was likely the most common infectious disease soldiers suffered from during the war, due in large part to its easy spread through contaminated water and food. Michael R. Gilchrist, "Disease & Infection in the American Civil War," *The American Biology Teacher* 60, no. 4 (1998), 260.

as "a most wretched and filthy town," wrote that sick soldiers were housed not only in tents but also in public and private buildings.[6]

Indeed, the 14th Georgia's time in western Virginia was most memorable not for combat but instead for the illness and death that befell its soldiers, who were unprepared for their fifteen weeks of service there. As Capt. Thomas C. Moore, the 14th Georgia's regimental adjutant, recalled in 1864:

> This was our first campaign remarkable in the history of the regiment for the sickness and sufferings we endured. We were *raw men*, ignorant of camp life, unused to exposures of wet and cold, and the fatigues of marching. We were encumbered with many things useless to the old soldier, and destitute of others since learned to be indispensable. We had to undergo the sickness always incident to camp life, and the season was an unusually wet one. Measels and mumps broke out and quickly spread through every company. While laboring under these diseases many took cold, and added to this, fever of a most malignant form made its appearance to an alarming extent. The medical department was unorganized, the supply of medicine wholly inadequate, and the accommodations for the sick of the very poorest kind. The consequence was disease and death were spread out on every hand. We left Lynchburg in the latter part of July, seven hundred and seventy strong, and of this number but one hundred and twenty reported for duty.[7]

Huntersville, for all its environmental challenges, was of great strategic value. It was the southern terminus of the Huttonsville-Huntersville Turnpike, a north-south feeder road to the region's most important roadway, the Staunton-Parkersburg Turnpike. The Staunton-Parkersburg Turnpike, in turn, connected the Shenandoah Valley, with its own strategic turnpike and bountiful crops, to the trans-Allegheny area of western Virginia. For the Union, the Staunton-Parkersburg Turnpike represented a potential invasion route southeast into the Shenandoah Valley and the rail line to Richmond. For the Confederacy, the Staunton-Parkersburg Turnpike posed a potential avenue of counter-attack against Union-held northwestern Virginia and access to the Baltimore & Ohio Railroad at

---

6. Arthur Howard Noll, ed., *Doctor Quintard, Chaplain CSA* (Sewanee, TN: University Press, 1905), 17.
7. Folsom, *Heroes and Martyrs of Georgia*, 145 (italics in original). Union intelligence estimates in late August 1861 stated that Lee and William W. Loring had 10,000 men at Huntersville, but that the troops were "sickly." *OR*, Ser. 1, vol. 5, p. 118.

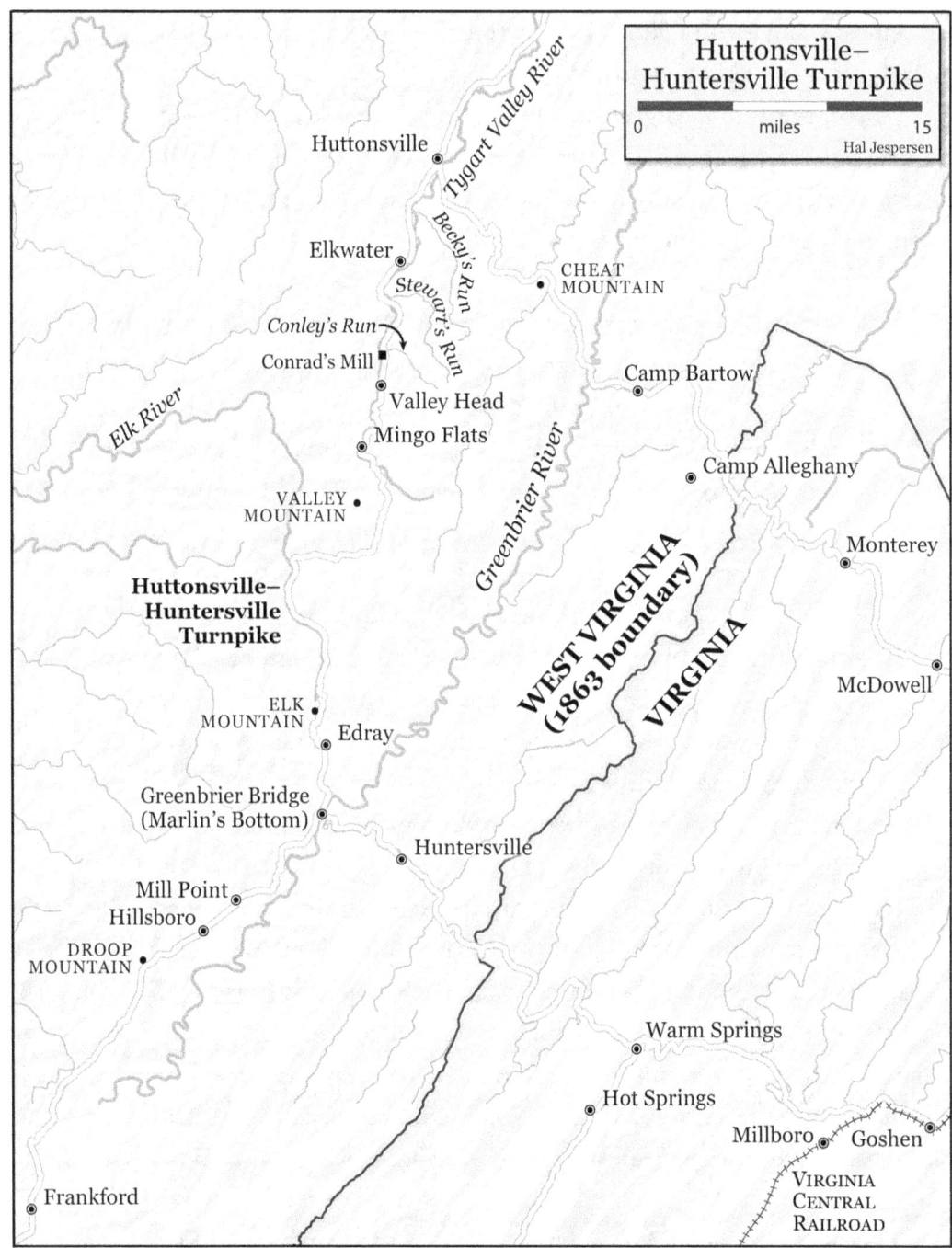

The Huttonsville-Huntersville Turnpike. This turnpike intersected with the Staunton-Petersburg Turnpike at Huttonsville. (Map by Hal Jespersen)

Grafton. Another critical road ran southeast from Huntersville through Warm Springs to the rail station at Millboro, Virginia.

By mid-July 1861, the Union army controlled the upper Tygart Valley River region in northwest Virginia. To block Confederate movement up the Huttonsville-Huntersville Turnpike, the Union army dug trenchworks at Elkwater, roughly seven miles south of Huttonsville. Union troops also constructed a fort on the summit of Cheat Mountain on the Staunton-Parkersburg Turnpike. The Federal troops, which included at least six companies of the 14th Indiana Infantry Regiment, dug entrenchments and cleared timber to provide an open view of the approaches to the fort, using the timber to build abatis. One of the earliest locations in the war where entrenchments were employed, the summit fort area included a parapet, blockhouses, and cabins for housing troops.[8]

The summit fort on Cheat Mountain. (Archives, West Virginia University)

Countering the Union forces in western Virginia was the Army of the Northwest, an awkward troika of three brigadier generals. William W. Loring commanded the Confederate units, including the 14th Georgia, on the two turnpikes, while the other brigadier generals, Henry Wise and John Buchanan Floyd, headed independent commands in the Kanawha Valley to the south. Loring was an experienced campaigner, a career soldier who had seen service in the Second Seminole War in Florida and who had lost an arm in the Mexican-American War. Wise and Floyd, however, had little to no military experience; rather, they were longstanding political enemies, both former governors of Virginia, who continuously bickered and tried to undermine each other's efforts in the Kanawha Valley.

---

8. Field entrenchments were used increasingly more often as the war progressed; in fact, the Civil War was the first American war where the armies made extensive use of entrenchments. Grady McWhiney and Perry D. Jamieson, *Attack and Die: Civil War Military Tactics and the Southern Heritage* (University of Alabama Press, 1982), 73. The summit fort also provided cabins large enough to house one-fourth of a company of soldiers. Earl J. Hess, *Field Armies and Fortifications in the Civil War: The Eastern Campaigns, 1861-1864* (University of North Carolina Press, 2005), 51.

This splintered command structure in western Virginia grew even more unwieldy in late July 1861 when Jefferson Davis ordered Robert E. Lee, his principal military advisor, to western Virginia to coordinate the efforts of the three brigadiers. Davis's orders gave Lee little power over the other three generals; as Civil War historian Clifford Dowdey notes, "Lee was faced with the nebulous task of 'coordinating' three prima donnas, without any authority over any of them."[9]

Lee traveled via Staunton and Monterey to Huntersville, arriving on August 3, just a few days after Loring had established his headquarters there. Loring gave Lee what historian Douglas Southall Freeman describes as a "surprised and distinctly cold reception;" after all, Lee had just appointed Loring to command of the Army of the Northwest two weeks earlier.[10] Lee had been pushing Loring since mid-July to go on the offensive in western Virginia, but Loring stalled, claiming he needed to build up supplies and establish a logistics train. Both the mountainous terrain and incessant rain that made bogs out of roads and trails made getting supplies to Pocahontas County a near impossibility. Loring's delay, whatever the reasons, gave illness time to spread and Union defenders additional time to strengthen.

When the 14th Georgia arrived in Huntersville on August 5, it marched into an area where illness was already rampant, in large part due to unusually heavy rain that had commenced falling in late July.[11] As Lee wrote his wife from Huntersville that same day, "The soldiers everywhere are sick. The measles are prevalent throughout the whole army, and you know that disease leaves unpleasant results, attacks on the lungs, typhoid, etc., especially in camp, where accommodations for the sick are poor."[12] To improve living conditions, the 14th Georgia moved on August 18, 1861, from Huntersville to Marlin's Bottom (now Marlinton, West Virginia) on the Greenbrier River. Over ninety men were left behind in Huntersville in "cold, wet, mudy (*sic*) tents."[13] But rain running on – and through – those tents caused them to mildew and rot.[14]

---

9. Clifford Dowdey, *Lee* (Stan Clark Military Books, 1991), 166.
10. Douglas Southall Freeman, *R. E. Lee: A Biography* (Charles Scribner's Sons, 1934) I:550.
11. One member of the 21st Virginia Infantry lamented that "it rained thirty-*two* days in August." Krick, *Civil War Weather in Virginia*, 31.
12. Jack Zinn, *R. E. Lee's Cheat Mountain Campaign* (McClain Printing Company, 1974), 69.
13. J. F. B., "Hardships and Sufferings of Our Troops – An Appeal to the Ladies of the South," *Savannah Republican*, November 1, 1861, https://access.newspaperarchive.com.
14. Kenneth W. Noe, *The Howling Storm: Weather, Climate, and the American Civil War* (Louisiana State University Press, 2020), 45.

The overall health of the regiment continued to worsen. Poor camp sanitation; deluges of rain; the onset of cold night temperatures; insufficient supplies; inadequate medical services; and green recruits, many of them from rural backgrounds and living in close quarters with strangers for the first time in their lives, were all factors that contributed to the outbreak of disease.[15] Living at higher elevations likely posed a greater challenge for the men of Company G, the only company in the regiment from southwest Georgia, than for the men in the companies from mountainous north Georgia.[16]

Sick troops not only deprived their unit of potential combatants but also drained food supplies and strained available medical services. One soldier in Company K wrote that when the regiment moved to Edray, a post office hamlet at the foot of Elk Mountain further up the Huttonsville-Huntersville Turnpike, on September 1, they left behind 363 men, including five from each company to tend to the ill, prompting one soldier to write home, "our regiment is scattered all over this country."[17] Many of the sick soldiers went to hospitals at Warm Springs, Virginia, and Rockbridge Alum Springs, Virginia, when there were sufficient transportation and personnel resources to move them.[18] Hall managed to avoid hospitalization in the fall of 1861, but he remained sick in his tent from August 19 until September 5. Those who remained well enough to work were tasked with trying to keep the roads passable.[19]

Lee moved his camp twenty-eight miles up the Huttonsville-Huntersville Turnpike to Valley Mountain, the Confederate front, where Loring eventually joined him in mid-August. Lee saw first-hand how debilitated his Confederate troops were, even writing his wife on September 1 that those on the sick list "would form an army" and that the constant

---

15. Contagious illnesses such as measles and chickenpox affected approximately half of all green soldiers, and surviving these diseases in a recruit's first encampment was critical to his becoming a "seasoned soldier." Kathryn Shively Meier, *Nature's Civil War: Common Soldiers and the Environment in 1862 Virginia* (University of North Carolina Press, 2013), 7. The lack of adequate medical services for the 14th Georgia in Pocohantas County was likely exacerbated when typhoid fever claimed the life of Assistant Surgeon George William Young on September 24, 1861.
16. The other nine companies and their home counties were Monroe (Company A); Wilkinson (Company B); Jasper (Company C); Cherokee (Company D); Forsyth (Company E); Johnson (Company F); Laurens (Company H); Butts (Company I); and Bartow (Company K).
17. William S. Smedlund, *Camp Fires of Georgia's Troops, 1861-1865* (Kennesaw Mountain Press, 1994), 119.
18. In November 1861, as many as 5,000 Confederate soldiers in western Virginia were sick in hospitals in the rear. Paul E. Steiner, *Disease in the Civil War* (Charles C. Thomas, 1968), 55. The hotel at Warm Springs, which prior to the war hosted visitors traveling to Bath County, Virginia, for its springs, was converted into a hospital that quartered over 450 men by October 1861. Bath County Historical Society, *Bath County Confederate Hospitals* (n.d.).
19. "From Gen. Donelson's Brigade," *Nashville Union and American*, Sept. 6, 1861, www.newspapers.com.

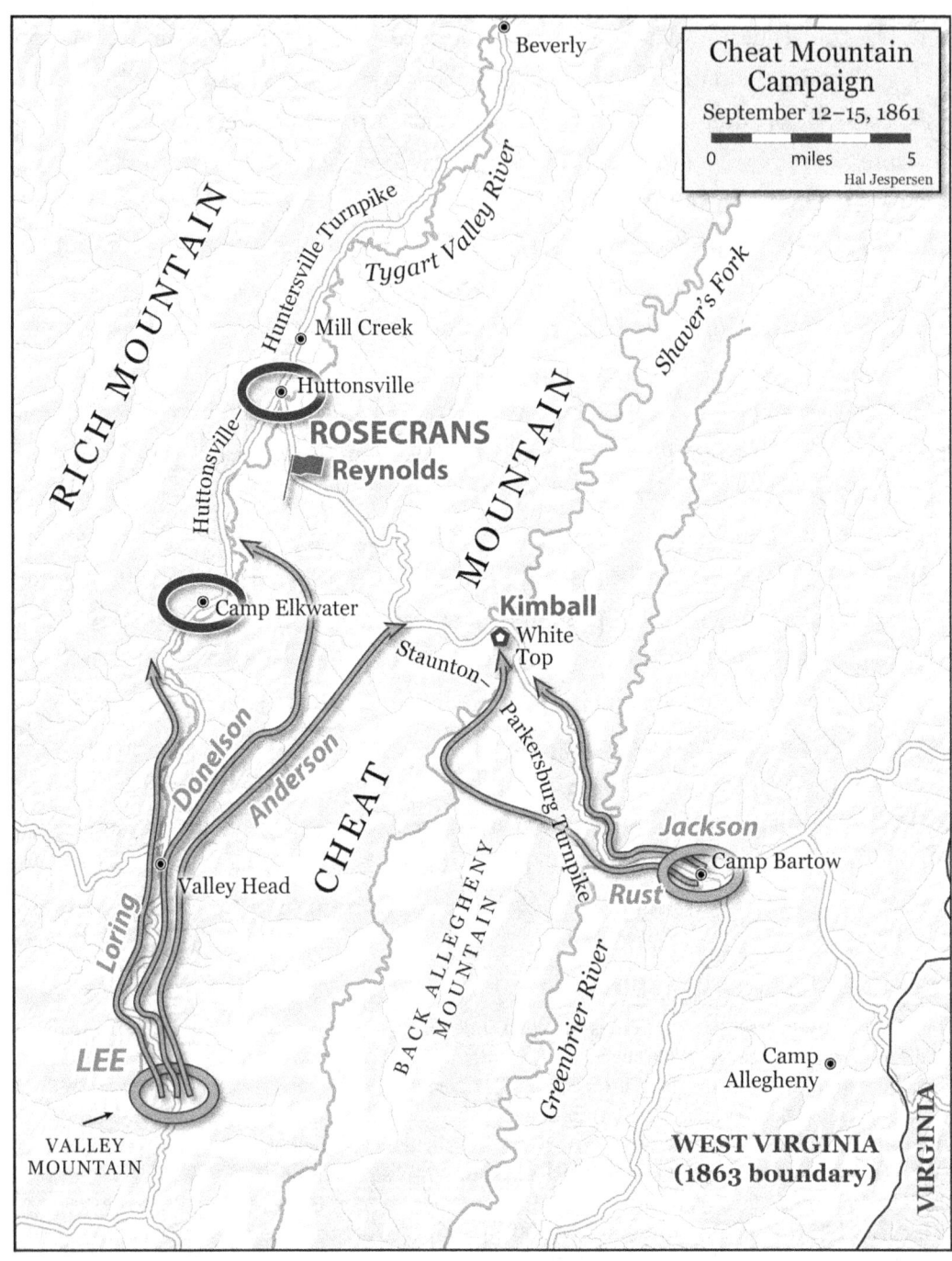

The Cheat Mountain Campaign of September 1861. Although assigned to Donelson's Brigade, the 14th Georgia likely did not accompany Donelson's Tennessee regiments further than Conrad's Mill, just north of Valley Head. (Map by Hal Jespersen)

rains, lack of shelter (other than tents), and impassable roads had "paralyzed" their efforts.[20] But the Confederate experience in western Virginia was a glimpse of the mortality from disease that both armies would incur as the war progressed. For every soldier who died from battle wounds, two died from disease in a war that would be "the last great armed conflict in the world fought without knowledge of the germ theory of disease."[21]

Nevertheless, the time had come for the Confederate troops to go on the offense. Lee developed an elaborate plan for simultaneous attacks against the summit fort on Cheat Mountain and the Union entrenchments at Elkwater, twelve miles north of Valley Mountain on the Huttonsville-Huntersville Turnpike. On September 8, 1861, Loring issued Special Order No. 28, dividing his 5,000 men into brigades. He assigned the 14th Georgia to Brigadier General (Brig. Gen.) Daniel S. Donelson's Third Brigade, which also included two Tennessee infantry regiments. The Third Brigade was to move up the Huttonsville-Huntersville Turnpike, just east of Tygert Valley River, and then attempt to swing in a counter-clockwise arc to attack the Union right flanks at Elkwater. This necessitated marching through heavily-wooded mountain terrain along Stewart Run and Becky Creek.

Brig. Gen. Samuel R. Anderson's Second Brigade, consisting of three Tennessee infantry regiments, was tasked with crossing the western slope of Cheat Mountain to cut the telegraph lines on the Staunton-Parkersburg Turnpike and to prevent reinforcements moving from Camp Elkwater up to the summit fort. The remaining troops in Loring's Huntersville division were to move up the Huttonsville-Huntersville Turnpike to Elkwater. To the east of Cheat Mountain, two brigades at Camp Bartow were tasked with attacking the summit fort some twelve miles to their northwest. Col. Albert Rust

---

20. Steiner, *Disease in the Civil War*, 55. Virtually all of the Confederate regiments on the Huttonsville-Huntersville Turnpike were similarly afflicted. Within three days of arriving at Huntersville, one hundred men in the 16th Tennessee Infantry Regiment were unfit for duty due to illness. John Savage, *The Life of John H. Savage* (Nashville, TN: *n.p.*, 1903), 91-92. One morning, more than five hundred men reported sick in the 16th North Carolina Infantry Regiment. George H. Mills, *History of the Sixteenth North Carolina Regiment in the Civil War* (Rutherfordton, NC: *n.p.*, 1902), 5. Union troops, who were generally better fed, better clothed, and better housed, did not suffer illness in western Virginia to the same degree as did Confederate troops in 1861 but they still suffered the misery caused by poor weather. Snow fell in mid-August on Cheat Mountain, and heavy rain in late September, the remnants of a hurricane, resulted in tents that were "waist high in water." Noe, *The Howling Storm*, 49-50.
21. Jeffrey S. Sartin, "Infectious Diseases during the Civil War: The Triumph of the 'Third Army,'" *Clinical Infectious Diseases* 16, no. 4 (1993): 580.

of the 3rd Arkansas Infantry Regiment, accompanied by a brigade of some 1,500 – 1,600 troops, was to approach the Union fort via a flanking path on an unguarded ridge that Rust had personally reconnoitered. The remaining troops in the assault on the east side of the summit, under Brig. Gen. Henry R. Jackson, were to march directly up the Staunton-Parkersburg Turnpike.

Rust, a former U.S. Congressman who had raised his own regiment just two months earlier, had asked Lee to permit him to lead the attack, which was scheduled for September 12; Lee, who knew that Rust was a friend of Jefferson Davis, agreed, despite the fact that Rust had no military experience.[22] Rust was to give the signal for other brigades to open their attacks. Jackson was to provide assistance as needed to Rust and then march his brigade over the Staunton-Parkersburg Turnpike to Huttonsville.

In retrospect, this five-column operation was overly-ambitious. Notwithstanding his sterling achievements in the Mexican-American War, Lee had never commanded a large force in the field. Still, if the plan had been executed correctly, it would "almost certainly strike and dislodge the Federals from their defenses on Cheat Mountain, at Elkwater, and along the Staunton-Parkersburg Turnpike."[23] But the weakest link of the plan was Lee's decision to grant Rust's request to lead the attack. As Jack Zinn wrote (and emphasized in his own italics), this "*was to prove the most costly and the most critical decision of the entire campaign.*"[24] In Douglas Southall Freeman's words, Lee's consent to Rust's request proved to be a "most expensive 'Yes.'"[25]

When the Huntersville brigades commenced their movement up the Huttonsville-Huntersville Turnpike in anticipation for the September 12 attack, the sick of the 14th Georgia – including Hall – were left behind. Anderson and Donelson moved off the Turnpike into the heavy woods to the east. The men of the 14th Georgia likely accompanied Loring's remaining troops up the Turnpike rather than following Donelson's two Tennessee regiments into the woods.[26] Regimental returns from five

---

22. W. Hunter Lesser, *Rebels at the Gate: Lee and McClellan on the Front Line of a Nation Divided* (Sourcebooks, 2004), 185.
23. David J. Eicher, *The Longest Night: A Military History of the Civil War* (Simon & Schuster, 2001), 115.
24. Zinn, *Cheat Mountain*, 84. David Eicher similarly contends that perhaps Lee's greatest error in his first campaign was "allowing an inexperienced commander without military training to play the crucial role on which all else depended." Eicher, *Longest Night*, 116.
25. Freeman, *R. E. Lee: A Biography*, I:561.
26. "Col Bonely's (sic) regiment, from Georgia, did not remain with us long, and did not participate in the marches and hardships we shall attempt to narrate." [Joseph G. Carrigan], *Cheat Mountain; or Unwritten Chapter of the Late War, by a member of the Bar* (Fayetteville, TN: Albert B. Tavel, 1885), 6.

companies of the 14th Georgia note that those companies left Edray on September 8th and marched to Conrad's Mill (also known as Coonrod's) via Big Spring and Valley Mountain; however, only 255 men were healthy enough to make the march.[27] They arrived at Coonrods on September 11. So did the rains after eleven straight dry days; as one soldier described the weather conditions, "the windows of the heavens were wide open, and rain in torrents fell as it never fell since before the flood."[28]

Despite a horrendous rainstorm on the night of September 11, all five columns were in place on the morning of September 12 but faced slick marching conditions and fog. Lee's planned simultaneous assault never launched because Rust never gave the signal, later claiming to Loring that he had found out from captured Union pickets that there were between 4,000 and 5,000 federal troops defending the summit fort.[29] He maintained that all of his field officers said that it would be "madness" to attack the fort, which Rust personally observed was defended by entrenchments and "heavy and impassable abatis."[30] Rust's failure to launch his assigned mission meant that Lee's other brigades, including those on the Huttonsville-Huntersville Turnpike, waited in vain for a signal that never came. Soldiers in Donelson's two Tennessee regiments did engage in minor skirmishes near Elkwater, but by the close of September 12, 1861, Lee had clearly not achieved either of his objectives – Union troops still held both Elkwater and the summit on Cheat Mountain. Blaming the weather, Lee wrote the governor of Virginia that if it had not been for the rainstorm on the night of September 11, he had no doubt his campaign would have succeeded.[31]

The 14th Georgia retreated to Big Springs, Virginia, arriving there on September 15. Two days later, Hall rejoined the regiment, only to be sent north on picket duty across

---

27. J. F. B., "Hardships and Sufferings of Our Troops – An Appeal to the Ladies of the South," *Savannah Republican*, November 1, 1861, https://access.newspaperarchive.com.
28. Noe, *The Howling Storm*, 48.
29. *OR*, Ser. 1, vol. 5, p. 191. Noe writes that Rust had heard "tall tales from prisoners that depicted the summit as a veritable Sebastopol." Noe, *A Howling Storm*, 49. Although some historians have interpreted Union reports as suggesting that there were only 300 Federal troops at the summit fort (later named Fort Milroy), Jack Zinn concludes, on the basis of multiple sources, that the evidence was "overwhelming" that close to 3,000 Union soldiers defended the fort. Zinn, *Cheat Mountain*, 150. Union records indicate that the 14th Indiana Regiment was joined at the summit by troops of the 24th Ohio Infantry Regiment and 25th Ohio Infantry Regiment.
30. *OR*, Ser. 1, vol. 5, p. 191.
31. R. E. Lee to John Letcher, September 17, 1861, Clifford Dowdey and Louis H. Manarin, eds., *The Wartime Papers of R. E. Lee* (Bramhall House, 1961), 75.

Valley Mountain. He wrote of how he had nothing to eat for two days and was subjected to constant rain, which caused the valleys to run with water "like rivers" and wash away men and teams of horses. According to regimental reports, the 14th Georgia, on orders from Col. William Gilham of the 21st Virginia Infantry Regiment, departed Big Springs on September 28 and arrived at Elk Mountain two days later. The Georgians remained at Elk Mountain until October 9, 1861, executing its assigned mission of blockading the Huttonsville-Huntersville Turnpike between Big Springs and Marlin's Bottom. The regiment then spent several days at Edray, where Hall suffered an attack of typhoid fever. The regiment arrived back at Marlin's Bottom on October 11 and moved to Huntersville on October 28.

Throughout its time in western Virginia, both the regiment and Company G experienced a great deal of churn in its officer ranks. Capt. Harris had finally joined the company in western Virginia in late September 1861 but aggravated his leg injury by walking eight miles over "mountains rocks and mud;" he was forced to take a room in Warm Springs, an appreciable distance from the company.[32] The Company Muster Roll showed Harris as absent on sick furlough in September and October 1861.[33] According to David Champion, the company was "captained" at Huntersville by a lieutenant from another company because Harris had moved into a hotel due to illness.[34] Command would have usually devolved to the Company G first lieutenant, Asa Giddens, but Giddens had resigned at Marlin's Bottom on October 2, 1861. Company G had two second lieutenants, but the junior of those, Robert Weeks, had died of illness at Huntersville in September 1861. Giddens's and Weeks's billets were gapped until mid-November 1861, when Terrell T. Mounger was elected First Lieutenant and John R.

---

32. "I have just landed in a road waggon (the only conveyance to be had at this place) from two miles this side of Big Spring, some sixty miles from here, where I caved in, the having, owing to the roads being so bad, to walk upon my broken leg and ankle some eight miles, over mountains rocks and mud. I am now in my room resting, having a very badly swollen ankle with a very pretty abscess upon it." William A. Harris, "War Correspondence, Sept. 22, 1861," *Albany Patriot*, Oct. 3, 1861, http://gahistoricnewspapers.galileo.usg.edu.
33. Civil War Service Records, Confederate Records, (www.fold3.com/image/35576463); Georgia Fourteenth Infantry, "Company Muster Roll Sept-Oct 1861" entry for William A. Harris, citing National Archives and Records Administration microfilm publication "Compiled Service Records of Confederate Soldiers Who Served in Organizations from the State of Virginia," M266, Roll 0285, Record Group 109, National Archives, Washington, D.C.
34. Champion, *Memoirs*, "Huntersville 1861."

Bozeman was elected junior second lieutenant. Thus, Company G likely spent several weeks in western Virginia, with 2nd Lieutenant William A. Johnston as its only elected company officer present.

The regimental command of the 14th Georgia was likewise in disarray. The regiment's second in command, Lieutenant Colonel (Lt. Col.) Whiteford Ramsay, submitted his resignation less than a week after arriving in Huntersville. Col. Brumby, at the age of fifty-one, had taken ill in Staunton and did not bear up well under the arduous conditions in western Virginia. He went to Richmond for several weeks at some point in late September or early October to ask that the regiment be reassigned.[35] The regimental major, Felix Price, would have been the logical choice to replace Ramsay as lieutenant colonel, but Price had been court-martialed in Monterey for "drunkenness and improper conduct towards a lady."[36] According to Lieutenant Patterson of Company E, Price was "under arrest for a long while" and "publicly reprimanded in general orders."[37] Patterson also maintained that once Price rejoined the regiment, he simply "continued to hover around the Regiment" until rejoining it in its march out of the mountains in November 1861.[38] Promotion to lieutenant colonel, effective September 1, 1861, appears to have gone instead to Company B commander Robert W. Folsom, a 26-year-old physician.[39]

---

35. During some of this period the 14th Georgia was subject to the orders of Colonel William Gilham of the 21st Virginia, according to Lieutenant Patterson of Company A and as stated in at least four company muster rolls. As Lieutenant Patterson wrote to his wife, "Brumby left us at a critical moment to the mercy of the stranger." Patterson to Wife and Children, October 4, 1861, "Incomplete Patterson Correspondence."

36. Josiah B. Patterson, Patterson to Wife and Children, December 10, 1861, "Incomplete Patterson Correspondence". As Patterson noted in a letter home, Captain Lester, his company commander, had to remain at Monterey, Virginia, in early August 1861 to serve as a witness at Price's court-martial. Patterson to Wife and Children, August 5, 1861, "Incomplete Patterson Correspondence."

37. Patterson to Wife and Children, December 10, 1861, "Incomplete Patterson Correspondence."

38. Patterson held little back in his opinion of Price, stating that Price was "totally destitute of every qualification that fits a man for a military leader" and had "forfeited the respect of the men so that no after conduct [could] regain their confidence." Patterson to Daughter, December 12, 1861, "Incomplete Patterson Correspondence."

39. Civil War Service Records, Confederate Records, (www.fold3.com/image/36000849); Georgia Fourteenth Infantry, "Company Muster Roll Sept-Oct 1861" and (www.fold3.com/image/36000872); Georgia Fourteenth Infantry, "Register of Roster of Confederate Officers," entries for Robert W. Folsom, citing National Archives and Records Administration microfilm publication "Compiled Service Records of Confederate Soldiers Who Served in Organizations from the State of Virginia," M266, Roll 0284, Record Group 109, National Archives, Washington, DC.

It was survival itself in western Virginia that provided Company G its greatest challenge in the fall of 1861. According to Patterson, the regiment was down to 250 men from the 750 who had departed Atlanta in July.[40] Capt. Harris's September 22, 1861, letter to the *Albany Patriot* from Warm Springs painted a bleak picture of the company's experiences in West Virginia.

> This is the last part of the world. Never wish a man in Hell, but in North-western Virginia a soldier paddling through this mud ankle deep, and he is in a mile of Hell. Empty wagons with four horses can scarcely get through. The soldiers only get a half ration a day... The army is awfully reduced by sickness, some 800 down with typhoid fever at Big Spring - 240 here, and all along the road sick men by the score. The 14th Georgia has some 200 men fit for duty at this time....
>
> In my company the sickness is severe. I have had the misfortune to lose several gallant soldiers. Lieut. R. J. Weeks, a gentleman and soldier, eager to meet the enemy, has met a worse enemy than Yankee bullets, viz: typhoid fever, and a few days ago he breathed his last calmly and serenely... I have also the painful duty to record the deaths of privates William Gunter, Manning McCraney, Pearson D. Brown, Fletcher Harden, of the Yancey Independents. One of my best soldiers, James Bass, shot his left hand off a few days since, with a Mississippi Rifle, by an unforeseen accident. He is doing pretty well. Many others of my company are quite sick. I am doing all in my power to remove them to these springs or to the Bath Alum Springs.[41]

As one Tennessean reported, many of the Georgia regiment under Colonel "Blomley" (sic) died at "Marlin Bottom;" indeed, "[m]en never died more rapidly, it seemed to us,

---

40. Patterson to Wife and Children, October 4, 1861, "Incomplete Patterson Correspondence."
41. War Correspondence, Sept. 22, 1861, Wm. A. Harris, *Albany Patriot*, Oct. 3, 1861, http://gahistoricnewspapers.galileo.usg.edu. A soldier in Company E corroborated Harris's statement of troop availability, writing home to his mother, "Our Reg[iment] is in exceeding discouraging circumstance at this time. We can muster only 2 hundred fighting men. The measles and typhoid fever having prostated (sic) stout framed and noble hearted men" Robert N. Rogers to Mother, September 5, 1861, *Crimson and Sabres: A Confederate Record of Forsyth County, Georgia*, ed. Don L. Shadburn (McNaughon & Gunn, 1997), 21. Private William Wood of Company F wrote home in November 1861 that of the 250 men who had enlisted with him, over half had died by October 1861. Mark A. Weitz, *A Higher Duty: Desertion among Georgia Troops during the Civil War* (University of Nebraska Press, 2000), 96.

than did these Georgians in Northwest Virginia. One-half of that regiment, no doubt, died while we were in those mountains."[42]

Following the failed Cheat Mountain campaign, Lee, Loring, and most of Loring's army moved to the Kanawha Valley in mid-September in support of General Floyd. Although some sources place the 14th Georgia under Floyd's command in the Kanawha Valley area of western Virginia, none of the available company records or personal accounts support such a movement. Rather, it appears that the men of the 14th Georgia, likely too infirm to travel south, remained on the Huttonsville-Huntersville line, part of a small force charged with monitoring the Union troops at Cheat Mountain."[43] The evidence that the regiment remained in the Huntersville-Marlon's Bottom area includes nine company muster rolls that show that those companies were at Huntersville for September and October 1861. Five of the company muster rolls provide narratives of their company movements, all of which were along the Huntersville-Huttonsville turnpike. Three personal accounts of the 14th Georgia in western Virginia – Hall's diary, Patterson's letters, and Champion's memoirs – also place the 14th Georgia squarely on the Huttonsville-Huntersville Turnpike between August and the end of October 1861.

Although the regiment had left Lynchburg "seven hundred and seventy strong," by this point in the Western Virginia Campaign, that number was greatly reduced when only "one hundred and twenty reported for duty."[44] This shockingly low number was corroborated by a Georgia newspaper, which reported that of 760 men previously in the regiment, only 125 were capable of performing duty as of October 23, 1861; one hundred had died, some fifty had been discharged, and thirteen commissioned officers had resigned.[45] Family and friends in Worth County who sent clothing and other goods

---

42. Carrigan, *Cheat Mountain*, 94.
43. In 1864 Regimental Adjutant Captain Thomas C. Moore wrote, "General Loring in command of the greater portion of the army, went down on the Gauly river, and the remainder left at Marlin's Bottom were under the command of General Donaldson (sic), of Tennessee – an officer long to be remembered for his kindness and courtesy." Folsom, *Heroes and Martyrs of Georgia*, 145.
44. Folsom, *Heroes and Martyrs of Georgia*, 145.
45. "Horrible Sufferings of the 14th Georgia Regiment," *The Central Georgian*, November 6, 1861, https://access.newspaperarchive.com.

to Company G surely had no frame of reference to comprehend the scale of losses within a unit that had yet to fire a shot in combat.[46]

The high percentage of sick troops almost certainly contributed, at least in part, to Lee's decision to abandon any thoughts of subsequent operations against Cheat Mountain. Physician Paul E. Steiner, writing on the impact of disease in the Civil War, contends that "communicable diseases helped greatly to defeat that Army of the Northwest," with nearly half of the men in Loring's nineteen regiments sick at the same time.[47] Historian James McPherson maintains that Lee failed in his Western Virginia Campaign "in part because illness incapacitated so many of his men."[48] Historian Kenneth Noe simply writes that "nature remained as much Lee's nemesis as the Union Army."[49]

Hall writes that "many a poor soldier saw his last day . . . and his remains left in the old bleak mountains." Some of those remains are still interred in Confederate cemeteries at Marlin's Bottom and Huntersville. Many more were transported to, and died at, the Confederate hospital at Rockbridge Alum Springs, Virginia. One can only imagine how much higher the casualties would have been if the 14th Georgia had been forced to "winter over" in western Virginia. However, orders to northern Virginia spared them that fate.

By November 1861, the Confederacy realized that continued operations in northwest Virginia were fruitless and gutted its army there, leaving only 4,500 troops to guard the passes over the winter. Loring kept some troops on the Monterey and Huntersville lines but otherwise disposed of his army by moving Donelson and the Tennessee regiments to reinforce Floyd and directing the remainder to travel to Staunton to await further orders.[50] The 14th Georgia, with little except casualties to show for its time in western Virginia, surely welcomed the change of duty. As one Milledgeville newspaper wrote in late November 1861, "the bleak mountains of Western Virginia [had] cost more in blood and treasure than they are worth."[51]

---

46. For example, in early November, almost ninety individuals in Worth County contributed clothing, blankets, coats, shoes, tobacco, red pepper, paper, ink, and envelopes to Company G. "Worth County Contributions to the 'Yancey Independents,'" *Albany Patriot*, November 7, 1861. https://gahistoric-newspapers.galileo.usg.edu.
47. Steiner, *Disease in the Civil War*, 53.
48. McPherson, *Battle Cry of Freedom*, 488. McPherson also attributed the failure of the Cheat Mountain campaign to difficult terrain, inexperienced officers, and the weather, with rain that fell almost daily starting in late July. Ibid., 322.
49. Noe, *The Howling Storm*, 48.
50. *OR*, Ser. 1, vol. 5, p. 938.
51. "The 14th Georgia Regiment," Milledgeville *Southern Federal Union*, Nov. 26, 1861, https://access.newspaperarchive.com.

Special Orders No. 222 of November 14, 1861, ultimately directed the 14th Georgia and the 16th North Carolina Infantry Regiment to march to Mount Jackson in the Shenandoah Valley and then travel by rail via Strasburg to Manassas to join Gen. Joseph E. (J.E.) Johnston's Department of Northern Virginia.[52] However, at least some portion of the regiment, including Hall, departed Huntersville between November 9 and 13 for Millboro, where boarded the railroad to Manassas Junction.[53] The regiment arrived on or about November 20, 1861, at Manassas Junction, where the Manassas Gap Railroad joined the Orange & Alexandria Railroad.

Once in Manassas, the 14th Georgia found itself initially assigned to garrison duties at Camp Pickens, the major supply depot at Manassas Junction on the road to Centerville.[54] They performed guard and fatigue duty at various sites around Manassas, which gave Hall the opportunity to visit what he called the "great Battle-ground." He also helped construct two or three local fortifications before the regiment moved as part of Col. Wade Hampton's brigade to the banks of the nearby Occoquon River. The winter of 1861-1862 would prove to be a welcome change of pace for the regiment.

Pocket Notebook Narrative of April 1, 1862

We left Lynchburg [July] 29th and proceeded on the cars Via Charlottesville Wayne[s]borough and arrive[d] at Staunton [July] 31st and there we left the Cars, and took up the line of march with our knapsacks on our backs and Proceeded over Several ranges of mountains and through deep ravines and Sometimes along the bed of a cold mountain stream for Several miles and over some of

---

52. *OR*, Ser. 1., vol. 5, p. 954.
53. "Special Correspondence from Col. Brumby's (14th) Regiment, November 16, 1861," *Southern Confederacy*, November 24, 1861, www.newspapers.com. The author, identified only as "Dixie," wrote that Colonel Brumby had gone ahead to Richmond.
54. *OR*, Ser. 1, vol. 51, pt. 2, p. 402.

the highest mountains in the Southern Confederacy. And the clouds would be below us, when we would strike camp at night we be so fatigued and exhausted that we would fall down on the ground and lie there till next morning and Sometimes on the mud and water.

We arrived at Huntersville Pocahontas County a Small village Situated in a muddy valley between two mountains and pitched our tents in a valley where there was nothing but mud August 5th. And there Some of our men were taken Sick and some died there. We received orders to march and on the 18th we took up the line of march and arrived on Greenbrier River the same day, and pitched our tents on an eminence between two mountains and there two thirds of the men in our reg[iment] was taken Sick and I was among that number and I came as near dying as any body ever did to live. A many a poor soldier saw his last day at that place and his remains left in the old bleak mountains.

I was taken Sick the next day after we got there the 19th. I had the measels and mumps and fever and was so I could not get out of my tent till about September 5th and all of that month I was so weak I could hardly walk and after I got so I could go about [I] was taken down with the camp Diarea and flux and it brought me verry low again but by the help of the Lord that watches over us day and night I was able to be up again but I had the Severest cough all the fall and winter that I ever saw anybody have.

The well portion of our regiment received orders to advance on the enemy on Cheat mountain the 5th or 6th of September and they left all the sick behind. They proceeded up near cheat mountain and the roads was so bad that we could not get supplies of provision to our men and they were all about to perish and we had to retreat back to Big Springs. I got so I could travel and I left Greenbrier River the 18th Sept. And I proceeded up and joined our regiment at Big spring and our reg[iment] sent out pickets 8 and 10 miles above Big Spring and I experienced the worst time that I ever Saw. I went out on Picket and had to cross Valley mountain for two days and nights without any thing to eat and it was raining as hard as it could pour all the time. And it had rain[ed] So much that the valleys were running with water like rivers and we had to wade water and it [was] cold and it run so swift that it washed away waggons and teams and drowned Several men and horses and before I got back to Big Spring our army had retreated back towards Huntersville and burned all our tents and part of our clothing and we lost nea[r]ly all our cooking utensils and the roads was so bad that we had to wade mud knee deep and some of our waggons and horses would bog up so that they never got out.[55]

We arrived back to Elk mountain and stayed there a week or two and we went down to Edray a neighborhood Post Office at the foot of Elk mountain and we stayed there three or four days and there I was taken with an attack of the Typhoid fever and was verry low for some time, and we left Edray and arrived at Greenbrier River and there we staid about two weeks and there we drew our first wages from the Confederate States which was $13.90 in money and $12.00 worth of clothing.[56]

---

55. The remnants of a Category 1 hurricane passing through western Virginia in late September contributed to the deluge of rain that caused great suffering by both Confederate and Union troops. Noe, *The Howling Storm*, 50.

56. This $12.00 was likely a clothing commutation allowance. As the war progressed, the Confederacy began to issue uniforms such as the ubiquitous "Richmond Depot Jacket," but many soldiers still bought their own clothing or relied on items sent from home, while others obtained clothing by plundering Union camps – and corpses -- after battle. Joseph T. Glatthaar, *General Lee's Army: From Victory to Collapse* (Free Press 2008), 174-175. Hall never mentions receiving or wearing any apparel item identifiable as part of a distinctive Confederate uniform, and he writes often of lacking both adequate clothing and shoes. The lack of sufficient footwear was the most glaring issue facing Confederate logistics, and one which Bell Wiley describes as the "most pervasive and the most keenly felt of all deficiencies." Wiley, *Life of Johnny Reb*, 119. The Confederacy was so desperate for shoes that it resorted to finding the solution within its army ranks: late in the war Private James C. Lunsford of Company G, a shoemaker by trade, was placed on detached duty to Columbus, Georgia, to make shoes.

We left Greenbrier River about the last of October and arrived at Huntersville the same day. We left Huntersville Nov 13th and after having to wade Several rivers and other Streams we arrived at Milboro Station on the Rail Road. We took the cars at Milboro and went by the way of Staunton Charlottesville Gordonville Orange Court-house, Culpepper Court-house and to Manassas and there we were attached to the Garrison and had to Guard the great Commissary Department Hospital Department and Armory Department and while I was there I visited the great Battle-ground of Manassas. Besides our guard duty we had to build two or three forts while we were at Manassas.

3

"MY FEET WAS SO SORE THAT I COULD SCARCELY PUT THEM TO THE GROUND" NORTHERN VIRGINIA TO THE PENINSULA: JANUARY – LATE MAY 1862

On January 5, 1862, Hall and the 14th Georgia joined other units of Hampton's Brigade near Bacon Race Church in Prince William County, Virginia, just southeast of Manassas Junction.[1] The brigade, which also included Hampton's Legion and two other infantry regiments, was tasked with performing picket duty on a twelve-mile stretch of the lower Occoquan River and guarding artillery batteries at potential river crossing points.

Joseph E. Johnston, commander of the Department of Northern Virginia, considered this area of the Occoquan as his most exposed position and, thus, the most likely site to be attacked by Union troops.[2] The 14th Georgia's sector was at Davis Ford, while Hampton's other regiments were at Wolf Run Shoals, Occoquan, and Colchester, Virginia. Lt. Col. James B. Griffin of Hampton's Legion wrote home that Hampton now had enough troops to ensure that the Union troops would get a "warm reception, wherever they may choose to cross the Occoquan."[3]

During January and February 1861, the 14th Georgia dug rifle pits and built breastworks as well as an artillery emplacement. Despite the fact that the regiment had to pitch its tents on snow-covered ground, Hall considered this a relatively comfortable

---

1. William S. Connery, *Civil War: Northern Virginia 1861* (History Press, 2011), 114; Rod Andrew, Jr., *Wade Hampton: Confederate Warrior to Southern Redeemer* (University of North Carolina Press, 2008), 87.
2. Andrew, *Wade Hampton*, 87.
3. Judith N. McArthur and Orville Vernon Burton, *A Gentleman and an Officer: A Military and Social History of James B. Griffin's Civil War* (Oxford University Press, 1996), 133.

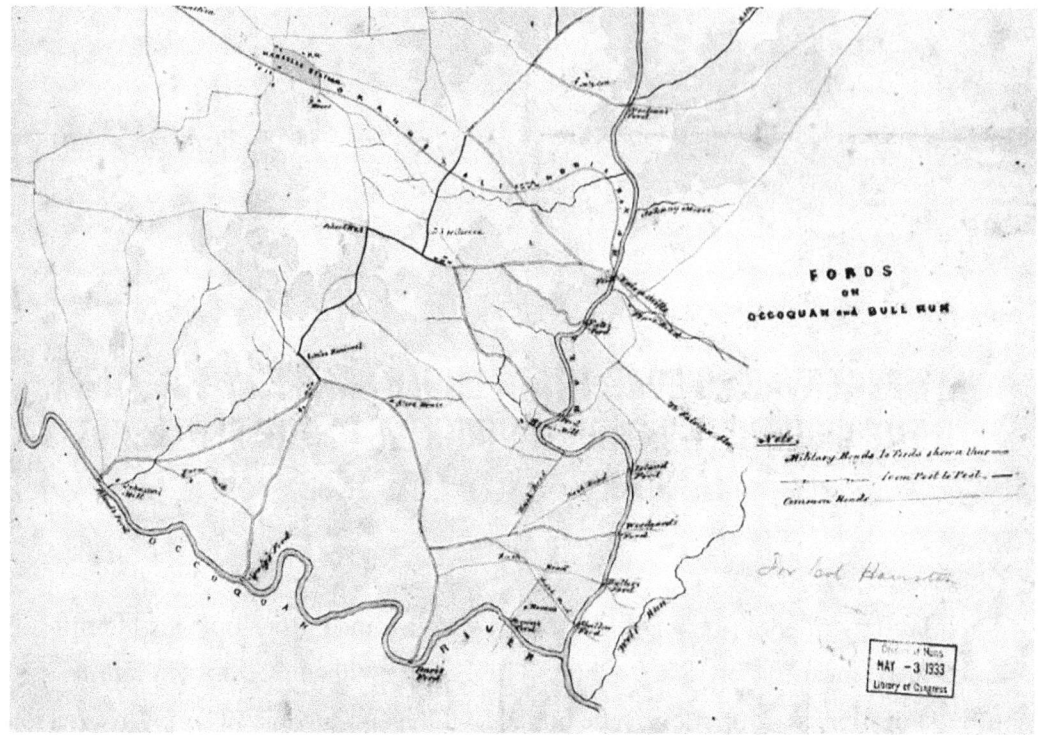

Map depicting the fords on the Occoquan. The 14th Georgia encamped at Davis Ford over the winter of 1861-1862. The 16th North Carolina Infantry, also in Hampton's Brigade, encamped at Wolf Shoals. (Library of Congress)

period for the regiment because wood and water were plentiful, and the soldiers' tents had chimneys, which not only provided warmth but also offered the option of cooking meals inside.[4] This assigned area was an important one, given that the regiment was tasked with defending both Davis Ford and the artillery batteries that guarded it. The 14th Georgia furnished pickets at Davis Ford around the clock, as well as fifty or sixty men for daily fatigue duty.

The regiment continued to experience personnel issues among its field commanders. On December 9, 1861, Felix Price was elected to replace Brumby, who had resigned on November 21. Lt. Col. Folsom refused to run for regimental colonel, which meant that

---

4. Hampton preferred his troops live in tents, thinking them healthier quarters than "miserable little huts." Edward G. Longacre, *Gentleman and Soldier: A Biography of Wade Hampton* (Rutledge Hill Press, 2003), 60. Although Hampton reported significant illness among his other troops, the 14th Georgia tolerated the conditions on the Occoquan without succumbing to the severe number of lives lost that it had experienced in western Virginia.

Price ran unopposed.⁵ Private William Rogers of Company E, who studied law before the war, pulled no punches in describing Price as a "miserable contemptible low flung lowlife vagabond" who was so drunk that he fell off his horse while drilling the troops.⁶ Patterson likewise wrote home that Price had often been drunk since the regiment arrived at Manassas Junction; on the day he assumed command, Price was "so drunk that he could not perform the simplest maneuvers in Battalion drill. Sober he is incapable of drilling a company much less of maneuvering troops in an engagement, Such is our Colonel."⁷ Two days later, Patterson described Price as "totally destitute of every qualification that fits a man for a military leader, and long since he has forfeited the respect of the men...."⁸

Bacon Race Church, which served as Hampton's brigade headquarters in early 1862. The 14th Georgia's encampment at Davis Ford was located some three miles from the church, which also served as a hospital and storehouse. (Photo Courtesy of Historic Prince William, Inc.)

The regiment discharged over seventy men for disability once it arrived in northern Virginia, including several from Company G. According to Patterson, only 530 men remained in the 14th Georgia by early December 1861.⁹ Although there are insufficient

---

5. Patterson to Wife and Children, December 4, 1861, "Incomplete Patterson Correspondence." Patterson predicted a dire future for the regiment if Price were elected, writing home that Maj. Price's "elevation will but ruin us."
6. Private William E. Rogers of Company E wrote, "The doom of this Regiment is sealed. The last ray of hope is gone. We are hence forth & forever to be the laughing stock of the army. The object of special ridicule, derision, & contempt.... The Reg. has been almost totally disorganized ever since it entered the service – it is now ruined beyond all hope unless Price be cashiered for his disgraceful conduct today. I forgot to tell you in mentioning his drunkenness that he fell off his horse. It would have been a fortunate circumstance if he had broken his neck." William E. Rogers, Letter to Father, December 9, 1861, in Shadburn, *Crimson and Sabres*, 23-24.
7. Patterson to Wife and Children, December 10, 1861, "Incomplete Patterson Correspondence."
8. Price failed "in a solitary instance" to "perform the duties of Major" or share the "hardships exposures or dangers" of the regiment in western Virginia. Patterson to Wife and Children, December 12, 1861, "Incomplete Patterson Correspondence."
9. Patterson to Wife and Children, December 10, 1861, "Incomplete Patterson Correspondence."

records to determine the exact number of men who died or were discharged by the close of 1861, Company G had lost at least one-fourth of their July 9, 1861, enlistees. In fact, no company within the regiment lost more men in western Virginia than did Company G, which accounted for almost one-third of the regiment's deaths during those fifteen weeks. As part of a recruiting effort to rebuild the regiment's numbers, Lieutenant Johnston of Company G returned to Worth County and enlisted some two dozen new recruits on March 4, 1862. The new recruits received a $50 bounty for enlisting.

Company G also continued to experience churn among its senior leaders. On January 28, 1862, Harris was elected to Price's former rank as major. That left a vacancy as captain of Company G, which First Lieutenant Terrell T. Mounger was elected to fill.[10] David Champion described Mounger as a "lovable character, gentle and sympathetic, commanding strict discipline, yet, loved by the entire company."[11] Mounger's brother-in-law, Robert Shine, who was the company's initial 4th Sergeant, was elected 1st Lieutenant. Both Mounger's and Shine's promotions dated to February 22, 1862.

Although there was snow on the ground during all of January and February, Hall was comfortable, passing "the cold Bleak winter of North Eastern Va better than [he] expected among the Snow Bleached hill of the Occoquan River." The regiment had a peaceful winter because the feared Union excursions across Davis Ford never materialized. Although the regiment had been in Virginia since late July 1861, the 14th Georgia still had not engaged Union troops in combat.[12]

The regiment's quiet life on the Occoquan changed suddenly in early March, however, when J. E. Johnston grew concerned that the approaching spring weather would spur Union commander General George B. McClellan to commence campaigning. Feeling over-extended and worried that he would not be able to hold at the Occoquan, Johnston elected to fall back forty miles to the Rappahannock River, abandoning Manassas and Centerville in the process. This movement, although unpopular with many in the South, dashed McClellan's plan for an amphibious landing on the Rappahannock in hopes of

---

10. Mounger was a Worth County physician who served briefly in the 4th Georgia Infantry before being promoted in November 1861 to 1st Lieutenant of Company G, 14th Georgia.
11. Champion, *Memoirs*, "The Green Brier River Raid."
12. In March 1862, Patterson wrote his daughter about a patrol where he hoped to be the first man in the regiment to fire upon the enemy. Patterson to Daughter, March 28, 1862, "Incomplete Patterson Correspondence."

outflanking Johnston and blocking the Confederate army from coming to Richmond's aid. McClellan opted instead for an amphibious landing at Union-held Fortress Monroe in Hampton Roads, followed by a westward advance towards Richmond seventy-five miles up the peninsula between the York River and James River.

After J. E. Johnston ordered his troops stationed south of the Occoquan to move to Fredericksburg, staff officers and commanders worked frantically to prepare to march on short notice.[13] That notice came on March 7, 1862, when the brigade was ordered to carry what it could and destroy the remainder. As Hampton wrote, "With the means at my disposal I moved, literally in the face of the enemy, four regiments of infantry, three batteries, containing 31 guns and gun-carriages, and 120 cavalry . . . over roads that were scarcely passable, a distance of 50 miles."[14] It was a Herculean effort by Hampton, whose division commander, Brig. Gen. William H. Whiting, wrote:

> The difficulties surrounding Colonel Hampton were indeed great. An extended line, insufficient transportation, an active and superior enemy in his front, incessant skirmishing all along his outposts; his army was watched and shelled from the enemy's fleet. Balloons had been up every day for some days previous on both sides of the Potomac, and from the activity of the enemy and the fact that the country people and negroes had got suspicion of the move it was considered certain that the enemy would attack at once. It is due to that distinguished, active, and vigilant officer to say that here, as everywhere, he conducted his brigade with consummate judgment, precision, and skill.[15]

In order to preserve public property, Hampton, faced with a shortage of wagons, reluctantly ordered his men to abandon their private baggage.[16] This distressed Hall because it meant having to repurchase those abandoned items at his own expense. Some of that loss, however, may have been attributable to poor packing on the part of the

---

13. McArthur and Burton, *A Gentleman and an Officer*, 168.
14. Andrew, *Wade Hampton*, 88.
15. *OR*, Ser. 1, vol. 5, p. 530.
16. According to Griffin, Hampton had received the order late on a Friday afternoon to start his wagons south that night and his troops at daylight the next morning. McArthur and Burton, *A Gentleman and an Officer*, 169. Hampton lamented the loss of private property to his soldiers, writing in his official report, "it seems to be a hard case to make the soldier bear a loss which was caused by no fault of his own." *OR*, Ser. 1, vol. 5, p. 534.

This map of the Eastern Theater shows the 14th Georgia's journey from the Occoquan to the Virginia Peninsula in March-April 1862. (Map by Hal Jespersen)

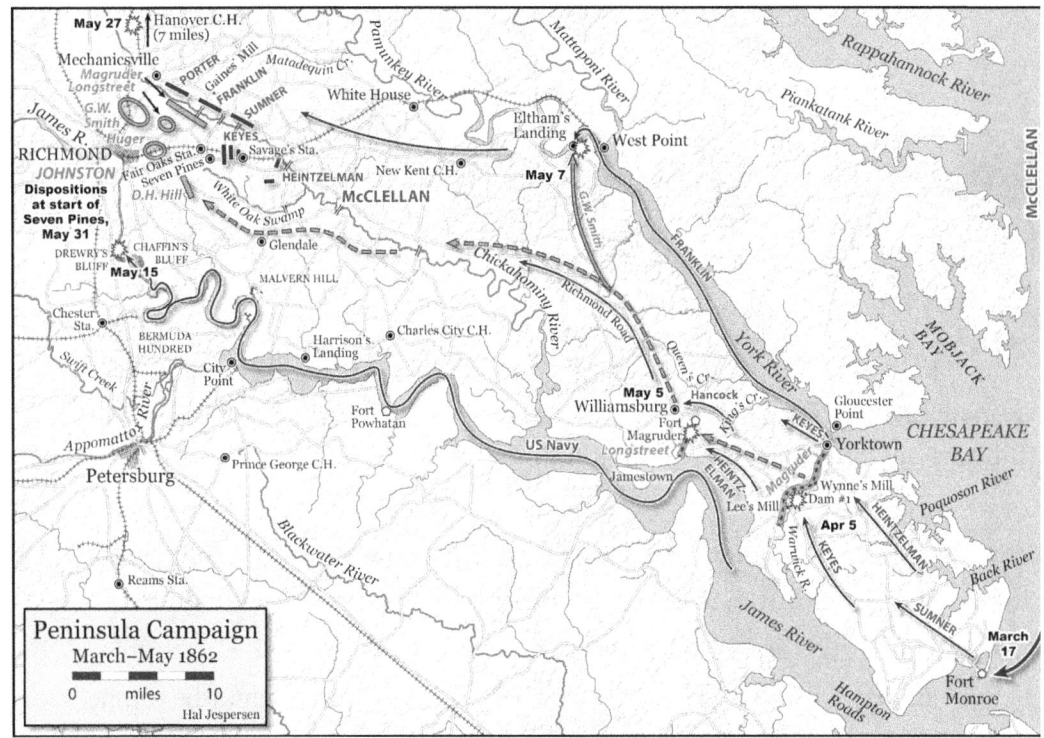

From mid-April until early May 1862, the 14th Georgia was encamped east of Halfway House, roughly midway between Yorktown and Williamsburg. (Map by Hal Jespersen, from *To Hell or Richmond: The 1862 Peninsula Campaign* by Doug Crenshaw).

regiment. The 16th North Carolina Infantry, with ten wagons, managed to move all its tents and equipment, but the 14th Georgia, with nine wagons, brought only their cooking utensils. Price claimed that he had to destroy his tents for lack of transportation.[17]

Company G, equipped with Mississippi Rifles, was one of two companies entrusted with serving as rear guard for the brigade's move to Fredericksburg.[18] Remaining at Davis Ford until noon, the rear guard did not catch up to the main body of the regiment until nightfall. Although many of Hall's comrades discarded items en route, Hall held

---

17. *OR*, Ser. 1, vol. 5, p. 535.
18. The Mississippi Rifle, more formally known as the US M1841, was the first U.S. Army rifle designed to use percussion caps rather than a flintlock. Eicher, *The Longest Night*, 410. Despite the age of its design, it was still a popular weapon early in the Civil War due to infantrymen's overall preference for rifles over smoothbore long arms.

Confederate fortifications at Yorktown (Library of Congress)

onto his knapsack and some of his clothing.

The regiment reached Fredericksburg on March 11, 1862, and encamped two miles out of town at Camp Bartow. One of the regiment's tasks during its four-week stay in Fredericksburg was to improve its drill techniques. As Private Will Rogers wrote after a review of the regiment by General Johnston, the "miserable thing known and distinguished as the 14th Geo. Reg. looked like a herd of cattle."[19] He went on to say that he would freely give the $60 in his pocket to be in a "good Reg."[20]

Hall started writing in his pocket notebook on April 1, 1862, while the regiment was at Camp Bartow. His first entry was a narrative reflection that began with his thoughts on Lincoln's election. He also began entries in two logs: one was a weather log and the other was "A Table Telling My occupation for the following days Commencing April 1st 1862." Each entry in the latter log was usually just a few words long. He discontinued both of these logs in May 1863.

Due to McClellan's change in strategy, Hampton's Brigade, which had been reassigned from Whiting's Division to Maj. Gen. Gustavus W. Smith's division in late March, did not remain long at Camp Bartow. As McClellan moved his Union troops by sea to Fortress Monroe, Johnston ordered most of his army further south to reinforce Confederate defenses around Richmond. Hall and his fellow troops in the 14th Georgia woke to a 3 a.m. reveille on April 8, 1862, and commenced marching south. Although some of Hampton's troops marched the entire route from Fredericksburg to Ashland, Virginia, the 14th Georgia rode part of the way by rail after marching from Camp Bartow to Milford Station on the Richmond, Fredericksburg, and Potomac Railroad just southwest of Bowling Green in Caroline County. Hall notes that during the three-

---

19. William N. Rogers to Mother, April 2 and April 5, 1862, Shadburn, *Crimson and Sabres*, 32.
20. William N. Rogers to Mother, April 2 and April 5, 1862, Shadburn, *Crimson and Sabres*, 32.

day march, they experienced snow, sleet, and cold rain. The roads had been torn up by wagons and artillery, leaving the men to walk knee-and-ankle-deep in mud and clay.[21] On the evening of April 11, the regiment rode by rail from Milford Station to Ashland Station, some fifty miles away.

On April 15, the regiment began a march from Ashland to Yorktown, a distance, according to Hall, of 86 miles. Hall found it noteworthy that the road he marched from New Kent Court House was the same road George Washington's troops had trod en route to Yorktown. Unlike the march out of Fredericksburg the week before, the 14th Georgia enjoyed "delightful" weather and "extra good" roads leaving Ashland. Hall described the area as the most beautiful he had ever seen.

Confederate sharpshooter. Hall served as a sharpshooter in May 1862 during the Confederate retreat towards Richmond. (*Battles and Leaders of the Civil War*, Yoseloff ed., 1956)

Union operations between the James River and York River in 1862, collectively referred to as the Peninsula Campaign, constituted the single largest campaign of the war.[22] The campaign began when McClellan disembarked tens of thousands of troops at Fortress Monroe commencing in late March and ended when he withdrew his troops from the peninsula in August 1862. It was extremely costly: one out of every four men who fought in the campaign became a casualty, either dead, wounded, captured, or missing.[23]

---

21. As Patterson wrote to his family, "You know I seldom yield to difficulties or complain of hardships But I will say this march was a tight paper." Patterson to Family, April 13, 1862, "Incomplete Patterson Correspondence."
22. Stephen W. Sears, *To the Gates of Richmond: The Peninsula Campaign* (Tichnor and Fields, 1992), xi.
23. Sears, *To the Gates of Richmond*, xii.

In its first few weeks ashore, McClellan's force moved slowly westward from Hampton Roads. Just east of Yorktown lay the Confederate defensive line of Maj. Gen. John McGruder, who was grossly outnumbered by McClellan's troops. But through clever use of ruses, McGruder bluffed McClellan, who spent the war perpetually convinced that he was outnumbered, into thinking that the Confederates had far more troops than they actually did. Rather than seizing the initiative and making a direct frontal attack, McClellan elected to besiege Yorktown, using the period between early April and early May to mount siege artillery.

The 14th Georgia, down to a strength of only 379 (making it the smallest infantry regiment in Hampton's Brigade of over 2,200 men), arrived in Yorktown on April 19, midway through the siege.[24] The brigade was kept in the rear of the Yorktown line, slightly east of Halfway House, Virginia, as part of Gustavus Smith's reserve force. Hall spent most of this period in camp, although he did spend guard duty on the line of battle in Yorktown. He saw a Union observation balloon aloft, and, from the wharf at Yorktown, he could see some of the Union blockading vessels.[25]

Johnston got the jump on McClellan by pulling back Confederate forces the day before the Union commander planned to unleash his siege artillery. Smith's division remained near Halfway House until May 4, at which point it accompanied the bulk of Johnston's troops in their retreat up the Peninsula towards Richmond. Hampton's Brigade served as the rear guard for the division.[26]

On May 4, Hall's regiment marched west to Williamsburg. Although they were continuously harassed by advancing Union troops, they did not participate in the battle of Williamsburg on the following day. As Johnston's army moved west, Smith's division was diverted, ordered to march north on the New Kent Church Road to Barhamsville to cover the Confederate flank closest to the York River.[27] As the regiment departed

---

24. *OR*, Ser. I, vol. 11, pt. III, p. 483.
25. Hall and Elsesser both make reference to the Union's use of balloons on the Peninsula. After convincing the Union army to establish a balloon corps, balloonist Thaddeus Lowe traveled to the Virginia Peninsula in April 1862. In addition to reporting the Confederate evacuation of Yorktown, he also observed the battles of Fair Oaks/Seven Pines and Gaines's Mill from the air. Joseph C. Scott, "The Infernal Balloon: Union Aeronautics During the American Civil War," *Army History*, No. 93 (Fall 2014): 13.
26. McArthur and Burton, *A Gentleman and an Officer*, 207.
27. Douglas Southall Freeman, *Lee's Lieutenants: A Study in Command*, vol. 1, Manassas to Malvern Hill (Scribner, 1970), 192.

Williamsburg, they marched through a soaking rain that Hall wrote had turned the road "half leg deep." The regiment spent the night of May 5 near Barhamsville, roughly five miles south of Eltham's Landing on the York River. The landing was across from West Point, the eastern terminus of the Richmond and York River Railroad. Johnston was concerned that after Yorktown fell, McClellan would send troops up the York River on a "large fleet of transports and 500 or 600 bateaux" to cut off the main body of Confederate forces heading west towards Richmond.[28]

Those concerns proved prescient when Brig. Gen. William B. Franklin disembarked 11,000 Union troops at Eltham's Landing on May 6. Brig. Gen. John B. Hood took his Texas brigade and most of Hampton's Brigade to counter Franklin's forces, which included four batteries of artillery. Although given multiple battle names (including the Battle of Eltham's Landing, the Battle of West Point, and the Battle of Brick House Point), the action, according to Stephen Sears, was more of a "heavy skirmish than a full-fledged battle."[29] According to Hall, the 14th Georgia was tasked with protecting a battery of light artillery, and although he was near enough to "hear the balls whistle," the regiment did not engage Union troops. Hood and Hampton's other men drove Franklin back to the river, permitting the main Confederate army to continue west without molestation. Union casualties, at 186, were far fewer than Hall's estimate of five to six hundred.[30]

After the skirmish at West Point, Hampton's Brigade resumed its trek towards Richmond. Following the old Williamsburg Stage Road, the brigade arrived at Baltimore Crossroads, some two miles west of New Kent Court House, on May 8. Hunger was a major concern for the regiment. Hall wrote that when the 14th Georgia resumed its march to Richmond at midnight on the night of May 7, he and his fellow soldiers were "as hungry as a herd of starved wolves" because they had not eaten in two or three days.[31]

Over the next few days, Hall served in what he described as the "line of battle" near New Kent Court House to protect the rear of the retreat. He was sent out on picket duty on May 14, and on May 15, he was "deployed as a sharpshooter on the line of the enemy." Hall's regiment camped outside of Richmond on May 18. In the days that followed,

---

28. OR Ser. I, vol. 11, pt. 1, p. 275.
29. Sears, *To the Gates of Richmond*, 85.
30. Sears, *To the Gates of Richmond*, 86.
31. Sears quotes a North Carolina soldier who likewise laments that Johnston's troops were hungry as wolves, a complaint that was "echoed by virtually every diarist and letter-writer in the army." Sears, *To the Gates of Richmond*, 88.

he stood brigade guard and picket duty, toured Richmond, and performed at least one scouting mission. The rain and swampy conditions made for miserable living, especially for men lacking adequate shelter. Patterson wrote home that after marching, they had "laid in water at night so much that we can say that we belong to the amphibious."[32]

McClellan followed slowly behind Johnston's army. After linking up with Franklin's forces at Eltham's Landing, McClellan pushed westward, finally reaching White House Landing, Virginia, where he set up his base of operations for a final push to Richmond along the Richmond and York River Railroad.

Company G's first lieutenant, Robert Shine, wrote his wife on May 30 that the company had experienced days without sleep and that scouting patrols had taken them "through some of the worst places in the world and in mud and water all the time."[33] This was likely the last letter that Shine wrote home: he was killed in battle at Seven Pines on the following day.

Pocket Notebook Narrative
Jan 5 – May 28, 1862

We left Manassas Jan 5th and arrived at Davis Ford on Occoquan River the same day and pitched our tents in the Snow. During the months of January and February the snow was on the ground all the time. At this place our Regiment had to furnish pickets to stand at Davis Ford all the time and it had to furnish 50 or 60 men every day for Fatigue duty. We cut down the forest around there about two or three hundred acres and threw up a large battery

---

32. Patterson to Family, June 5, 1862, "Incomplete Patterson Correspondence."
33. Maston O'Neal, *Prologue* (pub. by author, 1985), 130. Shine never had the opportunity to mail the letter. As he lay mortally wounded with his lower spine shot away, Shine asked the Union doctor who was tending to him to send the letter to his wife. The doctor was unable to do so until eleven years later. With the help of the postmaster in Warwick, Georgia, the letter was ultimately delivered to the man whom Captain Mounger's widow had married after the war. Shine's wife had died in the interim, so she never read her husband's last letter to her. Ibid., 131.

for artillery and dug rifle pits and throwed up breast-works and prepared a battle ground in general but they did not attack that point while we were stationed there but we were ready for them if they had a ventured out. We were better Situated there than any place we have been Since we have been in Service and we Stayed there longer than any place we had ever been stationed at before. Water and wood was verry handy and we had chimneys to all our tents and verry comfortable places to Sleep on and we passed off the cold Bleak winter of North Eastern Va better than I expected among the Snow Bleached hill of the Occoquan River. Here about the first of March we drawed wages the Second time from the C. S. A. I drawed $34.90 which was pay only up to the last of October 1861.

On the 7th of March we receved orders to destroy every thing we Possessed but what we could carry on our backs and march a forced march and on the 8th we started, after all of our tents, cooking utensils commissary Stores &c was destroyed. Our company and company (I) having Mississippi Rifle[s] were left behind as rear guards and we stayed down at the ford till near 12 o'clock waiting for the dastard Yankees but they did not come while we stayed and we took up the line of march after our regiment which we overtaken that night. The roads was so bad that our men throwed away nearly every thing they had. Some their knapsacks, and some their clothing but I made out to keep my knapsack and Part of my clothing. Every thing brings such an enormous price that it took nearly all our wages to recruit up again. We arrived at Fredericksburg Spottsulvania County Virginia the 11th of March and there we got tents and cooking utensils and there we were put in a Brigade with Hamtons Legion From South Carolina and the 16th North Carolina Regiment and the 19th Regiment Ga volunteers.

Fredericksburg is a verry thriving and enterprising City in the time of peace, and is distinguished for its manufactorys of Several kinds. There is such a great many implements of war manufactured there Such as bombs and shells of various kinds. It is at the head of navigation on the Rappahannock river. Steam boats and several kinds of sail vessels run up there daily.

On the 8th of April we left Fredericksburg and took up the line of march in a Southern direction and we traveled through the prettiest country I have Seen in Virginia. It is generally verry level and fertile producing the best wheat I ever saw. The 8th and 9th was the most disagreeable weather I ever have Seen. Cold rain and Snow and Sleet fell on us all the time and the road was from ankle to knee deep in mud and Stuff clay for the rain had been falling for Several days and the waggons and artillery had cut up the roads verry bad. All of our tents were behind and we had to stay out of nights and it [was] raining Sleeting and Snowing on us without any Shelter but what the trees afforded. On the 11th we arrived at Milford Station on the railroad and there we took the cars and arrived at Ashland 16 miles above Richmond that night. It is a verry beautiful country around there and puts me in mind of my dear old native Georgia, the Soil is light and Sandy in some parts and is intersected with pine and cedar groves. The country is admirable level around here and letting the eyes sight extend to a great distance. The wheat fields display a beautiful view extending a living green as far as the eyes can see.

We left Ashland and took up the line of march the 15th and we passed through in a South Eastern direction by the way of Hanover Courthouse New [K]ent Courthouse and Williamsburg. We passed through some of the prettiest Country that I ever Saw and what ad[d]ed to the Scene it was delightful weather our whole route and that the roads was extra good. I like my beloved Georgia better than any country but this is the most beautiful country I have ever seen.

We arrived at Yorktown on Saturday the 19th. It is Situated on York River near to where it empties into Chesapeake Bay and in the vicinity of Yorktown it is two or three miles wide. Large Ships and other vessels can land at the place. It is a beautiful view to behold the little Sail boats & Skiffs gliding over the Smoo[th] bosom of the waters. Yorktown is an old antiquated place and is noted in the Revolution as being the place where Cornwallis Surrendered his whole army which was the last engagement of that war and crowned our independence. The road that we marched from New Kent Courthouse to Yorktown is distinguished as being the road that Gen Washington marched his troops along to the memorial battle of Yorktown. At this place I was in the peninsular of Virginia.

The last day of May [April] our regiment was ordered down on the line to stand picket and that evening we marched down to take our Position but before we arrived there the order was countermanded and we marched back to our camps about 10 o'clock P.M. and next morning our reg was up and stirring at 3 o'clock. We sent off all our baggage such as tents, cooking utensils &c and that day till about 5 oclock P. M. we all remained in readiness to march at a moments warning and then we fell in and marched about one mile from camp and there we remained in line-of-battle all night and all the next day (the 3rd) and the following night not sleeping any only what we Slept with our arms at our side where we could get them in a moment and on the night of the 3rd all our Stores of ammunition and what cannon we could not get away was blown up and bursted and on the morning of the 4th we took up the line of march to bring up the rear of the retreat.

We arrived at Williamsburg 1 oclock P.M. 12 miles distance from Yorktown. The enemy pursuied us conti[nu]ously and that evening our cavalry attacked them and killed several and took a few prisoners. Next morning at 2 oclock we took up the march and it rained all day that day as hard as it commonly falls and the road was cut up so bad with waggons artillery and cavalry that the mud was half leg deep and it was the most tiresome to march imaginable (North Western va excepted). I had to throw away nearly every thing in my knapsack to get allong and a many a soldier threw away his knapsack and every thing he had. We arrived in about 5 miles of Westpoint that night and struck camps and dried our clothes and on the evening of the next day (the 6th) we heard that the yankees was landing heavy forces at Westpoint and we fell in lines and march down in about 2 miles of that place and stationed our artillery and remained in line of battle all night and the next day about 10 oclock our Brigade and one more attacked them in front and an engagement lasted about 3 hours and we drove them back to their gunboats with heavy loss while our loss was comparatively Small. Our regiment was not permited the pleasure of getting a crack at them. It was station[ed] to protect a battery of artillery and would have got into it if the engagement had become general but we was near enough to hear the balls whistle.

I forgotten to state that the rear of our army had a considerable battle with the enemy at Williamsburg on the 5th as my aim is principaly to note the events that comes in contact with our Brigade or regiment. There was a considerable loss on both sides as near as I can hear. The great difficulty with our men was they had to leave all our wounded at williamsburg and the[y] fell in the possession of the enemy.

At 12 oclock on the night of the 7th we resumed the march as hungry as a herd of starved wolves not having anything to eat in two or three days. We march on about 2 miles beyond New Kent Court House and Camped that night. We drew a little flour and a few pieces of hard bread about half rations.

On the evening of the 9th we were thrown in line-of-battle expected to be attacked but it proved to be a false alarm and about 6 oclock PM we marched 4 or 5 miles towards Richmond & struck camp and posting a heavy picket we taken a medium nights rest sleeping verry soundly for we had been deprived of that luxury for several nights.

On the 10th the enemy advanced in sight of us, and we were thrown in line-of-battle several times during the day but the enemy fell back a mile or two at the discharge of two peices of our flying artillery loaded with grape-shot. That night we advanced 3 or 4 miles Towards Richmond leaving Gen Hoods brigade to guard the rear.

On the 14th our company was Sent on picket near the enemies lines and that night we had a verry bad time it rained on us all night. Next morning the 15th verry soon we went out as Sharp Shooters and pretty regular fireing was kept up on both Side till near 12 oclock. The enemys balls whistled around our heads extensively Striking the trees in ever[y] direction but they did not hurt none of us but we wounded several of them. About 1 o'clock P.M. we quit our stand and rejoined our regiment which was on the act of marching and we resumed the march towards Richmond. We marched all that night till 3 o'clock A.M. and the raid was falling in torrents all the time through mud knee deep. We crossed the Chickahominy and rested from 3 o'clock till 7 A.M. and resumed the march and arrived at Richmond the 17th and camped about a mile from that Celebrated Metropolis.

On Saturday the 24th May our Brigade was ordered down on the enemies line on piquet [picket] and we march[ed] about 5 miles through the rain and mud half leg deep and we remained in line-of-battle all night and next morning we were deployed as skirmishers and remained till about 12 oclock but the enemy did not advance any and we were relieved and marched back to our camps.

On Monday the 26th our Brigade in the evening at about 7 oclock took up the march and marched back to where we were on the 25th and all that night the rain fell on us in torrents. The next day 27th our company was sent out as skirmishers on a Scout and we got a few shots at the enemy without much effort. After wading mud and water in a march knee deep all day we march[ed] back to our camps and arrived there about daylight the next morning of the 28th.[34]

Pocket Notebook Daily Entries
April 20 – May 23, 1862

Headquarters Hamton's Brigade
14 Ga Regiment
April 20th 1862

April 26, 1862

We are now in the Peninsula and arrived here yesterday evening after a force march of nearly one hundred miles. My feet was so sore that I could scarcely put them to the ground. We are now in a short distance of the enemy our pickets has skirmishes with them nearly every day. I saw the enemies balloon yesterday evening up in the air reconnoitering our force and fortifications and I stood at

---

34. Thayer included here a line and a half of typed periods in her manuscript, likely to indicate illegible writing.

Yorktown on the wharf and could See four of the Yankees Blockading vessels. The Confederate force in this vicinity is about 120,000 as near as I can conjecture. The Federal I cannot tell much about. I think there will be a great battle here before long but no one knows what will be the result but God above who knows all things and rules all, but I hope that it will be a decisive victory on our side and we may have a glorious independence waving over our beloved land once more.

Two or three evening ago I was detailed to go down on the River side on some business. It was a beautiful evening the sun shone with glorious red, over the broad expance of water and it was a beautiful view such as is rarely seen by our poor mortal eyes. York river is from 2 to 3 miles wide at this place and as I stood upon the Shore I could see far away into the blue waters of the Chesapeake Bay. Far away could be seen the sombre Blockading vessel of the enemy from day to day they stand as Sentinels in guarding the entrance of the Chesapeake into the Atlantic Ocean. The little Skiffs Barges and small sail vessels that sail about in York River is picturesque to behold in the rage of the setting sun.

4 o'clock PM, May 3, 1862

On the first day of May in the evening our regiment Started on picket down on the enemys line but before we got to our post the order was countermanded and we countermarched back to our Camps. The next day at 3 o'clock in the morning we packed up our baggage and sent it off with our waggons, and on the evening of the same day we fell into line with our knapsacks and our clothing what we could carry (burning up the remainder) and marched out in line of battle to await further orders and today the 3rd we are still in line of battle and have been anxiously expecting to throw our missile[s] at the enemy but have not had the opportunity yet. There is great preparations going on, on our side and I think it will come on before much longer. Our regiment is destitute of any thing to eat and is compelled to suffer if Something does not turn up before much longer.

7 o'clock PM, May 6, 1862

We are at this time in line of battle not far from West point expecting the enemy to attack us every moment. We have our Rifle[s] loaded ready to give them the contents on first sight. The enemy has been landing heavy forces at Westpoint all day.

10 o'clock AM, May 7, 1862

We are now at this time deployed as Skirmishers to protect a battery of light artillery. Our advance has open fire on the enemy and we are in anxious expectation of getting a crack at them before much longer.

5 o'clock PM, May 7, 1862

We have prove victorious by the help of God over the Yankees today. Our Brigade has done a good part in the Battle. We killed and wounded 5 or 600 of the enemy and taken between 50 and 1,00 prisoners, while the loss on our side was compareatively small. We drove them back to their gun-boats and routed them in every direction. It is remarkable that in every engagement we have with the Yankees, they can stand at a distance and shoot verry well but as soon as we begin to charge Bayonets on them they are certain to <u>run</u>.

May 13th 1862

<u>Reflections By the Way</u>

We are now at this time in camps about 20 miles each of Richmond (if camps it can be called). We have no tents but lie in the open air with our blankets Spread beneath the green trees which has just put forth their beautiful foliage.

Vegetation is about one month later here than it is in Georgia and every thing seems alive in the beautiful Spring. I always had an admiration of Spring and its beautiful flowers. It is with delight mingled with sadness, that I look on the pretty forest round about me. Instead of being the delight and pastime of the little birds and animals, it is the scene of devastation and death. The little bird is startled from the tree he has pearched and sung in all his life, by hearing the boom of the cannon and feel the stately oak give way beneath him rent asunder by the cannon balls. The little anamals is frightened and seek their dens by the thunder of resounding arms. B[ea]utiful wheat and corn fields is devastated and ruined. Such were my thoughts as I look around me and long for the time to come when I can enjoy beautiful spring in peace and hapiness and breathe the air of freedom I am striving to gain but never will I return to witness tyrannical opression and degradation. My blood may stain with crimson the green wheat or beautiful forest and my bones may whiten the hill or plain o[f] Virginia but I will fight on as long as life endures and hope that the great God and the father of our little republic may cause us to be Successful at that I may return home and find all safe with my dear friends.

May 23rd 1862

On Thursday the 22nd day of May 1862 I visited the city of Richmond for the first time The great metropolis of Virginia and the Capitol of the Confederate States. It is the great center of the opporations of the Confederate States. It[s] inhabitance [inhabitants] at this time is in great excitement for the enemy is near to the City in different directions and I think they will lay siege to it before many days longer but I hope they will be able to keep them out of it and never evacuate it as long as there is a man left of the Southern army to defend it.

4

"IT SEEMED LIKE TEN THOUSAND BULLETS PASSED OVER OUR HEADS"
SEVEN PINES/FAIR OAKS: MAY 31 – JUNE 26, 1862

The first true blooding of the 14th Georgia came on May 31, 1862, during the engagement that Hall referred to as the Battle of the Chickahominy. The common Confederate designation for the engagement was the battle of Seven Pines, named for a small grove east of Richmond and roughly a half-mile south of the Richmond and York River Rail line at the intersection of the Williamsburg Road and Nine Mile Road. The common Union designation was the battle of Fair Oaks, named for the rail station roughly a mile northwest of Seven Pines.[1] Hall and the 14th Georgia fought in Hampton's Brigade approximately a mile north of the Fair Oaks station.

As George McClellan continued to march west towards Richmond, he divided his five corps, keeping three to the north of the Chickahominy River to protect his supply lines along the railroad at White House Landing and sending two corps below the river. Johnston, with his back towards Richmond, devised an offensive operation against the two Union corps below the Chickahominy near Seven Pines. He divided his army into two wings, each roughly the equivalent of a corps. Hampton's Brigade was on the left flank in Gustavus Smith's left wing, making it the brigade closest to the Chickahominy River. Because Smith was in command of a wing, Whiting assumed command of Smith's division.

---

1. Indeed, the fighting at the two locations was so disparate that Brig. Gen. Edwin Sumner (perhaps in an effort to distance himself from the fighting at Seven Pines) advised the Congressional Joint Committee for the Conduct of the Civil War in early 1863 that these had been separate battles fought in two distinct places. Victor Vignola, *Contrasts in Command: The Battle of Fair Oaks, May 31-June 1, 1862* (Savas Beatie, 2023), xi, xiii.

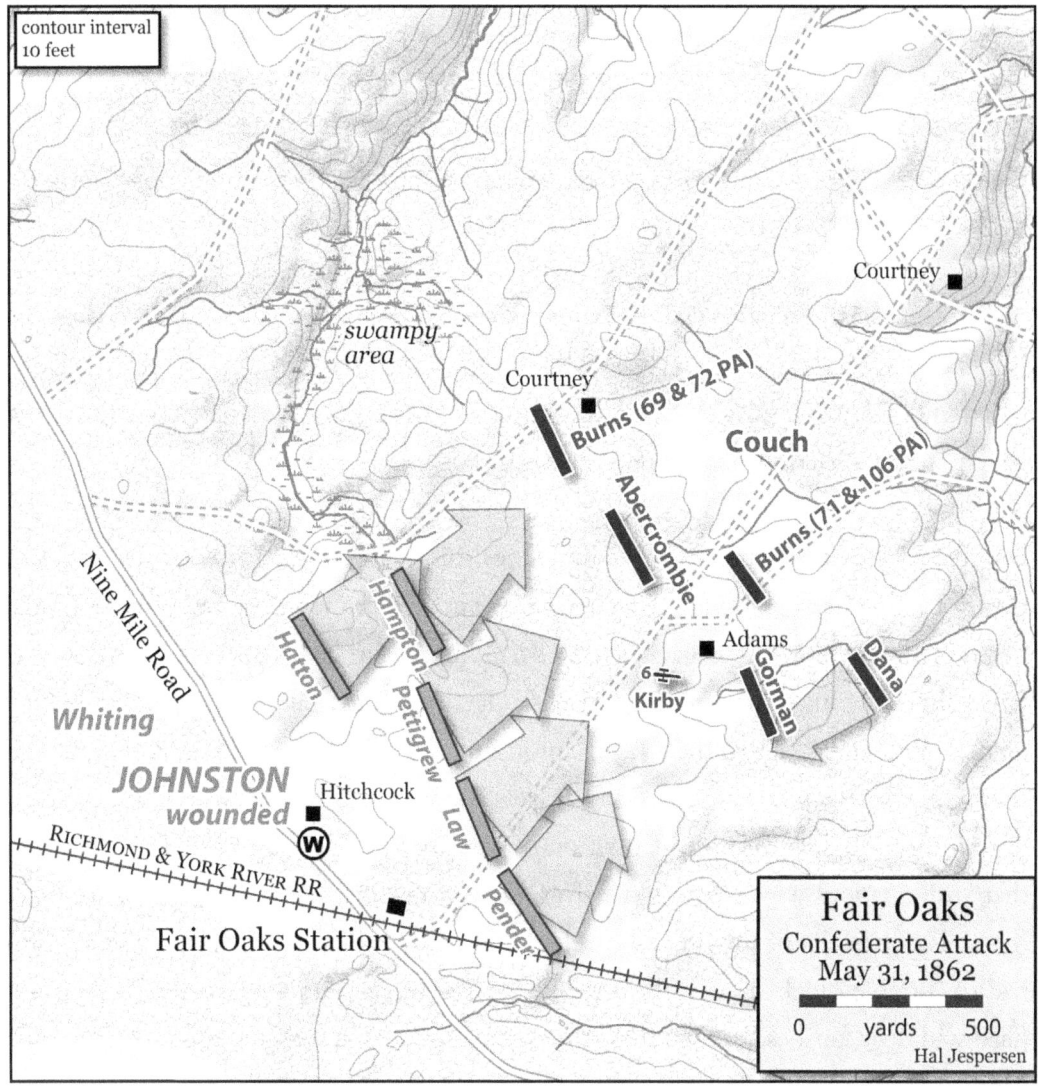

This map of the Confederate Attack at Fair Oaks shows Hampton's Brigade, which included the 14th Georgia, moving northeast from Nine Mile Road. (Map by Hal Jespersen, from *To Hell or Richmond: The 1862 Peninsula Campaign* by Doug Crenshaw)

Johnston planned to have over twenty of his army's almost-thirty brigades, coming from multiple directions, converge at the crossroads of Seven Pines east of Richmond. He gambled that McClellan's three corps north of the Chickahominy would be unable to join the battle because recent rains had swelled the river and washed away bridges, leaving Confederate troops in control of the remaining bridges. However, for a variety of reasons, including poor communications among the senior officers and a lengthy delay in the start of the Confederate attack, only nine brigades of the intended twenty-two Confederate brigades engaged in fighting that day, leading Stephen Sears to observe that "better than 30,000 men who were supposed to join the battle did not fire a shot."[2]

As Sears writes, "Few battles ever go entirely as their generals plan them, but seldom does a battle stray so far from its plan as Seven Pines on May 31, 1862."[3] What was supposed to be a coordinated Confederate attack along three lines turned into the separate engagements at Seven Pines south of the rail line and north of the rail station of Fair Oaks. General James Longstreet, who was supposed to move down Nine Mile Road to Seven Pines, marched down Williamsburg Road instead. In the process, he delayed or got entangled with units from other divisions.

When Confederate and Union troops finally engaged at Seven Pines, Hampton's Brigade, located the furthest north on Nine Mile Road, waited to be committed to battle. In the interim, Union Brig. Gen. Edwin V. Sumner, commanding II Corps north of the river, boldly began moving Brig. Gen. John Sedgwick's division over the Chickahominy on the fragile Grapevine Bridge, so named because grapevines helped hold the bridge's logs together. As a Union officer later wrote, the bridge was almost submerged by rushing water, and it was only the weight of the soldiers that kept it in place long enough to permit the division to pass over.[4] Once the Confederates realized that Union troops were crossing the river, Hampton's Brigade was dispatched to meet them. The mere act of moving up on the Union troops exhausted the Georgians, who had to "double quick" march three miles through wet terrain and wade a "large pond filled with logs, bushes, and water up the men's hips."[5] What ensued was the regiment's baptism of fire.

Facing Sedgwick's infantry and artillery without any artillery support of their own, Hampton's troops made multiple attacks in the late afternoon across "a low rise and through a patch of woods and across fields and through a swampy pond full of fallen

---

2. Sears, *To the Gates of Richmond*, 138.
3. Sears, *To the Gates of Richmond*, 138.
4. J. Gregory Acken, ed., *Inside the Army of the Potomac: The Civil War Experience of Captain Francis Adams Donaldson* (Stackpole Books, 1998), 87.
5. Patterson to Family, June 13, 1862, "Incomplete Patterson Correspondence."

tree trunks" that were "sleek as eels."⁶ The 14th Georgia was positioned on the left side of Hampton's Brigade, just behind Hampton's Legion. As one newspaper reported, "The Fourteenth charged up to within forty or fifty yards of the battery, where it received a most galling and destructive fire, and after delivering its own fire, fell back. Afterward, in conjunction with the other regiments composing the brigade, the Fourteenth made two successive and desperate charges upon the battery and finally fell back with the brigade."⁷ As Capt. Robert Folsom described the Union defenses to a Macon newspaper as presenting "the appearance of a living wall of flame, from the great number and rapidity of their discharges."⁸ In its first engagement of the war, the 14th Georgia learned how difficult it is for infantry without artillery support to make a frontal assault against infantry with artillery support.

The Union's Grapevine Bridge over the Chickahominy (Library of Congress)

Thomas C. Moore, later the regimental adjutant, elaborated on the 14th Georgia's actions at Fair Oaks as follows:

> Our first battle was that of Seven Pines. Unfortunately the regiment was put into action late in the evening, just before the close of that hard fought battle. The position attacked by us was an extremely strong one, and the disparity in numbers was greatly in favor of the enemy, much greater no doubt than was supposed by the commanding Generals; but our Brigade (Hampton's) composed of the Fourteenth and Nineteenth

---

6. Sears, *To the Gates of Richmond*, 137. Gustavus Smith wrote after the war that no artillery accompanied the advance "on account of the almost impracticable condition of the ground." McWhiney and Jamieson, *Attack and Die*, 123.
7. "The Charge of the Hampton Legion," *Southern Confederacy*, June 8, 1862, www.newspapers.com.
8. Folsom, Robert W., "Camp of the 14th Ga. Regiment, June 8, 1862," *Macon Telegraph*, June 17, 1862, www.newspapers.com.

Georgia, the Sixteenth North Carolina, and Hampton's Infantry Battalion, was ordered into action upon this strongly fortified line. The first and only order given after the formation of our line of battle was to charge, and the movement was executed in fine style, until we advanced into the woods filled with a dense undergrowth. Here the line became broken, but continued to advance until within less than fifty paces of the enemy's line, and immediately in front of one of his strongest batteries. At this moment the batteries of the enemy belched forth their thunders, showering a perfect hail storm of canister and grape into our lines, while a withering fire of musketry was poured upon us. An order to lie down was given, and it was then discovered that we were being flanked. Having no supports, or they not being up, the result was that the whole brigade retreated in disorder. It was rallied and again and again led to the assault with other troops, but the numbers and position of the enemy were too strong for us, and although the fighting continued until after dark, we failed to force the enemy from the field.[9]

Hampton's Brigade withdrew from the swampy battlefield and spent the night on the western edge of a clearing northwest of the rail station at Fair Oaks. When the battle recommenced to the south on June 1, Hampton's Brigade was not engaged but instead continued to anchor the furthest north position on Nine Mile Road.

Although both sides claimed victory at Fair Oaks/Seven Pines, the battle was soon dwarfed in strategic significance by the Seven Days' battles that followed four weeks later. The most significant outcome of Fair Oaks/Seven Pines was the fact that Joseph Johnston was wounded during the battle, which opened the door for Robert E. Lee to assume command of the Army of Northern Virginia. However, historian Craig Symonds contends that another consequence was that the battle unnerved McClellan. Seven Pines was the first battle where his troops had suffered major casualties, and the experience would make McClellan "even more cautious than usual" in the upcoming weeks.[10]

---

9. Folsom, *Heroes and Martyrs of Georgia*, 147.
10. Craig L. Symonds, *A Battlefield Atlas of the Civil War* (Nautical and Aviation Publishing, 1985), 31.

During the battle, Hampton took a Union bullet to his foot but remained on horseback while his surgeon extracted the bullet. With Hampton wounded, the 14th Georgia's Felix Price, as the next senior colonel, should have immediately assumed command of the brigade, but according to Lt. Col. Griffin of Hampton's Legion, Price "was separated by some means from his command."[11] It is difficult to imagine how a commander might be separated from his regiment on such a contained battle line, but Price, much to Griffin's disgust, eventually reappeared and assumed temporary command of the brigade. Griffin wrote his wife on June 5, 1862, that he was unwilling to go into combat under Price; in fact, he requested that Hampton's Legion be assigned to some other brigade until Hampton returned.[12] As events unfolded, Griffin himself was given temporary command of the brigade while Hampton recovered, and the 14th Georgia was transferred to Joseph R. Anderson's brigade.

One of the consequences of the fog of war is the inexactitude of casualty numbers due to faulty records on who participated and who survived; this is exacerbated by the fact that so many of the 14th Georgia's records for the period 1862-1864 did not survive the war. Newspaper accounts of battles, though based mostly on hearsay, are of some help in determining casualties, especially if the numbers are provided by a party responsible for calculating them. For example, a letter to the *Richmond Dispatch* from 1st Lieutenant R. A. Holt, the Acting Regimental Adjutant, likely offers the greatest accuracy for the 14th Georgia's casualties at Fair Oaks/Seven Pines. Holt reported that 486 officers and men went into action, with 12 killed, 54 wounded, and eight missing, bringing total casualties to 74.[13] As Holt described the action: "The Brigade arrived on the field about 6 o'clock P.M. after a double quick of 3 miles, and immediately formed in line of battle, and charged a masked battery situated in the woods on the left of the line, and to the left of the road. A large majority of the casualties of the 14th Georgia Regiment was caused

---

11. McArthur and Burton, *A Gentleman and an Officer*, 236.
12. McArthur and Burton, *A Gentleman and an Officer*, 236
13. Holt reported the following casualties in Company G: "Killed: Corporal James J. Goodman, regimental color bearer. – Wounded: Privates Levi T. Fowler, George W. Spring, Jackson J. Shiver, Thomas L. Wheelus, and Richard McElhannon, badly; First Serg't Thomas G. Westfall, Privates Elbert Baker, Romulus Weeks, John T. Jarkins, Thomas J. Deariso, James Deariso, Norman G. Gillis, and Nathan T. Calhoun, slightly. Missing: First Lieutenant Robert F. Shine, reported badly wounded." "List of Casualties in the 14th Regiment Georgia Volunteers, Col. F. Price Commanding, in the Battle of May 31, 1862," *Savannah Daily Morning News*, June 17, 1862, https://gahistoricnewspaptters.galileo.usg.edu.

by the enemy's first fire, which was delivered when the regiment had arrived within 30 yards of a hostile battery."[14]

Hall, who noted that Company G was on the extreme left of the regiment at its most exposed point, wrote that he was "right by" one man who was shot through his head; this was likely Corporal James Goodman, the only man from the company shot in the head (and apparently the regimental color bearer). Lieutenant Shine, much beloved by Company G, was mortally wounded during the action and was left on the battlefield.[15]

Hall summarized the action by stating that the 14th Georgia had made "three gallant charges, and was under a heavy fire of musketry and artillery 3 hours." He considered Seven Pines a "gallant victory" because some Union troops had been driven from their camps. Among the items taken from those camps were "one hundred barrels of Spiritious liquors" because, as Hall believed, "the Yankee commanders had to make their soldiers intoxicated to make them fight."

Following Fair Oaks/Seven Pines, the 14th Georgia changed camps several times, moving ever closer to Richmond. The men commenced a routine of days spent either in camp or on picket duty. Hall observed the first anniversaries of his enlistment in the Yancey Independents and his going into camp. He noted that he had not slept in a bed since.

Pocket Notebook Narrative
May 28 – June 29, 1862

About Sundown the same day [May 28] we took up the line of march from our camps (2 miles East of Richmond) and continued the march till about 3 oclock A.M. when we come to a halt and fell down by the side of the road and was soon asleep. We remained there till that evening and

---

14. "The Fourteenth charged up to within forty or fifty yards of the battery, where it received a most falling and destructive fire, and, after delivering its own fire, fell back. Afterwards, in conjunction with the other regiments composing the brigade, the Fourteenth made two successive and desperate charges upon the battery, and finally fell back with the brigade." "The Charge of the Hampton Legion," *Southern Confederacy*, June 08, 1862, www.newspapers.com.
15. Folsom, *Heroes and Martyrs of Georgia*, 147.

we took a new position about a mile from there where we remained till saturday morning the 31st. And we took up the line of march through mud and water which was caused by a thunder storm and a deluge of rain on Friday night. We marched on till about 12 o'clock that day and we was ordered to march double quick time in order to reinforce our army then engaged with the enemy on the Chickahominy.

When we were several miles off we could hear the thunder of the artillery and the roar of small arms Our Brigade was anxious to Send their missiles at the enemy. We doubled quicked about 6 miles and arrived at the Battle-field tired nearly out having to run through mud and water all the way it being a verry marshy tract of country in this region and continued rain for several days made it almost impossible. Our Brigade encountered a strong force of the enemy behind a thick peice of woods where they had entrenchments which they were behind and they had a heavy battery of artillery and they had their forces drawn up behind the Battery, and to the right and left at right angles. Hamtons Legion was in the advance of the Brigade and our regiment next and 16th North Carolina and 19th Georgia behind.

The yankee battery was belching forth bomb-shell and grape shot in a Rappid maner and we was ordered to storm the Battery and take it if possible and we charged it. The first charge I was up in 30 or 40 yards of the cannons mouths and they belching death and destruction at every moment. I could see the enemys flag a few yards from me. Our company is on the extreme left of the regiment and by the position of the enemy was in a more exposed point than any of the rest of the regiment. We raised our Rifles to our shoulders and took good aim and fired and as we pulled trigger the enemy cut in a murderous fire upon us in front and on our left making a cross fire. On our left several of our men fell to my right and left one was shot through the head right by me. We were ordered to fall flat on the ground which we done and it seem like ten thousand bullets passed over our heads trimming up the bushes in every direction. We loaded our peices and rose and fire[d] again, (the enemy was in pits.) We were ordered to fall back which we done and loading as we went. We turned and charged again with shouts that fa[i]rly made the earth tremble. Our brave boys went again.

We taken the Battery during the evening but the enemys force was so strong in their Breast-works that we could not hold it. A terrific firing was kept up on both sides till it grew so dark that we could not distinguish friend from foe, and it ceased for the night. We lay on our arms near the Battle field all night except detachments that was sent in to reli[e]ve the wounded. The contest was renewed the next morning gaining little advantage on either side till about 10 o'clock AM when the enemy sent in a flag of truce disiring a cesation of Battle to bury the dead which was done

The killed and wounded was heavy on both sides. The loss in our company was Corporal James I Goodman shot through the head killed dead on the field. Our 1st Lieutenant Robert F. Shine was mor[t]ally wounded through the body, private Geo W. Spring shot through the leg, private John I Shiver shot through the leg, Private . . . Macklehanon [Richard McElhannon] Shot through both legs, Elbert Baker shot in the shoulder. Thomas Whelus wounded in the back. Romulus Weeks shot in the arm and struck in the breast with a fragment of a bomb shell. James Deriso [Deariso] shot in the shoulder Slightly. [Sgt] T. G. Westfall Shot in the ear slightly. Total 1 killed and 10 wounded. The total killed and wounded in the 14th Ga 15 killed and about 50 wounded.

Our regiment did a gallant part on that day. It made three gallant charges, and was under a heavy duty of musketry and artillery 3 hours. All that witness[ed] this Battle and the Battle of Manassas stated that this was far more terrific than that Battle and it is given in by Generals writers and correspondent[s] that the latter part of this Battle was the most tremendious and terrific while it lasted of any since the war began. 3 or 4 of our Brigadier Generals was killed and several wounded. Col Wade Hampton commanding our Brigade wound in the foot. I am unable to tell the exact number of loss on either Side. Some say our loss was 2,500 while that of the enemy was 10,000 and others that of ours 3,000 and that of the Yankees about 8,000.[16]

We won a gallant victory over them is certain. Drove them back from the camps and fortifications and took a vas[t] amount of store[s] and camp equipage, tents, arms, ammunitions &c. including one hundred barrels of Spiritious liquors, which the Yankees carry with them all the time. The Yankees commanders had to make their soldiers intoxicated to make them fight. The wounde[d] on our side was taken to Richmond where they were well cared for by the patriotic ladies of that place who stood over them day and night administering like angels sent from heaven to their relief. In relation to my self I escaped unhurt by the help of God and I hope he may be with me to pass through as many more as it may be my fortune to get in to.

There was representatives from nearly every state in the Seceded in that memorial Battle. The Son of the proud old Georgia the empire State was foremost in the fray proudly and gallantly did they rally around their standard, the standard of their home and fire-sides, their wives and children and their Sweetharts and lovemates

---

16. Union casualties came to just over 5,000 out of 41,797 who fought; Confederate losses came to 6,130 out of the 41,816 who fought. Eicher, *The Longest Night*, 278.

rose conspicuous in their minds. Death appalled them not. Life has no charm if the marauders of our rights and liberty should conquer. Gallantly and nobly did they fight and charged up in defiance to cannons mouths which was sending forth fire and death at every moment. And there were also representatives from Florida the sunny and beautiful land of flowers. Oh m[a]y the dastard foe all bite the dust before they ever invade thy beautiful soil. Gallantly did her noble Sons respond [to] the Battle call. The 2nd Fla regiment was in the Battle on the 31st and gallantly did hold their position till their noble regiment lost nearly half their men. And gallantly did Alabamans hold their post. The 3rd Ala was cut out terably. South Carolina did nobly on that day. The 5th 6th regiment and several others fought noble on that day. So did Louisana Mississippi and Tennessee Virginia North Carolina Texas and lastly the oppressed but noble Marylander who is a refugee from their native State the land of their home and birth turned traitor unto Them.

Nothing of interest occured on Monday the Second day of June. Our Brigade still remained in line of Battle the 2nd and part of the 3rd, when we marched out a peice and camped and drawed Something to [eat] having not had anything in 3 or 4 days only what we got in the Yankee camp. On Friday the 6th our Brigade went out on piquet again. We remained on picket till the 4th and the Yankees throwing bombs among us every day but fortunately not hurting none of us. Details from our Brigade was throwing up entrenchments and Battlements night and day.

Late in the Evening of the 11th . . . . Brigade come and relieved us and we took up the march and took our position on the line to the N.E. of Richmond and about 4 miles from there. That night the full moon shone with great brilliantcy and its gentle rays fell on us poor soldiers as we tramped along through the mud and water and it seem to say "be of good cheer valiant men you are toiling in a just and holy cause and one that heaven will approve of", but about 12 oclock its gentle rays was totally obscured by a total eclips[e] which lasted over 2 hours.

About 8 oclock on the morning of the 12th we camped about 4 miles from Richmond where we remain till the 16th heavy details being made every day for piquet. On the 16th we taken our position higher up the Chickahominy and our regiment Stood picket 3 companies at a time on the Banks of the Chickahominy and here I drew my wages from the C.S. the amount of $44.00 which being for 4 months and up to Feb 28 1862.

Every two or three days I had to Stand picket in a luxurious wheat and oat field on the verry edge of the Chickahominy. The musquetoes was verry bad at night but we had a verry pleasant time in the day, it being fine weather nearly all the time. We could hear the enemy at all times just over the Creek from us but could not see them on account of the impentrable Swamp.

Pocket Notebook Daily Entries
June 5 – June 12, 1862

June 5, 1862
<u>Anniversary</u>

May 29 1862 was the first anniversary of my enlistment and is distinguish[ed] by me as being the day one year May 29, 1861 I put my signature down in defence of my dear beloved country to defend it as long as my life exist. I volunteered my services in the first company that left my native county and left all that was near and dear to come the scene of strife and bloodshed. I have been through various Scenes since then and have passed through sickness nigh unto death, and I have already been through one great Battle, and several Skirmishes, but by the protection of my dear Lord have passed through them all safe without a Scratch and hope and trust he may be with me in every one and be my guard and Shield and I may be permited to return home with peace and prosperity reigning o'er my country and peace and happiness with my dear friends.

June 5, 1862

June 5, 1862 is distinguish[ed] by me as being the first anniversary of my going into camp life. June 5th 1861 just one year ago from today I went into camp for the first time and I have not known the comforts of a house nor the luxury of lying on a bed since. I have a part of the time had a tent to stay in but it has been nearly two months since I have had a tent or any shelter but the dome of the heavens. Our campaign has been so active and near the enemy that it has been impossible to get transportation for tents. I have not got any thing but what I can carry on my back and double quick through mud and water from knee to waist deep. About one suit of cloth[e]s is all I can carry and them on my back. I go through drenching rains for two and three days at a time. My cloth[e]s get wet and stays so till air or sun drys them. I have several times lately been deprived of my sleep for several nights and have had to camp in watery places and lay down in the mud and water and have slept as sound as if I had been in a palace, and thanks be to the Almighty I have kept in as good health as ever I was in my life. The greatest Battle a historian has ever chronicled will take place in this vicinity before long and I hope it will be a decisive Battle and will decide this unholy war.

June 17, 1862

Fond are the recollections of happy scenes of the past, when brought to mind by stern realities of the present, far away from the happy scenes of childhood and every thing that is near and dear to me, and far sweeter are they made like scenes as the present. Our company and present has to stand picket on the Chickahominy in a beautiful field of wheat and oats that extends on all sides far away and its rich golden hue as the gentle breezes rustles its heavy laden ears with an abundant harvest put me in recollection of the past far away and gone, never to return. When I used to love to roam in the golden wheatfield and gather plums and berries among the hedges great is the contrast between now and then when I was surrounded by my dear friends and relatives and the comforts of life and was happy in my innocent childhood but now I am far away. War and Bloodshed has taken the place of peace and happiness thousands of homes is devastated and made desolate and thousands of dear ones has left their homes at their countrys call and have left to return no more but has nobly laid down their lives for their dear country. Their loved ones at home far away when the sad news reaches them. Their hearts is wrung in anguish and despair. But it is far better that they Should lay down their lives at the Sacrafice of their country and homes than to live and suffer Slavery and degradation below the beast of the forest. The tyrant Butlers hellish proclamation is enough to inspire the heart a stone to resist their base tyranny to the last day.[17] But the great God above never lets them that obeys him and stands on the right side in hour of tryal fall that upholds them with his omnipotent hand.

June 22, 1862

The Following is a list on roll of the Yancy Independent Co (G) 14 Regiment Ga Vols which was organized May 29th 1861 in the town of Isabella Worth County Georgia.[18]

Officers

Capt Wm A Harris - -	Major
1st Lieut Asa M Giddens - -	resined
2nd Lieut Wm A Johnston - -	x died Jul [62]
3rd Lieut Robert J Weeks - -	died September [61]

Non Commission[ed] Officers

1st Sergt Thomas G Westfall - -	w
2nd Sergt S H [Sylvanus Q.] Jordan	died Sept 62
3rd Sergt T [Thaddeus] M Bostick - -	3rd Lieut
4th Sergt R [Robert] F Shine - -	1st Let killed
1st Corp J [James] H Ford - -	5th Sergt w
2nd Corp James Bass - -	discharged
3rd Corp Lot [Lott] W Hill - -	killed
4th Corp James J Goodman –	killed

Privates – posts of honor

1	S [Salathiel] Adams	died
2	Harmon Bray	

---

17. This is likely a reference to Union General Benjamin Butler's May 1862 General Order No. 28 in New Orleans which said that any female who insulted or showed contempt to a Union officer or soldier would be treated as "a woman of the town plying her avocation."

18. Hall broke down the company roster by those who first enlisted, those who joined in September 1861 (mostly soldiers whom Harris recruited in late August 1861), and those who joined in March 1862 (recruited in Worth County by Lt Johnston). However, Hall's groupings are not entirely accurate. I have provided first names and corrected spelling where feasible. Hall also placed an "x" or a "w" after many of the names but I have removed those because he did not explain what those marks meant. Hall updated this list by noting some deaths that occurred after June 22, 1862.

	3	M [Malcolm] J Bass	dead oct 61
	4	T [Thomas] C Calhoun - -	killed
	5	N [Nathan] T Calhoun	
	6	Joseph Calhoun	dead oct 61
	7	Daniel Champion	killed
	8	Charley [Charles] Collier	discharged
	9	Jacob Chestnut	dead oct 61
	10	Bret [Brett or Britt] S [Samuel] J.	dead Sept 61
	11	Brown P [Pearson] D.	dead Sept 61
	12	Deriso [Deariso] James	died of his wounds
	13	Eady Edward	
	14	Exum B [Benjamin] E. T.	dead oct 61
	15	Ford R [Robert] G.	Substituted
	16	Ford J [John] J.	dis[charged] & returned
	17	Fowler L [Levi] T.	
	18	Fowler N [Nathan] J.	
	19	Fulton R [Robert] H.	
E 3rd Sergt w[19]			
	20	Gaughf [Goughf] Benjamin	died
	21	Gaughf [Goughf] G. [John] H.	died in Sept 61
	22	Gleaton D [Dudley] C.	discharged
	23	Green B [Bartley] C.	
	24	German [Germon] J [Joseph] B.	died in oct 61
	25	Hall G [George] W.	
	26	Hamilton Wm	discharged
	27	Hardin [Harden] J [John] F.	dead Sept 61
	28	Henderson M [Manassah]	discharged
	29	Hobby James	
E 4 corp			
	30	Hobby J [James] N.	discharged

---

19. Fulton was elected to 2d Lieutenant in September 1862, to 1st Lieutenant in October 1862, and to captain of Company G in May 1863.

31 Holiday [Holliday] E [Edward] G.   discharged
32 Holoman [Holamon] D[aniel] T. W. died oct 61
33 Hill H [Haskell] H.
34 Gunter W [William] J.   died Sept 61
35 Jerkins J [John] T.
36 Gillis N [Norman] G.   discharged
37 Jones J [Julius] M.   dis[charged] & returned
38 Johnson [Johnston] D [David] D.
39 Johnson Thomas   died oct 61
40 Kerce A [Albert] B.
41 Land W [William] L.
42 Lunsford J [James] W.
43 Massey A [Abel] C.
44 Massey G [George] W.
45 Massey S [Silas] M.
46 Massey R [Robert] B.
47 Mcrainey [McRaney, McCrainie,   died aug 61
    McCraney] R. M.
48 Mcrainey [McRaney, McCrainie,
    McCraney] G [George] W.
49 Meadows W [William] T.
50 Posey Wm
51 Quiet[t] H [Henry] C.
52 Rouse J [John] W.   died oct 61
53 Rodgers M [Martin] J.   died oct 61
54 Rodgers A [Asa] C.   died oct 61
55 Shiver Green   died Sept 61
56 Shiver W. J.   died Sept 61
57 Shiver J. J.
58 Smith J. C.
59 Stephens R [Rienza]   discharged
60 Tipton Thomas
61 Spring J [Joseph] L.
62 Spring G [George] W.

63 Sumner J [Joseph] L.

E 2 corp

64 (faded)[20]

65 Tabor A [Andrew] J.

66 Vicory [Vickery] Eli

67 Walker W [William] W.   died

68 Weeks R [Romulus]   killed

69 Whe[e]lus T [Thomas] L.   dis[charged] & returned

70 Williams B [Berrian] A.

71 Wiley Edward

72 Bozeman J [John] R.   E 3rd Lieut

73 Bozeman L [Luke] C.   discharged

74 Simmons Marion   discharged

75 Warren Lewis

77, 78 N [Nathaniel] B. Bostick J. C. Omooney [O'Mooney] both discharged

The following is a roll of recruits that came to Co[mpany] in Sept 1861

  1 Baker Elbert   killed

  2 Baker Nathan   died

  3 Champion David   elected Sgt

  4 Eady J [James] E.   discharged

  5 Hamilton David   killed

  6 Hobby William

  7 Hamock [Hancock] Jackson

  8 Dawkins [Dawson] Samuel

  9 Horn M [Michael] J.

10 Simpson M [Morris] F.

11 Simpson James   discharged

12 Simpson ? ? [Alexander]   died

---

20. The faded name may have been that of Thomas Tipton.

    13 ? ? ?
    14 ? ? ?
    15 ? ? ?   discharged
    16 Lane Wm   discharged
The following is a roll of recruits that come to Our Co
in April & May 1862
    Batey [Baty] Wm
    Derico [Deariso] T. J.
    Derico [Deariso] W. T.
    Ford G [Garry] G. [Green]
    Ford W [William] J.   discharged
    Gillis [William] Daniel
    Hobby Jesse
    Jones Isaac   died of his w
    Jeter J [Jeremiah] J.
    Kerce B [Barney]
    Kerce J [James O.]   killed
    Kerce J. M. [E. James M.]
    Haise [Hayes] John
    (three names faded)[21]
    Nichols C. M [Madison]
    Posey L [Littleton] P.
    Posey James
    Ross John
E corp
    Ridley Johnithan [W. Jonathan][22]   died

---

21. The faded names were likely William M. Harris, Daniel McCranie, and Valentine E. Potts.
22. Thayer noted here that two pages were "lost from diary." Those missing pages likely listed privates who enlisted on March 4, 1862, and whose last names began with a letter between S and Z, including Anthony Shiver, Henry Shiver, James Shiver; Napoleon Tabor, Daniel Thompson, Calvin Thompson, and Elihu Thompson – all of whom are shown on Hall's mid-July roster.

5

"I WILL TURN IT FROM A YANKEE TO A REBEL DIARY"
SEVEN DAYS: JUNE–JULY 1862

After Seven Pines, Lee reorganized the Army of Northern Virginia and placed the 14th Georgia in Joseph R. Anderson's Third Brigade in A. P. Hill's light division.[1] This realignment united the 14th Georgia with the 35th, 45th, and 49th Georgia Infantry regiments and the 3rd Louisiana Battalion. All four of the Georgia regiments would remain brigaded together through the end of the war, although they served under Anderson for only a brief period.[2]

Under Anderson's command, the 14th Georgia fought in three battles of the Seven Days battles around Richmond in late June 1862. These were Mechanicsville (Beaver Dam Creek) (June 26), Gaines's Mill (June 27), and Frayser's Farm (Glendale)(June 30), where

---

1. According to James Robertson, the term "light division" was a title Hill began using in June 1862. James I. Robertson, *General A. P. Hill: The Story of a Confederate Warrior* (Random House, 1987), 63. Hill's was not a "light division" in the strictest sense of the term. Although they did travel "lightly armed, lightly fed . . . march rapidly and fight frequently," they always fought as heavy infantry. A light division would have acted as more of a strike force acting independently of the rest of the army. Robert B. Broadwater, *Civil War Special Forces: The Elite and Distinct Fighting Units of the Union and Confederate Armies* (Praeger, 2014), 57-59.
2. Anderson, a graduate of the U.S. Military Academy, is best known as the superintendent at the famous Tredegar Iron Works in Richmond. He was commissioned a brigadier general in the Confederate Army in September 1861 but returned to the Tredegar Iron Works after resigning his commission in July 1862.

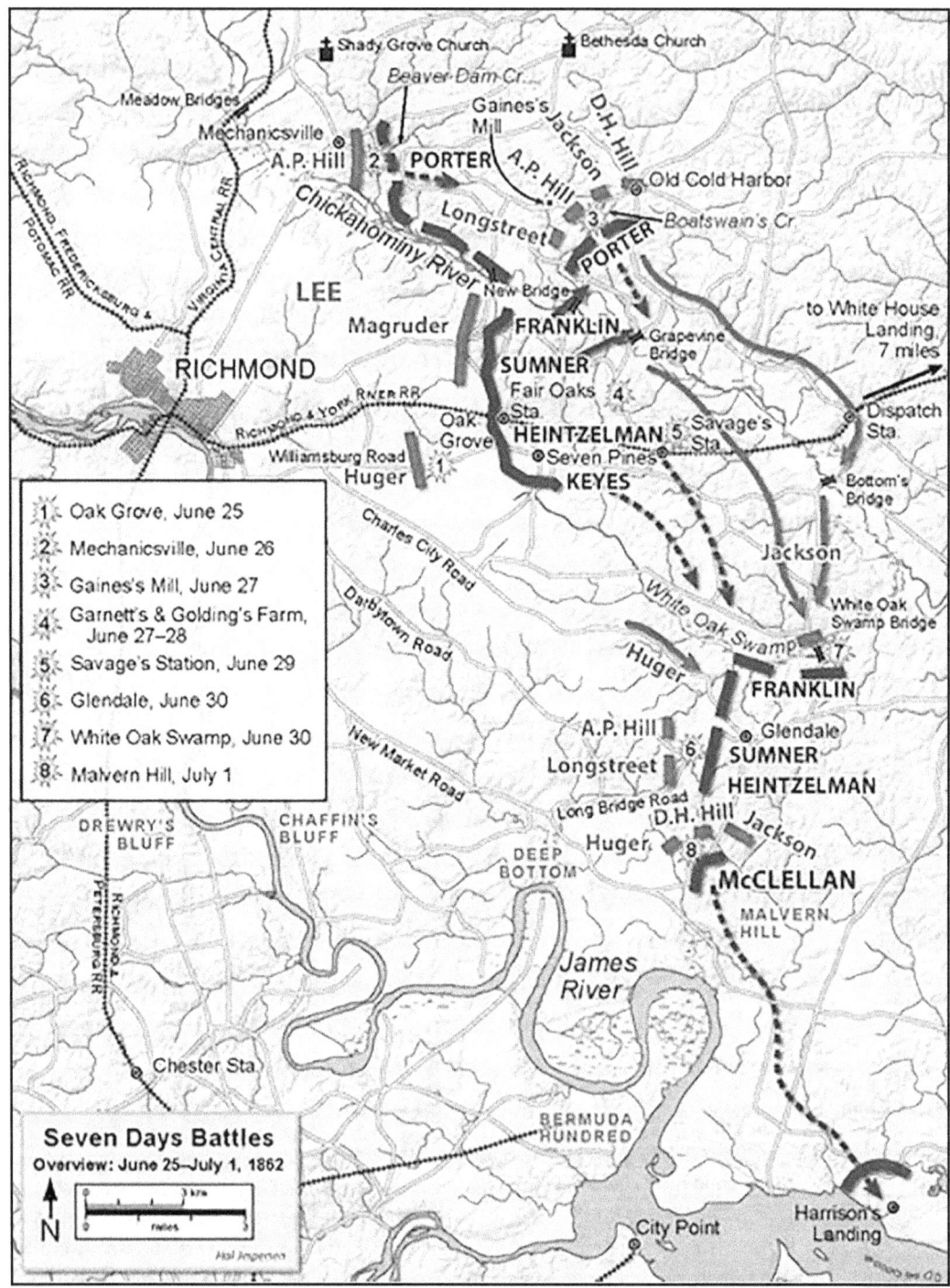

Hall's 14th Georgia regiment and Elsesser's 9th Pennsylvania Reserves regiment both participated in Mechanicsville (Beaver Dam Creek), Gaines's Mill, and Frayser's Farm (Glendale). (Map by Hal Jespersen)

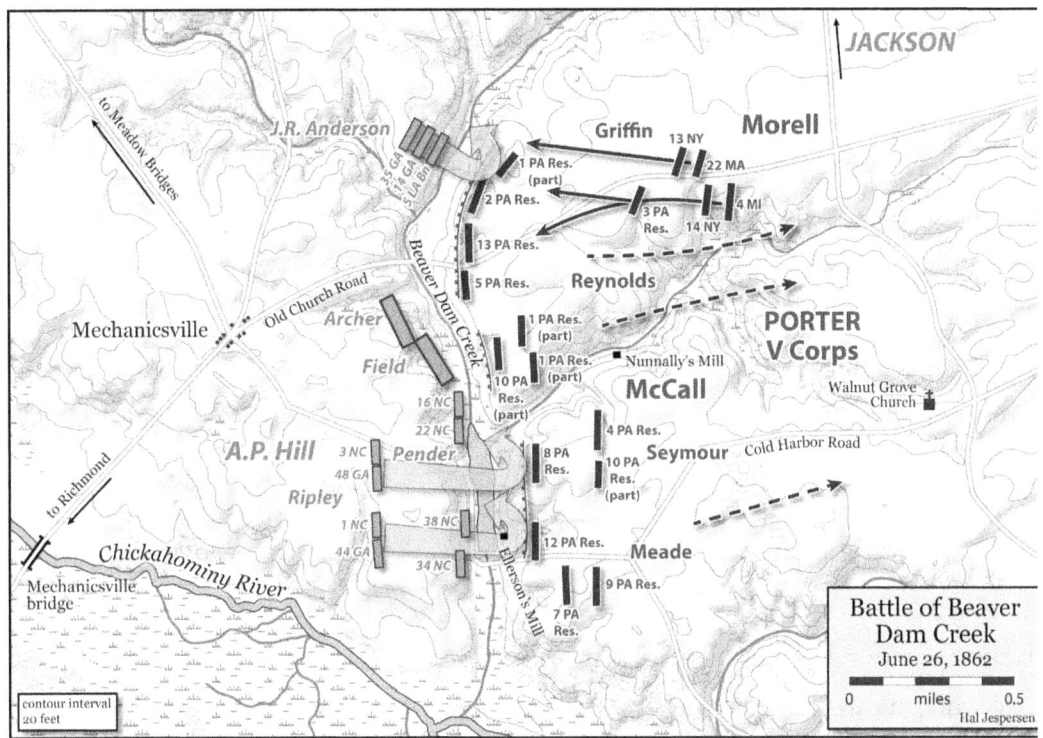

Soldiers of the 14th Georgia crossed Beaver Dam Creek well north of Hill's main assault near Ellerson's Mill. (Map by Hal Jespersen, from *Richmond Shall Not Be Given Up: The Seven Days' Battles, June 25—July 1, 1862*, by Doug Crenshaw)

Anderson was wounded slightly in the head, resulting in Col. Edward L. Thomas of the 35th Georgia assuming interim command of the brigade.[3] When Anderson resigned his commission a few weeks later, Thomas received permanent command of the brigade.[4]

---

3. Thomas, a Georgia native, gained military experience as a lieutenant in a company of the Georgia Mounted Volunteers during the Mexican-American War. "Mexican War Service Record Index," database and images, Fold3 (www.fold3.com/image/307214851; General Index Card, Edward L. Thomas, citing National Archives and Records Administration microfilm publication "Indexes to the Carded Records of Soldiers Who Served in Volunteer Organizations During the Mexican War, compiled 1899 - 1927, documenting the period 1846 – 1848," M616, Roll 0037, Record Group 94, National Archives, Washington, D.C. He received a commission to lieutenant for valor in combat, as well as an offer of a commission in the same rank in the U.S. Army. He declined the U.S. Army commission and spent the years prior to the outbreak of the Civil War on his Georgia plantation. Fox, *Red Clay to Richmond*, 6.
4. Anderson was reluctant to resign his command but felt, as did Lee, that he would better serve the Confederacy running the iron works. Charles Dew, *Ironmaker to the Confederacy: Joseph R. Anderson and the Tredegar Iron Works* (Yale University Press, 1966), 151.

The record of who was in actual command of the 14th Georgia in June and July 1862 is murky. In the absence of evidence to the contrary, a regimental commander is generally presumed to be present with his regiment – particularly during combat operations. In his brigade report on the actions at Mechanicsville, Gaines's Mill, and Frayser's Farm, Anderson refers to Robert Folsom as the commander of the 14th Georgia.[5] In Thomas's report on the battles, he likewise refers to Folsom and the 14th Georgia.[6] Moreover, the "org chart" for the Army of Northern Virginia for July 23, 1862, shows Col. R. W. Folsom in command of the 14th Georgia.[7] Thus, it appears likely that during the Seven Days battles, the 14th Georgia was commanded by its lieutenant colonel, not its colonel.

The Seven Days battles took place over a surprisingly small amount of acreage but resulted in over 36,000 casualties.[8] Some consider the first battle of the Seven Days battles to have been a relatively small action at Oak Grove on June 25, 1862, but others consider Lee's first offensive action at Mechanicsville as the start of Seven Days. A more contemporary view is that the fighting between June 25 and July 1, 1862, was just one large continuous battle that took place over seven days at different locations.[9]

The battle at Beaver Dam Creek on June 26, 1862, also known as the Battle of Mechanicsville, was the first major movement in Lee's planned offensive campaign against McClellan. The Union right flank was held by Porter's V Corps, the only corps McClellan had remaining north of the Chickahominy to guard the supply route to White House Landing; the other corps were south of the river, making their way to Union-held Harrison's Landing on the James River. Lee intended to supplement the troops already around Richmond with Maj. Gen. Thomas "Stonewall" Jackson's troops coming from the Shenandoah Valley to disrupt the Union supply line from White House Landing and to cut off Porter's V Corps. Porter had only half the troops that Lee did, but V Corps held an extremely strong, elevated defensive position across Beaver Dam Creek.

---

5. *OR*, Ser. 1, vol. 11, pt. II, p. 877.
6. *OR*, Ser. 1, vol. 51, pt. I, p. 117.
7. *OR*, Ser. 1, vol. 11, pt. III, p. 649.
8. Historian John Keegan, after driving the Seven Days battlefields, observed that maps, even those with scale legends, create an optical illusion that make the battlefields look further apart than they actually are. The distance between the Mechanicsville and Gaines's Mill battlefields is only three miles, with the remaining four battles spanning only a few additional miles. John Keegan, *Field of Battles: The Wars for North America* (Alfred A. Knopf, 1996), 228-229.
9. Glatthaar, *General Lee's Army*, 140.

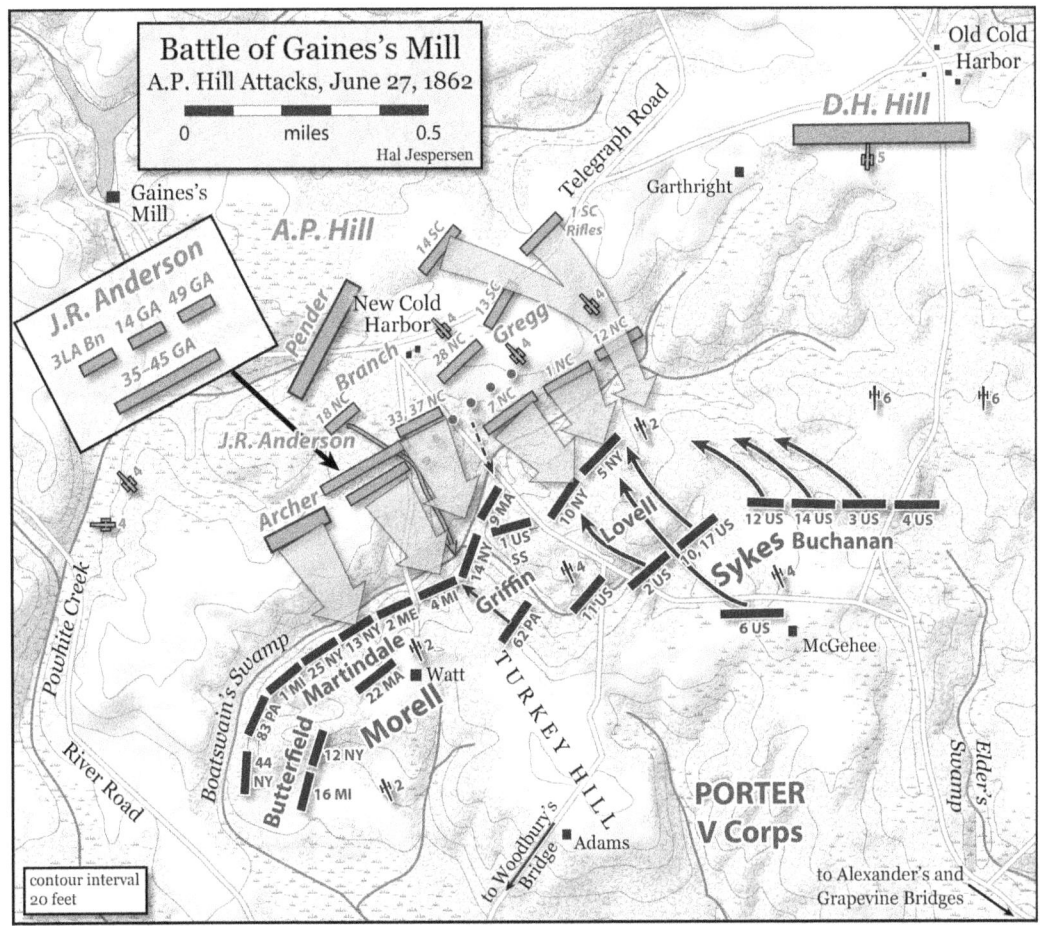

Hill's troops suffered heavy casualties in their afternoon assaults across Boatswain's Swamp. As Doug Crenshaw notes in *Richmond Shall Not Be Given Up*, "Of the 13,000 men Hill had marched up the Cold Harbor Road that day, more than 2,000 were slaughtered." (Map by Hal Jespersen)

Anderson's Brigade bivouacked the night of June 25 near Meadow Bridge and spent the following morning looking down over the Chickahominy River. Impatient with Jackson, who was running hours behind schedule, A. P. Hill, on his own volition, committed six brigades over the Chickahominy on the afternoon of June 26 to a frontal assault against Porter's V Corps across Beaver Dam Creek.

Hall's Company G and two other companies stood picket duty on June 26 and did not participate in the attack. The remaining seven companies of the 14th Georgia fought on the left flank of Anderson's Brigade, which was, in turn, on the left flank of Hill's forces. The Georgians faced an enemy force that was not only well-entrenched on the other side of the creek but also supported by "eighteen guns and abundant reserves."[10] Thomas personally led the 35th Georgia, seven companies of the 14th Georgia, and the 3rd Louisiana Battalion in an effort to cross Beaver Dam Creek, while the 45th Georgia and 49th Georgia remained in reserve.

The charging Georgians were under heavy fire as they attempted to cross the creek, which was fifty yards wide and up to four feet deep in places yet marshy with quicksand in others.[11] Folsom, who had been ill prior to the engagement, was wounded during the fighting, and only a few men from the 14th Georgia made it across the creek. Once across, Thomas's men put to flight some Union skirmishers but then saw that the main body of Union defenders was protected by a deep ravine, abatis, and rifle pits containing sharpshooters. Although Thomas requested reinforcements, none came, so he withdrew his troops back across Beaver Dam Creek.

Other Confederate units tried to cross the creek further down from the 14th Georgia. But as John Fox writes, "The men of the 35th and 14th Georgia and the 3rd Louisiana Battalion represented the only Southerners to place their feet on the enemy's eastern side of the creek during the late afternoon fight" on June 26, 1862.[12] In his brigade report, Anderson praised both Thomas and Folsom.[13] As to Folsom, Anderson wrote, "This officer was confined to his sick bed, but as soon as the order to move forward was given he got up and gallantly led his regiment, though laboring under the effects of the disease."[14] However, the battle was a clear tactical victory for the Union troops, who held their ground and suffered only 360 casualties. The Confederates suffered almost 1,500 casualties. It was arguably a strategic victory for Lee, however, because it contributed to McClellan's decision to forego a siege of Richmond.[15]

Private Jacob L. Elsesser's 9th Pennsylvania Reserves were in Brig. Gen. Truman Seymour's Third Brigade of Brig. Gen. George McCall's Third Division in Porter's V Corps. Elsesser was present at Beaver Dam Creek but positioned in reserve above the

---

10. Sears, *To the Gates of Richmond*, 203.
11. John J. Fox III, *Red Clay to Richmond, Trail of the 35th Georgia Infantry Regiment, C.S.A.* (Angle Valley Press, 2006), 60. The 14th Georgia had to wade through water that was "hip-deep across the swamp." Uzal W. Ent, *The Pennsylvania Reserves in the Civil War* (McFarland & Company, 2014), 60.
12. Fox, *Red Clay to Richmond*, 61.
13. Fox, *Red Clay to Richmond*, 64.
14. *OR*, Ser. 1, vol. 11, pt. II, p. 878.
15. McPherson, *Battle Cry of Freedom*, 467.

bridge at Ellerson's Mill, approximately a half-mile southeast of where the 14th Georgia crossed the creek. Anderson's Brigade bivouacked overnight west of Beaver Dam Creek, fully intending to resume battle in the morning. But with Jackson having finally arrived from the Shenandoah, McClellan ordered Porter to abandon his position east of Beaver Dam Creek just before dawn and move southeast to the high ground behind Boatswain Creek, near Gaines's Mill, roughly three miles to the south.[16]

In pursuit, the 14th Georgia marched over the abandoned Union gun pits and campsites. Hall and Patterson both recorded the enormous amount of supplies the Union soldiers had abandoned, including weapons, clothing, foodstuffs, and what Hall described as "in short ever thing pertaining to a camp."[17] Hall likely picked up Elsesser's abandoned diary at this point in the day. Hall wrote, "Following after the retreating enemy as he was burning up and leaving every thing he possess[ed] I thought I had as well preserve his diary as it certainly would have been lost so I will turn it from a Yankee to a Rebel diary." Elsesser's last entry was for Thursday, June 26, 1862. Hall's entries in Elsesser's diary commence with Friday, June 27, 1862. Although Hall had written a handful of dated daily entries in his pocket notebook, it was Elsesser's *Daily Pocket Remembrancer* that provided the framework for Hall's daily entries for the next thirty-three months.

Porter's troops spent the morning hours of June 27 building fortifications, digging rifle pits, and setting up batteries looking down over Boatswain's Creek. Again, the Union took advantage of superb natural defenses afforded by a deep ravine, a creek, and high ground on which to place artillery and sharpshooters armed with breech-loading rifles. A. P. Hill, whose troops arrived first, made the initial assault around 2:30 p.m. Lee had planned for both Longstreet and Jackson to join the battle by flanking the Union left and right, respectively, but again, Jackson was late. The brunt of the mid-afternoon assault fell to Hill, whose troops had to descend from a ridge, cross swampy terrain, and then attack three lines of Union defenders mostly arrayed uphill – under fire from Porter's artillery.[18]

---

16. The battle on June 27, 1862, is also sometimes referred to as the first Battle of Cold Harbor.
17. "Guns pistols Sabres Knapsacs Haversacks Canteens Shoes blankets overcoats Scattered all along the road indicated that the Yankees were in a hurry to get to some place of Safety." Patterson to Family, July 12, 1862, "Incomplete Patterson Correspondence."
18. Doug Crenshaw, *Richmond Shall Not Be Given Up, The Seven Days' Battles, June 25-July 1, 1862* (Savas Beatie, 2017), 41.

Over the course of the afternoon and early evening, Anderson's Brigade made three unsuccessful charges in what Clifford Dowdey called "one of the longest, hardest, most unsung actions of the war."[19] The Union line only broke hours later after Jackson arrived and Lee was finally able to get his divisions to attack en masse, with Hood's Texas Brigade finally penetrating Porter's center. As to the effort of Hill's troops over five hours of fighting, Longstreet wrote, "The troops of the gallant A. P. Hill, that did as much and as effective fighting as any, received little of the credit properly due them. It was their long and steady fight that thinned the Federal ranks and caused them to so foul their guns that they were out of order when the final struggle came."[20]

It was a brutal afternoon for the 14th Georgia. As Hall wrote, "We fought hard and desperate to drive the enemy from their breastworks and Batterys bullets and balls flying in showers among us, bombs and Grape shot flying thick and fast among us." The battle ended in the late evening, with the Union troops again in retreat, heading towards the James River. But the loss of daylight prevented Lee from capitalizing on his victory by pinning Porter against the river.

The six-hour engagement at Gaines's Mill was the largest Confederate attack of the war, involving more troops than the far more famous Pickett-Pettigrew-Trimble charge at Gettysburg a year later. Lee sent some 32,000 men forward in the final thrust but suffered over 8,700 casualties. Union casualties of 6,800 included 2,800 Federal soldiers taken prisoner. Between the frontal assault at Beaver Dam Creek and the unsuccessful charges at Gaines's Mill, Hill lost nearly a fourth of his division.[21] Hall wrote that there were as many as twenty-five dead men on a piece of ground only ten yards square and that the cries of the dying and wounded were "enough to melt the heart of a Stone."

Anderson's Brigade spent June 28 helping the wounded and burying the dead. It then marched south, spending the night at Atlee's Farm, making a wide swing to the west on Darbytown Road. This put them far afield from the June 29, 1862, battle at Savage Station. But Hill had his men in position by 11 a.m. on June 30, 1862, to participate in the battle at Frayser's Farm.

Lee still hoped to cut off a large portion of McClellan's troops from reaching the James River. As at Seven Pines and Gaines's Mill, the Confederates had a complex plan

---

19. Clifford Dowdey, *The Seven Days: The Emergence of Robert E. Lee* (Fairfax House, 1964), 221.
20. James Longstreet, *From Manassas to Appomattox* (Konecky & Konecky, 1992), 129.
21. Sears, *To the Gates of Richmond*, 226.

of converging lines that, for various reasons, never congealed at Frayser's Farm, a section of the larger battle of Glendale. Lee directed Longstreet and Hill, held initially in reserve to the west, to hold fire until they heard sounds of battle from Benjamin Huger's and Jackson's divisions to the east. Hall reported that the regiment waited for battle in a ravine with artillery "bombs" falling among them. In the late afternoon, Lee finally gave up on Huger and Jackson and ordered Hill and Longstreet to advance to the northeast. Just as at Mechanicsville and Gaines's Mill, Hill was again facing McCall's Division, which included Elsesser's 9th Pennsylvania Reserves in Seymour's Brigade.

Anderson's Brigade was the last Confederate brigade to engage at Frayser's Farm. Anderson placed the 14th Georgia and the 3rd Louisiana Battalion on the left side of Long Bridge Road and ordered his other regiments to the right side of the road. The 14th Georgia and the 3rd Louisiana moved out at a double-quick pace ahead of the three Georgia regiments on the right side of Long Bridge Road. Judging from the direction of enemy musket fire that Union troops were on the left side of the road, Anderson ordered the regiments on the right to join up with the 14th Georgia and 3rd Louisiana so as to form a parallel line to the enemy.[22]

Bayonet fighting at Frayser's Farm (*Harper's Pictorial History of the Great Rebellion*)

Hill had told Anderson that there would be a friendly brigade to his front, so Anderson had ordered his men to hold their fire until he could determine if the target was friend or foe. After Anderson's brigade crossed a fence in the darkness, they encountered a brigade or division whom Anderson suspected was the enemy. However, some of the Confederate troops were taken in by the unidentified troops calling out not to fire

---

22. *OR*, Ser. 1, vol. 11, pt. II, p. 879.

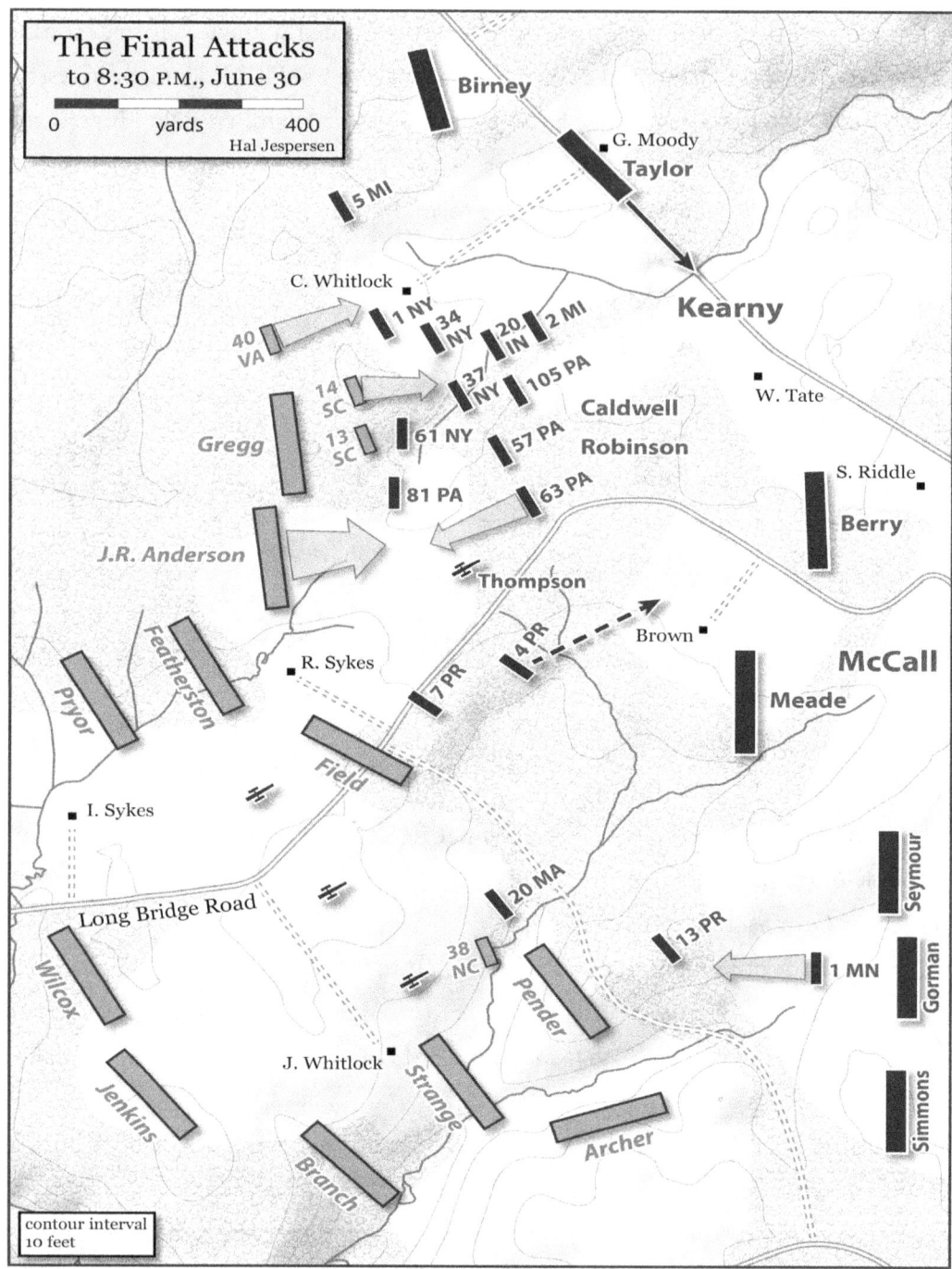

Confederate missteps at Frayser's Farm/Glendale resulted in one of Lee's greatest missed opportunities of the war. Other maps for this battle are contained in Chapter 14 to illustrate the actions of Elsesser's 9th Pennsylvania Reserves, which had withdrawn from the battlefield by the time the 14th Georgia was committed. (Map by Hal Jespersen, from *Richmond Shall Not Be Given Up: The Seven Days' Battles, June 25—July 1, 1862*, by Doug Crenshaw)

because they were friends. Anderson ordered his men to charge with bayonets at double-quick, but his troops were demoralized at the idea of firing on possible "friendlies." Some of Anderson's men realized that the voices they heard did not have a southern drawl, and all remaining doubt was removed when an enemy commander yelled "Fire," and Union troops delivered a strong fire to the left wing, primarily to the 45th Georgia. In the ensuing bayonet charge by the Union troops, Anderson was wounded in the forehead by a spent bullet, at which point Col. Thomas assumed temporary command of the brigade. Hill wrote the following year that he had instructed the 14th Georgia to cheer as loudly as they could in order to deceive the Union troops into thinking there were more fresh regiments; when the regiment did so, all firing ceased within five minutes, and the Union troops retired.[23]

The number of Union casualties was especially steep. "Piles of enemy dead, stacked two and three deep, covered the ground in front of the 3rd Louisiana, the 14th Georgia and the 45th Georgia."[24] As historian Brian Burton points out, the fighting at Frayser's Farm/Glendale was "some of the most savage of the war."[25] McCall, who was himself taken prisoner, suffered 3,000 casualties out of 9,000 men; A. P. Hill lost more than 4,000 out of roughly 14,000.[26] It was yet another strategic loss for the Confederates because Lee failed in his goal of surrounding and cutting off McClellan's run to the James River; as Douglas Southall Freeman wrote, it was one of the "great lost opportunities in Confederate military history . . . He had only that one day for a Cannae, and the army was not ready for it."[27] McClellan's men (minus McClellan himself, who was already at Harrison's Landing) again used the cover of darkness to race to the next defensive point, Malvern Hill, en route to the James River.

The battle of Malvern Hill, the final engagement of the Seven Days battles, on July 1, 1862, involved yet another series of frontal assaults over open fields by Confederate

---

23. *OR*, Ser. 1, vol. 11, pt. II, pp. 838-39.
24. Fox, *Red Clay to Richmond*, 74.
25. Brian K. Burton, *Extraordinary Circumstances: The Seven Days Battles* (Indiana University Press, 2001), 298.
26. Burton, *Extraordinary Circumstances*, 298.
27. Douglas Southall Freeman, *Lee: An Abridgement in one volume by Richard Harwell* of the four-volume *R. E. Lee* (Simon & Schuster, 1991), 214. At Cannae in 216 BC, Hannibal surrounded and destroyed the Roman army during the Second Punic War.

troops against a strongly-defended Union position, consisting of over 100 guns at the top of a 150-foot hill.[28] The casualty numbers, some 5,500 Confederates killed or wounded, reflect the futility of the assault, which had been executed in a disjointed manner that permitted the Union defenders to pick off attacking Confederates as each wave advanced. General Daniel H. ("D.H.") Hill later wrote that Malvern Hill was not war – it was murder.[29] Although held in reserve at Malvern Hill near the intersection of Darbytown Road and Quaker Road (later renamed Willis Church Road), the 14th Georgia was still subjected to incoming artillery fire. Hall described Malvern Hill as a "decided victory," likely because he believed the Confederates had driven the Union forces from their position and forced them to abandon their dead and many of their wounded. But from a strategic standpoint, Malvern Hill was only a blocking measure that enabled McClellan to finish moving his army and supplies to Harrison's Landing on the James River and under the protection of the Union gunboats.[30]

After Malvern Hill, McClellan pushed Lincoln for more men so he could resume the campaign against Richmond; Lincoln refused, astutely noting that even if he sent McClellan 100,000 men, the general would still claim he needed more. Moreover, rampant illness in the Union troops on the Peninsula also served as "an indirect but important factor" in whether to continue the campaign, given that one Union Corps commander reported that 20 percent of the army was sick.[31] McClellan and the Army of the Potomac were ordered back to northern Virginia by General Henry Halleck, the Union Army's new general-in-chief. Halleck had written McClellan that keeping his army in its current position "would almost destroy it in that climate. The months of August and September are almost fatal to whites who live on that part of the James River."[32] Thus did McClellan's vaunted campaign to Richmond end with a whimpered withdrawal to northern Virginia. McClellan emerged from the Seven Days Battles with his reputation as a fighter in shreds – he had made it to the outskirts of Richmond but did not complete the mission. Lee, contrarily, had stepped into command on short

---

28. McPherson, *Battle Cry of Freedom*, 469. Malvern Hill may have been the most famous use of artillery as a defensive tool during the entire war. McWhiney and Jamieson, *Attack and Die*, 112.
29. McPherson, *Battle Cry of Freedom*, 470.
30. McWhiney and Jamieson, *Attack and Die*, 112.
31. Steiner, *Disease in the Civil War*, 98, 142.
32. Steiner, *Disease in the Civil War*, 142.

notice, had molded the Southern forces into a better fighting force, and had saved the capital of the Confederacy.

Hall, from the perspective of the summer of 1862, described the Seven Days as "the greatest Battles the world ever saw." The Confederates suffered over 20,200 casualties and the Union over 15,855. Lee's forces had twice as many killed in combat, which is not surprising given the number of frontal assaults they made against strongly defended Union lines, but the Union suffered far more captured as prisoners.[33] A. P. Hill's division lost roughly 5,500 troops at Mechanicsville, Gaines's Mill, and Frayser's Farm.[34] Anderson's Brigade had roughly 1,750 men at the start of the Seven Days' Battles but suffered 563 killed or wounded.[35] As the war wore on, the South, with its much smaller population, could ill afford such high battle casualties.

In terms of casualties suffered by the 14th Georgia during the Seven Days battles, the regimental adjutant reported in 1864 that 24 men in the regiment were killed and 60 wounded, but the medical director for the Army of Northern Virginia submitted a report in 1863 that stated that the 14th Georgia (under an incorrect brigade) suffered 16 killed and 122 wounded.[36] In Company G, Privates Romulus Weeks and Benjamin Gough were both mortally wounded on June 27. The assistant regimental surgeon reported that George McCraney was severely wounded and that Sergeant J. Ford was slightly wounded in the shoulder.[37]

As in western Virginia, disease inflicted more casualties on the Peninsula than combat did.[38] Lieutenant William A. Johnston was admitted to Chimborazo Hospital # 3 in Richmond in May 1862 for dysentery but transferred to Lynchburg General Hospital # 1, where he died in late June 1862; Private Nathan Baker died of chronic diarrhea at Lynchburg on June 16, 1862; 2d Sergeant Thaddeus M. Bostick died at Richmond of diarrhea on July 22, 1862; 3d Sergeant Sylvanus Q. Jordan died of pneumonia at

---

33. Murray and Hseih, *A Savage War*, 188.
34. Robertson, *General A. P. Hill: The Story of a Confederate Warrior*, 95.
35. Folsom, *Heroes and Martyrs of Georgia*, 115.
36. Folsom, *Heroes and Martyrs of Georgia*, 148; *OR*, Ser. 1, vol. 11, pt. II, p. 505.
37. "Report of the Killed and Wounded in the 14th Georgia Regiment in the Battles for Richmond, on the 26th, 27th, and 30th of June, 1862," *Southern Confederacy*, July 16, 1862, www.newspapers.com.
38. For every soldier killed in combat during the Civil War, two died from disease, which was still a vast improvement over the Mexican-American War, where the ratio was a far more appalling seven to one. McPherson, *Battle Cry of Freedom*, 487.

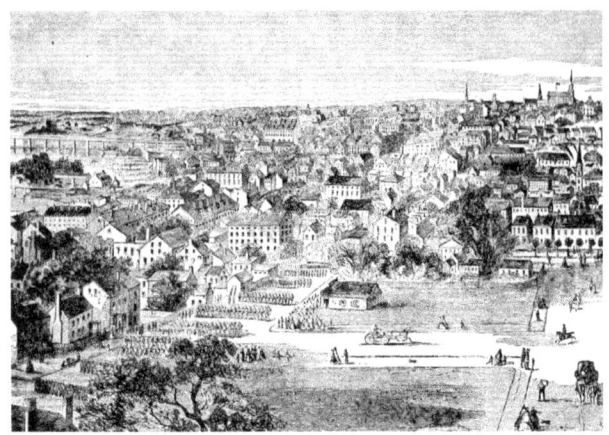

A sketch of Richmond from 1861. This was likely the first time in Hall's life that he had access to the resources of a city as large as Richmond, which, according to the 1860 U.S. census, ranked among the 25 largest cities in the United States. (Public domain: Charles Carleton Coffin, *Drum-Beat of the Nation* (New York, NY: Harper & Brothers, 1915)

Chimborazo Hospital # 2 in Richmond on August 19, 1862; and James M. Kerce died of typhoid fever in Chimborazo Hospital in Richmond on August 31, 1862.

As Patterson wrote on July 12th, "our Regt is entirely exhausted and worn out... I do hope for humanities sake they will let it retire and rest awhile at some healthy Camp."[39] Patterson got his wish, as the 14th Georgia spent several weeks in camp outside of Richmond. Food was plentiful, and there was ready access to the Richmond newspapers. Over the span of the Peninsula Campaign, Hall copied numerous pro-Southern songs and poems into his pocket notebook, many of which can be traced to contemporary Richmond publications.[40]

Hall was sick for much of July 1862, making him just one of tens of thousands of soldiers who fell ill during the Peninsula campaign. Much of the area contested during the Seven Days battles was on or near swampy ground. Men slogged through mud and often slept in standing water; hot, humid days alternated with cold rain. Camps were

---

39. Patterson to Family, July 12, 1862, "Incomplete Patterson Correspondence." Patterson had written home on July 12 that his health had been "very bad for several days owing to physical exhaustion and constant exposure in the swamps bordering on the Chickahominy." Apparently matters were even worse for another regiment in Thomas's Brigade, the 49th Georgia, where a company first sergeant reported that on June 1 his company was down to less than ten men and his regiment down to less than one hundred men due to "the effects of sickness and fatigue." Draughton Stith Haynes, *Field Diary of a Confederate Soldier* (Ashantilly Press, 1963), 5.
40. These entries and comments as to their likely sources are contained in Appendix B.

crowded and seldom far from freshly-dug graves and bloated dead horses. There was little access to fresh water, which forced men to dig for water or drink slime-covered surface water shared with wildlife. Hall likely did not grasp the epidemiological significance of his observation that the "musquetoes" were "verry bad at night."

Environmental factors had the ability to kill soldiers as effectively as combat. As of June 20, almost one-tenth of both armies were so sick as to be considered unfit for duty.[41] The major ailments included dysentery, chronic diarrhea, and "Chickahominy Fever," which was "neither typical malaria, true typhoid, nor pure scurvy, but appeared to be some variety of mixed complaint."[42] As environmental historian Kathryn Shively Meier writes, the "other enemy" in the Peninsula Campaign was "environment – the weather, climate, seasons, terrain features, flora, and fauna that [the soldiers] could not avoid, exposed as they were by lack of supplies, a pace . . . too slow on the Peninsula to avoid befouled soil and water, and swarms of disease-bearing insects."[43]

Hall fell ill on July 5 and was sent back to an "old camp" by his surgeon. In his narrative, he generally

Environmental conditions in the Chickahominy region caused an untold number of deaths in both armies. (*Battles and Leaders of the Civil War*, Yoseloff ed., 1956)

attributed his illness to fatigue from marching and "fighting day and night." But in several daily entries, he relayed that he had a very bad cough and was feverish and weak.

---

41. Sears, *To the Gates of Richmond*, 163. Sears also discusses the high number of general officers on both sides who became seriously ill from disease during the Peninsula Campaign, including a Union general who died of Chickahominy fever.
42. Dale C. Smith, "The Rise and Fall of Typhomalarial Fever: I. Origins, *Journal of the History of Medicine and Allied Sciences*. April 1982, 216.
43. Meier, *Nature's Civil War*, 45.

He rejoined the regiment on July 12, 1862, but only a few weeks later, he became so ill that he had to be hospitalized for the first time in his military service.

Hall included in his diary a muster of the company's strength on July 15, 1862, which consisted of 90 officers and enlisted men. Two major changes in the command structure occurred at the end of July. Lee promoted Edward Thomas as Anderson's replacement as brigade commander, and the brigade was transferred from Hill's Light Division to Stonewall Jackson's command in central Virginia. The brigade set out by train on July 31, 1862, for Jackson's headquarters at Gordonsville, Virginia, then a major rail station on the Virginia Central and the Orange & Alexandria Railroad railroads.

Pocket Notebook Narrative
June 25 – July 31, 1862

On the 25 of June our regiment was ordered off and left 3 companies on picket (one being ours) and we remained on picket till the evening of the 26 the day the great Battle commenced.

Our regt 7 companies was in the Battle on the 26th [Mechanicsville], and we was relieved off picket late that evening and joined them that night by crossing the Chickahominy two or 3 miles above Mechanicsville. On the morning of the 27th we took up the march and verry soon to meet the enemy which we found to be retreating. We come up with their rear 2 or 3 miles below Mechanicsville and began to see Signs of their hasty retreat. We fought and pursued them 6 or 8 miles passing their abandoned camps and fortification, passing thousands of arms, ammunition, commissaries knapsack, haver sacks and in short ever thing pertaining to a camp and a good many Sutters Stores was set on fire and burning as we passed them.

About 2 oclock we come up with the enemy in an overwhelming force behind Breast works and batterys and here the Battle [Gaines's Mill] become general and terriffic along a line of several miles. Our Brigade was in Gen. A. P. Hill's Division together with Gen Longstreets Division occupied the center. We fought hard and desperate to drive the enemy from their breastworks and Batterys bullets and balls flying in showers among us bombs and Grape shot flying thick and fast among us our brave boys regardless of all that continued with never tiring zeal. It was verry warm that day and a many a poor soldier fainted and give way lifeless on the field from exhaustion. Battery after battery we stormed and taken and at last completely routed the enemy from their works and set them completely to flight taking several thousand prisoners and all their wounded.

This Battle ended 9 or 10 oclock in the night. Next morning after taking a little rest I took a survey of part of the Battle Field and their was more dead men then I ever saw before. There were as many as 25 on a piece of ground ten yards Square. The most dreadful sight to behold their mangled Boddies some with their arms or legs torn off. Some with their heads completely gone and the cries of the dying and wounded displayed some of the horrors of war and was enough to melt the heart of a Stone. All that day our Brigade remained there and assisted in burrying the [dead]. Our men they was burried by digging a large pit and wraping them in blankets consigned as many of their poor bodies to a pit as it would hold. The dead of the enemy was buried by throwing a good quantity of dirt over them for we did not have time to burry them any better.

On the 29th our division took up the line of march and recross[ed] the Chickahominy at New Bridge on the nine mile road and on to the right of Seven Pine across the Williamsburg road 3 miles below Richmond and taken the Charles City Road leading down The James River. About 8 oclock P.M. we camped for the night. We resumed the march on the morning of the 30th and continued down the road at a slow pace. About 2 or 3 oclock we began to hear booming of cannon ahead of us and as we approached nearer at a quick march we could hear the roar of musketry.

As we neared the battle the bombs from the enemies Batterys began to whistle among us. Our Brigade filed out in to a thick ravine about a mile from the battle field and remained in line of Battle till near sundown and the shells falling among us at every instant. One bursted in the 49th Ga vol[s] and killed 2 or 3 and wounded several. At this instant we were ordered off to where the Battle was raging in quick time. About this time His Excellency President Davis passed us. There was a general shout our brave boys cheering him as he passed us in the road. "<u>On to the Battle Boys</u>" was the shout "<u>and drive the Robbers from our Sacred Soil</u>." And as we passed on we met many a poor fellow wounded but were in good Spirits for all some of them was nearly spent and one would say "<u>go on my brave comerade and revenge my wounds</u>."

When we arrived on the field the sun had set and we marched up in line of battle facing the enemy at a strong point of Breastworks the enemy had made by puling down a fence in the edge of a dense forest and piling up logs and old rubish of every kind. We had to charge through an open field. We began to fire on a line of the enemy that was out, the right of the main body. In the mean time it grew so dark we could not distinguish a man above ten steps from us and the Yankees a pooring a murderous fire upon us all the time. We resolved to drive the enemy from their strong position or die in the attempt. We come a charge and brought a shout that rent the air. We drove them through the wood panic stricken and scatered them with the four winds, and taken several hundred prisoners. Among them was Major Gen Mcall. This was a hard fought Battle but we gained a decided victory. We taken every piece of artillery they had on the field.

It is not my entention to give any account of the Battles only what I was witness to for any other part I knew not enough to give a detail, and no where in this Book have I put down any only what I was witness to for it is my aim to note what our regiment go through with and our Brigade as far as I knew.

The Battle ended about 9 oclock and our Brigade was the last that was engaged. The night was taken up by the litter bearers in bringing the wounded off the Battle and the Surgeons dressing their wounds as far as possible. The poor fellows crys and lamentations could be heard a good distance all around. We got verry little rest that night and next morning we marched about a mile and rested till Evening. About two oclock the rearing of artillery could be heard at intervals and ever thing was on the stir passing backwards and forward in double quick time and we knew that another great Battle had commenced. The artillery firing grew more fiercer every moment and towards night our Brigade was ordered to the scene of conflict and could distinctly hear roar of Small arms. Before this our brigade was marched up under a heavy fire of artillery and as we marched through a pine thicket that had been a field in cultivation once but had grown up in pines of all sizes from 2 feet in diameter to the smallest size.

I experienced a sight I never shall forget - cannon balls, bomb shells and grapeshot come thicker than hail cutting down and splitting and tearing all to a thousand peices, nearly every tree in the forest. Our Brigade did not get to fire a shot in this engagement [Malvern Hill] but they was under the fire of the enemy guns all the time. The reason we did not exchange a shot was there was too many of our men a head of us. Our commanders had more men under the enemies fire than could do execution.

It was the most terriffic cannonading and bombarding of any engagement during the war, and long after darkness has wraped her dark mantle around the terable scene it continued on with unabated fury. It was I dare say, 10 oclock in the night when it ceased. That was the 1st day of July and next morning the 2nd it commenced raining varry hard and continued through the day. Our Brigade was march[ed] through the Battle field that day and through them pines that was torn down so bad it look like it would have been impossible for a being to have been in there and escaped alive and it was over 3 or 4 miles square. We gained another decided victory here driving them from their position and they left all their dead behind and a great amount of their wounded.

The Yankees did not stop and take a stand no more till they got to James River, under cover of their Gunboats. Our army kept on their track till they got away down between The James & Chickahominy rivers, where their gunboats could run up both Streams. If they had attempted it we had them here in a verry narrow limit and it contrasted greatly with their possessions a little over a week previous, then they had unlimited Sway over a vast amount of teratory, from the James and Chickahominy to Pamunky and York Rivers and now they only possessed a verry narrow limit on the James River. They were in 3 miles of Richmond before the Battle commenced on the

26th of June, and now they were at least 30 miles nearest point of their army from the Confederate Capitol. This was on record having began June 26th and ended July 2nd having lasted 6 days and nights only ceasing long enough at intervals to pursue and overtake the retreating foe. The munitions of war that our men captured will do our government a vast amount of good. It was a great victory for the Southern Cause, and it Shows the Superiority of the Southerner over the niggard[44] yankee for that they had every material advantage over us that they could wish.

The 3rd and 4th of July we kept in close pursuit of them till they got to the river to their gunboats and they got in a position that we could not molest them any more for the present. On the 6th and 7th our regiment fell back in the rear to get Some rest from their toil and fatigues.

On the 5th I was taken sick from my over exertions to do my part and I was sent back to our old camp by the Surgeon where I remained till I got better and on the 13th I joined the regt in camp on the James River 5 miles below Richmond and by this time I had regained my health as good as ever for it was the fatigue of marching & fighting day and night that caused it.

Our camp at this place was very pleasantly situated, where we could go to the River to Bathe and on its banks grew more dewberries and huckleberries than I ever saw any where else and which was quite a luxury to us poor soldiers for we could take them and make pies and tarts which was a very palatable dish. We fared verry well during our stay at this place. We had plenty of good water to use and had verry good and nourishing food. The exorbitant prices of

---

44. "Niggard" is a Middle English word of Scandinavian origin for a cheapskate or stingy person. https://www.merriam-webster.com/dictionary/niggard

vegetables and all eatables in general kept us from indulging in much only what we drew. I will give a few of the prevalent prices in Richmond and vicinity during this period. Butter was $1.25 per pound Syrup $7.00 per gallon, pork 75 cents per pound candy $1.50 per pound black pepper $1.50 per pound. Course shoes was $10.00 per pair.

But we were doomed not to remain at rest and quietude long. On the 28th we got orders to cook three days rations and hold ourselves in readiness to march. On the 29th we got orders to march at 2 oclock that day but we did not get off until the 31st we marched to Richmond and it was raining drenching us to the skin at every step.

Remembrancer Daily Entries
June 27, 1862 – July 31, 1862

Friday, June 27, 1862

In the great battle and following after the retreating enemy as he was burning up and leaving every thing he possessed I thought I had as well preserve his diary as it certainly would been lost and so I will turn it from a Yankee to a Rebel diary and this day I never shall forget if I live a century it is unparrellel in the annals of American History.

Saturday, June 28, 1862

M fair. E cloudy & warm. This morning I took a walk over the Battle field or a portion of it and I walked over to where the enemy held such a strong position and there a sight that I am unable to find words to describe, came to my view. Thousands upon thousands of dead and wounded bodies torn and mangle[d] so that it was impossible to distinguish their countenance. Legions of the wounded Yankees fell into our possess[ion].

Sunday, June 29, 1862

Rain through the night. Partially cloudy and hot. We remain on the Battle field till 11 oclock and take up the march and cross the Chickahominy at new Bridge on the nine mile road and proceeded a little to the right of the seven pines and across the Williamsburg road in the direction of the James River and about dark we camped. This day was intensly hot.

Monday, June 30, 1862

Fair & Hot. This morning we marched on at a slow pace till about 3 oclock and we began to hear the booming of cannon ahead of us, and as we drew nigher we could hear the terriffic roar of musketry and about 4 oclock we arrived at the scene of the action. Our brigade was marching into it. We drove the enemy from thier position and gained another complete victory. The Battle ended about 9 o-clock P M.

Tuesday, July 1, 1862

M fair & warm. E cloudy & warm. Next morning I felt verry bad from fatigue and we tended to our wounded the night previous and burried our dead, and got some little rest & about 12 or 1 oclock P.M. another great Battle commenced about 2 miles from the one on Monday and it was kept up till 9 or 10 oclock in the night growing more fierce as the night advanced we drove the enemy away and kept on the Battle ground.

Wednesday, July 2, 1862

Hard rain. This day about 12 oclock P.M. we took up the march through the Battle ground of the evening previous and the most terrable sight I ever saw I witnessed hear which I cannot find words to describe. Thousand[s] of dead men and horses in every direction and some of them torn with bombs so you could not tell what they were. We marched two or three miles and camped for the night.

Thursday, July 3, 1862

Cool & cloudy with some rain. We took up the march in a south Eastern direction. We rested about 3 hours about the middle of the day and continued the march till 8 oclock P.M. and camped about 25 miles from Richmond. We have now got the Yankees drove up into a clost [closed] place and we still keep on pushing them to them to the wall and ere long will have them where they can neither back nor squall.

Friday, July 4, 1862

Fair & warm. This day is the greatest anniversary in American History. I use to love to enjoy it when I was at home with my dear friends but now I am far away and events of more vital importance to ourselves, is being transacted on this memorial day. 10 oclock A.M. Still at camp, about 1 oclock P.M. we marched in a south western direction till near night and camped and sent out pickets for the night.

Saturday, July 5, 1862

Fair & Hot. I was too sick to keep up with our regiment and I got a pass and started back to our old camps in company with Sergt [Sylvanus] Jordan and [Garry] Green Ford. We Had a verry bad time of it. I was verry sick. Our regiment took up the march in a southern direction.

Sunday, July 6, 1862

Fair & Hot. I arrived at our old camp today about 12 o'ck. It was verry hot. It has been 11 days since I left here before and I have been a fighting and a marching ever since, without ceasing. I have got a verry bad cough and hurting in my hip.

Monday, July 7, 1862

Fair and verry Hot & sultry. My cough hurts me verry much today. My hip and ankle is getting better. I hope I am able to join our regiment in a day or two for I am uneasy when I am away from them. I have not been away from them before in so long. Sent a letter home with account of the Battle.

Tuesday, July 8, 1862

Fair & Hot. At old camp sick with a verry bad cold and cough with some fevers, but hope I will be well in a few days. Its verry disagreeable weather here now. It is verry hot and sultry in the shade and if you under take to walk along the road the dust is intolerable.

Wednesday, July 9, 1862

Hot & sultry. I am some little better today. Continues hot and sultry. The farmers is busily harvesting their grain and making hay in this country. O how I long to be at home to eat vegetables water melons fruit &c but I have to stay away cut off from ever[y] luxury, but I am [in] a glorious cause.

Thursday, July 10, 1862

Fair Hot & dusty. I am still sick and I fear I am getting worse. Its verry hot dry and disagreeable weather.

Friday, July 11, 1862

M slow continued rain. E cloudy. Today I am verry sick. I had a verry hot fever part of the day, and I fell verry weak. We had a verry pretty little rain today which continued from soon in the morning till 12 oclock and it cooled the air and laid the dust considerable.

Saturday, July 12, 1862

Fair & pleasant. Today I feel some better and hope I may be able soon to join the regt. I have a verry bad cough but I hope that will soon wear off. It is fair as a silver bell today and is verry pleasant in the shade.

Sunday, July 13, 1862

Fair & Warm. I joined the regiment today 5 miles below Richmond on James River. The company was all in fine health & spirits. This day is just one year ago since our co[mpany] left Isabella Worth Co Ga on our way to Virginia. I hope this day one year hense will find us all safe at home and peace & prosperity breathing [o'er] our distracted country.

Sunday, July 13, 1862[45]

Anniversary 3rd[46]

This date July 13th 1862 is just one year since I left my native county for the seat of war, left my dear home with all its joys and comforts for a life of toils and privations, for a life of hardships unindurable, left all that near and dear to me for hardships in far off country but do I regret the day I left, the day my dear mother with grief and sorrow bid her dear son a last farewell. No, dear Lord forbid I should. Far from it I am proud today of being a soldier a <u>noble volunteer</u> in a noble cause one that will hold out and endure to the end, one that has proved its self to be a just cause. I have been through all kind of life since I left that dear home, have had on many a hairbredth escape from sickness and death. I have been [in] several great Battles and one that has not a parrallel in the worlds history one that lasted six days and nights without ceasing only long enough to pursue and over take the flying foe. It began the 26th of June and lasted till 2nd of July being Six days and Six nights that our brave boys fought without intermission. We were in glorious cause and we defeated and demoralized the greatest and grandest army that the world ever saw, and they had every material advantage of us that they could wish. My sincere hope and prayer is that July 13, 1863 may find us all safe at our homes in peace and

---

45. This dated entry is from the Pocket Notebook.
46. Hall observed anniversaries on the days on which he joined the Yancey Independents, when he went into camp in Worth County, when he departed Georgia, and when he swore allegiance to the Confederacy.

independence wafting over our dear but distracted country, and that we may enjoy the fruits of our toil and hardships.

Monday, July 14, 1862

Fair & Warm. I am somewhat getting over my sickness, although I feel verry bad this morning. I hope I may soon be as hearty as ever. It is verry warm today. Times is verry quiet. No news of importance. I do not think Mclelland can [not] get his army in fighting order in a month.

Tuesday, July 15, 1862

M fair & hot. E thunder & rain. Today is verry hot before noon and after noon several thunder clouds passes around but it rains verry little here. My health has returned in full vigor and I hope and pray to my heavenly Father and I may be keep it if every thing else deserts me. No news of importance.

Tuesday, July 15, 1862[47]

The greatest Battles the world ever saw beginning June 16 and lasting till July 2nd 6 days with out intermission and part of our troops still a fighting. A few days more will bring important and I hope decisive results. I hope and ernestly pray to my great Redeemer who has carried me safe through so many Battles and hair bredth escapes, that by Sept 4, 1862 a glorious peace and independence will be reigning over our unhappy country and all us poor soldiers who has fought so long and gallantly for her independence may return home to greet our long parted friends and relations and to reap the reward that is due us for our tolling and hardships. But alas a many a gallant brave is numbered with the dead. I hope God will have mercy on their poor souls and they may get a just reward in heaven.

---

47. This dated entry is from the Pocket Notebook.

The following is a roll of the strength of our company at present July 15th 1862. [48]

    Capt T. [Terrell] T. Mounger
    1st Lieut vacant R. [Robert] F. Shine   killed
    2nd Lieut vacant W. [William] A. Johnson died June 62
    3rd Lieut Thaddius M. Bostick   died Aug 62
    1st Sergt T. [Thomas] G. Westfall   E 3rd Lt
    2nd   S. [Sylvanus] Q. Jordan
    3rd R. [Robert] H. Fulton
    4th J. [John] T. Pierce
    5th J. [James] H. Ford
    1st corp J. [Joseph] L. Sumner
    2nd corp L. [Lott] W. Hill
    3rd corp James Hobby
    4th corp vacant J. [Julius] M. Jones   elected July 62
Privates
    11   Adams S [Salathiel]
    12   Baker Elbert
    13   Baker Nathan   died July 62
    14   Batey [Baty] W. [William] A.
    15   Bozeman L. [Luke] C.
    16   Calhoun T. [Thomas] C.
    17   Calhoun N. [Nathan] T.
    18   Champion Dan   killed Sept 62

---

48. Hall apparently made "upright" and horizontal marks of different sizes to indicate the extent to which a man participated in the battles beginning with Mechanicsville. He wrote, "In the above roll the longest horizontal mark denote the name it is against, was with the regt principally all the time during the late Battles that began on the 26th of June, those that has the shortest horizontal mark was with it only part of the time. Those that has the upright mark were not with us at all they were either at Hospitals, sick at old camp or strayed off on purpose to keep out of an engagement." Thayer included a "copiest's note" that it was "impossible to transcribe above mentioned 'marks'" on her typewriter. She did include the number "1" (or letter "l") and the letter "f" after many names on this July 1862 muster but does not indicate what the number "1" and the letter "f" stand for. Accordingly, I removed those notations.

19 Champion David
20 Deriso [Deariso] James
21 Deriso [Deariso] T. [Thomas] G.
22 Deriso W. [Michael W.]
23 Eady Edward
24 Ford R. [Robert] G.   e 3rd Lt July 1982
25 Ford G. [Garry] Green
26 Ford W. [William] J.
27 Ford J. [John] J.
28 Fowler [Levi] L. T.
29 Fowler N. [Nathan] J.
30 Gaughf Ben   died of his wound Aug 62
31 Gillis N. [Norman] G.
32 Gillis W. [William] D.
33 Green B. [Bartley] C.
34 Hall G. [George] W.
35 Haize [Hays] John
36 Hobbe Jesse
37 Harris Wm
38 Hamilton W. [William] J.
39 Hill H. [Haskell] H.
40 Jeter J. [Jeremiah] J.
41 Jerkins J. [John] T.
42 Jones J. [Julius] M.   e 4 corp July 1862
43 Jones Isaac
44 Johnson [Johnston] D. [David] D.
45 Kerce Barnet [Barney]
46 Kerce J. [James] M.
47 Kerce James
48 Kerce Albert B.
49 Land Wm. L.
50 Lunsford J. [James] C.
51 Massey G. [George] W.

52 Massey A. [Abel] C.
53 Massey R. [Robert] B.
54 Massey S. [Silas] M.
55 Meadows W. [William] T.
56 Mcrainey [McRaney, McCrainie, McCraney] G. [George] W.
57 Mcrainey []McRaney, McCrainie, McCraney] D. [Daniel] J.
58 Mcrainey [McRaney, McCrainie, McCraney] John   discharged
59 Nicholds [Nichols] M. [Madison]
60 Posey Wm.
61 Posey James
62 Posey L. [Littleton, Littleberry] B.
63 Potts V. [Valentine] E.
64 Quiet [Quiett] H. [Henry] C.
65 Ross John
66 Riddley [Ridley] J. [Jonathan]
67 Shiver J. [John] L.
68 Shiver Antony
69 Shiver Jehue
70 Shiver James
71 Shiver Henry
72 Shiver Manning   discharged
73 Simpson M. [Marion] F.
74 Smith J. [John] C.
75 Spring G. [George] W.
76 Spring J. [Joseph] L.
77 Tabor A. [Andrew] J.
78 Tabor N. [Napoleon] B.
79 Tipton Thomas
80 Thompson E. [Elihu] S.
81 Vicory [Vickery] Eli
82 Walker Wm. W.
83 Warren L. [Lewis] W.

84 Weeks Romulus
85 Wiley J. [Edward] E.
86 Williams B. [Berrian] A.
87 Whelus T. [Thomas] L.
88 Bray Harmon
89 Thompson Daniel
90 Thompson Calvin

Wednesday, July 16, 1862

Fair & Hot. Today is extremely hot and disagreeable even in the shade. I went in a bathing in James River which was pleasant and exhillerating and also I had some sport in gathering berries on the James. Dewberries & hucleberries grow in vast quantities along the country bordering its Banks. More than I ever saw anywhere else.

Thursday, July 17, 1862

M fair & Hot. E thunder Showers. To day we (our regt) goes out on picket 4 miles below our present camps. Have a verry pleasant time having a church to stay in. It rains verry hard in the evening.

Friday, July 18, 1862

M clo. E rain. We return to camp today. Its rather cool today and cloudy with some rain. I heard the news today of our Gunboat the "Arkansas" sinking and distroying several of the enemys Gunboats on the Mississippi.[49] Glorious for our little navy.

Saturday, July 19, 1862

Cloudy with some rain. I go out a berry picking today on the river and have a pleasant time of it, for it is always pleasant to me to ramble o'er the forest beside the majestic and renowned James River that is so full of Historic wonders. I also baked me some pies today that was verry good.

---

49. *CSS Arkansas* was an ironclad that ran through the Union fleet near Vicksburg.

Sunday, July 20, 1862

Cloudy with some rain. I went to the James today in company with several of boys and we had a good time a bathing in the River which is a verry good place. No news every thing quiet.

Monday, July 21, 1862

Partialy cloudy and warm. No news of importance every thing quiet. This day is one year ago Since the Battle of Manassas which was then a great Battle but it was a mere Skirmish to the Battles that has been fought lately around Richmond. I sent a letter home to my dear old mother today.

Tuesday, July 22, 1862

M fair. E cloudy & warm. To day I was detailed on Police in the city of Richmond and I had a very good view of the City and the statues of General Washington, Jefferson Maddison, Mason and Patrick Henry. Gen Washington is seated on his celebrated War horse. I returned to camp late in the evening exceedingly fatigued.

Wednesday, July 23, 1862

M cloudy & Warm. E a little rain. Today is just one year ago since I was mustered into the Service of the Confederate States of America and took the oath of Allegiance to defend and support its Government at all hazards which I have done, and will do to the end. Let Hords of the northern invaders come I will face them to the last.

Wednesday, July 23, 1862[50]

Anniversary 4th

July the 23 1861 I was mustered into the Service of the C.S.A. and taken the oath of allegiance to defend and support it to the last and if necessary die for it. [It] is one year ago from this day July 23 1862, one year I have been

---

50. This dated entry is from the Pocket Notebook.

for my dear country and I hope God will spare me Several to fight for it if necessary but I hope and pray that this year will end the Bloody Scene and that the new year 1863 will dawn with peace and happiness Settled over our beloved country. Enough blood has been Spilled, enough lives lost and too many homes made desolate already. Thousands upon thousands of poor Soldiers thousands of miles away from home and dear one[s], have laid down their lives in the cause of Liberty and Freedom never to behold them again only (I hope) where the angels stay. Take comfort dear mothers and wives with the thought that you will meet them on that Bright etherial land of heaven. I too, have a Dear Mother far away over a thousand miles from her Son and a many uneasy hour She passes I know for fear that her Son Battling in his countrys cause is no more. But I hope dear mother that we will meet and that soon.

Thursday, July 24, 1862

Cloudy & misty. To day I am verry sick awhile but I hope I will soon get over it. It is cloudy to day with fine mist falling in the fore noon and the atmosphere is oppressive. No news. Only rumors afloat. Yesterday 23rd we had an election for Brevet 2nd Lieut. Robert G. Ford was elected.

Friday, July 25, 1862

Fair & Warm. I feel better sound today although I do not feel well yet. It has cleared off today and the sky is as clear as a bell.

Saturday, July 26, 1862

M clo. E heavy rain. To day is very quiet in camp. Not a rifle seems to disturb the quietude. Afternoon it rain[ed] heavyly which cools the air considerably. No news only Col Morgan is making the Yankees verry uncomfortable in Kentucky by invading their country and capturing eleven cities and towns. "Huza" for Morgan.[51]

Sunday, July 27, 1862

Fair & Warm. I confine myself to reading before noon which gives me a good deal of Satisfaction. After noon I go to the James and have good time a bathing in it[s] lucid waters and swam across it twice being the first river I ever swam. I also picked some berries and made me a pie.

Monday, July 28, 1862

Fair & warm. We get orders today to cook three days rations and hold ourselves in readiness to march at short notice.

Tuesday, July 29, 1862

M fair & Warm. E cloudy. This morning we get orders to march at 2 oclock P.M. and send off our baggage before us and hold ourselves in readiness to march at a moment warning. We started but had to turn back to our old camp and remain there a day or two longer.

Wednesday, July 30, 1862

M rain. E fair & Hot. We still remain today there rises a considerable thunder cloud this and rains-in the evening I went to the river and taken my farewell bath in James River and its waters invigerated me to a great extent, for this evening is verry hot. We get orders to march tomorrow at 2 oclock P.M.

Thursday, July 31, 1862

Hard rain all day. A thunder cloud rised this morning and it continues raining all the day. A[t] 2 P.M. we start on our march regardless of the rain that pepers down on us all the time. We march to Richmond and take the cars and leave at 7 oclock P.M. on the Virginia Central Rail Road. We run all night.

---

51. This is likely a reference to then-Colonel John Hunt Morgan's raids in Kentucky. Ironically, July 26, 1862, was the date on which Morgan surrendered at Salineville, Ohio.

6

"I TAKEN THE SMALL POX"
CENTRAL VIRGINIA AND THE SHENANDOAH VALLEY:
AUGUST 1862 – MARCH 1863

The 14th Georgia arrived at Gordonsville on August 1, 1862, and encamped five miles from town. Although Hall had recovered enough to rejoin his company in mid-July, he became ill again shortly after arriving in Gordonsville. When his brigade marched off to Orange Court House on August 5, Hall was taken by wagon to the rail station in Gordonsville and transported by train to Lovingston in Nelson County, Virginia, where, on August 8, he was hospitalized for the first time in his military service. What Hall refers to as "Bellmonte Colledge Hospital" was likely Belmont House, a large

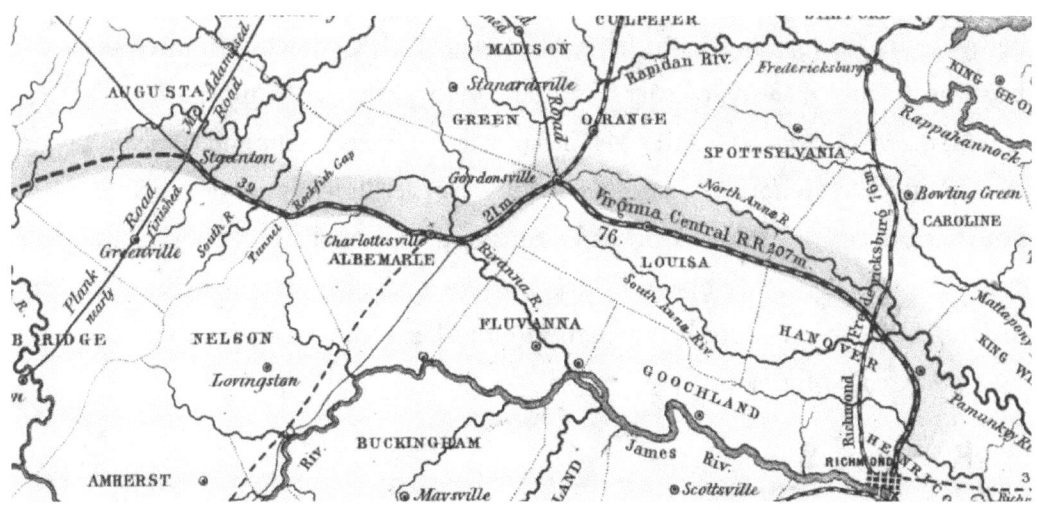

Hall traveled on the Virginia Central Railroad from Richmond to Gordonsville to Lovingston, Virginia. (Library of Congress, as cropped on Wikimedia Commons)

brick home a few miles northwest of Norwood, Virginia. Belmont served as a Confederate hospital during the war and still maintains a small cemetery for Confederate and Union soldiers who died at the hospital.[1]

While hospitalized, Hall celebrated his 21st birthday on August 21. In his diary, he laments that he had heard from his family only twice since leaving Georgia in July 1861 and not at all in the previous four months. He wrote of a vivid dream that one of his letters home, describing the battle at Seven Pines, was published in an Augusta newspaper.

Hall was released from the hospital on August 25, 1862, but was blocked from rejoining the 14th Georgia because Union troops occupied the territory between Gordonsville and his regiment. The local provost marshal in Gordonsville put him to work standing guard and performing police and fatigue duties. Consequently, Hall was not with Company G when it fought at Cedar Mountain on August 9; Second Manassas in late August; Chantilly (Ox Hill) on September 1; Harper's Ferry on September 13-15; and Shepherdstown on September 19. He rejoined his regiment for a few weeks at the end of September but took ill again in early October. After three weeks of being sick in camp, he miraculously survived over four months of hospitalization in Staunton, including several weeks in a smallpox hospital. During this period, he missed the battle of Fredericksburg on December 12-13, 1862, but finally regained his health sufficiently to rejoin his regiment on the Rappahannock in mid-March 1863.

Hall references most of these missed battles in either daily entries or as a narrative. On August 13, he wrote of his distress that he was not with his regiment, which he believed was "contending with the enemy." The 14th Georgia did indeed engage in battle on August 9, 1862, at Cedar Mountain, midway between Culpeper Court House and Orange Court House. After McClellan failed to take Richmond, Lincoln divided the Union forces in northern Virginia, leaving McClellan in charge of the Army of the Potomac but creating a new Army of Virginia under General John Pope. Lee wanted to strike a blow at Pope, then operating near the Blue Ridge Mountains, before McClellan had the chance to get settled in northern Virginia. Lee got his wish with the Confederate victory at Cedar Mountain.

---

1. Annie L. Harrower, "Architectural Description of Building Called Belmont," WPA Historical Inventory Project (Richmond: Virginia Conservation Commission, 1938). http://image.lva/virginia.gov/VHI/html/18/0457.html.

At Cedar Mountain, Stonewall Jackson defeated Union General Nathaniel Banks of the Army of Virginia. The 14th Georgia acquitted itself well in the battle, with Col. Folsom rallying both his men and elements of Taliaferro's Brigade, which had broken and were retreating through the 14th Georgia's line. Folsom waved the battle flag and, as several hundred men rallied around him, yelled that most stirring of all infantry cries, "Follow me." Folsom led the men approximately three hundred yards across the battlefield, fending off a Union cavalry charge before he collapsed.[2] Folsom earned the nickname "Cedar Mountain Folsom," and one Atlanta newspaper declared this the proudest day of the war so far for the 14th Georgia.[3] No members of the company were killed at Cedar Mountain, but Jesse Hobby and Isaac Jones were wounded.

Hall made multiple references to the second major battle he missed, that of Second Manassas, which was fought near the battlefield of First Manassas. Second Manassas was a tactical victory for the Confederates but not the "Waterloo" for Pope and McClellan that Hall had hoped. Stonewall Jackson, who, according to James McPherson, had "reverted from the sluggard of the Chickahominy to the gladiator of the Valley," added to the legend of his "foot cavalry" by having his corps of 24,000 men march at a hard pace some fifty-four miles in thirty-six hours around Pope's flank to raid the Union supply depot at Manassas Junction.[4] Before Pope could move his troops up to Manassas in response, Jackson's troops "swooped down on the mountain of supplies at Manassas like a plague of grasshoppers."[5] Moore, later the regimental adjutant, wrote that after many of the men marched to Manassas barefoot, ragged, and hungry, "[e]very man in the regiment filled his haversack with pickled beef, bacon, or pork, sugar and coffee, and took whatever else pleased him."[6]

---

2. Robert K. Krick, *Stonewall Jackson at Cedar Mountain* (University of North Carolina Press, 1990). 256-257. Krick writes that the 14th Georgia was initially commanded at Cedar Mountain by Felix Price but that Folsom assumed command when Price was wounded in the hand by a shell.
3. "Dixie," "Battle of Cedar Run," *Southern Confederacy*, August 21, 1862, https://gahistoricnewspapers.galileo.uga.edu. A. P. Hill wrote afterwards that "The Fourteenth Georgia, under the gallant Colonel Folsom, having become separated from the rest of the brigade by our fugitives, charged the advancing enemy and with brilliant success." *OR*, Ser. 1, vol. XII, pt. I, p. 215.
4. McPherson, *Battle Cry of Freedom*, 526.
5. McPherson, *Battle Cry of Freedom*, 527.
6. Folsom, *Heroes and Martyrs of Georgia*, 150.

In the battle of Second Manassas on August 28 through August 30, 1862, the South again gained a tactical victory but not a crushing blow. On August 28, 1862, Thomas's Brigade was positioned just south of Sudley Church behind an unfinished railroad entrenchment. It saw no action on August 28, but on the afternoon of August 29, it was in almost continuous combat, moving up and down the unfinished railroad and Groveton-Sudley Road relative to General Maxcy Gregg's brigade. Thomas's Brigade was in action again on August 30, mostly in support of two other brigades. According to the 14th Georgia's adjutant, the regiment lost eight killed and thirty-one wounded, but Company G emerged relatively unscathed.

Hall also missed the battle at Chantilly (Ox Hill) on September 1, 1862. Lee had sent Jackson in pursuit of the retreating Pope. Jackson's three divisions attacked two of Pope's divisions on September 1, 1862, in front of Little River Turnpike. The ensuing battle at Chantilly was fought mostly in the rain, which forced the combatants to resort to fighting with bayonets, musket butts, and even rocks. One-armed Union Maj. Gen. Philip Kearny was killed at Chantilly after wandering into Thomas's brigade lines.[7] Although the battle was a tactical victory for Jackson, he failed in his mission of cutting off Pope.

After Chantilly, Lee decided to shift his focus from defending Virginia and take the fight north into Union territory, a strategy that would ease the drain on Virginian resources, shift the strategic initiative, and perhaps obtain diplomatic recognition for the Confederacy in Europe.[8] Thomas's Brigade accompanied Lee on the

The main hall of the Virginia Institution for the Deaf, Dumb, and Blind in Staunton was converted early in the war to serve as a General Hospital. It already had 500 patients by August 1861. (Augusta County Historical Society)

---

7. Fox, *Red Clay to Richmond*, 111.
8. John Keegan, *The American Civil War: A Military History* (Alfred A. Knopf, 2009), 165.

march into Maryland, crossing over the Monocacy near Frederick, where Jackson split off to seize Union-held Harper's Ferry. Arriving at Harpers Ferry on September 13, Jackson directed his artillery to commence a bombardment on September 14. The Union garrison surrendered on September 15, netting Jackson's men over 12,000 Union prisoners, 73 artillery pieces, 13,000 small arms, and 200 wagons.[9] Company G was one of two or three companies in the 14th Georgia tasked with paroling Union prisoners. When Lee ordered A. P. Hill on September 17, 1862, to Sharpsburg, Maryland, fourteen miles away, Hill left Thomas's Brigade at Harper's Ferry to continue paroling the prisoners and disbursing the captured material. Consequently, the 14th Georgia did not participate in the battle of Antietam.

After completing its duty at Harper's Ferry, Thomas's Brigade rejoined Lee's army at Shepherdstown. As Lee was retreating to Virginia after the bloodbath at Antietam, A. P. Hill and Porter engaged in a small action at Boteler's Ford on the Potomac River at Shepherdstown. Hill's forces, which included Thomas's Brigade on the right flank, pushed Union troops back across the Potomac. As David Champion described the accompanying artillery battle, "Cannon balls exploded all around us; the shrapnel and cannister whipped the shrub oak in front of us to a frazzle."[10] David's brother, Daniel Champion, was killed within a few feet of him by an exploding shell.

Hall left Gordonsville on September 13, 1862, "resolved to go to my regt at all hazzards." Upon learning that the regiment was in Maryland, he and several other members of the regiment, including at least two officers, walked on the railroad tracks to Culpeper Court House and then on to Sperryville. The determined group passed through Front Royal on the evening of September 17, 1862, before crossing the Shenandoah River by boat. They camped outside of Winchester on the 18th, where they learned the regiment was opposite Shepherdstown. As Hall passed through Winchester on September 20, he saw many of the wounded from the battle of Antietam.

Hall finally reunited with his company on September 23, 1862, three miles north of Martinsburg. He wrote that the army "is in a bad condition at present, the most of

---

9. Ethan S. Rafuse, *Antietam, South Mountain & Harpers Ferry: A Battlefield Guide* (University of Nebraska Press, 2008), 225.
10. Champion, Memoirs, "Shepherdstown 1862."

it is barefoot and have not but one suit of clothing.[11] I have no shoes nor no clothes but what I have on my back. When I wash my clothes I have to go naked till I wash and dry them or put them on wet." On September 27, the men marched to a new camp at Bunker Hill, some ten miles north of Winchester. On September 29, Hall received his first mail in two months, including a letter from home. On October 1, the company held an election, at which Julius M. Jones was elected 5th Sergeant, David Champion was elected 4th Sergeant, and Elbert Baker was elected 4th Corporal. At the regimental level, Felix Price and William Harris both resigned from the 14th Georgia in the fall of 1862, which resulted in Folsom's formal promotion to full colonel. In Company G, Fulton was promoted to First Lieutenant and James H. Ford to Second Lieutenant to fill the vacancies created by the deaths of Robert Shine and Thaddeus Bostick.[12]

Hall had written in September that "health in war is half the battle and is one of the greatest riches ever bestowed on man." Little did he know how much poor health would affect him in the upcoming months. He took sick again on October 8 with a very bad cold and cough that turned into pneumonia, an ailment that killed as many as one out of every six soldiers who had it.[13] Fever set in two days later. This marked the end of Hall's daily entries until late January 1863. However, his narrative and daily activities log indicate that he remained sick in camp for about three weeks before being hospitalized at Winchester on October 30. Hall was transferred by ambulance to the Confederate General Hospital at Staunton in the middle of November 1862. En route to Staunton, he had to sleep on the floor of an old outhouse with only a single blanket for warmth.

While Hall was hospitalized in Staunton, his regiment marched from Berryville to Fredericksburg, Virginia, in twelve days, an impressive undertaking given the late fall snow and often rolling terrain. After encamping at Camp Gregg several miles south of Fredericksburg, they moved to Hamilton's Crossing in anticipation of battle. After

---

11. Lee had advised Jefferson Davis prior to entering Maryland that his men "are poorly provided with clothes, and in thousands of instances are destitute of shoes." R. E. Lee letter of Sept 3, 1862, to Jefferson Davis, Dowdey and Manarin, *Wartime Papers of R. E. Lee*, 293. Although Lee was able to scrounge up 1,650 pairs of shoes in Frederick, Williamsport, and Hagerstown, that number was not sufficient "to cover the bare feet of the army." R. E. Lee letter of Sept 12, 1862, to Jefferson Davis, Dowdey and Manarin, *Wartime Papers of R. E. Lee*, 305.
12. Folsom, *Heroes and Martyrs of Georgia*, 151.
13. Wiley, *Life of Johnny Reb*, 255.

McClellan's poor showing at Antietam, Lincoln replaced him with Ambrose Burnside, who was told in no uncertain terms that he was expected to move against Lee before year's end. But rather than engage the Confederate forces to the west, Burnside elected to move south from Warrenton to attack the city of Fredericksburg, which was only lightly defended in late November 1862. However, the pontoon boats that were needed to move Union troops across the Rappahannock River in Fredericksburg were delayed, which gave Lee ample time to build up Confederate defenses in and around the city.

Although the battle of Fredericksburg on December 13, 1862, is best known for the futile Union assault at Marye's Heights on the north end of the battlefield, what happened at the south end of the battlefield, at what became known as the Slaughter Pen, was the real turning point of the battle. Here A. P. Hill battled Union General John Gibbon's division across the Richmond, Fredericksburg, and Potomac railroad line just north of Hamilton's Crossing. When Gibbon's troops threatened to break James Lane's brigade line in the early afternoon, Lane requested Thomas's Brigade to come forward to assist. Moving forward of Lane's North Carolinians, Thomas's Brigade, with the 14th Georgia on the right flank, pushed the Union troops back across the tracks and routed them. For a portion of the battle, however, it seemed as though the 14th Georgia was fighting on its own because the other three regiments in the brigade were obscured from view.

The 14th Georgia was heavily battered at Fredericksburg, losing a third of its force.[14] One soldier wrote a Macon newspaper that the regiment went into battle with only 323 men and suffered 134 casualties.[15] Hall, who was relying only on hearsay information, wrote that 112 were killed or wounded in the regiment, numbers which were generally consistent with the adjutant's report.[16] Casualties in Company G included three killed:

---

14. Francis Augustin O'Reilly, *The Fredericksburg Campaign: Winter War on the Rappahannock*, Louisiana Paperback ed. (Louisiana State University Press, 2006), 212.
15. "The 14th Georgia in the Battle," *Macon Telegraph*, December 30, 1862, www.newspapers.com. This article was submitted by "G.E.K.," likely Private George E. Kelley of Company B, whose skill as a writer earned him an appointment later in the war as a court-martial clerk. Kelley's numbers are borne out by another article submitted to an Augusta newspaper, where "Jasper" wrote that in just 33 minutes of combat the 14th Georgia lost 134 out of 323 carried into action, or 41% killed and wounded (none missing). "Letter from Thomas Brigade," *Weekly Constitutionalist*, January 14, 1863, https://gahistoricnewspapers.galileo.usg.edu.
16. Thomas Moore reported that 24 men in the regiment were killed and 88 wounded, which is slightly lower than the newspaper accounts. *Folsom, Heroes and Martyrs of Georgia*, 151.

Thomas O. Calhoun, Corporal Lott W. Hill (died from wounds in January 1863), and James O. Kerce (died from wounds at Montgomery Springs, VA, on December 29, 1862). Lillian Henderson, chronicler of Confederate Georgia soldiers, wrote that Elbert Baker also died at Fredericksburg.[17] The wounded in Company G included Sergeant James Hobby, Norman G. Gillis, George W. Spring, Eli Vickery, Napoleon B. Tabor, Corporal Joseph L. Sumner, Joseph L. Spring, George W. McRaney, Green B. Wingate, and Littleton Posey. Although the exact number of casualties at Fredericksburg is unknown, Company G likely dropped below 80 officers and enlisted troops. One soldier wrote a lengthy narrative of the battle – and casualties – for the *Macon Telegraph*. He included a plea for blankets and shoes, lamenting, "The men in the Fourteenth Georgia Regiment are sadly destitute of blankets and shoes, and if not soon relieved must inevitably suffer vastly before the winter closes."[18]

By the time Hall arrived at Staunton in November 1862 he had developed bronchitis but began to recover due to what he deemed good medical care at the Confederate hospital.[19] However, in early December he contracted smallpox, which he wrote was "raging in terror in Staunton" at the time.[20] Smallpox, also known as the "speckled monster," was one of the most lethal diseases of the war, causing death in up to one-third of its victims.[21] A smallpox epidemic had erupted in Virginia in October 1862 and did

---

17. Lillian Henderson, *Roster of the Confederate Soldiers of Georgia, 1861-1865*. Vol. 2. (Longino & Porter, 1959), 381.
18. "The 14th Georgia in the Battle," *Macon Telegraph*, December 30, 1862, www.newspapers.com.
19. In the early years of the war, most of the patients at the General Hospital in Staunton, which numbered some 500 patients by August 1861, were treated for disease rather than combat wounds. Robert H. Moore II, *Gibraltar of the Shenandoah: Civil War Sites and Stories of Staunton, Waynesboro, and August County, Virginia* (Donning, 2004), 58. At one point, it filled to 1,300 before the wounded, who were brought in from throughout the Valley and as far as Richmond, were placed in tents in the groves above the rail depot and in individual homes. Charles Culbertson, *The Staunton, Virginia Anthology* (Clarion Publishing, 2013), 104-107.
20. Joseph Waddell, who kept a journal of life in Staunton during the war, wrote on November 12, 1863, that the number of smallpox cases prompted him to get re-vaccinated. On January 4, 1864, he observed that those who died from smallpox were buried at a separate cemetery. *Diary of Joseph Addison Waddell*, University of Virginia Library, https://valley.lib.virginia.edu/papers/AD1500
21. Thomas G. Cropley, "Dermatology and Skin Disease in the American Civil War," *Dermatology Nursing*, no. 1 (February 2008), 32.

not reach its peak until early in 1863.²² Both armies attempted to inoculate its soldiers against smallpox through a gruesome process where infected scabs were harvested for material that was administered through small cuts into the patient's skin. Cattle scabs were preferred, but if none were available, then human scabs were used; indeed, children sometimes were vaccinated at multiple locations on their arms so their scabs could be harvested.²³ Hall had been vaccinated in February 1862 while he was at Davis Ford but he nonetheless contracted smallpox ten months later. On December 6, 1862, he was transferred from the General Hospital in Staunton to the nearby smallpox hospital, which consisted of tents pitched near a pond that no one was allowed to approach any closer than one hundred yards.²⁴

After roughly twenty days in the smallpox hospital, Hall began to recover some of his strength and appetite. But around Christmas, he developed erysipelas, a contagious bacterial infection, in his foot and leg. Erysipelas was an especially painful disease because it ate tissue, leaving a swollen and discolored limb.²⁵ Hall was transferred from the smallpox hospital to the General Hospital on January 19, 1863, and as his health slowly returned, he was able to commence nursing duties on March 1, 1863.

Hall would not have witnessed the end of the war if the General Hospital at Staunton had not brought him through major life-threatening illnesses. But the hospital did more than provide medical treatment: it also provided the framework for a spiritual conversion of such power that it molded the next five decades of Hall's life. Although the diaries prior to January 1863 contain the occasional reference to God, the tone of the entries changed dramatically while Hall was in the General Hospital at Staunton. After surviving bronchitis, pneumonia, smallpox, and erysipelas in the span of only a few

---

22. Wiley, *Life of Johnny Reb*, 254. The worst epidemic in the Confederate Army occurred in the Army of Northern Virginia, shortly after the Antietam campaign in the fall of 1862. H. H. Cunningham, *Doctors in Gray: The Confederate Military Service* (Louisiana State University Press, 1986), 196. Of the cases treated in general hospitals in Virginia between October 1862 and January 1864, there was a 40% death rate. Ibid.
23. Terry Reimer, "Smallpox and Vaccination in the Civil War," posted November 9, 2004; accessed July 10, 2020, https://www.civilwarmed.org/surgeons-call/small_pox/
24. Samuel M. Quincy, *History of the Second Massachusetts Regiment of Infantry: A Prisoner's Diary* (George H. Ellis, 1882), 18.
25. Stanley B. Burns, "Civil War Disease and Wound Infection," PBS Learning Media Background Essay, accessed July 10, 2020, https://mpt.pbslearningmedial.org

months, it is little wonder that Hall turned to religion shortly after leaving the smallpox hospital. An entry on Sunday, January 25, 1863, is the first of over a hundred entries over the next twenty-seven months in which Hall wrote supplications to God, memorialized attendance at worship events, or otherwise referenced his Christian faith.

Rev. George Boardman Taylor, chaplain at the Confederate Hospital in Staunton, greatly influenced Hall's conversion in early 1863. (*Image courtesy of International Mission Board*)

Hospitals provided fertile ground for conversions. Confederate chaplains who helped attend sick and wounded soldiers not only conducted religious services but also provided spiritual counseling and distributed Bibles and religious tracts. The post chaplain at Staunton, Reverend George B. Taylor, D.D., maintained that early in the war it was difficult to get soldiers to listen to preaching; if they attended services at all, they were often distracted, smoked, or walked about.[26] But as the war progressed, men listened in earnest and more solemnly. Hospitalization provided men the time to engage in worship, to reflect on mortality, and to read spiritual material that "colporteurs" would distribute. Although colporteurs would occasionally charge money for religious tracts, such material was usually free for hospital patients.[27]

One of Taylor's most impactful accomplishments as post chaplain was establishing two large libraries for soldiers in Staunton. Some funding came from the Baptist Sunday School and Publication Board. Local citizens donated two or three bushels of books in response to Taylor's request for small Bibles and New Testaments for soldiers.[28] Hall appears to have taken enthusiastic advantage of the libraries. In early February 1863, he wrote that his mind was "calm and

---

26. J. Wm. Jones, *Christ in the Camp: Religion in Lee's Army* (Richmond, VA: B. F. Johnson & Co., 1887), 187.
27. Wiley, *Life of Johnny Reb*, 179.
28. H. Rondel Rumburg, *George Boardman Taylor: Chaplain – Pastor – Missionary* (Appomattox, VA: SBSS, 2019), 51; Jones, *Christ in the Camp*, 27.

serene and resting on the love of God" and that he had the opportunity while hospitalized to read "good books." The first book Hall mentions reading was Richard Baxter's *The Saint's Everlasting Rest* (1650). On February 26, he wrote that he was reading John Bunyan's *Pilgrim's Progress* (1678), hoping "by the blessings of the Lord I will gain good instruction from it." On March 9 and 10, he listed without explanation the titles of over ten Christianity-themed books, including collections of famous sermons; given that he expected to leave for his regiment soon, it is likely that Hall listed those titles as books he had already read or hoped to read in the future. Hall later reread *Pilgrim's Progress* – ironically, a book written by a former prisoner about a protagonist who is himself imprisoned – during his time as a POW at Fort Delaware. Hall's interest in the book is almost certainly attributable to Reverend Taylor, who wrote his own brother in 1862 that he had himself "lately been led to much heart-searching by *Pilgrim's Progress*."[29]

Taylor's father, Reverend James B. Taylor, Sr., also visited soldiers in the hospital at Staunton; he later wrote that these visits could be "peculiarly touching." As the senior Taylor relayed, "One man from Southwestern Georgia told me, with deep feeling, that out of 98 composing his company 24 were buried in Western Virginia."[30] Although Taylor did not name the soldier, this might very well have been Hall, who hailed from southwestern Georgia and had lost at least twenty-one of his company in western Virginia in the disastrous campaign there in 1861.

Hall was discharged from the hospital on March 13, 1863. "Taking the cars" from Staunton, he arrived by rail at Guinea Station south of Fredericksburg that same night. After rejoining his regiment, he immediately began attending worship services conducted by army chaplains, sometimes twice on Sundays. He also began attending weekday prayer services. Hall was fortunate to receive spiritual guidance from Chaplain John J. Hyman of the 49th Georgia, described as one of the best chaplains in the Army of Northern Virginia.[31] Hyman was "exceedingly popular" with his soldiers.[32] In visiting

---

29. Rumburg, *George Boardman Taylor*, 51.
30. William W. Bennett, *The Great Revival* (Philadelphia, PA: Claxton, Remsen & Haffelfinger, 1877). Although there was no specific date provided for this visit, Taylor did refer elsewhere in the letter to Stonewall Jackson in present tense, which suggests the letter was written prior to Jackson's death in May 1863.
31. "J. J. Hyman," Boykin, *History of the Baptist Denomination in Georgia*, 282; Bruce T. Gourley, *Diverging Loyalties: Baptists in Middle Georgia During the Civil War* (Mercer University Press, 2011), 118.
32. "J. J. Hyman," Boykin, *History of the Baptist Denomination in Georgia*, 282.

each of his four regiments, he sometimes prayed with soldiers four to six times a day.³³ At times Hyman was the only chaplain in Thomas's Brigade but was later joined by Baptist Edward B. Barrett, who was attached to the 45th Georgia, and Methodist minister Alexander. W. Moore, who served as chaplain of the 14th Georgia between August 1862 until just after the battle of Chancellorsville in May 1863.³⁴

Hall's return to his regiment coincided with the period of the first great revivals of the Army of Northern Virginia, which occurred along the Rappahannock River from September 1862 through May 1863.³⁵ But Hall's faith extended far beyond the end of the Rappahannock revival period – it was the fabric that draped the remainder of his life.

Pocket Notebook Narrative
1 August 1862 – March 1863

We took the cars at the Central depot and at 7 oclock P.M. we commenced flying to the Northward at a rapid

---

33. John Wesley Brinsfield, Jr., *The Spirit Divided: Memoirs of Civil War Chaplains: The Confederacy* (Mercer University Press, 2006), 201. By one chaplain's estimate, perhaps one in twelve soldiers in the Army of Northern Virginia were religious converts. Glatthaar, *General Lee's Army*, 240. As a former chaplain for the 13th Infantry wrote afer the war, "Brother Hyman, who was commissioned chaplain on the 1st of May, 1862, after serving for a time as private in the ranks of the Forty-ninth Georgia Regiment, was one of the most faithful and successful men we had, and though laid aside for a time by sickness (brought on by over-work), had the privilege of baptizing 238 soldiers, seeing 500 others profess conversion in connection with his labors, preaching about 500 sermons, besides many exhortations, lectures, etc., and distributing thousands of pages of tracts, and many Bibles and Testaments, and performing much other labor which may not be written here, but 'whose record is on high.'" Jones, *Christ in the Camp*, 307.
34. Jones, *Christ in the Camp*, 310.
35. Troy D. Harman, "The Great Revival of 1863: The Effects upon Lee's Army of Northern Virginia," accessed July 13, 2020, https://npshistory.com/series/symposia/gettysburg_seminars/8/essay5/pdf. Harman writes that regimental colonels favored an increased role in religion by their soldiers because Christianity "tended to make soldiers more loyal to the cause, faithful to duty, honest, and less susceptible to vices – which might become destructive – such as heavy drinking, gambling, and overuse of profanity." Moreover, for those who participated in revivals, "their lives changed as they became more sincere about service to country and about personal integrity. Because the issue of where each converted soldier would spend his eternity was settled, each of them perhaps was more apt to risk the dangers of the battlefield." Ibid.

speed. The train run all night and next morning about 7 oclock the 1st of August we arrived at Gordonsville Va 65 or 70 miles from Richmond at the Junction of the Orange & Alexandria R R with the Virginia Central R. R. We marched 3 miles below Gordonsville and camp[ed] till the next day and we went down two miles further and pitched our camps in a beautiful Shady forest of oaks and on the 4 [August] I was taken Sick with a high fever and on the 6 [August] our division was ordered off and they proceeded towards Orange Court House and I was sent to a hospital in Nelson County toward Lynchburg, beyond Charlottesville where I was verry sick and I remained there until the 26th when I started to rejoin my regt and got as far as Gordonsville and was stoped by the Provost Marshal it being verry difficult to get to my regt the enemy being between me and it and I remained there a brief period and done guard and police duty and while I remained there I will tell something of what my regt has been doing during my absence.

When They left me at Gordonsville they preceded up above Orange C. H. and on the Rapid Ann [Rapidan] River and above there on a branch of the Rappahannock. The[y] participated in the Battle of Cedar Run called by Some Cedar Mountain where they repulsed the enemy with great loss and drove the enemy before them. On the 9th of Aug. in this battle but one in our company was Seriously wounded and that was Isaac Jones.

The enemy kept up the retreat to the Manassas and on the 28 29 and 30th of Aug our forces gained a Signal victory over the Yankees with great loss on both Sides but far the worst on the enemys side. It is said that their losses is over fifty thousand while ours was over ten thousand. We taken about eight thousand prisoners and among the killed of the enemy was Several of their best Generals and millions of dollars worth of Commissary stores and clothing fell into our hands of which a great part was destroyed.

A train of cars over a mile in length was burned by General Jackson loaded with stores and supplies for the federal army.

Our army pursued the Yankees and near Fairfax C. H. they fought another Battle with the combined forces of Mclelland Pope and Burnsides and repulsed them again and drove them beyond the Potomac River and thither our army followed them and our victorious troops came to Leesburg and cross[ed] the Potomac into Maryland. Shout after Shout rent the air as they put their feet for the first time on the Maryland Shore. They proceeded into the verry heart of the country and burned and blew up the railroad bridges to cut off the enemy supplies and at Frederick City our regt stayed three or four days and proceeded by the way of Hager[s]town in a few miles of the line of Pennsylvania. Some of the citizens of Maryland received them with exclamations of joy and Showed our troops every kindness in their power and some was as strong Yankees as can be found in the New England States.

Part of our army recross[ed] the Potomac including our (A P Hills) Division at Williams Port and run the enemy out of Martinsburg and to Harpers Ferry and there transpired one of the most glorious achievement of the war, for our Side. It was the capture of one whole division of the Federal army including Sixteen thousand yankees and about four thousand [N]egroes together with all their arms and ammunition commissary stores and So forth. It was one of the grandest achievements that was ever accomplished. Our Brigade (Andersons) was left to guard the prisoners till they were paroled and the remainder of our division with the rest of the army proceed up the Potomac and in the vicinity of Sharpsburg Md.

On the 16th and 17th of September fought one of the fiercest Battle[s] that has ever been fought on the American continent. The worst part was fought on Wednesday the 17th beginning with the dawn of day and growing more feirce and terable as the day advanced. The antagonist Stood up hand to hand and gave back on neither side. Our true aim artillery played sad havoc in the ranks of the enemy mowing them down at every step but they kept their ranks filled up and continued to come. The Battle continued with terable vividness till late at night neither side gaining any considerable advantage. Dead men lay in heaps and piles. Next morning our army fell back and crossed the river at Shepherd[s]town on the Virginia side of the Potomac, and during the day and night the enemy in large forces crossed the river after them and on Saturday the 20th our Division had another terable battle on the bank of the river and near Shepherd[s]town and we defeated the enemy and drove them across the river again. One man in our company was killed and two wounded. Daniel Champion was killed with a shell.

Lines Worth the Memory of all young persons[36]

Keep good company or none

Never be idle.

If your hands cannot be usefully employed, attend to the cultivation of your mind.

Always speak the truth.

---

36. Various sources attribute many of these lines to Stephen Allen, Mayor of New York, who purportedly had written them in a notebook found on his person when he was killed in a steamboat explosion in 1852. "Excellent Maxims," *American Cotton Planter and the Soil of the South* 1, no. 1 (Jan. 1857), 21.

Make few promises.

Live up to your engagements.

Keep your own secrets, if you have any.

When you speak to a person, look him in the face.

Good company and good conversation are the sinues of virtue.

Good character is above all things else.

Your character cannot be essentially injured except by your own acts.

If any one speaks evil of you let your life be so that none will believe him.

<u>Drink no kind of intoxicating liquor</u>.

Ever live within your income.

When you retire to bed at night think over what you have been doing during the day.

Make no haste to be rich, if you would prosper.

Small and steady gains give competency with tranquility of mind.

<u>Never play at any game of chance</u>.

Avoid temptation, through fear you may not with stand it.

Earn money, before you spend it.

Never run into debt unless you have a way to get out again.

Never borrow if you can possible avoid it.

Do not marry untill you are able to support a wife.

Never speak evil of any one.

Be just before you are generous.

Keep yourself innocent if you would be happy.

Save when you are young, to spend when you are old.

Read over the above maxims at least once a week.

Guards & Guard Duty

There are several kinds of Guards and in different numbers. Regimental Guard is guard posted round one regiment of troops and it is equivolent to the commander of a regt or battalion whether he has guard or not around his command. Brigade guard is posted round a brigade, Division guard round a whole division. A Brigade is from 3 to 5 regiments but commonly only 4, there is from 5 to 10 Brigades in a division but commonly 6 or 7 owing to circumstances. The general rule for mounting guards is 8 oclock A. M. They are detailed from each company as thier name come on the roll and each one stands guard as his turn come beginning at the head of the roll and running through alphabetically.

The new guard forms into line two ranks at <u>Shoulder arms</u> and the command is given "<u>order arms</u>" or if at order arms the command is given "<u>Shoulder arms prepare to open ranks</u>" "<u>rear rank open order, march</u>" then the command is, "<u>rear rank right dress order arms inspection arms</u>." The[n] the guard makes a half face to the right, draw rammer, Spring rammer (that is inserting the rammer in the muzzle and letting it fall to the bottom of the barrel) and then come to a front face again, and the commanding officers commences the inspection, and at the same time the band commenses playing and continues until the inspection is completed and then the command is given "<u>Shoulder Arms</u>," "<u>close order march</u>," "<u>order arms parade rest</u>." Then the band marches up and down the line in front and plays then the command is given march in review, "<u>right face forward march</u>" and then the old guard is formed in front of the new, and the command is given to the old guard as the new guard marches in front of them "<u>present arms</u>" and the new guard forms on the right of the old and the old is dismissed, and the new is divided into three reliefs, the first relief of the new guard is posted and relieves the third relief of the old guard and the first relief stands two hours and the second relief go on post and relieves the first, and the third relieves the second and the first the third again, and so on for twenty four hours. Each relief stands eight hour in course of a day and night and no matter what kind of weather comes they have to stand their time out, through rain and snow, hot and cold.

Pocket Notebook Narrative
October 8, 1862

John L. Ross and Thomas L. Whel[u]s was wounded with peices of shells. From there our Brigade made its course towards Martinsburg, and nothing worthy of record befel it till I joined them. But now let me go back to where I left myself so unceremoniously at Gordonsville. I remained there till the 13th of Sept. When I jumped aboard the cars and resolved to go to my regt at all hazzards, and the cars did not run no farther than the Rapid Ann [Rapidan] river 15 miles above Gordonsville. The bridge across the river having been burnt by the Yankees and our men was building it but did not have it finished. From there I had to walk to the army then in Maryland. I left the station on the evening of the same day I left Gordonsville Sept. 13th in company with Lieut Davis of Co I[37] of our regt and Ajutant Tolerver of the 14th and several other members of the regiment and we walked on the rail road to Culpepper Court

---

37. This is likely a reference to Second Lieutenant John L. Davis of Company I. Davis was taken prisoner during the battle of the Wilderness and sent from Belle Plain to Fort Delaware on May 17, 1864, four days before Hall arrived. "Civil War Service Records, Confederate Records," Fold3 (www.fold3.com/image/35994391); Georgia Fourteenth Infantry, "File Record of November 3, 1914" entry for "John L. Davis" citing National Archives and Records Administration microfilm publication "Compiled Service Records of Confederate Soldiers Who Served in Organizations from the State of Georgia," M266, Roll 0288, Record Group 109, National Archives, Washington, D.C.

House, and from there we taken a turnpike that led in a North Western direction and we had a verry hard walk, but a verry cheerful time.[38]

On the evening of the 15th we come to Sperryville a small village at the edge of the Blue Ridge mountains and next morning we taken a northern direction and pass through Washington the county seat of Rappahannock county. Nothing worthy of notice happened to us till the 17th when we passed over the Blue Ridge there was a thick cloud a floating around us as we passed over it and as we desended to the valley below the Sun was a shining bright and beautiful. We passed through Front Royal that evening a small but beautiful town noted as being the place where Stonewall give the Yankees several drubings and where he started Banks and run him over the Potomac.

We crossed the Shennondoah River that evening in a boat the Bridges having been destroyed some time before. It is a beautiful clear stream with a rocky bottom. It runs nearly the whole length of the valley and emtys into the Potomac near Leesburg. On the morning of the next day we resumed our journey verry early, and passed through a beautiful country. On each side of the road there was a stone fence which will last forever.[39] We camped that evening in 3 miles of the city of Winchester, and before this time we were without anything

---

38. This is likely a reference to Addison Taliaferro, formerly 2d Sergeant, Co. I, who served as regimental adjutant from January 14, 1862, until April 1864. "Civil War Service Records, Confederate Records," Fold3 (www.fold3.com/image/35574189); Georgia Fourteenth Infantry, "File Record of November 3, 1914" entry for "Addison Taliaferro" citing National Archives and Records Administration microfilm publication "Compiled Service Records of Confederate Soldiers Who Served in Organizations from the State of Georgia," M266, Roll 0288, Record Group 109, National Archives, Washington, D.C.
39. Hall is likely referring to the Valley Turnpike, which had stone walls to prevent livestock from straying off the road. William J. Miller, *Mapping for Stonewall: The Civil War Service of Jed Hotchkiss* (Ellott & Clark, 1993), 51. This road, which was macadamized and ran most of the length of the Shenandoah Valley, became "one of the most important and heavily traveled roads in Virginia." Ibid., 163 n.2.

to eat and part of the time could not get any thing, for part of the inhabitance of this region is in sentiment strong for the union and part was noble and true to the South, and would devide with a poor soldier the last morsel the had. On the 19th [of September] we passed through Winchester, which has been in our hands and then the enemys several times. Gen Jackson has run them out of there 5 or 6 times and captured a great many waggons and comissary stores and munitions of war and then they have turned the joke on the old fellow about the same number of times.

The last time the Yankees was there they built a large fort on a commanding hill where I could see in every as far as the power of the eye could reach. When I was standing on the parapet I could see away to the east the Blue Ridge 20 miles distant and all the country between and to the west the Allighaneys, and away to the north where the two great ranges of Mountains extended into Maryland & Pennsylvania and seem like Sombre clouds a far off and to the South. The beautiful valley lies extended out as far as the eye can see. Inside the fort the Yankees blew up a magazine when they evacuated the place and the earth was torn up worse than I ever saw before.

That evening we heard our division was opposite Shepherd[s]town in Maryland and we set out for that place and that night we heard our army was falling Back on the Virginia Side of the Potomac, and the next day we met thousands of wounded that was able to walk on their way to Winchester that got wounded in the great battle that Sharpsburg Md. In Smithfield a small town that day we heard our division was making headway for Martinsburg and thither we turned our course and found our regiment about 3 miles north of that place.

On the 27th [of September] we left our camps and took

up the march Southwards through Martinsburg towards Winchester. The emence waggon trains and artillery delayed our progress and we were till nearly midnight a getting to our destination about 1 mile below a small village about half way between Martinsburg and Winchester called Bunkers Hill. At this place I was taken with the pneumonia and was not able to take any account of the movements of our Division. As near as I can tell about the middle of October they left me with some more sick of our regiment and our Division went on an expedition to destroy the track on the Baltimore and Ohio rail road. They were gone about a week and return[ed] to camp and I was verry sick about this time.

We only remained here a few days after that and they took up the march in a Southern direction carrying me in a waggon. The march was continued for 3 or 4 days and we camped near the Shennandoah River not far below Leesburg and from there I was taken to the hospital at Winchester about the first of November. I continued verry sick, and at Winchester I fared verry bad and came verry near dying but the Lord was with me and I was spared, but my sufferings was great. About the middle of November I was taken in an ambulance and started for Staunton 90 miles distant and on the way I had no where to lie at night only on the floor of some old out house and some time on the bare ground with only one blanket to lie and cover with, and the weather was severe and cold. When I arrived at Stanton, I had caught so much cold that my life was despaired of. By this time my disease had turned to the Bronchitis. At this hospital I was well cared for, had good medical attention and I soon began to recover. When on the 4th of Dec I taken the Small Pox, which was raging with terror in Staunton at this time. I lay verry low for 18 or 20 days when I began to gain my strength and appetite. I taken the Eresipelas in my foot and leg about

Christmas and it did not Get well till about the first of March 1863, and I continued to have pains in my brest and head the remainder of winter. The winter was cold and severe snow on the ground nearly all the time and the weather was more severe in March than any of the winter months.

Remembrancer Daily Entries
August 1 – December 31, 1862

Friday, August 1, 1862

Fair & hot. We arrived at Gordonsville this morning about 6 oclock and marched 3 or 4 miles below Gordonsville and camped and taken some rest and refreshment.

Saturday, August 2, 1862

Fair & hot. To day we move 2 miles lower down and camped being now 5 miles from Gordonsville. No news of importance. Everything quiet in this vicinity but I think there will be some stirring times in these regions before a verry great elaps of time.

Sunday, August 3, 1862

M partially cloudy. E rain. Today is slightly cloudy and pleasant and Serene. It is the holy day of the Lord, a day we are commanded to keep holy and refrain from worldly duty but in camps the day is barely kept by a majority of the soldiers. It is a bad place to keep the good day but I will try to do the best I can towards that important duty.

Monday, August 4, 1862

Fair & warm. To day I am taken with a verry high fever and is verry sick. We get orders to cook a days rations and hold ourselves in readiness to march.

Tuesday, August 5, 1862

Fair & Hot. I continue to be verry sick today with a hot fever.

Wednesday, August 6, 1862

Fair & hot. Thunder clouds pass. I am still verry sick today but not quite as bad as I was yesterday. Our Brigade got orders to march this morning at 5 oclock and all our baggage was loaded up, but the order was countermanded before we started. About 3 P.M.oclock our Brigade was called into line and marched off in a north western direction. I went with the waggon train to Gordonsville and arrived at night.

Thursday, August 7, 1862

Fair & Hot – Exceedingly. Today I am some better. Have verry little fever but a severe headache - at 1 oclock I took the cars and preceded via Charlottesville, to Livingston, Nelson Co Va and arrived there about dark in company with about 500 other was sent to Bellmonte Colledge Hospital 4 miles from the R R.[40]

Friday, August 8, 1862

Fair and exceedingly hot. This morning I have arrived at the hospital for the first time since I have been in the service and it is a verry dull place and I expect to leave here as soon as I get able to creep.

Saturday, August 9, 1862

Fair & verry hot. I am a little better today and think I shall soon be well and able to join my regiment which I expect is fighting the enemy by this time by what I can hear from them.

Sunday, August 10, 1862

M fair & hot. E a little rain. I have a very severe cough that troubles me so I can not sleep of a night. Otherwise I think I am mending.

---

40. Although Thayer typed "Livingston," this is likely almost certainly a reference to Lovingston, in Nelson County, Virginia.

Monday, August 11, 1862

Fair & hot. I feel verry bad this morning. My cough hurts me considerable last night.

Tuesday, August 12, 1862

M fair & Hot. E rain & hail. This morning I am verry sick. I cough so I cannot sleep of a night and of a morning I have a verry high fever.

Wednesday, August 13, 1862

Fair & warm. I am still very sick this morning. I fear there is some bad disease working me by my coughing so, but I hope not. My regiment is contending with the enemy, and by what I can hear has been for 4 or 6 days. I wish I was only well, and with them. May God watch over them and protect them till the end, is my prayer.

Thursday, August 14, 1862

Cloudy & warm. I continued to be verry sick. I have nothing to chronicle but I want to be with my regt verry bad.

Friday, August 15, 1862

Partialy cloudy & warm. I think today I am somewhat on the mend. I hope I will soon be able to get away from this monotions [monotonous] place.

Saturday, August 16, 1862

M cool. E fair & warm. I feel some what about the same. My cough is verry bad and hurts me terrable.

Sunday, August 17, 1862

M cool fair. E fair & warm. This morning I am verry bad off. Have a high fever and cough severely. Of evenings I feel a good deal better than I do in the morning.

Sunday, August 17, 1862[41]

I am now at Belmonte Hospital in Nelson County Va.

---

41. This entry is from the Pocket Notebook.

It was a Colledge in the time of peace and is situated in a pleasant part of the country intersected by Small mountains, branching off from the Blue Ridge and is a beautiful country in the time of peace. I am verry sick far away from the kind hand of my dear old mother and any relations or friends who could be so good to me in the time of Sickness, and who knows [n]ot that their dear Son and brother is lying Sick far away from them and longs to behold them once more. I have not heard one word from them in nearly four months, and I have never received but 2 letters from them Since I left my home and fireside to protect my unhappy country. Have never got a word or a line from them only twice during the long period of nearly 14 months. I do not know whether they are sick or well, alive or dead. Wi[s]h I could hear from them some time. I write to them once or twice every month and I do not know whether they get my letters or not but I hope and earnestly pray to God above that they do for many an hour of trouble and anxiety will they save my dear mother who can hear that her son who went to fight his country Battles and who will gain a name of undying fame in future ages -- is still in the land of the living. I dreamt of home and friend last night and a dream that I shall not forget in a long while and one that gives me a good deal of consolation.

  I dreamt of being at home and embracing my dear mother and friends and reciting to them the dangers and toils a far off country and I thought the children run to see me from every direction and of seeing the letters I sent home in mothers hands and one of my letters had been published in a paper in Augusta Ga. One that was dated June 7th in which I give them an account of the Battle of Seven Pines or the part taken by our regiment in that great struggle. I thought that I was at home to stay. It was the plainest dream I ever had and seemed that it was really so and "Oh! that it was true and I was with my dear friends today, and I sincerely hope that it will be so before many months longer, and that I may be at home and read this to them that I am writing now.

Monday, August 18, 1862

M cool. E fair & warm. I am about the same today I was yesterday. The mornings is cooler now than I ever saw for this season.

Tuesday, August 19, 1862

M cool. E fair & warm. I am some better today. My cough is not quite so bad nor my fever so high as it was.

Wednesday, August 20, 1862

M cool. E cloudy & warm. My cough has got a good deal better and my fever is not so high as they were and I hope they will keep getting lighter, till they do not come at all.

Thursday, August 21, 1862

M fair. E cloudy. I keep getting better I think but I am verry weak. I hope I will be able to join the regiment before much longer.

Friday, August 22, 1862

M cloudy & foggy. E clo with thunder. I feel about the same today I did yesterday. I am discontented and will continue to be so till I get to my company for I am uneasy all the time I am away from them.

Saturday, August 23, 1862

M cloudy. E thun & rain. I feel some better today and I think that I am mending and will soon be well I hope.

Sunday, August 24, 1862

M cloudy with a little rain. E clo & cool. Today I feel considerable better and think I shall soon be able to rejoin my regiment. It is verry thickly cloudy this morning and I [hear] there is going to be bad weather.

Monday, August 25, 1862

Fair & pleasant. Today is fair & pleasant. The sky is a beautiful blue. The sun shines calm and serene. I feel like I was nearly well and I went out in the country to buy me some bread to last me to my regt which is if what I hear is true nearly to Manassas. I will have a long way to walk to get to them. But I am resolved to try. Today is my birth day I am 21 years of age.

Monday, August 25, 1862[42]

<u>My Twenty First Birth Day</u>

August the 25th 1841 I was borned in the State of Alabama Talediga County. It was on that day that I first saw light in this world of wonders and wickedness, and hard and rugged was the path I had to follow and various have been the scenes and troubles. I have passed through from then till now little did I know at my first recolections what I would have to encounter in days to come. It is now August 25th, 1862. I am 21 year of age, the age that is considered that a youth becomes a man, and is free to do as the rights of a man allows him. I always looked to this day as to be a great day with me and with lofty expectations as to the career in life I was to begin, but my most sanguine hopes has been blasted and carried away as chaff before the wind. I am far away from all that is near and dear to me in a far off country, far away from my native State and county. Our country ravaged disordered and distracted and one of the most dire calmitys that ever happened has befell our dear beloved land. A war of the foulest kind a civil war where brother fights against Brother, Father against Son, husband against wife and thousands of our own countrymen and

---

42. This entry is from the Pocket Notebook.

kindred have already fell and stained the land that give them birth with their hearts blood. Thousands upon thousands of homes have been made desolate, and there is hardly a family but what has mourned the loss of some of its members and it still grows more terrible and destructive. God has blessed our arms with success and I hope and earnestly pray that he will continue with us to the end. We have drove them from every position they have brought against us, and we keep on the same way that we have for the last three months in one month more we will have off of the soil of Virginia. The Spirit of the South will never be broken till the last one of her sons be cold and motionless in death and <u>never no never</u> will we lay down our arms to the dastard felons till the last ones of the Sons of the Suny South has pored out the last drop of his lifes Blood and leave the land that was once happiness and prosperity bleak and desolate.

Tuesday, August 26, 1862

M cool. E fair & pleasant. Today I start to the regiment with hope that I can keep well to get to them for I hear that there is going to be a mighty battle before long. I get as far as the depot and stay for the night.

August, Wednesday 27, 1862

Cloudy & pleasant. I took the cars at Lovingston Station this morning at 8 ocl and arrived at Gordonsville about 12 oclock and here they inform me that I could not get to my regiment at present and the Provost Marshal detailed me to stand guard, for a few days.

Thursday, August 28, 1862

Cloudy & pleasant. Today I am on guard but I am not contented for I want to get to the company. I want to see the boys verry bad. No news. Only rumors. Things very uncertain.

Friday, August 29, 1862

Fair & pleasant. Nothing new. The weather is very dry and dusty.

Saturday, August 30, 1862

Cloudy & warm. Nothing new. I am on police duty today.

Sunday, August 31, 1862

M rain. E cloudy. This morning it rained verry hard for a while but did not last long. All through the day it was cloudy & drisly. I sent a letter home to my dear mother away in the Land of Flowers.[43]

Monday, September 1, 1862

M cloudy. E thunder & rain. This time one year ago I was in the mountains of N W Va lying verry Sick and I came nearer dying then than I ever did before. This evening there came some refreshing showers which will help to settle the dust and purified the air. I was on guard.

Tuesday, September 2, 1862

M cool & windy. E fa[ir] & pleas[ant]. This morning is very cool and begins to resemble autumn considerable the sky is clear and of a beautiful blue. Our arms has achieved another great victory on the plains of Manassas on the 28 and 29 of Aug. We gained the most complete victory that has been gained during the war.

Wednesday, September 3, 1862

M cool. E fair & pleasant. I have got the diarhea verry bad and it pains me verry much. News keeps coming in of the great victory we gained over the enemy. We completely routed them drove them before our victorious army in the utmost confusion and by this time a gr[e]at many of them

---

43. Rachel Holly moved from Worth County, Georgia, to Florida at some point prior to the end of August 1862. Hall often referred to Florida as "the land of flowers," a derivation of the English translation of the Spanish word "florida."

captured and the remainder completely demoralized. Today I am on fatigue duty.

Thursday, September 4, 1862

M cool. E fair & pleas. I feel verry bad today. The diarhea hurts me verry much and does not seem to get any better. The nights is cool and the days fair and beautiful. I want to be with my regiment verry much but I am not able a present to get to them.

Friday, September 4, 1862[44]

Another great Battle has been fought on the plains of Manassas, a great extent more terrible and fiercer than the one of July 21st 1861 and the rout of enemy more complete. God has blessed our arms with one of the greatest Victories that was ever achieved, the whole comb[ine]d forces of Mclellan, Pope and Burnsides, has been cut to peices and demoralized and our glorious army is now pursuing them and I hope ere this that the once grand armies of Pope and Mclelland has ceased to exist. On the 28 and 29 of August was the days the great portion of fighting was done but our men kept pursuing them. The last accounts, the twice stained field of Manassas with the blood of our heroic and noble Soldiers each time has been a glorious victory on our side and a disastrious defeat to the enemy. I think it will teach them a lesson they are not likely to forget. Manassas has prove[n] to be the Waterloo to Pope and Mclelland and our heroic and Noble commanders has imortal fame, and imperishable honors. Stonewall Jackson is the Washington of the [S]outh and I hope will live to see his dear country once more in peace and happiness.

---

44. This entry is from the Pocket Notebook.

Friday, September 5, 1862

Fair & pleasant. On Guard. Our army has gained a Signal victory in Kentucky on the Same day of the great victory at Manassas, and advices from there say that our men will soon have the enemy out of the state and our victorious army will soon have them out of Virginia.[45] I hope for we are in a fair way to do it. Have driven them over 75 miles in a few days.

Saturday, September 6, 1862

Fair & pleasant. Our army still advances and I hear a portion of it is in Maryland. I hope it is true. We have verry fine weather now on our wounded. It is fair and pleasant with cool moon-light nights.

Sunday, September 7, 1862

Fair & pleasant. Nothing new. My diarhea is nearly well and [I] want to get to my regt before long as I possibly can. On Fatigue.

Monday, September 8, 1862

Fair & pleasant. I hear today our army has entered Maryland. General Jackson's command and Gen. A. P. Hill and Longstreets Division has entered enmasse at Leesburg and is advancing on Baltimore to cut off the communication with the city of Washington. On Fatigue.

Tuesday, September 9, 1862

Fair & pleasant – windy. On Police. We have glorious news from every quarter today. Our army in Maryland is at the Relay House in nine miles of Baltimore when last hear[d] from and ere this is in that city I suppose.[46] Telegraphic news this evening bring news of the capture of the City of Cincinnatti by Confederate forces, and our troops is driving

---

45. This is likely a reference to the battle of Richmond, Kentucky, at the end of August.
46. The Relay House in Halethorpe, Maryland, was a stop on the Baltimore & Ohio Railroad.

the hessians out of Alabama and Tennessee. Glorious news indeed.

Wednesday, September 10, 1862

Cloudy & warm. Nothing new today. Only the confirmation of what was heard yesterday. The news comes in gloriously from every quarter for the Southern Confederacy. We are gaining ground and driving the foe from before from every point of the compass. On Guard.

Thursday, September 11, 1862

Cloudy & rainy. Nothing of importance. Our army is so far off that it takes a week to get straight news and then nothing that is reliable. Our commanders wished from some motive to keep their movements as secret as possible.

Thursday, September 11, 1862[47]

Great has been the change in our Situation from the 26th of June to the present time. Then the mighty hosts of Mcleland, had our army pen[n]ed in around the City of Richmond, with all our communication cut off from the outer world only from one way. Our supplies was limited to only what one rail road could bring in. Country produce of all kind got up to a price almost fabulous. Mcleland with the most numerous and best equiped army the world ever saw lay at his ease and said the Rebel Capital was surely his and he only wanted Some fine morning before breakfast to march in his countless hords and ensure its downfall and the capture and destruction of the rebel army and hundreds of his soldiers was so sure of success that they wrote home to their friends and relatives that the next time they heard from them the[y] would be in the doomed city.

But the God on high give Strength to our arms and one Thursday the 26th of June the memorial day never to be

---

47. This entry is from the Pocket Notebook.

forgotten as long as a Southern heart beats our noble and gallent vetreans marched against them. Seven days and nights did we fight and drive them before us completely routed and nearly annihilated the grand army and they Slunk away down some river under cover of their gunboats, and then again the first of August we marched against the mighty army of Pope which was soon joined by the combin[e]d forces of Mcleland and Burnsides. Our forces met them on Cedar run and completely routed them again and followed them up to the Plains of Manassas where they made their last stand and there the 28, 29 and 30 of Aug was fought one of the most terable battles that is recorded in the annals of history which ended in a disastrous defeat of the Federal army. Again our victorious army then proceeded to liberate Maryland, and they are now on its soil away in the interior threatening Baltimore and the Yankee Capital. As I Said, has [n]ot the change been great in a little over two months. Our cause is prosperous every where in Tennessee and Kentucky our army has been victorious and has advanced as far as the State of Ohio and the last accounts from there, the Queen city of the west was demanded to Surrender Cincinnati and ere this I expect it is in the hands of the Confederates.

Friday, September 12, 1862

Cloudy with some rain. Nothing new. Only I am gratified to say my health has returned in full vigor and I hope and trust to the <u>Supreme Being</u> that in future it may continue to be so, for health in war is half the battle and is one of the greatest riches ever bestowed on man.

Saturday, September 13, 1862

Partially cloudy & warm. This morning at 9 oclock I got on board the cars and started to my regt. It is a long and perilous journey but nevertheless I have undertaken it and hope I may get through safe but it's a long distance over 150 miles and I will have it to walk all but 15 miles. We arrive at Rapid Ann [Rapidan] River as far as the cars could go and taken it a foot 6 miles this evening.

Sunday, September 14, 1862

Partially cloudy & warm. Today we passed Culpepper Court House which looks barren and deserted. The marauders has shown their cloven foot here and it seem like it had been deserted for years. From there we taken the turnpike road toward Sperryville and before us could be seen mountains in vast heaps.

Monday, September 15, 1862

M cloudy. E fair & warm. We arrive at Sperryville today after a hard walk at the foot of the Blue Ridge. I feel verry tired and worn out and my feet is verry sore having to travel over a hard rocky road and I have got no shoes.

Tuesday, September 16, 1862

M fair & warm. E cloudy. We passed through the village of Washington where the court house of Rappahannock County is today and also Flint Hill a Small village and camped for the night verry fatigued and worn out.

Wednesday, September 17, 1862

M cloudy & foggy. E fair & pleasant. Today we passed over the Blue Ridge and passed through a thick cloud on top of the mountains and arrived at Front Royal and crossed the Shanandoah river in a boat and camp[ed] for the night in verry comfortable quarters.

Thursday, September 18, 1862

Partially cloudy & warm. This morning we started verry soon on the road towards Winchester. We are now in the great valley of Virginia between the Blue Ridge and Allighany Mountains which at this point is about 50 miles wide. We arrived in the evening in 3 miles of the City and camp for the night.

Friday, September 19, 1862

Partially cloudy & warm. This morning we passed through the city of Winchester which is a thriving place in peaceable times and we passed on to the Yankee fortifications where they built a large fort not long ago and when our forces run them away from there they blow up there magazine which made a Sign in the ground that was worth seeing. We took the road from Winchester to Shepherd[s]town and camped.

Saturday, September 20, 1862

Cloudy & pleasant. Today I met thousands of our wounded coming from Maryland where our forces and the enemy had a great Battle on the 16 and 17 inst. The poor fellows had a long way to walk or fall into the hands of the enemy. Every thing was in great confusion. Our army has fell on the South side of the Potomac and I can hear cannons in the distance.

Sunday, September 21, 1862

M cool & foggy. E fair & pleasant. Our army fought yesterday again and is crossing the river again today we hear. I am making my way to Martinburg and trying to over take my regt. We have been without any thing to eat for 3 or 4 days, only what we could pick up as we could get it. The weather is verry dry now and the roads is so dusty that you can scarcely travel them without being stifled with dust.

Monday, September 22, 1862

M cool. E fair & pleasant. Today I passed through Martinsburg. It is nearly as large as Winchester. The Baltimore & Ohio R R comes through this place. Our men has blown up all the bridges on this road and it will not do the enemy much more good during the war. I found my regt in the evening about 3 miles above Martinsburg and was verry glad to see my companions one more time and they were verry proud to see me.

Tuesday, September 23, 1862

M cool. E fair & pleasant. To day every thing seem[ed] quiet and still our army has camped and is taking a little rest for the first time in about two months but all our troops seem to be in good spirit. The poor fellows has had a hard time of it. We have been marching and fighting e[v]er since the begining of last spring. On fatigue duty today.

Wednesday, September 24, 1862

Cloudy & a little rain. The ground is dryer now than it has been before in two year, and the water is drying up rapidly. It rained a little today. I am now in the Great Valley of Virginia between the Blue Ridge on one side and the Allighanys on the other, running parillel to each other. The valley is a rich and beautiful country.

Thursday, September 25, 1862[48]

Camp 3 miles above Martinsburg Va. This is a beautiful autumnal day. The sky is clear and the sun shines balmy and serene. Autumn Seems to be set in, in earnest. This is one of those beautiful day[s] that brings to me memories of the past, when every thing was happy and contented and I was far away in my dear old native state and seeing the beautiful fields of cotton as white as snow and in my happy days thronged with youths of my own age. We used to pick the snowy down from the fruitful stalks. Then I was happy (if I had known it) fair & happy day did I see then but all that is gone, yes gone, I fear forever but I hope not. Hope is a great blessing and is always with me in my darkest hours. If our dear country is ever restored to peace then maybe happy days will return I hope to all of us.

I am now 3 miles north of Martinsburg in a few miles of the lines of Maryland and Pennsylvania. Our army is part of

---

48. This entry is from the Pocket Notebook.

it on the move and we will move in a day or two. Our army is in a bad condition at present, the most of it is barefoot and have not but one suit of clothing. I have no shoes nor no clothes but what I have on my back. When I wash my clothes I have to go naked till I wash and dry them or put them on wet, but I am in a just cause and one I hope God will reward.

Thursday, September 25, 1862

M a slight frost. E fair & Pleasant. Nothing new. Every thing quiet. We had a slight frost this morning. The first of this season. The remainder of the day was pleasant and beautiful.

Friday, September 26, 1862

M cool. E fair & pleasant. To day autumn seems to be set in in earnest and verry much resembles a day in October in my native country. We will leave this place tomorrow I expect. We have order[s] to cook up rations.

Saturday, September 27, 1862

M frosty. E fair & pleasant. This morning at 7 oclock we packed up and prepaired to march and we started but owing to delays of some kind we did not get off till about 12 and we marched toward Winchester, through Martinsburg and on to the village of Bunker Hill and camped about 2 miles below about 12 oclock at night verry tired and exhausted.

Sunday, September 28, 1862

M cloudy. E fair & warm. To day we fix our camp and draw rations and cook & eat for we got verry hungry yesterday. Every thing is quiet and still.

Monday, September 29, 1862

M frosty. E fair & pleasant. Nothing new. Only our mail arrive today for the first time in about two months and I received a letter from home which give me a great deal of

Satisfaction. Surrounded as I am by impending dangers all the time a word from the dear ones at home is a great comfort to me.

Tuesday, September 30, 1862

Partially cloudy & warm. Nothing of importance today. Every thing quiet. It threatens to rain but it does not come. The ground is verry dry and the dust intollerable.

Wednesday, October 1, 1862

Partially cloudy & warm. We have an election in our company to day for two Sergeants and one Corporal. J. M. Jones was elected 5th [Sergt.] and David Champion 4th Sergt. No news stirring. Elbert Baker is elected 4th Corporal.

Thursday, October 2, 1862

M cloudy & misty. E par[tl]y cloudy. Every thing Still & quiet, in this vicinity. We draw money today for two months wages and for Six months of clothing including the Second Six month[s]. $47.00 in all.

Friday, October 3, 1862

M foggy. E fair & warm. Today I am on Division guard. Division guard is guard round the whole division. An equal number of men is detailed from each regt and reports at one place and all forms together into three reliefs.

Saturday, October 4, 1862

Partially cloudy & warm. Nothing new. The weather is verry dry and dusty. It has not rained much for two months. The aspect of the clouds denote rain every day but it does not come and it is verry warm for the Season.

Sunday, October 5, 1862

Fair & cool. Nothing of importance. I write a letter home to my friend far away.

Monday, October 6, 1862

Fair & cool. We have two drills a day since we have been at this Station. Company drill before noon and Battalion drill after noon and dress parade[49] near Sun-set.

Tuesday, October 7, 1862

Fair M cool. E verry warm. We have verry favorable news for our cause, from Europe. Our army has gained the admiration of the world. France and Russia is talking of intervention but I doubt verry much of us getting aid from any quarter whatever.

Wednesday, October 8, 1862

Fair & warm. I had a verry bad cold and a Severe cough which pains me verry much in my head and throat It is verry warm and dry weather here now for the Season and no indications of rain.

Thursday, October 9, 1862

Nothing new. I continue to have a bad cold & cough.

Friday, October 10, 1862

M cloudy. E rainy. I have a fever and my cold grows worse. I received a letter from home which left the dear ones at home well which give me a great deal of satisfaction.

Saturday, October 11, 1862

M rain. E cloudy & cool. I am verry sick to day and my cough is severe.

Sunday, October 12, 1862

Cloudy & cool. I continue to be sick and have a severe headache but I hope I will soon be better by the help of the Lord.

Sunday, January 25, 1863[50]

I am at present Surrounded by verry wicked companions, a variety of Soldiers from different states and they are nearly all wicked profaners of the Lords Day and they all care more

---

49. This is Hall's only reference to a dress parade. In comparison, Elsesser makes over two dozen entries denoting dress parades, including an entry on May 7, 1862, that dress parades were required every evening.
50. This entry is from the Pocket Notebook. It is the first lengthy entry from the Notebook since September 25, 1862.

for worldly things than things of God. Oh Lord help me to withstand temptation and Turn my thoughts to thee always and let not Oh Lord the enfluence of wicked companions turn me from thee.

The Lord has been kind to me and carried me safe through many tryals and dangers and still my Hard heart rebels against his kindness. Give me a new heart Oh Lord, and help me to follow the narrow path that leads to everlasting life, and turn my thoughts from things of this world and purer and holier things above.

Remembrancer Daily Entries

January 1 – March 12, 1863

The Following that is wrote with ink is for 1863 with the day of the week designated.

In Gen Hospital Staunton Va. Snow Storm.

Wednesday, January 26, 1863

I began my diary again after a long while, and may the Lord continue my health till I return to my native home. I am not well at present. I have the Eresipelas & a disease in my head.

Thursday, January 29, 1863

Fair & cold. To-day has turned some warmer. The sunshines beautiful but the snow lies on the ground in heaps and has been lying for several days. I hope I may soon be able to rejoin my regiment which is now near Fredericksburg, and has been there since the great Battle in December.

Friday, January 30, 1863

M Snow. E fair. Nothing new. The weather is verry changeable. I am now gaining in Strength and flesh and hope I may soon be well. My leg is Swelled considerable from the Eresipelas.

Saturday, January 31, 1863

Par fair & cool. To day we hear good news if it only be true. That Northwestern States Indiana & Illinois are thinking Seriously about dividing from the Northeast & withdrawing their troops from the abolition service and also disruption is taking in several places in the north.

Sunday, February 1, 1863

Cloudy & wet. One month of the new year is past and gone never to return. Oh may the Lord cause this cruel war to close by the return of warm weather. That will be the happiest day a poor Soldier can See in this vile world, the day that he returns home to his kindred and friends.

Sunday, February 1, 1863

The Sabbath passes verry dull to me. I cannot serve the Lord and turn my heart to him as I ought to. Oh God I pray for a better heart, cause thy Spirit to rest on me all way. Give me a pu[r]er Spirit and help me to find the narrow path with here and there a traveler. I am Saddened at the wickedness of the world. When I look around me I See nothing but wickedness and my rebelious heart wants to go with the world. Oh Lord help me to Struggle through these difficulties through the blood of the Lamb. I have been reading a good Book today which I delight in and hope I may become as it teaches. The title of it is Baxters Saints Everlasting Rest. Oh that I may be as holy as the great and good man that wrote it and forever rest in the presence of the Lord.

Monday, February 2, 1863

Fair & cool. The News reached here today of the raise of the blockade at Charleston, by our naval forces at that place. I hope our little navy will Soon be Strong enough to clear the waters of the Yankees great [f]leets and boasted gunboats.

Tuesday, February 3, 1863

M Snow. E fair. Nothing of importance in this vicinity. I have pains in the Side of my head and my left ear had a rising in it about 3 months ago and is not well yet and I cannot hear any at all on that side.

Wednesday, February 4, 1863

M fair & cool. E clo[udy]. Nothing of importa[n]ce. It is Severely cold. The ice is verry thick. I feel verry bad today and unwell.

Thursday, February 5, 1863

Snow. It was Snowing this morning when I arose and is Snowing Still. It is verry fine & beautiful. The ground is perpetually covered in it from half leg to knee deep [at] This vicinity from the middle of Jan.

Friday, February 6, 1863

M cloudy. E fair & cold. Nothing of importance. It has Snowed so often and so much during the last and the present month that our army cannot do much.

Saturday, February 7, 1863

Fair & cold. I feel unwell to day. I have a head ache and cough.

Sunday, February 8, 1863

M fair & cold. E cloudy. I have a Severe cough and pain in my breast. I have not got over the pneumonia yet and I fear ther[e] is some lung disease working me.

Sunday, February 8, 1863[51]

Holy Bible book divine
Precious treasure thou art mine[52]

---

51. This entry is from the Pocket Notebook.
52. These are the first two lines of the hymn "Holy Bible, Book Divine." https://hymnary.org/text/holy_bible_book_divine_precious_treasure

Lay yourself treasure in Heaven where moth and rust doth not corrupt, and thieves do not break through and Steal. For where your treasure is there will be your heart also.[53]

Oh Lord! Teach me to think of thee always, and turn my mind from things of the world and keep my mind and meditations on heaven and thy Blessed word. I passed this Sabbath better than any previous one lately. I gained a good deal of comfort from reading a good book and in the afternoon heard a Sermon preached for the Benefit of the Soldiers in the hospital which I hope will be kept up throughout the army.

Monday, February 9, 1863

Cloudy & cold. Nothing of interest. My cough is some better.

Tuesday, February 10, 1863

Fair & cool. I feel verry unwell. Had a slight fever today. My mind is calm and Serene resting on the love of God. I see a great Satisfaction in reading good Books which I have a good opportunity for while I am here.

Wednesday, February 11, 1863

M Snow. E cloudy & wet. Nothing of interest.

Thursday, February 12, 1863

M fair. E cloudy & cool. Nothing new.

Friday, February 13, 1863

Fair & pleasant. I feel verry bad. Have a Severe head ache and a Slight fever.

Saturday, February 14, 1863

M cloudy. E fair & cool. Nothing uncommon.

Sunday, February 15, 1863

M rainy. E cloudy. I am gaining my health and Strength verry fast and hope I may soon be able to return to my

---

53. This is likely a paraphrase of Matthew 6:19-20.

regiment, If it is the will of the Lord, for I am getting anxious to see my companions in arms.

Monday, February 16, 1863

Fair & pleasant. Nothing of importance.

Tuesday, February 17, 1863

Snowing all day. We heard last night that the Northwestern State was a going into measures to Stop the war. I hope it is so but I fear it is all only idle rumors like Some we have heard before.

Wednesday, February 18, 1863

Cold & Rainy. My left ear continues to pain me verry much. It is now over three months since it first inflamed and it continues to discharge matter resembling an old running sore.

Thursday, February 19, 1863

M cold & clo[udy]. E fair & cool. Nothing to record.

Friday, February 20, 1863

Fair & cool with flying clo[uds]. Nothing worthy of record.

Saturday, February 21, 1863

M fair & cool. E cloudy. I feel verry bad with pains in my back and bre[a]st and my bowels pains me considerable.

Sunday, February 22, 1863

Heavy Snowing. It began to Snow last night directly after dark and continued till 12 oclock today. It is now a foot deep and over on level groun[d] and the clouds looks dark and lowring like it was going to continue.

Sunday, February 22, 1863[54]

I wish it to be the work of my life to be an instrument in Spreading the Glory of God and to bring Glory to his kingdom by influencing others to walk the narrow path that

---

54. This entry is from the Pocket Notebook.

leads to eternal life. Oh Lord put it in my heart and send thy blessed Spirit on me to pray always night and day, during my short pilgrimage here for the Spreading of thy glory in this wicked world. Grant Oh Lord that I may have the faith and Spirit of that Holy man of thee Mr. Muller.[55] From this day forward Strengthen my faith and love in thee And be with me in hours of temptation and tryal.

Monday, February 23, 1863

M Snow. E fair & cold. Nothing of importance.

Tuesday, February 24, 1863

Fair & cold. Nothing today.

Wednesday, February 25, 1863

Fair & cold. I have gained my strength considerable but I am weak yet & have a pain in my breast nearly constant. I hope I will soon be restored to my full health but I fear my lungs is so affected that my health never will be fully restored.

Thursday, February 26, 1863

Rainy & disagreeable. I am now reading the Pilgrims Progress. I hope by the blessings of the Lord I will gain good instruction from it and if it pleases God let me return to my home. I can read good books with better satisfaction.

Friday, February 27, 1863

Cloudy & cool. Nothing new. The ground is very Sloppy & muddy on account of the heavy Snows that has begun to melt.

Saturday, February 28, 1863

Cold & cloudy. Nothing of importance.

Sunday, March 1, 1863

M cold & rainy. E windy. I Sent a letter to my dear old Mother far away, and trusting the Lord I hope it will safely reach its destination and all will follow its precepts.

---

55. This may be a reference to George Muller, a British evangelical minister.

Today I commenced nursing for a while till I get able to stand field service.

Sunday, March 1, 1863[56]

It is a great comfort [to] me Surrounded as I am at present to pray to God for deliverance from Temptations, which verry often assault me on every Side. Evil and worldly minded companions is all the kind I have at present. And their hearts is hard to turn from the Sin they love to lavish in, Oh Lord thou are the only one that can turn their hearts from their wicked course. Do so Oh Lord for I fear many keep their hearts from thee until the last day. I gained a great comfort from reading the <u>Pilgrims Progress</u> during the past week and I hope I will be enabled to keep in mind what I learned therefrom and with my prayers, be a great comfort to me in hours of trial. And to never turn from the narrow way that leads the Celestial City[57].

Monday, March 2, 1863

Fair & cold. Nothing of importance.

Tuesday, March 3, 1863

M Snow Storm. E windy with flying clouds. The weather is verry changable now. It Snowed Soon this morning and then faird off about an hour and then come a Snow Storm which lasted about and hour and then faired off again.

Wednesday, March 4, 1863

Cold & windy with Scattering clouds. It is the coldest weather now that has been this winter.

Thursday, March 5, 1863

Cold & Severe.

Friday, March 6, 1863

Cold cloudy & windy. No news but we are waiting in

---

56. This entry is from the Pocket Notebook.
57. The "Celestial City" is a term John Bunyan used in Pilgrim's Progress to denote the concept of heaven.

suspense expecting to hear of the attack on Charleston Savanah or Vick[s]burg every day.

Saturday, March 7, 1863

Cloudy with a little rain.

Sunday, March 8, 1863

M rain. E fair & pleasant. I feel verry bad to day. I have a severe headache.

Monday, March 9, 1863

M rainy. E fair & cool.

Daggs Moral Science concordance of the Bible

Christian paradoxes

Pendletons Sermons

Steps toward Heaven, T. S. Arthor

Religious Encyclopedia

Comprehensive Commentary of the Holy Bible Bapt[ist][58]

Tuesday, March 10, 1863

Snow & Sleet.

Hesperian Harp

History of the reformation

Sermons By Andrew Fuller

Sermons By John Wes[t]ley

Websters unabridged Bible [D]ictionary[59]

Wednesday, March 11, 1863

M fair. E snow & wind. My trust is in the Lord and my hope is for things future in a Country not Seen by mortal eyes. I expect to start to my regiment in a day or two.

---

58. This book list likely refers in part to the follow publications: John L. Dagg's *Elements of Moral Science* (1860); J. M. Pendleton's *Short Sermons on Important Subjects* (1859); T. A. Arthur's *Steps Toward Heaven: Or, Religion in Common Life; A Series of Lay Sermons for Converts in the Great Awakening* (1858); and the *Comprehensive Commentary on the Holy Bible – Baptist Edition*, edited by William Jenks (1834).

59. This book list likely refers in part to the follow publications: William Hauser's *The Hesperian Harp: A Collection of Psalm and Hymn Tunes, Odes and Anthems*; Andrew Fuller's *The Complete Works of Andrew Fuller*, vol. 1: Memoirs, Sermons, Etc. (1845); and Noah Webster's *Dictionary* and King James Bible (1828).

Thursday, March 12, 1863

Cold & windy. Snow. Tomorrow I expect to start to my regiment for I want to see my company verry much.

Friday, March 12, 1863[60]

<u>P R A Y E R</u>

Before you enter into prayer, ask thy Soul these questions. To what end Oh my Soul art thou retired into this place. Art thou not come to discourse with the Lord in prayer. Is he present, will he hear the[e]? Is thy business slight, is it not concerning the welfare of thy soul? What words will thy use to move him to compassion? To make thy preparations, consider thou art but dust and ashes, and he is the great God, Father of our Lord Jesus Christ, that clothes himself with light as with a garment; that thou art a vile sinner, he is a holy God; that thou art but a poor crawling worm he is the Omnipotent Creater. In all your prayers for get not to thank the Lord for all his mercies. When thou prayest, rather let thy heart be without words, than thy words without heart. Prayer will make a man cease from his sin, or sin will entice a man to cease from prayer. The Spirit of prayer is more precious than treasures of gold and silver. Pray often; for prayer is the Shield to the soul, a sacrifice to God, and a S[c]ourge for Satan.[61]

The above was found among the writings of John Bunyan. O may the lord enable me to have a strong faith and as great patiences to bear tryal and suffering for His cause, as that holy man did.

---

60. This entry is from the Pocket Notebook.
61. The prayer to this point is from an unidentified edition of *Bunyan's Works: Bunyan's Dying Sayings*.

7

"FOR ALL WHO KNEW HIM ESTEEMED AND RESPECTED HIM HIGHLY"
VIRGINIA AND MARYLAND: MARCH – JUNE 1863

Once released from the hospital, Hall started back for his regiment on March 13, 1863, riding by rail from Staunton to Guinea Station, Virginia, a stop on the Richmond, Fredericksburg and Potomac Railroad. Thomas's Brigade encamped from late December 1862 through late April 1863 in winter quarters at nearby Camp Gregg. This camp, named for General Maxcy Gregg, a casualty of the battle of Fredericksburg, was eight miles east of Guinea Station and two miles from the Rappahannock River.[1] Hall arrived in camp on March 15 and remained there until the end of April, when the regiment moved west in preparation for the Chancellorsville offensive.

Life in camp resumed its usual routine. Hall spent his days rotating among picket duty, regimental guard duty, inspections, skirmish drills, and quiet days in camp. He continued to battle illness, though, as the camp experienced harsh weather. Above all, Hall focused on religion during this period in camp. April 12, 1863, proved to be one of the most significant days of Hall's war, if not of his entire life, because it was the date on which he was baptized by Chaplain Edward B. Barrett into the Missionary Baptist Church in the waters of the Rappahannock River. Hall's reflective entries for April 12 and April 13 burst with spiritual joy. He felt that he was not only a soldier in the defense of his country but now a Christian soldier as well.

---

1. Smedlund, *Campfires of Georgia's Troops*, 141.

Hall's entries for the remainder of the war made frequent references to different types of religious gatherings. A prayer meeting, usually conducted without a minister, featured scripture reading, hymn-singing, and a member of the group leading the others in prayer. Sunday divine services conducted by a chaplain or visiting minister usually included a sermon. Most services were conducted outdoors, even in inclement weather, with men standing in bare feet on snow-covered ground.[2] As music historian James Davis, who cites Hall's regular attendance at prayer meetings, writes, "winter encampment allowed soldiers to grapple with religious doctrine and forced them to consider their fates."[3] The relative slower pace of camp life, especially over the winter, afforded soldiers the opportunity to convene regularly. Hall often attended two or three sermons or prayer meetings per day, but his greatest joy appeared to be the latter.

Hall references attending services at a church named Liberty near his camp in late May 1863. This was likely Liberty Church, just southeast of Guinea Station on present-day Fort Walker in Caroline County, Virginia. Built in 1850, the brick structure is still in use as a chapel for special occasions at Fort Walker. (Photo courtesy of thechaplainkit.com)

The coming of spring meant the start of a new season of campaigning. Burnside, who lasted less than ninety days as commander of the Army of the Potomac, was replaced by Maj. Gen. Joseph Hooker, who hoped for an offensive that would either force Lee to retreat south or engage the Army of the Potomac in an open field showdown where the Union could take advantage of its superior manpower and artillery. What Hooker received instead was a thrashing at Chancellorsville.

---

2. Wiley, *Life of Johnny Reb*, 181.
3. James A. Davis, *Music Along the Rapidan: Civil War Soldiers, Music, and Community during Winter Quarters, Virginia* (University of Nebraska Press, 2014), 188.

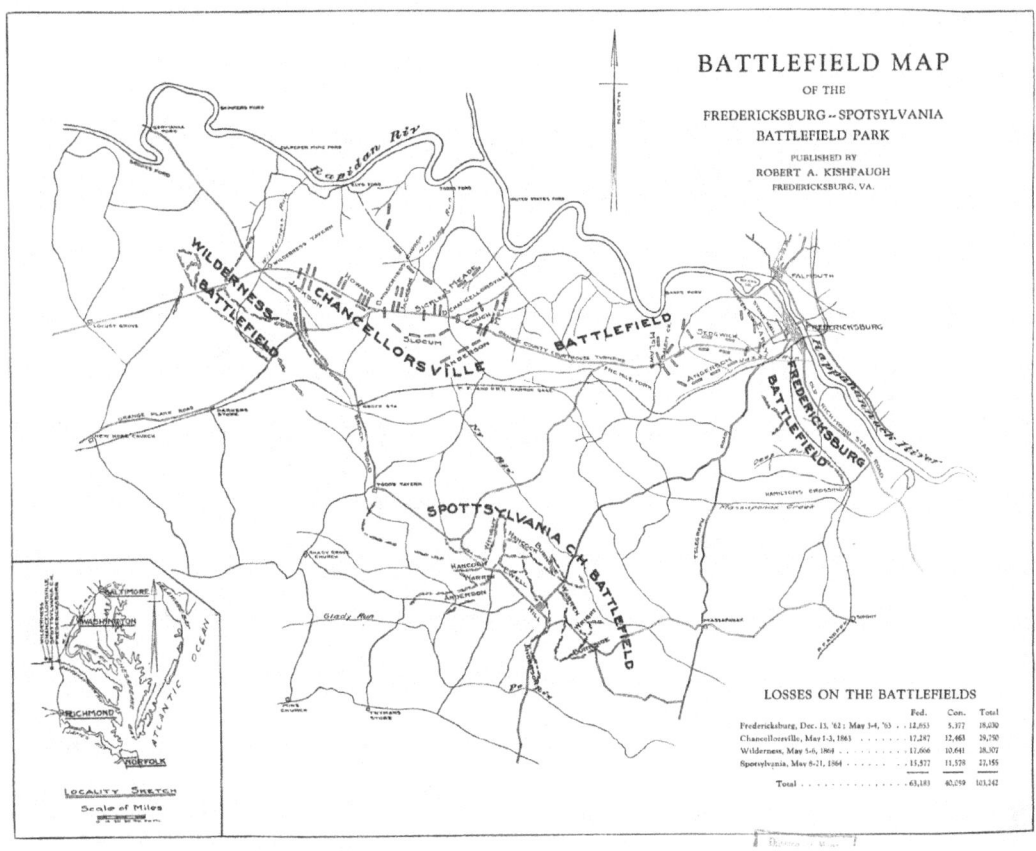

Three major battles – and many lesser skirmishes -- were fought in this relatively small triangle running from the Wilderness Battlefield east to Fredericksburg and south to Spotsylvania. (Library of Congress)

Having dispatched a sizable number of Longstreet's troops to southeastern Virginia to forage, Lee had roughly only half the number of troops on the Rappahannock as did Hooker by late April 1863. Hooker kept 40,000 men at Fredericksburg but moved 70,000 men ten miles west of Fredericksburg to Chancellorsville, where the Orange Plank Road and Ely's Ford Road converge with the Orange Turnpike. Lee, aware of Hooker's movement, left 12,000 troops under General Jubal Early at Fredericksburg and marched the remainder of his army, including Thomas's Brigade, west on May 1. After encountering Confederate resistance, Hooker made the extraordinary decision to pull back into the heavily thicketed Wilderness area, greatly reducing his numerical advantage over Lee and impeding effective use of his artillery. And then, inexplicably, "Fighting Joe" Hooker yielded the initiative by waiting for Lee to make the next move.

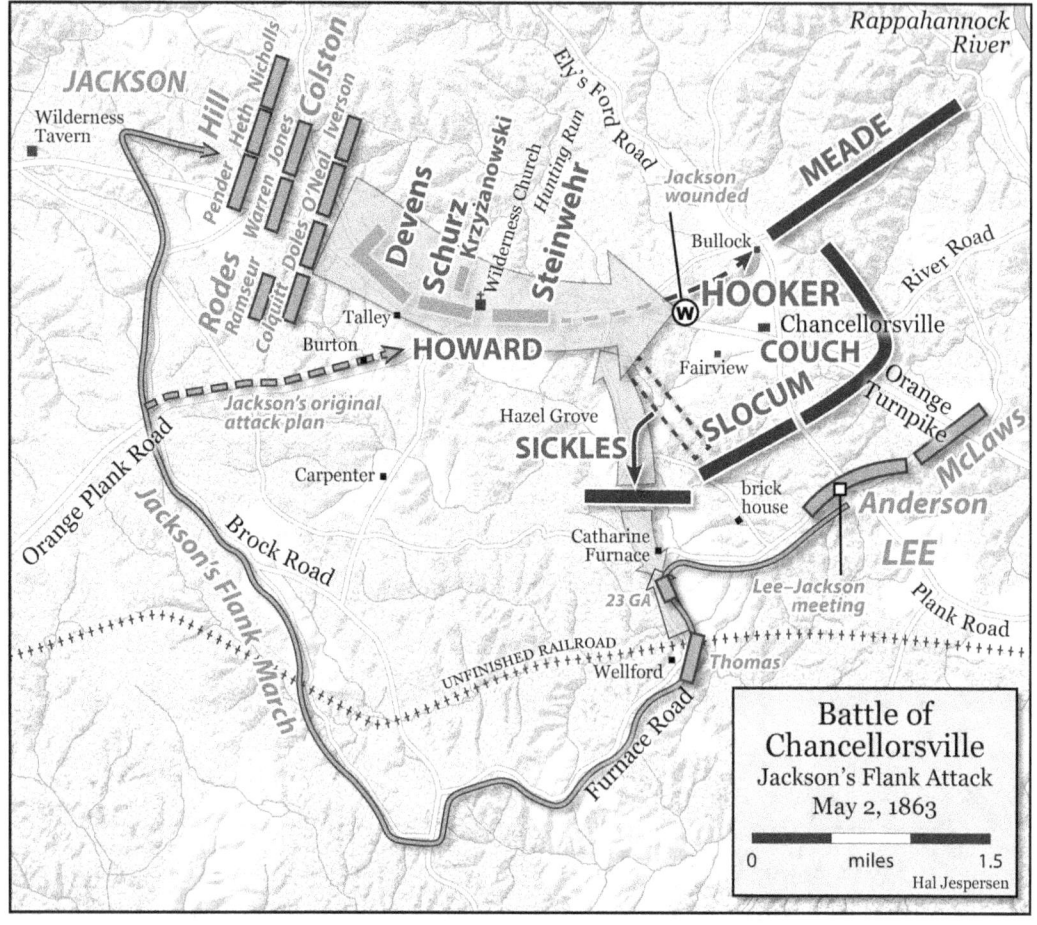

Thomas's Brigade, marching toward the end of Jackson's column, turned back to help the 23rd Georgia Infantry Regiment under attack at Catharine Furnace. It would take the brigade hours to catch up to Jackson's main column. (Map by Hal Jespersen)

Lee made arguably his greatest tactical risk of the war by splitting his forces yet again on May 2. Keeping only 13,000 troops with him at Chancellorsville, he sent Stonewall Jackson and his corps of roughly 30,000 troops along a narrow path on the Catharine Furnace road on a 12-mile march to flank Hooker from the west. As Hall wrote in his narrative, Generals Lee and Jackson were "wide awake enough for Hooker, and learnt his maneuvers before he could execute them." When Union troops saw a small portion of Jackson's men and artillery rolling to the southwest on the Catharine Furnace road, Hooker concluded that Lee was retreating. Jackson had the weather to thank in part for keeping the progress of his force unknown to the Union because the wooded paths that he used had been dampened by rain showers for several days previously, which meant his large column did not stir up a "betraying column of dust."⁴

Hill's division marched towards the end of Jackson's line, perhaps a reflection of the uneasy relationship the two men had at that point in the war. The men marched quietly to avoid detection by Union troops. Thomas's Brigade marched near the rear of the column to protect Jackson's wagons and over 100 cannons with limbers and caissons. In the late afternoon, when a small Union force from Hooker's center attacked the 23rd Georgia Infantry Regiment and threatened the artillery and wagon train at Catharine Furnace, the 14th Georgia – and eventually the remainder of Thomas's Brigade as well as Archer's Brigade – turned back to help the 23rd Georgia. As events unfolded, their assistance was not needed, so the two brigades hastened back to catch up to Jackson's main force.

Jackson's troops were strung out for almost ten miles on its flank march past Catharine Furnace. (National Park Service)

By this point, Jackson's lead element was hours ahead of Thomas's Brigade. As Thomas's Brigade labored to catch up, Jackson marched the main body of his troops east on the Orange Turnpike and maneuvered them into position for an attack on Maj. Gen. Oliver O. Howard's XI Corps, which had its arms stacked and was preparing its evening meal. Over the next two hours, Jackson battered the Union troops; as historian Edwin Bearss writes, the Confederate troops rolled up XI Corps "from west to east like a wet blanket."⁵ It was not until 8 o'clock that evening that the Confederate advance slowed to a halt due to darkness, heavy woods, and confusion in the ranks.

While Thomas's Brigade was moving to catch up on the afternoon of May 2, they were subjected to enemy artillery fire, and Hall was shocked and slightly wounded by

---

4. Krick, *Civil War Weather in Virginia*, 6.
5. Edwin C. Bearss, *Fields of Honor: Pivotal Battles of the Civil War* (National Geographic, 2006), 135.

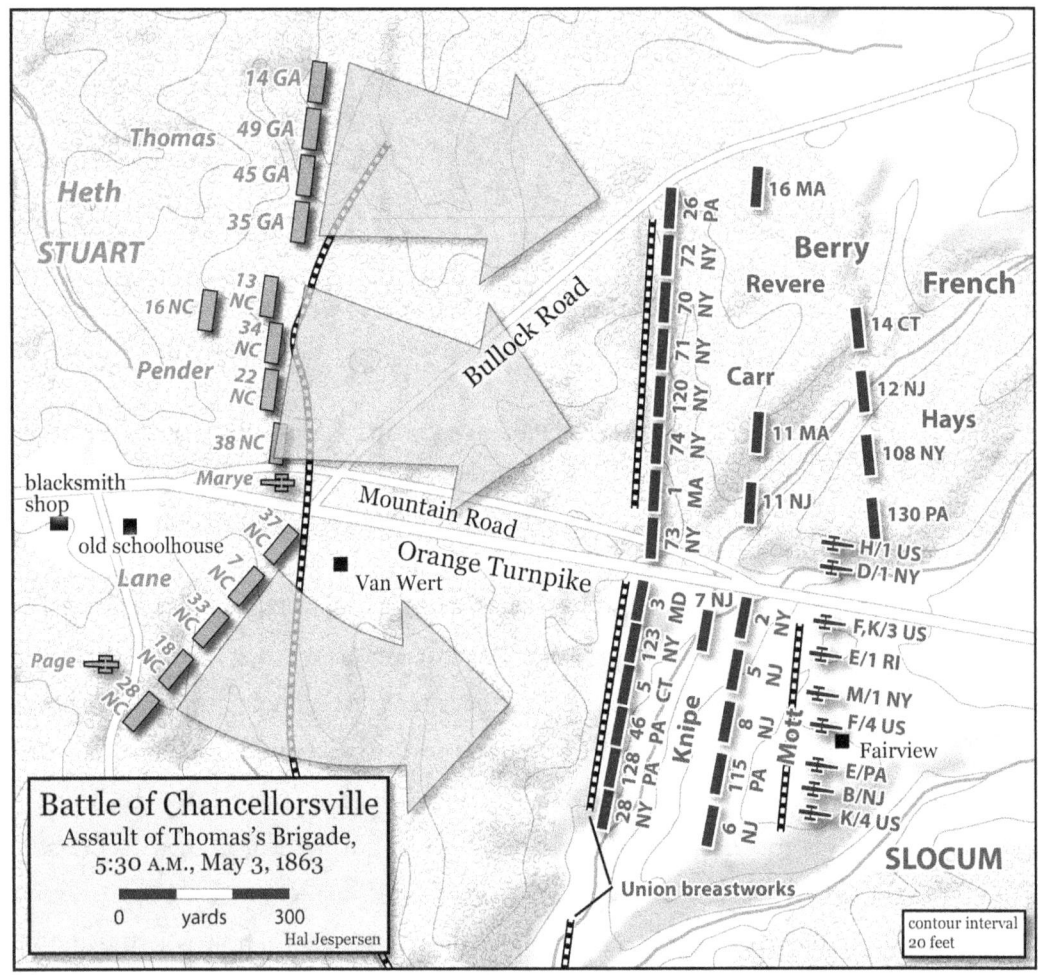

The 14th Georgia, situated on the far left of the Confederate line, suffered its worst combat casualties of the war at Chancellorsville. (Map by Hal Jespersen)

the explosion of a shell. By midnight, the brigade had caught up to Hill's division. They took position at the farthest north end of Hill's attack line opposite Maj. Gen. Daniel E. Sickles's III Corps.[6] The 14th Georgia was the most exposed at the left end of Thomas's regiments, at the top of a line of earthworks that ran north-south near the intersection of Bullock Road and the Orange Turnpike.

---

6. Hall has no daily entries in either the Pocket Notebook or Remembrancer for May 1 through 7. Thayer noted in the Remembrancer that those pages were already filled. However, in additional to a lengthy narrative in the Pocket Notebook, Hall also noted in his daily log (Appendix C) that he was in the line of battle on May 1, skirmishing and marching on May 2, in a "great Battle" on May 3, and skirmishing in line of battle on May 4.

The combat on May 3 at Chancellorsville, which produced over 17,000 casualties in just over five hours, may have been the bloodiest morning of the war.[7] At dawn, the Confederates unleashed a frontal infantry assault. As historian Earl Hess described the morning's battle, the thick vegetation prevented large formations from massing for attack, so the fighting "devolved into a series of violent charges by unsupported Rebel brigades with little artillery support."[8] The Union defenders had used the cover of darkness to erect crude breastworks overnight, which further impeded the Confederate assault. Hall wrote that the "roaring and terrific thunderings of battle" would make someone unaccustomed to combat believe that a "dozen thunder storms had met together to wage ten-fold destruction."

Thomas's Brigade, north of the Orange Turnpike with Bullock Road slanted across its front, charged through two lines of Union defenders behind breastworks, inflicting and suffering high casualties as they charged a third line.[9] The brigade initially faced units belonging to Brig. Gen. James B. Carr's and Brig. Gen. Joseph W. Revere's brigades in Maj. Gen. Hiram Berry's division, but once Berry himself fell, mortally wounded, Revere abandoned the battlefield, taking nine regiments with him back in the direction of U.S. Ford.[10]

Thomas's troops threatened to capture the remaining federal artillery at Fairview.[11] They got within 800 yards of Chancellor House but were countered by units of Col.

---

7. Murray and Hsieh, *A Savage War*, 263.
8. Hess, *Field Armies and Fortifications in the Civil War*, 182.
9. One article reported that Thomas's brigade "in their great ardor, forgot to fix bayonets, and carried their part of it at the point of the rifle." "Battles of the Rappahannock," *Southern Recorder*, June 16, 1863, https://gahistoricnewspapers.galileo.usg.edu. The regimental adjutant reported that "The Fourteenth Georgia performed their brilliant charge without having a single bayonet fixed." "The Sickles Brigade," *Philadelphia Inquirer*, June 9, 1863, www.newspapers.com.
10. Joseph Warren Revere, the grandson of Revolutionary War icon Paul Revere, was court-martialed for his actions in moving troops to the rear. Although charged with misbehavior to the enemy, he was found guilty of the lesser offense of conduct to the prejudice of good order and discipline by marching his brigade to a site about three miles from the scene of action. Revere was sentenced to dismissal, which Lincoln approved and ordered executed on August 10, 1863. General Order No. 282, War Department, August 11, 1863. Ultimately, Revere was permitted to resign in lieu of being dismissed. Steven W. Sears, *Chancellorsville* (Houghton Mifflin: 1996), 509.
11. Maj. Gen. James E. B. Stuart assumed command of Jackson's corps after Jackson was wounded. Stuart's "first line, numbering about 10,000 men, practically unsupported by artillery, had forced the Federal first line, manned by about 9,000 infantry, intrenched, and materially supported by artillery. The five regiments to which the assailants were now reduced seemed about to sweep away the last infantry protection on the right of the Federal artillery, and break in a surging mass on the flank and rear of the guns at Fairview, when their victorious progress was arrested by opposition from two directions." John Bigelow, Jr., *The Campaign of Chancellorsville* (Yale University Press, 1910), 353.

Samuel S. Carroll's and Col. Charles Albright's brigades.[12] As Brig. Gen. Henry Heth, temporarily in command of A. P. Hill's division after Hill was wounded, wrote:

> "Pender and Thomas, on the left, found the enemy posted behind a breastwork of logs and brush, immediately in their front, at a distance of about 150 yards. The breastworks were charged and carried, the men never hesitating for a moment, driving the enemy before them and pursuing him until a second line was reached, which was in like manner broken. A third line of the enemy was now encountered. After a desperate and prolonged fight, without supports or a piece of artillery to aid them, but on their part subjected to heavy artillery fire of from ten to twelve pieces, these gallant brigades fell back in order to the breastworks from which the enemy had been driven, and which they held until re-enforcements were brought up, when again the attack was renewed and the enemy driven from this part of the field of battle."[13]

Thomas, low on ammunition and vulnerable to counter-attack on his left, ordered his brigade back once he realized at the third line that he was subject to cross-fire, with no friendly troops in supporting distance to his right or rear. Corroborating Hall's claim that entire Union regiments and brigades were surrounded and taken prisoner, Revere's and Carr's brigades reported almost 200 missing after battle, including almost sixty troops from the 72nd New York Infantry Regiment alone.[14]

Over the course of the morning, Hooker, who had suffered a concussion when a shell hit the pillar he was leaning against at the Chancellor House, pulled his troops back from Chancellorsville. Lee had wagered and won, but at a high cost, with his greatest loss being the death of Stonewall Jackson, who died on May 10, 1863, after being shot by friendly fire during a night reconnaissance ride on May 2. Thomas's Brigade incurred 192 casualties at Chancellorsville, with seventy-five of those from the 14th Georgia, which suffered the most of the four regiments, with eight dead and 67 wounded.[15] One of those killed was the 14th Georgia's Lt. Col. James M. Fielder, who had been

---

12. Sears, *Chancellorsville*, 326.
13. *OR*, Ser. 1, vol. 25, pt. I, p. 891.
14. Sears, *Chancellorsville*, 481.
15. Sears, *Chancellorsville*, 496. The casualty rate for the 14th Georgia was approximately 40 percent and would have likely been much higher if Revere had not withdrawn nine Union regiments from the line of battle. Hall's regiment had over twice as many casualties as any of the other regiments in the brigade, which is not surprising given its position on the far left of the line.

promoted only four months earlier after William Harris resigned his commission due to poor health. Fielder fell several yards from the Union breastworks and died of infection a few days after having his leg amputated. Hall called him "kind and beloved."

Hall intensely grieved the death of his company commander, Capt. Terrell Mounger, who was wounded in his bowels at Chancellorsville on May 3 and died in a field hospital nine days later. As Thomas C. Moore noted in Folsom's *Heroes and Martyrs of Georgia*, Mounger was "a general favorite in the regiment, and his company was devotedly attached to him. . . . He died as he had lived, universally beloved by officers and men. A little mound upon the battle field of Chancellorsville is all that marks his resting place, but his comrades will ever cherish his memory."[16] Following Mounger's death, First Lieutenant Robert H. Fulton, who had begun the war as a private, was elected captain on May 12, 1863. Both Mounger and Fielder received recognition, on the Confederate Roll of Honor, for their valor.[17]

Company G soldiers wounded at Chancellorsville included William Land (shot severely through the knee), Robert B. Massey (shot in the arm/shoulder), and Henry C. Quiett (slightly wounded in the breast/side). Hall noted that he had been slightly wounded by a shell on May 2, although a casualty list submitted by the regimental adjutant to the press erroneously stated that Hall's finger had been shot off.[18]

In the aftermath of the battle, Confederate troops took advantage of supplies that the Union troops had abandoned, including blankets, food, and frying pans. Hall wrote that he feasted sumptuously on discarded beef, coffee, sugar, and crackers and slept that night under his "yankee tent and oil-cloth." The brigade remained on the battlefield

---

16. Folsom, *Heroes and Martyrs of Georgia*, 152. Captain Mounger's father, Lt. Col. John C. Mounger, 9th Georgia Infantry, located his son's grave and wrote his wife that he had put a small fence around it, erected a headboard, and prayed as he drew the dirt over the grave. Sears, *Chancellorsville*, 445.
17. The Confederate Roll of Honor was intended to recognize those officers, non-commissioned officers, and privates who "best displayed their courage and devotion on the field of battle." *OR*, Ser. 1, vol. 25, pt. I, p. 1051-1053.
18. "List of Casualties in the 14th Regiment Georgia Volunteers, Col. R. W. Folsom Commanding, in the Battle of the Wilderness, May 3, 1863," *Confederate Union*, June 9, 1863. https://gahistoricnewspapers.galileo.usg.edu. Although Hall mentioned being paralyzed in the hand and arm by an incoming artillery shell, he made no references in the diary or his pension application to having had a finger shot off; moreover, post-war photographs show all fingers present and accounted for. The adjutant may have confused Hall with Private Edward J. Wiley, who was admitted to Chimborazo No. 5 Hospital, Richmond, on May 4, for amputation of a finger.

until May 6, when it marched through mud back to camp south of Fredericksburg. The following weeks in camp were seemingly restorative for Hill's men after the ferocity of Chancellorsville. The 14th Georgia received a new battle flag, which prompted Col. Folsom to send the old "bullet-scared (sic) and shell-riven flag" as a gift to Georgia Governor Joseph Brown.[19] The brigade was on the march again in early June. Less than two months after Lee's zenith at Chancellorsville came his nadir at Gettysburg.

Pocket Notebook Narrative
March 13 – June 5, 1863

The 13 day of March I concluded I would go to my regiment and accordingly I got my discharge from the hospital and got on board the cars at Staunton and went from there to Hanover Junction and taken another train the same day and arrive[d] at Guin[e]as Station on the Richmond, Fredericksburg & Potomac R R the same evening about 8 oclock. I lay all night in the cars and suffered verry much from the cold. On the morning of the 14th I started a foot verry soon and arrived at the camp of our company about 9 miles from Guin[e]as Station and about the same distance from the City of Fredericksburg, and about 3 miles from the Rappahannock. I found the army in good health and spirits and was verry glad to see the boys in the company one more time. But I found a good many of them missing never to be seen more in this world of war and Blood shed. But I hope they have gone to a <u>better place</u> prepared for them by the Lamb that was slain and I hope died for them.

---

19. "Interesting Correspondence," *Confederate Union*, September 1, 1863, https://gahistoricnewspapers.galileo.usg.edu. An image of the regimental battle flag, current through Chancellorsville, is available at https://vault.georgiaarchives.org/digital/collection/flag/id/92/

I will now record, (as far as I know) what the movements of our regiment was during my absence after they left the place I left them at (which they did soon after). They crossed the Shenandoah river above Front Royal and crossed the Blue Ridge and proceeded by Orange C.H. [Court House] and from thence to the vicinity of Fredericksburg about the first of December, and there remained till the great Battle which took place the 13 & 14 December. In that engagement our regiment did a gallant part, and a many of its Heroic and noble members fell to rise no more till the Second coming of the Lord to Judge that world.

There was one hundred & twelve killed and wounded in our regiment out of three or four hundred carried in to the battle. The following was killed in our company Thomas O. Calhoun, corperal Lott W Hill and James O Kerce. The following was wounded Sergeant James Hobby, Norman G. Gillis, George W Spring, Eli Vicory [Vickery], Napoleon B. Tabor, corporal J. L. Sumner, Joseph L. Spring, George W Morainey [McRaney], Green Windget [Wingate] & L. B. Posey. Some of the above was so Bad that they will never be fit for Service any more. That Battle proved more disastrous to the Yankees than any before during the war, but it cost us the life of a many heroick and brave man.

From there our regiment marched to where they were camped when I found them and put up winter quarters and we did not have verry much duty to do. We had to stand picket once in every two weeks and stand regiment guard and work on the roads for they were so bad man or beast can scarcely traveled over them, and on the whole we fared better than might be expected in this bleak cold regions. There come a great many Snow-storms this winter. The snow lay on the ground nearly all the time, and March was about the worst winter month we had this winter, and the weather of

April was nearly as bad as March was in 1862. We remained in winter quarters till near the close of April when on the 28th our old camp was considered unhealthy. We moved out about 3 [miles] farther from the river and was puting us up verry comfortable quarters and on the 29th we received orders to march against them where they were crossing the Rappahannock below Fredericksburg and consequently we marched off double quick about 12 or 15 miles and taken our position. There was some shelling and Skirmishing, the 29th and 30th [December] during which time we remained in line of battle waiting for an attack from the enemy. But they did not cross the river below Fredericksburg with the intention of attacking us, but to draw our attention from their movements higher up the river.

But Gen-s Lee and Jackson was wide enough awake for Hooker, and learnt his maneuvers before he could execute them. And on the 1st of May before good day light we were marching at quick time up the river on the plank road in the direction of Orange Court House. On the night of the 1st we lay in line of battle in the worst swamp and thicket I ever saw in Virginia, and the pickets was skirmishing and throwing their leaded hail among us all night and the night was uncommonly chilly and cold and I was chilled to the bone. We were not permitted to take our blankets off to protect us from the cold for we know not what moment we would have to leave there and not have time to do them up. It was a night of deep anxiety to us, for at the dawn of day we were looking for the Battle to commence in earnest.

Next morning we sent out skirmishers which kept up a brisk fire till about 10 oclock, when we were relieved and marched off to take another position and we then performed a movement which discomfited the enemies plans considerable. Jacksons corps marc[h]ed round and attacked the enemy in the rear of his breast works, and a sharp Battle was fought on the evening of the 2nd which lasted till near 12 oclock at night. Our Brigade was in the rear protecting the artillery and waggon train, and we did not get into the Battle that evening, but we were under fire of the enemys artillery for a considerable time and I was shocked and slightly wounded by the explosion of a bomb-shell and I was unable to proceed any further that night or for two or three days after wards.

The moon shone bright that night and roaring of small arms and the booming of cannon and bursting of shell was grand and terrific. The shrieks and groans of the wounded and dying as I lay nearly insenceable [insensible] around me that night, displayed all the horrors of war and put feelings and imaginations through the mind that I never wish to experience again. There scattered over the fields and emence [immense] forest the Battle field encompassed lay thousands of poor wounded and dying soldiers far away from home and friends, writhing in the agonies of death with no one to speak a soothing word to their ears. They are perhaps thinking of their mothers and wives children and friends far away. Oh the horrors and agonies of war no one can tell, only those that have experienced it but I have one <u>friend</u> that is with me always and was with me <u>that night</u> to comfort and support me in the hours of tryal and distress and that friend is the living Lamb who has passed through the portals of death before me and I hope when my time comes to follow him without a murmer.

On the morning of the 3rd by the dawn of the first light of day the Battle was renewed with redoubled fury and the constant roar of Artillery drowned every other sound. The day was fair and warm but the roaring and terific thunderings of battle would have made one thought unacustom to Battle, that a dozen thunder storms had met together to wage ten-fold destruction where ever they went. The enemy was behind three strong lines of breast-works protected by the most thick and dense forest I ever saw, and they cut down the trees and brush and front of Their breast-works so that it was almost impassible but our brave men made charge after charge through the brush and fallen timber where the enemy thought our destructtion would be sure if we attempted to charge them, but soon found that no breastwork could turn a southern soldier who was fighting for homes and firesides. Onward our brave men went over them and the dastardly Yankees begun to fly for life and the ground was nearly covered with their killed and wounded, and whole regiments and Brigades give up and were taken prisoners.

The Battle raged with unabated fury when it began to subside and finaly died away in the vicinity where we was, but lower down the river we could hear it still raging between us and Fredericksburg, where it continued till night. We were sole possesors of the Battle Field and had the enemy hard pressed to the river where they were terror stricken and crossing to the opposite side as fast as possible. Thousands of them having left Their arms and accoutrements behind in our possessions, while the battle field was litterally covered with knapsacks, haver sacks, Blankets, oil cloths, frying pans over-coats and clothing of various kinds. Us tired and hungry soldiers feasted ourselves sumptiously on the Yankees well filled haver-sacks of crackers, beef coffee and sugar in Them.

There was some skirmishing and cannonading that evening and the next day, but the great fighting ceased on the 3rd, the enemies loss was terrable about 5 to our one but we lost many a brave and gallant man. Our devoted and well beloved Captain T. E. Mo[u]nger was mortally wounded and died a few days afterwards. His death was deeply mourned by not only our company but the whole regiment for all who knew him esteemed and respected him highly for no one could help liking his generous behaviour and noble conduct. This company in him suffered an irrepairable loss for this place can never be filled with one like him again. But I hope he has gone to a better place where war and blood-shed are no more and where peace and happiness dwells forevermore, and also our kind and beloved Lieutenant Colonel James M Fielder had his leg amputated and died a few days afterwards. His loss was deeply deplored by the whole regiment for we loved and respected him almost as a father. [H]e was tollerable well advanced in age. He was about 60 years old.[20] He was generous and kind to every one, and he done every thing that was in his power for the welfare and happiness of his men. He is a great loss to us and to his country. But I hope he is in a happier regions beyond the stars were there is no more war sorrow nor sighing, Sickness, pain nor death, by eternal happiness reigns, in the Presences of the once Slain, but now exalted Lamb for ever more.

The Following was wounded in our company, William Land Shot through the leg, Robert B. Massey shot in the shoulder, Henry C. Quiet slightly in the breast, and myself (George W Hall) Paralised in the hand and arm by a shell.

We remained on the Battle field near Chancellorsville, where we fought till May 6th when in a hard rain and muddy road. We commenced the march down the river towards Fredericksburg. I did not know the extent of the battle field

---

20. Fielder was actually only 46 years old at the time of his death. Robert K. Krick, *Lee's Colonels: A Biographical Register of the Field Officers of the Army of Northern Virginia*, 5th ed. (Broadfoot Publishing, 2009), 137.

till this evening, when I learned it stretched up and down the river from Fred[ericksburg] 15 miles in length and every where we could see the dead and mangled bodies of the enemy and some of them drifting along the hollows and in the gullies but the water that had collected in considerable quantities from the late rains. We marched till near dark and camped for the night wet and chilled to the bone. I stretch[ed] my yankee tent and oil-cloth and tried to get a little sleep, but not much fell to my lot that night, for the rain was so cold that evening and night that I remained cold and chilly all night. Next morning I felt verry sore and bad. We marched out 5 or 6 miles from Fred[ericksburg] on the rail road and we were glad of one more opportunity of resting our tired and weary limbs from the fatigues of the Terrable fighting and marching we just pass[ed] through. We only remained in them camps two or three days, and went to our camps we left the 29th of April and we remained there in peace and quiet and until June 5.

The trees had just put forth a beautiful foilage and the forest around our camp was beautiful indeed and we would meet every evening in a pleasant grove and have prayer meeting or preaching, praising the God that was so good to give us times to rest and have such beautiful groves to camp in. I was happier when I met around our rude seats to hear the beloved chaplains of our Brigade tha[n] I ever was before during this terrible and wicked war. The name of this camp and that where we were camped in the winter was Gregg. Both camps bore the same name and they both alike never will be e[r]aced from my memory as long as I live as happy days as my life affords I experienced there. It was there I fully resolved to turn from the wicked world Sin and Satan and take up my cross and follow the meek and lowly Jesus, and it has now been over four months since then and the true happiness and peace I have had since is worth more than all this wicked world to me, and that was indeed a hallowed spot of ground to me never to be forgotten as long as life endures.

Remembrancer Daily Entries
March 13 - June 4, 1863

Friday, March 13, 1863

Partially clo[udy] & cold. This morning I started to my regiment verry soon and took the cars at Staunton and arrived at Guineas Station at 8 oclock P. M.

Saturday, March 14, 1863

M cold & clo[udy]. E thu[nder] & hail. There come the largest hail here today that I ever Sa[w]. It covered the [ground] and did not melt for several hours.

Monday, March 16, 1863

M Snow. E fair & cold. Nothing new, only cannons can be heard towards Fredericksburg. I expect as soon as the weather will admit we will have another Battle here. I Sent a letter home.

Tuesday, March 17, 1863

Fair windy & cold. Nothing new only we could hear cannons in the direction of Fredericksburg.

Wednesday, March 18, 1863

Cloudy cold & windy. Lieutenant R. H. Fulton return from home on furlough today. On regimental G[u]ard.

Thursday, March 19, 1863

M cloudy & cold. E Snow. Today we hear of the Battle at Kellys-ford on the Rappahannock not far from Culpeper Court House. General Stuart after a severe engagement which lasted several hours defeated the Federals with severe loss and pursued them to the North bank of the Rappahannock.

Friday, March 20, 1863

Snowing all day. There is heavy snowing today. It began yesterday Evening and is continuing today.

Saturday, March 21, 1863

It continued Snowing till twelve oclock today and then turned some warmer and in the evening rainy. I was sick today with the diarhea and had a considerable fever with it.

Sunday, March 22, 1863

M cloudy & cool. E fair. To day I feel verry bad. My bowels hurts me very much and my headaches severely. The Lords will be done not mine but my prayer is to him that I may be fully restored health one more time if it is his Holy will.

Monday, March 23, 1863

Cloudy cold & windy. On Regimental Guard.

Tuesday, March 24, 1863

M cloudy. E windy & rain. Today I am verry sick. Have a high fever and the worst diarhea I ever had in my life.

Wednesday, March 25, 1863

M rainy. E par clo & windy. To day I feel some little better but I am verry weak and can scarcely walk.

Thursday, March 26, 1863

M rain & snow. E cloudy cool. I am considerable better of the diarhea, but I have a severe cough and hurting in in my breast. No News stiring.

Friday March 27, 1863

Fair frosty & cold. Fast day and humiliation and prayer for peace and happiness to be restored to our country.
Had a verry good sermon by our Chaplin and prayer for our country.

Saturday, March 28, 1863

Rainy & cold. Nothing new.

Sunday, March 29, 1863

Cloudy cold & windy. Every Thing is quiet. No news of any fighting an[y] where, but a dead calm foretells a storm. I expect we will hear of it from every quarter but I hope the Lord will be with us to the end.

Monday, March 30, 1863

Fair cold & windy.

Tuesday, March 31, 1863

Heavy snowing & sleet. No news.

Wednesday, April 1, 1863

Fair & cold severe wind. March came in like a lion and continued all through like a lion and went out like a lion, and was in the whole the worst weather I ever saw and April has come in not much better. We was on general inspection.

Thursday, April 2, 1863

Nothing of importance.

Friday, April 3, 1863

Fair & windy. The weather has turned some warmer and looks some what like spring, although the trees and foliage looks like the dead of winter.

Saturday, April 4, 1863

M cold & windy. E Snowstorm. Today is the coldest and most disagreeable weather I ever saw for the season. On Regimental guard.

Sunday, April 5, 1863

M snow storm. E cold, cloudy & windy. A snow storm begun yesterday evening and continued all night and today till 12 oclock. The snow has drifted very deep in some places. What a great contrast between here and my native home.

Pocket Notebook
Religious Reflection of
Easter Sunday, April 5, 1863[21]

This is the second Easter I have passed away from home, since I have seen any of my relations. Nearly two long years of war and bloodshed has come and gone, and still I am far away from home and friend but my best <u>friend</u> is with me no matter what land I am in he is always nigh, ready to help me at any moment, when I am in trouble and distress. He has already carried me safe through many danger toils and snairs and will carry me safe through as many more as it may be my lot to encounter, if only but prove faithful to his Sacred <u>word</u>.[22]

He has been merciful to me beyond measure, when my wicked heart turn from him as often as I am years old, and still he followed me with His precious mercies and did not cast me away. That great friend is the Lord and Savior Jesus Christ that died on the cross, that a poor worm like me might live. The precious Son of God died on calvary for me [but] still my wicked heart rebelled against his holy name. But I hope I may have faith as strong as a lion and patience to suffer any thing for His cause in the future, and I hope I may never turn one step from the narrow way that leads to his throne above and to life everlasting.

Monday, April 6, 1863

Cold & cloudy. No news. We had a Snow ball battle which was quite diverting and amused us verry much. Any thing to break the monoty [monotony] of the camp always please us exceedingly.

---

21. In a separate section of his Pocket Notebook, Hall recorded a series of religious reflections, mostly on Sundays, between early April and late May 1863.
22. This is likely a reference to the third stanza of John Newton's hymn *Amazing Grace*: "Through many dangers, toils, and snares, I have already come."

Tuesday, April 7, 1863

M fair & frosty. E cool cloudy & windy. Every thing quiet.

Wednesday, April 8, 1863

Cold & cloudy. Our regiment was on picket today on the Rappahannock and we had a verry cold time. Our pickets and the Federal pickets is only the bredth of the river apart and talk to each other on friendly terms, a great contrast between now and last year this time for then we shot at each other every night.

Thursday, April 9, 1863

M fair & frosty. E fair and cool. I have a verry severe cough on the account of taking cold last night on picket.

Friday, April 10, 1863

M fair & frosty. E fair & cool. Every thing still and quiet inthis vicinity. We hear of the news of the Yankees attack on Charleston.[23] Our guns sunk two of their iron clads while the loss on our side was only 3 or 4 men and one gun dismounted. On regimental guard.

Saturday, April 11, 1863

Fair & pleasant. Windy. It is verry fine weather to day and looks like spring will soon open. I have a severe cough.

Sunday, April 12, 1863

M fair & pleasant. E cloudy and a little rain. Had preaching by our chaplain.

Pocket Notebook
Religious Reflection of
Sunday, April, 12, 1863

A HOME OF REST

Far away in a sunbright clime, where sorrow, pain and death can never entered is rest for weary mortals. Blessed

---

23. The battle of Charleston Harbor, a Confederate victory, was fought on April 7, 1863. The Union Navy lost only one ironclad, USS *Keokuk*.

thought to earth's suffering children, Christian reader, when tossed to and fro, from us and weary alike of lifes cares and pleasures, how consoling the words of the blessed Savior "Let not your heart be troubled. In my Fathers house i[s] many mansions; I go to prepare a place for you, and will come again and receive you to my self, that where I am there ye may be also," Jesus knew that often verry often, we would be troubled tried and almost cast down, so he left <u>many</u> such precious promises to comfort [and] Sustain us; but best of all is the promise of eternal happiness and rest - - rest from all the vexations and cares of life. This thought cheers the dying saint. With an eye of faith he sees far beyond Jordan, the promised home, the heaven of rest, peace and joy; and his willing soul would fly away to be "forever with the Lord." Yet this mansion of rest is not for any and all - - only those who have believed in the blessed Savior and followed him through evil as well as good report, who like Paul, as the time of their departure draws near, can exclaim, "I have fought the good fight, I have finished my course, I have kept the faith; henceforth their is laid up for me a crown of righteousness, which the Lord the righteous Judge Shall give me at that day."

To any who love not the Lord Jesus, I would say, "Strive to enter in at the strait gate, for strait is the gate and narrow the way, that leads to that bright home, where the wicked cease from troubling and the weary are at rest."[24]

Camp Gregg Va
Geo. W. Hall

---

24. The "strait" gate appears to be a reference to Matthew 7:13. The last part of this sentence appears to be a reference to Job 3:17-19.

Pocket Notebook
Religious Reflection of
April 12, 1863

To day our chaplain delivered a good sermon, and we had verry good weather for the Services of God, and we all ought to be thankful for one more opportunity to meet in His name, thankful of the opportunity to hear one more sermon. In a few days at most, we will have to leave here perhaps to meet the enemy in another fierce struggle, and many of us may fall and be launched into eternity never to hear a sermon more or have an opportunity to ask God to forgive our many sins, and "alas many I fear will fall without the hope of ever seeing the Lord. It is a day long to be remembered by me, the Lord has been merciful to me, and has by the help of his holy Spirit turn[ed] me away from sin, I hope forever. To day I joined the Missionary Baptist Church and "Oh may the Lord Jesus be with me in hours of tryal and temptation and enable me to persevere in His holy name, and cause me never to falter nor turn away from his sacred word for any of the vanities of this world."]"[25]

Their was two more of our regiment [who] joined their names to the church today and "Oh may the Lord sent his holy spirit upon them and cause them never to turn back from the holy cause they have sought today, and forever may they persevere and His Holy name and when their pilgrimage is ended here may I meet them in that happy home above, where sin and sorrow is no more and chilling wing nor poisonous breath Is felt and feared no more.

---

25. This appears to be reference to Luke 13:24 and/or Matthew 7:14.

"Oh Lord may my faith be strengthen[ed] till nothing can turn it, be with me in the vally of the shadow of death cause me ever to remain ready to lay down my unworthy life here for thy Sacred cause, a thousand times if necessary. Cause me to keep the narrow way that leads to the Celestial City.

Monday, April 13, 1863

Cloudy & cool. Every thing quiet. Skirmish drill.

Pocket Notebook
Religious Reflection of
Monday, April 13, 1863

"Oh glorious day Oh happy hour, that turned my soul from Sin. April 12, 1863 will never be forgotten by me. Far away from my native state, this day is to be numbered with the happiest of my mortal life. In the Evening of this day, about five oclock might have been seen a scene a Solumn and impressive, on the Rappahannock river 5 or 6 miles below Fredericksburg that scene taken place. "Oh may it be deeply impressed on my heart so that I may never forget the least thing happened the last day of my life here below. A groupe might have been seen emerging from the different regiments in our brigade over the hills to a small pool of crystal water, where the cerimony of Baptism was to be performed, on two that I hope Henceforth and forever will be Christian soldiers as well as Soldiers in defense of their country. I am one of them Soldiers and Sergeant Johnston of Company (I) in my regement the other.[26]

---

26. This is most likely a reference to 1st Sergeant William A. Johnson of Company I. Like Hall, Johnson was captured at Spotsylvania on May 12, 1864, sent to Fort Delaware, and exchanged at Richmond in March, 1865.

"Oh may we prove faithful to our sacred trust, and our faith become so strong that nothing can turn it from the blessed course we have begun. And may the Lord Jesus be with us in times of temptation, and tryal, and may we persevere in the blessed work we have begun, and I hope and pray we may become instruments in the Lord['s] hands to spread his blessed word to every creature within our reach and proclaim on the house top what he has done for us and invite others to follow after. There is a many a Missionary Baptist belonging to this Brigade and the Lords work is persevering rapidly. "Grant Oh Lord that it may continue with an unceasing hand, and when that great day comes, when the Lord Jesus comes to taking his servants may we mount above the skies Shouting Glory forever more.

Tuesday, April 14, 1863

M fair & frosty. E partially cloudy & cool. Sent letter home to mother. Skirmish drill.

Wednesday, April 15, 1863

Cold wind & rain. No news stiring. Skirmish drill.

Thursday, April 16, 1863

M cloudy & cool. Nothing of importance. Skirmish drill.

Friday, April 17, 1863

Cloudy & cool. No news. Every thing quiet. Skirmish drill.

Saturday, April 18, 1863

Thayer note: [no room left on page as completely filled with writing of Union soldier]

Sunday, April 19, 1863

Fair & pleasant. We had a verry beautiful day and two good sermon by our Chaplain and the regiment went out in the evening to witness the ordinance of Baptism on a brother that joined the church today.

Pocket Notebook
Religious Reflection
of Sunday, April 19, 1863

The past week, has been the happiest week I have experienced during my existence in the vale of sorrow pain and wickedness here below. It has been a week of peace and contentment that I never felt before. Although a cruel and wicked war raged all around me, it has been a week of peace, peace of mind and happy contentment that I did not know was for poorer mor[t]als before. That peace and joy created by the Love of the Lamb that was slain. A peace and happiness not felt by any that serve Satan and grieve the Lord that sent his only beloved son to die for us all but still they slight him. This day above all, has been one of peace and happiness resting on his blessed word. It has been a beautiful and pleasant day beyond comparison with any that has been before this year. Fair and beautiful the blessed Savior seems to shine on us in holiness from above.

We had two Sermons from our chaplain Rev. Mr. Moore assisted by that able and true hearted brother, Mr. Barrret who labors day and night for the good of others. Two more in our regiment turned their backs to the world and joined the church of God, one the Missionary Baptist and the other the Methodist. The brother that joined the Baptist was Baptised this evening, by Rev. Barret at the same place that witnessed the ordinance of Baptism and on two happy individuals last Sabbath evening. The dear Lord has answered my prayer in many instances during the past week. I prayed that we might be permitted to remain here one more Sabbath and that it might be good weather and more might be added to the list that has set out for that that eternal home in the skies, and many others and he has answered them all. Oh may power dominion and glory be to his name forever. Amen.

Monday, April 20, 1863

Rainy & cool. Nothing new.

Tuesday, April 21, 1863

Cool & cloudy. Every thing quiet in this vicinity.

Wednesday, April 22, 1863

Cool & cloudy. And we go on picket on the Rappahannock and have wild onions for dinner and supper which sat verry well for vegetables of any kind would eat good to us now.

Thursday, April 23, 1863

Cold & rainy. We return off picket verry wet and cold for the weather was verry bad last night and this morning. Every thing quiet.

Friday, April 24, 1863

Cold rain & wind. No news stirring but it is the worst weather I ever saw for the time of year.

Saturday, April 25, 1863

Fair, cool & windy. On Regimental guard.

Sunday, April 26, 1863

Fair cool & windy. Had a good sermon by our chaplain.

Pocket Notebook
Religious Reflection of
Sunday, 26 April, 1863

One more week has flown, on the wings of Time, one more Sabbath has come and we were permited to assemble on the same hallowed spot, where we have met several sabbaths in succession for the worship and praise of God. The spot has become a sacred spot to me and a link in the chane [chain] of life. I never shall forget at this spot I hope my name was ordained in heaven to remain in letters of gold forever and Oh may I never dishonor that name but brighten it forever more. The Lord Jesus has been merciful to me beyond measure and does not forsake me in the hour of distress, but his precious promise is fulfilled, "as thy days so shall thy strength be," and oh may my future life as fruitful of peace and happiness and the last two weeks has been.[27]

Monday, April 27, 1863

Fair & pleasant. Nothing new.

Tuesday, April 28, 1863

Cloudy & some rain. Today we remove to a new encampment more convenient to wood &c.

Wednesday, April 29, 1863

M cloudy. E rain. To day just as we had commenced to fix us comfortable quarters we heard that the enemy was crossing the river and before we could prepare us any rations we were ordered to march and we double quicked about 15 miles verry soon. Rec'd letter from home.

Thursday, April 30, 1863

M rainy. E par fair. To day we remained in line of battle near Fredericksburg and some cannonading was carried on during the day. We prepare to change our position.

May 1, 2, 3, 4, 5, 6, 7, 1863

(Thayer note: "no entries, pages already filled")

Friday, May 8, 1863

Cloudy & cool. On Guard. Nothing new.

Saturday, May 9, 1863

Fair & pleasant.

---

27. This is likely a reference to Deuteronomy 33:25.

Sunday, May 10, 1863

Fair & pleasant. It is beautiful weather now and the trees has all put forth their leaves in splendor.

May 11, 12, 13, 1863

(no entries)

Pocket Notebook
Religious Reflection of
May 13th 1863

Once more I am permitted to write a few lines, by the help of the Lord I have passed through another series of Battles and at this time alive and well. God has been merciful to me and has answered my smallest prayer. Oh what sweet contentment those who have put their trust in the Lord and what advantage they have over the man of the world. Amid the roar and dread confusion of battle, they <u>stand calm</u> and collected knowing the God of Battles is with them and if they fall in the contest He will take them to His-self where wars famine and pestilence are felt and feared no more. Where no more sorrowing Sighing nor parting, but peace and happiness rest and enjoyment forever more. Oh may I never do any thing to turn me from that Bright home far away above the starry skies on that etherial region of light.

Thursday, May 14, 1863

M fair & warm. E cool & refreshing showers. Nothing uncommon.

Friday, May 15, 1863

Fair & pleasant. Skirmish drill. Had religious services in the evening by Rev Bro Hyman, chaplain of the 49[th regiment] and a member of co[mpany] B joined the church.

Saturday, May 16, 1863

(no entry)

Sunday, May 17, 1863

Fair & pleasant. I attended preaching in the 35th by Bro Hyman.

Pocket Notebook
Religious Reflection of
Sunday, May 17, 1863

One more sabbath of rest is granted us. I attended preaching in the 35[th regiment], and heard a good sermon by Rev Bro Hyman chaplain of the 49[th regiment] The Lord has blessed us with good weather for <u>His</u> services and his holy spirit is manifested among us and I hope he will continue to be with us to the end of this cruel war and cause it soon to come to a close before much longer. I hope he will have mercy upon us and cause peace to reign over this unhappy country and that I may be permited to return home to my parted friends and relations to speak the praises of God abroad and proclaim his name on the housetops and show the merciful and kind he has been to me in watching over and protecting me during this horrid and devastating war.

Monday, May 18, 1863

M fair & pleasant. E partialy cloudy. Nothing new. On regiment guard

Tuesday, May 19, 1863

Fair & pleasant. Every thing quiet.

Wednesday, May 20, 1863

Fair and pleasant. Our regiment goes on picket near our same old stand.

Thursday, May 21, 1863

Fair & warm. Return off picket have a mess of fish for dinner.

Friday, May 22, 1863

Fair & warm. Had prayer meeting in our regt.

Saturday, May 23, 1863

Fair & warm. Prayer meeting again. It has become verry interesting to many.

Sunday, May 24, 1863

Fair & warm. I attended preaching in the 49[th regiment] last night Sermon by rev Captain Harris.[28] Today I heard another sermon by him and we had prayer meeting in our regt in the evening.

Pocket Notebook
Religious Reflection of
Sunday, May 24, 1863

O now my dear breathren I bid you farewell
I'm going to travel to preach the gospel
I'm going to travel the wilderness through
Therefore my dear breathren I bid you adieu

May heaven protect you be Jesus your guide
On the walls of mount Zion may we still abide
Though we live at a distance you I never see
On the banks of cold Jordan acquainted we'll be

---

28. Thomas M. Harris served as regimental quartermaster for the 49th Georgia.

There all things are plenty like Eden in bloom
To those blissful mansions no sorrow can come
No sin nor temptation can enter that place
And there we shall join in a song of free grace

Adieu to affliction to trial and pain
I'm going to Jesus forever to reign
I'm going to Jesus – 'tis him I adore
With Saints and bright angels to dwell evermore

Live near to the Savior be fervent in Prayer
And while I am absent remember me there
That Jesus his gospel would crown with success
And my poor exertions to numbers would bless

And when we meet Jesus in mansions above
Where saints and bright angels are filled with his love
O then may I see these dear mourners appear
How glad we shall be to meet each other there[29]

Hark! the Jubilee is sounding
O! the joyful news is come
Free salvation is proclaimed
In and through Gods only son
Now we have an invitation
To the meek and lowly Lamb
Glory honor and salvation
Christ the Lord has come to reign

Come poor sinners cease from sinning
Seek the Lord without delay

---

29. This appears to be a version of the hymn, "A Minister's Farewell."

Christ the Savior is begining
Sin and guilt to wash away.
Golden moments we've neglected
Oh the times we've spent in vain
But the Savior long expected
Now appears on earth to reign

Happy children praise your Jesus
Love and praise him evermore
Free salvation should constrain us
To rejoice and to adore
Sound his praises round the nation
He is our exalted king
Glory honor and salvation
Let the saints forever sing[30]

The above beautiful hyms remind me of the home far away, for they were learnt to me by my dear old mother when I was quite small, and here in the confusion of war and bloodshed I had almost forgotten them. And I commit them to memory in writing. They remind me of child-hoods days past and gone never to return when I was near my dear Mother and other friends and knew not the wickedness of the world, nor how many of its afflictions and hardships I would have to pass through.

On the outset they seem unindurable and I was hard pressed down, by the troubles I had to encounter, almost unable to proceed not knowing which way to proceed, but now I have found relief. <u>My trust is in God and to him alone I look for aid and comfort. And to him I do not look in vain.</u> This

---

30. This appears to be a version of the hymn, "The Gospel Invitation."

world is full of sorrow and afflictions, pain and anguish, and why should we wish to live and remain here always were nothing but persecutions trials and Temptations surround those that love God. Why should we wish to stay here away from that happy home *and blest abode, a place of eternal rest high above the starry skies. Oh how I long to soar away and be at rest in the presence of the Lord where there is no more sorrow no more sighing no more wars famine and pestilence, but peace and happiness forever more. When Gods Children turns away from him he sends afflictions on them and takes away their joys of this world to make them look more to him and put their trust in him instead of things [in] this world. Oh dear Father when I turn away from thee in the least chastise greatly till [I] return to thy dear protection. Oh that my faith and love may become stronger and then I may be fully prepared for that glorious home above, and my Father calls me to his bosom. O! May I be ready, and willing waiting an anxious to Go.*

May 25, 26 1863

(no entries)

Wednesday, May 27, 1863

Cloudy & warm. No news. Prayer meeting.

Thursday, May 28, 1863

Fair & pleasant. Had a good sermon by Rev Capt Harris Q.M. of the 49th [regiment] this Evening at candle light. His text was 2 Chap 44 verse of Dan. No news.

Friday, May 29, 1863

Fair & warm dusty. Today was General review of our division on the river 5 miles from camp. Gens Lee Longstreet, A. P. Hill & Heath[31] was present. Another sermon by Capt Harris, in the evening.

---

31. This is a reference to General Henry Heth.

Pocket Notebook Entry for May 29, 1863

Second Anniversary of the organization of
Co (G) 14th reg Ga vols

The Second anniversary of my enlistment and the organization of our company May 29th 1863 is here upon us. The wings of time has brought around two long years upon us and still I am far away from home and friends and have never had the privilege of seeing my dear friends and connections since I left. I have been away from my dear old native home so long that I have almost forgotten how it looked and various are the scenes. Troubles and Tryals I have been through since that Time and "afflictions though they seem severe are oft in mercy sent, they stop the prodigals carreer and cause him to repent."[32] Though we are afflicted some times so that it seems we cannot bear them but they often bring good to us. They turn us from the vanities of this wicked world, and send our thoughts to more higher and noble things in that happy world above and to the Lord and God of all whom we should look to for every breath we breathe and every hour we live. Oh! Thanks and praise forevermore to the Lord and Savior Jesus Christ, for He has been merciful to me who sined against his holy will, all my days and he spared my unprofitable life and did not snatch me away in my sin and folly, for he would have been just in doing so, but he permitted me to live on in my sins till at last I awoke, and found my self on the brink of a frightful

---

32. This appears to be a version of "Afflictions, Though They Seem Severe" by John Newton.

precipice and at one step, only one step would land my soul in the everlasting death. But glory and praise to him forever I was brought to see the danger, and flee from the wrath to come before it was everlasting to late, and my future life be devoted to the glory and honor of his kingdom and the spreading of his blessed word forever and ever.

Saturday, May 30, 1863

Partialy cloudy & warm. Rev Mr Hyman chaplain of the 49th preached for us this evening. The spirit of the Lord seem to be manifested every where among us.

Sunday, May 31, 1863

Flying clouds & cool breezes. To day I attended church out in the country. The name of the church is Liberty about 3 miles from our camp. It reminded me deeply of happier days far away.

Pocket Notebook
Religious Reflection of
Sunday, May 31, 1863

One more Sabbath has come and still I [am] permitted to hear the word of God preached on the Holy day of the Lord. One today I heard a sermon at a church in the country and the scenes around brought deeply to my recollection Scenes of the past when I was far away at my dear old native home. I love to bring such scenes to remembrance happy days of childhood when I knew not the evils of the world that was in the future. Then our country was happy and every where was peace and prosperity. The Horro[r]s of war was unknown to me. I never once drempt what I would have to pass through. How I would tare my self away from home and friends and every thing I care for on earth, and be exiled away from them now nearly two long years, and the terable scenes I would have to pass through during that time.

But it is not ended nor may not be half through. I cannot tell when they will end nor no one but the Lord and he fore-sees all things and knows this minute what future has in store for me. Oh Gracious Lord cause this bloody strife to end and may I be permitted to read those lines I am writing now, when I am at home and peace is reigning o'er our beloved Land one more time and Grant Oh God that I may be an humble instrument in thy hands, to Spread thy glory to every creature within my reach and speak thy name on the house tops and lay down my unworthy life for thy cause if necessary and glory and praise be ascribed to thy dear name forever. Amen.

Monday, June 1, 1863

Fair & warm. We had a good sermon this evening by captain Harris and the Lord was with us and his holy Spirit seem[ed] to be upon us. Two more of our regt joined the church and are to be baptized tomorrow.

Tuesday, June 2, 1863

Fair and warm. Cool and gentle breezes. Prayer Meeting this evening the Lord is with us and I hope this blessed opportunity will last a long while and converts may be added to the list that has left the ways of the wicked till not one is left in our regt.

Wednesday, June 3, 1863

(no entry)

Thursday, June 4, 1863

Fair & pleasant. We go on picket. A Yankee Swam the river to us and went back, and two of our regt Swam over to them and returned with a late New York Herald.

8

"IT SEEMED THAT IT WAS IMPOSSIBLE FOR A LIVING CREATURE TO HAVE ESCAPED" GETTYSBURG: JUNE 5 – JULY 24, 1863

Bereft over the loss of his trusted "right hand" Stonewall Jackson, Lee reorganized the Army of Northern Virginia into three corps in the weeks following the battle of Chancellorsville. Longstreet remained in command of First Corps, Richard S. Ewell was promoted to lieutenant general and given command of Second Corps., and A. P. Hill was promoted to lieutenant general and given command of the new Third Corps. With Hill's promotion, the bulk of his division passed to Maj. Gen. William Dorsey Pender. Pender's Division included Thomas's Brigade, as well as the brigades of James Lane (consisting of North Carolina regiments), Alfred Scales (consisting of North Carolina regiments), and Abner Perrin (consisting of South Carolina regiments).

Coming off the bold victory at Chancellorsville with an army whose morale was at an all-time high, Lee decided the time was ripe to invade the North again. Ewell and Longstreet headed north on June 3, 1863, while Hill remained near Fredericksburg to mask the departure of the other two corps. Thomas's Brigade received orders to move out on short notice on the night of June 5. They marched north thirteen miles to Hamilton's Crossing, where they remained in line of battle for over a week.[1] Hall expected a Union attack, but Hill had simply moved the brigade in an effort to deceive the Union troops in Fredericksburg while Lee moved his other two corps north towards Pennsylvania.

---

1. Hill moved out on June 5 so quickly that the chaplains in Thomas's Brigade had to hastily finish an immersion baptism ceremony for forty-eight soldiers. Fox, *Red Clay to Richmond*, 174.

The monument at Gettysburg to Thomas's Brigade, erected in 1910, is located on West Confederate Avenue on Seminary Ridge. It states: "July 1. In reserve north of Chambersburg Pike on left of the Division. At sunset moved to position in McMillan's Woods. July 2. On duty in support of artillery. At 10 P.M. advancing took position in Long Lane with left flank in touch with McGowan's Brigade and the right near the Bliss House and Barn. July 3. Engaged most of the day in severe skirmishing and exposed to a heavy fire of artillery. After dark retired to this Ridge. July 4. At night withdrew and began the march to Hagerstown." The sign fails to note that a sizeable number of soldiers in the brigade were engaged on July 2 in very heavy skirmishing near the Bliss farm and with the 8th Ohio near Long Lane. (Photo by Mary Hall)

After Hooker deduced that Lee's army was on the march, there was no longer any need for Hill to remain near Fredericksburg. Third Corps marched west on June 16. As the men of Thomas's Brigade marched through Chancellorsville, they were assaulted by the smell of dead horses and half-buried, decaying bodies. The summer heat and humidity were so unbearable on June 17 and 18 that Hall reported that hundreds of men fainted and several died on the road; indeed, he stated that he "came verry near giving up" himself on the night of June 19th.

The 14th Georgia crossed the Potomac into Maryland on June 25 and then marched past Sharpsburg, seeing the battlefield there for the first time. The regiment camped near Hagerstown on June 25 but was sent back four miles on June 26 to protect artillery and the wagon train. That forced the men of the 14th Georgia to double-march on June 27 to catch up with the rest of the division crossing over into Pennsylvania. Once the division reached Cashtown, Pennsylvania, some eight miles from Gettysburg, the men were given time to recover after marching over 150 miles in twelve days.[2]

---

2. Robertson, *General A. P. Hill*, 204.

As of the end of June 1863, the Army of the Potomac had just over 93,000 men and a new commander after George Meade replaced Joseph Hooker on June 28, 1863. The Army of Northern Virginia had just over 76,000 men. The bulk of these armies were about to descend on the small college town of Gettysburg, which was surrounded by ridges and into which flowed, like wagon spokes, some ten roads, including those to and from Chambersburg, Fairfield, Emmitsburg, Baltimore, Carlisle, and Harrisburg.

Thomas's Brigade was over 1300 men strong on July 1, 1863, while the 14th Georgia's strength was between 324 and 351.[3] The morning of July 1, 1863, found the brigade marching east on the Chambersburg Pike towards the town of Gettysburg. They were posted at the rear of Pender's Division. Ahead of Pender was Heth's Division, which engaged Union troops near Herr's Tavern west of Gettysburg. As they neared Gettysburg, Thomas's and Lane's brigades were ordered to the north side of Chambersburg Pike, although Lane's Brigade did not remain there for long. As Pender's other brigades advanced east in support of Heth in the Herbst Woods on McPherson Ridge, Thomas's Brigade remained in reserve to support Pegram's artillery battalion in the open field on the north of Chambersburg Pike and west of Herr's Ridge Road.[4] Gottfried, who feels this was an example of Hill's mismanagement of troops during the battle, notes that this was "a strange use of a strong brigade, given the fact that the Federal troops in this sector were making no suggestion of taking offensive action."[5]

Thomas's Brigade remained west of Herr's Ridge Road until sunset, while Heth's and Pender's men drove Union troops off McPherson Ridge. Although never called upon for offensive action on July 1, Thomas's Brigade was subjected to incoming artillery.

Late on July 1, Thomas's Brigade rejoined Pender, assuming a position on Seminary Ridge, again in support of Pegram's artillery. On the morning of July 2, Pender's Division served as the northernmost division on Seminary Ridge, with Thomas's

---

3. Folsom, *Heroes and Martyrs of Georgia*, 115; Bradley M. Gottfried, *Brigades of Gettysburg: The Union and Confederate Brigades at the Battle of Gettysburg* (Skyhorse, 2012), 656. John and Travis Busey maintain that the 14th Georgia had 31 officers and 293 men. John W. Busey and Travis W. Busey, *Confederate Casualties at Gettysburg: A Comprehensive Record* (McFarland & Co. 2016), 365. The number 351 was obtained from The Interpretive Display on Unit Information at the Visitor's Center, Gettysburg National Military Park, viewed on August 21, 2018, and June 14, 2025. According to the same Interpretive Display, Thomas's Brigade had a strength of 1326, which is only one man off Busey's calculation of 1325.
4. The division assistant adjutant wrote afterwards that Hill retained Thomas's Brigade in that location "to meet a threatened advance from the left." *OR*, Ser. 1, vol. 27, pt. II, p. 656.
5. Bradley M. Gottfried, *Brigades of Gettysburg*, 657.

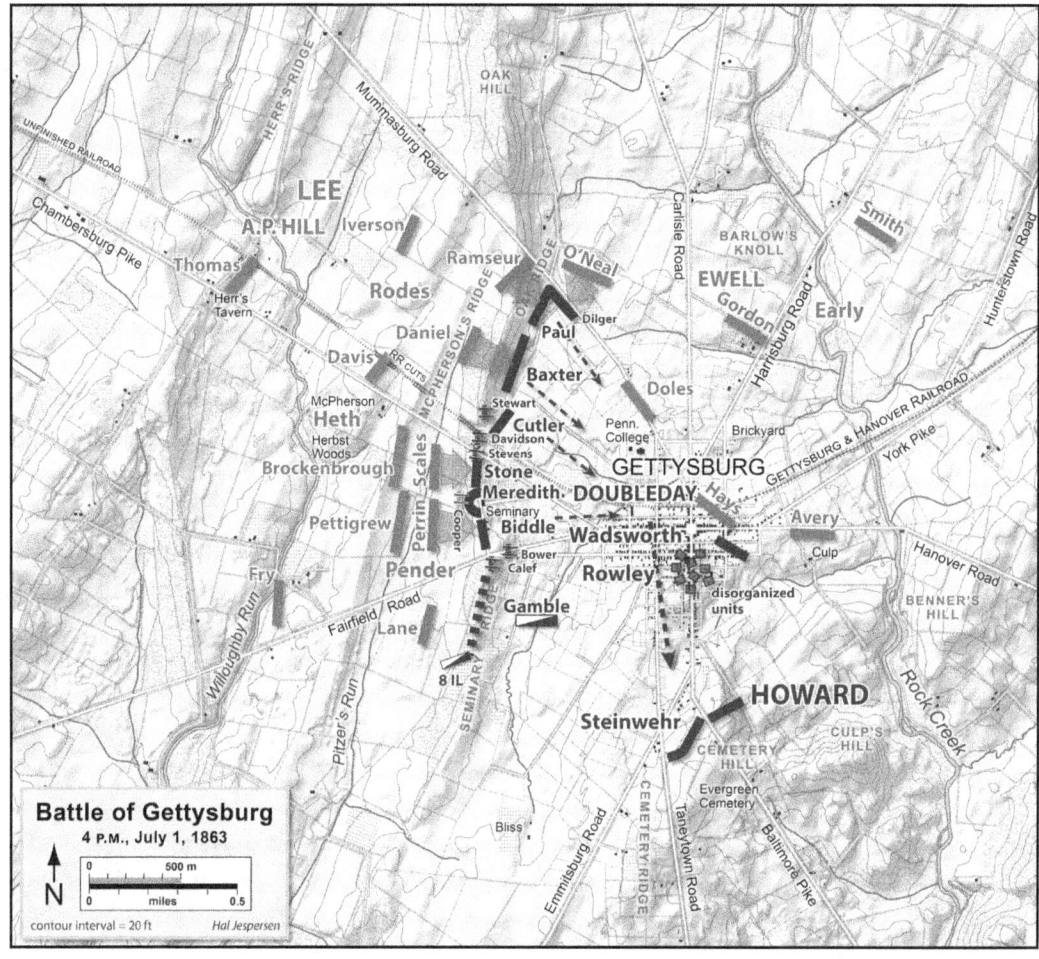

Thomas's Brigade remained on the north side of Chambersburg Pike during most of July 1, 1863. (Map by Hal Jespersen)

Brigade occupying the far left flank of Hill's Corps. In addition to being on the receiving end of brutal artillery fire, Thomas's Brigade played a significant role in the skirmishing over control of the Bliss farm on July 2. The 60-acre farm, which consisted of a barn, a farmhouse, and an orchard, lay almost equidistant between Confederate forces on Seminary Ridge and Union forces on Cemetery Ridge, "situated dead center in the no man's land between the opposing forces."[6] As Gettysburg historian Elwood "Woody" Christ writes, "The soldiers who could hold the house, barn, and orchard had an excellent

---

6. Elwood Christ, *"Over a Wide, Hot … Crimson Plain": The Struggle for the Bliss Farm at Gettysburg, July 2nd and 3rd, 1863* (Savas Beatie, 2022), 41, 86, 103.

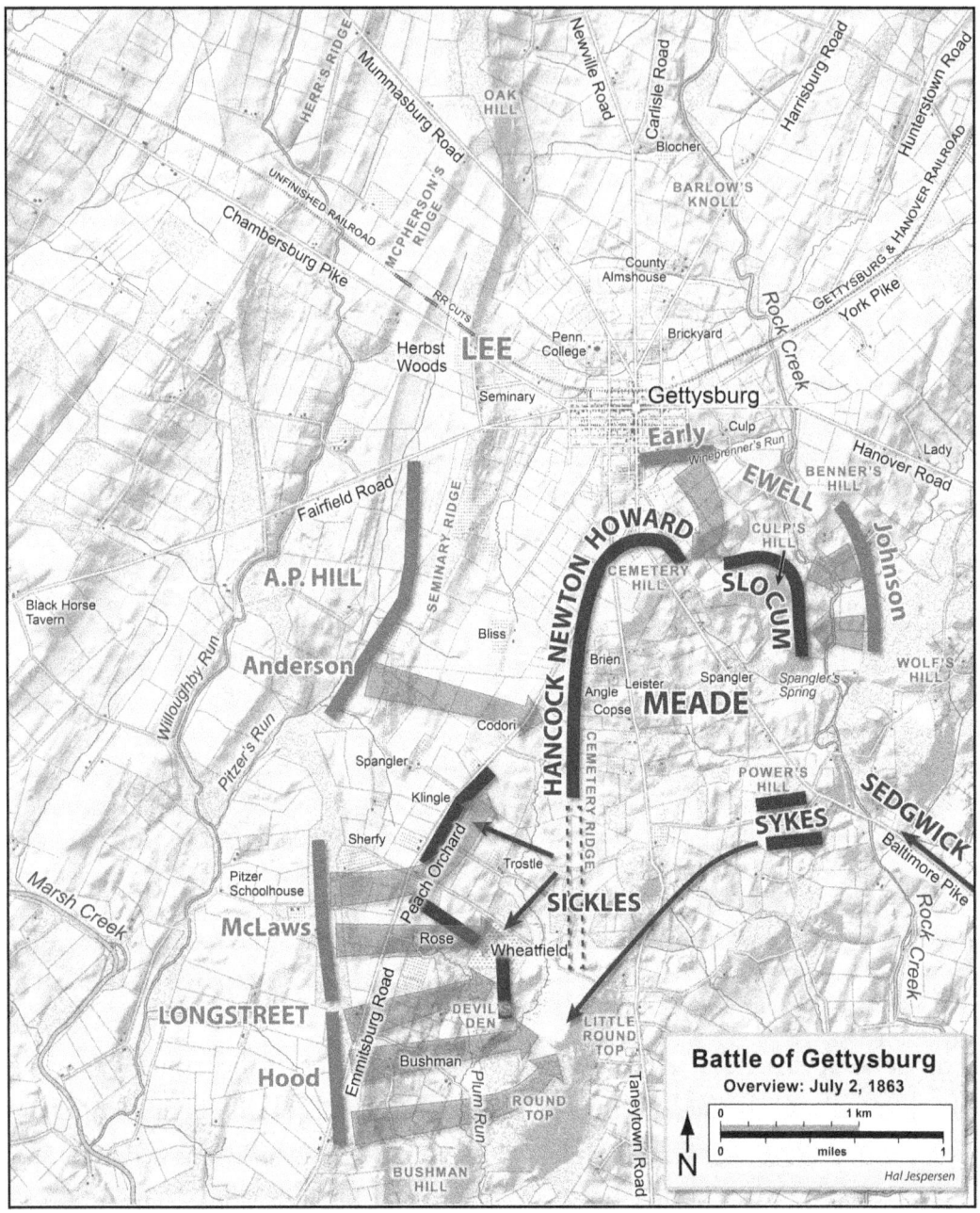

Shortly after dawn on July 2, 1863, Thomas sent troops out as skirmishers near the Bliss Farm in the no man's land between Seminary Ridge and Union troops on Cemetery Ridge. (Map by Hal Jespersen)

view of the opponent's main position and fortifications, could monitor their opponents activities more accurately, and any sharpshooters stationed there could rain havoc on

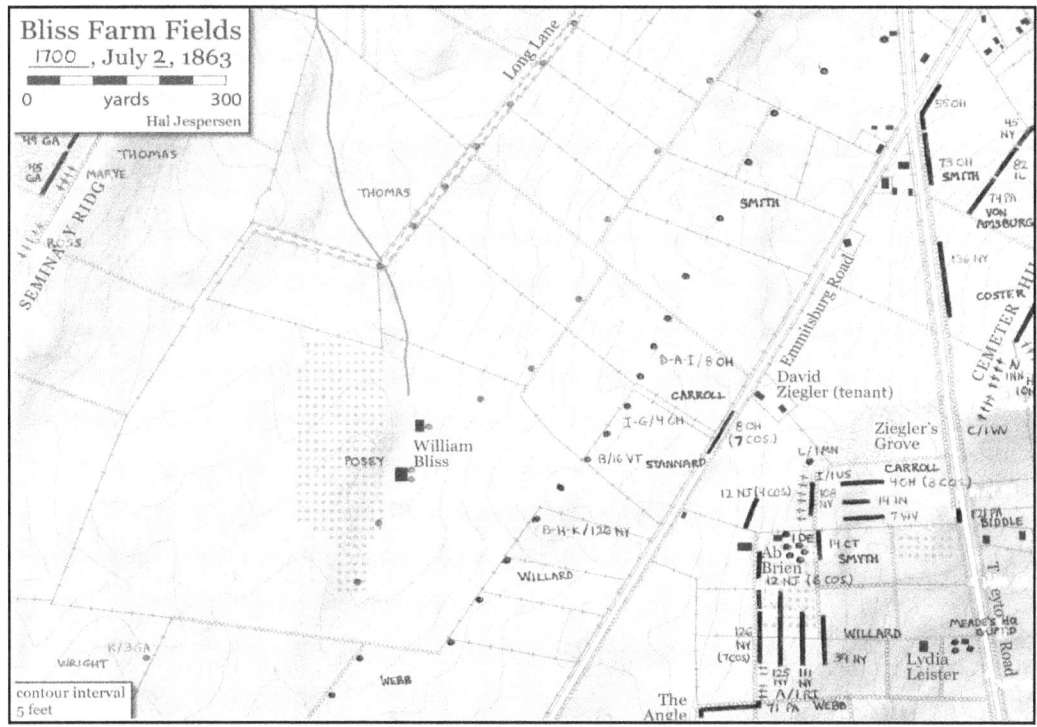

William Bliss's farm rested almost equidistant between the North Carolina Memorial on Seminary Ridge and the Copse of Trees on Cemetery Ridge. Thomas L. Elmore, a longstanding contributor to the popular online forum Civil War Talk, commissioned Hal Jesperson to prepare a map of the Bliss Farm Fields as the basis for a series of maps that Elmore annotated showing the fighting at the farm at various times between July 2 and July 4. On this map, Elmore notes that Thomas's Brigade had elements still on Seminary Ridge but also on Long Lane, then a farm road that ran due south from town to the edge of the Bliss orchard. Elmore's map also shows the position of the 8th Ohio Infantry Regiment, which at that point on July 2 straddled Emmitsburg Road before moving in its entirety west of the road and sending skirmishers closer to Long Lane. The small circles denote the likely location of skirmishers. (Map by Hal Jespersen; annotations by Thomas L. Elmore)

the enemy's troops all in relative safety."[7] The barn was the heart of the fighting at Bliss

---

7. Christ, "*Over a Wide, Hot... Crimson Plain*", 6. Christ's account of the fighting at Bliss Farm "remains the most reliable source of information about this small piece of a very large battle." Carol Reardon and Tom Vossler, *A Field Guide to Gettysburg*, 2nd ed. (University of North Carolina Press, 2017), 366.

Farm, in part because it provided an ideal location for Confederate sharpshooters to fire on Union artillery on Cemetery Ridge. Over the span of thirty hours, possession of the farm would change sides some ten times.

Some 2,160 Union soldiers fought on July 2 and July 3 to capture (and eventually destroy) the barn at Bliss Farm; over 2,300 Confederates – including an estimated 442 soldiers from Thomas's Brigade – fought to defend it.[8] Leaving several companies in each regiment behind to support the artillery on Seminary Ridge, Thomas ordered his early morning skirmishers to form a line near Long Lane, with the 49th Georgia situated the closest to the Bliss orchard. As Hall wrote, the 14th Georgia provided between three companies and half the regiment on the skirmish line, rotating troops throughout the day. One officer in charge of the 45th Georgia's skirmishers on July 2 said that the "skirmishing was the *heaviest*" he had ever heard of, "being almost equal to a pitch battle all the time."[9] It was on this skirmish line that Thomas's Brigade incurred most of its casualties.[10] Although the fighting at Bliss Farm paled in scale in comparison to Lee's main charge on the afternoon of July 3, estimated casualties still totaled over 800 men – enough men to fill approximately two regiments at that point in the war – with Union losses at 17% and Confederate loses at 20%.[11]

After William Dorsey Pender was wounded by artillery shrapnel at sunset on July 2, James Lane assumed command of the division. In the early evening of July 2, Maj. Gen. Robert Rodes, who was to join Maj. Gen. Jubal Early for an assault on Cemetery Hill, requested Lane to protect his right flank. Lane sent Thomas's and Perrin's brigades to Rodes's right. However, the attack was aborted, and by late in the evening on July 2, Thomas's Brigade, between Lane's and Perrin's brigades, rested "a short distance from

---

8. Christ, *"Over a Wide, Hot ... Crimson Plain"*, 81, 103. The primary Confederate unit committed to recapturing (and holding) Bliss Farm was the 1,300-man brigade of Brig. Gen. Carnot Posey, who remained so fixated on the farm that he failed to send sufficient men forward to protect the left flank of Brig. Gen. Ambrose Wright's brigade in the latter's *en echelon* attack on Cemetery Ridge in the late afternoon of July 2. Without Posey's support, roughly half of Wright's Brigade were killed, wounded, or captured. Bradley M. Gottfried, *The Maps of Gettysburg* (Savas Beatie, 2007), 210. Elwood Christ suggests that if Bliss Farm had not existed at all, then the Confederates "would have focused their attention on sustaining the en echelon attack on 2 July, and may have ... temporarily captured Cemetery Hill, if not force a Union retreat." Christ, *"Over a White Hot ... Crimson Plain"*, 87.
9. T. Conn Bryan, ed., "Letters of Two Confederate Officers: William Thomas Conn and Charles Augustus Conn," *The Georgia Historical Quarterly*, vol. 46 (1962), 189.
10. Gottfried, *Brigades of Gettysburg*, 657.
11. Christ, *"Over a Wide, Hot ... Crimson Plain"*, 108.

an orchard, near a brick dwelling and barn."[12]

What has become commonly known as "Pickett's Charge" (but should more accurately be referred to as Picket-Pettigrew-Trimble's charge) on Day 3 at Gettysburg – July 3, 1863 – is one of the best-known events in U.S. military history. Although Thomas's Brigade was relatively fresh and ideally situated to participate in the charge, they were not selected to provide the north end of the attack line. Instead, that mission fell to John Brockenbrough's brigade under James Pettigrew, who had assumed command of Heth's Division after Heth was wounded on July 1. Brockenbrough's brigade was under-strength and suffering from "poor morale and worse leadership;" in fact, on July 1, that brigade had "stopped in their tracks at the first enemy fire . . . and it was to be the case again on July 3."[13] As Bradley Gottfried writes, "The careless decision to align a small and inherently suspect brigade on the column's left flank" would prove to be "a costly mistake."[14]

Two Pender brigades were selected for the assault, but these – Lane's and William Lowrance's (formerly Scales's) brigades – were also questionable choices for July 3, given the casualties they had incurred fighting on Seminary Ridge two days earlier. Historian James Robertson suggests that Lee seemed to have simply selected those brigades because of their position in Pender's line.[15] Moreover, Lane's and Lowrance's brigades were placed under a new commander, Isaac Trimble, and positioned behind, rather than to the immediate left of Pettigrew's four brigades.[16]

As one of the two brigades in Pender's division not committed to the main assault, Thomas's Brigade spent July 3 engaged in heavy skirmishing in the morning and undergoing an oppressive artillery bombardment in the early afternoon. This included more skirmishing at nearby Bliss Farm, which changed hands repeatedly until it was finally set afire by Union soldiers in the morning of July 3. But Thomas's Brigade also renewed its skirmishing that morning with the 8th Ohio, which had crossed Emmitsburg Road on

---

12. *OR*, Ser. 1, vol. 27, pt. II, p. 666.
13. Sears, *Gettysburg*, 418.
14. Gottfried, *Maps of Gettysburg*, 254.
15. Robertson, *General A. P. Hill*, 220. Lowrance's (Scales's) Brigade had suffered a 63% casualty rate on July 1, including fifty-five of its officers. Stephen W. Sears, *Gettysburg* (Boston: Houghton Mifflin, 2003), 386-887.
16. As one commentator summarizes the command structure, "Trimble, belly-fire aggressive, eager to get into this fight before it began, not having commanded a unit in battle for ten months, now, mere hours before the attack, takes over two brigades who don't know him and whom he doesn't know." Stackpole Books, ed., *Gettysburg: The Story of the Battle With Maps* (Stackpole Books, 2013), 102.

the late afternoon of July 2 and had established a skirmish line on the west side of the road. At this location they occupied a broad, flat knoll at a higher elevation than Bliss Farm; in fact, it was the highest ground between Emmittsburg Road and Seminary Ridge.[17] After the entire 8th Ohio joined that skirmish line, they fired "volley after volley into the pesky Confederate troops from Thomas's Brigade."[18] According to Lane, the skirmishing in front of Thomas's position in the morning required at times "whole regiments to be deployed to resist the enemy and drive them back."[19] Thomas reported in his official report on the battle that his brigade had lost "many valuable men and officers in heavy skirmishing with the enemy."[20] Paying a heavy price for its aggressive skirmishing, the 8th Ohio had only some 160 men remaining by noon on July 3; its losses by that point were 4 killed and 41 wounded, including a captain, a lieutenant, and the regimental sergeant major.[21]

Confederates waiting for the end of the artillery duel at Gettysburg on the afternoon of July 3. (*Battles and Leaders of the Civil War*, Yoseloff ed., 1956)

---

17. Earl J. Hess, *Pickett's Charge – The Last Attack at Gettysburg* (University of North Carolina Press, 2001), 110.
18 Gottfried, *Brigades of Gettysburg*, 165. As John Fox notes, many of the 35th's casualties were attributable to men being captured as a result of the skirmishing on July 2 and July 3. Fox, *Red Clay to Richmond*, 187. A sampling of Lillian Henderson's regimental records suggests that over half of the men in Thomas's Brigade who were captured or went missing did so on July 2, but this varies by regiment: more men were captured or went missing on July 2 in the 14th Georgia and 49th Georgia and on July 3 in the 35th Georgia and the 45th Georgia.
19. *OR*, Ser. 1, vol. 27, pt. II, p. 666.
20. *OR*, Ser. 1, vol. 27, pt. II, p. 669.
21. *OR*, Ser. 1, vol. 27, pt. I, p. 462.

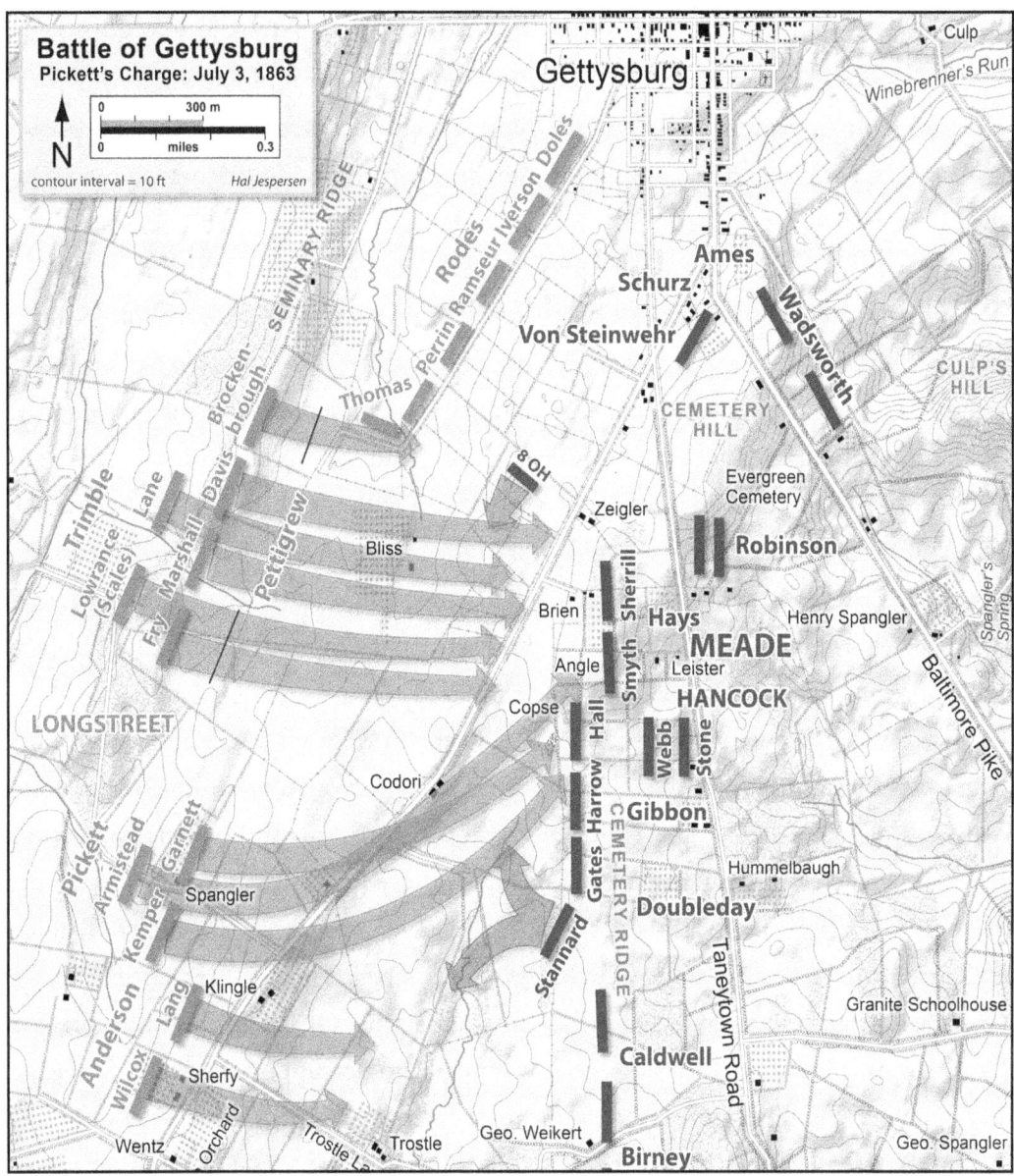

Thomas's Brigade on Long Lane was the brigade closest to the 8th Ohio after that regiment moved across Emmittsburg Road. It was also the closest Confederate brigade to the left flank of the Pickett-Pettigrew-Trimble charge on the afternoon of July 3. (Map by Hal Jespersen)

The prelude to the Confederate infantry charge on July 3 was the clash of over three hundred cannons, a duel opened by the Confederates in the early afternoon. Hall wrote of having to lay down during the artillery duel, with no shade to protect him; as he lamented, "no pen nor human words can describe the terrable and awful scenes we passed through yesterday and today." Although Hall thought the Confederate artillery had "done good execution" on July 3, the reality is that much of it flew over the Union infantry lines and landed in the Union rear. Moreover, some of the Confederate artillerymen had squandered ammunition in an effort to rid Union infantrymen from the barn on Bliss Farm.[22]

After the ferocious artillery barrage, the Pickett-Pettigrew-Trimble charge got underway in the mid-afternoon, with 13,000 men on a line almost a mile long. Things quickly collapsed at the left end of the line. Brockenbrough's Brigade in Pettigrew's (Heth's) division stepped off late and quickly gave way under Union artillery fire and an oblique line of musket fire by the 8th Ohio Infantry and skirmishers from the 125th and 126th New York; indeed, Earl Hess suggests that two of Brockenbrough's regiments may have advanced no further than Long Lane.[23] In comparison, the men in Joseph Davis's brigade may have moved out too quickly and out of alignment. They soon became so demoralized by both artillery canister and musket fire from the front and their flank to the point that many men turned back to Seminary Ridge.[24]

As Trimble brought up Lane's and Lowrance's brigades, awkwardly positioned behind Pettigrew, they collided with Davis's and Brockenbrough's retreating troops. Half of Lane's men executed a right oblique to maintain contact with Lowrance's men, but the remainder created a gap in the line when they moved to fill the area Davis's men had vacated. Lowrance's Brigade were so few that a lieutenant in the 38th North Carolina Infantry noted that they "were reduced to a mere skirmish line."[25] Lowrance, who was wounded in the charge, lamented in his after-battle report that Lane's and his brigades "were the only line to be seen upon that vast field, and no support in view. The natural inquiry was, What shall we do? And none to answer."[26] Many of the men of Lowrance's Brigade retreated without even waiting for orders. As Ed Bearss wrote about the charge on

---

22. Carmichael, *Lee's Young Artillerist*, 103.
23. Hess, *Pickett's Charge*, 188.
24. Sears, *Gettysburg*, 432.
25. Sears, *Gettysburg*, 434.
26. Sears, *Gettysburg*, 434.

July 3, the attack was over in far less time than in the 1993 movie *Gettysburg*.[27]

The battle of Gettysburg has left historians with more topics and questions for debate and speculation than likely any other battle in American history. Two such questions pertain to Thomas's Brigade, although neither can be answered with any great degree of certainty. The first is why the brigade, whose troops were relatively fresh and who had performed so aggressively at Chancellorsville, was not committed to shore up Lee's disarrayed left. As Bradley Gottfried argues, "Because Thomas's Brigade occupied the right of Long Lane, they had an unobstructed view of the Pickett-Pettigrew-Trimble charge, particularly the destructive fire thrown against Brockenbrough's Brigade and the artillery on Cemetery Hill and by the 8th Ohio, which flanked it. With better leadership, it is conceivable that Thomas's fresh brigade could have been thrown forward to thwart the destructive actions of the Ohio regiment."[28]

A steady brigade like Thomas's arguably would have provided a far more stable left flank to the charge than Brockenbrough's did.[29] Stephen Sears says the fact that Pettigrew's left fought without support was "symptomatic of the indifferent planning applied to the left wing of the attack."[30] In fact, four of the six brigades in the left wing of the line had been routed or "stopped cold by the Federals" at some point in the previous two days of combat.[31] Thomas's Brigade, with its hardened veterans of Gaines's Mill, Cedar Mountain, Second Manassas, and Chancellorsville, would have provided a much-needed mainstay on the left. Moreover, Thomas's men, as well as those in Stephen Ramseur's and George Doles's brigades to Thomas's left, "were exactly what one in command of such a maneuver as Pickett's Charge would have wanted to have coming up behind the initial assault: fresh

---

27. Bearss, *Fields of Honor*, 201. James McPherson described Pickett's charge as representative of the overall Confederate war effort, displaying "matchless valor, apparent initial success, and ultimate disaster." McPherson, *Battle Cry of Freedom*, 662.
28. Gottfried, *Brigades of Gettysburg*, 657.
29. Philip Thomas Tucker takes a contrarian view by maintaining that anchoring Brockenbrough on the left flank was a sound decision on Lee's part, in part because it meant they would sacrificially take the brunt of the enfilading Union artillery fire on Cemetery Hill, rather than the "best combat units to the south that would form the battering ram. . . ." Phillip Thomas Tucker, *Pickett's Charge: A New Look at Gettysburg's Final Attack* (Skyhorse Publishing, 2016), 143-144.
30. Sears, *Gettysburg*, 419.
31. Sears, *Gettysburg*, 419.

troops that had not been previously engaged."³² Perhaps Thomas's Brigade was being saved for a second wave if needed to exploit "any triumph of the first."³³ Perhaps the brigade was held in reserve in the event of a counter-attack.³⁴ Or perhaps the answer is as simple as that suggested by James Hessler and Wayne Motts, that the brigades on the left end of the line might have been "forgotten, as one more example of Confederate communication breakdowns that plagued Lee's army throughout the battle."³⁵

The second inquiry, related to the first, is whether any of the men of Thomas's Brigade, whose line was only a few hundred yards from Union troops, joined the charge at the left end of the Pettigrew-Trimble line, with or without express orders to do so.³⁶ Thomas's Brigade was the brigade closest to Brockenbrough's Brigade on the left flank of the assault line. According to John Bachelder's 1863 birds-eye view of the battle, Thomas's Brigade sat on Long Lane, with the 49th Georgia at an oblique to the assault line facing the Bliss farm, with Thomas's other regiments – the 45th, 14th, and 35th – running north in that order.³⁷ Elwood Christ suggests that as Pettigrew's and Trimble's men shifted south, the gap to Thomas's line widened, and that eventually Thomas's troops "found it impossible to support the advancing gray lines," which "permitted the 8th Ohio and other Yankee troops to enfilade Pettigrew's line."³⁸

Thomas gave no indication in his after-battle report that any of his regiments participated in the charge. No official report suggests that any regiment in the brigade joined the charge. The brigade historian and adjutant wrote that the brigade had not participated in the battle of Gettysburg "except in very heavy skirmishing, and in being

---

32. Richard Rollins describes Thomas's Brigade as one of the five brigades and one regiment that were "the missing pieces of the puzzle of Pickett's Charge" and maintains that "[I]n the secondary literature on Pickett's Charge, the men in Long Lane seem to have disappeared." Richard Rollins, "The Second Wave of Pickett's Charge," *Gettysburg Magazine* 18 (1988), 105.
33. Sears, *Gettysburg*, 359.
34. One newspaper article said that Thomas may have been kept in place to "meet a threatened advance on the left." "Review of the Pennsylvania Campaign, Army of Northern Virginia, February 24, 1864," *Richmond Dispatch*, March 9, 1864, www.newspapers.com.
35. James A. Hessler and Wayne E. Motts, *Pickett's Charge at Gettysburg: A Guide to the Most Famous Attack in American History* (Savas Beatie, 2015), 82.
36. *OR*, Ser. 1, vol. 27, pt. II, pp. 668-669.
37. Bachelder, John B. "Gettysburg battle-field. Battle fought at Gettysburg, Pa., July 1st, 2d & 3d, by the Federal and Confederate armies, commanded respectively by Genl. G. G. Meade and Genl. Robert E. Lee." Boston and New York: Jno. B. Bachelder, 1863. Map. https://www.loc.gov/item/2007630421/.
38. Christ, *"Over a Wide, Hot . . . Crimson Plain"*, 79.

subjected to one of the most awful artillery fires ever witnessed."[39] The regimental adjutant and historian for the 14th Georgia simply noted that the regiment was engaged in the battle and suffered forty-four casualties (eleven killed and thirty-three wounded).[40] As Hessler and Motts further suggest, perhaps the most logical answer as to why Thomas did not charge on his own initiative might have been because his brigade was "opposed by a strong Union skirmish line," which included the 8th Ohio.[41] That regiment engaged not only Thomas's skirmishers commencing at 6 a.m. but also Pettigrew's men in the afternoon charge.[42]

Some of Thomas's veterans claimed long after the war that the troops from the brigade joined the Pickett-Pettigrew-Trimble charge. David Champion of Hall's Company G wrote that the company next to theirs joined Pickett's division, which was actually hundreds of yards down the assault line.[43] Private John A. Andrews of Company I of the 14th Georgia made the extraordinary claim that he was wounded with Brig. Gen. James Kemper at the stone wall, but it is difficult to reconcile the distance factor between Thomas's Brigade and where Kemper was on the right flank of Pickett's division. Andrews, who was on picket duty at the start of the charge, claimed that he joined the charge on the direct order of the officer in charge of the picket detail, whom Andrews said "had been taking a little

---

39. Folsom, *Heroes and Martyrs of Georgia*, 119.
40. Folsom, *Heroes and Martyrs of Georgia*, 153.
41. Hesler and Motts, *Pickett's Charge at Gettysburg*, 83. Hessler and Motts invite readers to consider, however, whether three or four thousand Confederate infantrymen, from Thomas's Brigade and others to its left, would have even made a difference to the battle's outcome on July 3, 1863.
42. Thomas F. Galwey, then a 17-year-old brevet captain in Company B of the 8th Ohio, wrote in his diary, "We found ourselves, a single regiment of less than three hundred men, two hundred yards in front of the main Federal position. Seemingly a forlorn position for us but, as it turned out, destined to play an unexpectedly vital part in the defense of the salient angle which Meade's line of battle made just behind us." Thomas F. Galwey, *The Valiant Hours: Narrative of "Captain Brevet." an Irish-American in the Army of the Potomac* (Stackpole, 1961), 116.
43. Champion, Memoirs, "Gettysburg." Pickett's Division was nowhere near Thomas's Brigade but Champion may have just labeled all of the units in the charge as part of Pickett's Division, much the same way the action is often referred to as "Pickett's Charge" rather than "Pickett-Pettigrew-Trimble Charge." For an excellent discussion on the objectivity of history and the subjectivity of memory, see Carol Reardon's *Pickett's Charge in History and Memory* (University of North Carolina Press, 1997).

stimulant, which I suppose made him feel like fighting."[44]

Yet another post-war claim was that of Private George Washington Nichols of the 51st Georgia Infantry, who wrote in his 1898 memoirs that "one of the most desparate (sic) and fruitless charges of the whole war was made on the evening of the third day by General Pickett . . . and Thomas', Wrights', and Wilcox's brigades of Georgians."[45] Cadmus Wilcox, however, had no Georgians at Gettysburg; in early July 1863, he had only Alabama regiments in his brigade and they fought almost at the far right of the Confederate line. These inaccuracies undermine any trust that might be placed in Nichols's claim that Thomas's Brigade participated in the charge.

The only significant claim during the war that Thomas's Brigade had participated in the charge on July 3 was an assertion in Folsom's *Heroes and Martyrs of Georgia* that Lt. Col. William McCulloh had led the 35th Georgia Infantry in the "memorable charge of Picket (*sic*) and Heth" after hearing Thomas order the brigade forward in the wake of a nearby brigade.[46] However, this claim – in a chapter that was apparently penned by McCulloh himself -- contradicts Thomas's official report. Moreover, casualty numbers for both Thomas's Brigade and the 35th Georgia would surely have been significantly higher if the regiment, rather than just a handful of men, had intentionally joined the afternoon charge. Thomas's three-day losses, however, were so low that only one Confederate brigade

---

44. John A. Andrews, "Georgians Were in Pickett's Charge: Fourteenth Georgia Scaled the Hights (sic) at Gettysburg in Battle That Decided the Civil War," Jackson (Ga.) *Progress-Argus*, March 27, 1925 (reprinted as "Centennial in Review" on April 8, 1965). In May, 1921, when he was 76, Andrews wrote his "war record," in which he claimed that he was wounded on the afternoon of July 3 in Pickett's charge and laid in a wheat field until retrieved by an ambulance driver. Carole E. Scott, "The Butts County Boys' War: The Stories of Benjamin Lewis McGough and John Oliver Andrews," accessed July 19, 2020, https://sites.rootsweb.com/~cescott.butts.html.
45. G. W. Nichols, *A Soldier's Story of His Regiment (61st Georgia) and Incidentally of the Lawton-Gordon-Evans Brigade Army Northern Virginia* (n.p., 1898), 117. Nichols also wrote of the day's artillery attack, "No one that fought in this terrible battle or heard the thunder of artillery and the explosion of the shells can ever forget it. I heard a responsible man of Thomas' Georgia brigade, who was wounded and captured in this battle, and is now an eminent minister of the gospel, say that the ground around the enemy's battery was nearly covered in fragments of shells, and that it was the worst sight he had ever seen." Ibid., 118.
46. Folsom, *Heroes and Martyrs of Georgia*, 140.

suffered fewer casualties at Gettysburg than did his Georgians.[47] The fact that the 35th Georgia suffered more casualties than any other regiment in the brigade was most likely attributable to its proximity to the 8th Ohio Infantry.[48] According to the 8th Ohio's commander, his regiment took over 200 prisoners at Gettysburg, although at a high cost, with the Union regiment incurring almost 50% casualties.[49]

Perhaps some of Thomas's men were indeed swept up by the enthusiasm of the charging line. Perhaps some charged with their comrades in nearby brigades simply because they were weary of passively ducking artillery under a scorching sun; indeed, John Fox persuasively points out that their position behind a wooden fence was "an infantryman's worse nightmare."[50] Perhaps some moved forward as skirmishers during the oblique attack on Brockenbrough's and Davis's brigades by the 8th Ohio, who likely fired on Thomas's ranks as well. But there is simply not sufficient evidence on which to conclude that Thomas's Brigade – or any regiment in the brigade – joined the Pickett-Pettigrew-Trimble attack.

Both sides spent an uneasy July 4 tending to the dead and wounded and speculating as to the intentions of the other. Some southerners were hopeful that Meade would initiate an attack so that the Confederates could flip the tables, but Meade, who had only been in command of the Army of the Potomac for one week, had had enough. So had Lee, who was short on ammunition and had lost seventeen general officers (out of fifty-two) as casualties. Lee decided to return to Virginia in a deliberate withdrawal.[51]

At some point on July 4, Hall passed through Gettysburg, likely en route to Fairfield

---

47. Gottfried, *Brigades of Gettysburg*, 657. The Interpretive Display on Unit Information at the Visitor's Center, Gettysburg National Military Park, viewed on August 21, 2018, and June 14, 2025, states that Thomas's Brigade suffered 264 casualties (34 killed, 127 wounded, and 103 captured). Those numbers conflict with the strength and casualty numbers on the 1910 brigade monument, which states that 34 were killed, 179 were wounded, and 57 went missing, for a total of 270 casualties. Hall's 14th Georgia suffered the lowest percentage of casualties in the brigade, at 14.81% of its pre-battle strength of 31 officers and 293 men. Busey, *Confederate Casualties at Gettysburg*, 365.
48. Gottfried, *Brigades of Gettysburg*, 165. As John Fox notes, many of the 35th Regiment's casualties were attributable to men being captured as a result of the skirmishing on July 2 and July 3. Fox, *Red Clay to Richmond*, 187.
49. *OR*, Ser. 1, vol. 27, pt. I, p. 462.
50. Fox, *Red Clay to Richmond*, 186.
51. Eric J. Wittenberg, J. David Petruzzi, and Michael F. Nugent, *One Continuous Fight: The Retreat from Gettysburg and the Pursuit of Lee's Army of Northern Virginia, July 4-14, 1863* (Savas Beatie, 2013), 39.

Road, and lamented the condition of the town. He sympathized with the townspeople, writing that Confederate troops should not have destroyed the homes of helpless women and children even though the "yankees desolated a many a happy home in the South, but that is no reason we should do theirs so."

The route out of Gettysburg back to the safety of Virginia entailed roughly forty miles of marching to reach Williamsport on the Potomac River. Uncertain how much effort Meade would put into pursuing or attempting to cut off the retreat, Lee disbursed his troops and wagons in different directions. The army's supply wagons and the bulk of the infantry, including Hill's Third Corps, took Fairfield Road over Jack Mountain, through the Monterey Pass on South Mountain, and then to Waynesboro, Leitersburg, Hagerstown, and Williamsport, where most crossed the Potomac. When Hill's Third Corps moved out, Pender's Division, which included Thomas's Brigade, was in the front. The march was a miserable experience, with howling winds, incessant rain, and mud so thick and high that it sucked shoes off the feet of the marchers. Ewell, who wanted to renew battle with Meade, brought up the rear guard.

The Army of the Potomac learned in the early morning hours of July 5 that the Army of Northern Virginia was on the move. Concerned first and foremost about protecting Baltimore and Washington, Meade moved his army south but remained east of the mountains; by the time he reached Frederick (almost due south of Gettysburg) and then moved west to Middletown, Lee was already at Hagerstown and Williamsport. Union cavalry, however, harassed Lee's retreating forces, not only at his main column but also the Confederate ambulance train, which was attacked in Greencastle, Pennsylvania.

Hall was ill during most of the passage back into Virginia, again running a fever and having gastro-intestinal issues. Exhaustion from the three days of battle and the evacuation march only worsened his condition. Hill's column marched all night,

The retreat from Gettysburg. (*Battles and Leaders of the Civil War, Yoseloff ed., 1956*)

stopping briefly at Fairfield and Waynesboro. It reached the base of South Mountain on the evening of July 5. On July 6, Longstreet's corps replaced Hill's corps at the front of the infantry column.

That night Hill and his men camped just east of Hagerstown, at Leitersburg. Lee had ordered his engineers to build a pontoon bridge at Falling Waters on the Potomac, but while this time-consuming task was undertaken, he created a defensive line west of Hagerstown, with Hill's corps at the center; Pender's Division was on the left.[52] By this point, Meade had multiple corps formed on a line south of Hagerstown to Sharpsburg. It was decision time for Meade: should he attack Lee, who had his back to the Potomac River, or not? Meade solicited his commanders in council for advice. The majority voted against attacking Lee, and Meade, much to Lincoln's dismay, could not bring himself to make an assault that most of his commanders were not willing to support.[53]

There was, however, one last significant engagement in the Gettysburg campaign, that being the battle of Falling Waters on July 14, 1863. Fitzhugh Lee's Confederate cavalry brigade passed over the pontoon bridge there prematurely, which left Heth's and Pender's divisions on the north shore of the Potomac River without any cavalry screen for protection. Heth's Division, likely due in part to exhaustion, thought approaching cavalrymen were Confederates but they were instead the 6th Michigan in George Custer's brigade making a charge with sabers drawn. Although the combat only lasted a few minutes, it resulted in a fatal gunshot to James Pettigrew, one of only two Confederate deaths in the engagement. Some 230 soldiers in what Sears calls "John Brockenbrough's brigade of unfortunates" were captured.[54] Pender's Division, which had been about to cross the pontoon bridge, was sent back to help Heth's men. Lane, who had sixty-five men captured on July 13 and July 14, later wrote that the retreat from Hagerstown was even worse than the retreat from Gettysburg.[55] Hall wrote of the intolerable mud on the march.

After shepherding his army across the Potomac, Lee moved his army approximately sixteen miles to Bunker Hill, where Hall had camped the previous fall. The men were

---

52. Gottfried, *The Maps of Gettysburg*, 286-287.
53. Gottfried, *The Maps of Gettysburg*, 286-287.
54. Sears, *Gettysburg*, 492. When Brockenbrough retreated, he reportedly had left his aide, a captain, to lead the brigade in combat. Wittenberg, *One Continuous Fight*, 292-293.
55. *OR*, Ser. 1, vol. 27, pt. II, p. 667.

in terrible shape. On July 14, Hall wrote the following: "We camped 3 or 4 miles from Martinsburg hungry and fatigued having not eat anything in nearly 3 days, and nearly all our army was barefooted and nearly naked." While at Bunker Hill, the men learned that Pettigrew and Pender had both died of their wounds. Lee had planned to move his army east into Loudon County but, while he waited for high water on the Shenandoah to subside, Meade's cavalry blocked the passes over the Blue Ridge.[56] Lee then ordered his army to Culpeper Court House, and Meade eventually moved his army back to the north bank of the Rappahannock.[57] Both armies then settled in to regroup after their enormous losses at Gettysburg.

Pocket Notebook Narrative
June 5 – July 14, 1863

About 11 P.M. of June 5th we were aroused from our slumbers in order to fall into line immediately. We scarcely had time to do up our things and we marched off in the direction of Fredericksburg. We marched the remainder of the night and arrived at Hamiltons Crossing a little before daylight and taken up the R R towards Fredericksburg and formed line of Battle along the R R and sent out Skirmishers on the river, but there was no fighting done by us but higher up the river there was Skirmishing for 5 or 6 days where the Yankees had crossed the river but down where we were the river Seperated our pickets from the enemy and several of the yankees swam over to us and brought us papers and coffee and then returned to their own side. We remained in line of Battle over a week expecting to fight

---

56. Walter H. Taylor, *General Lee: His Campaigns in Virginia, 1861-1865* (University of Nebraska Press, 1994), 219.
57. Wittenberg, *One Continuous Fight*, 348.

every day and there was some shelling across the river nearly every day but none that done any damage.

What the designs of the [yankees] were in making this demonstration I cannot tell, but they re-crossed the river a day or two before we left, and not much sign of them could be seen on the opposite side of the river. Our army left there on the morning of June 16th, and taken the road that led to the Battle field of Chancellorsville, & crossed the Rapid Ann [Rapidan] river at Elys ford and camped for the night and cooked up rations and started again next morning by light, and the night of the 17th we camped 8 miles from Culpeper C. H. [Court House] and 18th beyond there 8 or 9 miles.

During the 17th and 18th [of June] the weather was so hot and we marched so hard that hundreds of our men fainted and several died on the road. I came verry near giving up myself the night of [the] 19th. We camped 4 miles from Flint Hill near the Blue Ridge. 20th we camped on the Blue Ridge in a thunder cloud so dark we could hardly see our way. 21st we passed through Front Royal and waded the Shenandoah river and camped 6 miles beyond on the Winchester turnpike. 22nd we camped near Berryville and remained there until one P M. 23rd and resumed the march through Berryville and 10 or 15 miles beyond and camped for the night, and 24th we marched through Smithfield and cross the Baltimore and Ohio R. R. and camped in two miles of Shepherd[s]town on the Potomac river.

At 10 A. M. we marched again and waded the Potomac at Shepherd[s]town and arrived in Maryland and pass through Sharpsburg and the Battle field of last year and camped about half way between the Potomac and Hagerstown. The rain fell all night and nearly all next day. We marched at daylight again and when we arrived in two miles of Hagerstown our regt was sent back to guard some wagons, and we never got back to where brigade till late that night. The 27th [of June] we started by daylight passed through Hagerstown and got into Pennsylvania, about 10 A. M. and camped near Chambersburg that night. We marched farther that day than we had before on this campaign and I was so tired and sore that it would have been impossible for me to have went much farther and my feet had swelled considerable next day.

The Quarter-Masters of our army put forth all their energies to press all the horses and beef cattle they could, and they gathered them up in great numbers. They got beef enough to last our army for several months, and our old broke down Artillery and waggon horses were dismissed and good ones put in their places.[58]

The Cumberland valley in Pennsylvania was the part we were in at this time. It is the finest and richest country I ever saw and no signs of the devastating war was seen here. Every thing looked as though war had never been in a thousand miles of it. The vandal foe had laid wast[e] to the beautiful fields of Virginia and other states of our beloved South, while their own country lay as peaceful as if there had been no war. But I guess [the] region our army visited felt something of the weight of war, something they will not soon forget.

At daylight on the morning of the 30th [of June] we march again in an eastern direction across the Blue Ridge and camped at the fort. It rained all day; the 1st of July we marched again and soon after we cleared our camps

---

58. Many of the horses commandeered in Pennsylvania were unsuitable for military service; according to one artilleryman, they were "big, fat, and clumsy unfit for the quick movements and long, forced marches." Peter S. Carmichael, *Lee's Young Artillerist: William R. J. Pegram* (University of Virginia, 1995), 95. A significant number of those horses were left behind in their home state when Lee retreated to Virginia after Gettysburg. Ibid.

we began to hear the boom of cannon ahead of us and as we advanced it became more distinct. About 10 A. M. we formed line of Battle each side of the road and advanced through woods and fields swamps and brier thickets and presently shells began to fall and burst among us. We got orders to march by the right flank. We marched up and lay down in rear of one of our batterys that was firing at the enemy while part of our division advanced and attack the enemy. The roar of Battle becomes constant and almost deafening. We can see the Yankees flag flying in the breeze. Onward our brave goes with a yell that seems to rend the air. We can see the Yankees in the edge of the woods. See the thick clouds of smoke that flies forth and their numerous Batterys belched forth fire and death into our ranks. Onward our brave boys goes with a shout. The enemys colors disapear and soon our men disappear also in the woods, the enemy flying before them. The thick colums of smoke ascends and hides the rays of the sun. Before this time bombs was falling and exploding among our regiment but they now ceased. Our men had cause[d] them to speedily retire. Towards sunset the firing of small arms ceased. The enemy retired beyond the city of Gettysburg to a high and commanding position, placing their artillery on a hill where I suppose they had previously threw up earthworks to protect it; and the front line of their infantry were protected by a stone fence.

About sun set our brigade marched up and taken position on the front line, and while we were forming the enemy threw grape shot and cannon balls at us as thick as hail, but they done little damage. A grape shot struck me on the foot and made it smart and ache a little. We lay in line of Battle that night. The night was unusually still. No sound disturbed dead silence that reigned over the terrable Battle field where a few hours before the thunders of artillery and roar of small arms, and the shouts of antagonist[s] as they rushed madly forward upon each other and the shrieks of the wounded and dying could have been heard several miles but now all was still and silent. Save once and awhile a stray gun shot from some out post picket.

There was a many an anxious heart that night for the result next day. We sent out skirmishers verry soon next morning about half our regiment at a time and when they fought till they got out of ammunition and then the other half would go out. Our artillery had taken its position the night before. They kept up a rapid and concentrated all day from both side, and the most terrable cannonading that I ever saw or heard was done this day and the next 2nd and 3rd of July it seemed that ten thousands shells would explode in an instant mowing down trees like a harricane and tearing up the earth in every direction. It seemed that it was impossible for a living creature do have escaped. Artillery horses were killed in heaps. Shells burst so near to me they threw dirt over me but I escaped unharmed though several in our regiment was killed and Severly [wounded].

This continued from soon in the morning till dark each side keeping the same position until the night before. At night our brigade got a new supply of ammunition. Gen Longstreets corps fought terrable and lost a great many today on our right and also Gen E[w]ell on our left. (Ours) Gen Hills corps occupied the center. That night we advanced our infantry about half a mile and taken our position along a fence in an open field. Our artillery kept the same position. There were some picket firing nearly all night. The morning of the 3rd we went at it again verry soon and the cannonading nearly like it was the day before. We were between our artillery and the enemy's and what time we were not engaged with the enemy we had to lie flat on the ground and it seem[ed] the hotest day I ever experienced. There was no shade to protect us at all. The vertical rays of the sun pored down upon us and the explosion of so much gunpowder het [heated] the air and rendered the heat more hot than it would have been otherwise. About 3 oclock P.M. our corps charged the enemy in order to try to rout them from their strong position, but we had to charge them so far across the old field, and the weather was so hot a great many of our men fainted and the remainder were exhausted so we had to fall back to our old position. Our artillery done good execution that day. It silenced all the enemys batterys but one and it was protected by fortifications so they could have no affect on it.

That night we fell back to the position we occupied on the 2nd. By that time it was day light the morning of the fourth. It commenced raining hard directly after day, and the Battle was suspended. There was skirmishing all day but no fighting of any consequence. I was in part of the town that day and saw some of the havoc the Battle had made on it. Some of the finest buildings I ever saw tore to peices and demolished by cannon balls and shells and our troops had taken Shelter in some of them out of the rain, and the most desolating sight I ever saw, I saw there. All the furniture had been torn down and trampled underfoot, ward robes bureaus, sofas trunks, and librarys, torn open and their contents Scattered in every direction. Our troops done to[o] bad there for they ought not to have destroyed the homes of helpless women and children. The Lord will not approve of no such. It is true the yankees desolated a many a happy home in the South, but that is no reason we should do theirs so, for the dear Savior taught us to do good for evil and not evil for evil. But they are few and far between who do this.

We remained there till after dark the following night and commenced the retreat. The night was dark and the rain was falling hard. The mud was deep in the road that it was with difficulty we got along at all. I had to stop several times and feel for my shoes in the mud, and several lost their shoes burried so deep in the mud that they never found them. About daylight we halted. I was verry sick a while from the excessive fatigue I had been through. We had not had any sleep for the last 3 days and nights and we try to sleep a little but we were so wet and chilly we could not sleep much. We left there about 12 A.M. and recrossed the Blue Ridge and camp that night about midnight, and remained there after 12 next day, the 6th and marched again, and passed through Waynesboro a beautiful town and cross line of Pennsylvania and Maryland and camp for the night verry hungry and tired. The 7th [of July] we marched by light again[,] passed through Hagerstown and our cavalry had fought the enemy the evening before and run them away. We camped two miles from Hagerstown. We remained in camp till the 10th and the enemy was getting rather to[o] clost to us. Our wagons was sent on and we formed line of battle and skirmished with them in order to let all our waggons sick and wounded cross the river and on the night of the 13th & morning of the 14th we evacuated Maryland and crossed the Potomac Some at Williamsport and some 4 miles below on a pontoon bridge. The evening of the 14th we camped 3 or 4 miles from Martinsburg hungry and fatigued having not eat anything in nearly 3 days, and nearly all our army was barefooted and nearly naked. The 15th we marched through Martinsburg and camp at Bunker Hill our old camp ground of last year.

Remembrancer Daily Entries
June 5 – July 24, 1863

Friday, June 5, 1863

Partially cloudy & warm. We return off picket. To day two years ago I first commenced camp life at Isabella Ga.

Saturday, June 6, 1863

(no entry)

Sunday, June 7, 1863

Partially cloudy, cool winds. Sent letter to Wm L Land.[59] Today we are in line of Battle at the same place we were yesterday. There is some skirmishing and cannonading on our left. The enemy is this side of the river in large force near Fredericksburg. We look for a great Battle soon.

Pocket Notebook
Religious Reflection
Sunday, June 7, 1863

The Sabbath has once more dawned upon us and found us in quite different circumstances to what we were in last, and what next Sunday may bring forth no one can fathom the deep and terrable struggles we may have to pass through before that time, but Him whom I put my trust in and lean on for safety. He knoweth all things and Oh God of Battles, be with us, and nerve our hearts to pass the terrable ordeal trusting in Thee we can fear nothing; amid the roar of battle when the missiles of death fly thick and fast how Sweet is the christians peace of mind Trusting to their Fathers will knowing if they are taken away, they will go to that bright home above and see the face of that dear

---

[59]. Land, a soldier in Company G, had been wounded in the leg at Chancellorsville. In early June 1863 he was likely still in the hospital or home on furlough. He was present at the surrender at Appomattox on April 9, 1865.

Lamb that died for them. What unworthy creatures we poor mortals are to fear death so much, when that dear Jesus did not hesitate to lay down his life for us. O! Dear Lord make me willing to lay down my unprofitable life to come to thee at any time thou seest fit to take me away. What is in this wicked world that I am so loath to leave it, nothing but sin temptations and tryals is here while I go to eternal happiness and everlasting life.

We are at this time in line of battle on the old battle ground of the 13th of December last, hourly expecting another great Battle perhaps more terrible than that was, and we know not what the dark future has in store for us, but the Lord knoweth and if we put our trust in his divine will what have we to fear. He will be with us if we only do his <u>will</u> and if we fall, it will not be without his <u>will</u>, and he will receive us in that <u>Home of eternal rest</u> where we will be done with this cruel war, which was brought on by a wickedness. Thy will be done dear Father not mine, I lie passive in thy hands do with me what so ever thou willest. Oh! what blessed hope is the hope of the children of God. I earnestly wish all that had that hope, but alas how few they are.

Monday, June 8, 1863

Night cool. Day fair & pleasant. We still remain in line of Battle today. Nothing worth[y] of notice transpires along our lines. We have out skirmish[ers] on the river and the enemy is in plain view. Sent letter home.

Tuesday, June 9, 1863

There is some cannon firing on the left today, but the great battle has not commenced yet. Night cool. Day fair & pleas[ant].

Pocket Notebook

Wednesday, June 10, 1863
(no daily entry)

<u>On picket on the banks of the Rappahannock June 10, 1863</u>

I am now in a pleasant shade, in a few feet of the waters edge of this famous river which will maintain a name in history as long as the world stands. It [is] verry narrow here scarcely 100 yards wide and only the width of it separated us from the enemies pickets, and there is no swamp and either side and we have a plain view of each other. They seem to [be] verry tired of the war and do not want to fight against us any more. Two of the 2nd Vermont reg<u>t</u> swam over to us to day, and exchange papers. Pickets acts quite often different from what the[y] did last year for then we were shooting at each other every sight of each other we got but now we visit each other and in peace and friendly terms, talk upon various Topics. But when we meet in Battle we are quite changed. Then each party tries to take the others life and slay as many of his own kindred and country men as he can, but I hope it will not be so always.

Thursday, June 11, 1863
Cloudy & a little rain. We still remain in line of Battle. Nothing worth of notice takes place. We still look for a great battle to be fought here and that before long.

June 13, 14, 15, 16, 17, 18, 19, 20, 21, 1863
(no entries)

Monday, June 22, 1863
Fair & pleasant. We resumed the march this morning soon & turned off the turnpike to the right and arrived near Berryville and camp for the night and cook two days rations. The weather is fine for marching.

Tuesday, June 23, 1863
Fair & pleasant. Today at 1 oclock we marched again

down through Berryville and in a northern direction towards Shepherdstown on the Potomac. We marched till dark and stacked arms and spread our blankets & endeavored to take a little rest.

Wednesday, June 24, 1863

Par cloudy & pleasant. We marched again at daylight and through Smithfield and crossed the Baltimore and Ohio Rail Road and camped in a mile or two of the Potomac near Shepherd[s]town and cook two days rations and tomorrow we will cross into Maryland I expect & from thence to Pennsylvania.

Thursday, June 25, 1863

M clo E rainy. Today at 10 A.M. we commence crossing the Potomac and by 12 nearly [all] our division was across. We passed through part of the Battle field and took the turnpike toward Hagerstown and pass through another village and camped for the night. The rain fell all night.

Friday, June 28, 1863

Rainy all day. We commenced the march this morning in the rain. The road was verry muddy. We marched till near 12 oclock when our reg[iment] was sent back 4 miles to protect the rear of our artillery & waggon train and the remainder of the division goes on and leaves us in the rear. We cook two days rations.

Saturday, June 27, 1863

At daybreak this morning we were up and gone. We passed through Hagerstown Md, which is a nice place and proceeded on at a rapid march so as to be enable to over take the division. About 10 A. M. we crossed a small river and landed on the Pennsylvania shore. We passed through Waynesboro and 3 more towns in Penn that I did not learn the name of. Late in the evening we camped. My feet was so sore I could hardly put them to the ground.

Sunday, June 28, 1863

We remain in camp today. Have inspection of arms. My feet is verry sore and swelled considerable but I hope and trust in the Lord that I will be able [to] bear up and stand all I may have to pass through for I have to live a hard life now, but trusting in God I hope it will not last always but will end some time. We are now 7 or 8 miles from Chambersburg where I expect we will start. Preaching by Bro Hyman. Tomorrow part of our forces already and I think we will not turn back till we get to Harrisburg the Capitol of this state and I doubt of us getting any more rest till next winter. This is the finest country I ever saw and if the inhabitan[ts] could not hear from the war and our army had never come here they would not know that any war was going on at all. Every thing is as cheap as in time of peace and there looks like there is enough wheat here to sup[p]ly the world.

Monday, June 29, 1863

Cloudy & pleasant. We still remain in camp today and cook two more days rations. We drawed flour, beef, Syrup, Sugar and salt. Nothing worth of notice transpires. Our army is pressing in provision[s] and horses by the whole sale and some of the finest horses I ever saw.

Tuesday, June 30, 1863

Hard showery weather. We march again at daylight and ma[r]ched over the mountains in an eastern direction and passed through the village of Greenwood and camped on the side of a mountain and cook one days rations. It rains verry hard.

Wednesday, July 1, 1863

Warm and some rain. This morning verry soon we march towards Gettysburg and leave all our waggons behin[d]. We hear the report of artillery in front and know that the enemy is near. We march double quick and form line of battle on each side of the road, and advance about a mile.

By this time (11 oclock) the Battle has begun by Gen Heaths division in front of us. The enemys Batterys throw shell all around us and our Batterys just in front of us keep up a continual roar. Our men charge and drive the enemy before them. A fierce Battle continues till near sunset and ceases for the night. Our division takes position on the front line and send out a strong line of Skirmishers.

Thursday, July 2, 1863

Par cloudy & hot. This morning at daylight the Skirmishers commence a rapid and continued fire in front of us. Our artillery takes position and opens on the enemies Batter[ie]s. The artillery commence roaring from both sides. We lie down in front of Battle to keep the enemys Batterys from having Such affect on us. Cannon balls, bombs, grape and canisters fall thick and fast around us and among us killing and wounding several of our regt. Every hour or two we relieve Skirmishers, keep out three companies from our regiment all the time. The fighting is not verry heavy only with artillery in the center but on the right & left the small arms roar with increased fury. The Battle continues near 10 oclock at night. We get no rest nor sleep this night.

Friday, July 3, 1863

Fair & intensely hot. At day light the Battle in commenced again and continues all day. With a continued roar the firing of artillery and bursting of shell is kept up with intense fury all day. No pen nor human words can describe the terrable and awful scenes we passed through yesterday and today. Cannon balls and shells threw dirt all over me and killed and wounded a great number of our regiment. We accomplished nothing toward driving the enemy today. We charged them several times but their position was to[o] strong for us. The air was so hot that a great number of our men fainted. I came verry near it myself.

Saturday, July 4, 1863

Rain all day. We continue in line of battle today but there is verry little fighting. I feel sick and bad from the exposure & and fatigue I have passed through. To night at dark we commence retreating. The enemys cavelry in the rear of us and about to capture all our waggons. We march all night through mud and water nearly knee deep and rain falling in torrents.

Sunday, July 5, 1863

Rainy and muddy. We halt this morning at daylight and rest till about 3 oclock and march again till near 12 oclock at night and camp fatigued and exhausted. I was verry sick awhile but by the help of the Lord I was enable to keep up. We recross the mountains. We passed through where the Yankee cavalry taken a good many of Gen Ewells wagons.

Monday, July 6, 1863

Cloudy with some rain. We rested awhile this morning and I eat some of the best cherries I ever saw. At three oclock we marched again and passed through Waynesboro, and crossed Mason's & Dixons line and arrived in Maryland again. We camped about 10 P.M.in 3 miles of Hagerstown.

Tuesday, July 7, 1863

Cloudy & warm. At daylight we marched again through Hagerstown and our cavalry and the Yankees had a Battle yesterday evening and our men whiped them and run them plum away. We camped before 12 A. M. The Potomac is so full on account of the rain that has fell lately that we cannot cross. We cook 2 days rations.

Wednesday, July 8, 1863

M heavy rain. E cloudy. We remain in camp. Inspection of arms.

Thursday, July 9, 1863

M foggy. E fair & warm. I was verry sick today with pains in my bowels and I vomited considerable. We cook two days rations more, in order keep two days in our haversacks all the time.

Friday, July 10, 1863

Fair & Hot. I continue sick. Have a high fever. There is a fierce cannonading in the direction of Hagerstown. Today our wagons is sent 2 miles farther on and we hold ourselves in readiness to march at a moments warning.

Saturday, July 11, 1863

Cloudy & warm. Today we marched out in line of Battle not far from where we were camped and threw up breast works and sent out Skirmishers. There was not much [f]ighting today but the enemy is near in heavy force.

Sunday, July 12, 1863

M cloudy & warm. E rain. We still remain in line of Battle and send out skirmishers.

Monday, July 13, 1863

Rainy and sultry. This day two years ago our company left Isabella Worth County Georgia for the seat of the war and I never have had the privalidge of seeing home or any of its dear ones since. We remained in line of Battle till after dark and commence falling back. We continue marching all night. Every thing in confusion. We cross the Potomac at Williamsport and part of the army at a pontoon bridge 4 miles lower down. Rainy all night. Mud intollerable.

Tuesday, July 14, 1863

M cloudy & warm. E rain. It was late in the day before all our troops got across the river. The Yankee cavalry attacked our rear and produced a good deal of confusion but a few volleys and shells made them skedaddle. The mud was bad. We camped & drew something to eat for we were all verry near famished, having not had any thing in two days. It rained so we could hardly cook.

Wednesday, July 15, 1863

Cloudy & hot & sultry. We marched this morning soon & passed through Martinsburg and on towards Winchester. We camped at Bunkershill tired and worn out. My feet is so sore that it is with difficulty I walk at all and I have been sick all day, but by the help of the Lord I have been enabled to keep up.

Thursday, July 16, 1863

M cloudy & warm. E rain. Our regiment had to go on picket this morning 3 miles back the way we come but we were in a pleasant place and all got as many rasberries and dewberries as we wanted.

Friday, July 17, 1863

Warm & rainy. We return off picket. It rains considerable. My feet is verry sore.

Saturday, July 18, 1863

Cloudy & warm. We clean up our guns and have inspection of arms, draw two days rations of flour, but what we draw for two days we can eat in one and we also get about half as much beef as we can eat and not half enough salt to season it.

Sunday, July 19, 1863

Partially cloudy & warm. Our chaplain preached for us and also Bro Hyman in the evening. I get another bate of berries.

Monday, July 20, 1863

Par cloudy & warm. I went to the creek this morning to wash, and before I got ready to leave orders came to leave and I put my clothes on wet and fell in and we marched off but halted in about 2 miles and camped in a better place near where we camped last October.

Tuesday, July 21, 1863

Fair & hot. To day at 12 oclock we received orders to march. We fell in and taken the turnpike towards Winchester. We passed through Winchester and camped two miles on this side and it took us half the night to draw our rations and cook them.

Wednesday, July 22, 1863

We marched again at daylight. Crossed the Shenandoah on pontoon bridges and camped near Front Royal, verry tired and sore. We drew one quarter of a pound of flour to the man to last a day. Partially fair & hot.

Thursday, July 23, 1863

Par fair & Hot. We march again at daylight through Front Royal and across the Blue Ridge and camped near Flint Hill and cooked two days rations.

Friday, July 24, 1863

At daylight we marched again and about 9 oclock we began to hear cannon and we marched a mile or two and shell began to fall amongst us but it did not last long. It was only a small cavalry force of the enemy. We captured their cannon and part of them and put the rest to flight. We cross two branches of the Rappahannock and camped for the night. The weather was extremely hot today. We suffered considerable from heat.

9

"IT WAS THE MOST SOLUMN SCENE I EVER SAW."
VIRGINIA: JULY 25 – DECEMBER 31, 1863

Some three weeks after the march from Gettysburg, Hall and the 14th Georgia encamped near Culpeper Court House and learned they had received a new division commander, Maj. Gen. Cadmus Wilcox.[1] Other than Hill's impetuous assault at Bristoe Station and Meade's half-hearted Mine Run Campaign, the remainder of 1863 was essentially a time for both armies to recover from the Gettysburg campaign. Lee had entered Pennsylvania with over 70,000 men but suffered over 22,800 casualties. Meade had suffered almost as many casualties in his force of over 89,800.[2]

Hall's diary entries through the end of 1863 reflect the calmer, restorative pace of camp life in central Virginia, with drills, picket duty, and inspections punctuated by false alarm marches and the occasional skirmish. Hall appears to have attended prayer services almost every day, occasionally listening to three sermons in a single day. Many of his entries reflect a day that began with battalion drill and ended with an evening prayer service. Regimental prayer meetings rotated among the various units, which gave Hall the opportunity on Sundays to attend services conducted by chaplains from other regiments.

---

1. Wilcox, a North Carolinian and arguably the U.S. Army's pre-war expert on riflery, was a West Point graduate who, like Thomas, had made a name for himself for bravery during the Mexican-American War. Ezra J. Warner, *Generals in Gray: Lives of the Confederate Commanders* (Louisiana State University Press, 1959), 337. Lee had considered giving the division to Thomas but was concerned that it might be an unpopular move given that three of the four brigades in the division were from the Carolinas. Fox, *Red Clay to Richmond*, 194.
2. Wittenberg, *One Continuous Fight*, 27.

Hall noted that a revival began in the brigade on August 15, 1863. This post-Gettysburg period was the second great revival period in the Army of Northern Virginia. But this Rapidan revival of late 1863 differed from the Rappahannock revival period earlier in the year; not only were the Rapidan revivals on a much larger scale, but participation was likely due in no small part to a sense of the need for repentance after Confederate losses at Gettysburg and at Vicksburg. Many in the ranks believed that those losses "were the results of God's punishment for ongoing sins in both Lee's army and the Confederate nation."[3] These purported sins had little to do with actual military service; rather, they were primarily camp amusements such as dancing, profanity, frivolity, gambling, breaking the Sabbath, and, not surprisingly, consumption of alcohol.[4] If soldiers wanted victory over the enemy in battle, they first needed a victory over sin in camp.

The message that the Army of Northern Virginia had sinned came from Jefferson Davis himself. On August 13, 1863, Lee issued General Order No. 83, announcing that Davis, acting on behalf of the Confederate people, had designated August 21 as a "day of fasting, humiliation, and prayer." Like a "safety standdown" in today's military, all military duties on August 21 were to be suspended except as "absolutely necessary." Brigade and regimental commanders were requested to arrange for divine services suitable to the occasion to be performed in their respective commands. Lee's language left little doubt as to his belief that he and his army had let down God.

> "Soldiers! We have sinned against Almighty God. We have forgotten His signal mercies and have cultivated a vengeful, haughty and boastful spirit. We have not remembered that the defenders of a just cause should be pure in His eyes; that our lives are in His hand and we have relied too much on our own arms for the achievement of our independence. God is our only refuge and our strength. Let us humble ourselves before Him. Let us confess our many sins and beseech Him to give us a higher Courage, a purer patriotism and more determined will. That He will convert the hearts of our enemies; that He will hasten the time when war

---

3. Harman, *The Great Revival*, 113.
4. Harman, *The Great Revival*, 115.

with its sorrows and sufferings shall cease, and that He will give us a name and peace among the Nations of the earth."[5]

On Davis's day of fasting, humiliation, and prayer, Hall attended three sermons and prayer meetings. Through this broader revival period, Hall took great joy in seeing how many of his comrades joined the church, claiming that "although a war of death and destruction surrounds us we have happy days now." Gardiner Shattuck maintains that Confederate armies were "the most religious fighting units ever," surpassing even Cromwell's Roundheads in the English Civil War some two hundred years earlier.[6] Indeed, estimated conversions in the Confederate armies topped 100,000, with ten percent of Lee's Army of Northern Virginia converting during the 1863-1864 revival period.[7]

Desertion and executions also formed a significant theme in Hall's life during the post-Gettysburg period. On July 30, 1863, Hall wrote that three hundred North Carolinians had deserted the night before to head home. Desertion had been a serious issue in the Army of Northern Virginia long prior to Gettysburg. A soldier who deserted not only left his unit with one less combatant, but his departure ate into the resolve of those who remained to serve, especially those who had been conscripted rather than enlisting through their own volition. Those who deserted made it even more difficult for those who stayed with their units to get furloughs to go home. Deserters heading home usually had to live off the countryside, which meant plundering scarce food supplies. Once the deserter was back home, those in the community who knew the soldier had deserted often found themselves split by competing loyalties. Some deserters never went home; instead, they went to the Union lines, where they were welcomed for any information they could provide.[8]

---

5. Army of Northern Virginia General Order No. 83, accessed July 23, 2020, https://leefamilyarchive.org/9-family-papers/74-general-orders-no-83-1863-august-13
6. Gardiner H. Shattuck, Jr., *A Shield and Hiding Place: The Religious Life of the Civil War Armies* (Mercer University Press, 1987), 96, 99.
7. Shattuck, *A Shield and Hiding Place*, 96, 99.
8. For example, during the raid on Moorefield and Fort Mulligan at Petersburg, West Virginia, by Thomas's Brigade in late January 1864, a Confederate deserter told Union forces that Early was moving towards Moorefield. *OR*, Ser. 1, vol. 33, p. 38. Ella Lonn wrote that a deserter betrayed Lee's three-column strategy at the Wilderness. Ella Lonn, *Desertion during the Civil War* (University of Nebraska Press, 1998), 103-104. Glatthaar provides several other examples of engagements where deserters provided advance information to the Union. Glatthaar, *General Lee's Army*, 408-409.

The study of desertion in Confederate ranks is an inexact science due in large part to incomplete records and the hazy line between desertion (absence with the intent to remain away permanently) and the lesser offense of unauthorized absence (sometimes referred to as "French leave"). An estimated one out of seven soldiers in the Army of Northern Virginia deserted at some point during the war. Georgia ranked fourth in officer desertions (79) and sixth in enlisted desertions (6,797).[9]

Second only to Virginia in the number of troops provided to the Confederacy, North Carolina had far more desertions than any other state, with 428 officer desertions and 23,694 enlisted desertions.[10] By the spring of 1863, Lee was complaining to his Secretary of War about frequent desertions from the North Carolina regiments, which would soon incur the most deaths of any Southern state at both Chancellorsville and Gettysburg.[11] Pender reported that in one month during the spring of 1863, at least 200 soldiers had deserted from the 24th North Carolina.[12] Hall wrote that "great numbers" of North Carolinians had deserted at Gettysburg and "went to the Yankees," although it would have been difficult for him to know with certainty which soldiers had willfully deserted and which ones may have simply been captured. Many Confederate soldiers deserted not out of fear of combat but rather to resolve issues at home, such as anxiety over the safety and health of loved ones or to help plant or harvest crops; for those soldiers, "desertion was as much a response to the home front as to the battlefield."[13]

---

9. Lonn, *Desertion during the Civil War*, 231. Most of the deserters from Georgia were from the Army of the Tennessee rather than the Army of Northern Virginia, and came from northern Georgia, the area of the state most threatened by Union occupation. Samuel B. McGuire, "Desertion," *The Civil War in Georgia: A New Georgia Encyclopedia Companion* (Athens: University of Georgia Press, 2011), 157.
10. Lonn, *Desertion during the Civil War*, 231.
11. In mid-May, 1863, thirty-two soldiers from one company of the 37th North Carolina deserted, taking with them all of their weapons and equipment. D. Scott Hartwig, "'Never Have I Seen Such a Charge: Pender's Light Division at Gettysburg, July 1," *High Water Mark: The Army of Northern Virginia in the Gettysburg* Campaign: *Programs of the Seventh Annual Gettysburg Seminar* (National Park Service: 1999), 40. http://npshistory.com/series/symposia/gettysburg_seminars/7/essay3.pdf
12. Philip Gerard, "Deserters and Outliers," *Our State Magazine*, accessed July 23, 2020, https://www.ourstate.com/deserters-outliers/. Over 300 deserters came from the Branch-Lane brigade alone. Michael C. Hardy, *General Lee's Immortal: The Battles and Campaigns of the Branch-Lane Brigade in the Army of Northern Virginia, 1861-1865* (Savas Beatie, 2018), 304.
13. Weitz, *A Higher Duty: Desertion Among Georgia Troops during the Civil War*, 1.

In Thomas's Brigade, desertions were minimal but unauthorized absentees were "returning by the multitudes," which more than doubled the size of the brigade.[14] Most soldiers who took short unauthorized absences voluntarily rejoined their units, anticipating only a mild punishment upon their return, such as extra duties, restriction to camp, or forfeiture of pay.[15] But for those who took longer absences or were returned involuntarily, execution was the ultimate sanction and it was usually carried out in a manner to serve as a deterrent to others.[16] Although an execution meant there was one less soldier to fight for the South, as Confederate Surgeon Spencer Glasgow Welch wrote, "there was no other way to put a stop to desertions."[17] In fact, Welch, in a comment of unexpected severity from someone who healed lives, lamented that the executions had not started sooner. In an odd twist on words, he wrote, "It is most unfortunate that this thing of shooting men for desertion was not begun sooner. Many lives would have been saved by it, because a great many men will now have to be shot before the trouble can be stopped."[18]

Hall notes on September 19, 1863, that two North Carolinians of Lane's Brigade had been shot for desertion.[19] The 14th Georgia witnessed the execution of one of its

---

14. Folsom advertised a reward of $30 each to whomever returned two named deserters (neither from Company G), to the nearest Conscript Camp. One of the soldiers was alleged to have "deserted in the face of the enemy on the 12th of December last" (during the battle of Fredericksburg) and was rumored to have returned to Georgia. "$30 Reward. H'DQ'S 14th Regiment GA VOLS," *Southern Confederacy*, February 4, 1863, https://gahistoricnewspapers.galileo.usg.edu. The ad provided the soldier's name, age, height, complexion, hair color, and eye color. However, the detail that he was wearing "grey pants and jacket, and cap" likely did little to narrow the field of suspects.
15. Glatthaar, *General Lee's Army*, 409.
16. Death by firing squad was the usual method of execution, although Ella Lonn reported an event in February 1864 where twenty-two deserters in North Carolina were hanged. She was skeptical of one story that reported that a deserter had been crucified. Lonn, 59, 61. Regardless of method, executions occurred during the Civil War more frequently than in any conflict in U.S. history. Drew Gilpin Faust, *This Republic of Suffering: Death and the American Civil War* (Vintage, 2008), 27.
17. Spencer Glasgow Welch, *A Confederate Surgeon's Letters to His Wife* (Neal Publishing 1911), 58.
18. Welch, *A Confederate Surgeon's Letters*, 79-80.
19. These men belonged to the 33rd North Carolina. For the execution, the brigade was formed in three sides of a square. While the band played the "dead march," the two condemned soldiers were marched with their spiritual advisors to two stakes where the men were tied and blindfolded. Twenty-four men served as the firing squad, with half of the guns loaded with blanks to ease the consciences of the executioners. Hardy, *General Lee's Immortals*, 310-11.

own, along with a North Carolina soldier from Scales's Brigade, on September 26.[20] Hall wrote that the men were "shot to death with musketry" and "it was the most solumn scene I ever saw." The soldier from the 14th Georgia was Company B's Private Romulus Dixon, who had been sentenced to death on September 1, 1863, for leaving the regiment for two days during the battle at Chancellorsville and for feigning a wound (and forging a surgeon's certificate of disability) at Gettysburg.[21] Although sentenced to die for cowardice, Dixon, according to one witness, refused a blindfold and "died without a quiver."[22] Dixon died instantly after being struck by six balls but the North Carolinian was struck only once and lingered in death. Afterwards, the troops were marched past the corpses as a measure of deterrence.

As to military operations, the latter part of 1863 was relatively quiet in comparison to the spring and summer months. Lee had wanted to launch another major offensive in late 1863 but Jefferson Davis had other priorities. Ultimately two brigades from Longstreet's corps were sent to assist General Braxton Bragg in Tennessee. Lee did run a small offensive campaign, the Bristoe Campaign beginning in early October. Meade's army was encamped less than twenty miles from Lee, who thought that turning Meade's right flank would force the Army of the Potomac to withdraw closer to Washington and leave the Culpeper–Orange line to Lee. Lee marched his troops from their encampment on Clark's Mountain over the Cedar Mountain battlefield, and then to Warrenton, hoping to turn Meade's flank. But Meade deduced Lee's plans and began withdrawing his forces to the northeast to protect Washington. Hill caught up to the Union rear guard at Bristoe Station and, without waiting for support, attacked what he thought were isolated Union troops of III Corps and V Corps. Hill realized he had walked into a trap when II Corps troops emerged from behind a railroad embankment. Hill's failure to conduct adequate reconnaissance resulted in a Union victory and almost

---

20. Surgeon Welch wrote his wife that on September 26, there were also seven more executions from Lane's Brigade. Welch, *A Confederate Surgeon's Letters*, 79. Welch was tasked afterwards with dissecting two of them. Ibid., 80.
21. Fox, *Red Clay to Richmond*, 202-203.
22. Fox, *Red Clay to Richmond*, 202. Dixon's reputation within the brigade was that he was a "gambler and reckless character" but appeared resigned to his fate. Jeffrey C. Lowe and Sam Hodges, eds., *Letters to Amanda: The Civil War Letters of Marion Hill Fitzpatrick, Army of Northern Virginia* (Mercer University Press, 1998), 90.

1,900 Confederate casualties, nearly one man every two seconds of the engagement.[23] Wilcox's Division, minus the 35th Georgia which was guarding a wagon train, marched double quick time but arrived at the end of the engagement, too late to assist Hill but just enough time to undergo Union artillery fire.[24]

A few days later Thomas's Brigade commenced tearing up the rail lines of the Orange & Alexandria Railroad, beginning in Warrenton and ending at the Rappahannock Bridge, where they tossed track iron into the river. Working in torrential rains, the brigade, as Hall wrote, "camped as wet as drowned rats." The destruction of the railroad continued the next day. However, the cool rainy conditions presaged illness for Hall, who developed a fever and a cough that lingered for almost two weeks.

Denying the enemy of the use of the rails was a new element in warfare. This image shows the tracks of the Orange & Alexandria Railroad after they were destroyed by Confederate forces. (Library of Congress)

Although the 14th Georgia had changed camp numerous times over the previous three months, Hall believed in early November that the regiment had finally settled into their winter quarters. The regiment had already commenced building oak shanties for the winter in one location but wound up returning to the

---

23. Robertson, *General A. P. Hill*, 239. Robertson noted that notwithstanding the debacle at Bristoe Station, the campaign itself was a strategic success because Lee had forced Meade to retreat and the Confederates had wrecked miles of the Orange & Alexandria Railroad. Ibid., 239-240.
24. Douglas Southall Freeman describes Hill's actions at Bristoe Station as the most badly managed battle that had ever been fought by the Army of Northern Virginia. Freeman, *Lee* (Harwell abridgment), 352.

camp area they had occupied just prior to the start of the Bristoe Campaign. The brigade moved even further east in late November, marching on the Orange Plank Road towards Fredericksburg for Meade's Mine Run campaign, where Meade considered mounting an offensive to close out the campaigning year; however, the Union troops took so long to get in place that Lee had time to fortify his position. Thomas's Brigade did not take part in the small battle at Mine Run on November 27, 1863, but instead remained in line of battle at the edge of the Wilderness.

On December 3, the brigade marched back to the "comfortable quarters" they had left the previous week at Clark's Mountain near Orange Court House. By December 9, Company G had settled into what Hall described as "verry warm shanties." But less than a week later, Hall's expectations for a comfortable winter were dashed when Thomas's Brigade received short notice to march on December 15, 1863. Lee had temporarily detached the brigade to the command of Maj. Gen. Jubal Early, whom Lee had tasked to deal with pesky Union General William Averell, whose cavalrymen were wreaking havoc raiding the Shenandoah Valley. Averell appeared to be heading south to Salem, Virginia, a major rail station on the Virginia and Tennessee Railroad that the 14th Georgia had passed through in July 1861 en route to Lynchburg. On the night of December 15, 1863, all four of Thomas's regiments took the cars on the Alexandria and Orange Railroad to Gordonsville, where they changed trains and then rode on crowded Virginia Central Railroad cars through Charlottesville and Staunton to Buffalo Gap. The Virginia Central rail cars were so overloaded that some men were forced to ride in open cars.

Joseph Waddell of Staunton noted in his journal on December 15 and December 16, 1863, that trainloads of soldiers had been arriving in Staunton; he surmised that the troops passing through "must be intended to cut off the retreat" of Union soldiers who had destroyed the Virginia and Tennessee Railroad in Salem, but none of the officers he spoke with had any knowledge of where they were headed.[25] Waddell added that "it was distressing to see many of our poor fellows who had just arrived, without blankets and overcoats. As a mass they were dirty, ragged and badly clad, but lively as usual, extracting fun from everything."[26]

---

25. Waddell, *Augusta County: Diary*, https://valley.lib.virginia.edu/papers/AD1500
26. Waddell, *Augusta County: Diary*.

Early was too late to intercept Averell and prevent the Union sacking of Salem. In the span of only six hours at Salem on December 16, 1863, Union forces had cut the telegraph wires, demolished a water station and turntable, set fire to the depot and several bridges, tore up rail track, and destroyed supplies.[27] Early hoped to intercept Averell on the Union cavalryman's return north. All four of Thomas's regiments rode the rail cars from Buffalo Gap back to Staunton, where the 14th Georgia and 45th Georgia disembarked and the 35th Georgia and 49th Georgia rode west to Millboro.

The 14th Georgia spent a cold night outdoors in a bitter wind in Staunton before finding some old houses for shelter.[28] On December 19, 1863, the 14th Georgia and 45th Georgia rejoined the other two regiments at Millboro, which the men of the 14th Georgia had last seen as they were winding up the calamitous Western Virginia Campaign two years earlier.[29] Early again failed to intercept Averell, however, due in part to poor weather that slowed Early's infantry but also to Averell's unexpected decision to take a westerly route up a portion of the Huntersville-Huttonsville Turnpike in what had just become the new state of West Virginia several months earlier.

Having just missed Averell, Thomas's Brigade rode by rail from Millboro back to Staunton on December 20, 1863. However, their stay in Staunton lasted less than a day. When news came that another Union force was raiding Harrisonburg, the brigade marched over thirty-five miles north from Staunton in a bitter, driving winter wind, only to find the Union troops exiting Harrisonburg just as Thomas's troops arrived. The regiment then marched nine miles to camp at New Market. Hall wrote that by the time they got to camp, he could barely put one foot in front of the other.

Hall spent Christmas encamped at New Market, where he attended Sunday worship, possibly at Smith Creek Baptist Church, on December 27, 1863. He spent the last days of the year marching up the Shenandoah Valley, sleeping at night in the cold open air. As Hall's last words for the year, he wrote: "The last of 1863. It's gone never to return." The new year would prove to be even more eventful for Hall than 1863 had been.

---

27. Mark A. Snell, *West Virginia in the Civil War: Mountaineers Are Always Free* (History Press, 2011), 117; Robert N. Thompson, "William Averell's Cavalry Raid on the Virginia & Tennessee Railroad," *America's Civil War* (November 2000), accessed July 24, 2020 at https://www.historynet.com/william-averells-cavalry-raid-on-the-virginia-tennessee-railroad.htm
28. Thompson, "William Averell's Cavalry Raid."
29. Fox, *Red Clay to Richmond*, 221.

Remembrancer Daily Entries
July 25 – December 31, 1863

Saturday, July 25, 1863

Par fair & hot. We marched again at day and arrived in two miles of Culpeper Court House and camped.

Sunday, July 26, 1863

M fair & warm. E thun & rain. There come a thunder cloud last night and good rain which cooled the air verry much. Today is not as hot as yesterday was. We remain in camp & and attend preaching in the 20th N.C. regt. The Lord is good to us in letting us rest and hear his blessed word once and a while.

Monday, July 27, 1863

M cloudy & warm. E rain. Today about 10 oclock we got orders to march to a new and better camp a mile or two distant where we arrived and camped and drew two days rations and there is more Blackberries here than I ever saw.

Tuesday, July 28, 1863

M par fair & warm. E rain & thunder. Every thing quiet and us poor tired and worn out Soldiers is taking a good rest, but it will not last long for there is not much rest for us during this cruel and wicked war, but there is better day for us in a house not made with hands.

Wednesday, July 29, 1863

M par cloudy & warm. E thunder & rain. We still remain in camp. The weather is warm and showery. Nothing new. Every thing quiet. We get orders to have roll call three times a day and post regimental guard.

Thursday, July 30, 1863

Nothing new only about 300 North Carolinians deserted last night and started home. Great numbers of them deserted and went to the Yankees at Gettysburg.

Friday, July 31, 1863

Fair & hot. On Regimental guard. Nothing of importance. We get orders to cook up rations and be ready to move. Capt Fulton that was wounded at Gettysburg returned this evening.

Saturday, August 1, 1863

Fair and extremely hot. At 4 or 5 oclock this evening we get orders to march. We march out in an old field North of Culpepper C H [Court House] and remain till near midnight and then march into a piece of woods and cook rations.

Sunday, August 2, 1863

Fair and Hot. It was day this morning before we got our rations cooked. We remained in camp till near 12 A.M. and then marched one or two miles and filed out in the woods and stayed there the remainder of the day. The weather seems the Hotest I ever experienced. Brother Hyman preached a good sermon for us this evening.

Monday, August 3, 1863

Fair & hot. We fall in verry soon this morning and march through Culpeper C H [Court House] and in direction of Orange C.H. [Court House]. About 12 A.M. we file out into the woods to rest for the weather is so hot several of our men fainted with heat on the road and we are now on the Battle field of Cedar Run which was fought Aug 8 1862. We left there about 4 P.M. and marched till dark and camped and had two days rations and we had to set up nearly all night to cook and I felt verry [ ] from the excessive heat.

Pocket Notebook
Monday, August 3, 1863[30]

Once more we are in camps permited by the blessings of God to hear his dear name preached and to meet around our beloved chaplain each evening at the going down of the great orb of day, to worship and send up thanks and adoration to <u>Him</u> that sends us those beautiful evening and gives us time and opportuneity to meet here. The happiest hours of my life, is the hours [of] our humble prayer meetings. The hardships, toils and dangers of this unholy war seems to be forgotten and my mind and soul soars away to that bright and happy home above. My thoughts are no longer bound to the beggarly elements of the world, but go away to things not seen by mortal sight, things that perish not but are eternal. Oh! Those blissful hours, how happy they are. A happiness is mine I knew not a few months ago. Bro Moore preached for us before noon and the Chaplain of the 10th Ala after noon.

Tuesday, August 4, 1863

M cloudy & hot. E thunder clo. At 5 A.M. we march again. We cross Rapid Ann [Rapidan] river and camped near Orange Court House in a beautiful peice of woods. I am sick and have a fever and severe cough this evening.

Wednesday, August 5, 1863

M fair & hot. E thunder clouds. I continue verry sick from the excessive fatigue I have been through for the last

---

30. This appears to be the last dated entry in Hall's Pocket Notebook. All of Hall's entries after this date were written in the *Remembrancer*.

few days but I hope the Lord will soon restore me. Prayer meeting in Co[mpany] A.

Thursday, August 6, 1863

M fair & Hot. E thun showers. I feel a good deal better this morning. I write a letter home to my dear old mother. It rains a cool and refreshing shower in the evening. Prayer Meeting in co B.

Friday, August 7, 1863

M fair & Hot. E thun & rain. Every thing quiet. I wash my cloth[e]s.

Saturday, August 8, 1863

M fair & hot. E thun & rain. Nothing new. Prayer meeting in company C.

Sunday, August 9, 1863

Fair & warm. This day is beautiful. The sky is clear and blue. We have divine services before noon and after noon. Our chaplain and chaplain of the 10 Ala regt preached for us and the spirit of the Lord seemed to be with us.

Monday, August 10, 1863

Fair & hot. Nothing new. Prayer meeting and preaching before and after noon.

Tuesday, August 11, 1863

Fair & Hot. Every thing still and quiet in this vicinity. We have [a] verry interesting prayer meeting in our regt every evening and the Lord seems to be with us.

Wednesday, August 12, 1863

Fair & hot. E thunder. We have brigade inspection. Preaching and Prayer meeting in the evening.

Thursday, August 13, 1863

M cloudy & rainy. E rainy. Nothing new. Preaching by Bro Hyman.

Friday, August 14, 1863

M fair & hot. E thun & rain. We go on picket on the

Rapid Ann [Rapidan]. Have a verry pleasant time. My whole trust is in the Lord and the sweet consolation and peice of mind is worth ten thousand times more than any thing in this wicked world.

Saturday, August 15, 1863

Fair & Hot. Return off picket. Have divine service. The spirit of the Lord is with us. A revival has commenced in our brigade. I hope will spread from heart to heart till all receives joy and peace.

Sunday, August 16, 1863

M fair & Hot. E thun & rain. We have service before and after noon. Nine of our Brigade joined the church today. Although a war of death and destruction surrounds us we have happy days now.

Monday, August 17, 1863

No news. Every thing quiet. We have a verry interesting prayer meeting this evening. The Lord is with us. Fair & warm. Company & s[k]irmish drill.

Tuesday, August 18, 1863

Fair & warm. We have divine service before noon. A reverend old gentlemen a captain in the 42 Miss regt preached for us. We get orders from Gen Lee to furlough seven men from the regiment. Prayer meeting. Two drills.

Wednesday, August 19, 1863

Fair & warm. Nights cool. I attend the ordinance of baptism. 6 were baptised from Wrights Brigade. Preaching afternoon. The happiest prayer meeting we ever had. 8 of our regt joined the church. Two drills.

Thursday, August 20, 1863

Fair & warm. Nothing new. On Brigade guard. Prayer meeting at night. Sent letter Home.

Friday, August 21, 1863

Fair & warm. A day of fasting humiliation and prayer.

Had 3 sermons and prayer meetings. I hope [God] will answer our prayers and send us speedy deliverence.

Saturday, August 22, 1863

Fair & Hot. We had another verry interesting prayer meeting. The Holy Spirit is certainly with us. 6 or 7 more united with Gods people. This is one of the most Happy times of my life.

Sunday, August 23, 1863

This morning I attended the ordinance of baptism. Eleven were baptized from our brigade. We had three good sermons and the last one at night was the most interesting I ever witnessed in my life. It was enough to melt the heart of a brute much less mans and I wish such happy scenes would last all my life.

Monday, August 24, 1863

M fair & Hot. E thun & rain. Every thing quiet. Battalion drill in the evening on account of rain. We had no prayer meeting.

Tuesday, August 25, 1863

M hot. E thunder & rain. Today I am 22 years of age. Nothing new.

Wednesday, August 26, 1863

Fair & cool. Bat[talion] drill. No news. A good little prayer meeting. Lieutenant Abbett joined the church.[31]

Thursday, August 27, 1863

Fair & cool. On Brigade guard. Prayer meeting in the evening. No news.

Friday, August 28, 1863

Fair & pleasant. Preaching & prayer meeting. Four more joined the church of God. His holy spirit is certainly with us. Bat[talion] drill.

---

31. This is likely a reference to Armstead Abbott, first lieutenant of Company D, 14th Georgia.

Saturday, August 29, 1863

Fair & cool. E some rain. Nothing new. Bat[talion] drill. We have a little prayer meeting in co[mpany] D.

Sunday, August 30, 1863

Fair & cool. A beautiful day though rather cool. We had two good sermons. My mind was calm and serene and I hope spent the day in honor and glory of my blessed Master. Prayer meeting in co[mpany] H.

Monday, August 31, 1863

Fair & pleasant. Every thing quiet. General muster. Bat[talion] drill. Prayer meeting in co[mpany] C.

Tuesday, September 1, 1863

Fair & cool. No news. Prayer meeting in co[mpany] D. General review of our Division.

Wednesday, September 2, 1863

Fair & pleasant. Every thing quiet. No new movements. Bat[talion] drill. Prayer meeting in the evening at the stand. It was quite interesting.

Thursday, September 3, 1863

Fair & pleasant. On regimental guard. Another Happy little prayer meeting.

Friday, September 4, 1863

Partially cloudy & warm. Prayer meeting. Bat[talion] drill. Every thing still and quiet. Not a ripple disturbs the calm serenity.

Saturday, September 5, 1863

Fair & pleasant. No news. The weather is dry and dusty. An interesting little prayer meeting at night.

Sunday, September 6, 1863

Fair & pleasant. We had two good sermons and two of the happiest prayer meetings I ever had the pleasure of attending.

Monday, September 7, 1863

Fair & pleasant. We have a good sermon at night by Reverend Mr. Wells. Bat drill.

Tuesday, September 8, 1863

Fair & warm. No news. Every thing still and quiet. Mr Wells preaches for us again at candle light. Bat drill. Recd letter from home.

Wednesday, September 9, 1863

Fair & warm. Prayer meeting at night. Bat drill.

Thursday, September 10, 1863

Cloudy & pleasant. On regimental guard and Brigade review. Prayer meeting but I was not present.

Friday, September 11, 1863

Cloudy & warm. General review of our corps. The ground is powerful dry and dusty. Gens Lee, Hill, Wilcox, Andersen and Heath was present.

Saturday, September 12, 1863

M fair & warm. E thunder and rain. I attended the ordinance of baptism. 42 were baptised.

Sunday, September 13, 1863

Thunder & rain. We had two good sermons to day but the last one was interrupted by the rain.

Monday, September 14, 1863

M cloudy. E fair & warm. We had quite a disturbance. Last night after prayer meeting we first received order to get ready to move at a moments warning. We then received orders to cook one days rations and about midnight we got orders to be ready to march this morning at day light, and at day light we received orders to strike tents but we did not leave. After noon we drew 3 days rations and were ordered to cook them. Received a letter from Mother immediately. We can hear a rapid fire of cannon in the direction of Rapid Ann [Rapidan] station which lasted till dark. We have a verry interesting meeting to night. Rev Mr Wells preached for us. 3 united with the church.

Tuesday, September 15, 1863

M cloudy. E fair & warm. We still remain in camp expecting to leave at any moment. Have prayer meeting. 2 joins the church. Every thing seems quiet. We double our pickets on the river.

Wednesday, September 16, 1863

M foggy. E par cloudy & warm. At 6 oclock this morning our regt and the 35th goes on picket on the river. The enemy does not seem to be verry close only in small bodies of cavalry and their designs is unknown at present but I think they are trying to draw our attention from other points.

Thursday, September 17, 1863

Cloudy & rain. We return off picket. Have prayer meeting at night. 3 more joined the church. Every thing apariently quiet.

Friday, September 18, 1863

M hard rain. E par fair. The rain fell with violence today harder than it has rained in a long time before. On regimental guard. At 9 oclock P.M. we get orders to cook one days rations. Prayer meeting.

Saturday, September 19, 1863

Cool & cloudy. Some rain. Nothing new, only 2 North Carolinians of Leanes [Lane's] brig was shot for desertion. Prayer meeting at night.

Sunday, September 20, 1863

Fair & cool. Preaching by Bro Moore. Two happy little prayer meetings in the evening.

Monday, September 21, 1863

Fair & cool. Every thing quiet. Wrote letter home.

Tuesday, September 22, 1863

Fair & cool. At 2 oclock this morning we got orders to be ready to march at daylight and at daylight we started up

Rapid ann [Rapidan] river and marched up 6 miles from camp. We could hear the boom of cannon and soon heard that Gen Stuart was engaged with the enemy near Madison C. H. [Court House]. It drew nearer till evening the enemy tried to surround Gen Stuarts cavalry force but they cut their way out and whiped the enemy and drove them back taking several hundred prisoners. Their was fighting all along the lines today. Our regt went on picket on the opposite Side of the river and looked to be attacked every minute.

Wednesday, September 23, 1863

M frost. E fair & cool. This morning we are relieved off picket by the 35th and return and join the Brig[ade] on the south side of the river, and in the evening we march out 2 or 3 miles and camp. We had frost this morning the first this year.

Thursday, September 24, 1863.

M cool. E fair & pleasant. To day we march back to our old camp and remain an hour or two and march to new camp higher up the river and camp in a beautiful place. Good news from Gen Bragg.[32] The weather is pleasant beautiful and reminds me of day past and gone.

Friday, September 25, 1863

M cloudy. E fair & cool. On guard, guarding cornfield. Have roasting ears for breakfast, beans, for dinner and pumkin for supper.

Saturday, September 26, 1863

Fair & cool. Today our Brigade marches out and witnesses the execution of two deserters shot to death with musketry. It was the most solumn scene I ever saw.

Sunday, September 27, 1863

M frosty. E fair & cool. Bro Pope preached for us at night.

---

32. This is likely a reference to the Confederate victory under Braxton Bragg at Chickamauga, Georgia, on September 19, 1863.

Monday, September 28, 1863

M cool & fair & pleas. We go on picket on the Rapid Ann [Rapidan]. Have quite a pleasant time. Every thing still and quiet. We have beautiful moon light night.

Tuesday, September 29, 1863

M cool. E fair & Pleas. We return off picket. Attend meeting. Bro Hyman preaches.

Wednesday, September 30, 1863

Fair & pleasant. Nothing of importance. Prayer meeting in our regt.

Thursday, October 1, 1863

Partially cloudy. On regimental guard. Prayer meeting but I could not attend.

Friday, October 2, 1863

Cool & rainey all day. Nothing of importance.

Saturday October 3, 1863

Fair & pleasant. Bro Hyman preaches for us. Two of our regt joins the church.

Sunday, October 4, 1863

Fair & Pleasant. Our regt goes on picket. 7 cavalry men are baptised by Bro Hyman. I gained a great consolation from the word of God.

Monday, October 5, 1863

Fair & very cold. I received a letter from my dear Mother far away yesterday evening. We return off picket. Prayer meeting.

Tuesday, October 6, 1863

Fair & cold. Nothing of importance. Prayer Meeting.

Wednesday, October 7, 1863

Cloudy & cool. E rain. Today we held elections for Governer, Congress, Senators, and reprasentatives. Sent letter home. Nothing new. Only it is rumored we will leave here before long.

Thursday, October 8, 1863

Fair & cool. This morning we get orders to cook 3 day rations and hold ourselves in readiness to march. Prayer meeting.

Friday, October 9, 1863

M fair & frost. E cool. This morning at daylight we march, cross the river and march in a N Western direction. Camp verry cautiously in the evening near Madison C. H. [Court House}. Camp fires are forbiden till after dark and then verry small. We have a little secret prayer meeting.

Saturday, October 10, 1863

Cool & cloudy. E little rain. We resume the march at daylight, move cautiously and avoid high eminenses and open places where troops can be seen from a distance, wind about in a circuitous rout[e], the greater part of the day through thick woods and old fields making a wide trail as we go. We crossed Robertson river and camp for the night.[33]

Sunday, October 11, 1863

M frost. E fair & beautiful. At 7 oclock A.M. we march again in a northern direction in the same manner we did yesterday, cross another small river, cross the turnpike leading from Culpeper C.H. [Court House] to Front Royal. Our advance surprises yankee pickets several times during the day and capture some of them. We camp 6 or 8 miles west of Cul[peper] C. H. [Court House] and cook 2 days rations. Have to set up nearly all night. We hear the enemy is retreating in the direction of Manassas, and I expect we will pursue them tomorrow.

Monday, October 12, 1863

M cool. E fair & pleasant. We resumed the march soon

---

33. This is likely a reference to the Robinson River, a tributary of the Rapidan River in Madison County, Virginia.

this morning, cross Hazel river. Move in the same maner we did the two previous days except with less caution. We camp near a small village called Amosville [Amissville]. Our regt goes on picket. We have a cold time.

Tuesday, October 13, 1863

M frosty. E par cloudy. We march at daylight, cross the Rappahannock river. March at quick time. Pass through old yankee camps all day. Camp near Warrenton, and cook two days rations. Set up all night nearly.

Wednesday, October 14, 1863

M cool & cloudy. E a little rain. We pass through Warrenton which is a beautiful village. Hear cannon and musketry ahead of us. We march verry hard, pass a village called Greenwich, where some of the enemy was camped last night. Cannon is firing rapidly in front of all the time. We march double quick. Meet wounded men and prisoners constant. We file left, form a line of Battle. The bombs fall thick amongst us. We see the dark lines of the enemy ahead of [us]. Nights shades gathers over the scene. The flashes like a thunder cloud. The shells bursting in the air is a scene pen cannot describe.

Thursday, October 15, 1863

M cloudy. E rainy & mudy. The cannonading continued till a late hour last night. The morning the enemy had disappeared, and cannonading in the direction of Centreville soon told they had retreated thither. We remain in line of battle and cook two days rations till nearly night and fell in and marched to the railroad near Bristol [Bristoe] Station in a few miles of Manassas junction and marched down the R. R. till about 11 P M. The mud was intolerable. We camp. The rain fall slow but steady.

Friday, October 16, 1863

Cool & hard rain. We march at daylight, pass Catlett

Station and at Warrenton junction our division commences tearing up and destroying the Orange & Alexandria R R which was hard and muddy work. The rain falling in torrents constant, in the evening there arose a thunder storm and the hardest rain I have ever seen in Va. We adjourned from destroying the R. R. and camped as wet as drowned rats. The earth was covered with water (the country being verry flat) and it was a long time before we could get fire started to warm and dry ourselves for we were shaking like we had an ague.

Saturday, October 17, 1863

Fair & cool. We resumed tearing up the R R again this morning and continued till we got to the Rappahannock and camped before night, and cook two days rations. About 2,000 yankee prisoners passed us taken near Manassas. To day was fair but the ground verry muddy.

Sunday, October 18, 1863

Fair & cool. We got ready to march this morning but had to wait for a bridge to be built across the river, and we started once but turn back and stayed in camp all night on account of the bridge haven broken down.

Monday, October 19, 1863

M cold & rainy. E fair & cool. We were awakened before day this morning by heavy rain, and we were soon drenched to the skin and shivering like we had an ague. 8 or 9 oclock we started wading mud and water over knee deep. We stoped along standing in the road till after 12 A.M. before we cross the river. We camp 3 or 4 miles from where we crossed the river. Drawed two days rations of flour, beef & salt. I have got a cold and cough that is verry bad.

Tuesday, October 20, 1863

Par cloudy & cool. I am verry sick today with a severe cold & cough and headache. We remain in camp. Capt Harris preached for the Brigade today.

Wednesday, October 21, 1863

Fair & cool. I continue sick. Have a considerable fever. A chaplain in Mcgowins [McGowan's] Brigade pre[a]ched for us today. We draw 3 day rations of flour beef & salt.

Thursday, October 22, 1863

Par cloudy & cool. I feel some better to day than I did yesterday.

Friday, October 23, 1863

M clo & cool. E cold rain. Nothing of importance. I continue to have a verry bad cold & cough and fe[e]l verry bad.

Saturday, October 24, 1863

Cold rainy & windy. The weather is cold, wet and disagreeable. If we attempt to warm by a fire the smoke nearly sufocates us. We draw 2 days rations of flour Bacon & salt.

Sunday, October 25, 1863

Fair cold & windy. Nothing new. The weather and smoke is verry disagreeable.

Monday, October 26, 1863

Fair cold & windy. On regimental Guard. We draw 2 days rations of flour, beef & salt. [S]end letter home. We hear cannonading in a northern direction.

Tuesday, October 27, 1863

Cloudy windy & cold. My cough continues as verry bad and troubles me verry much. Nothing of importance.

Wednesday, October 28, 1863

Fair cold & frosty. We draw 3 day rations of flour beet & salt. Bat[talion] drill. My cold & cough is verry bad.

Thursday, October 29, 1863

Fair & frosty. No news stiring. Battalion drill.

Friday, October 30, 1863

Par cloudy cold & windy. My cough is terrable. I have a light fever every morning. Bat[talion] drill.

Saturday, October 31, 1863

M cold & rainy. E fair. Gen Muster day. We draw 2 days rations of flour beef & salt. The wind blows verry Hard and cold from the north tonight.

Sunday, November 1, 1863

Fair & cold. On regimental Guard. Our chaplain delivered us a good sermon. The evening is warmer & beautiful.

Monday, November 2, 1863

Fair frosty & cold. We draw 2 months wages $22.00. We draw one days rations of flour & bacon.

Tuesday, November 3, 1863

M cold. E fair & pleas. We draw 3 days rations of flour, beef & salt. Bat[talion] drill.

Wednesday, November 4, 1863

M cold. E fair & pleas. Nothing of importance. Bat[talion] drill.

Thursday, November 5, 1863

M frosty. E fair & pleasant. We go on picket our regt this morning on the Rappahannock.

Friday, November 6, 1863

Cold & windy. We return off picket. Move to new camps about 5 miles distant near Culpepper C. H. [Court House]. Commence winter quarters.

Saturday, November 7, 1863

M frosty. E cold & windy. We draw 4 days rations of flour one of beef.

Sunday, November 8, 1863

M fair & cold. E cloudy. We lay down to sleep last night as we thought in peace and security. Our regt had commenced building Shanties out of oak logs and had several already up ready to put on the roof. About midnight orders come to get ready to move immediately before daylight. We march out and form line of battle a mile or so from camp and remain all day. The enemies cavalry attacked part of our division and was repulsed. At dark we march again all night in the weather severly cold. Passed through Culpepper C H.

Monday, November 9, 1863

M cold & cloudy. E snow. We halt this morning 2 hours before day and rest till daylight. March again cross Robertson [Robinson] river march on cross Rapid Ann [Rapidan] river to our old camps we left Oct 9. Verry tired and hungry not having eat anything since Saturday. We also had snow the first this season and we draw 3 days rations of beef and cooked and eat. We suffered verry much from cold on this march, some of us entirely barefooted. I do not expect we will stay here long as the enemy is following us.

Tuesday, November 10, 1863

Fair cold & windy. Nothing of importance. We draw 2 day rations of flour beef & salt.

Wednesday, November 11, 1863

Fair cold & windy. Every thing appears quiet. The weather is cold & severe.

Thursday, November 12, 1863

Fair & cool. We draw 3 days rations of flour & salt. 2 of bacon.

Friday, November 13, 1863

Fair & pleasant. We get orders this morning to cook 2 day rations and be ready to march at a moments warning.

Saturday, November 14, 1863

M fair & warm. E rain. Everything quiet. Gen Ewells corps had an engagement with the enemy yesterday. We have not heard the particulars.

Sunday, November 15, 1863

M rainy. E cloudy & cool. Our regt went on picket this morning and we was wet to the Skin by a cold rain. About

3 PM our division was in commotion and marched out preparatory to leaving when the order was countermanded.

Monday, November 16, 1863

Fair & cool. We return off picket with the expectation of leaving soon but when we arrived in camp every thing was quiet. Draw 2 days beef, flour & salt.

Tuesday, November 17, 1863

Fair & cold. Nothing new.

Wednesday, November 18, 1863

Par cloudy & cold. On regimental guard. I attend prayer meeting in Co[mpany] C. Drew 2 days flour bacon & salt.

Thursday, November 19, 1863

Fair & cool. Nothing of interest.

Friday, November 20, 1863

M fair. E cloudy. Draw two months wages. Draw 2 days flour beef & salt.

Saturday, November 21, 1863

Hard rain all day. We go on picket. Have a wet disagreeable time on the Rapid Ann [Rapidan].

Sunday, November 22, 1863

Fair & cool. Return off picket. Received letter from home last Thursday. Draw 1 day of flour & beef.

Monday, November 23, 1863

Fair & cool. Nothing New. Draw 2 days rations of flour Beef & salt.

Tuesday, November 24, 1863

Rainey & cold. All quiet.

Wednesday, November 25, 1863

Fair & cold. Draw 3 days flour & salt 2 bacon 1 beef. Recd letter from R. R. Jenkins.[34]

---

34. This is likely a reference to Royal R. Jenkins of Worth County, who served as a lieutenant in the 10th Georgia Battalion but resigned his commission in September 1863.

Thursday, November 26, 1863

Cold & frosty. About 9 oclock tonight we get orders to cook 1 days rations and be ready to march at a moments warning. Near midnight we get orders to cook all we got and march at 4 oclock A.M.

Friday, November 27, 1863

Cold & severe weather. At 4 A.M. we march. The ground is frozen. March through Orange C.H. [Court House] in the direction of Fredericksburg on the plank Road. We march hard all day. Hear the boom of cannon ahead of us. All the evening, near sun set we file out, form line of Battle right and left of the road. Hear rapid skirmishing in front and see Scores of wounded passing to the rear.[35]

Saturday, November 28, 1863

Cold & rainy. We remained in line all night. Before good light this morning We march toward the rear about 2 miles from line of Battle and commenced breastworks. Remain an hour or two. March again to the front about a mile from line of Battle again and build breastworks all day and the cold rain falling fast.

Sunday, November 29, 1863

Cold cloudy & windy. In line of Battle expecting to be attacked today. We are in a wilderness. The undergrowth nearly unimpenetrable. My trust is in the Lord of Host.[36]

Thursday, December 3, 1863

Par cloudy & cold. At 5 oclock A.M. We march again. Pass Orange C H to our old camps we left last Friday. We were verry tired, sore and worn out, and glad to get back to our comfortable quarters once more.

---

35. This is likely a reference to the Mine Run campaign.
36. Thayer typed a line of periods across the page here, perhaps to signify illegible entries for the period November 30 through December 2, 1863.

Friday, December 4, 1863

Fair & cold. Our reg[iment] goes on picket. Every thing quiet. We [hear] Gen Braggs army has been defeated.[37]

Saturday, December 5, 1863

Fair & cold. Return off picket, draw 2 days rations of flour & beef. Nothing new.

Sunday, December 6, 1863

Fair & cold. The weather is cold and severe. Send letter Home.

Monday, December 7, 1863

Cold freezing Severe. Send letter to R R J.[38] Every thing still & quiet.

Tuesday, December 8, 1863

Fair frosty & cold. Nothing of importance.

Wednesday, December 9, 1863

Fair frosty & cold. We are now verry comfortable Situated. All the co[mpany] has verry warm Shanties.

Thursday, December 10, 1863

Fair, cold, frosty & windy. This is a day set apart by Gov Brown for fasting Humiliation & prayer. We have two prayer meetings.

Friday, December 11, 1863

Cloudy & cold. Our regt goes on picket to Barnets ford on the Rapid Ann [Rapidan].

Saturday, December 12, 1863

Rainy & cold. Return off picket.

Sunday, December 13, 1863

M rain. E fair & pleasant. Last night John D. Hale one of our companions in arms departed This life after a Short

---

37. This is likely a reference to the Union victory at Chattanooga, Tennessee, in late November, 1863.
38. This is likely a reference to Royal Jenkins.

and Sudden illness.[39] He was only sick 24 hours. His Spirit has flown into a world unknown.

Monday, December 14, 1863

Cold rainy & Stormy. I visited Orange C[ourt] H[ouse] today. All quiet.

Tuesday, December 15, 1863

Fair & cold. Our regt was detailed to work on the Streets of Orange C. H. and was ordered to cook rations and get ready to march.

Wednesday, December 16, 1863

Cloudy & cold. At 4 oclock yesterday evening we marched to Orange C. H. and after standing about in the cold till about 10 P.M. we left on the cars. At Gordonsville we changed trains and after being delayed a considerable time in the cold we left on the Va Central R.R. We run at a verry Slow rate being over loaded. We passed Charlotsville just before daylight and Waynesborough & Staunton and at buffalo Gap we remained Stationary all night. The car Boxes was crow[d]ed so we passed an uncomfortable night.

Thursday, December 17, 1863

Cold rain & Sleet. We return to Staunton. Get off the cars march out 2 miles and camp in the ice and pass a cold disagreeable. It Sleets all night.

Friday, December 18, 1863

Fair windy & cold. Draw 3 rations of flour 1 of bacon. About 10 A.M. we march again to Staunton. Remain Standing in the cold till night. Draw 1 ration of hard bread and a large Supply of clothing. We remain out Standing in the cold wind half the night and nearly freeze to death. Part of the brigade leaves on cars. Our regt takes possession of Some old houses and Stand around large fires the remainder of the night.

---

39. This is likely a reference to Company G's Private John D. Hayes/Hays, who died on December 13, 1863.

Saturday, December 19, 1863

Cloudy windy & cold. About 2 P.M. We leave on the cars and arrive at Milboro 40 miles from Staunton. At dark we march out and camp. Draw 2 rations of hard bread 3 of Bacon. The Weather is severe.

Sunday, December 20, 1863

Fair windy & cold. We hear that the yankees we started up here after have all retreated back towards the north west and at 11 oclock A.M. We take the cars and arrived back in Staunton at 3 P M. March out on the turnpike towards Winchester 3 miles and camp & received orders to march at 4 A.M.

Monday, December 21, 1863

Cloudy windy & cold. We had Scarcely got to Sleep last night when we were roused up in at 1 oclock A.M. We marched at a rapid force march, pass Mt Sidney before day. Pass Mt Crawfor[d] after day, Harrisonburg in the evening. The Yankees run out of Harrisonburg on one Side as we marched in on the other. It is the most beautiful & thriving enterprising town in the valley and We pursued the Yankees till night and camped 9 miles from New Market, having marched 31 miles to try to overtake the yankee robbers, for they were Robbing and plundering every [ ] in the valley. They came across and if we could have caught them they would have payed dearly for their whistle. My feet was so sore I could scarcely put them to the ground and the cold weather had nearly used me up. When we got to Camp I could hardly put one foot before the other.

Tuesday, December 22, 1863

M cloudy & cold. E a little Snow. We march again at 11 A.M. Pass New Market and camp. The yankees continued to Skedadle.

Wednesday, December 23, 1863

M Snow. E fair, windy & cold. We draw 1 ration of hard bread & bacon. 2 rations of pork & flour. At 3 P.M. we march again cross a Small river & camp at a Gap in the Shenandoah mountain.

Thursday, December 24, 1863

Fair & cold. We remain in camp. I have a Severe cough.

Friday, December 25, 1863

Cloudy & cold. Christmas Day and the 3rd Christmas I have passed in this cruel war away from home and loved ones. We move to another camp a half a mile from New Market. A dull time to us, in the cold wind among the ice.

Saturday, December 26, 1863

Fair & cold. I go out foraging and get butter, milk and cabbage. Have a dinner that is good to the tast[e] of a poor soldier. A luxury we seldom have. We fair a good deal better in regard to Something to eat in the valley then we did with the main army.

Sunday, December 27, 1863

Rainy & cold. I attend preaching at a church in New Market before & after noon.

Monday, December 28, 1863

M rain. E sleet. The weather at present is cold wet and disagreeable and we are out in it all the time without any tents or Shelter what ever but lie out in the open air.

Tuesday, December 28, 1863

Fair frosty & mild. About 11 A.M. we march up the valley, pass Mount Jackson and camp. Draw 2 days rations beef.

Wednesday, December 29, 1863

M cold & frosty. E mild. March against 10 A.M. Pass Woodstock and camp. My feet is verry sore. Pass Edenburg.

Thursday, December 31, 1863

Cold rain all day. March again at 8 A.M. Rains on us all. Camp near Strasburg. The last of 1863. Its gone never to return.

10

"TODAY I DRAW MY FURLOUGH"
VIRGINIA AND FLORIDA: JANUARY 1 – APRIL 1864

Hall's new year commenced with Thomas's Brigade still detailed to Maj. Gen. Jubal Early's command in the Shenandoah Valley. The next two months would be filled with incessant marching up and down the Shenandoah Valley in bitter winter conditions, often in deep snow. But February 1864 would bring Hall a long-awaited furlough home.

Hall rang in the new year encamped on Fisher's Hill two miles south of Strasburg. Many of Thomas's men lacked shoes in near zero-degree weather that Hall noted was the coldest the area had experienced in five years. Thomas marched his brigade north from Fisher's Hill towards Winchester to guard recently-captured supplies, but then dispatched the 14th Georgia and one other regiment back south to prevent Union troops from crossing the Shenandoah River at Strasburg. Hall's company was one of two assigned to picket duty but they rejoined the regiment before it returned to Fisher's Hill. Hall noted in his diary that he had no tent, which speaks to the hardiness of the men in the brigade. Early observed how well Thomas's men, despite being from Georgia, endured the heavy snows and harsh temperatures.[1]

The 14th Georgia had certainly toughened up considerably from its early days in western Virginia in late 1861; one reason may have been improved rations in the Valley.

---

1. "The men had no tents and their only shelter consisted of rude open sheds made of split wood, yet, though Thomas' was a Georgia brigade, they stood the weather remarkably well and seemed to take a pleasure in the expedition, regretting when the time came to fall back." Jubal A. Early, *Memoirs: Autobiographical Sketch and Narrative of the War Between the States* (Konecky & Konecky, 1994), 333.

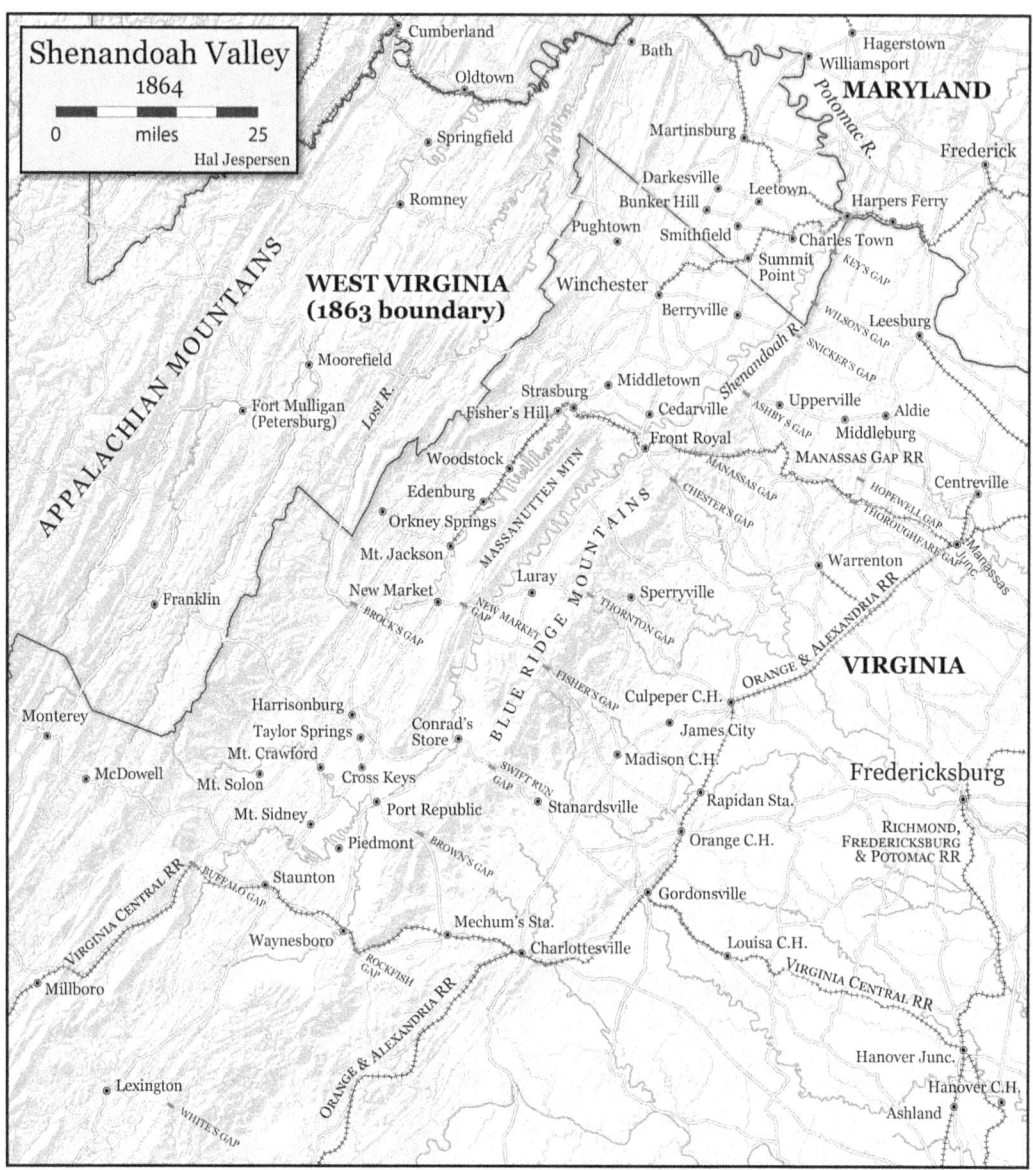

The 14th Georgia spent almost three months marching north and south on the Valley Turnpike between late December 1863 and March 1864. Later designated as U.S. Route 11, the pike was one of the first macadamized roads in Virginia. (Map by Hal Jespersen)

But the men still had their limits. On January 9th, the regiment began a march past New Market and Harrisonburg to a camp near Staunton. This was an exhausting march of over seventy miles in four days and resulted in two-thirds of the brigade falling sick or becoming exhausted. As Hall wrote on January 12, 1864, "We lay in the snow every night and marched . . . through it all day." He grew so sick in mid-January 1864 that he missed a Sunday church service, but he was recovered sufficiently on the following day to march with the regiment back towards Winchester. They halted at Taylor Springs, a camp a few miles east of Harrisonburg. Hall hoped the regiment would remain at Taylor Springs for the remainder of the winter but their stay lasted only a week. Although Hall was not one of the six men in Company G to receive furloughs home that week, he did receive a paycheck for $148, which consisted of $22 in wages, $50 from the county, and $76 for clothing.

Thomas's Brigade departed Taylor Springs on January 27, 1864, to join Early's other units for an expedition into West Virginia. Hall was in bad shape, weak from diarrhea and pain in his feet and legs. Early planned to lead a raiding party on Moorefield and Petersburg, the site of Fort Mulligan, a Union garrison. It was a brutal mountain march with Hall noting that they crossed the same creek "20 or 30 times."

The brigade's 80-mile march, through the pass at Orkney Springs into Lost River Valley, put them in Moorefield, within eight miles of Petersburg. While at Moorefield, Early learned that a Union supply train was approaching Petersburg on the following day. Early dispatched his cavalrymen, under Brig. Gen. Thomas L. Rosser, to capture the train. Rosser's men overwhelmed a large number of Union defenders in seizing the wagon train, which netted the Confederates over fifty intact wagons of supplies.

Early planned an assault on Fort Mulligan, in Petersburg, for February 1, 1864. Thomas's Brigade split at Moorefield, with the 49th Georgia taking the road directly to Petersburg while Hall's 14th Georgia and the remainder of the brigade marched through fog along an old mountain trail covered in underbrush. However, the Union troops at Fort Mulligan had learned from a deserter and from a captured prisoner that Early was at Moorefield and planned to attack Petersburg the next morning. As Hall described the Union response, they "smelled a mouse" and evacuated Fort Mulligan, taking most of their stores with them.[2] Early's surprise attack proved to be no surprise to the Union defenders. According to one soldier in the 35th Georgia, some of the Union soldiers even left behind their wives as they were in "a big hurry to get off."[3] However, Early's men

---

2. *OR*, Ser. 1, vol. 33, p. 38.
3. Fox, *Red Clay to Richmond*, 229.

celebrated Rosser's capture of the fifty wagons of commissary supplies, which included bacon, sugar, and coffee.

After Thomas's Brigade destroyed portions of the Fort Mulligan magazines and shelters, they returned to Moorefield on February 1, while Early sent Rosser to cut the Baltimore & Ohio Railroad and to collect livestock. On February 4, Early's force began its march back to the Shenandoah Valley. Rosser's livestock raid had been a success, and as Early later wrote, the abundance of provisions, the "luxury of a little coffee taken from the enemy, and the kind hospitality of the people of Moorefield rendered this winter campaign into the mountains a most pleasant episode" for his men.[4] The 14th Georgia was the advance guard of Early's column on the march, which put them in the enviable position of walking in front of 1,200 cattle and 500 sheep, rather than behind them, as the other regiments were forced to do. Hall described the view of the valley from his mountain-top vantage point as the most beautiful he had ever seen, with the fields and farmhouses bringing back memories of "happier scenes of by gone days."

After camping near Mount Jackson and at New Market, the regiment returned to its camp at Taylor Springs on February 7, 1864. Hall moved to a new camp less than a week later. He described the weather during his time there as "the coldest and most disagreeable" he had ever experienced in his life, likely due in large part to being forced to sleep without a tent on the north side of a mountain.

The 14th Georgia relocated to Orange Court House at the start of March 1864, but Hall did not accompany them. On February 22, he drew a furlough and waited impatiently until February 26 for it to be processed so he could depart.[5] Furloughs were granted throughout the war, usually to provide a soldier time to recover from a wound or illness or on humanitarian grounds such as illness in a family member back home. But commanders often begrudged granting furloughs due both to the ensuing loss of manpower and a general fear that soldiers permitted to return home might not return to their units. Later in the war, furloughs were expanded as a means of rewarding merit and discouraging desertion, but Lee's late-1863 plan of one furlough per one

---

4. Early, *Memoirs*, 337.
5. Hall does not state how he was selected for a furlough but if his company used a lottery system, it may have simply been through sheer luck.

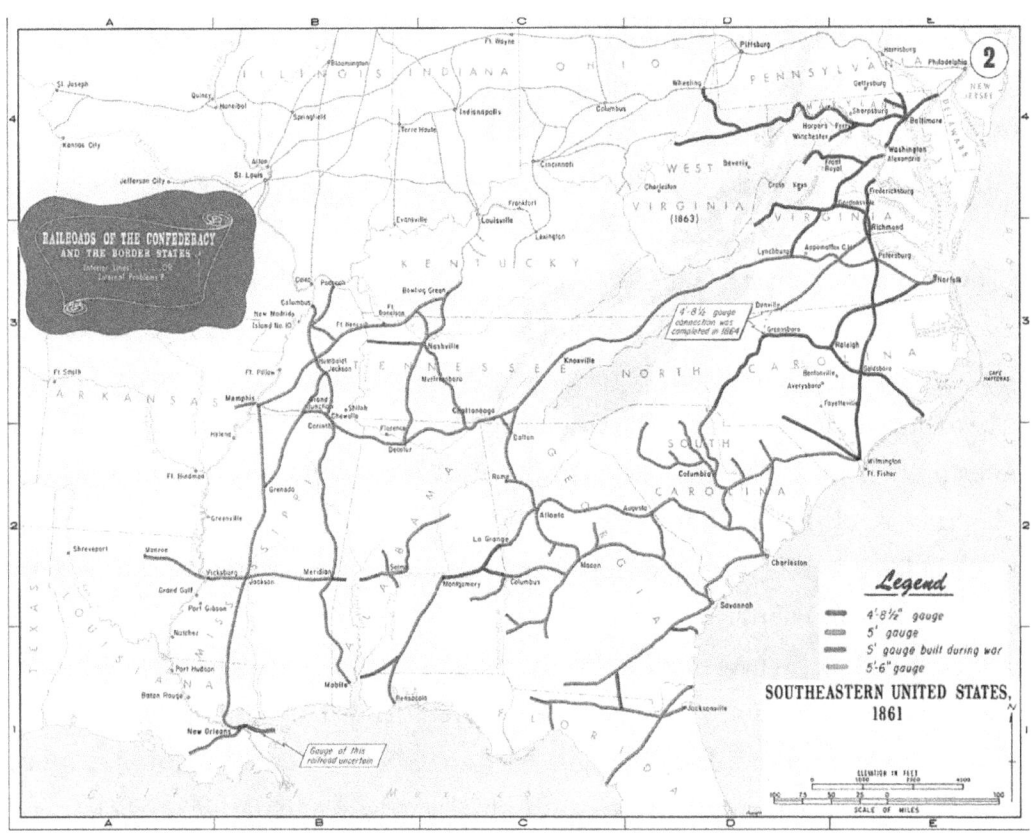

The Civil War was the first U.S. war to utilize railroads on a large scale to move troops and supplies. The "cars" took Hall to war in 1861, moved him around Virginia for almost three years, carried him home on furlough in 1864, and then again home after his release from Fort Delaware. (Wikimedia Commons, Map of the main railroads of the Confederacy, 1861, published as The West Point Atlas of the Civil War, U.S. Military Academy)

hundred men was "a solution so paltry that it was almost worthless."[6] By mid-January, Lee expanded furlough numbers to twelve per one hundred men.[7] Most furloughs for non-medical reasons were of thirty days' duration but the scheduling and travel options from Virginia to points south (and back again) were unpredictable. Hall's journey to northwest Florida took over a week. After a blister-inducing 25-mile walk to Staunton

---

6. Glatthaar, *General Lee's Army*, 412; R. E. Lee letter of Aug 17, 1863 to Jefferson Davis, Dowdey and Manarin, *Wartime Papers of R. E. Lee*, 591.
7. Glatthaar, *General Lee's Army*, 225.

on February 26, 1862, he received his transportation documents and caught a train to Richmond on the following morning. He traveled by rail to Petersburg, Virginia, and Weldon, North Carolina, to Wilmington, North Carolina, where he crossed the Cape Fear River in a steamboat. He took another train south through Augusta, Georgia, to Savannah, Georgia, where he spent the night at the Soldiers Wayside Home. On the following morning, March 1, he took a car on the Savannah, Albany & Gulf Railroad to "No. 17," a station in Dixie, Georgia, just a few miles north of the Georgia-Florida state line. From the station at Dixie, he took a stage coach to Monticello, Florida. On March 2, he took a railcar from Monticello to Quincy, Florida, with a dinner stop at Tallahassee. Seven miles outside of Quincy, he spent the night at the home of a wealthy gentleman who had recently moved from Georgia. Hall arrived home to the embrace of his family around March 4, 1864, after crossing several streams of "clear crystal water," a geologic feature of that area of northwest Florida.

Feted while at his new home in Liberty County, Hall was welcomed by his family's neighbors and entertained at social events. He attended a wedding where, as the only young man present, beautiful girls "vied to see which could pay [him] the most attention." As Hall observed, "Such days as this is rarely seen in the life of a Soldier and will be long remembered."

Hall spent the night of March 12 at the home of a Mr. McNair, likely John G. McNair of Liberty County, Florida. McNair was the father of Private John A. McNair of Company L, 1st Florida Reserve Infantry.[8] On March 13, 1864, Hall attended church with "some very accomplished young ladies" and had "a pleasant time." Although Hall did not name any of these "accomplished young ladies" in his diary, this was likely the day on which he met his future wife, Amanda M. E. Mobley, at Mt. Elon Baptist Church in nearby Wakulla County.[9] Two days later he crossed the river "into Wakulla" and stayed the evening with "some beautiful young ladies," where he met a fellow soldier also on furlough from the Army of Northern Virginia.[10]

---

8. John A. McNair, 1844-1875, https://www.findagrave.com/memorial/95418500/john-a-mcnair
9. John A. McNair was one of the witnesses to the wedding of George Washington Hall and Amanda M. E. Mobley in July 1865. McNair married Amanda's younger sister Elender Vasti "Ellen" Mobley in 1869.
10. This was likely Reed M. Bentley, with whom Hall traveled back to Virginia several days later. In the spring of 1864, Bentley was serving in Company M of the 2d Florida Infantry, in Perry's Brigade in the Army of Northern Virginia. After the war, he resided in Sopchoppy, Florida, where Hall served as a preacher.

Hall split the remainder of his time in northwest Florida between Wakulla County and his home. As he prepared to take a "sad farewell" of those he loved, he vowed to stand "like a wall of fire to the dastard foe" and "die any death to protect home and loved ones." On the morning of March 20, Hall departed from "his old homestead and dear ones" for Quincy. Traveling with Reed Bentley, Hall boarded a train in Quincy and arrived at Monticello later in the day. Again he took a stage coach to No. 17 at Dixie, Georgia, on the rail line, and from there to Savannah. While in Savannah on March 23, Hall had his "Photograph drawn to Send to dear ones." Hall then took the railroad to Petersburg, Virginia, passing through Columbia, Charlotte, and Raleigh en route. He left Raleigh on March 27, spent March 28 in Richmond, and took the train to Orange Court House on the following day to rejoin his brigade, which had returned to Wilcox's Division in early March 1864. He had to walk three miles to find his company, which was in "fine health and Spirit" and glad to see his safe return. Although it was cold and raining in torrents, Hall celebrated having a "cheerful fire and a warm Supper" awaiting him in the "Snug log cabin" that his mess had erected.

Hall returned to the Rapidan area to find that religious revivals were still going strong. On Good Friday, April 8, 1864, Hall attended three prayer meetings and one sermon. Religion continued to play a major role not only in Hall's life but throughout the Army of Northern Virginia, as evidenced by revivals in 32 of that army's 39 brigades.[11] But Hall's social life also expanded after his furlough. He began writing home more frequently and started socializing with friends in Perry's Brigade, likely Reed Bentley and Amanda Mobley's brother Robert S. Mobley of the 5th Florida Infantry.[12] Hall is candid in describing how much those friendships meant to him.

The quiet days in Company G's camp were about to come to a close as May brought the start of spring campaigning for 1864. Little could Hall anticipate how much his life would change in only a matter of weeks.

---

11. Joseph Wheelan, *Bloody Spring: Forty Days that Sealed the Confederacy's Fate* (Da Capo, 2014), 32.
12. The 5th Florida Infantry, which was also in Perry's Brigade, had been formed in Tallahassee in the spring of 1862. One company came from Liberty County, where Hall's family had moved to, and another from Wakulla County, where the Mobleys lived.

Remembrancer Daily Entries
January 1 – April 30, 1864

Friday, January 1, 1864

Fair, windy & cold. We remain in camp on a high hill 2 miles from Strasburg. The weather is extremely cold. We draw 2 days pork, flour & salt.

Saturday, January 2, 1864

Fair windy & cold. At 8 A. M. we march again, pass Strasburg & Middletown in 13 miles of Winchester. Camp. Our company goes on picket. We hear the enemy is advanc[ing] in two directions, from Front Royal and Winchester. It is affirmed by citizens that the weather was colder last night than in 5 years before.

Sunday, January 3, 1864

Cloudy & cold. Last night near midnight our regt and the 49th marched back to Strasburg to hold a point on Shenandoah river at the northern termination of Shenandoah mountain. Our co[mpany] and co[mpany] J remain on picket till 2 P.M.& join regt at the above named place. Draw 1 day hard bread & pork.

Monday, January 4, 1864

Heavy snowing all day. Today we join the Brig[ade] at the camp we left the 2nd inst. Snows on us all day. We have no tents, draw 1 ration hard bread 1 flour 2 of beef.

Tuesday, January 5, 1864

M cloudy. E fair Windy & cold. The snow lies on the ground nearly a foot deep. We remain in camp. I am nearly sick, draw 2 rations pork 1 hard bread. Everything quiet.

Wednesday, January 6, 1864

Cloudy & cold. We have elections today for county officers at home. I go out foraging on a pass. The people of this valley are the kindest and most benevolent of any place I have ever known. Draw 1 ration flour.

Thursday, January 7, 1864

M cloudy & cold. E snow. Draw 2 rations of pork. Nothing of importance.

Friday, January 8, 1864

M snow. E fair & cold. Another heavy snow fell last night on the one that fell the 4th inst. Draw 1 ration of flour & pork.

Saturday, January 9, 1864

Fair windy & cold. We march this morning at 8 oclock and the Snow is so deep we can Scarecely get along. We pass Woodstock & Edenburg and camp in the Snow not far from the latter place. Draw 1 ration of flour & pork. My right hip hurts me & is verry sore from marching in the Snow.

Sunday, January 10, 1864

Fair windy & cold. We march again at 8 A.M. Pass Mount Jackson & New Market and camp 6 miles from the latter place. Draw 2 rations of flour & pork.

Monday, January 11, 1864

Fair windy & cold. March again at 6 A.M. Pass Harrisonburg & camp at Mount Crawford. Draw 2 rations of flour 1 of beef.

Tuesday, January 12, 1864

Par. cloudy & cold. March again at 8 A.M. Pass Mount . . . . Camp in 2 miles from Staunton having marched 70 miles in 4 days and nearly 2 thirds of our Brigade is worn out and sick. We lay in the snow every night and marched through it all day.

Wednesday, January 13, 1864

Fair & cold. Nothing new. Draw 3 rations of flour & pork.

Thursday, January 14, 1864

Fair & cold. Windy. I feel Sick to day have a fever & Severe headache.

Friday, January 15, 1864

Cloudy a little snow. I feel verry unwell and I fear I Shall be sick.

Saturday, January 16, 1864

Par cloudy & cold. Draw 3 rations of flour & pork & beef. I continue verry Sick.

Sunday, January 17, 1864

Par cloudy & cold. The Blessed Lord day. I am too Sick to attend preaching But I would have been glad to have done so.

Monday, January 18, 1864

Cloudy & cold. I feel verry bad to day but some better. Get orders to march. Draw two 2 rations flour & pork. We are going to march again toward Winchester.

Tuesday, January 19, 1864

Cloudy with some snow. We march at 8 A.M. Pass Mount Sydney and camp 2 miles from Mount Crawford. The wind blew cold and Severe in the evening.

Wednesday, January 20, 1864

Partially cloudy & cold. March again at 8 A.M. Pass Mount Crawford & Harrisonburg, turn east and camp near Taylor Springs 4 miles from Harrisonburg and I hope we will remain here the remainder of the winter. What we will do, time will only Show.

Thursday, January 21, 1864

Cloudy & cold. We remain in camp. Every thing quiet.

Friday, January 22, 1864

Fair & cold. Beautiful. I wash my clothing. Six men get furlough from our company, they will start home soon.

Saturday, January 23, 1864

Fair & cool. Fine weather. Nothing new.

Sunday, January 24, 1864

Fair & beautiful. I attend preaching in the country. We draw money. I drew County $50. Monthly wages $22. For clothing $76.

Monday, January 25, 1864

Fair & pleasant. Delightful. We hear we are going to move our camps and go into winter quarters but I think it is doubtful chance about us going in to winter quarters this winter.

Tuesday, January 26, 1864

Fair & pleasant. We received orders last evening to cook two days rations and march this morning at 8 oclock but we remain to day to await Shoes.[13]

Wednesday, January 27, 1864

Nights cool. Days fair & pleasant. We march this morning at 8 oclock, by Harrisonburg and pass New Market and camp. I am verry weak from a diarhea I have had for Several days, and it was with extreme difficulty that I marched today at the rapid rate we had to go. My feet and legs pained me so bad that I could not lie still nor sleep much. I received a letter from my dear friends far away last evening.

Thursday, January 28, 1864

Nights cool. Days fair & pleasant. We march again at 8 A.M. At Mount Jackson we turn to the left, direct towards the Aleghany mountains. We march for several miles along a muddy road, cross a small mountain and camp at the foot of another rugged High mountain. I am verry tired and worn out but feel better than I did yesterday.

---

13. As Lee wrote the Confederate Quartermaster General on January 30, 1864, "The army is in great distress for shoes and clothes. Every inspection report painfully shows it, artillery, cavalry, & infantry." R. E. Lee letter of Jan 30, 1864 to Alexander R. Lawton, Dowdey and Manarin, *Wartime Papers of R. E. Lee*, 665.

Friday, January 29, 1864

Nights cool. Days fair & pleas. At 8 A.M. we resume the march, cross over a high Steep mountain. Wind along a muddy road and cross one creek 20 or 30 times, to through the gaps of two more mountains and after dark we camp in a narrow lonesome valley between two lofty mountains. Pass the night verry uncomfortable.

Saturday, January 30, 1864

Cloudy & cool. At 5 A.M. One hour before daylight we march again over a high craggy mountain along a narrow muddy road. We march for several miles along the top of the mountain and the cloud was so dense around us we could scarcely see our way. As we descend to the valley beneath we leave the cloud above us and march for several miles along an uninhabited tract of country with[out] approaching the habitation of a single human being. In the evening we approach a large river that winds along through the mountains resembling a monster Serpent. We follow its windings for a few and cross it on a temporary bridge and camp as the dark mantle of night begins to draw her folds around us. In 8 miles of Petersburg West Va, the place of our destination having marched over 80 miles in 4 day[s] over mountains and the ruggedest road I ever saw. Our Brig[ade] is all the troops that is in these regions except one brigade of cavalry. The object of this campaign is to capture a garrison of Yankees at Petersburg. They are strongly fortifyed and we hear the cavalry has cut off their waggon train and captured a large amount of commissary stores, and tomorrow we advance on the place and I hope the Lord will enable us to prove successful.

Sunday, January 31, 1864

Cloudy & a little rain. We march again at daylight. One regt the 49th take the road direct to Petersburg. The remainder of the Brig[ade] goes on old blind trai[l] along the top of a cragged mountain. Some places so steep and the undergrowth so thick that it was with extreme difficulty that we made our advance. A thick fog enshrouded the mountains and lay heavily in the valleys which was very favorable to our movements for the enemy could not have seen our approach, nor would not have known we were about till we would have been on them but we were too late. They had Smelled a mouse and Slipt out last night at midnight and Skedadled but we made safe their waggon train and a large amount of commissaries consisting of Bacon, flour, pork crackers, Sugar, coffee, beans, and several other articles to[o] numerous to mention, besides clothing and forage for horses. We destroyed their fortifications and winter quarters, taken several prisoners, and march back and camped where we camped last night. I stood guard all night which was verry disagreeable being verry much fatigued.

Monday, February 1, 1864

Cloudy & a little rain. This morning we march again a river which we found out to be a South branch of the Potomac on the Winchester turn pike, pass through Moorefield and camp two miles from that place. We have about 60 of the enemies waggons we captured. All the remainder was destroyed as they were in the mountains and it was impossible to get them away.

Tuesday, February 2, 1864

Par cloudy & cool. We remain in camps and draw rations of beans pickled pork, sugar, coffee, salt, black pepper, & meal. Our cavalry is driving large herds of beef cattle & sheep down from the mountains from the vicinity of Romney. They had an engagement with the enemy today.

Wednesday, February 3, 1864

A light fall of snow. At 12 oclock today we go on picket on the river near the turnpike leading from Morefield to Romney. At dark we get orders to follow our regt that is gone on advance guard and camped at the foot of the mountains. The night is dark and cold, the old trail we had to march wound around through the mountains and it was with great difficulty that we found our way to where the regt was encamped. After wandering and falling over the rocks and skining our shins we arrived at camp near midnight.

Thursday, February 4, 1864

Fair & cold. At daylight this morning our regt begins to ascend the mountains. The order that we was to march was our regt as advance guard, next to us the waggon train, next the beef cattle & sheep (which were several hundred head,) next our Brig or the remaining 3 regiments and last, Gen Rosser's Brigade of cavalry. Before our regt had gain the top of the mountain we could hear the boom of cannon in the valley below, near the hour of noon. We had marched several miles along the top of the mountain. Our regt was ordered back near 5 miles to protect the cattle or reinforce our brig in case they became engaged but before we began to descend the mountain we were informed all had become quiet. The yankee cavalry under the command of Averill did not care to pursue us, and we proceeded on quietly and were not molested any more. Our regt camped at Lost river, the remainder of the brig[ade] on the mountain.

Friday, February 5, 1864

M fair & cold. E cloudy. We march at Sunrise. Our regt over the mountains towards Mount Jackson. The waggon train proceeds through Brooks Gap and down the valley to Harrisonburg. As we descend the last range of mountains between us and the Shenandoah valley the most beautiful view

I ever saw presents its self to us. The wide extensive valley dotted over with a hundred towns and villiages. The broad fields and beautiful farm houses extending away from Winchester to Staunton, brings vivid to my memory happier scenes of by gone days. We march a good distance to day. We camp at dark in two miles of Mt. Jackson, verry much fatigue[d].

Saturday, February 6, 1864

M cloudy. E Cold rain. We march at 8 A.M. Pass Mount Jackson and camp at New Market. Draw rations and cook. The cold rain is verry disagreeable.

Sunday, February 7, 1864

M Snow. E fair & cold. At 8 A.M. we march again down the turn pike, pass Harrisonburg near Sunset and arrive at our camps We left Jan 27th. Verry much fatigued and worn out.

Monday, February 8, 1864

Fair windy & cold. We remain in camp and I hope they will let us rest a week or two.

Tuesday, February 9, 1864

Fair & cold. Nothing of importance.

Wednesday February 10, 1864

Fair frosty & cold. Nothing New. 3 of our company starts home on furlough. Sent letter home yesterday to my dear friends.

Thursday, February 11, 1864

Fair frost & cold. Every thing quiet. I wash today.

Friday, February 12, 1864 Friday

Partially cloudy & cold. We move to new camp.

Saturday, February 13, 1864 Saturday

M cold. E fair & pleasant. We hear cannonading east of the Blue Ridge.

Sunday, February 14, 1864

Fair windy & cold. The winds blows severe.

Monday, February 15, 1864

Snow. Nothing new.

Tuesday, February 16, 1864

M snow storm. E cold & severe wind.

Wednesday, February, 17, 1864

Hard cold wind. The weather for the last two days has been the coldest and most disagreeable I ever experienced in my life. We are encamped on the north side of a mountain without any tents and the cold wind is so severe we can hardly live.

Thursday, February 18, 1864

Fair & severely cold. Gen Lee has whip[p]ed the yankees again and run them to Centerville.

Friday, February 19, 1864

Fair & severely cold. Nothing New.

Saturday, February 20, 1864

Fair & cold. The weather has somewhat moderated to day but verry cold yet.

Sunday, February 21, 1864

Fair & cold. E cloudy. Rev Mr. Stuart of Terrill Co Ga preached for us.[14]

Monday, February 22, 1864

Partially cloudy & cold. To day I draw a furlough.

Tuesday, February 23, 1864

Fair & cold. I wash my clothing to be ready to visit my dear friends far away.

Wednesday, February 24, 1864

Cloudy windy & cold. Nothing of importance.

Thursday, February 25, 1864

Fair windy & cold. I am anxiously await[ing] the return of my furlough with not a verry great amount of patience.

---

14. This is likely a reference to Thomas H. Stewart, a Methodist missionary appointed to Lee's Army of Northern Virginia. Fox, *Red Clay to Richmond*, 247.

Friday, February 26, 1864

Fair windy & cold. My furlough came at 10 oclock A.M. I started for Staunton 25 miles distance. I arrived near dark. My feet was severely blistered. I got my transportation and passport to Richmond and then endeavored to take a little rest.

Saturday, February 27, 1864

Fair windy & cold. I took the cars at 6 oclock and arrived at Richmond at 7 oclock P.M. and got my transportation ticket in full and at a late hour retired to rest preparatory for the long journey ahead of me to visit home and loved ones far away in the land of beautiful flowers.

Sunday, February 28, 1864

Fa[i]r and cold. This morning at 5 oclock I leave Richmond on the cars. At Petersburg I change car and arrived at Weldon, N.C. about 3 P.M. Change cars again and arrived at Wilmington next morning at 4 oclock.

Monday, February 29, 1864

Fair & pleasant. Cross Cape Fear river in a Steamboat. Take the cars again. Change cars at [K]ingsville, S.C. after dark and change again at Branchville near midnight and arrived at Augusta Ga at daylight next morning.

Tuesday, March 1, 1864

Fa[i]r & pleasant. Take the cars at 8 A.M. and change again at Millen Geo. Arrive at Savanah at 5 P.M. Rest during the night at the Soldiers Side Way Home.[15] Take the cars on the S. A. & G. R. R. at 8 A.M.[16] Arrive at No 17 near 10

---

15. The Savannah Wayside Home, formerly the Pavilion Hotel, provided meals and lodging for soldiers traveling on furlough. Announcement, *Savannah Republican*, March 7, 1863, https://gahistoricnewspapers.galileo.usg.edu.
16. This is the abbreviation for the Savannah, Albany & Gulf Railroad.

P.M. and take the Stage Coach and arrive at Monticello Fla at daylight next morning.[17]

Thursday, March 3, 1864

Leave Monticello on the cars at 9-1/2 A. M. and go at a rapid Speed through the land of flowers. Tarry at Tallahassee an hour and get a good dinner at the Side way home. Arrive at Quincy on the cars at 4 P.M. and walk out and 7 miles from Quincy and remain all night with a wealthy gentleman that recently removed from Georgia. Passed the night verry pleasantly but longing to be with the loved ones at home.

Friday, March 4, 1864

M fair & pleasant. E clou. At Sunrise I start again, pass through a beautiful Country, level as a plain. Cross several beautiful Streams of clear crystal water, and arrived at Home and embraced the loved ones after an absence of nearly three long years. I found them in fe[e]ble health but hope the Dear Lord will soon restore them.

Saturday, March 5, 1864

Cloudy & a little rain. Several neighbors came to see me today. They were proud to see me. This is a fine country.

Sunday, March 6, 1864

Fair & pleasant. I remain at home. My feet is verry sore yet but I enjoy my Self with the dear ones at Home.

Monday, March 7, 1864

Fair & pleasant. Nothing of importance. The weather is delightful. Vegetation is springing forth and beautiful flowers in every direction.

---

17. The town of Dixie, Georgia, in Brooks County, was initially known as Number 17, its station sequence on the Savannah, Albany & Gulf Railroad. Kenneth K. Krakow, *Georgia Place-Names: Their History and Origins* (Winship Press, 1975), 62.

Tuesday, March 8, 1864

Fair & pleasant. Nothing New.

Wednesday, March 9, 1864

M cloudy. E thun & rain. Heavy rain fell today.

Thursday, March 10, 1864

M cloudy. E thun & rain. Summer rain clouds.

Friday, March 11, 1864

Par fair & beautiful. Today I had the pleasure of being at a wedding or infair [infare]. I was the only young man there and the place was thronged with beautiful girls and they all vied with each other to see which could pay me the most attention. Such days as this is rarely seen in the life of a Soldier and will be long remembered.

Saturday, March 12, 1864

Fair & pleasant. Nothing of importance.

Sunday, March 13, 1864

Fair & pleasant. I stayed at Mr McNairs last night and went to church today with some verry accomplished young ladies, has a pleasant time.[18]

Monday, March 14, 1864

Fair & pleasant. I passed last night verry pleasant and joyous and returned home this morning and some other ladies came to visit me. At home time flies rapid.

Tuesday, March 15, 1864

Fair & pleasant. I remain part of the day at home and in the evening cross the river into Wakulla and stay with some beautiful young ladies and a Soldier a relative of theirs had just got home on furlough from my army in Virginia and I was verry glad to form his acquintance.[19]

---

18. Hall wrote in the July 9, 1885, issue of the *Florida Baptist Witness* that he had met his wife during the war at Mt. Elon Baptist Church.

19. This was likely a reference to Amanda Mobley's brother, Private Robert Mobley, Company C, 5th Florida Infantry, Perry's Brigade.

Wednesday March 16 1864

M cloudy & cool. E fair. This day passed off happy and joyous as any day of my life.

Thursday March 17, 1864

M cold & frosty. E windy. I remain with the same party last night I did yesterday and night before. And it was with Sorrow deeply felt I bid them a last farewell this morning till after I go to the cruel war again. But I hope and Sincerely trust the good Lord and God of Battle will enable us all to meet when this cruel war is over.

Friday, March 18, 1864

M cold & frosty. E fair. I crossed the river again today to visit some friends and we cut a bee tree and had a pleasant time and I took leaf [leave] of some more beautiful young ladies and recrossed the river and tarried all night with some dear friends.

Saturday March 19, 1864

Fair & pleasant. Today is the last day I have to stay at home. Tomorrow I take a sad farewell of those I love and speed my course for the old Dominion where I will stand like a wall of fire to the dastard foe and I will die any death to protect home and loved ones.

Sunday, March 20, 1864

Fair & pleasant. Last night I stayed with Home and loved ones for the last Time perhaps till this cruel war is over, and I hope and Sincerely pray that the Blessed Lord will Spare us all to meet again when Sweet peace and happy contentment reigns tryumphant o'er our beloved Sunny South one more time. At 10 A.M. we parted deeply impressed with Sorrow but I hope we will soon meet again with glad and Joyful hearts. The loved ones looked after us till we disappeared from their view. I turned and cast a last look at the old homestead and dear ones as they stood taking the last sight of me. Then a curve in the road and we disappeared from each others view. What my thoughts were at the feelings of my poor heart no Tongue can tell or pen describe. Had I not received so much kindness, respect and attention and happy enjoyment by which I formed the acquaintance of so many new friends, I might have left without the pang I felt at parting. But I hope we will all meet again and I believe we will if we will only serve the Lord and keep a strong faith. We arrived at Quincy late in the night and did not rest much.

Monday, March 21, 1864

Heavy rain all day. Before day me and R. M. Bentley my friend and companion got our transportation from Quincy to Savan[n]ah and at daylight we bid farewell to Mr Bentley, my friends father, and to Quincy and were soon flying along at a rapid speed. As we crossed the Oclockney [Ochlockonee] River my thoughts soared away down the river for my dear friends and loved ones, live on each side of the Oclockney in Wakulla and Liberty Counties.[20] My thoughts and mind were absor[b]ed till the first thing I knew we were at Tall[a]hassee. We remained [in] the capital of the land of Flowers one half hour. Dark clouds lay heavily in the Zenith and the cars sped there onward course. The rain began to fall in Torrents and continued till near night. At Monticello we took the Stage coach, and were soon across the Florida line. My thoughts were I cannot describe. We arrived at No 17 on the S. A. & G. R. R. We remained there all night.

Tuesday, March 22, 1864

Rainey and cool. At daylight we got aboard the cars, and arrived at Savannah after dark and tarried all night at the Soldiers wayside home. I got to sleep and soon dreaming Sweet dreams of home and loved ones.

---

20. Hall's mother and step-father resided in Liberty County; Amanda Mobley resided in Wakulla County.

Wednesday, March 23, 1864

Fair & cool. We had to remain till 4 P.M. We taken a stroll through the city and I had my Photograph drawn to Send to dear ones, and wrote letter home. At 4 P.M. we took the cars again on the Ga central R.R. We arrive at Millen at 11 P.M. Got a good supper, at 2 A.M. We started again.

Thursday, March 24, 1864

Fair & cool. We arrived at Augusta directly after daylight and left there at 2 A.M. at Branchville S.C. We changed cars again, pass Kingsville and arrive at Columbia, the capital of South Carolina after dark. Change cars, run all night, arrive at Charlotte North Carolina near 8 A.M.

Friday, March 25, 1864

Cold rain, Sleet & Snow. We remain at Charlotte nearly all day. Pass a disagreeable day. Leave there near night run all night.

Saturday, March 26, 1864

Fair & cold. We arrive at Raleigh the capital of North Carolina near 11 A.M. Remain there all day. Take a stroll through the city, purchase Some little articles. Remain at the wayside Home all night. The temperature of the weather is several degrees colder here, than at my fair Sunny home far away. Pass a Somewhat comfortable night.

Sunday, March 27, 1864

Fair & cold. Leave Raleigh at 6 A.M. and arrive at Weldon at 4 P.M. There we change cars again and leave half past five P.M. and arrive at Petersburg in the old Dominion at 1 A.M. One week ago today since I left home and loved ones. I am now far away from them, but the Lord will be done not mine.

Monday, March 28, 1864

Fair & cold. At 3 A.M. we leave Petersburg and arrive at Richmond near daylight and we remain in the metropolis and capitol of the Confederate States all day and night and visited various parts of the city. Today my furlough expires, we tarry all night at the Georgia Soldiers wayside home and dream of dear ones far away.

Tuesday, March 29, 1864

Cold rainy & disagreeable. At 6 A.M. we take the cars on the Va central R R. Change at Gordonsville and arrive at Orange C. H. near 4 P.M. The rain is falling in Torrents and verry cold. I got [a] considerable wetting before I arrived at my Brigade. I found them camped 3 miles distant and ever in fine health and Spirit, and were all glad to see me return safe. I found a cheerful fire and a warm Supper awaiting me in a Snug log cabin my mess had erected.

Wednesday, March 30, 1864

Cold and rainy. Nothing of importance. Sent 2 letters off. The weather is cold and disagreeable.

Thursday, March 31, 1864

Cloudy & cold. Sent 2 letters off. The roads is all in bad condition and the recent heavy snows and rains will probily delay the opening of the Spring campaign. Our army is in fine health and spirits.

Friday, April 1, 1864

Cloudy and cold rain. On regimental guard but the rain causes us to be dismissed.

Saturday, April 2, 1864

Heavy snowing. It comenced snowing last night and contin[u]ed nearly all day. Sent one letter off. Every thing quiet.

Sunday, April 3, 1864

Cloudy cold & windy. We go on picket on the Rapid Ann [Rapidan]. Have a cold disagreeable time. Today is two weeks Since I left home an[d] loved ones. Write letters Home.

Monday, April 4, 1864

Snows and sleets all day. We return of[f] picket.

Tuesday, April 5, 1864

Snows & sleets all day. Write letter. Everything quiet.

Wednesday, April 6, 1864

M rain. E Fair & pleasant. Nothing of importance.

Thursday, April 7, 1864

Fair & cool. I visit Orange C.H. [Court House] and Perrys Brig[ade], meet with several friends and an old acquaintance I have not seen before during the war, pass a verry agreeable day, and mail some books to the loved ones at home. Get Back to camp at dark.

Friday, April 8, 1864

Partially fair and cool. A day of fasting humiliation and prayer. I attend 3 prayers meetings and one sermon, a verry Solum occasion and I hope we will all profit by it and the blessed Lord will hear our prayers and deliver us.[21]

Saturday, April 9, 1864

Cold & rainy. Nothing new. It rains all day. The ground is inte[n]sely wet and the rivers overflowing their banks.

Sunday, April 10, 1864

M fair. E thun & cool. Nothing of importance.[22]

Monday, April 11, 1864

Cloudy & cool. I attend prayer meeting. Every thing still & quiet.

Tuesday April 12, 1864

Fair & cool. This day is the first anniversary of my joining the church of Church of Christ. The Blessed Lord has spared me to see another year, and I am in the best of health. To his Dear name be ascribed all the honor and

---

21. Jefferson Davis declared a national day of "fasting, humiliation, and prayer" for April 8, 1864. Wheelan, *Bloody Spring*, 32-33.
22. The brigade observed Easter with a meeting on April 10 where Chaplain Hyman and Rev. Thomas H. Stewart preached. Fox, *Red Clay to Richmond*, 246.

glory forever. Where I will be at the expiration of another eventful year He alone can Tell, but I hope & pray this cruel war will be ended, and I shall be at home with loved ones.

Wednesday, April 13, 1864

Fair windy and cool. We go on picket. Have a verry agreeable time.

Thursday, April 14, 1864

Par cloudy & cool. Return off picket. Our regt has election for ensign.

Friday, April 15, 1864

Fair & cool. Company drill, Brigade inspection, Batalion drill &c. Every thing quiet.

Saturday, April 16, 1864

Cold & rainy.

Sunday, April 17, 1864

Par cloudy & cool. I visit Perry Brig[ade] and spend the day with friends that I cherish as dearly as any friends on earth and I was with one that had just returned from home, and I heard from loved ones, one more time.

Monday, April 18, 1864

M frosty. E par cloudy. Co drill, inspection of Co ammunition.

Tuesday, April 19, 1864

M frosty. E par cloudy. Bat drill, and co drill. Every thing quiet.

Wednesday, April 20, 1864

M frosty. E par cloudy. Bat[talion] drill before and after noon. Indications of rain or snow.

Thursday, April 21, 1864

M frost. E par cloudy. Bat[talion] drill before and after noon. All quiet.

Friday, April 22, 1864

Fair and cool. E cloudy, rain. I am on regimental guard. Bat[talion] drill before & after noon.

Saturday, April 23, 1864

Fair and pleasant. Breezes. We have division review. Our Division is in better fighting trim than at any time previous during the war and all is in excellent health and spirit. After review our co[mpany] and co[mpany] D goes on picket at our same position on the Rapidan.

Sunday, April 24, 1864

M fair & pleasant. E cloudy. Return off picket. The weather is delightful. I attend preaching. Have a good sermon.

Monday, April 25, 1864

M fair & pleasant. E rain hard. Ever thing quiet in this vicinity. Battalion drill before and afternoon.

Tuesday, April 26, 1864

Fair & pleasant. Bat[talion] drill & Brig[ade] drill. The weather is beautiful.

Wednesday, April 27, 1864

Fair & pleasant. E windy. I visit Perrys Brigade Andersons Division and spend the day with some of my best and most beloved friends, and I had a most pleasant time which almost seemed like being with dear friends at home.

Thursday, April 28, 1864

Fair & cool. I remained all night last night with Co C 5th Fla and returned soon this morn.[23] We have two Bat drills, and a good little prayer meeting at night.

Friday, April 29, 1864

Fair & pleasant. Two Bat[talion] drills and Brigade drill. Prayer meeting at noon.

Saturday, April 30, 1864

Cloudy & cool. Some rain. Gen muster & inspection. Every thing quiet.

---

23. This was Robert S. Mobley's company.

11

"SO ENDS THE MOST EVENTFUL DAY OF MY LIFE"
VIRGINIA: MAY 1 – MAY 12, 1864

While Hall was in Florida, the war in the eastern theater entered a new dimension with the promotion of Ulysses S. Grant in rank to lieutenant general and in billet to general-in-chief of the Union armies. No longer would the goal of Union armies be to simply capture Richmond or other Confederate territory; rather, Grant set out to destroy Lee's armies in a multi-faceted campaign that would prevent the Confederates from shifting troops among fronts and theaters, as it had done most recently by Longstreet's temporary assignment to Braxton Bragg's forces in the west. As general-in-chief, Grant had a broad strategic vision, developing a master plan of simultaneous offensive actions against Lee in the east in central Virginia, in the Shenandoah Valley, up the James River to Richmond, and, in the west, land operations against Atlanta and a joint army-navy operation at Mobile, Alabama.[1] But the singular distinguishing characteristic Grant brought to the table was a shift in attitude from the "fight and recover" approach of his predecessors. According to Gordon Rhea, "[g]one were the days of short battles followed by months of leisure to refit and regroup; under Grant, Union armies were to engage their foes and hold on like bulldogs, fighting until they had destroyed the secessionists' capacity to resist."[2]

---

1. Wheelan, *Bloody Spring*, 20.
2. Gordon C. Rhea, Foreword, Alfred C. Young III, *Lee's Army During the Overland Campaign: A Numerical Study* (Louisiana State University, 2013), vii. Grant also benefited from the growing gap between the North and South in numbers of available troops and industrial resources. Symonds, *A Battlefield Atlas of the Civil War*, 81. Symonds notes that Grant even reduced garrison strength in order to put more Union troops in the field.

The Wilderness, located west of the 1863 Chancellorsville battlefield, was the site of the first direct confrontation between Lee and Grant as well as the initial engagement of Grant's Overland Campaign. On May 4, 1864, the Army of the Potomac, with three infantry corps (II Corps under Winfield S. Hancock, V Corps under Gouveneur K. Warren, and VI Corps under John Sedgwick), crossed the Rapidan River at two different fords to draw Lee into battle in central Virginia. Meade still commanded the Army of the Potomac, but now he had the general-in-chief with him in the field rather than back in Washington. Union troop strength also included 20,000 men in Ambrose Burnside's IX Corps, which was not technically part of the Army of the Potomac because Meade was junior in rank to Burnside.

Lee was outnumbered roughly two-to-one, but the rugged topography of the Wilderness diminished the utility of Grant's far superior troop strength and artillery, a similar impediment to the one Hooker encountered a few miles east at Chancellorsville the previous May.[3] Once Lee sussed Grant's intentions, he ordered Ewell's Second Corps and Hill's Third Corps to the Wilderness, an eighteen-mile march for Ewell but a twenty-eight-mile march for Hill's men coming from Clark's Mountain. Hoping to surprise Grant, Lee ordered Ewell to march down the Orange Turnpike while Hill marched down the Orange Plank Road. Longstreet's First Corps, having just returned from the western theatre, had encamped near Gordonsville, ten miles from Orange Turnpike and some forty-two miles from the Wilderness. Intersecting both the Orange Turnpike and the Orange Plank Road in the Wilderness was Brock Road, which the National Park Service has described as perhaps the "most important intersection of the entire war."[4] The Union needed physical control of the intersection in order to proceed southeast towards Richmond.

On the morning of May 4, the 14th Georgia and the rest of Cadmus Wilcox's division marched out of their encampment north of Orange Court House with Hill's

---

3. The Wilderness, which Gottfried calls a "living quagmire," was 70-square miles of thick second-growth scrub pine and other reforestation that grew up to replace virgin timber that had been cut down years before to feed local iron smelting furnaces. Bradley M. Gottfried, *The Maps of the Wilderness* (Savas Beatie, 2016), 22. Whether the topography of the Wilderness gave Lee a major tactical edge remains a matter of debate; after all, he had to fight through the underbrush and in poor visibility just as Grant did. Adam H. Perry, "Reconsidering the Wilderness's Role in Battle, 4-6 May 1864," *Journal of Military History*, No. 82, April 2018, 413-438.
4. Virtual Tour Stop, Brock Road-Plank Road Intersection, accessed July 25, 2020, https://www.nps.gov/frsp/learn/photosmultimedia/wildvritual.htm

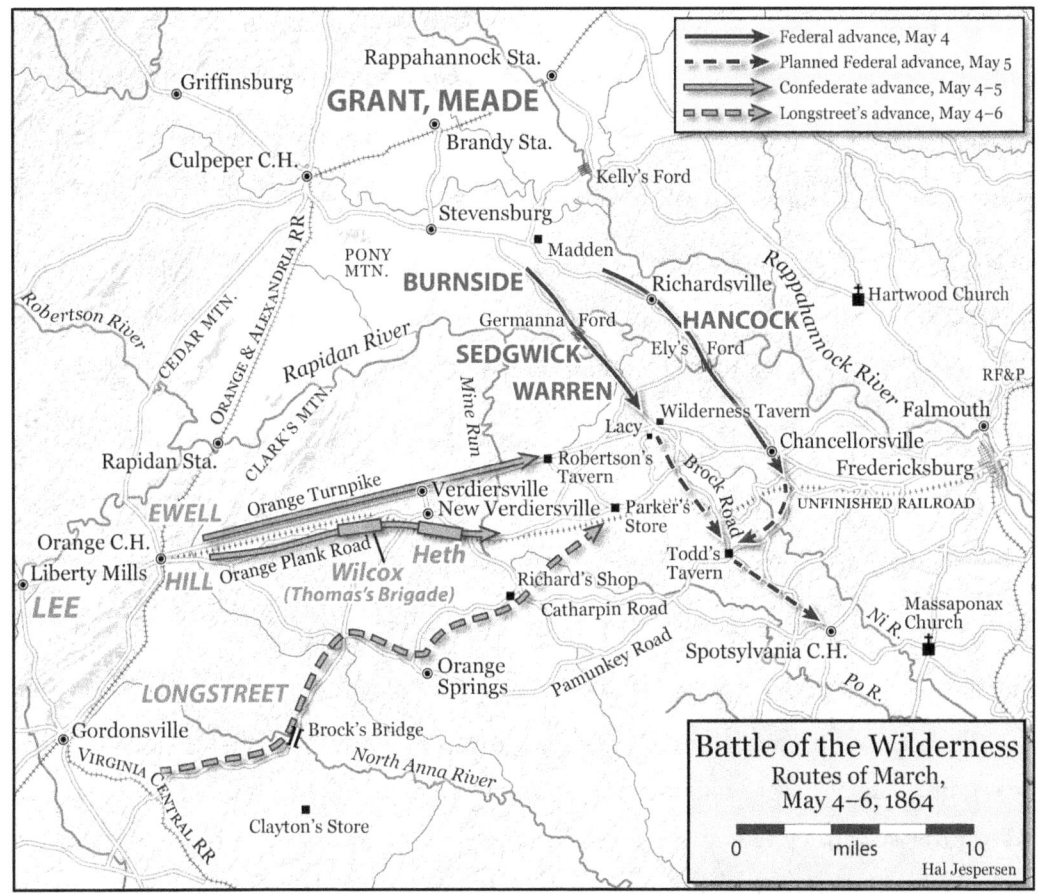

Route of Thomas's Brigade from Orange Court House east on Orange Plank Road. (Map by Hal Jespersen)

Third Corps down Orange Plank Road, camping on the night of May 4 near New Verdiersville. Hall cooked that evening for his mess but still spent a "sweet hour in meditation & prayer near midnight." On the following morning, Hill's corps resumed its march down Orange Plank Road towards the intersection with Brock Road, with Heth's division marching about a mile ahead of Wilcox's Division.

After some early skirmishing, the major combat on May 5 commenced when Ewell clashed with Union V Corps troops on Orange Turnpike. Some two miles to the south, Hill's lead troops in Third Corps on Orange Plank Road closed on the Brock Road intersection. Hancock's II Corps was well south of the intersection, which meant that if Hill could take Brock Road, he could cleave Meade's army in two and isolate Hancock's II Corps, or he could march north to attack Warren's V Corps and relieve pressure on

Ewell. Meade, however, realized his vulnerability at the Brock Road intersection and rushed Getty's division from VI Corps to defend it, while also ordering Hancock to hasten to the intersection.

Lee, in mid-afternoon on May 5, ordered Wilcox's division north from Orange Plank Road to bridge the gap with Ewell. To do so, the division had to march north through two miles of rugged underbrush and brambles towards Ewell's right flank, which was commanded by Brig. Gen. John Gordon. Hall wrote that they marched through an old field, a dense thicket of undergrowth, and a swampy, boggy ravine. Lane's Brigade led the line north, followed by Thomas's Brigade, with Scales's and McGowan's brigades remaining near Chewning Farm. Lane's battalion of sharpshooters, which moved out in advance, engaged a large body of Union troops, capturing over 140 of them.[5] Lane's and Thomas's brigades reached Jones's Field just north of the Chewning Farm, and Wilcox himself advanced far enough north to meet up with Gordon at Higgerson's Field.[6] The two commanders had barely commenced talking when Wilcox heard musket fire through the woods and hurriedly rejoined his two lead brigades.

When Lee dispatched Thomas's Brigade north to connect with Ewell's right flank, he was unaware of the growing threat posed to Heth on Orange Plank Road at the Brock Road intersection. Heth's division faced not only Getty's division but was about to be grossly outnumbered by Hancock's II Corps, which meant that Heth's division would be engaging a total of three Union divisions. Wilcox's division was the only immediate reserve, which forced Lee to choose between continuing to close the gap with Ewell or recalling Wilcox's four brigades to support Heth. Lee chose the latter.

Scales and McGowan, closer than Lane and Thomas to Orange Plank Road, reached Heth first. Scales moved east to the right of Orange Plank Road and McGowan fought from the center to relieve two of Heth's brigades. However, there was no immediate help for Col. John Stone's Brigade, which occupied Heth's far left. Stone's men, having withstood at least a half-dozen charges against their line, had expended most of their ammunition. Just as one of Stone's regiments prepared to attack with bayonets, Thomas's Brigade showed up in relief. Lane joined Scales on the right side of the Confederate line.

---

5. Hardy, *General Lee's Immortals*, 265. Hall writes that the number of prisoners was "several hundred."
6. Cadmus M. Wilcox, "Lee and Grant in the Wilderness," in *The Annals of the War Written by Leading Participants North and South*. ed. Alexander K. McClure (Philadelphia: Philadelphia Times Publishing, 1879), 492; Gottfried, *Maps of the Wilderness*, 110.

The Union army, however, had dispatched four brigades toward the left flank and rear of the Confederate line, manned only by Thomas's Brigade. As Bradley Gottfried writes, this was "[p]erhaps the greatest threat to Lee's line" because "[i]f these four brigades hit Thomas's Brigade's flank, the entire Rebel line would be rolled up and defeated."[7] Thomas's Brigade now formed a line to Orange Plank Road, facing the approaching Union brigades at an oblique angle, with the 14th Georgia closest to the Union brigades. Hall wrote that they maintained their ground against "3 times our number." It was vicious fighting, with one Confederate soldier writing that it was "butchery pure and simple . . . a mere slugging match in a dense thicket of small growth, where men but a few yards apart fired through the brushwood for hours, ceasing only when exhaustion and night commanded a rest."[8]

Hill had no more regiments to commit in Thomas's support but he did have the 150 men of the 5th Alabama Battalion, who had been guarding prisoners in the rear. That battalion let loose with sufficient clamor and noise in the encroaching darkness that the attacking Union force under Brig. Gen. James S. Wadsworth stopped in its tracks, unsure of how many Confederate troops it faced. The Union army's attack stalled. Thomas's good fortune was a missed opportunity for the Union troops; as Murray and Hsieh note, if Wadsworth had acted more decisively, he could have destroyed much of Hill's corps.[9]

Gottfried describes the fighting on May 5, 1864, at the Wilderness as "slaughter on a horrific scale at close quarters," with scant artillery fire but unceasing musket fire for hours.[10] According to James McPherson, May 5-6 saw "the most confused and frenzied fighting the war had yet seen."[11] As McPherson writes, this fighting took place "in these dense, smoke-filled woods where soldiers could rarely see the enemy, units blundered the wrong way in the directionless jungle, friendly troops fired on each other by mistake, gaps in the opposing line went unexploited because unseen, while muzzle flashes and exploding shells set the underbrush on fire to threaten wounded men with a fiery death."[12] As at Second Manassas, the Union troops at the battle of the Wilderness

---

7. Gottfried, *Maps of the Wilderness*, 118.
8. Gottfried, *Maps of the Wilderness*, 128.
9. Murray and Hsieh, *A Savage War*, 372. Murray and Hsieh also note that with another hour of daylight Hancock might have crushed both Heth and Wilcox "but again the Army of the Potomac was a day late and a dollar short." Ibid.
10. Gottfried, *Maps of the Wilderness*, 128.
11. James M. McPherson, ed., *The Atlas of the Civil War* (Skyhorse: 2022), 141.
12. McPherson, *Battle Cry of Freedom*, 725.

engaged in piecemeal assaults and, just as at Second Manassas, they failed.. Ewell had stood his ground and Hill, whose 15,000 men had held off 40,000 Union troops, delivered "one of the war's most brilliant defensive efforts."[13]

However, the integrity of Hill's line had all but ceased to exist toward the end of May 5; the men had been "fragmented into clusters" and were "huddled behind logs, rocks, and jerry-rigged earthworks in every direction."[14] As James Robertson writes, the two armies had not pulled apart after the battle ended; rather, "they simply stopped fighting where they were, with remnants of regiments and brigades facing in every direction all over the Wilderness and nobody quite knowing where friends or enemies might be."[15] Heth's Division had become intermingled with Wilcox's Division, which made both commanders uneasy about their positions relative to each other for fear of friendly fire and of weakening of their lines.[16] When the two division commanders suggested to Hill late on May 5 that they reform their lines astride Orange Plank Road, Hill rebuffed their concerns, telling Wilcox and Heth that Longstreet would be in position to relieve them before dawn and they should let their men sleep. Wilcox sought out Lee around 9 p.m.but before he could express his concerns about the front line's lack of stability, Lee reassured Wilcox, as had Hill, that Longstreet was en route to replace Hill's troops on Orange Plank Road.

Lee's and Hill's reassurances did not assuage Wilcox's concerns. Shortly before daybreak, Wilcox ordered pioneers to start felling trees to construct an abatis, but the early hour and the threat of close enemy fire prevented the pioneers from continuing.[17] The exact location of Thomas's Brigade as dawn approached on May 6 is subject to debate; it is indisputable that the brigade fought north of Orange Plank Road on May 5 but where they were at dawn on May 6 is far less clear. The strongest evidence supports

---

13. Gottfried, *Maps of the Wilderness*, 128.
14. Gordon Rhea, *The Battle of the Wilderness: May 5-6, 1864* (Louisiana State University Press, 1994), 276.
15. Robertson, *General A. P. Hill*, 260. David Champion wrote in his post-war memoirs that when he set the picket line for the 14th Georgia that night, one of the men reported that the Union troops were just a few feet away. Champion reported this to Colonel Folsom who said he would "do his best to have the line straightened during the night," but was told by "higher officers" it would be put in "proper position" the next morning. Champion, *Memoirs*, "Battle of the Wilderness, 1864 ."
16. Heth and Wilcox likened their lines to a "worm fence, at every angle." William L. Royall, *Some Reminiscences* (Neale Publishing Co., 1909), 30.
17. Hardy, *General Lee's Immortals*, 269; Leigh Robinson Address to Seventh Annual Reunion, Virginia Division of the Army of Northern Virginia Association, Richmond, VA, 1877, in J. William Jones, *Army of Northern Virginia Memorial Volume* (Richmond: J. W. Randolph & English, 1880), 228.

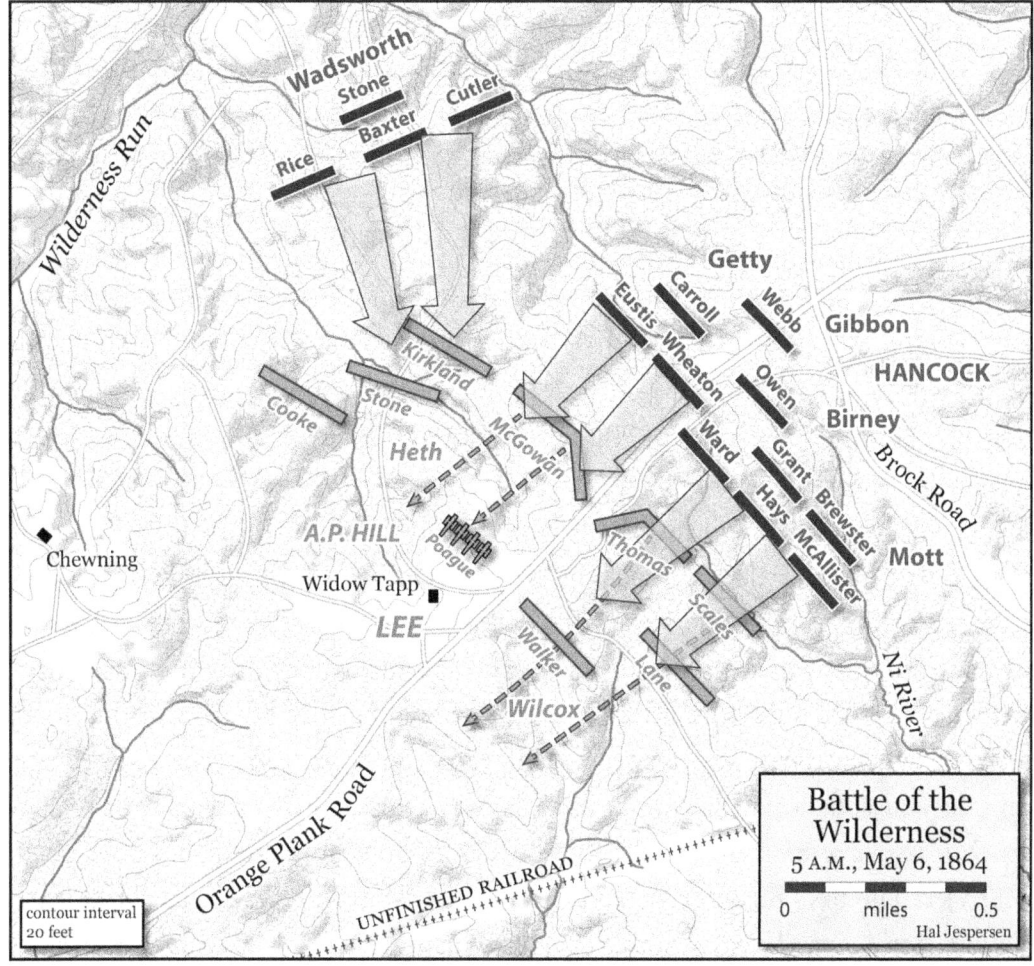

Although most of Thomas's Brigade was likely south of Orange Plank Road at the time of the Union attack, the 14th Georgia may have been north of the road or even straddled it. (Map by Hal Jespersen)

the conclusion that McGowan's Brigade was on the north side of Orange Plank Road and Thomas's men to the immediate south of the road.[18] However, it is also possible that

---

18. Gottfried addresses the inconsistencies in the sources in Footnote 2 to his Map Set 14, noting that Gordon Rhea places Thomas on McGowan's right; Edward Steere places Thomas to the right of Scales's brigade on the south side of Orange Plank Road; and Frank O'Reilly places Thomas on the left side of Wilcox's line, where it had fought on the night of May 5. Gottfried, *Maps of the Wilderness*, 142-143, 277. J.F.J. Caldwell, an officer in McGowan's brigade, wrote that his brigade's right rested on the road and Thomas's was immediately to the right of the road. J.F.J. Caldwell, *The History of a Brigade of South Carolinians* (Philadelphia, PA: King & Baird, 1866), 131.

Thomas's Brigade straddled Orange Plank Road, with the 14th Georgia remaining on the north side; Hall wrote that he maintained "nearly the same position all night" and a company commander in the 14th Georgia recalled that the regiment remained north of the road.[19] By morning, Thomas's and McGowan's brigades formed a small salient across Orange Plank Road. Hall wrote that their lines "extended into the enemys nearly in the shape of a V or horse shoe."

Many of Hill's men, still low on ammunition, stacked arms and slept out of exhaustion in the belief that Longstreet would arrive before dawn. But dawn did not bring Longstreet and First Corps – instead, it brought a frontal and flank assault by over 30,000 Union troops against Hill's men on Orange Plank Road. The Union forces, some thirteen brigades strong, attacked with the rising sun at their backs. Hall wrote that the Union soldiers attacked in three columns which provided cross-fire from the front, right flank, and rear. Hill had only "eight battered Rebel brigades in two divisions, fewer than 9,000 men in various states of readiness and disarray."[20] As James Robertson writes, Heth and Wilcox had been "strangely unprepared" for the possibility of a dawn attack; even if the lines were still in disarray, waking the men before daylight would have arguably improved their preparedness for the Union onslaught.[21] Ultimately the generals were at fault.[22]

Wilcox's division was routed. Scales's Brigade retreated through Lane's lines, which left Thomas's Brigade exposed to a flank attack on the right; as Hall wrote, with ammunition low and the right flank nearly all captured or killed, Thomas's Brigade reluctantly fell back, too.[23] Before 6 A.M., Hill's line on Orange Plank Road had

---

19. Fox, *Red Clay to Richmond*, 249.
20. Gottfried, *Maps of the Wilderness*, 144.
21. Robertson, *General A. P. Hill*, 262.
22. Hill, Lee, Heth, and Wilcox arguably all remain responsible to some degree for the lack of preparedness in the Confederate front lines on Plank Road when Hancock attacked at dawn. Robertson, *General A. P. Hill*, 262. Historian James L. Morrison, Jr., provides a harsher critique, declaring that even a "moderately diligent corporal could be expected to organize his position and maintain contact with neighboring units" and suggesting that Heth and Wilcox should have disobeyed Hill's order; the attendant reprimand or court-martial for doing so would have been "far better" than to "risk disaster." James L. Morrison, Jr., introduction, *The Memoirs of Henry Heth*, ed. James L. Morrison, Jr. (Greenwood Press, 1974), xlviii.
23. As a member of McGowan's brigade wrote, "For some reason or other, that [Thomas'] brigade broke. The enemy may have struck their flank, or overlapped them, or they may not have been well in line." Caldwell, *History of McGowan's Brigade*, 125. One soldier in the 35th Georgia wrote that the brigade had to "turn tale and get up or the last one of us would of bin taken prisoner." Gottfried, *Maps of the Wilderness*, 146.

collapsed in an assault that happened so rapidly that many Union troops never fired their weapons. Heth maintained decades later that if Wilcox and he had been in line of battle on the morning of May 6, they could easily repulsed the Union attack, enabling Longstreet and Hill to drive Grant back across the Rapidan.[24]

Thomas's Brigade retreated about a half-mile to a position near Lt. Col. William T. Poague's artillery battalion at Tapp Field, close to where Lee was located. As Poague opened fire on Hancock's advancing men, Longstreet's First Corps troops finally made their appearance, rolling back the Union assault on Orange Plank Road, both through a frontal assault and a later flanking maneuver that took advantage of an unfinished railroad bed to the right. Thomas's Brigade, having regrouped behind Poague's artillery, again marched northeast and built emplacements just south of Chewning's Farm. However, in mid-afternoon on May 6, Longstreet was wounded by friendly fire, which took the steam out of the Confederate assault.[25] Although Lee attempted a late afternoon attack against Hancock's breastworks, he did not have the troops to push through, leading some to believe it was a "flagrant lapse of judgment" from a man described by Heth as the most "belligerent" man in the Confederate army.[26]

Fighting continued sporadically until late on May 6, but the sounds of the dying continued all night as wounded men roasted to death in fires that broke out in the underbrush. On May 7, both armies considered their next move. As Ed Bearss described the battle, the Wilderness was a "bloody tactical draw;" Grant had failed to deal Lee a decisive blow but Lee had failed to force Grant back across the Rapidan River.[27] The Union still controlled Brock Road, but instead of retreating and regrouping as so many of his predecessors had done, Grant elected to press on, hoping to fight Lee in open terrain.[28]

---

24. Morrison, *Memoirs of Henry Heth*, 185. Heth also believed that Lee never forgave him or Wilcox for their "awful blunder." Ibid.
25. Major General Richard H. Anderson assumed command of First Corps. Lee, aware that Hill was ill, placed Early in temporary command of Third Corps, which resulted in Gordon taking command of Early's division and Colonel Clement A. Evans taking command of Gordon's brigade.
26. Rhea, *Battle of the Wilderness*, 402.
27. Bearss, *Fields of Honor*, 297.
28. Chris Makowski maintains that the Brock Road/Orange Plank Road intersection was the real turning point of the Civil War, because "there was, quite literally in Grant's view, no turning back. Instead, Grant turned left and south in the first of a series of left-and-south maneuvers that finally jumped the James River and settled into the siege of Petersburg." Chris Makowski, "The Turning Point of the War: The Wilderness, not Gettysburg," Post July 4, 2013, accessed July 25, 2020, https://emergingcivilwar.com/2013/07/04/the-turning-point-of-the-war-the-wilderness-not-gettysburg/

Although the exact numbers are in dispute, both the Union and the Confederate armies suffered staggering losses at the Wilderness.[29] The Union army, thanks to the North's much higher population, was better able to absorb such losses, whereas the Confederacy's pool of potential recruits continued to diminish; as James McPherson writes, "The South was scraping the bottom of the manpower barrel."[30] At the end of April, Thomas had requested, but never received, the transfer of a Georgia infantry battalion to his brigade because he was down to only "1,297 muskets."[31] At the Wilderness, the brigade suffered 406 casualties, almost one-third of its strength; the 14th Georgia suffered seventy-four casualties, with seven killed in action, thirty-two wounded in action, one wounded and captured, and thirty-three missing in action.[32] The most critical casualty for the 14th Georgia was the death of its commander, Col. Robert Folsom, who was shot in his side and his chest on May 6 during Hancock's

Confederate entrenchments on Orange Plank Road. (Library of Congress)

---

29. Union losses are generally accepted to have been just over 17,600, although that number may have been falsified to soften the blow to morale. Rhea, *Battle of the Wilderness*, 435. Confederate losses range from 7,750 to 11,400 casualties. Eicher, *The Longest Night*, 671.
30. McPherson, *Battle Cry of Freedom*, 718. The Confederacy was likewise scraping the bottom of the logistics barrel by mid-1864. One Union private wrote after the war that the many dead Confederates he saw near Brock Road, who were poorly clad, poorly shod, and had inferior arms, showed the "direful poverty of the Confederacy." Frank Wilkeson, *Recollections of a Private Soldier in the Army of the Potomac* (G. P. Putnam's Sons, 1886), 70.
31. Fox, *Red Clay to Richmond*, 247.
32. Young, *Lee's Army during the Overland Campaign: A Numerical Study*, 302. Young's Introduction provides an excellent explanation on the difficulty in assessing accurate numbers of Confederate casualties due to poor record-keeping. Ibid., 3.

dawn attack. Folsom died in a field hospital two days later.³³ Lt. Col. Richard P. Lester assumed command of the 14th Georgia.

Grant's and Lee's next stop was Spotsylvania Court House, where Hall would lose his freedom on May 12, 1864. Grant, still wanting to interpose the Union army between Lee and Richmond, raced to get to Spotsylvania first. Lee won - Confederate troops arrived shortly before the Union forces marching down Brock Road.

Although best remembered for the carnage of May 12, 1864, the battle of Spotsylvania (sometimes referred to as the battle of Spotsylvania Court House) was actually a series

Confederate entrenchments at Spotsylvania (Library of Congress)

of engagements between May 8 and May 20. The terrain at Spotsylvania was a mixed bag, with heavily wooded and marshy areas but still enough open field area to permit increased utilization of artillery and even cavalry by both sides. The heart of the battle, on May 12, 1864, raged over a salient in the Confederate line known as the "Mule Shoe," the scene of almost twenty-four hours of close combat with swords, bayonets, hatchets, and musket butts. But it was also very much a musket battle as well, with some soldiers each firing in excess of three hundred rounds.³⁴

---

33. Folsom, *Heroes and Martyrs of Georgia*, 154. Although Robert Folsom's tombstone at Hollywood Cemetery in Richmond shows his date of death as May 24, 1864, various registry cards in his National Archives records corroborate a date of death of May 8, 1864. Civil War Service Records, Confederate Records, (https://www.fold3.com/image/20/36000864); (https://www.fold3.com/image/20/36000868); (https://www.fold3.com/image/20/36000875), entries for Robert W. Folsom, citing National Archives and Records Administration microfilm publication "Compiled Service Records of Confederate Soldiers Who Served in Organizations from the State of Virginia," M266, Roll 0284, Record Group 109, National Archives, Washington, DC.
34. Chris Mackowski and Kristopher D. White, *A Season of Slaughter: The Battle of Spotsylvania Court House, May 8-21, 1864* (Savas Beatie, 2013), 90.

Thomas's Brigade marched to Spotsylvania Court House on May 9, arriving around noon at the intersection of Brock Road and Fredericksburg Road. During the afternoon, they moved north to the left of the Fredericksburg Road, near a brick kiln, and they began constructing breastworks.[35]

Thomas's Brigade remained in that location, with Scales's Brigade to its right, near the courthouse village, through May 10. Burnside's IX Corps had moved down Fredericksburg Road, centered near the Beverley Farm slightly east-northeast of Wilcox. Hall reported fierce fighting to his left on May 9 and 10.[36] But Thomas's Brigade also had fighting of its own on those two days; Hall wrote that Union forces charged his breastworks several times in succession but were repulsed each time. This may have been an initial attack to test Confederate strength at the right end of Lee's line or a reference to the fighting on May 10 when Union IX Corps artillery fired on Wilcox's men before commencing what John Fox describes as "several half-hearted Union assaults."[37] Gordon Rhea maintains that Grant's failure to fully commit IX Corps against Wilcox, at the time the only Confederate division near Fredericksburg Road, was the most tragic of all the Union's missed opportunities on May 10.[38]

On May 11, Hall and the 14th Georgia moved a short distance to their left, with Union artillery shells falling all around them in the morning. A small Union force demonstrating near Shady Grove Church Road near the Po River prompted Lee to order Early (now the Third Corps commander in Hill's absence) to reinforce the Confederate line at Shady Grove by the morning. Accordingly, Early had Wilcox send two brigades, Thomas's and Scales's, west on Shady Grove Church Road to support William Mahone's division, which had already withstood one Union attack near that road the day before.

---

35. As James McPherson writes, "By this stage of the war the spade had become almost as important for defense as the rifle," with soldiers constructing "elaborate networks of trenches, breastworks, artillery emplacements, traverses, a second line in the rear, and a cleared field of fire in front with the branches of felled trees (abatis), placed at point-blank range to entangle attackers." McPherson, *Battle Cry of Freedom*, 728.
36. On May 10, for example, Union Colonel Emory Upton employed blitzkrieg-like tactics to temporarily break through the western edge of the salient. Upton had to fall back, but his initial success prompted Grant to consider that if twelve regiments could break through the salient breastworks, an entire corps could do far more. Grant found his answer on May 12.
37. Fox, *Red Clay to Richmond*, 259.
38. Gordon C. Rhea, *Battles for Spotsylvania Courthouse and the Road to Yellow Tavern, May 7-12, 1864* (Louisiana State University Press, 1997), 181.

Hall wrote that in the afternoon, he moved "several miles" to the left on a road muddy from rain and that he passed Perry's Brigade, which had been posted with Mahone but was then reassigned to a site near the Spotsylvania Court House. Perhaps Hall spotted his friends Mobley and Bentley as the two brigades passed each other on Shady Grove Church Road, with Hall marching to the west and his friends to the east.

Lee's most critical decision on May 11, 1864, would prove disastrous to the Army of Northern Virginia. Faced with conflicting intelligence reports, he miscalculated Union intentions. Erroneously concluding that Grant was moving east towards Fredericksburg, Lee, anticipating a need to move east in response, ordered the removal of over twenty artillery pieces, many of which supported Maj. Gen. Edward Johnson's portion of the Mule Shoe salient. Johnson protested their removal but, as James McPherson writes, "Too late the guns were ordered back – just in time to be captured by yelling bluecoats as fifteen thousand of them swarmed out of the mist and burst through the Confederate trenches."[39]

The skies released a torrential amount of rain on the evening of May 11 and into May 12. When it appeared that suspected Union activity near Mahone at Shady Grove was only a feint, Wilcox recalled both Thomas's and Scales's brigades in the early morning hours of May 12. It was fortuitous for Lee that Wilcox did so, because the Union made two major pre-dawn fog-covered attacks on May 12, with the largest scale fighting occurring at the Mule Shoe. Hancock's II Corps attacked Ewell's Second Corps corps at the apex of the Mule Shoe. As David Champion wrote after the war, Hancock poured through the gap "like bees into a sugar barrel."[40] Rodes's division held the left sector of the salient, Edward Johnson's division held the right, and at the bottom center was Gordon's (formerly Early's) division in reserve, intended to support either side as needed. As Hancock's men broke through the apex and moved down the salient on the right, they captured two thousand prisoners, including generals Edward Johnson and George H. Steuart, one of Johnson's brigade commanders. Many of Johnson's men, surprised by the aggressiveness of the Union assault, found that overnight rain had wet the percussion caps on their loaded muskets, rendering them useless.

As Hancock's II Corps men advanced down the right side of the Mule Shoe, Potter's Division of Burnside's IX Corps Co advanced on the salient from the east. As the

---

39. McPherson, *Battle Cry of Freedom*, 729.
40. David Champion, *Memoirs*, "Spotsylvania Court House."

Union troops poured down the interior of the Mule Shoe breastworks, the Confederates cobbled together piecemeal attacks from almost every available unit, including Clement Evans's brigade (formerly Gordon's Brigade), a brigade of North Carolinians, scattered survivors from Johnson's division, and men from both Rodes's and Wilcox's divisions.[41] As James Lane led his North Carolinians forward, he was joined by two of Wilcox's other brigades, those of Scales and Thomas.[42] Wilcox had good reason to respond to his left; although he was well-fortified with artillery facing Burnside, the Union push inside the salient posed a danger of enfilade fire.[43] Thomas and Scales "deployed behind Lane and slightly to his left, bridging the gap northward to Gordon."[44] The 14th Georgia occupied the far left of Thomas's line, which placed it closer to the Mule Shoe than the other regiments in the brigade. As Gordon Rhea writes, "Lane, Scales, Thomas, and scattered units from Evans pressed Potter slowly back," after which "Thomas continued ahead, battering Potter."[45]

Hall is very specific in his entry for May 12 that Thomas's Brigade assisted Gordon's (now Evan's) Brigade, which "had retaken our works and drove the enemy back 4 or 5

---

41. Shelby Foote, *The Civil War: A Narrative Red River to Appomattox* (Random House, 1974), 219. Foote wrote that Wilcox was free to assist in Gordon's counterattack because the early morning attack by Burnside had been so ineffective; there had been no penetration of Wilcox's lines, and Burnside's divisions were "made up of greener, less determined men than the veterans under Meade." Ibid.
42. Freeman, *Lee* (Harwell abridgment), 385-86. As Early wrote in his memoirs, "A portion of the attacking force swept along Johnson's line to Wilcox's left, and was checked by a prompt movement on the part of Brigadier General Lane, who was on that flank." Early, *Memoirs*, 355. According to Freeman, "On the right of the salient, Gordon with the help of part of Wilcox's Division of the Third Corps drove the enemy almost to the apex." Douglas Southall Freeman, *Lee's Lieutenants* (Scribner, 1944 renewed 1972 by Inez Godwin Freeman) 3:408.
43. Dowdey, *Lee's Last Campaign*, 208. Dowdey wrote that Gordon, with help of Wilcox's regiments, pushed the enemy outside of the works. Ibid., 211.
44. Rhea, *Battles for Spotsylvania Courthouse*, 253.
45. One area of the battlefield where the 14th Georgia almost certainly was *not* present at on May 12, 1864, was near the site of the post-war 15th New Jersey Infantry Regiment monument. The 15th New Jersey long maintained that it had seized the flag of the 14th Georgia on May 12, and, in 1909, the state erected a monument to "mark the portion of the Confederate line held by the 14th Georgia Regiment, and assaulted May 12, 1864, by the 15th Regiment, New Jersey Volunteer Infantry." However, the 14th Georgia was nowhere near the 15th New Jersey on the left side of the Bloody Angle. No one, at the time the flag was seized, identified it as the 14th Georgia's; in fact, a New Jersey newspaper, a week after the battle, identified it as coming from a Tar Heel (North Carolina) regiment, which makes far more sense given that Dodson Ramseur's North Carolina brigade did engage in hand-to-hand combat with New Jersey troops. Peter S. Carmichael, "We Respect a *Good* Soldier, No Matter What Flag He Fought Under: The 15th New Jersey Remembers Spotsylvania," in Gary W. Gallagher, ed., *The Spotsylvania Campaign* (University of North Carolina Press, 1998) 222, n34.

hundred [likely yards] to their breast works."⁴⁶ Sergeant J. J. Tibbots of Company K of the 14th Georgia recalled how the order came about:

> Just before we got into our breastworks there came a courier to Col. Paul Lester and gave him a paper, then, he turned in his saddle and gave the command – about! face, right shoulder shift! Arms double quick, march! We went about one mile down the road and halted, ordered arms, fixed bayonets and charged with a yell! The Yanks had gotten our works and all of Johnson's division that was in the works, and we took the works from them and drove back into their works, and they had five lines firing on our half line.⁴⁷

Thomas's and Scales's men hurried a half mile, according to Hall, "through a dense wilderness of undergrowth, sometimes through marshes and ponds" higher than the soldiers' knees. Hall specifically references fighting alongside the 13th Georgia Infantry of Evans's (Gordon's) Brigade. He said the 14th Georgia joined the 13th Georgia, with their combined strength still less than a single regimental line. Hall continued, "We engaged 3 strong lines of the enemy and fought them in less than 50 yards of their lines for nearly two hours under the most terrible fire I ever saw. I fought at the colors of the gallant 13th, our Noble boys falling killed and wounded all round me." As Earl Hess describes the action, Thomas's and Scales's brigades "filled the gap between Lane and the right flank of Gordon's Reserve Line, and supported Lane's Tar Heels by driving Griffin out of the captured segment of the Third Corps trench."⁴⁸ According to Jeffrey Wert, the addition of Thomas's and Scales's brigades not only intensified the fighting, but also proved decisive.⁴⁹

---

46. Rhea, *The Battles for Spotsylvania Court House*, 246.
47. J. J. Tibbets, "The Battle of Spotsylvania C. H. May 12, 1864," *Reminiscences of Confederate Soldiers and Stories of the War*, vol. IX, 172-173. A veteran of the 35th Georgia recalled after the war that Thomas' Brigade "participated in retaking the works lost by Johnson's division, advancing with Gordon's brigade in its charge against our own breastworks, and following the enemy within a short distance of their own, which was in a pine thicket." W. T. Irvine, "Old 35th Georgia," Atlanta *Sunny South*, May 2, 1891, https://gahistoricnewspapers.galileo.usg.edu. David Champion also wrote that the regiment "came on the ground at double quick to support Gordon in his charge." David Champion, *Memoirs*, "Spotsylvania Court House."
48. Earl J. Hess, *Trench Warfare under Grant & Lee: Field Fortifications in the Overland Campaign* (University of North Carolina Press, 2007), 69-70. Simon Griffin was a brigade commander in Potter's Division in Burnside's IX Corps.
49. Jeffry D. Wert, *The Heart of Hell: The Soldiers' Struggle for Spotsylvania's Bloody Angle* (University of North Carolina Press, 2022), 121.

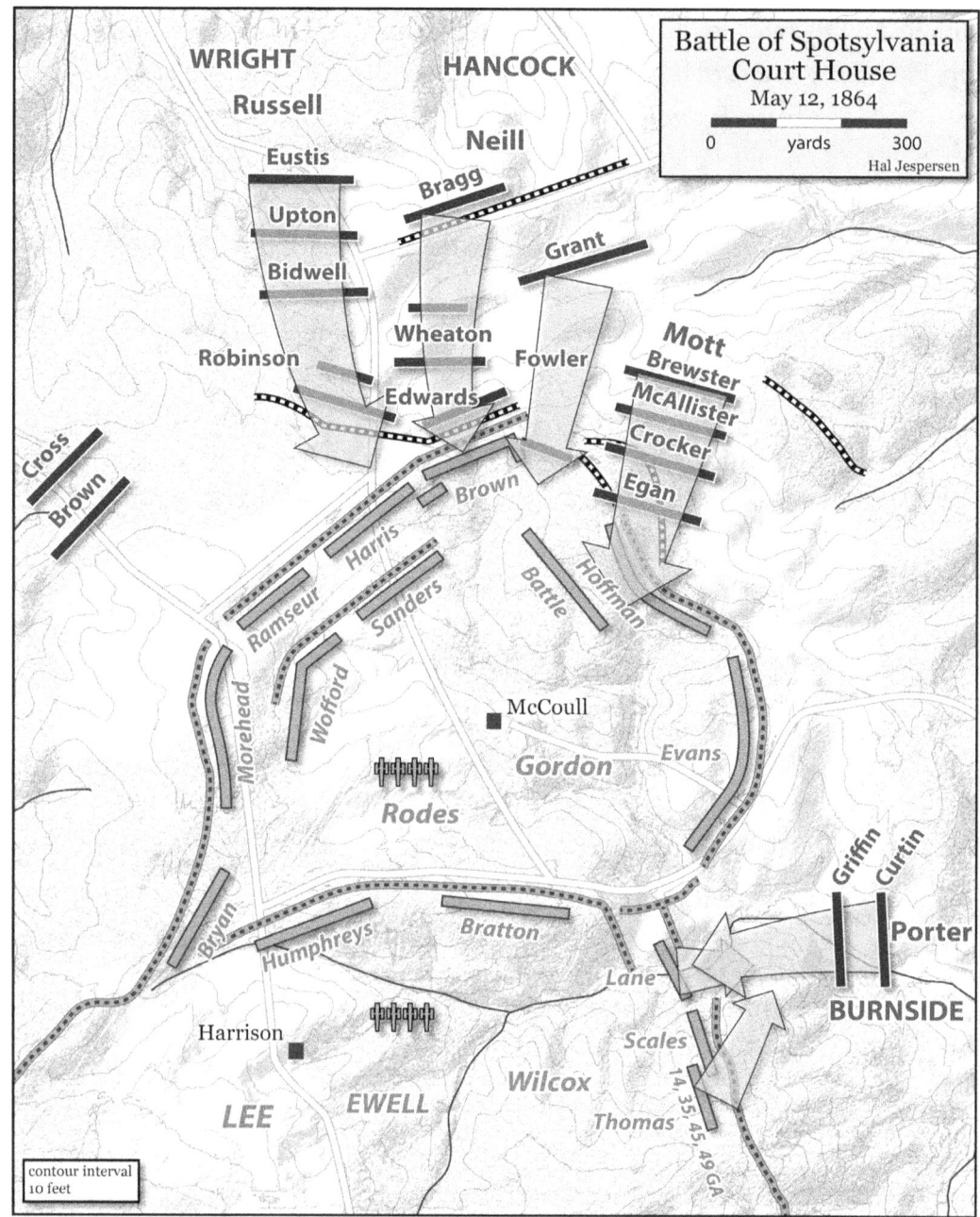

Thomas's Brigade not only countered attacks by Burnside's men but also supported Gordon in pushing back the Union troops in the Mule Shoe. (Map by Hal Jespersen)

As the combined Confederate firepower repulsed Burnside's attack, many of Wilcox's division climbed over their breastworks and chased the Union troops under a terrible fire from muskets and artillery. Hall wrote they had a steep bluff to go down and a wide ditch, three or four feet deep with mud and water, to cross in a field in full view of the enemy in less than a hundred yards of their lines. After getting flanked and their line weakened, Hall and his comrades had to climb back up the bluff and work their way back through the ditch. Hall wrote that very few of the regiment were able to pass those obstacles before they were killed or taken prisoner.[50] Hall wrote that it was the Lord's will that he was one of the latter.

Hall and the other prisoners from the 14th Georgia were hurried to the rear by their captors, likely troops from IX Corps because they took the prisoners to that corps' headquarters, where Hall saw Burnside and several other general officers. The rain began to fall in torrents again, with Hall writing eloquently that the thunders of the heavens were mingling with the thunder of battle. While under fire from incoming artillery shot, Union guards separated wounded prisoners and marched Hall and the other non-wounded prisoners through mud two or three miles to another location. The group halted for the night on Orange Plank Road, the same road which Hall had traveled on a year earlier en route to Bullock Road and which had been the source of such vicious fighting just a week before in the Wilderness. Hall fell asleep in the mud and rain.

Hall credits God's will with the fact that he was taken prisoner rather than killed. Indeed, his faith served him well at Spotsylvania, giving him courage in combat: "I resigned my self into His hand and trusted alone in His Almighty Power and I feared not the missiles of death although they mowed down my comrades by scores in every direction." He attributes his survival to God: "The Lord was with me and preserved me for without His aid I could never have escaped death." Hall would lean into that faith to get him through the following nine months of captivity.

Hall ends his entry for May 12 with the sentence, "So ends the most eventful day of my life and what I have sketched is only a faint outline." Hall's active role in the war effectively ended on May 12, 1864, with his capture at Spotsylvania. Some three hundred miles away the war effectively also ended for Jacob Elsesser, whose enlistment expired that day.

---

50. Thomas's Brigade incurred 184 casualties at Spotsylvania, with the 14th Georgia accounting for the highest number of casualties in the brigade (68). The regiment suffered eighteen killed, twenty-four wounded in action, ten wounded and captured, and sixteen missing in action. Young, *Lee's Army During the Overland Campaign*, 303. Among those killed was First Lieutenant Josiah B. Patterson, whose letters home in 1861 and 1862 provide so much insight into the struggles the regiment faced in Virginia early in the war.

Remembrancer Daily Entries
May 1 – 12, 1864

Sunday, May 1, 1864

M cloudy. E fair & pleasant. Preaching before and after noon prayer meeting at night. Two of my friends from the 5th Fla pays me a visit.

Monday, May 2, 1864

M fair. E thunder storm. The Signs of the times indicates that the campaign will commence before another week expires. Important events will Transpire ere long no doubt. There came a feir[c]e thunder storm this evening which we learn was a snow storm on the mountains.

Tuesday, May 3, 1864

Cloudy, windy & cool. We go on picket on the Rapidan. I received two letters, and wrote one.

Wednesday, May 4, 1864

Fair & pleasant. We return off picket at our usual hour of being relieved. Every [thing] appearing as quiet as usually, although we had heard the evening previous that the enemy were crossing the river. We had scarcely arrived back at camp and got our breakfast when we received orders to march immediately. The drums resounded and echoed from the various brig[ade] and regt from every direction, thier hoarse monotious [monotonous] sound be token and war[n]ed us to prepare, for batter [battle]. Near noon we marched through Orange C.H. thence down the plank road toward Fredericksburg. Late in the evening we camp near Mine Run, where we offered Meade Battle last Dec. Cook two days rations. I get hardly any sleep sitting up in order to cook for my mess, but the Lord is with me and I spend a sweet hour in meditation & prayer near midnight. I put my whole trust in him and I believe He will Shield guard and protect me from all harm and I believe He will be with me on the field of Battle. Trust in God.

Thursday, May 5, 1864

Fair & warm. At daylight we march again. Our cavalry skirmish along in front of us for several miles. Part of our corps becomes engage[d] with the enemy before noon. Our division files out to the left of the plank road, form line of Battle and march through an old field and through a dense thicket of undergrowth and through a swampy boggy ravine. We halt a few minutes and take breath when the order comes down the line "march by the right flank," and in order to close up we double quick a considerable distance, charge in line of battle through another dense peice of wood when we capture several hundred prisoners, Without our brigade being engaged. The time this movement was executed was brief indeed, for we march back nearly the way we came for two or three miles, to where our men are warmly engaged near the road. We march in cool and calm, my whole trust in God. I resign myself [e]ntirely into His hand. I fear not for the Lord of Host[s] is with me with His strong arm. Verry soon the enemy's balls are whistling around our ears. Soon the cheers and Shouts of our boys sounds above the thunders of Battle. Soon the sharp crack of our rifles add to the already terrible roar and bloody carnage. We maintain our ground against 3 times our number. The contest rages with unabated fury till dark. We still maintain nearly the same position during the night.

Friday, May 6, 1864

Fair and warm. At daylight the battle was renewed. Our lines and the enemy was not but a few yards apart, during the night and our lines extended into the enemys nearly in the shape of a V or horse shoe & when the Battle begun this morning, the enemy advanced in 3 colum[n]s cross firing on our Brig[ade] from 3 directions from the front, right flank and rear, & we withstood the terrable fire for a considerable time and had nearly exhausted our ammunition when our right flank was nearly all captured or killed. We were ordered to fall back which we reluctantly done. Gen Longstreet and his gallant corps came to our relief and we were permited to fall to the rear and rally our shattered forces. Our Noble Col Robert W Folsom was mortally wounded and died soon afterwards. 5 or 6 of my company was killed or taken prisoners and several wounded. The Battle raged nearly all day. The remainder of time we were not fighting, we were building breastworks.

Saturday, May 7, 1864

M cloudy. E fair & warm. We taken a new position and changed that 3 or [4] times and lay in line of Battle. Last night the Battle continued in fierce conflict on the right and left. Our Brig[ade] was not engaged today, except Skirmishing. I received letter from A.M. which gave me a great consolation.[51] After night we move up over a mile to the right.

Sunday, May 8, 1864

Fair & warm. We remain in the line of battle till after noon when we ascertain the enemy has all moved to the right in the direction of Fredericksburg & we march several miles to the right. The Battle has raged hot and heavy near Spottsylvania C.H. [Court House]. We remain in line of Battle during the night what time we are marching.

---

51. This is likely a reference to Amanda Mobley.

Monday, May 9, 1864

M cloudy. E fair & warm. At daylight we march again in a curcuitous route. We arrive at Spottsylvania C.H. near noon and form lines and change positions. The remainder of the evening a fierce Battle rages on our left and some on the right Again today. After dark we move over one mile to the right below the C.H. [Court House].

Tuesday, May 10, 1864

Par cloudy & warm. We remain where we were last night till about 10 A. M. when we move back to the court House. The enemys shells fall among us all the evening. The Battle rages with renewed vigor just a little to the left of us. The enemy charges our breastwork several times in succession and were repulsed each time with terrable slaughter and were driven several miles on the left.

Wednesday, May 11, 1864

M cloudy. E thunder & rain. Heavy skirmishing was continued in front of us at entervals all night last night. This morning we moved a short distance to the left. The enemys shells fall all among us before noon. Afternoon we moved several miles to the left. The road is rendered verry muddy by the rain. We pass Anderson's Div. Perrys Brig[ade]. The Battle rages with contested fury at various points along the line. The rain continues nearly all night. After dark a considerable time we halt but get scarcely any rest.

Thursday, May 12, 1864

M foggy. E Thunder and rain. We pass a chilly disagreeable night. Before daylight we march back the way we came last evening. Heavy firing commences a short distance to the left of the Court House. Before good light we march to the court House, halt a few moments and we get news that the enemy under cover of the dense fog (which lay heavily on the earth till near noon) had surprised our forces and brake through our line carrying our left flank before them. Our Brigade was sent in to the relief of Gen Gordons Brig[ade] who had retaken our works and drove the enemy back 4 or 5 hundred [ ] to their breast works. They had sustained a heavy loss and after our Brig[ade] had advanced over a half mile through a dense wilderness of undergrowth, sometimes through marshes and ponds over our knees, we cross[ed] our breast works and advanced several hundred yards under a terrable fire of grape canister shells and minies balls. We had a steep bluff to go down and a wide ditch to cross in a field in full view of the enemy in less than a hundred yards of their lines. A good number of our men were shot down before we arrived.

The 14 Ga joined the 13 Ga and the ranks of both regts were thin[n]ed so that both did not make a line as strong as one regt. We engaged 3 strong lines of the enemy and fought them in less than 50 yards of their lines for nearly two hours under the most terrable fire I ever saw. I fought at the colors of the gallant 13[th], our Noble boys falling killed and wounded all round me. The Lord was with me and preserved me for without His aid I could never have escaped death. I resigned my self into His hand and trusted alone in His Almight Power and I feared not the missiles of death although they mowed down my comrades by scores in every direction.

In the meantime our line had become so weak it began at length to give way before the murderous and heavy fire of three lines of the [ ] besides they had flanked us on the right, that steep bluff was to be ascended ere we could get any distance from the view of the enemy. Besides a wide deep ditch 3 or 4 feet in mud and Water verry few of our regt were able to pass those obsticles before they were killed or taken prisoners. It was the Lords will for me to be with the latter.

20 or 30 of my regt was taken at the same time and hurried to the rear by our uxultant captors. We saw the full positions of the enemy and know what they had employed against us. As we pass out we see Gen Burnsides & several other general officers. We halt a few minutes at Burnsides Head-Quarters. The rain begins to fall in torrents, the thunders of the Heaven mingling with the fierce carnage and thunder of Battle. The elements seemed to have caught the angry contagion from the fierce clash of resounding arms & hoarse accents of death from the Battle field. Shells from our Batteries begin to fall & and burst near us. We are carried on farther to the rear, halt again. The rain chills us to the bone. They have separate[d] the wounded from the well. Soon they hurry us on through the mud 2 or 3 miles and we remain there, till near dark, and start again & go through mud & water in some places over knee deep at a slow pace, behind a waggon train. A little before day we halt on the plank road near Chancellorsville, lie down exhausted in the mud and rain and soon I am unconscious of my ill-fated position. So ends the most eventful day of my life and what I have sketched is only a faint outline.

12

"I SIGH AND PRAY FOR DIXIE"
FORT DELAWARE: MAY 13, 1864 – DECEMBER 1864

On the morning of May 13, 1864, Hall woke up feeling sick and exhausted, almost surely more uncertain about his future than on any other day of the war. Union escorts from a New York regiment marched him towards Fredericksburg. The group arrived in town on May 15 and commenced marching again at sunrise on May 16. Hall and new escorts, Union cavalrymen, crossed the Rappahannock over a pontoon bridge and arrived in mid-afternoon at Belle Plain, a steamboat landing on Potomac Creek that served as a forward supply base for Union forces. Only a dozen miles from Fredericksburg, its multiples wharves provided a critical water route up the Potomac to Alexandria, some eight hours up river, and fed into the Chesapeake Bay downriver.[1] One unique feature of the area around Belle Plain was the "Punch Bowl," a series of ravines that provided a natural prison yard for Confederate prisoners of war. Hall noted that cannons on the hills overlooking the prisoners threatened the Confederates with "instant destruction" to ensure they remained quiet and well-behaved.

Over 7,500 Confederate prisoners were processed through the Punch Bowl in mid-May 1864 and dispatched by steamers at Belle Plain to Union prison camps.[2] The majority were sent to Point Lookout in southern Maryland, and many of those were transferred soon thereafter to Elmira, New York. Hall avoided both Point Lookout and Elmira;

---

1. U.S. Army Center of Military History, *Wilderness-Spotsylvania Staff Ride Briefing Book* (n.d.), 10. Belle Plain is often referred to as Belle Plains. I use the name reflected in the *Official Records.*
2. William A. Frassanito, *Grant and Lee: The Virginia Campaigns 1864-1865* (Charles Scribner's Sons, 1983), 57.

instead, he was sent to Fort Delaware, Delaware, on Pea Patch Island on the Delaware River. Providing his name and rank, Hall was mustered by his captors on May 17. On the following day he boarded a steamboat, and then a "large Steam frigate," for the trip to Fort Delaware. Accommodations were cramped, with five to seven hundred Confederates crowded on the lower deck, in suffocating conditions with no room to lie down.[3] At one point the frigate ran ashore, requiring a tow from two tugs and a steamboat. After getting lost in a fog, the frigate finally landed Hall at Pea Patch Island on May 20. Hall was searched for contraband but permitted to keep his diaries. Once his in-processing was completed, he was assigned a division, a unit for administrative accountability.

The "Punch Bowl" at Belle Plain: Confederate troops captured at Spotsylvania on May 12, 1864. ((Library of Congress)

Ships at the Belle Plain landing, May 1864. The steamboats may have been those used to transport prisoners of war down the Potomac River. (Library of Congress)

---

3. Roger Pickenpaugh, *Captives in Gray: The Civil War Prisons of the Union* (University of Alabama Press, 2009), 90.

What to do with prisoners of war is an issue as old as warfare itself. Gone were the days of simply executing captives, selling them into slavery, or holding them for ransom. Instead, the emergence of the law of armed conflict in Western warfare meant that captors needed to afford those captured certain protections, such as housing, food, and medical care. Implementing those protections often became unwieldy as the scale of warfare grew to battles involving tens of thousands of combatants. Such battles could mean potentially thousands of prisoners of war for the victorious army to both guard and maintain. During the Civil War, the Union held approximately 220,000 Confederate prisoners; the Confederacy held about 200,000 Union prisoners.[4] Many of the captured on both sides were wounded men who could not be removed during battle, which meant the army who ultimately claimed the field also claimed responsibility for the care of the enemy wounded.[5]

Prisoners of war posed both a logistical and political issue for armies. One of the easiest alternatives was for the two sides to simply exchange prisoners after the battle, a practice long recognized in Western warfare. However, this practice proved unwieldy with large numbers of prisoners. Moreover, it briefly left Lincoln in a delicate political position. The practice of exchanges was one that existed between sovereign states, a status which Lincoln was not prepared to afford the Confederate States of America. At the same time, he did not wish to treat every captured Confederate soldier as a traitor to the Union, which was a capital crime. The compromise was to establish an exchange cartel between the Union and what was considered another army – but not a separate government.[6]

The initial exchange cartel, named the Dix-Hill Cartel after the Union and Confederate major generals who negotiated it, went into effect in July 1862. Prisoners were to be exchanged on the James River near Richmond or at Vicksburg.[7] Each prisoner of war held relative value based on their rank. Enlisted personnel and officers

---

4. William Best Hesseltine, *Civil War Prisons: A Study in War Psychology* (Frederick Unger, 1930), 2. Almost one of every six Confederates was captured over the course of the war. Glatthaar, *General Lee's Army*, 327.
5. The largest single loss to the Confederacy occurred at Gettysburg, where some 12,000 Confederates were captured, including almost 7,000 wounded officers and enlisted men. Glatthaar, *General Lee's Army*, 327.
6. Brian Temple, *The Union Prison at Fort Delaware: A Perfect Hell on Earth* (McFarland & Company, 2003), 14.
7. R. Hugh Simmons, "Parole & Exchange," *Fort Delaware Notes,* 51 (2001), 9.

would be exchanged one for one with prisoners of the same rank. However, exchanging a higher-ranked prisoner for a lower-ranked one required consultation with a table almost as complex as foreign currency conversion. A brigadier general could be exchanged for twenty privates but a major could be exchanged for only eight privates. Pending the exchange, prisoners could be released on parole, a status where they promised to not to raise arms for their army again until the exchange process was completed. Again, the sheer number of prisoners made this part of the process essentially unenforceable, so both sides began holding prisoners in military forts and prisons until the exchange process was completed.

Fort Delaware, on Pea Patch Island in the middle of the Delaware River, had been built to protect the water approaches to Wilmington and Philadelphia. George McClellan, then a captain of Engineers, served as one of its first construction officers in the early 1850s. Legend has it that Pea Patch Island came into creation after a ship carrying a cargo of peas ran aground on a sandbar in the Delaware River; the peas sprouted and over time, the sandbar became an 80-acre swampy island as material dredged from the river was added to the vegetable-rooted sandbar. When its first garrison assumed duties there in 1860, Fort Delaware was still undergoing final stages of construction. The fort was a massive polygonal structure, with walls up to thirty feet thick and thirty-two feet tall. The structure covered six acres and was surrounded by a moat, twelve feet deep and thirty feet wide, that provided defensive protection as well as a conduit for waste from the fort to be sluiced into the Delaware River. Fort Delaware was state-of-the-art for 1860, and at seventy-five ground acres, it was the largest fort in the United States for its time. But when the United States entered its next war, Fort Delaware, with its capacity for over 150 guns, never fired a shot in battle; rather, this mighty defensive bastion was reduced to service as a prison camp.

Fort Delaware was an ideal location for a prisoner of war camp. Escapees from the island would have to swim at least a mile across the current to reach either the New Jersey or Delaware shores. The fort's location on the Delaware River offered easy access for supply ships, convenience as a prisoner exchange point, and security due to the unlikelihood of attack by either the Confederate army or the Confederate navy. Use of the fort as a prison camp was first proposed in 1861, in part because of overcrowding at Fort McHenry but also due to concerns about housing pro-Southern prisoners in Baltimore. The Fort Delaware garrison was likely unhappy with the change in mission.

Aerial view of Pea Patch Island in the 1960s. (Library of Congress)

Fort Delaware received its first prisoners in 1862. The Dix-Hill Cartel worked relatively smoothly at this juncture in the war and prisoners departed Fort Delaware "at a record-setting pace."[8] However, the cartel program lasted less than a year, collapsing due to abuse of the parole system and the Confederate Congress's authorization in May 1863 for its army to enslave or execute captured Black soldiers and their white officers.[9] Between the collapse of the cartel and the explosion in numbers of prisoners from Gettysburg and Vicksburg, Fort Delaware was soon bursting at the seams, with over 12,000 prisoners; in fact, due to its prison population, Pea Patch Island was, at times, the largest city in Delaware.[10]

One of the immediate logistical issues involved in maintaining a prison population this large was housing, an issue that entailed not only putting roofs over heads but also providing a means of monitoring and controlling prisoners. Fort Delaware was the only Northern prison that confined not only all ranks from private to general but political prisoners as well.[11] Where a prisoner lived at Fort Delaware was almost entirely dependent

---

8. Dale Fetzer & Bruce Mowday, *Unlikely Allies: Fort Delaware's Prison Community in the Civil War* (Stackpole Books, 2000), 74. In July 1862, there were 3,434 prisoners but by January 1, 1863, there were only 17. Ibid., 87. However, the number skyrocketed later that year, especially after the battle of Gettysburg.
9. Moreover, Grant believed that the Confederacy was recycling its parolees back into combat without waiting for the exchange process to be completed. Some of the Confederates captured at Chattanooga in November 1863 had been paroled after Vicksburg and Port Hudson several months before. Temple, *The Union Prison at Fort Delaware*, 26.
10. Fetzer and Mowday, *Unlikely Allies*, 108.
11. During the war, Fort Delaware held a total of over 450 political prisoners, many of whom were confined after Lincoln suspended the writ of habeas corpus; few ever went to trial. The most well-known of the political prisoners was Rev. Isaac Handy of Maryland, who spent sixteen months at Fort Delaware for allegedly making disloyal comments.

on his status or rank; indeed, the cliché "rank has its privileges" proved a bitter reality to incarcerated privates. Senior officers and political prisoners were usually housed inside the fort itself. Lieutenant McHenry Howard, a staff officer to Brig. Gen. Steuart, admitted that he had access to special privileges and advantages due to his status.[12] At one point, senior officers were permitted to walk around the island freely, although that privilege was amended in May 1864 to require the company of a guard.[13]

Junior officers and enlisted soldiers had their own wooden barracks out in what was called "the pen." These barracks, plus a hospital, were northwest of the fort and enclosed by a tall plank fence. The eight-acre compound was divided into two areas, the larger sector for enlisted men and the smaller for officers.

Enlisted prisoners at Fort Delaware occupied rectangular plank buildings that were uniformly 24 feet wide and, for those built in 1863, anywhere from 211 to 519 feet long.[14] Hall described the interior of the barracks as having tiered wooden sleeping scaffolds arranged like berths on a ship. A wood-burning stove sat in the center of the barracks. The enlisted men were assigned to divisions. A senior prisoner in a division was usually a sergeant.[15]

---

12. McHenry Howard, *Recollections of a Maryland Confederate Soldier and Staff Officer under Johnston, Jackson and Lee,* (Williams & Wilkins Co., 1914), 305. Howard was a Maryland political blue-blood: one grandfather had served as governor (and had a county named for him) and the other grandfather was Francis Scott Key (which may explain "McHenry" as Howard's first name). Evan Phifer, "Reminiscences of an Exiled Marylander," *Military Images,* vol. 35 No. 4 (Autumn 2017), 68-70. After his capture at Spotsylvania, Howard was provided a horse to ride for a portion of the way to Fredericksburg and had a seat in the main saloon of the river steamboat that took him down the Potomac River. General Albin Schoepf, the Fort Delaware garrison commander, apparently took a particular liking to Howard because he not only permitted Howard's family to visit but hosted the family in his quarters as dinner guests. Moreover, it was at Schoepf's suggestion that Howard claimed that he had rheumatism in order to obtain a medical exchange in late October 1864. Howard, *Recollections of a Maryland Confederate Soldier,* 328, 332.
13. Howard, *Recollections of a Maryland Confederate Soldier,* 331. Colonel William W. Ward of the 9th Tennessee Cavalry Regiment wrote in his diary that he was "paroled to the island" and permitted "unlimited freedom of movement around the island from reveille to retreat." Rosenburg, ed., *For the Sake of My Country,* 16, 25.
14. Joel Citron, *Confederate Prisoners at Fort Delaware: The Legend of Mistreatment Reexamined* (McFarland, 2018), 73-74.
15. The sergeant's duties included leading the prisoners into meals, ensuring the barracks were cleaned every morning, getting the sick to the hospital, distributing mail, and reporting to the Union lieutenant in charge of the enlisted prisoner barracks. In return, the sergeant was entitled to choose his own bunk. William H. Runge, ed., *Four Years in the Confederate Artillery: The Diary of Private Henry Robinson Berkeley* (Virginia Historical Society, 1991). Berkeley commenced his imprisonment at Fort Delaware less than a week after Hall sailed south to Richmond.

FROM A YANKEE TO A REBEL DIARY

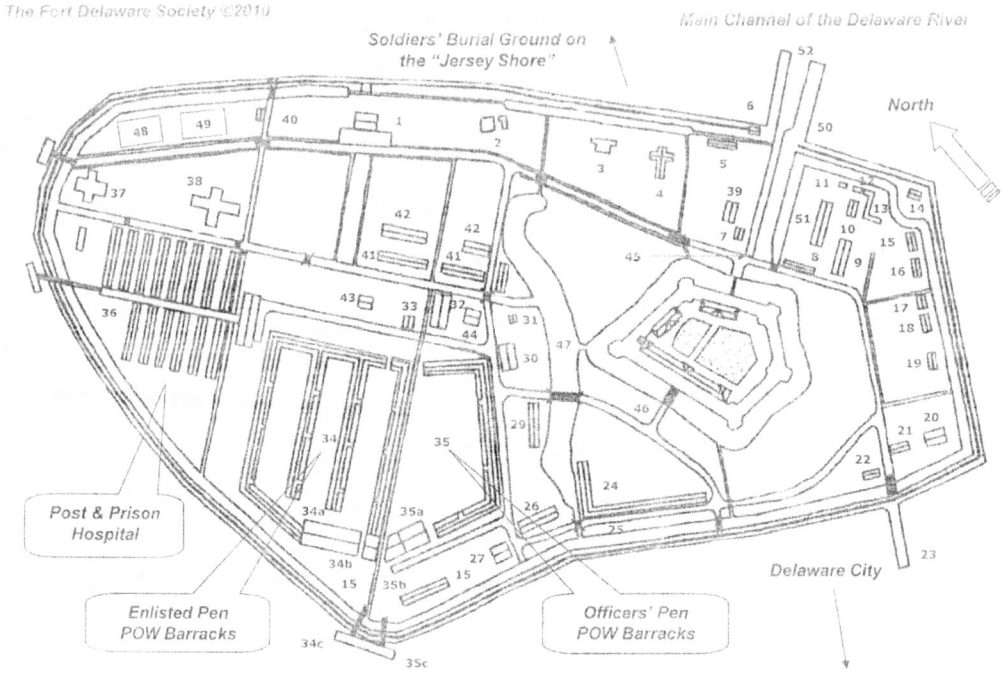

Military Prison on Pea Patch Island
U. S. Army Engineer's Map – June 1864
(See Map Key on Reverse Side)

Map Key
Military Prison on Pea Patch Island
June 1864

1	Post Commander's Quarters	30	Prison Bakery
2	Chaplain & Staff Quarters	31	Garrison Officers Ice House
3	Post Surgeons Quarters	32	Garrison Officers Hospital
4	Trinity Chapel	33	Officers Guard House (Prison Staff)
5	Laborers' Shanty	34	POW Enlisted Men's Prison Barracks
6	Pump engine house	a	Enlisted Prison Mess Hall
7	Lime house & rigging loft	b	Enlisted Prison Kitchen
8	Cement shed	c	Enlisted Latrines ("The Rear")
9	Carpenter shop	35	POW Officers & Civilian Detainee Prison Barracks
10	Blacksmith shop	a	Officers Prison Mess Hall
11	Coal house	b	Officers Prison Kitchen
12	Old Iron shed	c	Officers Latrines ("The Rear")
13	Sutler's store	36	Post & Prison Hospital
14	Ordnance Sergeant's Quarters	37	Contagious Ward
15	Sutler's store	38	Hospital Surgeons Quarters
16	Laborers & laundresses	39	Garrison Officers Gymnasium
17	Laborers & laundresses	40	Hay Barn
18	Laborers & laundresses	41	Infantry Barracks
19	Officers Mess	42	Infantry Officers Barracks
20	Officers Quarters & Boarding House	43	Store House
21	Teamsters & Boatmen	44	Officers Guard House (Post Security)
22	Shanty & storehouse	45	Sluice Gate to the moat
23	Civilian Dock to Delaware City	46	Fort Sally Port
24	L-shaped Infantry Barracks	47	Island drainage ditches
25	Laundry Sheds	48	Union Cemetery Plot
26	Cart Shed	49	Confederate Cemetery Plot
27	Stable & Barns	50	POW, Quartermaster & Commissary Dock
28	Granary	51	Commissary Store & Shed
29	Prison Commissary Storehouse	52	Sluiceway to sluice gate & moat

The Fort Delaware Society ©2010

Hall's barracks are at location 34. Location 34a is the enlisted prison mess hall. Location 34c is the latrine over the water. (Map and legend courtesy of the Fort Delaware Society)

At times, prisoners were permitted only a single blanket. Rain leaked through the roof and in the winter, snow blew on the berths through holes in the weather boarding. Hall lamented that there were only two stoves to heat 500 men. Men who lived on the top tier, the "high livers," dealt with leaks while the "floor men" on the lower tiers were the most uncomfortable due to "dripping from higher men and breathing in the dampness from the wet ground under the open, badly constructed floor."[16] Hall was apparently a "high liver" at one point because in late November, 1864, he fell from the top bunk to the floor and was "rendered insensible for nearly an hour."

Hall wrote on his first full day on the island that the water was very bad. As he grew sick in mid-July, he noted again how poor the water was and maintained that its use was contributing to "contagious diseases . . . raging violent." Obtaining fresh water was always a challenge for those who lived on Pea Patch Island. Because of the island's water table, wells were not available to provide water suitable for drinking. Instead, rainwater was collected from the roofs of the barracks into two wooden tanks but often in insufficient quantity for the number of prisoners on the island; moreover, in the summer when there was little rain, the water quickly became putrid and stagnant.[17] Prison officials arranged for water to be brought by boat from the Brandywine River, but it was reportedly unfiltered and often left sandy sediment in the water cisterns.[18] Diarrhea brought on by the poor water put additional strain on the capacity of the "sinks," the toilet sites that ran just offshore where waste dropped directly into the river.

Interior of a reconstructed enlisted prisoner barracks. (Photo by Michael G. Hall)

---

16. Temple, *The Union Prison at Fort Delaware*, 41.
17. Temple, *The Union Prison at Fort Delaware*, 45.
18. Temple, *The Union Prison at Fort Delaware*, 35.

Food was also in short supply for the prisoners, unless they were officers or political prisoners, many of whom grouped their resources to form a mess where they purchased food from a sutler or received boxes sent to them by Northern sympathizers. Some higher-ranking prisoners in the fort had their meals cooked and served to them, either by a Union soldier (possibly a prisoner himself), or for a while, by a Black woman who was hired to cook and wash. To kill off bugs in the drinking water ("wiggle waggles"), officers, who were permitted to keep liquor in their rooms, mixed their water with whiskey or brandy that they purchased from the sutler.

Enlisted men who had private funds to pay the high prices demanded by the prison sutler could purchase food to augment their prison rations; otherwise, they ate only their standard rations. Hall wrote early on in his stay at Fort Delaware that what he got to eat was "more scant" than he ever had to live on before.[19] Prisoners at Fort Delaware received two meals a day, and Hall wrote that he got more for one day's ration when he was with the army than he got in three days at Fort Delaware. The morning meal usually consisted of a small piece of bread (likely cornbread) or a handful of crackers and a small piece of beef or bacon. Dinner usually duplicated breakfast but with the addition of a bit more meat and soup. With a rare display of cynicism, Hall wrote that the short rations reduced illness and death because prisoners were not given enough food to cause them to become ill from eating too much, which meant that the prisoners avoided the fever and other diseases brought on by indigestion. On November 2, 1864, he wrote that twice a day his meat ration was a piece of lean boiled beef the size of a man's thumb, that he received four to six ounces of bread a day, and that some days he had a half pint of soup.

---

19. Another prisoner wrote that his rations consisted of one-fourth of an eight-ounce loaf of baker's bread twice a day, and that there was only enough meat provided for "one good mouthful" with the occasional Irish potato added. W. H. Bland to G. W. Nichols, December 20, 1897 in Nichols, *A Soldier's Story of His Regiment (61st Georgia)*, 234.

At times he received no soup or meat.[20] Hall's hunger apparently never abated; when he reached the eight-month mark in his confinement, he wrote that he suffered more from hunger than he ever thought he was capable of enduring. Hall lamented the quantity of food but not its quality, which other prisoners had reported (often long after the war) was fit only for a pigsty or trough.[21] Nor is there any indication in Hall's diary that he was ever reduced to eating rats, as others reported doing.[22]

What was frustrating for Hall was not only that he was hungry but that those around him who had money ate so much better; as he expressed his feelings, "It is the most miserable life to live & always be hungry & also to see a plenty of good things to eat all around you every day & for it to be impossible for you to get any of them." Even a prisoner who was a colonel lamented that "If it were not for what we purchase we could not live."[23] Although prison documentation suggests that adequate food may have been

---

20. The issue over living conditions, including rations, at Fort Delaware has prompted vigorous debate in Union prison camp historiography. Joel Citron, for example, analyzes the question of inadequate rations through a detailed examination of commissary records and rations reports. Citron, *Confederate Prisoners at Fort Delaware*, 39-56. The suspect trustworthiness of post-war accounts, which might have been influenced by inaccurate recall or "Lost Cause" bias, compelled James Gillespie to intentionally disregard eyewitness accounts written after 1865. James M. Gillespie, *Andersonvilles of the North: The Myths and Realities of Northern Treatment of Civil War Confederate Prisoners* (University of North Texas Press, 2008), 3. Gillespie concluded that prisoner diaries generally did not contain "many complaints" about the food at Fort Delaware but he does not cite Hall's diary as a source. Ibid., 191.
21. Samuel Harding wrote that the evening soup contained maggots and was "an indescribable olla podrida of soups of every kind and reminds one irresistibly of the sty and the trough." W. Emerson Wilson, *Fort Delaware in the Civil War* (Fort Delaware Society, n.d.), 7 (by count). Another wrote that the soup contained "rotten water, rice hulls, white worms half an inch long, (dozens of them in every pint of the stuff), grit, nails, hair, etc. with now [and] then a grain of corn, or perhaps occasionally a teaspoonful of rice." J. G. deRouhlac Hamilton, "The Prison Experiences of Randolph Shotwell: II. Fort Delaware," *North Carolina Historical Review*, vol. 2, no. 3, July 1925, 340.
22. Captain John Swann wrote that shortly after his arrival he heard "Rat call! Rat call!" A Union sergeant then tossed rats among the prisoners, who "scrambled for the rats like school boys for apples." Elizabeth Cometti, ed., "Excerpts from Swann's 'Prison Life at Fort Delaware,'" West Virginia Department of Arts, Culture, and History, *West Virginia History*, vol. 2 no. 2 (January 1941): 120-141 and no. 3 (April 1941): 217-230. lhttp://www.wvculture.org/history/journal_wvh/wvh2-1.html. Isaac Handy wrote of a lieutenant from Texas who made "a fine mess for supper" after a rat hunt which netted so many rats they had to be carted off in a wheelbarrow. Isaac W. K. Handy, *United States Bonds or Duress by Federal Authority: A Journal of Current Events During an Imprisonment of Fifteen Months, at Fort Delaware* (Baltimore: Turnbull Brothers, 1874), 601.
23. Rosenburg, *For the Sake of My Country*, 64. In contrast, Howard wrote that he ate better in prison (with the senior officers) than he had in the field, noting that at his first meal at Fort Delaware he had genuine coffee, condensed milk, and ice cream. Howard, *Recollections of a Maryland Confederate Soldier*, 307.

purchased for the prisoners, that did not necessarily mean it wound up in the prisoners' serving cups. One prisoner wrote after the war that he suspected that a sizable amount of the food was being siphoned off by prison officials, cooks, and cookhouse sergeants who made "large sums by selling extra rations to those officers who can purchase."[24] Hall provides no information in support of this allegation.

Hall had no money to augment his rations by purchasing food from the sutler; in fact, he was so strapped for funds that he was reduced to selling his meals for stamps to he could write home and to his regiment.[25] His frustration is understandable. But, as in so many other circumstances during the war, he turned to his faith. "Those of the prisoners who were fortunate enough to have green backs in their possession when captured & also those who have friends or relative[s] inside the Federal lines, have every thing they want in abundance but us who have no friends nor money are in a deplorable & lamentable condition but the Blessed Lord bears me up & reminds me that this is not my rest and & if I only prove faithful, I will soon secure an everlasting home where I will never hunger nor thirst any more."

As the war progressed, the North and the South accused the other of treating their prisoners of war inhumanely while defending their own practices. The debate still rages over whether Fort Delaware, in particular, was – or wasn't – "hell on earth" or "the Andersonville of the North."[26] Hall's entries rebut the sentiment of a Philadelphia newspaper article in 1863 that made captivity at Fort Delaware sound like good living, claiming that "rebel prisoners" lived in "spacious and comfortable wood barracks" and were provided "good food" and the opportunity to bathe in the Delaware.[27] But the reality for Hall was that the barracks were poorly heated in the winter; the food was

---

24. Hamilton, "The Prison Experiences of Randolph Shotwell," 342.
25. Hall wrote home in early June and September 1864, but did not receive a letter from "home and loved ones" until the end of September. The June letter advising them of his location likely never arrived.
26. The infamous Confederate prison camp at Andersonville is regarded as the benchmark for living conditions for prisoners of war during the Civil War. For both sides of the debate over whether Fort Delaware was the worst Union prison camp, compare Citron's *Confederate Prisoners at Fort Delaware* with Temple's *The Union Prison at Fort Delaware*.
27. "The Rebel Prisoners: Their Quarters in Fort Delaware," *New York Times*, July 16, 1863, accessed through ProQuest Historical Newspapers and originally published on July 14, 1863, in the *Philadelphia Bulletin*. The article described the private soldiers as "generally ignorant men of the 'poor white trash' class," a fourth of whom were unable to even sign their name; the article also wildly claimed that most were "well supplied with Confederate money."

often provided in insufficient quantity; and by January 1865 he was barefoot and nearly naked. Procuring clean water was beyond his control. He makes no mention of ever bathing in the Delaware River, which would hardly seem invigorating or healthy given all the waste that went into the river. As one former prisoner wrote, "What location could have been more admirably unhealthy than those ten acres of reclaimed swamp, in the middle of, and five feet below the level of a broad river, whose waters still percolated through the thin levees, and permeated the black porous soil until in rainy weather the island seemed a plot of mud?"[28] Even a Union surgeon declared Fort Delaware an "utterly unfit location for a prison."[29]

Not surprisingly, the prisoners at Fort Delaware suffered a high rate of disease. Over a single three-month period, diarrhea, dysentery, pneumonia, scurvy, typhoid, and other illnesses claimed more than twelve percent of the prison population.[30] Altogether, over 2,500 Confederate prisoners died at Fort Delaware, many from a smallpox epidemic that hit the prison in late 1863. Confederates maintained that deaths at Fort Delaware were due to lack of decent food, overcrowding, and the swampy terrain, but the Union blamed inadequate vaccination and the poor condition that the men were in when they

Prisoners walking under armed escort at Fort Delaware. (Isaac Handy, United States Bonds or Duress by Federal Authority: A Journal of Current Events During an Imprisonment of Fifteen Months, at Fort Delaware, Wikimedia Commons)

---

28. Hamilton, "The Prison Experiences of Randolph Shotwell," 332-333.
29. Temple, *The Union Prison at Fort Delaware*, 49.
30. "Confederate Burials in the National Cemetery," Department of Veteran Affairs, accessed August 8, 2020, https://www.cem.va.gov/cem/pdf/InterpretiveSigns/ConfederateBurials-TheFortDelawarePrison.pdf

were captured.[31] Still, the nine percent death rate at Fort Delaware was lower than that at many other Union prison camps, such as the twenty-four percent death rate at Elmira, New York.[32] And none of the death rates in Union camps matched the twenty-nine percent death rate at Andersonville.[33]

Hall kept a low profile at Fort Delaware. Despite his earlier medical history, it appears he never became sick enough at Fort Delaware to warrant medical attention, much less hospitalization. His diary reveals no evidence of any disciplinary action or maltreatment by guards, although he did reference almost unbearable rules. But he still suffered from a loss of freedom and lived an existence full of tedium and uncertainty. Hall dealt with those issues the same way he eased those concerns in camp: through prayer meetings and services. It did not take Hall long to seek out Christian brethren among his fellow prisoners; in fact, he attended a prayer meeting on his second full day on the island. He worried that his family at home and his "brothers" in his company would think he was dead because it looked impossible that anyone would have survived what he had gone through before he was taken prisoner. It is evident from his entries that he took great comfort from his faith, and he considered his happiest hours those he spent in prayer meetings. When he wasn't in prayer meetings or sermons, he spent his time "reading & meditating on the word of God, the greatest portion of the day." He also visited other parts of the prison barracks to talk to other faith-filled prisoners. Hall reread Bunyan's *Pilgrim's Progress*, now from the perspective of a prisoner himself. He wrote that "it has been a great comfort & consolation to me during my troubles, sore trials & afflictions." Just as Bunyan, the author, and Christian, the protagonist in Bunyan's book, used faith to help them endure confinement, so did Hall.

---

31. Temple, *The Union Prison at Fort Delaware*, 94.
32. Michael P. Gray, *The Business of Captivity: Elmira and Its Civil War Prison* (Kent State University, 2001), 153-154; James I. Robertson, Jr., "The Scourge of Elmira," *Civil War History* 8, no. 2 (1962): 80. Point Lookout transferred thousands of its prisoners to Elmira, including four of Hall's company comrades: Corporal Abel Massey (who died of pneumonia in December 1864) and Privates William D. Gillis, William T. Meadows, and Andrew J. Tabor. The prisoners at Elmira certainly faced winters far more brutal than those in the mid-Atlantic.
33. "Guards Death Rate," National Park Service, accessed August 7, 2020, https://www.nps.gov/ande/learn/historyculture/guardsdeathrate.htm

Remembrancer Daily Entries
May 1864 – December 1864

Friday, May 13, 1864

Continued rain. I awoke this morning feeling Sick and bad. Not having rest[ed] a good nights rest in 10 nights I was nearly exhausted for want of sleep and from fatigue and exertion and my clothing being wet so long I felt like I had an ague. The Battle raged all day yesterday & nearly all night for we could hear the roar of small arms nearly all night. I sent up an earnest silent prayer to Him who holds our destiny in his hand for our deliverance. In the evening we march towards Fredericksburg, march through the camps of the enemys reserve, Artillery & cavalry & an emmence waggon train. We halt in 2 or 3 miles of Fred. & remain all night.

Saturday, May 14, 1864

Showery wet weather. We hear fierce & rapid cannonading today & I would give any thing I possess in this world to be with my company & know the causualleties [casualties] of our regts & Brig[ade] inside our lines in the Dear Sunny South once more. Near dark we march back a mile & remain all night in the mud. My whole trust is in God & I believe He is with me.

Sunday, May 15, 1864

Continued hard rain. We move again this morning & march to Fred[ericksburg]. We are as hungry as poor rebels generally ever gets to be able to travel not having eat anything since we were captured only a few old dry hard crackers.³⁴ We remain here all day & get a little sugar & coffee. There is an immence number of the enemys wounded at this place. The once prosperous & thriving city of Fredericksburg is deserted & laid waist. The fine dwellings and public edifices has become the habitation of wild birds of prey. The heart sickens to witness the scene of desolation & it tells a tale of suffering & heart rendering anguish that no pen can describe. I pray earnestly for our dear country.

Monday, May 16, 1864

Par cloudy & showery. We march about sunrise pass through the city & cross the Rappahannock on pontoons. Our guard from the Battlefield to Fred[ericksburg] were a detachment of the 8th N. Y. regulars who were in the Mexican war.³⁵ But here we changed & a body of Penn cavalry escorted us to Belle Plains Landing, on the Potomac, where we arrive about 2 P.M. & march into an enclosure surrounded by guard[s] & there is six or eight thousand Rebel prisoners here at present, on an area of 40 or 50 achers [acres], principally in a small valley surrounded by high hills, very well adapted to the purpose. On the hills are cannon pointing over us with their dark brassen throat threatening with instant destruction if we do not keep quiet. There is prisoners here from Va., N.C., S.C., Ga., Ala., Miss, La. & Tenn. But more from N.C. than any other state.

Tuesday, May 17, 1864

Par cloudy & showery. A large portion of the prisoners left

---

34. William Sharp, Company B, of the 14th Georgia, was also captured at Spotsylvania on May 12, 1864. He confirmed in testimony on June 21, 1864, to the U.S. Sanitary Commission that he received only four crackers a day until he arrived to his transport ship at Belle Plain. *Narrative of Privations and Sufferings of United States Officers and Soldiers while Prisoners of War in the Hands of the Rebel Authorities*, U.S. Sanitary Commission (Philadelphia: King & Baird, 1864).

35. Although Burnside's IX Corps included the 8th New York Regiment, the reference to "regulars" who were Mexican-American War veterans suggests Hall was escorted by the 8th U.S. Infantry, which served as Provost Guard for the IX Corps.

here to day & we will leave soon. I suppose for some region unknown to us & what our fate may be the Lord alone knows. But He will be with all who put their trust in no matter where they go. Oh it is sweet when we are forsaken by the world & misfortunes press us on every side to put our trust in God & know that He will be with us & forsake us never while we put our whole trust in Him. We draw pork & hard bread sugar & coffee. We are mustered. Our names & rank taken preparating to leave this point.

Wednesday, May 18, 1864

Par cloudy & thun showers. We embark today near noon. First we take a Steamboat which carries us out to a large Steam frigate & we are put on board. Some of our men were crow[d]ed into the hold where they nearly suffocated. Several fainted & would have died if our capters had [not] permitted them to be taken on deck where they could get fresh air. We had to remain crowded together so thick we could scarcely sit down with our feet & legs doubled up under us without any air being able to reach us only what came down through the hatch way, for 2 nights & nearly 3 days. My sufferings were more intense than ever before for the same length of time, and those terrable tedious hours will be vivid in my memory as long as life shall last.

The rout[e] we sailed was down the Potomac to Chesapeake Bay & thence down that Bay to the Atlantic Ocean. On the morning of [May] 19 a little before day we run a ground near the Va shore on a sand bar & were unable to get away till late in the evening. 2 steam tugs & one larger steam boat came to our relief & towed us out of the Sand. We were soon sailing down the Chesapeake again & verry soon we came to the broad Atlantic & soon the land of old Virginia was lost to our view. With a deep drawn Sigh I cast a last farewell look on the land of my Childhood Home

& loved ones, perhaps never to behold it again. My fe[e]ble pen cannot describe the language of my heart, if I had space. I Sent up a Silent heartfelt prayer to Him who hold[s] our destiny in His hands to be with the dear ones far away. I committed them all into His care & I believe He will guard them & protect them from all harm & He will deliver our dear country from the desolation that now seems to press it to the earth in His own good time, & I believe I will return & see them all again. Oh it will be a joyful time & a happy hour, when I meet all those I love so dearly, who perhaps now mourn me as dead.

We passed near Fortress Monroe & sailed in a northern [route] on the Atlantic. Another dreadful night passed & we hailed day with joy. On the morning of the 20 we came near being lost & consequence of a heavy fog which lay dense on the bosom of the ocean. A steamboat came to our relief & we were piloted into the right direction. We sailed into Delaware Bay & arrived at our destination a short time after dark & we were verry glad to get where we could breathe fresh air & straiten our legs. We landed on Fort Delaware Island & after we were searched & inspected & such articles as we were not allowed to retain, taken from us, we were marched into the Barrack of Fort Delaware & it was a great relief to get where we could lie down to rest & sleep once more, out of the foul air of the hold of that old frigate.[36]

Saturday, May 21, 1864

Par cloudy & warm. This morning I have the opportunity to viewing our Situation. Fort Delaware is an Island near the Northern termination of the Bay of the same name. The State of delaware is on one side of us & New Jersey on the

---

36. Hall appears to have covered the events of Thursday, May 19, and Friday, May 20, in his entry for Wednesday, May 18.

other. The city of Philadelphia is Situated on Delaware river a short distance above here. Our prison consists of long rows of Barracks built of rough lumber about 20 feet wide with bunks of sleeping scaffolds arranged somewhat after the same manner of sleeping berths on board a vessel at sea. The confines of our prison is limited to a small area of ground between the barracks. Perhaps from one to three acres. The water we use is verry bad & what we get to eat is more scant than I ever had to live on before. I hope & pray, night & day, for us soon to be delivered out of here. The Lord alone can help us.

Sunday, May 22, 1864

Par cloudy & warm. No one knows the tediousness & troubles of a captivity confined to a small island & a much smaller compass inside the prison walls of which we are confined & we could pass the time off more congenial to our feelings if we could get enough to subsist on but we could eat all we get in 2 days at one meal & we draw more for one days ration in Dixie then we get here in 3. But the Lord is with us & I hope will saunctify our troubles to our good & soon deliver us.

Monday, May 23, 1864

Fair & warm. Today our squad the last that arrived at this place was divided every state to its self. We have a happy little prayer at night. The Lord can be with us & bless us here, as well as any where else for He is present every where. I have committed every thing into His kind hand & Almighty care. My dear ones at Home far away who I pray for night & day I commend them all to His care, that He may guard them & protect them from all harm & turn their hearts to Him in deep Sorrow & distress & live devoted to the cause of Christ, pure & undefiled by the stains & polutions of this wicked world of sin. The Loved ones at Home

I expect mourn me as dead for my company & regiment no doubt thinks me no longer among the living for it looked almost impossible to any rational creature, for me ever to escaped from the place alive where I was taken prisoner. But God was with me & preserved me as He has done numerous times before. All honor glory & praise be ascribed to His dear name forever. I would give any thing in my power to know the condition of my company for I fear the largest portion of them was killed. They all feel as Brothers to me & I had much rather be with them today in line of Battle fronting old Grant, ready to strike for the dear Sunny South, Home & loved ones & every thing I hold dear on earth than to be here in this loathsome prison. But the will of God be done, not mine. He will deliver me & my beloved country also in His own good time. My trust is alone in Him.

Tuesday, May 24, 1864

Fair & warm. Nothing unusual. We have another prayer meeting at night. I get acquainted with several Brethren of the Church from several different states of the confederacy.

Wednesday, May 25, 1864

Cloudy par hot & sultry. I attend preaching near noon & we have another happy little prayer meeting. The languishing hours of our imprisonment in this awful & dreary place passes away more pleasant & sweetly than I anticipated. God is with us & if He will always be with us with His all-abounding love & dispel our gloom by His dear presence, prisons will palaces prove & He can make us happy no matter where we are or what circumstances we placed in.

Thursday, May 26, 1864

Rain all day. Nothing of material importance transpires today. What we pass through one day we have to encounter ever day. I spend my time in reading & meditating on the word of God, the greatest portion of the day. Part of my time I spend in walking up & down & visiting various parts of the prison barracks & conversing with several pious brethren I have formed the acquaintaince of since I have been here & we spend several pleasant hours together. The humble followers of Jesus Christ are like Free Masons. They soon become acquainted & known to each other wherever they go & we can administer to each others wants in several little ways to make each other comfortable & happy and resigned to our unhappy fate.

There is a large number of prisoners here that have been here since the battle of Gettysburg & some have been here for a much longer period than that. Some having been here nearly two years & there are prisoners here from every part of the army & from every state in the Confederacy. There are some there that was captured beyond the Mississippi river in Ark, Missouri & Texas & various other places & you can see among them men of every grade trade or profession, occupation or pursuit & they follow various occupations here in prison on this small island. There is some of the finest & fanciest articles manufactured here by prisoners that would surprise the outer world to see them & it would seem verry mysterious & surprising indeed to some to imagine How such things could be produced with the material & implements they have to work with. But the ingenious human mind naturally seeks employment when cut off & isolated from the remainder the world & hense it can contrive & invent numerous objects as articles of imployment especially when they can Better their deplorable conditions by so doing. I will mention a few of the various little articles of merchandise manufactured here by prisoners here such as ladies fans, tooth brushes, finger rings, ear rings, breast pins, beside an enumerable number of various other articles, which they could never have contrived or thought of producing in more favorable circumstances.[37]

Friday, May 27, 1864

Rainy & cool. Every things goes on as usual. I have a strong desire to hear from my regt & Co[mpany]. How many of them is alive after the terrible & protracted blood struggle they have been through. The Battle had been raging over 2 week. The last reliable news we received the scene of bloodshed, But we will never know the position nor true state of our army as long as we remain here. But I pray night and day for the Lord of Hosts to be with them & our little Confederacy & I believe He will.

Saturday, May 28, 1864

Cool windy & cloudy. All remaining the same.

Sunday, May 29, 1864

Fair & pleasant. My heart seems unusually oppressed with Sorrow & Sadness this blessed sabbath day, as I contemplate the past & reflect on my deplorable condition, & the aspect of affairs around me. Only a few Sabbaths ago I [was] with my near & dear friends & loved ones at my dear Sunny Home far, far away. Lofty mountains rise & unfathomable deep waters, Swelling tides & mighty rivers rise & flow between me & them & they know not where I am or whether I am yet alive among the living & I am cut off from all communication with them. I cannot hear from them nor them from me. I am exiled isolated & cut off from

---

37. McHenry Howard refers to some of these items as "Confederate Jewelry." He said that some of the items were sent to wives and sweethearts at home or given to the ladies who donated food and clothing, but in either event, they brought in a "helpful amount of money to the artificers." Howard, *Recollections of a Maryland Confederate Soldier*, 330. Other items made were musical instruments such as violins and banjos. A photograph of several of these items is the cover page of the February 1990 issue of *Fort Delaware Notes*, accompanied by K. A. Pippin's article, "Jewelry Making at Fort Delaware During the War Between the States," at pages 2-4.

all I cherish or hold dear on earth without any insurance under Heaven that I will ever hear from them or behold their dear faces again.

I am on a desolate island in the hands & power of a crue[l] unmerciful & remorseless enemy & what ill fate may be in store for me I know not. <u>It is terrible enough all ready</u>. But if every thing is torn from me on earth, O thank God I am not forsaken yet for I have a friend that if I will only prove true to Him, He will never forsake me, no matter where it may be my lot to go or what my circumstances may. He is a friend that sticketh closer than a brother, an all powerful friend that can come to my relief if I was in the Strongest & most impenetrable & strongly guarded prison on the globe. That Friend can cause the most strongest prison walls to yeild to His touch & crumble to the earth in an instant & that Almighty & ever present Friend is the Lord God of Hosts & He is with me here in this prison & will deliver me, when His all-wise purpose of bringing me here is accomplished, for perhaps He laid His chastening rod on me & cause[d] me to be transmited into the hands of a cruel & vindictive foe, to bring me close to Him & turn my affections from objects of this world & place them more strongly on eternal & imperishable objects of that noble & Happy world above.

The immence throng of human beings & the various character of the multitude that I associate with daily, does not tend to create or produce a devotional feeling for there is wickedness & vice practiced here among the prisoners I regret to say of nearly every form & kind that they are in their present Situation capable of committing but thank God among the evil there is some good, Some pure & undefiled virtue & holiness that remains untarnished by the crime & wickedness that Surrounds it. I have become acquainted with a good number of Sincere & devoted followers of the Meek & lowly Jesus & with them I Spend the greatest part of my time, & we pass several hours of Sweet peaceful conversation together about the things of God & how to promote the advancement of His cause to the greatest of our ability & the hours of trouble & sorrow cause by our captivity is to a great extent alleviated thereby. I can almost invariably tell a Christian from others & can single them out from among this vast multitude by their neat & ordily [orderly] appearance & calm resigned countenance.

We have preaching somewhere among the barrack 2 or 3 times a week & there is a little prayer meeting in nearly every division every night besides a more extensi[v]e prayer meeting that is appointed in a different division each night in succession till it goes round to each div. & then begining & going the round again & a revival is begining to Spring up a[l]ready & several mourners are enquiring the way to Christ & I hope & pray earnestly that it may spread & widen till it embraces the intire island & the strong holds of Satan be torn down & Sin & crime exterminated by all coming to the blessed Saviour & embracing his boundless love & mercy & set their faces towards the New Jerusalem.

Monday, May 30, 1864

Fair & warm. We pack up & move out of our barrack in order that they may be cleaned up & scoured out. The weather is extremely warm & Sultry. Yesterday was the 3rd anniversary of the organization of my company which was organized May 29 1861. No reliable news is received here as to what our army is doing in Va or where it is. We here that Gen Lee has the Strongest Position he has ever had & is on the South Anna river.[38] We also hear that Grant has lost over one hundred thousand of his best men since

---

38. Grant's Overland Campaign was far from over after Spotsylvania. The 14th Georgia participated in battles at Jericho Mills on the North Anna and Cold Harbor between May 23 and June 3, 1864. The regiment then participated in the siege of Petersburg and fighting around Richmond from June 1864 until April 1865.

he crossed the river the 3rd of this month.[39] That is an immence loss to lose in such a short time & is more than our [e]ntire army we brought against him.

Tuesday, May 31, 1864

Fair & extremely warm. They make us move out of our barracks again today to white wash them over afresh. This day two years ago the Battle of Seven Pines was fought, which was the commencement of Mclellans boasted attempt to take the Rebel Capitol & the Federal army has been making desperate attempts to get the[re] ever since before that time under various leaders & they have expended thousands of millions of money & hundreds thousands of their best men have been sacrificed to this insane object of trying to enslave a free people but thanks be to the Lord of Hosts they have failed in their wicked designs & with God on our side they will never succeed & I sincerely believe He is on our side & that our cause is just in His sight & that eventually & speedily he will deliver our dear Sunny South, from its vile enemies & restore sweet peace & independence to our beloved land.

Wednesday, June 1, 1864

Thunder & hard rain. Every thing goes on as usual but I sigh & pray for Dixie & for loved ones at Home Sweet Home far far away.[40]

Thursday, June 2, 1864

Cloudy with some rain.

---

39. Grant's total casualties between May 5 and June 18, 1864, came to 66,000. Lee's casualties came to 35,000. Wheelan, *Bloody Spring*, 343. The 14th Georgia's casualties came to 171. Young, *Lee's Army During the Overland Campaign*, 302. The regiment's highest casualties during the Overland Campaign were incurred at the Battle of the Wilderness.

40. On June 1, 1864, Fort Delaware had 8,126 prisoners present. Fetzer and Mowday, *Unlikely Allies*, 152. Between June 1, 1864, and February 1, 1865, the monthly prisoner count ranged between 7,622 and 9,174. Ibid.

Friday, June 3, 1864

Fair & warm. The weather has been rather cool for the season. Since I have been here the nights is cold enough to sleep comfortable under a blanket & during the day a gentle breeze is stirring nearly all the time blowing generally from off the Bay which renders our Situation more indurable which exposed to every ray of the sun as this island is without a continued breeze.[41] The intense heat would be more than we could scarecely bear. The sickness & mortality of deaths is greatly lessened among the prisoners by our rations being so short for there is no danger of sickness by eating to[o] much for we just get enough to keep us a live & hence a great many fevers & other diseases caused by indigestion is avoided.

Saturday, June 4, 1864

Partially fair & windy. Nothing of interest transpires here one day more than another. The dull monotony that seems to hangs over us like some terrable & dense fog is never dispersed. The close confinement & strict almost [u]nbearable disciplined rules we are subjected to goes verry hard with one who has been used to liberty all his life but my whole trust is in God & my earnest prayer is to Him day & night that He will send us speedy deliverance & I believe He will not forsake us if we will trust all in his almighty power.

Sunday, June 5, 1864

M rain. E cloudy & cool. This Sabbath passed away dull & heavily. A heavy rain fell last night & the black mud is over our shoe quarters when we step out of the barracks & we have to confine our selves the narrow limits of our barracks, the [e]ntire day. But I spend the day in reading & meditation on the word of God & thereby gain a great comfort & consolation & we have a happy little prayer meeting at night.

---

41. The island was barren of trees which might otherwise have provided shade and breeze.

Monday, June 6, 1864

Par fair & warm. E thunder & rain. Our army in Va has been engaged with the enemy again near Mechanicsville & coal [Cold] Harbor[42] a terrible battle last three days but we cannot tell How they succeeded for we never get a true statement here of any thing relative to the army or any thing about our dear beloved Sunny South. Also Gen Johnson has been feircely contending against the enemy under Gen Sherman for several days.[43]

Tuesday, June 7, 1864

M cool. E fair & pleasant. The news papers states that during the month of May Seventy two thousand men were killed dear on the Battle fields of Virginia alone between Grant & Lee. Such is the terrable character of the gigantic [war] now waged on one hand for Liberty peace & to protect Homes & loved ones & every thing we hold dear on earth. On the other hand for booty & plunder & to subjugate & tyrannize over a people thats sworn to be free & with the help of God we will be free at no very distant day. 72,000 killed dead on the immence field of slaughter besides what has & will die of wounds, according to the aggregate ratio commonly in a battle as many or more dies of wounds after being removed to hospitals as there is killed on the field, which will amount to the immense number of 150,000 deaths cause by this unholy war in one short month, in Virginia alone, besides elsewhere.

Wednesday, June 8, 1864

Par fair & warm. Today I sent letter home with an earnest

---

42. This is likely a reference to the Battle of Cold Harbor near the site of the Gaines's Mill battle in 1862 in Mechanicsville, Virginia.
43. This is likely a reference to the Atlanta Campaign.

prayer that it may reach its destination safely.[44] It will have to be sent through by flag of truce & will have to pass through [v]arious and & many difficulties to reach the dear ones its is intended for & I hope & pray it may go safe for it will relieve them from the great trouble & anxiety I know they must be in on my account for there is no doubt but what they think me dead or that some terrible & unfortunate fate has beffallen me.

Thursday, June 9, 1864

M hard rain. E fair & warm. Nothing of interest.

Friday, June 10, 1864

M par cloudy & cool. E windy & cool. I feel unwell to day & I fear I shall be sick.

Saturday, June 11, 1864

Fair windy & cool. E cloudy. Good & cheering news comes in for our cause from every part of the scene of war showing that the Lord has not forsaken us & will soon deliver us if we will only hold faithful to Him & to ourselves. I have a considerable fever today & my head verry bad.

Sunday, June 12, 1864

Par fair & cool. One month ago today I fell into the hands of the enemy on the terrible 12 May. The most extensive & deadly contested Battle was fought that the annals of the world has ever recorded. I continue verry sick with a fever & severe headache. Gen Stonewall Jacksons father-in-law preached here yesterday & today.[45]

Monday, June 13, 1864

M cool. E par fair & warm.

---

44. Prisoners were permitted to send letters of one page. Correspondence was screened to ensure that it pertained only to personal matters

45. Rev. George Junkin, a Presbyterian, was president of Washington College (now Washington and Lee) when Jackson was an instructor at Virginia Military Institute. Jackson married Junkin's daughter Elinor, who died giving birth in 1854.

Tuesday, June 14, 1864

Fair & warm. Nothing uncommon.

Wednesday, June 15, 1864

M cloudy & cool. E fair & warm. This morning one of the prisoners a mere boy stab[b]ed another prisoner & inflicted a severe wound from which he died immediately. I am still unwell but some what mending.

Thursday, June 16, 1864

Fair & warm. Our little prayer meetings progresses regular in our Division every evening & we have preaching occasionally & a good many are enlisting under the banner of the Lord Jesus.

Friday, June 17, 1864

Fair & warm.

Saturday, June 18, 1864

We hear today that part of the prisoners here are going to be paroled or exchanged. Two Divisions start out but return again to their barracks.

Sunday, June 19, 1864

Fair and warm. I have a severe fever today. Nothing of importance transpires.

Monday, June 20, 1864

Fair & warm. We are taken out & examined & searched again today. Our little prayer meetings is forbiden by the guard, but there [a]re a blessed privalidge to us yet that cannot be easily taken from us by all the enemys in the world & that is praying in Secret & sweet meditations with God that the outer world knows not of & the blessed Lord Jesus will not forsake us though the world does.

Tuesday, June 21, 1864

Fair & extremely warm.

Wednesday, June 22, 1864

Fair & Hot & dry & dusty.

Thursday, June 23, 1864

Par cloudy & warm. Every thing goes on as usually.

Friday, June 24, 1864

Fair & hot. Last night a considerable rain fell here.

Saturday, June 25, 1864

M par cloudy. E fair & hot.

Sunday, June 26, 1864

M fair & sultry. E cloudy with a swift breeze & thunder clouds pass round at a distance. This morning a number of confederate officers from this Island embark on board a Steamer & leave here to go I know not where, but I hope & earnestly pray to the God of hosts who holds our destiny in His hands, that some means may be devised ere long for us all to get away from this dismal place & never see it more hence forth & forever.[46]

Monday, June 27, 1864

Par cloudy & windy.

Tuesday, June 28, 1864

Par fair & cool.

Wednesday, June 29, 1864

Fair & cool.

Thursday, June 30, 1864

M cloudy. E a little rain.

Friday, July 1, 1864

Fair & Hot. E thun & rain.

Saturday, July 2, 1864

Par fair & Hot.

Sunday, July 3, 1864

Fair & cool. Several of the prisoners has escaped from here during the past week, by swimming the bay. Some by the

---

46. Hall was likely referring to the "First Fifty," a group of generals and field officers selected to go to Charleston, SC, for possible exchange.

aid of canteens and in consequence thereof all our canteens were confiscated today in the same manner are knives were not long since.[47] I am willing to let them take the last thing I possess even to the clothes off of my back, if we will only set me down safe in Dixie. I attended a happy & interesting little prayer meeting at night. I gained a great comfort & consolation by reading & meditation on the blessed word of God.

Monday, July 4, 1864

Fair & pleasant. The guns of fort fire to a salute at noon which was answered from other forts & batteries in the vicinity & my thoughts were at home & loved ones in the dear Sunny South far away.

Tuesday, July 5, 1864

Fair & warm. We here various news & rumors & the prospect is brighter for our cause than it has been for a long time past. The light of hope & success gilds the horizon & I hope & earnestly pray will ere long be shining in the Zenith.

Wednesday, July 6, 1864

M par cloudy. E fair & warm.

Thursday, July 7, 1864

Before noon fair & warm. Afternoon cloudy & sultry with thunder. Various rumors are afloat.

Friday, July 8, 1864

Par cloudy & hot.

Saturday, July 9, 1864

Par cloudy & windy. This day 3 year ago our regt received

---

47. One newsworthy escape from Pea Patch Island occurred in August 1863 when six men made life preservers by tying four canteens around each man and swimming downriver. One man who wore eight canteens drowned because he was not an expert swimmer. Three of the men eventually made their way to Richmond. "Escape of Prisoners from Fort Delaware," *Richmond Dispatch*, August 28, 1863, www.newspaper.com. Handy wrote that on July 3, 1864, each of the divisions was inspected for escape contraband and three thousand canteens were seized to avoid their being used for escapes. Handy, *United States Bonds*, 468. The unfortunate consequence of this seizure was the prisoners no longer had canteens to use to retrieve water from cisterns, an especially cruel outcome during the summer months.

the first marching orders & therefore we commenced drawing wages from that day.

Sunday, July 10, 1864

A.M. fair & warm. P.M. cloudy & extremely sultry. The air last night felt more hot & [o]pressive that any night I have experienced this year.

Monday, July 11, 1864

Fair & intensively hot. I have the severest cold & cough I have had in [a] long time. I have been suffering from it from over a week & it seems to get worse. The earth is very dry here at present. There has not been a good rain for several weeks.

Tuesday, July 12, 1864

Today two months ago I was captured & I hope and earnestly pray that the Lord will devise some means for us to be exchanged & get away from this place & return to our native Sunny South before two months has passed away for I had rather be at any place I have ever seen no matter how mean that place may have been than to be here. Par cloudy hot & sultry.

Wednesday, July 13, 1864

A.M. pleasant and P.M. warm. Various rumors & dispatches are afloat here. Some say our army has possession of Baltimore & in six miles of Washington & others say they are Pennsylvania & others that they have captured several thousand prisoners, but nothing is confirmed & therefore I will not put any confidence in any report till I am satisfied of its reality & confirmation. I can only wish & pray for the long hoped for period.[48]

---

48. Hall may have been referring to Early's 1864 campaign on Washington, DC, and/or Brigadier General Bradley Johnson's and Major Harry Gilmore's cavalry raids around Baltimore. Johnson's mission was to reach Point Lookout to release prisoners, but he was recalled before reaching southern Maryland.

Thursday, July 14, 1864

Fair & Hot.

Friday, July 15, 1864

A.M. fair & cool. P.M. par clou & warm. Our army is falling back out of Maryland with it is affirmed by northern papers, enough supplies to last it 12 months & the Federals give it in as the most remarkable & celebrated raid that has ever been perpetrated. It is stated that when they marched through the Baltimore the citizens give our boys any thing they wanted and every thing they carry away.

Saturday, July 16, 1864

Fair & warm.

Sunday, July 17, 1864

A.M. cool. P.M. fair & warm.

Monday, July 18, 1864

A.M. cool. P.M. fair & warm. Last night I was verry sick & I feel verry unwell today. Besides I have had a severe cold & cough for more than three weeks. The weather is verry changable here. The nights are cold & the days hot & therefore a great amount of sickness is caused. The water we have to use is verry bad, worse than any I've ever saw used before & the use of it bring on various diseases. Besides contagious diseases are raging violent here small-pox, measles, mumphs, itch & hooping cough. A great many are dying daily, far away from home & friends in a strange land, with no one to speak a kind or soothing word of comfort in the gloomy hour of death. Sons of the Sunny South you are laying down your life for the cause of freedom & if no one seems to care for you in this world if you have only given your hearts to God & trusted in the merits of the blood of the dear Saviour & have made your peace, calling & election sure your are far better off to die & go home to Jesus than those that still remain here. Your troubles &

sorrows are over, you will never hunger or thirst any more. Blessed are all who die in the Lord.

Tuesday, July 19, 1864

A.M. fair & warm. P.M. cloudy & warm.

Wednesday, July 20, 1864

A.M. fair & warm. P.M. cloudy with indications of rain

Thursday, July 21, 1864

Cloudy & pleasant. Last night there fell a light shower of rain, which cooled the air considerable.

Friday, July 22, 1864

Par cloudy & verry cool for the season.

Saturday, July 23, 1864

Par cloudy & cool.

Sunday, July 24, 1864

Cloudy with cool winds.

Monday, July 25, 1864

M rain. E fair & windy. It began to rain last night near midnight & continued till near noon today. The weather is extremely cool for the season. Several prisoners escaped last night by swimming the Bay. A good many has escaped at various times during the summer. It is a dangerous adventure, having a long distance to swim. Besides some are caught & brought back.

Tuesday, July 26, 1864

Fair & warm.

Wednesday, July 27, 1864

Par fair & warm.

Thursday, July 28, 1864

Fair & Hot. This morning our division was all sent out to unlade a boat of lumber, which was hard labor for us till near noon. Afternoon we were transferred from Div[ision] 17 to Div[ision] 7 which was done in order to get the prisoners of each state together. Div[ision]s No 7 and 8 are occupied exclusively of Georgians. In all there are 900 or 1000 Georgians on the island.

Friday, July 29, 1864

Par fair & hot.

Saturday, July 30, 1864

Fair & hot.

Sunday, July 31, 1864

Fair & hot.

Monday, August 1, 1864

Fair & extreamely hot. The last 3 days & night has been the warmest weather that has been here before this summer.

Tuesday, August 2, 1864

M fair & hot. E thun & rain.

Wednesday, August 3, 1864

M par cloudy & sultry.

Thursday, August 4, 1864

M rain. E cloudy & warm.

Friday, August 5, 1864

Par fair & warm.

Saturday, August 6, 1864

Fair & verry hot.

Sunday, August 7, 1864

Fair & Hot. We have a prayer meeting in our div[ision] every evening & those precious hours of prayer & praise are the most blessed & sweetest hours of my captivity. All my tryals, troubles & afflictions seem to be forgotten & it seems like the blessed Saviour come down & comforts me & bears me up & tells me not to faint but bear up through all faith fully. For my light afflictions here which are but for a moment will work out for me a far more exceeding & eternal weight of glory. That will be my reward in that day when the last loud trump[et] shall sound & He come to make up His jewels.

Monday, August 8, 1864

Hazy cloudy & warm. I sold my dinner for a stamp to write home to loved ones far away & I earnestly pray that the little missive will safely reach its intended destination, safely.

Tuesday, August 9, 1864

Par cloudy & warm.

Wednesday, August 10, 1864

Fair & hot.

Thursday, August 11, 1864

Fair & intensely hot. This day is the warmest day we have had here this summer.

Friday, August 12, 1864

Hazy cloudy & hot. This day three months ago I was captured near Spotsylvania Court House.

Saturday, August 13, 1864

M foggy. E fair & hot.

Sunday, August 14, 1864

Fair & hot.

Monday, August 15, 1864

Par clo & warm.

Tuesday, August 16, 1864

M par cloudy indications of rain.

Wednesday, August 17, 1864

M fair & hot. E thunder wind & rain.

Thursday, August 18, 1864

Cloudy with a little rain.

Friday, August 19, 1864

Cloudy & pleasant.

Saturday, August 20, 1864

Cloudy & pleasant. Night cool.

Sunday, August 21, 1864

M rain. E par cloudy. Time seems to pass off slow & the hours drag heavily along. I have now been here over 3 months & it seems like ages since I first came into those gloomy & dreary prison walls. We do not get enough of the subsistence of animal life to satisfy the cravings of hunger. I have been hungry nearly all the time I have been here & I have almost forgot how one feels who get a plenty to eat. It is the most miserable life to live & always be hungry & also to see a plenty of good things to eat all around you every day & for it to be impossible for you to get any of them. Those of the prisoners who were fortunate enough to have <u>green backs</u> in their possession when captured & also those who have friends or relative inside the Federal lines, have every thing they want in abundance but us who have no friends nor money are in a deplorable & lamentable condition but the Blessed Lord bears me up & reminds me that this is not my rest & if I only prove faithful, I will soon secure an everlasting home where I will never hunger nor thirst any more.

Monday, August 22, 1864

M par cloudy & warm. E light showers of rain.

Tuesday, August 23, 1864

Par cloudy & warm. All the enlisted prisoners of war were ordered out & searched again today.

Wednesday, August 24, 1864

M cloudy. E par clo & warm. I have just finished reading Bunyans Pilgrims Progress which I delight in more than I am able to express and it has been a great comfort & consolation to me during me troubles, sore trials & afflictions & my most earnest hearts desire & prayer to my Prince is, that I may follow the way marked out therein, & at last when I come to the river with no bridge I may be able to go over rejoicing & enter in through the Beautiful Gate into the Celestial City in tryumph, & dwell with my beloved Master forever who gave His Life that a poor worthless worm like me might live forever.

Thursday, August 25, 1864

Par fair & pleasant. This is my birth day I am 23 years of age. This is the fourth birth-day I have seen since I have been in this cruel war, far away from home & loved ones.

Friday, August 26, 1864

Par cloudy & warm.

Saturday, August 27, 1864

M rain. E fair & warm.

Sunday, August 28, 1864

Fair & warm.

Monday, August 29, 1864

Par fair & pleasant.

Tuesday, August 30, 1864

M cool. E pleasant.

Wednesday, August 31, 1864

M cool. E fair & pleasant.

Thursday, September 1, 1864

Fair & pleasant.

Friday, September 2, 1864

Fair & pleasant. The weather is delightful now. The beautiful blue sky calm & serene & the warm balmy sunshine fell enliving & envigorating & all seems more beautiful & lovely by contrast with my present life, shut up in those gloomy prison walls, & I sigh when bygone days rushes on my memory, days when I was free & happy. Oh sweet days will you ever return to gladen this poor heart again? Yes a secret moniter within this sighing breast seems to whisper, only prove faithful to thy sacred trust & I will [ne'er] forsake thee. Trust in Me & I will deliver thee saith the Lord. Thy will be done not mine for thou knoweth what is best for me dear Lord.

Saturday, September 3, 1864

Cloudy & pleasant.

Sunday, September 4, 1864

Rainy & cool.

Monday, September 5, 1864

Rainy & cool.

Tuesday, September 6, 1864

Rainy & cold. The rain has been falling unceasingly for 3 days & nights & the air as cool as winter & we can scarcely get out of the barracks for the mud in the streets. We hear that Atlanta Geo has been captured which, if true, is the most serious disaster to our cause that has happened during the war.

Wednesday, September 7, 1864

Par cloudy & cool.

Thursday, September 8, 1864

M fair. E par cloudy.

Friday, September 9, 1864

Cloudy & pleasant.

Saturday, September 10, 1864

M rain. E fair & pleasant.

Sunday, September 11, 1864

Rainy & cool.

Monday, September 12, 1864

Cloudy, windy & col[d]er than I ever saw before for the season. The air is nearly at freezing point. This day four month ago I was captured.

Tuesday, September 13, 1864

Cloudy & cool.

Wednesday, September 14, 1864

M cloudy & cool. E rainy. I forgot to state until now that I sold my breakfast one day & din[n]er next day & thereby got enough money to write to the loved ones at home once more & also to my regt & I wrote on [the] 10th & sent them off the 12th earnestly praying that the good Lord may conduct them safe to thier greatly desired destination.

Thursday, September 15, 1864

Fair & pleasant.

Friday, September 16, 1864

Fair & pleasant. The weather has been beautiful & delightful for the last two days.

Saturday, September 17, 1864

Fair & pleasant. Beautiful moon light nights.

Sunday, September 18, 1864

Par cloudy & cool. 6 or 700 sick, wounded & disabled prisoners left here this morning on a steamer bound for the sweet Sunny South.[49] They were paroled & probily will be exchanged soon. I would have given any thing in my power to have been one of that number but the Lords will be done not mine. He knows what is best & probily will devise some means for my deliverance ere long.

Monday, September 19, 1864

Fair & pleasant.

Tuesday, September 20, 1864

Fair & ple[a]sent.

Wednesday, September 21, 1864

Par fair & pleasant. Last night another body of Confederate prisoners arrived here from Washington numbering something over 100. They were captured at different times from 12 months back to the present time.

Thursday, September 22, 1864

M cloudy. E fair & pleasant.

Friday, September 23, 1864

M rain. E fair.

---

49. The actual number was higher than Hall's estimate. Some 953 sick or disabled prisoners were sent to Confederate authorities at Venus Point on Jones Island west of Fort Pulaski on the Savannah River. Fetzer and Mowday, *Unlikely Allies*, 152; R. Hugh Simmons, "Prisoner of War Delivery Places on the James River in Virginia," *Fort Delaware Notes*, 55 (2005), 12.

Saturday, September 24, 1864

M rainy. E par cloudy. Last night I had a remarkable dream of home & loved ones, which I sincerely hope I will realize some day, not far distant.

Sunday, September 25, 1864

Cool & windy. The fort here fired a salute of 100 guns last evening in honor of a victory acheived over Gen Early, by Sheridan near Strasburg in the Shenandoah Valley & also, a heavy rain fell here late in the evening & faired off cool.[50]

Monday, September 26, 1864

Fair & cool.

Tuesday, September 27, 1864

Fair & pleasant.

Wednesday, September 28, 1864

M par cloudy. E a little rain.

Thursday, September 29, 1864

M rainy. E par fair & pleasant. Another steamer left here today for Dixie with a cargo of Sick & disabled prisoners, numbering about 6 or 800 & I hope & earnestly pray the time is not far distant when we will all be delivered from here.

Friday, September 30, 1864

M rainy. E cloudy windy & cool. Thanks be to the Lord on high I received a letter from home & loved ones far away in the dear Sunny South which was the greatest consolation I have experienced during my captivity on this dreary island. May the good Lord continue his mercies to them & supply both their spiritual & temporal wants is my earnest & constant prayer.

Saturday, October 1, 1864

M cloudy & cool. E cold rain.

---

50. This is likely a reference to the battle of Fisher's Hill, south of Strasburg, Virginia, on September 22, 1864.

Sunday, October 2, 1864

Cool & rainy.

Monday, October 3, 1864

Cloudy & cool.

Tuesday, October 4, 1864

Rainy & cool. I have scarcely had the pleasure of beholding Sun moon or stars in 6 or 7 days. A cool slow steady rain has been falling nearly all the above named period & the black mud on this island has become stirred up so deep we can hardly walk out of the barracks without miring up. Late this evening we beheld the sun.

Wednesday, October 5, 1864

M par fair. E cloudy.

Thursday, October 6, 1864

M foggy & rainy. E cloudy.

Friday, October 7, 1864

Fair & pleasant.

Saturday, October 8, 1864

Fair & cool.

Sunday, October 9, 1864

Windy & cold. Par cloudy. The cold wind seemed col[d]er today than I ever experienced for this season.

Monday, October 10, 1864

Fair windy & cool

Tuesday, October 11, 1864

Fair & cool.

Wednesday, October 12, 1864

M cloudy & cool. E rainy. Today five months ago I was captured.

Thursday, October 13, 1864

Fair & cool.

Friday, October 14, 1864

Par cloudy windy & cool.

Saturday, October 15, 1864

Par cloudy & cool.

Sunday, October 16, 1864

Par cloudy & cool.

Monday, October 17, 1864

Fair & cool.

Tuesday, October 18, 1864

Fair & cool.

Wednesday, October 19, 1864

Fair & cool. The last 3 days the weather has been beautiful & pleasant in the sunshine & bring vivid to my memory happier days [t]hat are past & gone.

Thursday, October 20, 1864

Par cloudy & cool.

Friday, October 21, 1864

Par cloudy & cool.

Saturday, October 22, 1864

Rainy & cool.

Sunday, October 23, 1864

Par cloudy & cool.

Monday, October 24, 1864

Cloudy & cool.

Tuesday, October 25, 1864

Fair & cool.

Wednesday, October 26, 1864

M rain. E windy.

Thursday, October 27, 1864

Cloudy & cool.

Friday, October 28, 1864

M rain. E windy.

Saturday, October 29, 1864

Fair & windy & cool. I sent a letter my regt today.

Sunday, October 30, 1864

Fair & cool. Sent letter to home & loved ones which I hope & earnestly pray will [reach] its destination soon.

Monday, October 31, 1864

Fair & cool.

Tuesday, November 1, 1864

Fair & cool.

Wednesday, November 2, 1864

Cloudy & cool. Today we were hyked out, & all that had two blankets one was taken from them & all that had none one was given them.[51] We have 2 stoves to 500 men & yesterday they give us coal for the first time. Our meat rations now will average a peice of lean boiled beef the size of a man thumb twice a day. Our bread rations is from 4 to 6 ounces a day & some days we get half pint of soup. To day we got none & some days we get no meat.

Thursday, November 3, 1864

Cloudy & cold.

Friday, November 4, 1864

Cold rainy & windy.

Saturday, November 5, 1864

Cloudy windy & cold.

Sunday, November 6, 1864

Frosty fair & cold.

Monday, November 7, 1864

Rain all day.

Tuesday, November 8, 1864

Cloudy & warm. Today the great presidential election is

---

51. One prisoner called taking extra blankets "the most shameful act of barbarity of recent date. No matter how many blankets a man may have brought with him, or purchased from the sutler with his own money, he is striped (sic) of all but one single one! Altho' it is a well known fact that in these open barracks no man could sleep comfortably under even three blankets, and lying upon as many more." Temple, *Union Prison at Fort Delaware*, 126.

held in the North which is to decide the destiny of a nation now envolved in one the feircest & bloodiest wars that was ever recorded in the annals of history. George B McClellan & Abraham Lincoln are the candidates. Lincoln is sure to be elected.

Wednesday, November 9, 1864

Warm & rainy.

Thursday, November 10, 1864

Cloudy & warm.

Friday, November 11, 1864

Fair & cool.

Saturday, November 12, 1864

Cloudy & cool. This day 6 months ago I was captured & am still a prisoner on a dreary island but I hope & earnestly pray that the Lord will provide a way for me to get away from here before long.

Sunday, November 13, 1864

M snow. E cloudy & cold.

Monday, November 14, 1864

Cloudy windy & cold.

Tuesday, November 15, 1864

[no entry]

Wednesday, November 16, 1864

Cloudy & cold.

Thursday, November 17, 1864

Cloudy & cool.

Friday, November 18, 1864

Rainy & cool.

Saturday, November 19, 1864

Cloudy & cold.

Sunday, November 20, 1864

Rainy & cool. This day six months ago I landed at this place & have not breathed the air of freedom since.

Monday, November 21, 1864

Rainy & cold. Gloomy weather.

Tuesday, November 22, 1864

A little snow.

Wednesday, November 23, 1864

Fair windy & cold. Last night & today the weather had been colder than any time before this season.

Thursday, November 24, 1864

Par fair & cold.

Friday, November 25, 1864

Fair & cold.

Saturday, November 26, 1864

Par cloudy & cold. A little rain at night.

Sunday, November 27, 1864

Cloudy & cool.

Monday, November 28, 1864

Fair & cool.

Wednesday, November 29, 1864

Par cloudy & cool. I caught the heaviest fall night before last I ever experienced in my life before. I fell from the top bunk to the floor which rendered me insensible for nearly an hour, but by the help of the Lord I am nearly well.

Thursday, December 1, 1864

Par cloudy & cool.

Friday, December 2, 1864

M cloudy. E cold & rainy.

Saturday, December 3, 1864

Cloudy & cool.

Sunday, December 4, 1864

Par cloudy & cold.

Monday, December 5, 1864

Fair & cool.

Tuesday, December 6, 1864

Cloudy & cool.

Wednesday, December 7, 1864

Rainy & cold.

Thursday, December 8, 1864

Par cloudy windy & cold.

Friday, December 9, 1864

Par cloudy windy & cold.

Saturday, December 10, 1864

Snow.

Sunday, December 11, 1864

Cold & cloudy.

Monday, December 12, 1864

Par cloudy windy & cold last night & today. The weather was as cold as I ever saw or even colder.

Tuesday, December 13, 1864

Par cloudy & severely cold.

Wednesday, December 14, 1864

Cloudy & cold.

Thursday, December 15, 1864

M cloudy. E snow.

Friday, December 16, 1864

Cold & sleety.

Saturday, December 17, 1864

Cloudy wet & cold.

Sunday, December 18, 1864

Cloudy & cold.

Monday, December 19, 1864

Rainy & cold.

Tuesday, December 20, 1864

Par cloudy & cold.

Wednesday, December 21, 1864

M snow. E cold rain.

Thursday, December 22, 1864

Cloudy windy & cold.

Friday, December 23, 1864

Par cloudy & cold.

Saturday, December 24, 1864

Par cloudy & cold.

Sunday, December 25, 1864

Christmas fair & cold. This is the fourth Christmas I have passed far away from home & loved ones.

Monday, December 26, 1864

Rainy & cool.

Tuesday, December 27, 1864

Rainy & cold.

Wednesday, December 28, 1864

Cloudy & cool.

Thursday, December 29, 1864

M snow. E fair cold & windy.

Friday, December 30, 1864

Par fair & cold & windy.

Saturday, December 31, 1864

Heavy snowing. 1864 leave us today never to return. I am far away from home & loved ones with no probibility of seeing them in a long long time.

13

"IT WAS A JOYFUL TIME FOR US TO BE SET AT LIBERTY ONCE MORE & BREATH[E] THE AIR OF FREEDOM"
FORT DELAWARE AND HOME: JANUARY 1 – MARCH 28, 1865

Hall's prayer for the new year on January 1, 1865, was that "this cruel war" would end and that all would be "safe at home in the dear Sunny South." Although that prayer would be answered in 1865, the year began poorly for Hall and the other prisoners on Pea Patch Island. It had snowed on December 31, 1864, leaving snow deep on the ground for the new year. Hall wrote on January 2 that he was "barefooted and nearly naked," both of which surely compounded his discomfort from the elements.[1] The early snow was followed by an ice storm, which disabled one of the two water boats used to bring drinking water from the Brandywine River.[2] On January 13, Hall again lamented that he was "now destitute of shoes & nearly naked for clothes." He had no money to pay a sutler for clothing nor outside sources to turn to for help.

The first step towards Hall's freedom occurred on January 20, 1865, when Division 7 was closed and he was moved to Division 6. Then, on February 8, he learned that all Georgia prisoners captured at Spotsylvania were to be paroled. On February 28, he watched between one thousand and twelve hundred prisoners leave. And then on March 6, Hall

---

1. Citron, *Confederate Prisoners at Fort Delaware*, 85. The U.S. Army had supplied a substantial amount of clothing to prisoners in 1863 but after autumn of that year, there was "little mention of the prisoners receiving clothing from the U.S. Army." Ibid., 79. Even Commandant Schoepf noted in January 1865 that clothing was insufficient and that some of the prisoners were "too thinly clad for such exceedingly cold weather." Ibid., 87.
2. Fetzer and Mowday, *Unlikely Allies*, 129.

learned that his time had arrived: he would be leaving Fort Delaware the following morning.

Shortly after sunrise on March 7, Hall lined up for examination and embarked on his southern-bound ship by 9 A.M. The trip south was apparently less eventful than the one that brought him to Delaware, because he simply notes that on the morning of March 10 he landed on the James River and proceeded to Richmond. At Camp Lee, a local training area named for famed Revolutionary War cavalryman Henry Lee, Hall received his parole documents and Special Order 226 from Headquarters, Department of Richmond, authorizing him a sixty-day leave of indulgence, at the expiration of which he was to return to his command. Endorsements on those orders, which were dated March 18, 1865, show that Hall received $50 at Camp Lee for rations for twenty days and transportation in kind to Barnett, Georgia.

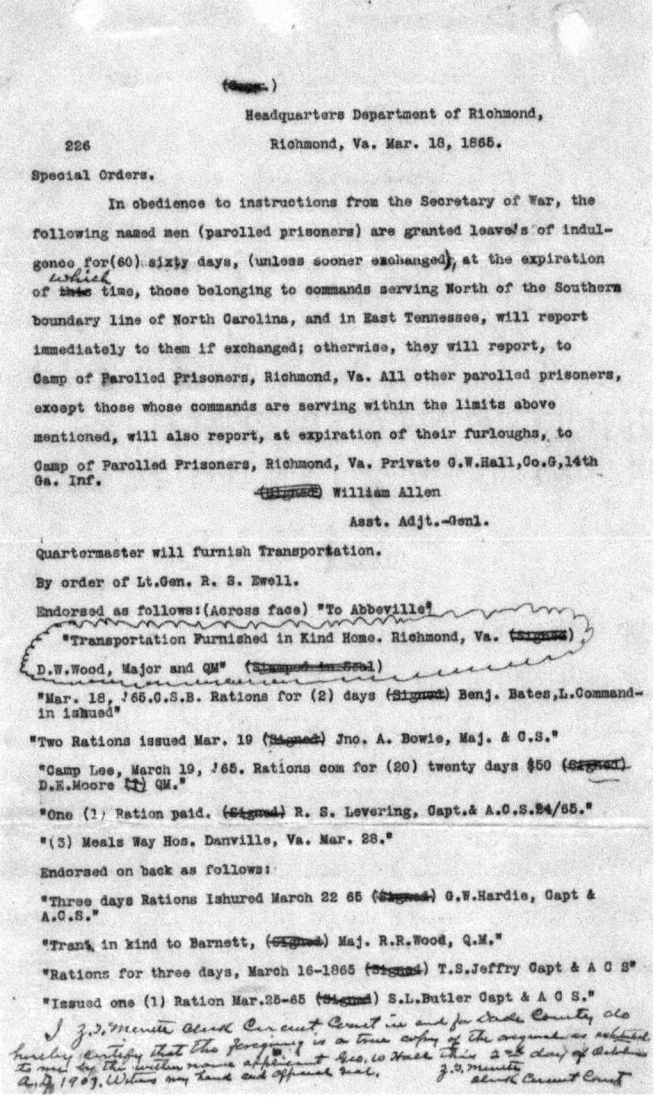

Hall submitted his 1865 leave of indulgence orders with his pension application to show his status at the end of the war. (Image from George W. Hall pension file, Florida Memory.com)

Hall's trip home to northwest Florida took roughly ten days, undoubtedly slowed by unreliable rail travel so late in the war and the need to avoid Union troops in the Carolinas. Several segments of the trip involved marches over forty miles in duration, which were likely a great physical challenge after nine months in the confines of Fort Delaware. Another segment of his trip home took him to Albany, Georgia, where he met up with one of his lieutenants, the first member of his company he had seen since his release from Fort Delaware.[3]

Hall took the stage from Albany to Bainbridge, Georgia, but when he learned the stage would lay over until the following day, he decided to simply walk. He arrived at Quincy on March 27 and on March 28, he arrived home "verry Badly worn out & exhausted."

Remembrancer Daily Entries
January 1 – March 28, 1865

Sunday, January 1, 1865

Fair & cold. The snow lies deep on the ground. The 1st day of the new year find[s] me in prison in the cold bleak north, but I hope & pray to the blessed Lord that the news years day of 1866 may find this cruel war ended and all of us safe at home in the dear Sunny South.

Monday, January 2, 1865

Par cloudy & cold. I am barefooted & nearly naked & see no probility of getting any clothing.

Tuesday, January 3, 1865

Par cloudy & cold.

Wednesday, January 4, 1865

M snow. E fair & cold.

Thursday, January 5, 1865

Par cloudy & cold.

---

3. This was likely Thomas Westfall, who had resigned his commission in April 1864 and resumed duties as Worth County Surveyor.

Friday, January 6, 1865

Rainy & cool.

Saturday, January 7, 1865

M snow. E cold & cloudy.

Sunday, January 8, 1865

Par cloudy. Windy & cold.

Monday, January 9, 1865

Cloudy & cool.

Tuesday, January 10, 1865

Rainy & cool.

Wednesday, January 11, 1865

Par fair & cold.

Thursday, January 12

Fair & cold.

Friday, January 13, 1865

Par fair & cool. Yesterday was 8 months since I was captured & long weary months I have passed a captive & have suffered more from hunger than I ever thought I was capable of enduring & I am now destitute of shoes & nearly naked for clothes.

Saturday, January 14, 1865

Rainy & cool.

Sunday, January 15, 1865

Par clo & cold.

Monday, January 16, 1865

Fair & cold.

Tuesday, January 17, 1865

Windy & snow.

Wednesday, January 18, 1865

Cloudy & cold.

Thursday, January 19, 1865

Fair & cold.

Friday, January 20, 1865

Par cloudy & cold. The 7 division is shut up today & we are put into the 6 & 8. I go in the 6th.

Saturday, January 21, 1865

Heavy snowing all day.

Sunday, January 22, 1865

Cloudy & cold.

Monday, January 23, 1865

Cloudy & cool.

Tuesday, January 24, 1865

Fair & extremely cold.

Wednesday, January 25, 1865

Fair & cold. Yesterday & today has been colder than any weather this winter. Every [ ] is frozen up from morning till night.

Thursday, January 26, 1865

Fair & severely cold.

Friday, January 27, 1865

M snow. E fair windy & cold.

Saturday, January 28, 1865

Fair & cold windy.

Sunday, January 29, 1865

M snow. E fair & cold.

Monday, January 30, 1865

Cloudy & cool.

Tuesday, January 31, 1865

Par cloudy & cool.

Wednesday, February 1, 1865

Fair & cool.

Thursday, February 2, 1865

Fair & cold.

Friday, February 3, 1865

Snow.

Saturday, February 4, 1865

Cloudy & cool.

Sunday, February 5, 1865

Fair windy & cold.

Monday, February 6, 1865

Cloudy & cold.

Tuesday, February 7, 1865

Heavy snowy all day.

Wednesday, February 8, 1865

Fair windy & cold. Today all Georgia prisoners captured at or near Spottsylvania were paroled & I was among that number & feint hope is revived within the breast of us poor prisoners, of breething the air of freedom in our dear Sunny South once more.

Thursday, February 9, 1865

Fair & cold.

Friday, February 10, 1865

Cloudy & cold.

Saturday, February 11, 1865

Fair & cold.

Sunday, February 12, 1865

M heavy snowing. E snow storm. The most severe weather I ever saw I experienced today.

Monday, February 13, 1865

Fair windy & cold. Severe freezes.

Tuesday, February 14, 1865

Fair & calm & some warmer than before.

Wednesday, February 15, 1865

Par cloudy & cool.

Thursday, February 16, 1865

Par fair & cool.

Friday, February 17, 1865

M cloudy. E rainy.

Saturday, February 18, 1865

Cloudy & cool.

Sunday, February 19, 1865

Fair & cool. I have been a prisoner on this island 9 months today but I hope & believe I will soon get away from here.

Monday, February 20, 1865

Fair & cool.

Tuesday, February 21, 1865

Fair & cool.

Wednesday, February 22, 1865

Par cloudy & cool. The weather has been the warmest & mildest for over a week it has been before this winter.

Thursday, February 23, 1865

Rainy & cool.

Friday, February 24, 1865

Rainy & cool.

Saturday, February 25, 1865

M cloudy. E warm & hard rain.

Sunday, February 26, 1865

Fair & pleasant.

Monday, February 27, 1865

Fair & cool.

Tuesday, February 28, 1865

Cold & snowy. Yesterday about 1000 or 1200 left here for Dixie on exchange. They were Missoureans Tennesseans & Marylanders.

Wednesday, March 1, 1865

Cloudy & cool.

Thursday, March 2, 1865

Rainy & cool.

Friday, March 3, 1865

Continued rain.

Saturday, March 4, 1865

M Rainy. E fair & pleasant. This day one year ago I arrived at home on furlough a day long to be remembered by me. We are expecting to leave for Dixie every day.

Sunday, March 5, 1865

Fair & cool.

Monday, March 6, 1865

Fair & cool. This evening we received the glad tidings that another boat of prisoners would leave here tomorrow at 7 A.M. & that Georgia would be among that number.[4]

Thursday, March 7, 1865

Fair & cool. This morning we were called out soon after daylight & examined & by 9 oclock A.M. we were on board the vessel that sailed soon afterwards. Our voyage only lasted 3 days & nights. On the morning of [the] 10th we landed on the James river & came inside our lines & proceeded on to Richmond.[5] It was a joyful time for us to be set at Liberty one more & breath[e] the air of freedom in our dear Sunny South. At camp Lee near Richmond we all received our paroles & leaves of absence to visit our home & loved ones.

On the morning of the 12th I left Richmond on the cars. The R.R. was out of repairs. The cars proceeded at a slow rate. We passed Danville Va in the evening on the 13th. On the 14][th] we arrived at Saulsbury [Salisbury], N. C. The

---

4. In March, 1865, 1,038 prisoners at Fort Delaware were delivered or exchanged. Fetzer and Mowday, *Unlikely Allies*, 152.
5. W. H. Bland, a private in the 61st Georgia, wrote that all 1,000 privates from Georgia were paroled and, along with ten Georgia officers, boarded the ship on the morning of March 7, 1864. They were underway by 11 A.M. During the three-day trip, six prisoners died and were buried on the banks of the James, having finally returned home to the south. The remaining prisoners were taken up the James to a landing near Richmond and marched to Camp Lee, Virginia, where they drew money and clothing, in addition to their documentation for a sixty-day furlough. W. H. Bland to G. W. Nichols, December 20, 1897, in Nichols, *A Soldier's Story of His Regiment (61st Georgia)*, 235.

15th we arrived at Charlotte & on the 16th we arrived at Chesterville [Chester] S. C. & from there Newberry Court House. I had to march 50 miles over a bad muddy road & so much rain had fell recently the river had over-flowed their banks & I was compelled to wade at several places. On the 19[th] I took the cars at Newberry & arrived at Ab[b]eville the same evening & from there I had to march to Washington Ga, where I arrived on [the] 21[st]. My feet & legs was verry sore not having marched much since I left prison. It was with difficulty that I could bear my feet to the ground.

Next morning, I then traveled a short distance on the cars from Washington to Barnets on the 22nd & from Barnets to Milledgeville.[6] I had to march again 45 miles. I arrived at Milledgeville on the 25th & took the cars from Midway to Macon the same evening. On the 25th I left Macon on the S. W. R. R. & passed my old native county where I was raised & arrived at Albany that evening near 4 oclock & met up with one of my Lieut the first one of my company I have seen since I came through the lines. I remained all night at Albany & next morning left there on the Stage & arrived at Bainbridge at 12 oclock next morning. The stage from some cause lay over there till next day & I concluded I could get home quicker to walk from there & the 27th I arrived at Quincy. On the 28th I arrived at Home Sweet Home verry Badly worn out & exhausted.

---

6. This is likely a reference to Barnett, Georgia, in Warren County, which anchored a spur line to Washington, Georgia.

14

THE DIARIES OF PRIVATE JACOB L. ELSESSER

Jacob Elsesser was born in Brumath, near Strasbourg, in the Alsace region of France, on March 27, 1828. His parents, Jacob (Senior) and Salome, emigrated to Philadelphia, Pennsylvania, when the younger Jacob was only a few months old. The family settled in Philadelphia, where the elder Jacob worked as a miller and Salome as a midwife. Jacob entered local politics and served as a Philadelphia street commissioner.[1] When Jacob, Senior died during a trip to New Orleans in 1849, young Jacob and his mother moved to Pittsburgh via a stage coach trip over the old Pennsylvania turnpike. In later years, Elsesser reveled in telling stories of the journey.

After a short stay in Pittsburgh, Jacob and his mother moved to Stewartstown, which was incorporated in 1868, as Etna, Pennsylvania. Having served as an apprentice to a bootmaker in Philadelphia, Elsesser opened a boot making shop in Stewartstown. He also began reading law with a local attorney, traveling by canal boat to the attorney's office in Pittsburgh and returning home on the weekends. When his mother became ill and died, however, Elsesser was forced to abandon his plans to become a lawyer. He returned to boot making, often mending or replacing the shoes of "Corn Planter Indians" who traveled by raft on the Allegheny River to Pittsburgh.[2]

---

1. Thomas Cushing, ed., *A Genealogical and Biographical History of Allegheny County, Pennsylvania* (Genealogical Publishing Co., 1975 reprint), 453.
2. This is likely a reference to members of the Seneca tribe in northwestern Pennsylvania who rafted lumber down the Allegheny River to Pittsburgh and beyond.

Jacob Elsesser became a naturalized citizen in 1850, sponsored by Daniel Hieber, who became his father-in-law three years later when Elsesser married Hieber's daughter Mary Salome. During this period, Jacob began operating a grocery store in addition to repairing shoes. Perhaps taking a cue from his father's civic engagement, he commenced his first term as the elected magistrate (justice of the peace) in Shaler township.[3] Jacob and Mary had four children before the Civil War erupted, but the eldest child died before her second birthday.

In 1854, a fast-moving cholera outbreak swept through Pittsburgh and its environs, claiming the lives of hundreds of victims. Elsesser was one of three men in Etna who tended to the sick and dead. The *Pittsburgh Press* praised Elsesser for laboring "unflaggingly and heroically to help the stricken men and women around him. The whole village [of Stewardstown] was in a state of terrible panic, and the responsibility for caring for the dying and dead devolved almost entirely on Mr. Elsesser and two other dauntless souls."[4]

Elsesser responded to a different call to service on May 1, 1861, when he enlisted in Company B of the 9th Pennsylvania Reserves. His enlistment was for a term of three years. Although he was never promoted beyond private, his diary entries show that he was regarded with a rare degree of responsibility and respect that junior enlisted

Although he never rose above the rank of private, Elsesser was entrusted by Company B with multiple responsibilities usually undertaken by a non-commissioned officer or second lieutenant. His diary references numerous instances where he socialized with officers and shared quarters with his company commander. (*Battles and Leaders of the Civil War*, Yoseloff ed., 1956)

---

3. "Justice of the Peace in Etna Has Held Office Fifty Years," *Pittsburgh Press*, February 2, 1908, www.newspapers.com
4. "Justice of the Peace in Etna Has Held Office Fifty Years," *Pittsburgh Press*, February 2, 1908, www.newspapers.com

personnel seldom experience, likely due to his age (33 when he enlisted), education, reputation, and status as a justice of the peace in his western Pennsylvania community.

Elsesser maintained at least two diaries during, or pertaining to, the Civil War. One was the 1862 *Daily Pocket Remembrancer* that Hall converted to his own use in late June 1862. Elsesser also wrote a 32-page "Diary of Co. B, 9th Rgt., P.R.C.," which was handed down within his family. Although the 1862 *Daily Pocket Remembrancer* gives an intimate glimpse into Elsesser's life, the "Diary of Co. B" reads more like a command history than a personal diary; for example, it lacks many of the references to family and friends that are found in the 1862 daily entries.[5] Elsesser, who performed a variety of quartermaster and clerical jobs for the company, apparently also served as *de facto* company historian, writing a brief history of Company B for the commanding general of the Pennsylvania Reserves Division in late February 1864. This company history may have formed the basis for his *Diary of Company B*.

The entries in both the 1862 *Daily Pocket Remembrancer* and the *Diary of Company B* reveal that Elsesser had a very close relationship with officers, quite unlike that which most privates experienced during the Civil War (or, indeed, in most armies, whether in war or peace). For example, in May 1862, he shared quarters with then-company commander Capt. Emil von Sothen, with whom he had a "social Tea together" and on a different date, a "social nap." On January 14, 1864, he wrote of a "Social Tete-a-Tete at our Quarters" with "Capt. F. Lieut. B and Capt. W of Co. H. present."[6]

The combined contents of the two Elsesser diaries not only provide information about Jacob Elsesser's war but also a basis for comparison with George Washington Hall's war. When reading the Elsesser 1862 entries, one cannot help but draw contrasts between the two men's access to food, clothing, and support from home during the first six months of the year. Elsesser sent and received mail on a regular basis, rarely went hungry, appears to have had sufficient clothing (indeed, an actual uniform), and had the finances to ship money and items home by Adams Express, a commercial shipping

---

5. A photocopy of the handwritten *Diary of Company B* shows that the entries from 1861 through late 1863 are relatively tidy but the entries beginning in late 1863 have strike-outs and writing in the margins, suggesting those pages may have been a draft that Elsesser intended to rewrite.
6. This is likely a reference to Company B's Captain Henry Fuhren and 1st Lieutenant Charles Becker, and Company H's Jacob Winans. Elsesser also noted that on May 13, 1862, he was "friendly entertained" by General Ord and his "O.S." (likely a reference to the rank/billet of Orderly Sergeant).

carrier. Hall often lamented during the war about being barefoot but Elsesser wrote in May 1862 that the men in his regiment were required to have two pairs of shoes and at least two pairs of socks.

The 9th Pennsylvania was one of fifteen regiments in the Pennsylvania Reserve Division, which Richard J. Sommers of the U.S. Army Heritage & Education Center describes as "one of the great combat divisions in American history."[7] The Reserves had unusual roots, having been formed as the Pennsylvania Reserve Volunteer Corps (PRVC) by the commonwealth's governor, Andrew Curtin. The PRVC initially consisted of thirteen infantry regiments, later augmented with light artillery and a cavalry regiment. The thirteen infantry regiments were numbered one through thirteen but when they were mustered into federal service in July 1861, they were designated the 30th through 42nd Pennsylvania Volunteer Infantry regiments. Consequently, Elsesser's unit was designated as Company B of both the 9th Pennsylvania Reserves and the 38th Pennsylvania Volunteer Infantry.

The thirteen infantry regiments were divided into brigades in the Pennsylvania Reserve Division, one of the few Union divisions consisting of soldiers from the same state. Curtin appointed Maj. Gen. George A. McCall, an 1822 graduate of West Point and a veteran of the Mexican-American War, to serve as initial commander of the Reserves. Subsequent division commanders included two of the most noteworthy Union general officers of the war, Major Generals John Reynolds and George Meade. Meade, in fact, was promoted to command of the Army of the Potomac in late June 1863 from his billet as the Reserves' division commander.

The 9th Pennsylvania Reserves regiment consisted of ten companies, including Company B, the "Garibaldi Guards," formed in Pittsburgh. The initial regimental commander was Col. Conrad Feger Jackson.[8] Company B's first commander was Francis (Frank) Hardtmeyer, a physician, who resigned his commission in December, 1861. Command then passed to Emil von Sothen, who was dismissed on July 15, 1862, after

---

7. Richard J. Sommers, Foreword to *The Pennsylvania Reserves in the Civil War: A Comprehensive History*, by Uzal W. Ent (McFarland, 2014), vii.
8. Jackson was promoted to brigade command and to brigadier general in July 1862. He was killed in action at Fredericksburg on December 13, 1862. He was succeeded in command of the 9th Pennsylvania Reserves by Colonel Robert Anderson.

fleeing during battle at Mechanicsville, Virginia, on June 26, 1862. For the remainder of the company's existence Company B was commanded by Capt. Henry Fuhren.

Company B entered Camp Wilkins, near the old Allegheny County Fairgrounds, for training on May 1, 1861. On June 11, they left Camp Wilkins for Camp Wright, near Oakmont, Pennsylvania. They remained there until late July, when they traveled to Camp Curtin at Harrisburg, Pennsylvania. There they drew their weapons, blankets, and knapsacks before riding by rail to Baltimore and then on to Washington, D.C. Elsesser and his regiment were mustered into federal service on July 28, 1861. In September, the 9th Pennsylvania Reserve regiment was assigned to the Third Brigade of McCall's Division. Brig. Gen. Edward O. E. Ord assumed command of the brigade from Col. John S. McCalmont in mid-November 1861.

The 9th Pennsylvania Reserves remained at various camps in the Washington area, initially at Tenleytown, for the next several months as they trained, stood picket duty, and erected fortifications to strengthen Washington's defenses. On August 21, the regiment (and its division) passed in review at Bailey's Crossroads, Virginia, for President Lincoln, the Cabinet, and Maj. Gen. McClellan, who staged this as his first large-scale review.[9] The division moved briefly into Virginia in early October, crossing the Potomac River at Chain Bridge before moving on to Langley, Virginia. McClellan sent McCall's Division to Dranesville, Virginia, on the Leesburg Pike to conduct reconnaissance, after which it remained in the Dranesville area.

Although most units in Virginia, on both sides, were in winter quarters by mid-December, 1861, foraging and perimeter patrols never stopped for the season. Elsesser saw his first combat on December 20, 1861, when several companies of the 9th Pennsylvania Reserves engaged then-Brig. Gen. J.E.B. Stuart and a mixed band of roughly 1,800 Confederate cavalrymen and infantry, accompanied by four artillery pieces, on a foraging raid near Dranesville. Stuart was intruding on the Pennsylvania Reserves' own foraging area. Elsesser wrote in his Company B diary that the Union troops under Ord engaged the Confederates "and in 1 ¾ hour whipped them badly. We killed 172 rebels. Captured about 100 stand of arms, their Caisson also fell into our hands we have 4 killed and 14

---

9. Davis, William C. *Lincoln's Men: How President Lincoln Became Father to an Army and a Nation* (Free Press, 1999), 52.

wounded."[10] After the battle Elsesser gave his blouse to the surgeon "so that he could ease the pain of one of the Enemies, who was mortally wounded." Dranesville was the Army of the Potomac's first victory of note and the men who participated were cheered by their fellow soldiers when they returned to camp. Those who participated were relieved of duties for three days and given full rations of "coffee, crackers, and cartridges."[11]

In April 1862, the regiment moved to Manassas Junction, where it occupied Camp Pickens, Hall's campsite from several months earlier. Shortly thereafter, the regiment moved to Catlett's Station, Virginia, where it remained until May, when the regiment marched to Falmouth near Fredericksburg. In early June, the regiment boarded transport steamers at Belle Plain and two days later arrived at the Federal supply compound near White House Landing, Virginia, on the York River. Arriving in time for the Seven Days battles around Richmond, the 9th Pennsylvania Reserves participated in the same battles as did the 14th Georgia, at Mechanicsville (Beaver Dam Creek), Gaines's Mill, and Frayser's Farm (Glendale). McCall's division of Pennsylvania Reserves, which began arriving at White House Landing, Virginia, on June 10, were, according to Stephen Sears, well-trained with good morale and "had promise of being formidable fighters."[12]

In the battle of Mechanicsville at Beaver Dam Creek on June 26, 1862, the 9th Pennsylvania Reserves, part of Truman Seymour's Third Brigade, stood brigade reserve behind the 12th Pennsylvania Reserves near Ellerson's Mill, roughly just over a mile downcreek from where the 2nd Pennsylvania Reserves were holding the 14th Georgia at bay. Even though the 9th Pennsylvania Reserves was not engaged in combat at this point, Capt. Sothen ran away from the company; purportedly a former aide to the King of Hanover, Sothen supposedly "double-quicked" to the rear when a shell exploded

---

10. Ord reported 50-75 Confederate dead, which was much closer to Stuart's report of 45 dead than the 172 claimed by Elsesser. Ent, *History of the Pennsylvania Reserves*, 35. The Reserves suffered eight men killed, sixty-one wounded and two missing. Ibid. One soldier in Company B, Private John Schmidt, was wounded in the engagement and ultimately discharged on Surgeon's Certificate in June 1862. Samuel P. Bates, *History of Pennsylvania Volunteers, 1861-5* (Harrisburg, PA: D. Singerly, State Printer, 1869), I:797.
11. Ent, *History of the Pennsylvania Reserves*, 36.
12. Sears, *To the Gates of Richmond*, 156, 202. Although Sears maintains that the Pennsylvania Reserves had not seen combat before, this was not true of Elsesser's company, which had fought at Dranesville in December 1861.

Union defenses at Ellerson's Mill. (*Battles and Leaders of the Civil War*, Yoseloff ed., 1956)

over Company B and he "was never to be seen again."[13] Late in the engagement, the regiment marched to a position in support of the 12th Pennsylvania Reserves, where it suffered continuous heavy fire.

Company B went out that night as skirmishers. In the early morning hours on June 27, McClellan directed V Corps commander Fitz John Porter to have McCall's division abandon its position at Beaver Dam Creek and fall back several miles to Gaines's Mill. McCall directed Seymour's Third Brigade to leave last and delay the expected Confederate onslaught. Seymour, in turn, assigned the 9th Pennsylvania Reserves as the rear guard. When Confederate forces resumed attacking the Union rifle pits at daybreak, Conrad Feger Jackson sent troops to relieve those in the rifle pits until the main body of the brigade could be withdrawn. The 9th Pennsylvania Reserves remained in place until about 7 a.m. and then cautiously pulled back while being subjected to incoming shot and shell for the first mile of its retreat. The regiment suffered sixteen casualties that morning, including two killed. It is likely that the men of Company B had no opportunity to pack up camp before they pulled back, which left Elsesser's diary abandoned for Hall to claim as the men of the 14th Georgia swept through the Pennsylvanians' former campground. June 26, 1862, was Elsesser's last dated entry in the *Daily Pocket Remembrancer*.

After arriving at Gaines's Mill, the 9th Pennsylvania Reserves initially served as reserve but in the late afternoon, they – along with other regiments in the Pennsylvania Reserve Division – were detailed piecemeal as needed along the Union line. The 9th Pennsylvania Reserves shifted to support the 62nd Pennsylvania Infantry Regiment and

---

13. Chris Rasmussen and Jim Owston, *History of The Ninth Pennsylvania Reserve Corps*, accessed August 4, 2020, http://www.9thPennsylvania Reserves.org/Library11.htm. Sothen was discharged on July 15, 1862.

the 9th Massachusetts Infantry Regiment. The 9th Pennsylvania Reserves had to traverse a swampy ravine while it was being raked by Confederate musket fire. Advancing at charge bayonet position, the regiment joined the 62nd Pennsylvania and the 9th Massachusetts in repeated charges which devolved into a series of counter-attacks. Charles Becker, then a sergeant in Company B, reported that the last Confederate charge was not until 9 p.m.[14] After the battle, a Confederate tactical victory, tapered off, the 9th Pennsylvania Reserves crossed the Chickahominy River with the remainder of V Corps.

Company B's next action was at Frayser's Farm (Glendale) on June 30, 1862.[15] Samuel Bates, who wrote a history of the Pennsylvania Reserve Division shortly after the war ended, describes the 9th Pennsylvania Reserve's combat here as the fiercest that the regiment had yet encountered.[16] For much of the afternoon of June 30, McCall's division, in its third battle in five days, took on, almost single-handedly, Longstreet's and A. P. Hill's divisions. At least one commentator has questioned the combat preparedness of the Pennsylvania Reserves, as Brian Burton maintains that the Union troops at Frayser's Farm, although the "most exposed to the enemy attack," were simply not ready for battle due to casualties and physical exhaustion.[17]

Battle of Glendale--Contest around General McCall's Cannon. (Public domain: from Rev. J.J. Marks, *Peninsula Campaign in Virginia, or Incidents and Scenes on the Battle-Fields and in Richmond*.)

McCall's division had 5,000 infantrymen arrayed behind five batteries at Frayser's Farm, with Meade's

---

14. Ent, *Pennsylvania Reserves in the Civil War*, 72.
15. Bates, *History of Pennsylvania Volunteers*, I:796. Bates refers to this action as the battle at Charles City Cross Roads. Charles City Road intersects Long Bridge Road just north of Frayser's Farm.
16. Bates, *History of Pennsylvania Volunteers*, 788.
17. Burton, *Extraordinary Circumstances*, 249. Burton points out that the division had lost twenty percent of its strength and had made a strenuous march with very little food and sleep. Ibid., 301.

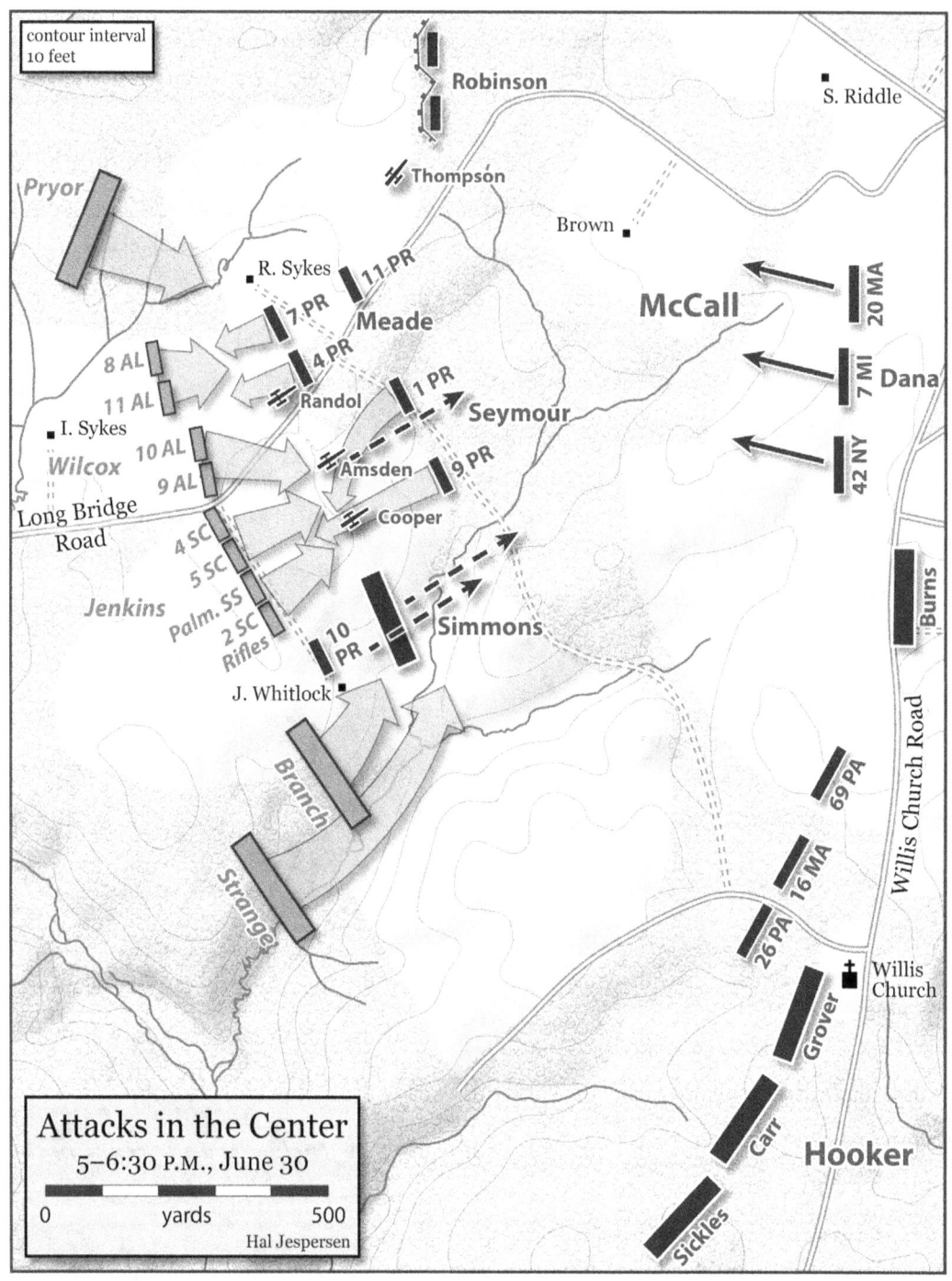

Meade's Pennsylvania Reserves took heavy casualties defending Cooper's and Randol's batteries. (Map by Hal Jespersen, from *Richmond Shall Not Be Given Up: The Seven Days' Battles, June 25—July 1, 1862*, by Doug Crenshaw)

Brigade on the left of Long Bridge Road and Seymour's brigade on the right, covering the terrain between Long Bridge Road and the Whitlock farmhouse. The 9th Pennsylvania Reserves in Seymour's brigade was situated behind the six guns of Capt. James H. Cooper's Battery B of the 1st Pennsylvania Light Artillery. Opposing the Pennsylvania Reserves were the combined forces of James Longstreet and A. P. Hill. Longstreet, in ordering Micah Jenkins's brigade to silence Cooper's guns, anticipated that Jenkins's sharpshooters would simply shoot the gunners without prematurely starting a general engagement. However, Jenkins interpreted the order as direction to advance on the battery and sent the bulk of his South Carolina brigade moved forward shortly before 4 p.m. As Burton writes, Jenkins set up his brigade for "horrendous" losses, sending infantrymen to charge artillery in an open field.[18]

As Jenkins's Brigade charged, Cooper's guns were defended by the men of the 1st Reserves rather than the 9th Pennsylvania Reserves, which had, in the interim, been dispatched further on the Union left towards Whitlock farm. Jenkins's men made multiple charges and finally seized the guns after the combat devolved into bayonet thrusts and hand-to-hand combat. The 9th Pennsylvania Reserves hastily returned to its original position and, with the help of the guns of Alanson Randol's battery, drove Jenkins's men back. However, Jenkins attacked again, reinforced by two Alabama regiments from Cadmus Wilcox's Brigade. The Union artillerymen in Cooper's battery were forced to retire without their artillery because they had no horses to move the guns. Nevertheless, the 9th Pennsylvania Reserves continued to fight at the battery position.

The 14th Georgia was Hill's last regiment to be committed to the battle at Frayser's Farm and likely entered the fray well after the 9th Pennsylvania Reserves retired. Still, it is possible that at Frayser's Farm, Elsesser and Hall were present at Frayser's Farm within a half-mile of each other. Although Lee was not successful in breaking and holding the Union line at Glendale, McCall's division paid a steep price of some 1,600 casualties. McCall himself was captured, Meade was wounded in his arm and side, and Seymour wandered off the battlefield in a daze. Every regiment in McCall's division "retired or broke at some point" during the battle.[19] In the fight for Cooper's battery, the 9th

---

18. Burton, *Extraordinary Circumstances*, 277.
19. Sears, *To the Gates of Richmond*, 301. The Pennsylvania Reserves incurred almost twenty percent of the Union Army's entire casualties during the Seven Days battles. Burton, *Extraordinary Circumstances*, 387.

Pennsylvania Reserves had seventeen men killed, eighty-four wounded, and thirty-six missing. In Elsesser's Company B, two men were killed in action, one man died from wounds incurred during battle, three others were wounded and discharged pursuant to Surgeon's Certificate, and one, a sergeant with whom Elsesser had shared quarters, went missing in action.

Neither the 9th Pennsylvania Reserves nor the 14th Georgia fought in the Confederate trouncing at Malvern Hill on the day following Frayser's Farm. After McClellan's forces, including the 9th Pennsylvania Reserves, reached the safety of the Union gunboats at Harrison's Landing, they remained there until mid-August 1862 while McClellan belabored Washington for more troops to continue the campaign for Richmond. Life at Harrison's Landing was both restorative and crippling; the Army of the Potomac was able to rest and replenish their supplies but was subjected to occasional incoming artillery fire and could not shake the illness that heat, humidity, terrain, and insects inflicted on both armies throughout the campaign. The Army of the Potomac found itself camping near swampy terrain. As then-Sergeant Charles Becker of Company B wrote, the drinking water was "awful and sickness is spreading rapidly. The heat here is fearful and the smell of those infernal swamps poisons the very air we breathe."[20]

While at Harrison's Landing, Brig. Gen. John Reynolds, who had been captured at Gaines's Mill, returned from his brief time as a prisoner of war and replaced McCall as division commander. Conrad Feger Jackson was promoted to brigadier general and placed in command of Third Brigade to replace Truman Seymour, who was transferred to command of First Brigade. Lt. Col. Robert Anderson was promoted to command the 9th Pennsylvania Reserves.

The Pennsylvania Reserve Division left the Peninsula for Aquia Creek in northern Virginia via Fortress Monroe in mid-August to join Pope's Army of Virginia. The 9th Pennsylvania Reserves, which stood picket duty from August 10-16, 1862, was one of the last units to leave the Peninsula. Once the regiment landed at Aquia Creek, it boarded trains for Falmouth, near Fredericksburg. There was scant time for rest as the regiment

---

20. Charles Becker Narrative, July 16, 1862, in Ent, *The Pennsylvania Reserves in the Civil War*, 104. According to Kathryn Shively Meier, the plummeting health of the Union troops at Harrison's Landing contributed to the decision to withdraw the Army of the Potomac in mid-August. Meier, *Nature's Civil War*, 45.

was almost immediately ordered to march towards Manassas and imminent battle with Stonewall Jackson, whose corps now included the 14th Georgia. The 9th Pennsylvania Reserves arrived on August 28; as Bates wrote, "This forced march of five days without adequate supplies or provisions, with the enemy hanging on flank and rear, proved one of the most exhausting which [the regiment] was ever their lot to endure."[21]

On August 29 and August 30, 1862, the 9th Pennsylvania Reserves fought in the battle of Second Manassas, although not in the vicinity of Thomas's Brigade. On August 30, due to poor planning by Pope, the Reserves were, for a time, the only Union division facing Longstreet's newly-arrived 28,000 men.[22] As Elsesser wrote in his Company B diary, "Fought again, and being on the extreme left, and left uncovered by support we had to give way under a destructive fire." Conrad Feger Jackson suffered a ruptured blood vessel during the fighting. Col. Martin Hardin of the 12th Pennsylvania Reserves assumed brigade command but was wounded himself and succeeded in command of the brigade by Col. Kirk of the 10th Reserves, who, when wounded himself, passed command of the brigade to Lt. Col. Anderson of the 9th Pennsylvania Reserves. Command of the 9th Pennsylvania Reserves devolved to Maj. James Snodgrass. Third Brigade suffered 287 casualties at Second Manassas. Company B suffered four men killed. Several days later it returned to Arlington Heights near the District of Columbia, where it had been encamped four months previously. As Bates writes, "A little more than four months before, the Ninth had left this neighborhood a strong regiment, full of vigor and buoyant with hope; it was now again upon the same ground, reduced by killed, wounded, and sick to nearly one-half its former numbers, and the survivors worn and exhausted with almost constant marching and fighting."[23] The regiment rested for two days and then marched to Monocacy Creek, where it remained until marching to Turner's Gap on South Mountain on September 14, 1862.

Lee's victory at Second Manassas had helped spur his decision to invade Maryland. While Stonewall Jackson (and Thomas's Brigade) moved on Harper's Ferry, Elsesser's next action was at South Mountain on September 14, 1862. By this point, Anderson had resumed command of the regiment as Col. Thomas Gallagher assumed command

---

21. Bates, *History of Pennsylvania Volunteers*, I: 789.
22. Ent, *The Pennsylvania Reserves in the Civil War*, 119.
23. Bates, *History of Pennsylvania Volunteers*, I: 790

of Third Brigade in Conrad Feger Jackson's absence. The 9th Pennsylvania Reserves engaged Rodes's Brigade in a hard-scrabble fight across ravines and ridges at Frostown Gap, roughly a mile north of Turner's Gap. One private in Company B died of wounds incurred at South Mountain. Ten men altogether died in the 9th Pennsylvania Reserves, and thirty-three were wounded. When Gallagher was wounded during the battle, Anderson again assumed brigade command, leaving twenty-five-year-old (and future U.S. Congressman) Capt. Samuel Dick of F Company in temporary command of the 9th Pennsylvania Reserves.

The worst fighting of the war to date for the Pennsylvanians was to come just a few days later at Antietam, the single bloodiest day of combat in American military history. Of the 84,000 men who fought at Antietam, almost 29% became casualties. One out of five men in the Pennsylvania Reserves at Antietam became a casualty.[24]

In the early morning hours of September 17, 1862, the 9th Pennsylvania Reserves, still under command of Capt. Dick, with its right near Hagerstown Pike, marched with Meade's Pennsylvania Reserves division into famed Miller's cornfield, located between Hagerstown Pike and the East Woods.[25] Possession of the cornfield would soon change hands some six times in less than three hours. A key Union objective was the Dunker Church, well south of the cornfield at the intersection of Hagerstown Pike and Smoketown roads.[26]

As it reached the northern edge of the cornfield, Anderson's Third Brigade, including the 9th Pennsylvania Reserves, stopped at a fence and positioned their muskets using the wooden rungs to steady their aim. Once the Confederate troops of the 1st Texas Infantry Regiment in Hood's Brigade charged to within thirty feet, the Pennsylvanians

---

24. Ent, *The Pennsylvania Reserves in the Civil War*, 157
25. Reynolds temporarily relinquished command of the Pennsylvania Reserves Division on September 12, 1862, to Meade after Pennsylvania Governor Curtin demanded that Reynolds command the 75,000 militia Curtin had called out to defend Pennsylvania against Lee's incursion. Ent, *The Pennsylvania Reserves in the Civil War*, 130
26. As James McPherson observes, "Many cornfields were the scene of fighting during the Civil War, but this one was ever after known as *the* Cornfield." James M. McPherson, *Crossroads of Freedom: Antietam* (Oxford, UK: Oxford University Press, 2002), 117-118. "After the battle was over, every stalk of corn in the northern part of the field was cut as closely as could have been done with a knife, and the slain lay in rows as precisely as they had stood in ranks." William H. Powell, *The Fifth Army Corps (Army of the Potomac): A Record of Operations during the Civil War in the United States of America, 1861-1865* (New York: Putnam's Sons, 1896), 275

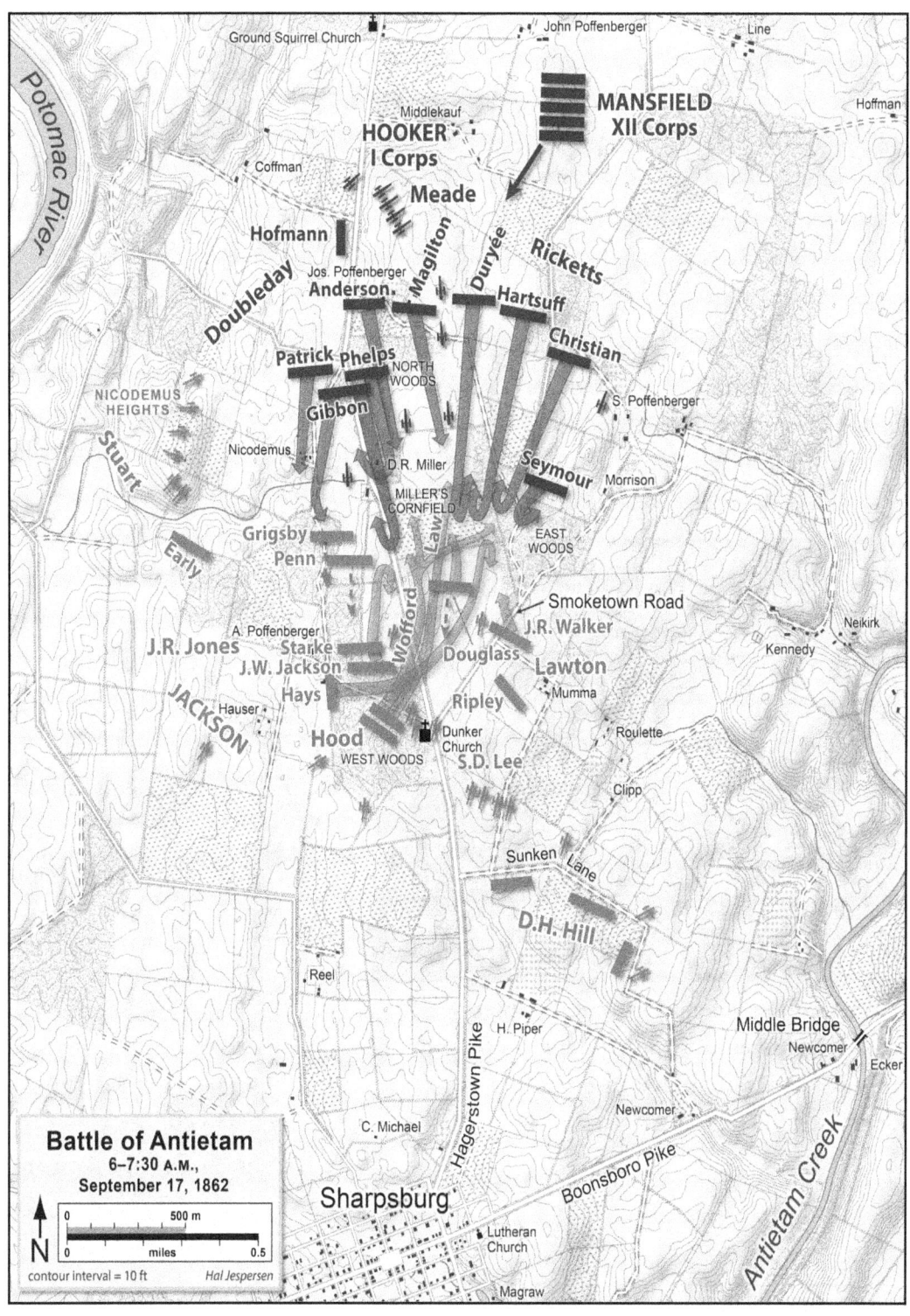

An early morning attack brought the 9th Pennsylvania Reserves into battle with the 1st Texas Infantry in Miller's Cornfield. (Map by Hal Jespersen)

Union troops advancing through Miller's cornfield at Antietam (*Battles and Leaders of the Civil War*, Yoseloff ed., 1956)

```
              U.S.A.
         FIRST ARMY CORPS
  ANDERSON'S BRIGADE, MEADE'S DIVISION
  LIEUT. COL. ROBERT ANDERSON, 9TH PENNA.
         RESERVE, COMMANDING.
              ORGANIZATION.

         9TH PENNSYLVANIA RESERVES
        10TH PENNSYLVANIA RESERVES
        11TH PENNSYLVANIA RESERVES
        12TH PENNSYLVANIA RESERVES

            (SEPTEMBER 17, 1862.)
   ANDERSON'S BRIGADE ADVANCED FROM THIS POINT ABOUT 6:30
  A.M. IN SUPPORT OF GIBBON'S, PHELPS' AND PATRICK'S BRIGADES OF
  DOUBLEDAY'S DIVISION, MIDWAY BETWEEN THE NORTH WOODS AND
  THE D. R. MILLER HOUSE, THE 10TH REGIMENT WAS SENT TO THE
  WEST ABOUT 700 YARDS TO PROTECT THE FLANK OF THE UNION LINE
  AGAINST A THREATENED ADVANCE OF THE ENEMY. THE THREE
  REMAINING REGIMENTS BECAME ENGAGED WITH THE ENEMY IN THE
  NORTH EDGE OF THE CORNFIELD SOUTH OF THE MILLER HOUSE.
                                              NO. 24.
```

Antietam Battlefield Historical Tablet No. 24 commemorating Anderson's Brigade, Meade's Division, between 6-9 A.M. on September 17, 1862.

opened fire. Between musket fire and Union artillery, the western edge of the cornfield turned into what Ethan Rafuse describes as a "slaughter pen."[27] The 1st Texas, which had bolted forward on its own through the cornfield, suffered a staggering casualty rate of 82%, including some eight colorbearers.

The 9th Pennsylvania Reserves, which saw three of its color bearers cut down in the action, likely pushed further south than any other regiment in Third Brigade, but Anderson's men were eventually driven back by Confederate reinforcements from a brigade of Georgians and North Carolinians.[28] As Uzal Ent writes, the Pennsylvania Reserves were "pretty much out of the fight" by 10 a.m., withdrawing to the North Woods after being relieved by units of another corps.[29] According to Elsesser, Company B lost three killed in action and

---

27. Rafuse, *Antietam, South Mountain & Harper's Ferry*, 50.
28. Phillip Thomas Tucker, *Miller Cornfield at Antietam: The Civil War's Bloodiest Combat* (History Press, 2017), 148.
29. Ent, *The Pennsylvania Reserves in the Civil War*, 156.

four wounded so severely that they were discharged pursuant to a Surgeon's Certificate. First Lieutenant John Longbein was among those killed. The regiment lost, according to Elsesser, sixteen killed and sixty-seven wounded.[30] Overall, the three infantry brigades of Pennsylvania Reserves suffered 550 casualties at Antietam.[31] Governor Curtin lamented that the division had entered federal service with over 15,000 men, but after Antietam, it could not muster four thousand.[32] Some companies had no officers remaining, forcing sergeants into company command.

In the weeks that followed the bloodbath at Antietam, the 9th Pennsylvania Reserves moved from Maryland back to the Potomac region. Its next major action was the Battle of Fredericksburg on December 13, 1862. Ambrose Burnside, now in command of the Army of the Potomac, had divided his army at Fredericksburg into three "grand divisions." The 9th Reserve regiment, in Conrad Feger Jackson's Third Brigade, Meade's Division, Reynolds' I Corps, was assigned to Franklin's left grand division.[33]

Franklin tasked Reynolds's I Corps with the assault against Stonewall Jackson's corps on Prospect Hill, near Hamilton's Crossing. Reynolds, in turn, selected Meade's division of 4,500 Pennsylvania Reserves, one of the smallest in the entire Army of the Potomac, to lead the assault against the south end of Stonewall Jackson's line. The 9th Pennsylvania Reserves were detailed as flankers and skirmishers for Conrad Feger Jackson's brigade.

As Bates described the 9th's engagement at Fredericksburg:

> The Ninth regiment occupied a position on the left flank of the division, and was thrown forward on the skirmish line. As it advanced near the foot of the hill to the left of the railroad, the firing became very severe, and in compliance with orders it was marching directly by the line, when it was ascertained that its supports had obliqued to the right and were out of supporting distance. The regiment then took shelter behind an old fence and ditch, which answered the purpose of rifle-pits. Here the men

---

30. Ent reports seventeen killed and sixty-six wounded. Ent, *The Pennsylvania Reserves in the Civil War*, 158.
31. Ent, *The Pennsylvania Reserves in the Civil War*, 158.
32. Ent, *The Pennsylvania Reserves in the Civil War*, 160.
33. During the fighting at Antietam, Meade had replaced Hooker as corps commander after Hooker was shot in the foot. Reynolds later assumed command of the corps and Meade assumed command of the Pennsylvania Reserve Division. Conrad Feger Jackson, having recovered from his health issues at Second Manassas, resumed command of the Third Brigade.

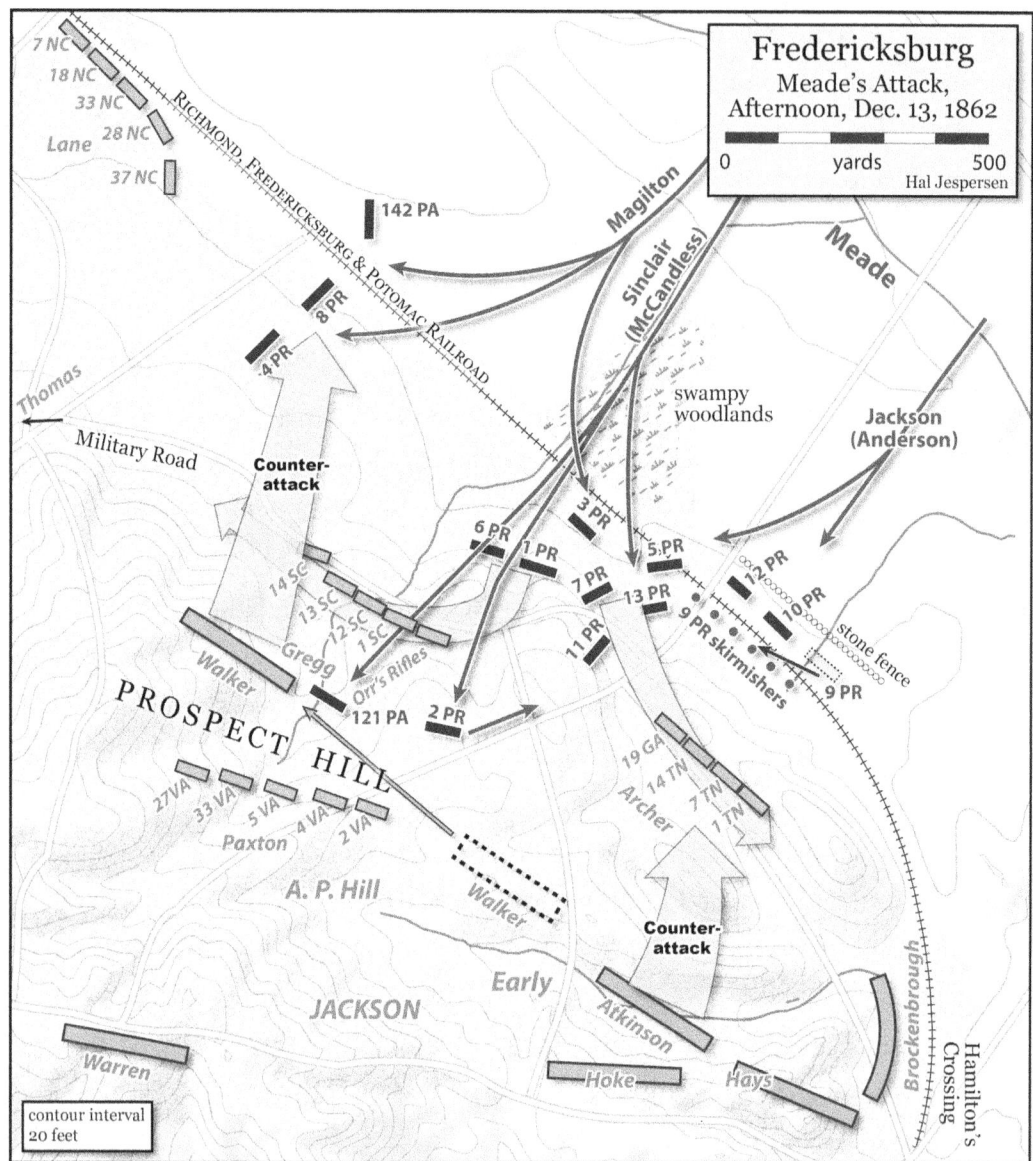

The 9th Pennsylvania Reserves fought as skirmishers on the rail line in Meade's attack at Fredericksburg. Elsesser's brigade commander, Conrad Ferger Jackson, was fatally wounded during the battle. (Map by Hal Jespersen)

did excellent service picking off the rebel sharp-shooters and the gunners from a battery commanding the left flank of the division. This battery had been inflicting terrible slaughter upon our forces, but it was completely silenced by the sure marksmen of the Ninth. This position was held until it was ascertained that the remainder of the division had fallen back to the batteries, when the order was given to retire. But as soon as the breast work was abandoned, and the men were out from cover, a terrific fire from the enemy's infantry, and from his battery, which had been held in check, was opened upon them. In the meantime, a detachment of his infantry had been moving around to the left under cover of the woods, and had gained a position within a short distance of its left flank, ready to dash out and capture it. But the withdrawal was timely and successfully made. The loss was nine killed, twenty-seven wounded, and sixteen taken prisoners.[34]

Notwithstanding Bates's intimation that the 9th Pennsylvania Reserves made a deliberate withdrawal of their own volition, historian Frank O'Reilly writes that Archer's Brigade and Brockenbrough's Brigade made a frontal assault on the 9th Pennsylvania Reserves, which held the Confederates at bay by musket fire for a time. But the 9th Pennsylvania Reserve's line finally gave way when Hoke's Brigade turned the Pennsylvanians' left flank.[35] Although the Pennsylvania Reserves had penetrated Stonewall Jackson's line, they were unable to hold it long. Franklin, who should have committed more of his readily available troops to the initial assault, compounded his error by failing to send troops to Meade's aid, enabling Confederate reserves to successfully counter-attack and drive Union soldiers out of the woods near Prospect Hill.

The percentage of Meade's division lost as casualties at Fredericksburg rose to an astronomical 41 percent: 1,853 out of 4,500, including 175 killed.[36] The Third Brigade suffered the most casualties in the division, including Conrad Feger Jackson, who was shot while attempting to rally his men. Elsesser recorded in his Company B diary that his regiment lost forty men in the battle. As the only Union division to even break through the Confederate line, the role of the Reserves at Fredericksburg was one of their greatest commitments of the war.[37] As Frank O'Reilly writes:

> Contrary to all the historical attention lavished on the December 13 action around Marye's Heights and the stone wall, these Confederate defenses did not determine the outcome of the Battle of Fredericksburg.

---

34. Bates, *History of Pennsylvania Volunteers*, I:791.
35. O'Reilly, *The Fredericksburg Campaign*, 224.
36. Ent, *The Pennsylvania Reserves in the Civil War*, 184.
37. Gottfried, *Brigades of Gettysburg*, 269.

The Federals suffered predictable losses against them without one soldier even reaching the Southern lines, much less penetrating them. The decisive factor of the battle focused on the fighting around Prospect Hill. George Gordon Meade's Pennsylvania Reserves fought the true Battle of Fredericksburg, as opposed to the dramatic and compelling slaughter of Federal troops that took place on the Federal right.[38]

On December 18, 1862, the 9th Pennsylvania Reserves moved to an encampment near Belle Plain, where George Washington Hall was held captive seventeen months later. Except for a brief unsuccessful foray for Burnside's weather-doomed "Mud March" on January 20, 1863, the 9th Pennsylvania Reserves remained in winter quarters through early February 1863, when they embarked at Belle Plain for duty in Washington, D.C. The regiment hoped that duty in the Washington and the Alexandria area would be a time to recruit new troops to the Reserves, but it turned out to be months of dangerous picket duty, provost assignments, and harsh weather. However, its assignment to Washington spared the regiment from fighting the battle of Chancellorsville in May 1863.

The 9th Pennsylvania Reserves enthusiastically rejoined the Army of the Potomac in late June 1863 as Lee's second invasion of the north – this time to the Pennsylvania Reserve Division's home state - became imminent. Both Reynolds (I Corps) and Meade (V Corps) sought the Pennsylvania Reserves for their respective corps, but Meade won out. The division's delight at again serving under Meade deflated somewhat when Meade was promoted to command the entire Army of the Potomac on June 28, 1863. Brig. Gen. Samuel Crawford replaced Meade in command of the Pennsylvania Reserves in May 1863, with the exception of one brigade which remained behind in Northern Virginia during the Gettysburg Campaign. Col. James Fisher, untested in battle as a brigade commander, commanded the Third Brigade, which included Elsesser's 9th Pennsylvania Reserves.

The Third Brigade joined V Corps near Frederick on June 28, 1863, the day on which Meade was promoted to command of the Army of the Potomac. Elsesser's regiment crossed the Pennsylvania state line on the afternoon on July 1, as the battle

---

38. Frank A. O'Reilly, "Busted up and Gone to Hell": The Assault of the Pennsylvania Reserves at Fredericksburg." In *Blood on the Rappahannock: The Battle of Fredericksburg*, edited by Theodore P. Savas and David A. Woodbury, *Civil War Regiments: A Journal of the American Civil War*, Vol. 4, No. 4 (1995), 23.

of Gettysburg was already underway. The men marched hard to get to Gettysburg, traveling roughly seventy miles in just over three days in rainy conditions and on slippery roads. They arrived between 6 and 7 a.m. on July 2, 1863, having had barely any sleep over the previous three days.

Meade sent the two brigades of the Pennsylvania Reserves to strengthen the left flank of the Union V Corps line on Little Round Top south of Gettysburg. Brig. Gen. Gouverneur Warren had already hastily ordered Brig. Gen. Strong Vincent's and Brig. Gen. Stephen Weed's brigades to Little Round Top after realizing that there were no Union combat troops there. Those brigades, which included Joshua Chamberlain's famed 20th Maine Infantry Regiment, had already turned back waves of attacking Confederates on Little Round Top before the Pennsylvania Reserves arrived.

After Crawford sent McCandless's First Brigade, along with the 11th Pennsylvania Reserves, into battle near Plum Run, he dispatched Fisher's remaining regiments to the Round Tops. By the time these regiments maneuvered over the rocks and brush of the north slope, the bulk of the fighting there was over but the appearance of fresh Union troops may have contributed to the withdrawal of the Confederate attackers. However, a raging debate ensued between Chamberlain and Fisher as to which regiment(s) took the lead in gaining possession of Big Round Top on July 2, 1863: Chamberlain's 20th Maine or Fisher's 5th and 12th Pennsylvania Reserves.[39]

Big Round Top from entrenchments on Little Round Top. (Library of Congress)

---

39. As Bradley Gottfried wrote, the "real battle began after the war, when Fisher and his men took on the 20th Maine about what really happened on the night of July 2, 1863." Gottfried, *Brigades of Gettysburg*, 278-79.

Notwithstanding the Chamberlain-Fisher debate, it is uncontroverted where Elsesser's 9th Pennsylvania Reserves were on July 2, 1863: they assumed a position, with the 10th Pennsylvania Reserves, in the "saddle" between the two Round Tops. They moved forward overnight and constructed a wall from loose granite, which helped shield them from Confederate sharpshooters in the Devil's Den directly in front of them. Elsesser's Company B diary entries for Gettysburg for July 2 make no mention of combat for the 9th Pennsylvania Reserves and note only that on July 3 the regiment constructed stone walls. The battle of Gettysburg may have decimated many other regiments during three days of fighting, but the 9th Pennsylvania Reserves escaped with only a handful of men wounded, none of whom were in Company B.[40]

Troops of the Pennsylvania Reserves prepare for the grand sword presentation for General Meade (Library of Congress)

As Meade tracked Lee during the Confederate withdrawal to Virginia, the Pennsylvania Reserves crossed the Potomac on July 17 and had a relatively uneventful few months to recover from their foray into their home state. Elsesser notes that on August 28 the division held a "Grand sword presentation" for their beloved Meade, who received a sword, sash, belt, and golden spurs. Meade, in thanking the division, said that no division in the Army of the Potomac was entitled to claim more credit for its "uniform gallant conduct and for the amount of hard fighting" as did the Pennsylvania Reserves. He singled out the service of the privates in particular.

During the recuperative period after Gettysburg, Elsesser also found it noteworthy to mention the execution of five soldiers of the 118th Pennsylvania Infantry Regiment

---

40. Fisher's brigade suffered only three percent casualties at Gettysburg compared to twenty-six percent in Vincent's brigade and thirteen percent in Weed's brigade. Bradley M. Gottfried, "Fisher's Brigade at Gettysburg: The Big Round Top Controversy," *Gettysburg Magazine* 19 (1998), 84.

on August 29. These men were deserters who had collected bounty money for enlisting. One corporal in Company C of the 9th Pennsylvania Reserves wrote home that executions were the only way to stop desertions.[41] The unit history for the 2nd Reserves noted that after the "culprits" graves were filled up, "the troops marched back to their camps with their bands playing merry tunes."[42]

The remainder of 1863 was otherwise relatively uneventful for the 9th Pennsylvania Reserves.

Alfred Waugh sketch of the execution of five deserters. Both Union and Confederate armies required soldiers to stand in formation to witness executions as a means of deterrence. (New York Public Library/ *Campfire and Battlefield*)

Elsesser wrote only that he was on picket during A. P. Hill's ill-advised attack at Bristoe Station on September 14, 1863, although other Pennsylvania Reserve regiments did see combat during the engagement. Elsesser made multiple references to marching at the end of October, likely as part of Meade's aborted Mine Run Campaign. Although newspapers later maintained that Elsesser had been wounded in combat at Mine Run, he simply described the injury as a "slight tap on the leg" as he lay in line as a skirmisher on November 27, 1863.

The 9th Pennsylvania Reserves spent a relatively peaceful winter. Their winter camp was near a rail line that gave them a reliable means of receiving the Civil War equivalent of "care packages" from home. However, life in winter camp was not without its risks. Union troops in Virginia lived under the almost-constant threat posed by marauding guerillas who often preyed on pickets, patrols, or men who simply wandered too far from friendly lines. Elsesser referred to numerous incidents where Union troops, particularly

---

41. Ent, *The Pennsylvania Reserves in the Civil War*, 229. Bates lists nine men as deserters in Elsesser's Company B. Bates, *History of Pennsylvania Volunteers*, I: 796-97.
42. Ent, *The Pennsylvania Reserves in the Civil War*, 229.

the "Bucktails" of the 13th Pennsylvania Reserves, were poisoned, hanged, or had their throats cut by guerillas.[43]

As the war rolled into 1864, a debate arose over when the Pennsylvania Reserves' three-year expiration of service would occur. Not surprisingly, many of the troops maintained that the end of their enlistment fell on the third anniversary of when they were mustered into state service; however, a number of senior officers and officials at the War Department maintained that the three-year obligation did not commence until the Pennsylvania Reserves were mustered into Federal service. The "Federal" alternative would have pushed the 9th Pennsylvania Reserve's expiration of obligated service from early May to late July, 1864. However, the earlier date, which Meade had supported, eventually won the day, at least for Elsesser's regiment. The 9th Pennsylvania Reserves were the first of the Pennsylvania Reserves regiments to muster out.

Thus, on May 4, 1864, as the rest of the Army of the Potomac was preparing to cross the Rapidan to commence its spring campaign at the Wilderness under its new general-in-chief, Ulysses S. Grant, the 9th Pennsylvania Reserves were wending their way home. They rode by rail from Brandy Station, Virginia, to Pittsburgh, via Alexandria, Washington, and Baltimore. Elsesser wrote in his Company B diary that he mustered out on May 12, 1864 – the same date that George Washington Hall was captured at Spotsylvania.

During the war, the 9th Pennsylvania Reserves suffered a total of 187 casualties, although that figure did not include any who may have been captured. Six officers and 131 enlisted men were killed or mortally wounded, and one officer and forty-nine enlisted men died from disease.[44] Out of the ninety-seven men on Bates's roll of Company B, only twenty-eight were mustered out on May 12, 1864: three officers, seven non-commissioned officers, and eighteen privates. Ten others who had enlisted later in the war, including six who had reenlisted on Christmas Day, 1863, transferred to the 190th Pennsylvania Volunteers on May 3, 1864. The remainder had been either killed or mortally wounded in combat; discharged for medical reasons ("on Surgeon's Certificate"); met accidental death; transferred to the Veteran's Reserve Corps; deserted; or in Andrew Sende's case, discharged through a writ of habeas corpus.[45] In stark contrast to the over thirty men who died from disease in Hall's Company G, no member of Elsesser's Company B is identified as having died from disease.

---

43. The "Bucktails" of the 13th Pennsylvania Reserve Regiment were so named because they wore deer tails in their caps.
44. Frederick H. Dyer, *A Compendium of the War of the Rebellion* (Dyer Publishing Co., 1908), 1581.
45. Bates, *History of Pennsylvania Volunteers*, I: 796-97.

In 1890, a granite monument to the 9th Pennsylvania Reserves was dedicated at Gettysburg National Military Park. It depicts a soldier, cap in one hand, the other hand wrapped around the barrel of his musket, standing with his head bowed over a comrade's grave. The reverse of the monument reads as follows:

The Regiment arrived on the field July 2nd about 5 p.m. with 377 officers and men and soon after moved to this position and held it until the close of the battle with a loss of five wounded.

Recruited in the counties of Alleghany, Beaver and Crawford.

Mustered in State Service April & May 1861.
Mustered in U.S. Service July 28th 1861.
Mustered out May 12th 1864.

Total enrollment 1090

Killed and died of wounds 6 officers 108 men.
Died of disease & etc. 1 officer and 53 men.
Wounded 18 officers and 294 men
Captured or missing 2 officers 98 men
Total loss 572.

Mechanicsville
Gaines' Mill
Charles City Cross Roads
Malvern Hill
Gainesville
Groveton
2d Bull Run
South Mountain
Antietam
Fredericksburg
Gettysburg
Bristoe Station
Mine Run

Monument at Gettysburg National Military Park to the 9th Pennsylvania Reserves. The monument is located at the foot of Little Round Top near the intersection of Warren and Sykes Avenues. (Lithograph by Julius Bien)

Daily Pocket *Remembrancer* for 1862
J. L. Elsesser Co. B, 9th Regt. PR.C.

Wednesday, January 1, 1862

Take up my Quarters, with Sergeants [Charles] Ulrick Shendel [E. Von Schendel] & [Florian] Epple. Inspection of arms and Knapsacks. On guard at Camp. Relieved off guard, and attend to the wood Squad. Today our Captain treats the whole Company to a Sour Crout dinner. Cold.

Thursday, January 2, 1862

Receive Letter from home. Colonel Jackson presented with a fine Sword, Sash, and Belt, as a token of Esteem, by the Officers of his Regiment, upon which affair the entire Regt. is drawn up in an appropriate manner, the Address on behalf of the Regt. is made by Rev Pyatt, Chaplain. Cold and fair.

Friday, January 3, 1862

Nothing of importance. Cold.

Saturday, January 4, 1862

Co. B on picket, return with two prisoners. Cold.

Sunday, January 5, 1862

[no entry]

Monday, January 6, 1862

Snow falls during the night. We hear of the Report of Genl. Thomas Treachery. All Furloughs refused. Snow.

Tuesday, January 7, 1862

Today our Pay rolls are made out and signed, today I draw a blouse from Company, for the one given to the Dr. at the fight of Drainville, so that he could ease the pain of one of the Enemies, who was mortally wounded. Cold.

Wednesday, January 8, 1862

Nothing of importance. Cold.

Thursday, January 9, 1862

Boing [Richard Boeing] & Wallbruch [Henry Walbruch] go home on Furlough. Rec'd letter from home. Rec'd letter from Jno McKee.[46] Rain.

Friday, January 10, 1862

On Fatigue duty, and make distribution of wood to the Regiment. Make out my report and hand it over – All right.

Saturday, January 11, 1862

Nothing new. We lay in our tents as contented as Birds being warm inside, and cold outside.

Sunday, January 12, 1862

Today we get our Flag back, a great turn out. Senator Grow of Pa. make the Speech and A. G. Curtin, Esq. Governor of Pa. replies.[47] We have Brigade Drill and review. Cold & wet.

Monday, January 13, 1862

Sent Letter to McQuaide.[48] Cold.

Tuesday, January 14, 1862

A. Smith of Co. A died this morning of his wounds.[49] His Body will be sent home. Snow.

Wednesday, January 15, 1862

The Body of A. Smith sent home. An escort accompanies the remains to Washington. Cold.

Thursday, January 16, 1862

Get my Boots soled & heeled ($1.00). On Fatigue duty at Camp. Sent a Letter to John Louder. Fine.

Friday, January 17, 1862

On guard duty. Today the Dr. vaccinates the whole Regt.

---

46. John McKee, a baker in Etna, served in Company C, 9th Pennsylvania Reserves.
47. Galusha A. Grow was Speaker of the U.S. House of Representatives, not a Senator.
48. This is likely a reference to Dr. Andrew McQuaide, a physician, of Etna.
49. Private Alex. Smith died of wounds incurred in the engagement at Dranesville on December 20, 1861.

To Night at 10 oCl P.M. a great firing is heard. It is our fleet, testing the Batteries of the Enemy along the Potomac. The firing is kept up till morning. Fine.

Saturday, January 18, 1862

Our Division gets orders to march. Rec'd Letter from home – rain.

Sunday, January 19, 1862

No church today. Rain.

Monday, January 20, 1862

C. [Charles] Becker goes home on Furlough.[50] Our Camp is very muddy – got shaved by P.[Philip] Pastro. Rain.

Tuesday, January 21, 1862

Get Bread. Firing of heavy Cannon in a distance. Go after wood – snow.

Wednesday, January 22, 1862

Bread – Sent Letter home. Cold.

Thursday, January 23, 1862

Nothing new.

Friday, January 24, 1862

Paymaster came here today. Pays out $26.00.[51] On wood duty. Cold.

Saturday, January 25, 1862

Visited 8th Regt. Met Jas. Lumpkin, Jos. Wegman & others. Took Dinner with Tompkins, saw McCormick of Sharpsburgh today. Frobugh and Hunter of Etna call & see us at our camp. Cold & wet.

Sunday, January 26, 1862

Co. A on Picket. Sent $10 home. Rain.

---

50. Charles Becker was a sergeant in January 1862 but later promoted to Second Lieutenant and First Lieutenant.
51. The amount of $26.00 appears to have been Elsesser's basic pay. His diary entries reference multiple other payments in this amount. In contrast, Hall's pay as a Confederate private was $11 per month prior to the summer of 1864, when it was bumped to $18, although by that point Hall was at Fort Delaware.

Monday, January 27, 1862

Rec'd Letter from Major Hamm.[52] Sent Letter to Jno. E. Louder. Rain.

Tuesday, January 28, 1862

Nothing new.

Wednesday, January 29, 1862

Sent $10 home. On Fatigue duty. Get Likeness taken ($1.00). Got Box to [send] it ($1.00). Sent Likeness home.

Thursday, January 30, 1862

Bought 1 lb Butter, also a Frank Leslie.[53] Sent it home. Rain & muddy.

Friday, January 31, 1862

Sent Letter to Revd Dethlefs.[54] Rain.

Saturday, February 1, 1862

Fixed my coat, and put Pockets in. Snow.

Sunday, February 2, 1862

Sent Letter to G. Mertz. Rain.

Monday, February 3, 1862

Rec'd Letter from home.

Rec'd Letter from Gschwend.[55]

Rec'd Papers from Gschwend. Snow.

Tuesday, February 4, 1862

Haul wood for Tent. Rain.

Wednesday, February 5, 1862

Sent letter to Jno. Cammer. Fine.

Thursday, February 6, 1862

On Fatigue duty. Rain.

---

52. Then-Major John Hamm served in Company I, 74th Pennsylvania Infantry.
53. This is likely a reference to *Frank Leslie's Illustrated Newspaper*.
54. Rev. Dethlefs was the pastor of Elsesser's church, the German United Evangelical Lutheran Church of Centerville, more commonly known as the First Congregational Church of Etna. https://www.findagrave.com/memorial/117416071/matthias-frederick-dethlefs
55. Charles Gschwend was a toll collector in Etna.

Friday, February 7, 1862

On Guard duty. Sent Letter home, together with three valentines. Rain.

Saturday, February 8, 1862

Sent Valentine to Boerzler. Rain.

Sunday, February 9, 1862

Boecht goes home on Furlough.[56] Fine.

Monday, February 10, 1862

Went after wood. Capt. returned from home. Fine.

Tuesday, February 11, 1862

Went after wood. Snow.

Wednesday, February 12, 1862

Co. B goes on picket. Have a good time. Snow.

Thursday, February 13, 1862

Releived off Picket. Fine.

Friday, February 14, 1862

Rec'd Letter from Louder. Wrote Letter to Gschwend. Rain.

Saturday, February 15, 1862

Sent Letter to Gschwend. Regt Drill. Dress Parade. Boecht comes back. Snow.

Sunday, February 16, 1862

No Meeting. Snow.

Monday, February 17, 1862

Good news from Fort Donelson.[57] Rain.

---

56. This is likely a reference to then-Sergeant Lewis Brecht.
57. Elsesser's good news regarding the capture of Fort Donelson was anything but a happy turn of events for brothers John D. Warden and William R. Warden of Company A, 41st Tennessee Infantry, both of whom were taken prisoners at Fort Donelson and sent to Camp Morton, IN. John Warden was my great-great-grandfather on my mother's side; he was exchanged after approximately seven months and returned to service near Vicksburg in the fall of 1862. William Warden died shortly after arriving at Camp Morton and is buried at Crown Hill Cemetery in Indianapolis.

Tuesday, February 18, 1862

Sent Letter home with one to Louisa. Got Tea and some Tobacco from home pr hands of John Jiebert, who was home on Furlough.[58] Get a cap from Company. Rain.

Wednesday, February 19, 1862

Writing in my Diary. Rain.

Thursday, February 20, 1862

Wrote Letter for the Capt. Bur[k]hart of Co "K" died today, he was from Butler.[59] Took dinner with Howenstein.[60]

Friday, February 21, 1862

Went after wood. [John Longbein] Langbein went home on furlough. Lubald went home on Furlough. Fine.

Saturday, February 22, 1862

Washingtons Birthday. Sent Letter home. The Regt turned out in full. Had the Farewell Address read by our Chaplain.[61] Rec'd a large Box from Otto Hartung as a present for the Company.[62] Fair.

Sunday, February 23, 1862

Attended meeting. Joseph Wegman visited our Camp, he took supper with us. John Jiebert gave me a call. Spent social Evening with Lieut [Henry] Fuhren. Sent val. to Boertzler[63]. Rain & muddy.

Monday, February 24, 1862

Great storm. The wind sweeps many tents off from our [camp] and the 12th Regt.

---

58. This is likely a reference to John D. Hieber, Elsesser's brother-in-law, who at the time was a sergeant in the 139th Pennsylvania Infantry.
59. Private Baxter Burkhart of Company K died at Camp Pierpont, Virginia, on February 19, 1862.
60. Howenstein began the war as a private in Co. G, 9th Pennsylvania Reserves but transferred to the 6th US Cavalry in October 1862.
61. This is likely a reference to George Washington's Farewell Address of 1796.
62. This is likely a reference to Charles Otto Hartung, an Allegheny County druggist.
63. This is likely a reference to John H. Boertzler, who lived on the same street in Etna as did Elsesser. Boertzler, regarded as one of the oldest residents of Etna, was employed by Elsesser's father-in-law, Daniel Hieber, as a wagonmaker and, like Elsesser, was active in civil office. Obituary, John H. Boertzler, *Pittsburgh Post-Gazette,* June 15, 1913, www. newspapers.com.

Tuesday, February 25, 1862

Rec. Marching Orders to pack and be ready at 9 oCl A.M. tomorrow. Dress parade. I draw new Pants. Fine.

Wednesday, February 26, 1862

Brigade Drill. Lew Ghreiner goes home on furlough.[64] Orders to march with 3 days rations. We pack and Box every thing. I box Hat, uniform &c and send them home by Adams Express. Rain.

Thursday, February 27, 1862

Wrote Letter to Howenstein. Sent papers home. Rec'd Letter from Jno Cammer. Sent Letter home. Fair.

Friday, February 28, 1862

Wood duty. Inspection of arms by Genl Ord. Cold.

Saturday, March 1, 1862

March as far as Chain Bridge in full uniform. Rec'd Letter from home. Fair.

Sunday, March 2, 1862

On Guard duty. Rec'd Letter from McQuaide. Sent Letter home.

Monday, March 3, 1862

Wrote Power of Attorney for William Nicholson. Snow.

Tuesday, March 4, 1862

Bayonet Drill. Fair.

Wednesday, March 5, 1862

Went on Picket duty. Fine.

Thursday, March 6, 1862

Bayonet Drill. Cold.

Friday, March 7, 1862

Rec. Letter from home. Box safe at home. Cold.

Saturday, March 8, 1862

Sent Letter home. Cold.

---

64. This is likely a reference to Private Lewis Schreiner of Company B.

Sunday, March 9, 1862

Inspection, Dress parade. Sent letter to Gschwend. Evening Service.

Monday, March 10, 1862

Ready for marching. Fair.

Tuesday, March 11, 1862

Several Regts pass our Camp. Centerville evacuated, Manassas also. Fair.

Wednesday, March 12, 1862

Saw Wm Rawie, H. Ochmler, and List of Etna. We found 3 [Mississippi] Vol dead on our picket line. One man got killed by a shell which he found and throw it on the ground, thereby exploding. Fair.

March, Thursday 13, 1862

Took dinner with Howenstein. Had chicken. Sent letter home. Rec'd Letter from Wm Howenstein. Thos Reed of Co. G died at the hospital in Camp. He was from Connelsville. Regt Drill. Fair.

Friday, March 14, 1862

Regt Drill. Fair.

Saturday, March 15, 1862

Order to march, pack up and leave Camp at 4 oCl P.M. Arrive at Falls Church at 3 oCl A. M. March towards Alexandria. Encamp 3 miles beyond the City, openly encamped at Camp Misery. Rain.

Sunday, March 16, 1862

Still encamping at what we call Camp Misery. Still raining like fury and nothing to cover ourselves with. Rain.

Monday, March 17, 1862

Rec'd Letter from home. Rec'd Letter from Gschwend. Strole around the near Neighborhood, and find the country very fine, with few exceptions. Still raining. Rain.

Tuesday, March 18, 1862

Rec'd Letter from home. Rain.

Wednesday, March 19, 1862

Sent letter home. Rain.

Thursday, March 20, 1862

Met Bernhard Shell. He is in the 35th Regt in Schimelpfeing. Also met Schachleiber. Rain.

Friday, March 21, 1862

Stay all night at the 35th. Have good warm quarters, and are treated to a good breakfast. Rain.

Saturday, March 22, 1862

Stay all night at 35th Regt. Have good supper and a good Break-fast. Rain.

Sunday, March 23, 1862

Wesley Hannah pays us a visit. Rain.

Monday, March 24, 1862

Sent Letter home. Rain.

Tuesday, March 25, 1862

Grand Review at Munson Hill by Genl. McDowell . There are 70000 under arms. We have our Reveiw at the Seminary where Genl. McClellan has his Headquarters. Fine.

Wednesday, March 26, 1862

Sent Letter home. Have general washing day. Fine.

Thursday, March 27, 1862

My 34th Birthday. Washing day, sent Letter home.

Friday, March 28, 1862

Regt Drill. Get our Company Due Bills settled. Rain.

Saturday, March 29, 1862

Rec'd from Capt. Sothen the Sum of 33-25/100 for due Bills leaving still a balance of about 45.00 due us by the Company Dept. Rain.

Sunday, March 30, 1862

Get one of the Sibly Tents from a deserted Camp, move

into it and live high. Have a stove and fixins. We live high on acct of getting plenty of eatables from the various deserted Camps. Our men also get Coats, Pants, Shoes &c.

Monday, March 31, 1862

Company drill. Visited Alexandria, bought knife and steel for the Company. Visit the Marshall House, the slave pen, the wharf, the Post Office and different Hospitals, also the Government shops.[65] Found the City strongly guarded by our Troops. Rain.

Tuesday, April 1, 1862

No News. Fair.

Wednesday, April 2, 1862

No News. Washing day. Fair.

Thursday, April 3, 1862

Rec'd Letter from home. Today I give Capt. Sothen the money of due bills for him to hold in trust for the company. We buy a Mess Chest out of the money, a kitchen knife and a steel, also get the Box made by [John] Bandi, pay him $2.00. Rain.

Friday, April 4, 1862

Inspection & drill. Fair.

Saturday, April 5, 1862

Inspection & drill. Fair.

Sunday, April 6, 1862

Send Letter home. Send a Letter to Gschwend. Got a Letter from Nich. Klein of Sharpsburgh, he is in the Hospital at Alexandria. Fair.

Monday, April 7, 1862

Washing day. Make out the Company clothing account, and also a Requisition for shoes, &c. Snow.

---

65. In May 1861, Colonel Ephraim Ellsworth, commander of the 11th New York Volunteer Infantry Regiment, was shot dead by the proprietor of the Marshall House as Ellsworth was attempting to remove a Confederate flag from the roof.

Tuesday, April 8, 1862

Fix Knapsacks and arrange every thing for marching. Snow.

Wednesday, April 9, 1862

Rec. news of the Battle at Corinth. A Salute of 100 guns are fired at Washington. Snow.

Thursday, April 10, 1862

No News.

Friday, April 11, 1862

Leave Camp at 6 oCl A.M. March to Fairfax C. H. Rest a few minutes, then march on, make 16 miles and encamp open. This proves a hard march, being warm, and the roads mud up to the Ancles [ankles], poor water along the road & scarce --

Saturday, April 12, 1862

Start at 6 oCl A. M. Arrive at Centreville at 2 oCl P.M.View the various fortifications. Arrive at Manassas at 5 oCl P.M.Encamp open for the night. Take a fine view of Centreville and its fortifications, also the fortifications around Manassas. Fair.

Sunday, April 13, 1862

Rec'd Letter from home. Fix up our camp. Have a prayer meeting. This is a pretty fair spot, and near the Junction, where we can view the Forts at [Manassas] Junction, also the Battle Field of Bull Run. Fair.

Monday, April 14, 1862

Leave Camp at 8 oCl A. M. and occupy Camp Pickens (Rebel Camp). This camp is built of logs, and it is the best camp for accomodations we ever had, since we left Camp Wright. We find a Shell concealed in one of the Chimney places. Paymaster calls and pays off, $26.00. This place is rather swampy and unhealthy. Fair.

Tuesday, April 15, 1862

Buy a loaf of Rye Bread for 20 cts. Spend the day in walking around and seeing the Batteries at Manassas &c.

Find all the Buildings in ruins, the rail road partly torn up and one Loco-motive blown up. Fair.

Wednesday, April 16, 1862

We picket all around, and send out Scouts in every direction. Three Bucktails poisened and one found with the Throat cut, the tail off the Cap in his mouth. Fair.

Thursday, April 17, 1862

Regtl Drill, Co[mpany] Drill. In the Evening, all those who were not at regular drill are compelled to drill one hour with their Knapsacks on, as a punishment. Fine & warm.

Friday, April 18, 1862

March from Camp at 6 oCl A.M. with two days rations. Leave Manassas and march toward Warrenton. Arrive at Manassas Gap at 12 oCl M. Wrote Letter, and enclosed $10 but can not send it home. Make a distance of 15 miles and encamp open (Camp Caslet).[66] This Camp lies along the Manassas R. Road, and about 6 miles from Warranton Station, is a hard looking place, and a rebel Cavalry (Hampdons Legion) once encamped here. Their Chimneys are still standing together with the Stable. A Union Farmer gives us plenty of Straw.

Saturday, April 19, 1862

Co. B goes on Picket. Sent Letter & $10 home. Rains all day again and making it unpleasant to be on picket duty. Rain.

Sunday. April 20, 1862

No News. No Meeting.[67] Rain.

Monday, April 21, 1862

Clean our Guns. Another Bucktail found with his throat cut. Rain.

---

66. This is likely a reference to Catlett's Station.
67. Given that this was Easter Sunday, the absence of a prayer meeting seems unusual.

Tuesday, April 22, 1862

Co B on scouting duty. I make out Requisition for Clothing. I have a severe touch of the Rheumatism. Rain.

Wednesday, April 23, 1862

We expect to march. Cook 3 days rations. Fair.

Thursday, April 24, 1862

Co[mpany] inspection. Make out the Muster Roll of Comp. B. Some Contrabands are brought in.[68] Buy medicine for the Rheumatism 25 cts pr Bottle. Fair.

Friday, April 25, 1862

No Mail since the 19th, Bull Run Bridge having been washed away. Our men in bad humour about the mail.

Saturday, April 26, 1862

Co[mpany] B on picket. We scout the woods, bring 12 prisoners in to Genl Ords Headquarters. Take dinner at a Farmers house. He tells us of the bad treatment from the hands of Bl[ ]kers men and the Garibaldi Regt in particular.[69] Our Company highly complimented by Major Snodgrass for their civilities while on picket. We are releived by Co[mpany] A. The first Brigade marches off to day. Fair.

Sunday, April 27, 1862

No meeting. Inspection of Arms & Regt at 10 oCl AM. No mail yet, take medicine, get hair cut & shaved. Dress Parade by the whole Brigade. Fair.

Monday, April 28, 1862

Second Brigade marches off, I buy some blk. Tea. We expect to march every moment. Fair.

---

68. "Contraband" was the term used to describe enslaved persons who escaped to Union lines during the war.
69. This is likely a reference to the 38th New York regiment, nicknamed the Garibaldi Guard, in Brig. Gen. Louis Blenker's Brigade.

Tuesday, April 29, 1862

Get Beef Tongue for rations. Rec'd Letter from home, with $5 enclosed. Finish the Muster Rolls for Co[mpany] B. Rain.

Wednesday, April 30, 1862

Mustering & Inspection on Camp ground by Col. Jackson, Co[mpany] B Color Guard. Issue clothing for Co[mpany] and give out some Shoes, Caps, Pants & Blouses

Thursday, May 1, 1862

Issue Clothing, Shoes and Socks for the Company Take Supper with Andrew Sende, as it is this day one year since Company B went into Camp Wilkins at the City of Pittsburgh.[70] Receive marching orders with 3 days rations. The Regimental Pioneers are sent ahead of the Regt to repair the roads and Bridges. Towards evening a heavy Shower springs up. It rains all night very hard. We pack every thing ready for the morning. Cloudy and rain.

Friday, May 2, 1862

We leave Camp at 6 oClock AM. Companies B and G are the Advance Guards. The roads are in a very bad condition, owing to the late rains. The Bridges are mostly flowed away, and in some instances, we are obliged to throw away the part of the Contents of the Wagons, in order to get along. The 9th Regt in the advance Guard followed by the 10th and 6th Regts. We march to a distance of 13 miles, toward the Town of Fredericksburgh, and lay over for the night. Co[mpany] B and G go on Picket duty immediately. Weather fine and warm.

---

70. Andrew Sende was likely the youngest soldier in Company B. He had enlisted at the age of 19 with Company B on May 1, 1861, and served honorably until he was discharged on July 24, 1863, pursuant to a writ of *habeas corpus* issued by the U.S. District Court for the Western District of Pennsylvania because he was well under the minimum age to enlist (21). Chris Naylor, "'You have the body': Habeas Corpus Case Records of the U.S. Circuit Court for the District of Columbia, 1820-1863," National Archives *Prologue*, Fall 2005, vol. 37, no. 3, accessed August 4, 2020, https://www.archives.gov/publications/prologue/2005/fall/habeas-corpus.html

Saturday, May 3, 1862

We march again at 5 oCl AM. The 6th Regt. in the advance and the 10th in the rear. The roads are somewhat better, but still soft and muddy. We have the Battery (Eastons) along with us.[71] We to day pass over some of the finest Country in this Section of the Country. The People seem to be very hospitable and generous, but as usual some are secessh – We march 13 miles towards Fredericksburgh and stop for the day, arriving at the camping ground at about 3-1/2 oCl P.M. Our rations having been thrown off the wagon we have nothing to eat up. Warm.

Sunday, May 4, 1862

March again at 5 oCl A.M. toward Fredericksburg. Pass by Wal-worth at 8-1/2 oCl. and arrive the Picket lines at 9-1/2 where we meet the portion of the 8th Regt. We get into Falmouth at 10 oClock A. M. The roads are still getting drier. The 9th regt in advance. The Blacks are astonished at hearing music, the people seem delighted. We unfurled the Regt Flag and cheer upon cheer is made as we pass through the Town. After we march 2 miles farther we encamp, having marched 14 miles. We are in sight of Fred[e]r[ic]ksburg. Sent letter home. Rain and changeable.

Monday, May 5, 1862

We draw Rations today for the Company. Our Artillery and some Infantry & Cavalry cross the River at Fredericksburgh, to hoist the Flag, and test the feelings of the inhabitants. They have a small Skirmish in crossing, but they accomplish their object. I make a list for another Shoe issue, and at the same time make out a Requisition. Attend to the Clothing accounts. This Evening we draw 2

---

71. Captain Hezekia Easton commanded Battery A of the 1st Pennsylvania Light Artillery. He was killed at Gaines's Mill the following month.

days rations ahead, to have ready for march. Fine and fair. Rain at night.

Tuesday, May 6, 1862

I buy a peice of Mutton for 25 cts. Make a good Soup, and attend to the Shoe Business. Draw 15 pr Shoes, buy a [f]rying pan for 62 cts. Sergt Becker arrives here from home. The Regt. on dress parade. Good news from Yorktown, the Enemy evacuated that place today. One of our Cavalry Pickets was fired at by one of the Enemy but missed. He returned the compliment by killing the offender. Fair and warm.

Wednesday, May 7, 1862

I draw my portion of Government Paper, Envelopes & Sealing Wax. Companies are ordered to drill twice a day, and dress Parade in each Evening. Buy a Dress Coat for 25 Cts. As the weather is fine I wash my clothing. The 6th Regt. detailed on Guard duty on Rail Road. I finish the quarterly account for Clothing in Books. Our O. S. [orderly sergeant] goes over into Fredericksburgh, and purchases some smoking Tobacco, and other things. It rains through the night. Fine.

Thursday, May 8, 1862

The Whip o Will is busy through the night and Keeping up his noise. The Wood dig is commencing his opporation on the Bhoys- We move our Camp to about one and half mile off. We now have a fine Camp ground, and Board Houses. I make my Quarters with Capt. Sothern, and find every thing right. The water here is plenty and good. Fine and warm.

Friday, May 9, 1862

Today the 9th Regt. discover a Tobacco Warehouse, and leave been had from Genl. Ord, each Soldier carries away as much Tobacco as he desires. I rec'd a Letter from home with a likeness of my Mary, enclosed. We get a full supply of Beef to day, about 150 Head of Cattle are brought into our

Camp. Our bhoys enjoy them-selves highly here. We still get some Good news. The 13th Regt comes into Camp. They lost five men, being captured by the Va. Gurillas, one having, after being shot, made his Escape. Warm.

Saturday, May 10, 1862

This morning we fix up our Tent with Cedars. The P. O. Dept. is transfured to our quarters. I am the receiver of all Company Letters. Today I accept the Quartermaster Dept. for the Co. as the Company has been asking the Captain to induce me to take charge of it. Two of the 13th New York Vol. found the[ir] Throat cut near Fallmouth. One was hanging in a Tree by the Heels. Weather fine ---

Sunday, May 11, 1862

Today we raise a Flag, on the Regtl. Flagstaff. The Regt. turn out and Prayer i[s] offered by the Regt. Chaplain, singing and music. <u>Send Letter home</u>. Draw Sugar, Candles, Beans, Coffee & Crack for the Company. We receive Orders to draw and cook two days rations to be ready for moments march, as the Pickets opposite were driven in. Take Supper with And. Sende. Our Col. is commanded to join the Regt. again, and releaved off duty at building Bridge. Six Prisoners brought in, one a first Lieut of the C. S. Artillery. The 88th Regt. comes into Camp. Our pickets across the river are driven in. Good news from Norfolk & the Merrimac.[72] Fair and cool.

Monday, May 12, 1862

Draw Shoes from Commissary (13) pair. Send Letter to C. Gschwend. Write to Maj. Wade for Capt. Sothen. To day some fifteen Pris. brought in, also some of our Cavalry were brought in, being found outside of the Picket

---

72. This was likely a reference to the destruction that week of the Confederate ironclad CSS *Virginia*, constructed on the hull of the former USS *Merrimac*.

line. This Evening Capt and I have a social Tea together. I send C. Gschwend a piece of Col. Taylors Saddle Cloth. Contrabands are today pouring into our Camps, having escaped the Enemies picket lines. No signs of the approach of the Rebels yet, Alls well! We throw Shell over the town of Fredericksburg to show them what we could do, if we wished. Fine and warm.

Tuesday, May 13, 1862

Our Company does not go on Picket, it being detailed by Genl Ord for other purposes. Today we have Regimental drill twice. Draw fresh Beef from Commissary. <u>Send Letter</u> & a piece of Saddle Cloth to my wife. Sent for some striping stuff. Clean up all my Accoutrements, and go to Genl Ord. Am friendly entertained by him and his O.S. I stay there for several hours and report myself at quarters again. The Weather being hot the Capt and I take a social Nap together. 13 prisoners brought in, among them 5 Females, the[y] were brought in by our Pickets. Warm.

Wednesday, May 14, 1862

This morning is rather cloudy and indicates rain. Co[mpany] B goes out on Picket, they were specially instructed to keep on sharp look-out. I am ordered to remain in Camp and attend to the O.S. duty and Provision Return. I draw fresh Beef and Salt from Commissary. Our Cavalry bring in some Contrabands which they picked up on the line, they hail from Manassas. Steady rain from 6 oCl AM.

Thursday, May 15, 1862

Make out Requisition for Beef and everything necessary. It rains all day. I take a scatch [sketch] of our Mess for the purpose of sending it home. The Company has Drill. As they come home they bring home Contrabands, also some flying Squirrels and grey Squirells. Our O.S. is taken sick, while on picket. Rain steady.

Friday, May 16, 1862

This morning I attend to the Books of the Company, make out a Requisition for Shoes, Shirts, Blouses, drawers, Socks & Pants and attend to recordin[g] Orders and other Doc. from Regimental and Brigade Head Quarters. Buy a Newspaper. Hang out our clothes to dry from the wet from yesterday. Take supper with Sende, have fresh Fish, which were caught in the Creek in the Picket line. Two prisoners brought in by our pickets. Stay up till 11-1/2 P.M. writing. Fine and Fair.

Saturday, May 17, 1862

Draw Salt Beef, and other things. Have Company drill in the morning. Regimental Drill in the afternoon. This Evening Genl Ord informed his Command that he had been ordered away, and Genl Seymour takes his place. The different Regiments turn out to meet him and bid him farewell. He takes farewell of the 9th Regt, and our men feel greatly dejected at his departure. Today still busy in making out Book Accts. Make Hash for Supper. Fair & warm.

Sunday, May 18, 1862

The Weather is fine this morning, the Birds sing loud and long. I close my Acct. Books. Have Hash for Breakfast. Draw Salt Pork from Commissary. Today a Flag of Truce is sent to our lines by the Enemy. We have a good Sermon at the dress Parade of the 6th Regt. Today each Soldier is ordered to have on hand two pair of shoes, and at least two pair of Socks. Cloudy and rain-like.

Monday, May 19, 1862

Today we had Regimental drill. The Capt. went to Falmouth, and Fredericksburgh. We put up a gymnastic pole. John Seibert comes over to see us.[73] Two of the 14th New York are shot by some un-known person from the opposite side of the river. They died on the spot. At the time they were guarding some Flour at the river. We expect to march soon. Strict orders are given to have light out at Tap, and Card playing is strictly forbidden. Fair and warm.

Tuesday, May 20, 1862

Today we started out for Review. We had a fine one, about three miles from Camp. Our new Brig. Genl. Seymour and Genl McCall were pleased with us. Genl McCall openly plauded Co. B. as one of the best Companies in the field and spoke highly of them to Brig. Genl Seymour. Phillip Pastre returns from the Hospital, having been there only two days. And. H is removed to Genl. Hospital.[74] Today I draw Pants for some of our men. Very warm.

Wednesday, May 21, 1862

Wrote Letter to John E. Louder. We have Brigade drill and Review. We draw Pants. I make out a Requisition for four days rations. Have Company drill & Dress Parade. Buy a Limburger Cheese and lend Sende $1.00. Hear of the death of Fred Rall & Capt. Brunn who fell at Williamsburgh.[75] We give a Fatigue Squad for building the Rail Road Bridge.

Thursday, May 22, 1862

Have Company drill this morning, and a grand Review in the after-noon, in which the 12th Regt takes part. George Eiffler and Brinkman comes over from Fredericksburgh on a visit. News from McClellans Corps, they being only 10 miles off Richmond. Morning fine -- Afternoon Rain --

---

73. This likely a reference to John D. Hieber, Elsesser's brother-in-law.
74. This is likely a reference to Andrew Hoell of Company B.
75. Private Fred G. Rawl and Captain Jacob Brunn, both of the 70th New York Infantry, had enlisted from Pittsburgh. Both were killed on May 5, 1862, in action at Williamsburg.

Friday, May 23, 1862

Today there is a grand Inspection of Wagons and Horses, Harness &c. Have a gran[d] Review, where the President, Genl Ord, McCall and McDowell were present. The review took place about 6 miles from Camp. Had a visit paid by Capt. Senk of Alleghaney, and Ruthmiller formerly of our Company and Burkhart also, they both belong to Shields Division and Artillery. Morning fair, after-noon rain.

Saturday, May 24, 1862

Today have Co[mpany] drill. I draw Shoes from the Commissary. Capt Sothen takes sick. Sende and I buy some nice Liver and we have a good meal. We get orders to keep ready for march. Expect good news from McClellan. Morning fair, afternoon rain.

Sunday, May 25, 1862

This morning we have Company inspection, Orderly Call - - Orders that we draw 4 days rations. I make out a Requisition for it, and draw them. There is an Explosion takes place in Fredericksburgh, Killing some people, caused by a Magazine. Orderly Call. 1 days cooked rations in Haversacks. We expect to leave as Shields Division has left already, & the 1st and 2nd Brigade has orders also. We hear that Bank's retreated to Winchester, but do not believe it. Rec'd two papers from Gschwend. <u>No letter yet from Home</u>. Fine weather.

Monday, May 26, 1862

Receive marching Orders, to march immediately. We pack up every thing and in the course of an hour we leave Camp (10 oCl AM). We march about 5-1/2 miles and rest there, until we get further orders. We directly make preparations for encamping for the night, a fine place, and still in sight of Fredericksburgh. I send my Great Coat home through Adams Express, pay 25 cts for shipment to Fredericksburgh. <u>Still no Letter</u>. Evening rain.

Tuesday, May 27, 1862

Cloudy and rain. Busy making a good Shelter for Capt and myself. We build a large one, to hold 5 persons, to wit, Capt, myself, [John] Bandi, [Henry] Peoples and Sende. I make out a List for Clothing. Last night I took severe Cramps in the legs which disables me today from walking about any. Regimental Drill & Dress Parade. News of Genl Banks retreat to the town of Winchester. Rains previous night.

Wednesday, May 28, 1862

Send Letter home and $1.00. Get news from Ord, beating the Enemy at Caslet, our men at Fredbg [Fredericksburg], working ordered to the Balt. & Ohio R. Road. We still fix up our quarters. Have Regtl Drill & Company Drill. One of Eastons Battery gets drowned at the river while bathing. Fine & warm.

Thursday, May 29, 1862

Today I walk out of Camp in Company with Peoples. We pass Genl McDowells Head-Qtrs and go down to the R. R. where we see the Contrabands working, unloading Corn & oats. Company & Regimental Drill. No Mail today. Washing day. We expect to march again. Fine & hot.

Friday, May 30, 1862

Company Drill – Fresh Beef today. The Weather is fine all fore-noon but in the afternoon it begins to rain very hard and continues on till Evening. Send Letter to C. Gschwend. It rained all night. Our Guard load their Guns, and are made stronger. Spend the Evening with Howenstein & Nicholson. Buy a loaf of Bread. Fine & warm.

Saturday, May 31, 1862

Still raining hard. Fresh Beef. Have Inspections by Col. Our Cavalry come home and bring in some prisoners. They have been over the river to a distance of 15 miles, and hit upon McClellan Scouts. Buy 3 loaves of Bread @ 5 cts pr loaf, buy 3 pkgs Tob[acco]. Rain.

Sunday, June 1, 1862

Have meeting this morning. The whole Regt is ordered to march in Companies to the place of worship. Make out a report of Clothing Ammunition, &c. In the Evening the Pay Master comes into Camp, expect to get money tomorrow. Through the night it rains, and lightnings, and the air is very warm & suffocating. We can hardly sleep. Fair & warm.

Monday, June 2, 1862

Paymaster pays off today. I send $20 home pr Adams Express. Our Cavalry comes in with some prisoners. Sende and I go to town and buy some Bread & Lemonade. Take a good walk around Falmouth. Fair & warm.

Tuesday, June 3, 1862

Have Co[mpany] Drill & Regimental Drill in the forenoon. I attend to making out the receipts for our men who are sending their money home. A great storm comes on just as we have Regtl Drill in the Afternoon, blowing away the roofs of most of our quarters, and one of Co[mpany] D is seriously hurt by a Tree falling on him. Our Capt nearly cuts his finger off with a Hatchet. I get a Letter from Chas. Gschwend, but <u>no news from home</u>. It rains hard, and we are washed out of home, our clothes & Blankets are [w]ringing wet. Good news from McClellan. Fair & warm.

Wednesday, June 4, 1862

It has rained all night, and is still pouring down. Geo. Adler leaves us to join the Artillery. I get my receipt from Adams Express. The Bridges across the river are mostly torn away by the freshet. The proposition is made to Brig. Genl Seymour to act as the Governor of Fredericksburgh and to have the 9th Regt to patrol the City. It rains all day. <u>No Mail.</u> Rain.

Thursday, June 5, 1862

We detail men for repairing the Bridges. It has rained

all night. H. Peoples detailed on Bridge duty. I make out Invoices for Guns &c – I make out Description List also. Adler returns from Artillery. It rains all day. Draw Shoes from Commissary. Get Letter from home. Dress parade. I send Letter to Mr. Howenstein. I put stripes on my Dress Coat. Rain.

Friday, June 6, 1862

Send Letter home -- $1.00 in money and the receipt of Express Co. Buy a Plug of navy Tobacco .50 cts. Make out Requisitions for 3 days – rations. Regimental Drill and dress parade. Gov. Curtin has ordered the names of the Battles to be placed on the Flags of the Pa. Regts. who participated in them. All papers to the Town of Fredericksburgh refused. Buy a pound of cheese 25 cts. Cloudy.

Saturday, June 7, 1862

Co[mpany] Drill. We expect to move the Camp. Jno. Werkman [Workman] receives his Sentence of Court Martial, which is 7 days guard, with Knap-sack and Blanket & Clothing. I go to Falmouth for purchasings. This Evening I get the Stripes from my Mary. Cloudy.

Sunday, June 8, 1862

Have meeting. Inspection of Arms. L. Boecht [Lewis Brecht] reduced to 2 Sergt.[76] We have marching Orders, expect to join McClellan at Richd. Meet Nich. Brannon, he is in the 4th Cavalry Regt. Put stripes on my Pants. Buy a box of [ ] and some Paper Wrappers & Envelopes. Fine.

Monday, June 9, 1862

Co[mpany] Drill, Regt Drill, and at dress parade we are informed to join McClellan, to be ready next morning at 7 oCl AM to get shipped. Great Joy in Camp at the

---

76. Lewis Brecht was promoted to second lieutenant in April 1863 and assumed command of Company F.

news. Bandi, Brietlach [John Christ. Breitlauch] & Fuchs [Frederick Fuchse] on the sick list. We pack up tonight yet. I send a Paper (Christian Banner) home. It rains through the night. Cloudy.

Tuesday, June 10, 1862

We leave Camp at 7 oClock AM. It rains all day. The roads are in very bad condition. We march 7 miles to the boats, and are wet through & through. We build a large Fire and dry ourselves as well as we can, lay out open for the night. The last of the 2nd Reg[iment] goes off on the Steamer Jno. Brooks. Rain.

Wednesday, June 11, 1862

This Morning I am greatly troubled with the Rheumatism, from being wet yesterday. We build huts to spend another fine day. The Weather looks as if it would be a fine warm day. Fine.

Thursday, June 12, 1862

The Artillery Wagons are shipped today together with some Cavalry Horses and Men. The Steamer Propellar Buena Vista and the Steamer Columbia take them south. Our Boys go to the river and fish, catch plenty Eels and Catfish. The 12th Regt goes off. Fine.

Friday, June 13, 1862

Write Letter home. Make out a Requisition for two days rations. Lay of the clothes today, take a walk with Lieut Fuhren along the river where we take a good wash. Today I buy 25 cts worth Lemons to take on the Boat with me, also ½ doz. Eggs, 15 cts. The 10th & 6th Regt leaves today. The Steamer Georgia and several Schooners arrive, and we hope to get away tomorrow. Dress Parade. Make out for rations for 2 days. Send the Letter off home. Fine & warm.

Friday, June 14, 1862

We get up at 3 oCl A. M. Get ready and go on board the

Steamship Georgia and leave at 6 oClock.[77] The Slaves & Owners along the opposite shore great us with cheers, the Band playing Star-Banner & Dixie. -- Saturday -- Pass the Blockade at 10 oCl AM. Have a fine view of Yorktown with its fortifications. Pass several rebel Batteries along the river. Have eat nothing since yesterday morning but a few Crackers & Water or Lemonade. Pass West Point, and along the whole Neighborhood pass the beautiful Steamer Commodore. We arrive at White House Landing at dark and encamp about a mile from it, throw out Camp guard. Fine & warm.

Saturday, June 15, 1862

This morning make out requisitions for three days rations, get Coffee for Breakfast. <u>Send Letter home</u>. Get orders to march, leave Camp at 11 oCl AM. March 4 miles along R. Road and encamp for the day. The march were hard and hot, the men nearly give out. Upon arriving Co. B & A go on picket. We picket on a place where two days before a party of Garillas attacked 25 of our Teams, and burnt the wagons and took 100 Mules. It rains all night, and we expect an attack any moment. This day is the first day that I felt sick. I suffer severe Headache and through the night take cramps severely. Hot & [ ]

Monday, June 16, 1862

This morning is cool and windy, the sun shines brightly. We go off Picket at 6 oCl AM go over to Camp, and start off again on a march. We start, march only 6 miles and encamp. We march along the R. Road. Pass Lonsales Station, and go as far as Dispatch Station, where we turn

---

77. Bates confirms that the regiment embarked on SS Georgia and arrived at Mechanicsville on June 19, 1862. Bates, *History of Pennsylvania Volunteers*, 786. However, in Elsesser's *Diary of Company B*, he wrote that the regiment embarked on the steamer "Forrest City."

into Camp. We are now 13 miles from Richmond. I buy a pound of dried Beef for 25 cts. Boecht, Kaufli [Martin Kauffley], Schreiner [Lewis Schreiner], Kinple [Christian Kimple] went out on a scout, and have not returned yet. They return through the night, minus Knapsacks. No drums, or any kind of noise are allowed here; after throwing out our Guard, we retire to rest. Cool.

Tuesday, June 17, 1862

This Morning we turn out for review, but as a heavy firing is heard not very far off, no review takes place. We are ordered not to leave Camp, and be ready to fall in at any time, without Knapsacks. I make out a Req for 3 days rations. We turn out in the Evg. again for review, but again we are dissapointed. We get Orders to march at 6 oCl AM. I make out requisition for two days rations. We draw Sea Horse.[78] Fine & warm.

Wednesday, June 18, 1862

We get up at 3-1/2 oCl AM. and fall into line. We march from Camp at 6 oCl. and march 12 miles toward Hanover Court House. It is a hot and dusty march, and we do it in short metre. I met James Tomkins and found him unwell. We pass the 62d Regt. (S. W. Blacks).[79] We encamp near the Chicohominy river, our Battery firing Shell rapidly across the river. We are not allowed to leave Co[mpany] Quarters. Here it is very dangerous for Pickets to be. We are now 6-1/2 miles from Richmond. Hot.

Thursday, June 19, 1862

We get orders to march at 6 oCl AM. owing to certain movements of the Enemy on the opposite Side of the river.

---

78. This is likely a reference to salted beef.
79. Col. Samuel W. Black, a Pittsburgh native and former governor of Nebraska territory, was killed weeks later at Gaines's Mill.

We leave camp, march a counter march in order to fool the Enemy. We locate about a mile from the old camp in the Woods. We lay in line of Battle, the 9th in front. We here look for fun every minute. We are on the Petersburgh Road, near Mechanicsville, at Old Turners Mill. I take charge of the mill and put guard over it through the day, it is the property of Dr. Allison. His Slaves make corn cakes for us. One of the 7th Louisiana Tigers come over to us. He is fired at by his own men, but not hit. Hot.

Friday, June 20, 1862

Our Regt. goes on picket this morning at 3 oCl. We start out without taking Breakfast. We picket in a thicket where we can easily see the Enemies picket, their Batteries &c. The 10th Regt are picketing to our right, the[y] turn out only 4 Co[mpanies] today. The Enemy is shelling today very rapid, but to no purpose. Our Batteries open and silence theirs in a short time. Shells fly right over our heads all day. Several Baloon assentions are made by our Professor.[80] I receive a Letter from home, money all right. Also one from Gschwend. We do not get releived tomorrow, but must stay a day longer. We move Camp today. I get some papers from Gchswend. Hot.

Saturday, June 21, 1862

Nothing occurred through the night. Fine morning, up to 9 oCl. no Shelling heard. In the afternoon one of the 10th Regt kill one of the Enemy, on the river Shore. There is a great firing of Musketry and heavy Cannon not far off,

---

80. Thaddeus Lowe billed himself as a professor but from all accounts, he never matriculated with a college degree. During his time aloft in the Peninsula, he reported campfires he saw from the air to help him pinpoint Confederate positions and then sent reports by telegraph. He provided the first information that the Confederates were abandoning Yorktown. James Robertson, *The Untold Civil War: Exploring the Human Side of War* (National Geographic, 2011), 206-207; Broadwater, *Special Forces*, 69.

an Engagement has taken place no doubt. We shell out a Battery and a Headquarters of Cavalry, firing through the night, and we suppose the Enemy has moved from our presence, (Get Letter from home, Get Letter from C. Gschwend, also several [   ]. Fine.

Sunday, June 22, 1862

No sign of relief yet. No sign of any shelling today, all quiet. Get releived from Picket by the 8th at 3 oCl. P.M. We form in this woods and pass out unobserved. Send Letter home. All unusually quiet today. No meeting. Hot.

Monday, June 23, 1862

We leave Camp, and move to about one mile farther off, in order to avoid Shelling and avoid much sickness. We are hardly there when we are called under arms. We proceed two miles and engage the Enemies pickets, Kill three of them, and we throw Shell from three of our Batteries among the rebel Camps. After Shelling two hours we return to Camp, and eat a hearty dinner. We can see the Church towers of Richmond plain from our Camp. There is Shelling going on all day along our lines. It rains hard all night. It is one of the hardest rains yet. Our Baloons goes up today, they fire at it. Cloudy.

Tuesday, June 24, 1862

This morning at 2 oCl we are called to fall into line, expecting an attack. We stand under arms untill 8 oCl AM when we retire. Today there is great firing on our picket line. We suppose the Enemy is trying to drive our picket in. I get some Powders from Dr. for the Diahrea. I buy 50 cts worth chewing Tobacco and 50 cts worth of smoking Tob[acco]. The firing continues up to late in the Evening. Our Batteries are in position. Richmond appears to be burning. Peoples & I have some fried Beefsteaks for Supper, cost each 15 cts. This Evening the Enemy throw Shells into our Camp. They burst right over us, but do no damage. It rains. Our Balloon goes up today, they fire at it. Cloudy.

Wednesday, June 25, 1862

Pat. & Walt Grubbs call and see me. Their Regt. lies near ours. Today we expect four new 34 lb Guns. Yesterday Eveg. the 12th cross the Creek and chase the Enemy. No firing yet this morning. At noon we are ordered under Arms. We stack in front, and keep in Camp. Take powders from Dr. Feel very bad, owing to cramps which I took through the night. The 63rd in a fight today. John Ford is killed and others are either killed or wounded. They out-flank the Enemy and capture two camps from them. Orders for cooking 3 days rations and to be ready at any time. Fair.

Thursday, June 26, 1862

Called under arms this morning at 10 oCl. Stay under them during the day. There is no firing today up to [ ]. I take medicine, feel very sick, would like to write but am unable to do so, from weakness. Fair.

15

AFTER THE WAR: TWO MEN SERVING THE BETTER GOOD

REV. GEORGE WASHINGTON HALL

While hospitalized in Staunton in February, 1863, Hall determined to commit his life's work to spreading the glory of God and "influencing others to walk the narrow path that leads to eternal life." After the war he made good on that promise by becoming a Baptist preacher. After obtaining certification of membership from Red Oak Baptist Church in Worth County, Georgia, Hall began officiating at Mount Elon Baptist Church in Sopchoppy, Florida, in April 1866.[1] He was ordained by that church in 1867. Likely recalling how important religious reading material had been to him during the war, Hall obtained a grant from the American Baptist Publication Society in 1868 for books for his congregation. In 1870, he oversaw the construction of a new church building.

On July 24, 1865, Hall married Amanda M. E. Mobley, whom he had met at the Mount Elon church while he was on his 1864 furlough. The Halls initially lived in Sopchoppy, where their first three children were born: Mary Ida (1866), Burwell Adoniram Judson ("B.A.J.") (1867), and Robert Erastus (Eric) (1871).[2] The Halls moved to Concord, Florida, in 1872, where Hall served as pastor of multiple churches in Gadsden County and helped establish Corinth Baptist Church in Hosford, Florida.[3]

---

1. Mount Elon Baptist is still an active church near Sopchoppy, Florida.
2. Mary Ida was Leta McGregor Thayer's mother. Robert was my grandfather. Burwell was named after Amanda's father, Burwell, and Adoniram Judson, a noted Baptist missionary to Burma (now Myanmar).
3. Corinth Baptist is still an active church. It celebrated its 150th anniversary in 2021.

The Halls' fourth child, Willis Washington Hall, was born in 1874 in Concord. The family moved in late 1875 to Putnam County, Florida.

Hall's journaling habit continued after the war. A post-war diary held by the family shows the date of February 10, 1869, on the inside cover. The first nine pages contain grammar rules, with a reference to Richard Morris's *English Grammar*. Hall then includes a few dozen diary entries from late 1871 through mid-January 1872, followed by over two dozen pages of a chart of dates from 1872 through 1876. Each entry in this section contains information on preaching engagements, including the Bible book and verse of his sermons, the dates of the sermons, and the locations where he delivered them. In addition to preaching at his regularly-assigned churches, Hall also preached at numerous other churches, at schoolhouses, and even at the homes of Baptist families. He was also active in regional Baptist associations, at times hosting and serving as moderator at their annual meetings.

In 1877, Hall served as a pastor at Eliam Baptist Church in Melrose, Florida. The family built a house in Melrose, where daughter Minnie Viola was born (1877) and son Robert later procured his first position as a teacher.[4] From Melrose, Hall, usually riding by horseback or driving a horse and buggy, preached across the breadth of northern and central Florida. The published minutes of his local Baptist ministers' association minutes show that in just over nine months of 1876-1877, Hall traveled 2,126 miles and preached 132 sermons for a salary of $225.[5] Hall also served several years as association treasurer and often represented the association as a delegate to the Baptist State Convention. En route to serving as a delegate to the Atlanta Baptist Convention in May 1884, Hall stopped in Americus, Georgia, visiting his uncle, Dr. John E. Hall, and "reviewing the scenes of his boyhood."[6]

---

4. After several years as a teacher and high school principal, my paternal grandfather Robert Hall was elected as county Superintendent of Schools for Dade County, Florida, in 1905, a position he held through 1920. E. V. Blackman, *Miami and Dade County, Florida: Its Settlement, Progress and Achievement* (Victor Rainbolt, 1921), 177. In 1916 Robert Hall worked with William Jennings Bryan and local civic officials on plans for a local college, which reached fruition when the University of Miami was chartered in the mid-1920s. Charlton W. Tebeau, *The University of Miami: A Golden Anniversary History, 1926-1976* (University of Miami Press, 1976), 4-5.
5. "Report of Rev. G. W. Hall," *Proceedings of the Twenty-First Annual Session of the Santa Fe River Baptist Association* (Jacksonville, FL: 1877), 17.
6. "Personal Paragraphs," *Americus Weekly Recorder*, May 9, 1884.

By 1881, the extent of Hall's reputation as an evangelical preacher was such that his biography was featured in *The Christian Index's History of the Baptist Denomination of Georgia*, the second half of which is a collection of biographies of prominent Baptist ministers from various southern states. Hall's biography includes much of the information noted elsewhere in this book, with one passage acknowledging how far he had moved beyond the limited advantages of his childhood:

> "He is a good preacher, using excellent language, and being remarkably systematic and clear, for one whose educational advantages have been limited. He is a prudent, calm, self-possessed man, whose influence in the family and social circle is good. Few men of like opportunities have been more useful; few, under similar circumstances have had their labors more blessed."[7]

The biography also notes that between the end of the war and 1881, Hall had served as pastor at approximately twenty churches in Florida. However, it is difficult to compile a list of all of the churches where Hall served as pastor, due both to the size of his circuit and the fact that some of his churches may have been "quarter-Sunday" churches, holding preacher-led services only one Sunday a month.

Hall's next ministerial calling was to create a program to bring religious education to children. First named to the new State Board of Missions in 1880, Hall was appointed in 1884 to serve as the first

This line sketch accompanies Hall's biography in *The Christian Index's History of the Baptist Denomination of Georgia*. The sketch may have been based on the photograph that Hall had taken of himself on furlough in 1864.

---

7. Boykin, *History of the Baptist Denomination in Georgia*, 242. Three of Hall's war-time chaplains – George Broadman Taylor, Edward B. Barrett, and J. J. Hyman – are featured in the biographies as well.

state Sunday school missionary.[8] He wasted little time instituting Sunday school programs throughout north Florida. The following year he reported to the state convention that 260 services for children had been held; 31 mission bands and 18 Sunday schools had been organized; and 359 religious books had been sold.[9]

Hall kept a grueling pace in his travels. For example, during one visit to Madison County over a 22-day period in the spring of 1885, Hall was scheduled for two commitments a day in seventeen different communities. The *Florida Baptist Witness* newspaper encouraged attendance, promising

Hall's post-war diary contains records of his missionary travels, sermons, Bible study lessons, and notes of English grammar rules.

that "the children will be delighted by his sweet songs; the older ones will be benefited by his words of counsel; and we are sure that those who hear Bro. Hall once, will want to hear him again."[10] One history of Melrose, Florida, describes him as the "Missionary on Horseback."[11]

Using the pen name of "Uncle Hall," Hall wrote a regular column for children in the *Florida Baptist Witness* in the mid-1880s. The Florida Baptist Historical Society notes that Hall's column was very popular. He not only provided the children with spiritual guidance and stories of his travels, but also responses to their letters. He addressed the

---

8. Donald S. Hepburn and E. Earl Joiner, *Favored Florida: A History of Florida Baptists Volume One 1784-1939* (Florida Baptist Convention, 2013), 201.
9. American Baptist Publication Society, *American Baptist Year-Book, 1884* (Philadelphia, PA: American Baptist Publication Society, 1884), 29.
10. "Appointments," *Florida Baptist Witness*, April 30, 1885.
11. Zonira Hunter Tolles, *Bonnie Melrose: The Early History of Melrose, Florida* (Storter Printing, 1982), 249.

children as his nieces and nephews, providing news of the churches he visited, thanks to the families he met, and personal encouragement to those who wrote about sick relatives or were new to Mission Bands.[12] In its June 18, 1885, issue, the newspaper called Hall a "zealous and efficient missionary," and declared that from the letters the newspaper received, Hall was "leading many of the young to the Redeemer."[13] In a July 1885 column, Hall wrote that he had just returned home after a ten-week absence, during which he had traveled 1,015 miles by horse and buggy. The range of his travels from Melrose extended as far south as Kissimmee, Florida.

One of Hall's particularly poignant columns in the *Florida Baptist Witness* was one where he wrote of his visit to his old church at Sopchoppy, where he had "found the girl, Amanda M. E. Mobley, who became [his] wife about twenty years ago." He wrote of how she had to fill the place of both mother and father to their children, training them and looking after home affairs, because he had been "absent in pastoral and missionary work for about three-fourths of [his] time during all of these years." Hall called Amanda "the greatest blessing" he had ever had, and he asked the children who prayed for him to also pray for "Aunt Hall, who enables [him] to go and tell them about Jesus."[14]

Portrait of George Washington Hall (Photo courtesy of Mary Jeanette Howle)

Hall's faith prompted him to take an enormous financial gamble in 1887. Because so many ministers, like Hall, had little, if any, college education, Baptist leaders in Florida developed plans to establish a college.[15] Henry A. DeLand, a New York manufacturer

---

12. The Florida Baptist Historical Society summarizes Hall's contribution by noting that he "served as a pastor, state missionary, Sunday School worker and children's work organizer in North and Central Florida in the late 1800s."
https://floridabaptisthistory.org/2020/11/23/biographies-h/ (accessed March 20, 2022).
13. "Rev. G. W. Hall," *Florida Baptist Witness*, June 18, 1885. Hall on at least one occasion also held children's meetings just across the Georgia state line in Decatur County.
14. "Journeying," *Florida Baptist Witness*, July 9, 1885.
15. Hepburn and Joiner, *Favored Florida*, 217.

who wintered in Florida, pledged his financial support if the proposed Baptist college was established in the town he had founded. The state convention accepted DeLand's offer and even promised to name the college after him. The college opened in 1885, but when the State Board of Missions found itself unable to raise the $10,000 they had promised to contribute, it appeared DeLand would withdraw his offer if that money was not produced in two months.[16] Hall was one of thirteen men who signed a $10,000 promissory note in March 1887, which made all of them individually liable for the money if churches came up short on donations. As Florida Baptist historians Donald Hepburn and E. Earl Joiner write, "Those men – whether unwittingly or with a high degree of confidence that the churches would eventually donate the $10,000 – took the State Convention's responsibility on themselves as individuals."[17] This was an extraordinary risk on Hall's part, who was not off the hook financially for this note until 1890, when the State Convention ratified the note.[18]

The Hall family, circa 1890. Front: George Washington, Minnie, and Amanda Hall; back: Willis, Mary Ida, Burwell, and Robert Hall.

Hall remained active as a traveling preacher in north Florida through at least 1891. However, at some point during the decade, he apparently ceased service as an active church pastor, perhaps because his medical history of rheumatism and grueling travel schedule had taken their toll. This was not the end of his ministry, however. He moved to Rudden, Georgia, in 1899, where he and Amanda lived with their son Willis and daughter Minnie, both of whom taught at a local academy. On several occasions Hall traveled to south Georgia counties on mission work. His post-war journal contains

---

16. Hepburn and Joiner, *Favored Florida*, 222.
17. Hepburn and Joiner, *Favored Florida*, 222.
18. DeLand College's name was changed to Stetson University in 1889 in reflection of John Stetson's emergence as the school's primary financial benefactor. Hepburn and Joiner, *Favored Florida*, 226. A photograph of the promissory note is reproduced in Hepburn and Joiner at page 222.

George Washington Hall's tombstone at Miami-Dade Cemetery reads "Forever with the Lord." Amanda, who died on October 1, 1928, is buried with her husband. (Photo by J. Rowan at https://www.findagrave.com/memorial/40272044/george-washington-hall)

several dozen pages of Bible-based lessons he wrote in Rudden for daily family worship.

While visiting a half-brother in Miami, Hall became so charmed with the town that he, Amanda, and three of their children moved there in 1902. Although no longer active in a pastoral ministry, Hall still did "a great deal of missionary and ministerial work."[19] On Sunday afternoons, Hall, likely recalling how much worship had meant to him when he was a prisoner, conducted religious services in the Dade County jail. Sponsored by the Women's Christian Temperance Union, he also ministered to sailors and to the poor and destitute of all races in the Miami area. He returned to Georgia in 1904 and 1905 on evangelical missions.

By 1907 Hall's health rendered him too disabled to work. He applied for, and received, an annual $100 Florida state pension for Confederate veterans. Among the extensive documentation he filed in support of his application was his 1865 furlough orders, a certified duplicate of which was submitted in his package to show that he was not in deserter status at war's end.[20] He also had to list his assets, which after four decades of preaching consisted of only $100 in personal property.

Hall died on June 8, 1911, at the age of 70, of a "long lingering illness" described as a "general breakdown."[21] The *Miami Herald* wrote that he had made "a great many friends" and that he was always "kind, gentle in manner, and did a great deal of good, especially in missionary work."[22]

---

19. "Rev. G. W. Hall died this morning after two weeks illness," *Miami News*, June 8, 1911, www.newspapers.com.
20. Soldier's Pension Claim Under the Act of 1909, G. W. Hall, State of Florida Archives, https://www.floridamemory.com/items/show/179592
21. "Rev. G. W. Hall died yesterday," *Miami Herald*, June 9, 1911, www.newspapers.com. Hall was reported in the local news as "very ill" on May 30, 1911. *Miami News*, May 30, 1911, www.newspapers.com
22. "Rev. G. W. Hall died yesterday," *Miami Herald*, June 9, 1911, www.newspapers.com..

JACOB L. ELSESSER

Unlike Hall, Jacob Elsesser did not start a new life after leaving military service; he simply resumed his old one in Etna, Pennsylvania. He reclaimed his office as magistrate at the next election after the war and then ran for reelection – and won – every five years until his death in 1909. He was believed to be the oldest living public official in Pennsylvania when he turned eighty, enjoying the longest tenure in government service. According to one Pittsburgh newspaper, Elsesser rose from being one of the earliest settlers of Etna to being one of the best-known men in Allegheny County.[23]

Jacob Elsesser with his daughter Amelia Mell in Etna. (Photo courtesy of Mel Truman)

Elsesser's office was the front room of his residence. He kept all of his commissions on his office wall but was reported to be the proudest of his army discharge certificate. Life as a Pennsylvania justice of the peace likely kept Elsesser busy with the routine legal issues such as marriages, deeds and wills, but on occasion a newsworthy event would intrude. One such example occurred in 1908, when Elsesser made the Pittsburgh newspaper after a woman blamed him for her husband being jailed for disorderly conduct. The irate wife marched into Elsesser's office, deposited her two-year-old baby on Elsesser's desk, and said, "You have my man in the lockup, you can have my baby, too." With that, the woman left the office. Elsesser gave custody of the baby to neighbors of the irate wife.[24]

Elsesser was active in veterans' groups for the remainder of his life. He was a charter member of Grand Army of the Republic (G.A.R.) Post No. 38 named for General George Custer and founded in 1876. Elsesser served in various positions in the post, including commander, adjutant, and quartermaster.[25] His pride in his post was evident in

---

23. "Justice of the Peace in Etna has held Office Fifty Years," *Pittsburgh Post*, Feb. 2, 1908, www.newspapers.com.
24. "Mother Leaves Babe on Squire's Desk: Blamed Justice Elsesser for Arrest of Husband – Party at House was Raided," *Pittsburgh Press*, June 29, 1908, www.newspapers.com.
25. "Fifty Years a Justice of the Peace in Etna," *Pittsburgh Daily Post*, Apr. 11, 1904, www. newspapers.com.

Monument in honor of Union soldiers from Etna and the surrounding area. The monument, erected by Jacob Elsesser's G.A.R. post, is located in Greenwood Cemetery, Allegheny County, Pennsylvania. (Photo provided by Mel Truman)

a letter he submitted to G.A.R. Headquarters in which he described the post's hall. It contained "two cleverly executed imitation Napoleons" and large pictures depicting the "Last Fight of Custer" and the "Prison-Pen of Andersonville."[26] Elsesser was also a member of the Union Veteran Legion No. 1. He hosted reunions of Civil War veterans every three months in his office, and "94 old soldiers" would come from a radius of 15 miles to have their pension papers signed in his office.[27] Elsesser himself received a $12 monthly pension for his service during the "late war of the rebellion."[28]

In 1908, Elsesser marked his 50th year of service as justice of the peace, a milestone of such significance that it was reported as far away as Kansas. As one article claimed, "He proved his courage during war and plague."[29] When Squire Elsesser died the following year on February 8, 1909, he was well into his eleventh commission as justice of the peace. His death certificate stated that he died of old age and exhaustion. On the occasion of his death, his G.A.R. Post, No. 38, issued the following proclamation:

RESOLUTIONS OF RESPECT

Whereas we have again been called upon to submit to the will of the Supreme Commander in the calling away by death our beloved comrade Past Commander Jacob L. Elsesser; and

Whereas, While we bow in submission to the will of Him who doeth all things well, we deeply

---

26. "Pennsylvania," *Washington National Tribune*, Aug. 23, 1883, www.newspaperarchive.com.
27. "'Squire for Over 50 Years," *Pittsburgh Press*, Oct. 16, 1904, www.newspapers.com.
28. "Allegheny County: Pensions Granted under the Act of June 27, 1890," *Pittsburgh Daily Post*, Feb 25, 1894, www.newspapers.com.
29. "'Squire Jacob L. Elsesser Expects to Receive his Eleventh Commission as His 80th Birthday Present," *Pittsburgh Press*, Feb. 2, 1908, www. newspapers.com.

feel his loss, not only as a true and honored comrade of the Grand Army of the Republic, but as an honored and respected citizen of the community wherein he lived; therefore,

Resolved, that his death has deprived us of a faithful and honest servant of the organization and the community at large of a faith and upright citizen.

Resolved, that we hereby extend to the sorrowing widow and her family our heartfelt sympathy in the hour of their bereavement and pray that what is loss to them is to him unspeakable gain.

Resolved, That a copy of these resolutions be transmitted to the family and also be inserted in our local papers and spread at large upon our minutes.

Elsesser was survived by his wife Mary, who lived until 1916, and three daughters, Elizabeth Caroline Schultz, Amelia Mell, and Mary Emma Sandrock, wife of Conrad Sandrock and mother of Charles A. Sandrock.[30] Charles Sandrock, Jacob's grandson, was only four when his father died. In a letter to C. P. Thayer in 1929, Sandrock said that Jacob had raised him after his father's death. "My father died when I was very young and my grandfather raised me. Naturally I had the very deepest of love for him and at the time of his death and his properties were divided among his children, I asked if I might have his Civil War diary which I knew he prized greatly." At the end of the diary, Jacob had written in pencil, "A citizen once more."[31]

Elsesser is buried at the First Congregational Church Cemetery in Etna, Pennsylvania. (Photo by Mary Hall)

---

30. Two of Elsesser's five children predeceased him; in addition to the daughter, Henriette Caroline, who died in 1855, his only son Johann "John" Daniel Elsesser died in 1901 at the age of forty.
31. C. A. Sandrock to C. P. Thayer, March 2, 1929. Copy in possession of Mary T. Hall.

APPENDIX A

"IT SEEMED ONE WAY I COULD CONTRIBUTE SOMETHING TO THE HISTORY OF OUR COUNTRY" – THE STORY BEHIND THE THAYER MANUSCRIPT

Mary Leta McGregor Thayer, who preferred to use Leta as a first name, was born in Melrose, Florida, in 1898 to Mary Ida Hall McGregor, George Washington Hall's eldest child, and Mary Ida's husband, Archibald G. McGregor. The family moved to Miami within a few years of her birth. Leta, who was George Washington Hall's oldest granddaughter, was twelve years old when he died. She recalled him "with much affection and delight" as a "jolly kind of person" who loved to sing and who had a memorable long white beard.

In August 1924, Leta married Clarence Putnam Thayer of Brockton, Massachusetts. The couple honeymooned in Havana, Cuba, before moving to Puerto Rico in September 1924. In August 1928, they left Puerto Rico for Miami, where they stayed for a month with Leta's parents before moving to Waterbury, Connecticut. During that Miami visit, Leta borrowed George Washington Hall's two diary volumes from her uncle Willis W. Hall, who had been given the books upon his father's death in 1911. Leta took the books with her to Connecticut and then, several months later, to New Orleans. During this period she typed the manuscript.

J. L. Elsesser's name on the flyleaf of the *Daily Pocket Remembrancer* sparked Leta's curiosity. In late December 1928, she wrote the U.S. War Department; the Bureau of Pensions for the U.S. Department of the Interior; and the Adjutant General for the Commonwealth of Pennsylvania requesting information on J. L. Elsesser. The War Department responded on January 4, 1929, stating that Elsesser had served from July 27, 1861, until May 12, 1864, in Company B, 9th Pennsylvania Reserves. Winfield Scott,

Commissioner of the Bureau of Pensions, reported that Elsesser had died on February 8, 1909, and advised that his widow, Mary, had received his pension at 331 Butler Street, Etna, until her death on May 28, 1916. A clerk at the Pennsylvania Adjutant General's Office provided an official certificate of Elsesser's service. Leta included copies of these replies and the certificate of service in her bound manuscript containing her transcription of the diaries.

Leta McGregor Thayer, second from left; Amanda Mobley Hall, far right. Robert E. Hall and his wife Lena stand next to Amanda with two of their children, Robert E. Hall, Jr. and Jean Hall. Perhaps my father did not find wearing a sailor suit to his liking because he eventually served several years in the Florida National Guard in the 1930s, followed by over thirty years of service in the U.S. Army.

In early January 1929, Clarence Thayer, Leta's husband, wrote municipal officials in Etna for information on Jacob Elsesser. The borough clerk, J. C. Armstrong, replied that he had known Jacob Elsesser very well and that the Elsessers were an old family in the borough of Etna. Armstrong forwarded Thayer's letter to Jacob's grandson, Charles A. Shadrock. Shadrock wrote Charles Thayer the following in response:

> Dear Sir: I received from our borough clerk, Mr. Armstrong the letter concerning my grandfather's Civil War diary which he lost in battle. My father died when I was very young and my grandfather raised me. Naturally I had the very deepest of love for him and at the time of his death and his properties were divided I asked if I might have his Civil War diary which I knew he prized greatly. I have it still in my possession and I am very interested in your discovery of the lost diary. My mother is still living but up in years. Mr. Armstrong is a very dear friend of our family and knew I would be interested so he gave the letter to me a short time ago.[1]

---

1. C. A. Shadrock to C. P. Thayer, March 2, 1929.

Shadrock then recited several entries from the *Diary of Co. B.* He wrote Thayer that Elsesser had served the entire enlistment without a furlough or being injured, and that in pencil at the end of the diary Elsesser had written, "A citizen once more." Thayer suggested to Shadrock that the diaries of both men were so interesting that he thought there "might be a possibility of having them published, making a story and bringing in both the Union and Confederate soldier." It would take almost one hundred years to make this happen.

Leta returned Hall's two diary volumes to her uncle Willis during a family visit to Miami in the summer of 1931; this was likely the last time she saw the books. In 1935, the Thayers moved to Miami, where Leta and her husband both spent many years working in municipal government jobs. Leta wrote the University of Georgia in the summer of 1952 to ascertain their interest in acquiring Hall's diaries. The university replied that it would be pleased to house the diaries in their new library that was nearing completion. But in 1953, Leta, surely with great disappointment, wrote the university that her uncle could not locate the diaries. After Willis's death in 1967, Leta wrote the University of Georgia again, to advise that there was still no sign of the diaries. She offered the university a copy of her bound manuscript, which the university accepted. She likewise provided a bound copy of the manuscript to the Library of Congress in 1970. As she wrote the Library of Congress in 1969, contributing the bound manuscript "seemed one way [she] could contribute something to the history of our country."[2]

Leta Thayer died on July 14, 1984, in Sumter County, Georgia, and is buried at Eliam Cemetery in Melrose, alongside George Washington Hall's mother, Rachel Holly. Nieces lovingly recall Leta as a woman ahead of her time, possessing great confidence, a stately appearance, and keen intellect. She left copious notes on family genealogy and, more specifically, on her preparation of the Hall diary manuscript.

Two of the most interesting documents in Leta's files are letters in 1943 to and from noted Civil War historian Bell Wiley, then an infantry captain serving at the Army War College in Washington, D.C. Leta had just finished reading Wiley's *Life of Johnny Reb* and gently chided Wiley for failing to discuss Confederate prisoners of war in his book. She closed her letter by asking for Wiley's guidance on disposition of the Hall

---

2. Leta McGregor Thayer to Exchange and Gift Division, Library of Congress, December 22, 1969.

diaries. Wiley wrote back soon thereafter that he had planned on a chapter on prison life in *Life of Johnny Reb* but cut it because the book had become too bulky. He explained that it would be easier for him to advise her on the disposition of the diaries if he knew more about their content, so he asked her to loan him a copy of the typed manuscript, promising to take good care of it and "not keep it long." But there is no indication that Leta ever followed up on his offer.

The following pages contain the authenticating and organizational documents which Thayer included in the bound manuscript. The final page in this appendix is her index to her manuscript. She had divided the manuscript into five sections, each with its own pagination commencing at page 1.

MEMORANDUM, AFFIDAVIT, AND INDEX PREPARED BY LETA MCGREGOR THAYER

MEMORANDUM

This transcript is the original typewritten copy of the Civil War diaries of George Washington Hall. The Affidavit given on a separate page speaks for itself.

Attention is called to the entries made by the Union soldier, E. J. (sic) Elsesser of Pennsylvania, and his war record as reflected by the letters and official record. Refer to the Index.

The diaries were kept mostly in pencil, some pages being very faded with age, with some apparent water damage. The spelling, punctuation and abbreviations were copied as written. Pagination was made at the time of copying, an apparent effort to correlate the entries and dates written in the two books. These separate numberings of pages are set out in the Index and at the beginning of each division.

Examination of the entries made by Private Hall in his diaries will show that he used both his own and the one originally belonging to the Union soldier, alternately. There seems to be an over-lapping of dates. Further efforts have been made to cross-index these, but it would seem that the dates are not as important as what was written. It is not known whether the various poems and songs were copies or whether these were original compositions written by Private Hall.

Listed in the books were the names of many individual soldiers so it is possible that those who are searching historical records will be able to make use of this information.

Described in the diaries were details of camp life, descriptions of battles, treatment in prison, deprivations and hardships under which he existed. He wrote vividly of his own conversion and baptism while in the midst of battle. His is a telling testimony to the goodness of God and of his unwavering faith in Him, to continue throughout his life.

It is hoped that those who have occasion to read this record will do so with a realization that goodness, loyalty to his family, his State and The Cause were paramount in his thinking and so woven together throughout his life that his oldest granddaughter, who transcribed the diaries many years ago and who has assembled this record, remembers him as he visited her family many times when she was a small girl, with much affection and delight.

Mrs. C. P. Thayer (Leta McGregor Thayer)
50 N.W. 44th St.
Miami, Florida 33127
December 1, 1969

STATE OF FLORIDA)
COUNTY OF DADE)

AFFIDAVIT

Personally appeared before me, the undersigned authority, LETA MCGREGOR THAYER, who deposes and says:

That she is the granddaughter of George Washington Hall, who enlisted in the 14th Georgia Volunteers of the Confederate States of America in Worth County on May 29, 1861. He served the entire four years of the war, including one year he was held in a Federal prison on Ft. Delaware Island.

At the end of hostilities, he returned to his family, then living near Tallahassee, Florida. He married Amanda Melvina Elizabeth Mobley and they had five children. He died in Miami, Florida in 1912, having served about 45 years as a Baptist minister in both Georgia and Florida.

That her grandfather had kept a diary, using two little note books. Upon his death, these were left in the possession of his son Willis W. Hall. That she borrowed these books in 1928 and made one typewritten copy, returning the original diaries to her uncle. At the time of his death in 1968, the books could not be found among his papers and have never been located.

That she still has the original typewritten copy which she made in 1928 and believes that it has some value for its historical content.

That this affidavit is being made for the purpose of the establishing the fact that the two diaries did exist, that she had these in her possession in 1928, that she read the books and did make the copy that she now has in her possession.

That this affidavit is being attached to the original typewritten copy, as a permanent part of the record.

/s/ Leta McGregor Thayer
                    AFFIANT

Sworn to and subscribed before me this
26 day of November, 1969.

/s/
NOTARY PUBLIC STATE OF FLORIDA AT LARGE

INDEX

Diaries of George Washington Hall, 14th Georgia Volunteers, Confederate States of America – 1861-1865

VOLUME I
Section (1)   Pages 1 – 72
    Diary begun April 1, 1862, with entries through April 18, 1863. Last pages (58-72) are weather tables and notations of daily activities.

VOLUME II
Section (1)   Pages 1 – 23
    This is the diary of J. L. Elsesser of the Union Army, which was lost on battlefield and found by Private Hall. See Volume I, page 23; also Volume II, Section (2), Page 1. January 1, 1862 – June 26, 1862.

VOLUME II
Section (2)   Pages 1 – 15
    Entries made by Private Hall
    June 27, 1862 – October 12, 1862

VOLUME II
Section (3)   Pages 1 – 35
    Entries began January 23, 1863 (after a long stay in Military Hospital) and end December 31, 1863.

VOLUME II
Section (4)   Pages 1 – 49
    Entries began January 1, 1864 and end March 7, 1865.

APPENDIX B
POEMS AND SONGS

Hall included many songs and poems in his pocket notebook. Thayer noted in her Memorandum that she did not know whether these were copied or original compositions. Thanks to online search engines, I have found that the likely sources for most of the poems were newspapers, which suggests that Hall simply copied them, with some minor alterations, into his notebook.[1] Other entries in his pocket notebook were lyrics to popular war songs such as "Dixie." Although he wrote his name below many of these entries, only one entry contained the notation "By G. W. Hall." This was the short two-stanza poem titled "Far Away in the Deep Blue Sea," likely written near Yorktown around April 24, 1862.

Most of these entries were made while Hall was located on the Virginia peninsula and had access to Richmond newspapers. He made his last entries of this nature in March and April 1863.

---

1. Faith Barrett included an assessment of these poems in her book on Civil War poetry. In analyzing some of the themes of these poems, she attributes the likelihood of authorship to Hall based on what she described, but did not specify, as "textual evidence." Faith Barrett, *To Fight Aloud is Very Brave: American Poetry and the Civil War* (University of Massachusetts Press, 2012), 60-68.

THE SOLDIERS SONG[2]

1st

We are volunteers for the war, boys
We are in for the end of the fight
We will conquor a glorious peace, boys
Or die in the cause of the right
Through the summers scorching heat, boys
Through the winters sleet and snow
Though we hunger thirst and freeze, boys
We will stand like a wall to the foe.

2nd

We are here at our countrys call boys
We will stay till our work is done
Till the final blow is struck, boys
And our independence won
We will never lay down our arms boys
Whatever the danger and toil
While a foemans gun is heard boys
Or his footprint stain our soil

3rd

We have many dear ones at home boys
And sometimes we almost despair,
When we think of the hardships here boys
And the joys and comforts there;
But what would be a home and friends boys
And what would be a sweetheart or wife
If the falst-hearted tyrant should win boys
And we should be bondsmen for life.

4th

No we will never submit boys,
And never will we go back,
With the flush of shame on our cheek boys
And the yankees on our track
When the last great battle's won boys
And never a day before
Will we return to our homes boys
And the loved ones greet once more

George W. Hall
April 24th 1862

---

2. These appear to be the lyrics to "The Volunteers" attributed to "An Old Soldier" in *No.3 Southern Flag Song Book* (Vicksburg, Mississippi: H. C. Clarke, 1863).

FAR AWAY IN THE DEEP BLUE SEA

As I strayed out from the
    lonesome camp
And away from the weary hum
As down by the waters Side I stamp
From the noisesome tap of the drum

Far away in the deep blue sea,
I looked with wandering eyes
And thought how the world would
    seem to me
Far across the waters wise

By G. W. Hall

"DIXIE" – THE BELOVED LAND[3]

Come all ye gallant Southern band
And rush to arms for Dixie Land
Look away away away, in Dixie Land

We'll drive the invader from our Shore
And Shout for freedom evermore
Look away away away in Dixie Land
        Chorus

Oh I am bound for Dixie away away
In Dixie Land to take my stand
To live and die for Dixie
Look away away away, down South
  in Dixie

Mclelland now a force employs
To march against our Dixie boys
Look away &c

But though a million round him gather
He'll share the fate of Fuss and Feathers
Look away
        Chorus

He says he'll march strait through
  our towns
Down to the utmost Southern bound
Look away &c
        Chorus

But his course we will retard
With <u>Johnston</u>, <u>Lee</u> and <u>Beauregard</u>,
Look away &c
        Chorus

Then every hero take your stand
To die for the beloved land
Look away &c

And then we'll fight them man to man
Before well crouch the Northern clan
Look away &c
        Chorus

---

3. Hall wrote in his pocket journal that he visited Richmond on May 22, 1862. The lyrics to this version of "Dixie" and to "The Flag of Virginia" were published in the *Richmond Dispatch* that same day, one above the other in the same column. The only variation to "Dixie" in Thayer's transcript was the substitution of the words "away, away" in the chorus for "O, ho, O, ho" in the newspaper.

THE FLAG OF VIRGINIA[4]

Virginias flag – no eagle yet
Soars with unfettered pinion
Above the fowlers Snare more free
Than the flag of the Old Dominion.

While on the breeze of heaven it floats
Our souls with rapture fill;
We'll fight beneath its sacred shield
Till death our hearts Shall Still.

The brightest star that Sheds its light
O'er heaven azure dome
To us Shall e'er Seem half so bright
As that which marks our home.

In childhood, Youth, or manhood prime
Our Motto Still Shall be
Sic Semper Tyrannis
The Watchword of the free.

Fanatics may our rights assail
But, with true hearts, and brave
Our enemies we will drive back
And Still our flag shall wave.

And when amid the battles din
The chord of life doth Sever
We'll catch from dying lips the strain
"Virginias flag forever"

If round her flag, 'mid stormy scenes
Destruction seems to hover
The God of battles with his shield
Virginias heed Shall cover

In time to come throughout out land
From every vale and mountain
Will float the ensign of the free
Our own Virginia flag

June 17th 1862

---

4. This poem was published in the *Richmond Dispatch* on May 22, 1862. www.newspapers.com

TO ONE BRAVE YOUNG SPIRIT WHO GIVE HIS LIFE IN HIS COUNTRY'S CAUSE[5]

Brave gallant youth we deeply mourn
Thy fate tho' glorious yet how sad,
Torn from Lifes threshold, while its joys
Filled thy young heart with fancied glad

Thy daring spirit led thee on
To battle for thy countrys good
To save thy mother from a wrong
Thy Sisters from a tyrants mood

Cold duties rein you proudly spurned
And rushed with ardor to the field
Resolved to crush th' insulting foe
Or in the van thy spirit yield

The order "Charge" rang on the air
And as the word fell on the ear
Ten thousand forms to battle hied
That recked not danger knew not fear

Among the one so debonair
The brightest form mid all the throng
True valor beaming in his eyes
And on his lips the warrior song

"Charge! my boys, for our mothers dear
To save our sisters from the foe
Alas! the words died on his lips
The warrior met the fatal blow

And realing, from his steed he fell
A star from honors lofty dome
His Smile lit face bespeak full well
Fond thoughts of <u>loving ones</u> at home

His noble soul hath winged its flight
His hallowed memorys left with friends
Take comfort from his glorious death
An unmixed grief God never sends

Rest martyred soldier, rest in peace
Beneath the flower enamelled sod
Thy form in Holy wood now sleeps
Thy soul we trust is with thy God

Geo. W. Hall
July 14th, 1862

---

5. This poem was printed as "Lines on the Death of the Brave Young Soldier, S. Demitt Mitchell," in the *Richmond Daily Dispatch* on July 12, 1862. www.newspapers.com

THE STARS AND BARS[6]

Above us our banner's waving
The hope of the brave and the free
We must watch must gard and defend
'Till the minions of tyrany flee

With swords and good rifles we'll meet them
On the Hill the vale and the plain
And though they may come like the locusts
We'll fatten our land with their slain

Then shout for the stars and the Bars
Three cheers for the Bars and the stars
A nation has Sworn to defend them
They'll die for the Stars and the Bars

Brave sons of the South are now ready
Each bosom is burning to save
Our land of bright sunshine and flowers
From the tread of the Northern Slave

And mothers though bending in anguish
Thus nobly cry out to their sons
"Go meet the invader with firmness
And true be the aim of your guns

    Then shout &c

Far better to live in a desert
The blue sky our canopy too,
Than wearing the chains of those demons
The Selfish fanatical crew
Far better to perish with honor,
Far better to go to the grave
And better to die as a freeman
Than live as a northerner's Slave

    Then shout &c

        Geo W Hall
        July 21st 1862

---

6. The first verse of this was printed on commercially-produced stationery used by Confederate soldiers during the war. J. Edward Lee and Ron Chepesiuk, ed., *South Carolina in the Civil War: The Confederate Experience in Letters and Diaries* (McFarland, 2000), 120.

AFTER BATTLE – A WAR SONG[7]

On yesterday, untrodden lay
The fields now tramp'd and gory,
We met the foe, we laid them low,
Bereft of life and glory.

The Battle's fought, the victory's bought
We will not say too dearly;
Though many a brave, lies in his grave
Whose life we mourn Sincerely.

Better to fall, by Sword or ball
Where wounds and fame are showered
Then live to meet, at woman's feet,
The Scorn that waits the coward.

Though dead, they live, who freedom give
In death, to unborn ages;
Their names enrolled, in glittering gold,
Shall grace our histories pages.

In after years, with glistening tears,
Their sons shall read the story,
Of how they fought, and what they wrought
And in the fair fame glory.

George W. Hall
August 3rd 1862

---

7. This song is of unknown origin.

DEAREST SPOT OF EARTH TO ME IS HOME[8]

To have "been to the wars" is a life-long honor, increaseing with advancing years, while to have died in defence of your country will be the boast and glory of your children's children
The dearest spot on earth to me
Is home Sweet home
The fairy land I long to See,
Is home Sweet Home.
There how chained the Sense of hearing
There where hearts are so endearing
All the world is not so cheering
As home Sweet home

The dearest spot on earth to me,
Is home Sweet Home,
The fair land I long to see,
Is home Sweet home.
There my dear old mother stays
There I have seen happy days
There my joys and pleasures lays
At home Sweet home

The fair land I long to see
Is home Sweet home

Geo W Hall
August 10th 1862

---

8. Although there are some lyric variations, this appears to be closely-related to a song titled *Dearest Spot of Earth to Me is Home*. Wrighton, William Thomas; Weiland, Francis; and Gaw, Robert M., "Dearest Spot of Earth to Me Is Home" (1857). Historic Sheet Music Collection, 51. https://digitalcommons.conncoll.edu/sheetmusic/51

MY SOLDIER[9]

Is my darling sadly dreaming
On his lonely watch to night
Of the home where happy faces
Beamed with Such a lovely light
Does he hear the merry laughter
Hear the old sweet songs again
Feel the gentle touch of fingers
Softly charming heart and brain
Ah! too dimly Ah! too sadly,
Die the smiles and songs of yore,
Till God sends the dreaming soldier
To our longing hearts once more.

Is he lying sorely stricken
Fever scorched on lip and brow
Murmering faintly names of dear ones
Dear ones all unanswering now
Shrieking out each ghastly vision
Dark with dread or mad with pain
Visions such as haunt the chambers
Of the sick bewildered brain
God have pity on my darling
Give those sad beseeching eyes
Slumbers such as used to bless them
Morning such as used to rise.

Is my darling daring nobly
Where the battle thunders peal
Fiery eyed and gallant hearted
Darling onward steel to steel
Or with front of stern defiance
Does he breast the foemans sway
Standing where the headlong billows
Break and sink with scattered spray
God protect him God preserve him
Or, from earths poor, faint existences
Raise him to heavens perfect health

Aug 10 1862

---

9. This poem was published in Editor's Table: "My Soldier," *Southern Literary Messenger* 34 no. 4 (April 1862), 271-272. https://quod.lib.umich.edu/m/moajrnl/acf2679.0034.004/277:10?

THE SOLDIERS SONG

When the war began to rage, I was doing verry well.
\With my friends all around young and old;
It was a short time ago that I bid farewell,
And embarked with the brave and the bold.

Chorus

Oh soldier, poor soldier hungry and cold
Though poor I'll return to my home far away
So farewell to the brave and the bold

It was a hard thing to part from the little ones at home
That was playing on the yard round the door.
And my wife cried aloud as I started away,
Saying farewell, I shall see you no more,

I dreamed I was at home, on the old orchard treat,
The little ones so gay it did seem
As I reached forth my hand to pluck the apple over my head
Disappointed I awoke from a dream.

Cold wet and hungry I sleep on the ground
When those visions of happiness came
Alas I awoke by the drums rolling sound
And my friends calling out for my name

I marched night and day for my country's right and wealth
Through rain snow and cold with delight
Alas sad misfortune has ruined my health
So my fond friends at home all good night

Chorus & ct

Oct 7th 1862
George W. Hall

THE YANKEE STAMPEDE[10]

Air "Root Hog or Die"
Now listen to a story that I'm going to relate
It happened near by Richmond in the old Dominion State;
T'was a stampede of the Yankees down the Chickahominy,
Big Yank little Yank root yank or die
Chorus
Mclellan, Seward and Greely
with all their Yankee cunning
Will never live to wipe us out,
we are not the stock for running
And, I'll tell you the reason why
Dixey will be Dixey root hog or die

To Richmond on to Richmond's been the Yankees constant cry
They said that they would have by the middle of July - -
But you see that their predictions all turned out to be a lie
For Lee and Stonewall Jackson made them root hog or die

Lee and Stonewall Jackson together put their wits
And verry shortly after threw the Yankees into fits
Lee pitched into the center and Stonewall on the sly
And down the river went the Yanks, root hog or die

Quite early in the morning on the thirty-first of May,
I guess you all remember that memorible day
When Hill of Carolina thought the Yankees rather nigh
He soon made them mark time root hog or die

---

10. These lyrics are similar to those in sheet music for "Root Yank or die!" at the Library of Congress. *Root Yank or die! Air-"Root hog or die."* www.loc/gov/item/amss.cw201550/

Mclellan wrote to Lincoln not far from our lines
That he fought the rebel devils at a place called Seven Pines
He fixed it all up nicely, but wound up with a lie,
For every body knows we made him root hog or die.

Mclelland he was bothered in regard to our course
He was also quite uneasy for fear we'd reinforce
Oh how little was he thinking that Lees chicane-ry
Would soon make him double quick root hog or die

From before the city the Yankees broke pell mell
And flew down the river like two forty on a shell
When they got the sight of rebels 'twould done you good /
to see them fly
It was quick, quick, double quick root hog or die

Lower down the river Mack thought he'd make a stand
But after some hard fighting found he couldn't stand his hand
So onward went Mclellan down the Chickahominy
Crying to his hirelings, root hog or die

General Stonewall Jackson is a terror to the yanks
He regularly used up Fremont, Shields and also Banks
Go it Stonewall Jackson and make the feathers fly
Make Yankee doodle, doodle-dom root hog or die

Now I'll tell you Uncle Samuel we'll have you understand
To get back Cousin Sallie you never, never can
For she's opposed to union, so Uncle Sam good-bye
Dixie will be Dixie root hog or die

Oct 8th 1862
Geo. W. Hall

A SONG[11]

From the bright sunny South
When in peace and content
The years of my boyhood I
    carelessly spent
From the broad spreading plains,
To the deep flowing streams,
Ever dear to my memory,
Ever seen in my dreams

I left the refinements and comforts of life
Through dangers of bloodshed
Privations and strife
I have counted the cost
Have plighted my word
I have shouldered my musket
And belted my sword

My father looked sad when
He bid me depart
My mother embraced me
In anguish of heart
My beautiful sisters look pale in
    their wo[e]
They kissed me and blessed me
And told me to go.

Oh father dear father for me do not weep
For in some foreign mountains
I expect for to sleep
Through the dangers of war
I expect for to share
Through sickness and death
I expect for to bear

Oh sisters, dear sister, I can not see
    your wo[e]
Your tears and your sorrows
They trouble me so
Oh! now I must be gone
And here I cannot stand
For I am going in defence
Of my own native land

O mother dear mother
For me do not weep
For [y]our kind advice I forever
    shall keep
You taught me to be brave
From boyhood to a man
Now I am going out to fight
For my own native land

---

11. The lyrics here are almost identical to several versions of the bluegrass banjo classic "Bright Sunny South." As an example, see the lyrics to Sam Amidon's Bright Sunny South. https://genius.com/Sam-amidon-bright-sunny-south-lyrics

From my sisters and my parents
I once had to part
From my friends and my sweetheart
That are dear to my heart
I never shall forget when I took them
By the hand
And started in defence of my own
    native land

I left a fair maiden my heart polar star
More beautiful than others
More precious by far
When I gave her my hand
Not a word could I say
Though I gave her a kiss
And I hastened away

Oh the time will soon come
Oh how long it will be
When from Union and Yankees
Our country will be free
When wars are o'er and our
Troubles are all done
Then we'll look for our loved ones
And hasten home

Time points to a day
When this conflict shall cease
And victory befall us by
    permanent peace
When From Northern invaders
Our country will be free
Then I'll look for the loved ones
Now weeping for me

               Camp Gregg
               Mar. 18. 1863

WHEN THE WAR IS OVER

'Twas summer eve; the twilight dreamy hour
Like a sweet memory o'er the senses stole
The birds were nestled in their leafy bower
And night her train was gathering up to roll
Her darkened curtains round the dewy earth
'Twas then <u>She</u> laid her small white hand in mine
And as her gentle sight to words give birth
She softly whispered, "I am ever thine!

I pressed her then to name the happy hour
We'd stand together at the altars side
To say how long before the orange flower
Would crown her there my fair young loving bride
She said whilst kindled up her blue eyes bright
Had breathed within an inspiration bright
"Not soon but when the war is over love"

Thy country is thy bride till she shall stand
Stand proudly mid the nations of the earth
Till gentle peace come smiling o'er the land
And direful woes give place to joy and mirth
Strike till the presence of a dastard foe
Our hopes of happiness no longer mars
And if no more I'll see the here below
<u>I'll meet thee in the world beyond the stars</u>

Camp Gregg
April 6 1863

THE SOLDIERS FAREWELL[12]

Hark! The Tocsin is sounding my comrade
Bind your knapsacks away let us go
Where the flag of the freeman is waving
March to vanquish the ruffian foe

Chorus

Ho for Liberty Freedom or Death boys
That's the watchword, away let us go,
To the Sound of the drum and the bugle
March to vanquish the ruffian foe

Farewell to the scenes of my childhood
To my mother who's praying for me
She would weep if the son of her bosom
From the face of a foeman should flee

Farewell to the home and the hearth stone
Where my sisters are weeping for me
Oh the foot of the spoiler shall never
Stain the home of the brave and the free

Adieu thou beloved of my bosom,
For your soldier, love, shed not a tear
But beseech the great Lord of the battle
To protect him and all he holds dear

---

12. This song is contained in *Southern War Songs – Camp-Fire, Patrotic & Sentimental*, collected and arranged by W. L. Fagan (New York: M. T. Richardson, 1889). Fagan wrote in the introduction that many of the songs had been gathered from Southern newspapers.

Adieu honored father who taught me
For the right of a freeman to stand
To resist his rod, the oppressor,
Shakes in wrath o'er my dear native land

Oh, my country, Thou home of my loved ones
You, the tyrant would seek to enslave
Sweep you from the face of creation
Wake, freemen our country to save

Hear the threats of that ruthless banditti
Who for booty and beauty would fight
Shall they sweep our loved South from creation
No! her sons will arise in her might

Sweep The South from the face of the earth, boys
We can sweep too, oh land of my birth
For our homes and our alters, and dear ones
We the ruffians, can sweep from the earth

Adieu to the church, where the Christian
For the soldier and Sabbath will pray
But the Bible and Chaplain go with us
And Jehovah, our God is our stay

When the old British lion oppressed us
<u>He</u> with <u>Washington</u> went to the field
Unto him we will look in the battle
And will strike till the enemy yield

                        Camp Gregg
                        April 18 1863

APPENDIX C
HALL'S DAILY LOG: APRIL 1862 – MAY 1863

A Table Telling my occupation for the following days Commencing April 1st 1862[1]

APRIL 1862

1	detailed with waggons that haul hay
2	on Regimental Guard
3-7	in camp
8-10	on the march from Fredericksburg to Millford Station and on the 11th
11	at 6 P.M.we took the cars at Millford Station and arrived at Ashland Station that night in all 50 miles
12-14	in camp at Ashland
15-19	on the march from Ashland to Yorktown the distance of (86) eighty Six Miles
20-23	in camp at Yorktown
24	on Fatigue
25-30	in camp

MAY 1862

1	in camp
2	M in camp E in line of battle
3	on Guard in line of battle
4	on the march from Yorktown to Williamsburg
5	on the march from Williamsburg to the vicinity of West Point
6	M in camp on the march and in line of battle close to West Point
7	in the Battle of West Point
8	on the march from the vicinity of West Point to New Kent C H
9	in line of battle 2 miles from New Kent C H
10	in line of Battle protecting the rear of the retreat
11-12	in camp
13	on guard
14	M in camp E sent out on picket
15	deployed as a sharpshooter on the line of the enemy
16-17	on the march to Richmond
18	in camp near Richmond
19	on Brigade Guard
20-21	in camp

---

1. Dates of consecutive similar events, such as "in camp," have been compressed in the date column.

22	in the City of Richmond		21	on picket on the Chickahominy
23	in camp		22-24	in camp
24	M in camp E go out on picket our whole Brigade		25	on picket on the banks of the Chickahominy
25	on picket on the enemies line		26	on picket and on the march
26	M in camp E in the march		27	in the great Battle
27	on a scout and skirmish on the line of the enemy		28	in camp on the Battleield
28	M march back to camp		29	on the march
29	in the woods		30	in another great Battle
30	in camp			
31	in the Battle of the Chickahominy			

JUNE 1862

1	In line of Battle near the Battle Ground
2	in line of Battle and on the march
3	in camp with some marching
4-5	in camp about 5 miles of Richmond
6	M in camp E go out piquet
7-9	on picket outpost duty
10	Work on Battery
11	on picket out post duty
12	on the march and in camp
13-14	in camp 4 miles from Rich[mond]
15	on Guard
16	on the march & in camp
17	In camp
18	on piquet on the Banks of the Chickahominy
19-20	in camp

JULY 1862

1	in another great Battle
2	in the rain and on the march
3	on the march
4	in camp & on the march
5-6	Sick on my way to camp
7-12	Sick in camp
13	I join the regiment
14-16	in camp
17	on picket
18	return off picket
19-21	in camp
22	on Police in Richmond
23-28	in camp
29	start to march but turn back
30	in camp
31	on the march and on the cars

AUGUST 1862

1	on the cars and on the march
2	We camp 5 miles from Gordonsville
3	in camp

4-5	Sick in camp
6	I start to hospital
7	I took the cars for Livingston
8	I arrive at Bellmonte colledge Hospital
9-24	Sick at hospital
25	I prepare to leave the Hospital
26	I start to my regt
27	on my way to the regt
28	on Guard at Gordonsville
29	in camp at Gordonsville
30	on police duty at Gordonsville
31	in camp at Gordonsville

SEPTEMBER 1862

1	on Guard
2	in camp
3	fatigue duty
4	in camp
5	on guard
6	in camp
7-8	on fatigue
9	on police
10	on guard
11-12	in camp
13-21	on the way to my regt
22	I arrive at my company
23	on fatigue
24-25	in camp
26	on the march
27-30	in camp

OCTOBER 1862

1-2	in camp
3	on Division guard
4-8	in camp
9-29	sick in camp
30-31	Sick in Hospital at Winchester

NOVEMBER 1862

1-15	Sick in Hospital at Winchester
16-19	In ambulance on the Road to Staunton
20-30	Sick in Hospital at Staunton

DECEMBER 1862

1-4	Sick in Hospital at Staunton
5	Carried to Small Pox Hospital
6-31	Sick in Small Pox Hospital

JANUARY 1863

1-18	Sick in Small Pox Hospital
19	Transferred to General Hospital
20-25	Sick at General Hospital
26-31	Sick in General Hospital

FEBRUARY 1863

1-28	Sick in General Hospital

MARCH 1863

1-12	Sick in General Hospital
13-14	on the way to the reg

15-17	in camp	26-27	in camp
18	on regimental guard	28	we move our camp
19-22	in camp	29	on the march & in line of battle
23	on regimental guard	30	in line of battle
24-27	sick with diarhear		
28-31	in camp		

APRIL 1863

MAY 1863

1-3	in camp	1	on the march & in line of battle
4	on regimental guard	2	Skirmishing & marching
5-7	in camp	3	in a great Battle
8	on picket	4	Skirmishing & in line of battle
9	return of picket	5	in camp on the Battle ground
10	on regimental guard	6	on the march
11-21	in camp	7	on the march
22	on picket	8-13	in camp
23	return off picket		
24	in camp		
25	on regimental guard		

APPENDIX D
HALL'S WEATHER LOG: APRIL 1862 – MAY 1863

Weather Table Commencing
April 1st 1862

1	Morning fair & cool Evening cloudy
2	Cool and thick cloudy
3	Fair and pleasant weather
4	Fair and pleasant Delightful weather
5	M. rain, E cool & cloudy
6	Fair & pleasant windy
7	Cool & cloudy E snow
8	Cold & rainy
9	Cold & rainy E sleet & snow
10	M snow E fair & cold
11	Fair & cool & frosty
12	Fair & cool & frosty
13	Cool & cloudy
14	Cool & cloudy
15	M rainy E cloudy
16	fair & pleasant
17	fair & pleasant
18	fair & pleasant gentle breezes
19	cloudy & warm
20	rainy
21	wet & rainy
22	rain & thunder clouds
23	M fair & frosty E. fair & windy
25	cool & cloudy with some rain
26	cold and rainy
27	cool and cloudy
28	M cool & clo E fair
29	M fair E cloudy
30	cool & cloudy

MAY 1862

1	cool and rainy
2	M cool & cloudy E fair
3	M partial clo E fain thunder heads
4	fair with some clouds
5	a hard perpetual rain all day
6	fair cool & windy flying clouds
7	M cool E cloudy
8	M cool E fair and pleasant
9	fair & pleasant
10	fair & pleasant
11	fair & pleasant beautiful weather
12	fair & pleasant beautiful weather
13	Fair & warm
14	M cloudy E rainy
15	Hard perpetual rain
16	Hard perpetual rain
17	M fair E cloudy
18	Fair & warm

19	cloudy & rainy	14	fair and warm
20	fair & warm E thun shower	15	M fair & warm E thun shower
21	fair & warm	16	fair & pleasant
22	M fair & warm E thun shower	17	M cool E fair & pleasant
23	M clo E fair & warm	18	M fair E rain
24	Rain Rain	19	fair and warm
25	M clo & cool E partialy fair	20	fair and pleasant
26	M cool & clo E hard perpetual rain	21	fair and warm
27	M continued raining E partialy fair	22	fair and warrm
28	Fair & plesent	23	M fair & warm E heav. thun. show.
29	Fair and pleasant	24	M cloudy E thunder showers
30	cloudy & wet	25	fair & pleasant
		26	fair & warm
		27	fair & warm
		28	M fair E. cloudy & warm
		29	partially cloudy & Hot
		30	Fair & Hot

JUNE 1862

1	M cloudy & misty E thunder clouds
2	M cloudy thunder clouds & some rain
3	M fair and warm E hard rain
4	continuous rain verry hard E clo & windy
5	cloudy & cool with some rain
6	cloudy & cool with some rain
7	M partially cloudy E thunder show
8	cool & cloudy
9	cool & cloudy
10	Hard continued raining
11	Partially fair and cool
12	fair and warm
13	fair and warm

JULY 1862

1	M fair & warm E cloudy
2	verry hard rain
3	cool & cloudy some rain
4	Fair & warm
5	Fair & Hot
6	Fair & Hot
7	Fair & Hot
8	Fair & Hot & sultry
9	Fair & Hot & sultry
10	Fair & Hot & dusty
11	M rain E cloudy
12	fair & pleasant
13	fair & warm

14	fair & warm		14	cloudy & do
15	M fair & hot E thun & rain		15	partially cloudy & do
16	fair & Hot		16	M cool E fair & warm
17	M fair & hot E thunder shower		17	M cool E fair & warm
18	M cloudy E thunder shower		18	M cool E fair & warm
19	cloudy with some rain		19	M cool E fair & warm
20	cloudy with some rain		20	M cool E fair & cloudy
21	partially cloudy & warm		21	M fair E fair & cloudy
22	M fair E cloudy & warm		22	M cloudy & foggy E thunder
23	M cloudy & warm E some rain		23	M cloudy E thunder & rain
24	cloudy & misty		24	M cloudy a little rain E clo & cool
25	fair & warm			
26	M cloudy E heavy rain		25	fair & pleasant
27	fair & warm		26	M cool E fair & pleasant
28	fair & warm		27	cloudy & pleasant
29	M fair & warm E cloudy		28	cloudy & pleasant
30	M rain E fair & hot		29	fair
31	hard rain all day		30	cloudy & warm
			31	M rain E cloudy

AUGUST 1862

1	fair & hot			
2	fair & hot		**SEPTEMBER 1862**	
3	M partially cloudy E rain		1	M cloudy E thunder & rain
4	fair & warm		2	M cool & windy E fair & pleasant
5	fair & hot			
6	M fair & hot E thunder clouds		3	M cool E fair & pleasant
7	fair & exceedingly hot		4	M cool E fair & pleasant
8	fair & exceedingly hot		5	fair and pleasant
9	fair & exceedingly hot		6	fair and pleasant
10	M fair & hot E a little rain		7	fair and pleasant
11	fair & hot		8	fair & pleasant
12	M fair & hot E rain & hail		9	fair & pleasant windy
13	fair & warm		10	cloudy & warm
			11	cloudy & rainy

12	cloudy with some rain	10	M cloudy E rainy
13	particularly cloudy & warm	11	M rain E cloudy & cool
14	particularly cloudy & warm	12	cloudy & cool
15	M cloudy E fair & warm		
16	M fair & warm E cloudy	**JANUARY 1863**	
17	do cloudy & foggy E fair & pleasant	28	Snow storm
		29	fair & cold
18	partially cloudy & warm	30	M snow E fair
19	particularly cloudy & warm	31	fair & cool
20	cloudy & pleasant		
21	M cool & foggy E fair & pleasant	**FEBRUARY 1863**	
22	M cool & foggy E fair & pleasant	1	cloudy & wet
		2	fair & cool
23	M cool & foggy E fair & pleasant	3	M snow E fair
		4	M fair & cold E cloudy
24	cloudy & a little rain	5	continued Snow
25	M a slight frost E fair & pleasant	6	M cloudy E fair & cold
26	M a slight frost E fair & pleasant	7	fair & cold
27	M a slight frost E fair & pleasant	8	M fair & cold E cloudy
28	M cloudy E fair and warm	9	cloud & cold
29	M frosty E fair and pleas.	10	fair & cold
30	partially cloudy & warm	11	M Snow E cloudy & cold
		12	M fair E cloudy & cool
OCTOBER 1862		13	fair & pleasant
1	partially cloudy & warm	14	M cloudy E fair & cool
2	M cloudy & misty E partially clo	15	do rainy E cloudy
3	M foggy E fair & warm	16	fair & pleasant
4	partially cloudy & do	17	Snowing all day
5	fair & cool	18	cold & rainy
6	fair & cool	19	M cold & cloudy E fair & cool
7	fair, M cool E warm	20	fair & cool E cloudy
8	fair, M & warm	21	M fair & cool E cloudy
9	fair, M & warm	22	heavy Snowing

23	M Snow E fair & cold
24	fair & cold
25	fair & cold
26	rainy & disagreeable
27	cloudy & cool
28	cold & cloudy

MARCH 1863

1	M cold & rainy E windy
2	fair & cold
3	M snow storm E windy
4	cold & wind with scattering clouds
5	fair cold & severe
6	cold cloudy & windy
7	cloudy with a little rain
8	M rain E fair & pleasant
9	M rainy E fair & cool
10	Snow & Sleet
11	M fair E snow & wind
12	cold & windy snow
13	partially cloudy & cold
14	partially cloudy & cold
15	cold & cloudy E thunder & hail
16	M Snow E fair & cold
17	fair windy & cold
18	cloudy cold & windy
19	M cloudy & cold E snow
20	Snowing all day
21	M snow E rainy
22	M cloudy & cool E fair
23	cloudy cool & windy
24	M cloudy E windy & rain

25	M rainy E par cloudy & windy
26	M rain & snow E cloudy & cool
27	fair frosty & cold
28	rainy & cold
29	cloudy cold & windy
30	fair cold & windy
31	heavy snowing & sleet

APRIL 1863

1	fair & cold severe wind
2	fair & cold & windy
3	fair & cold & windy
4	M cold & windy E snow storm
5	M snow storm E cold cloudy & wind
6	cold & cloudy
7	M fair & frosty E cloudy & windy
8	cold & cloudy
9	M fair & frosty E fair & cool
10	M fair & frosty E fair & cool
11	fair pleasant & windy
12	M fair & pleasant E a little rain
13	cloudy & cool
14	M fair & frosty E par cloudy & cool
15	cold wind & rain
16	cloudy & cool
17	cloudy & cool
18	fair & pleasant
19	fair & pleasant
20	rainy & cool
21	cool & cloudy

22	cool & cloudy
23	cold & rainy
24	cold rain & wind
25	fair cool & windy
26	fair cool & windy
27	fair & pleasant
28	cloudy & some rain
29	M cloudy E rain
30	M rain E partially fair

MAY 1863

1	fair & pleasant
2	M fair E cloudy
3	fair & pleasant
4	cloudy & some rain
5	M fair & pleasant E thunder & rain

APPENDIX E
ELSESSER'S DIARY OF CO. B 9TH REGT. P.R.C.

Diary of Co. B 9th Regt. P.R.C.[1]

1861

May 1	Entered Camp Wilkins
June 11	Left Camp Wilkins for Camp Wright.
July 23	Left Camp Wright under Orders from War Dept.
July 24	Received our Guns and Accoutrements at the Camp Curtin at Harrisburgh. Also got our Blankets and Knapsacks.
July 25	Arrived at Baltimore at 12.M. Marched through the City to the depot, where we took the cars for Washington at 11 oCl. P.M.
July 26	Arrived at Washington at 4 oCl A.M. Same day marched to Camp Jackson, a distance of 6 miles.
July 28	Mustered into the U.S. Service
Aug. 4	Paid $25 33/100
Aug. 5	Marched to Camp Tennaly, having the enemy in our front about 4 miles.
Aug. 6	The Regt. marched to the Potomac, Co. B left to the guard Camp.
Sep. 17	Co. B detached and ordered into Fort Pennsylvania.
Sep. 19	Rec. Payment $16.32
Sep. 23	Returned to Regiment by permission of Genl. McCall.
Nov. 8	Rec'd. Payment $26.00
Dec. 20	Left at 5 oCl A.M. Met the rebel pickets at 12 oCl.M. Marched to Drainesville where we met the enemy, consisting of Calvary Artillery and Infantry. We engaged there and in 1 ¾ hour whipped them badly. We killed 172 rebels, captured about 100 stand of arms, their Caisson also fell into our hands we have 4 killed and 14 wounded.

---

1. Transcription notes: Mel Truman typed the contents of the diary from the handwritten original that was handed down within his family. I provided some additional edits.

1862

Jany. 4	We have the first snow.
Jany. 6	More snow.
Jany. 24	Paid $26.00
Fby.	Snow + rain
Fby. 24	Great storm in Camp, most of the tents carried off, and trees rooted. Several in the 3d Regt. Killed and wounded
Fby. 25	Marching Orders.
Fby. 26	Marching Orders countermanded.
March 10	General movement of the Army. Our Div. moves, except our Regt. which remain at Camp under marching orders
March 15	Moved at 2 oCl pm under heavy rain, made out to get to Falls Church, where we built fires in order to dry our clothes.
March 16	Marched toward Alexandria
17 – 18	Rain
19,20,21	Rain
March 22	Fair. We go into Camp Misery.
March 25	Grand Review by Genl. McDowell.
Apl. 1-9	Snow and rain, We have no Tents but manage to get a few from other Camps
Apl. 11	We leave Camp Misery (glad of it) at 6 oCl A.M. Get to Fairfax C.H. at noon and at 5 oCl P.M. we encamp for the night within 3 miles of Centreville.
Apl. 12	March to Manassas Junction
Apl. 13	Palm Sunday we rest.
Apl. 14	We go into the rebel Camp "Pickins" same day paid off. $26.00
Apl. 18	Moved again to Catlett station, it being 10 miles from Manassas.
May 2	Left Catlett again, marched all day.
May 3	Marched again all day to Hartwood
May 4	Marched to Falmouth, and beyond we encamped.
May 10	We moved Camp, went into Camp "Ord", which we fixed up nicely
May 18	Genl. Ord bid us farewell, and we are under Genl. Seymour
June 11	We march again to the Rappahannock - it rains all day hard.

June 13	Get shipped on board Steamer Forrest City
June 15	Arrive at White house - camp all night.
June 16	March again to Tunstall Station. Co. B go on picket.
June 17	March to Dispatch Station.
June 18	March to Mechanicsville.
June 19	Co. B go on Picket. Our picket line are close together, but we mutually agree not to fire at each other.
June 21	We (9th) with Battery go down and open upon the rebels, we drive their pickets in, and kill several of them. We have only one man wounded, but we capture Clothing and Eatables which the rebels in a hurry leave behind.
June 26	4 oCl P.M. the Enemy attacks us in great force, we hold our ground, Capt. Sothen runs away from the Co. The firing becomes heavy, and is kept up till night at 9 oCl. Co. B goes out as Skirmishers during the night.
June 27	Battle renewed at daybreak, and the Pa. Reserve get orders to hold our ground at all hazards. We fall back at night. It was here where we held Stonewall in check with a greater force than ours, and where one Regt. (12th) repullsed the rebels 4 times. We kept the ground, and in the morning the fight was commenced again, our men again in the fire, as no reinforcements could be spared. One killed 5 wounded.
June 29	We fight at Gaines Mill,[2] the fight lasts all day, but owing to confusion, the fire ceases early in the evening.
June 30	We fight again. We lose 3 killed 13 wounded
July 1	Fight again, the rebels lose heavily. It rains hard. We go to Harrison Landing.
2 -3 -4	We lay quiet and draw Clothing.
Aug. 1	The Rebels shell our Camp during the night, Killing many. Also we have many Horses Killed, but we open on them with heavy pieces,

---

2. Elsesser's date here is incorrect: the battle of Gaines's Mill was on June 28, 1862. The regiment did not participate in the battle on June 29, 1862, at Savage's Station, just south of Gaines's Mill.

Aug. 10	We go on Picket on the opposite side of the James River, where we stay till the 15th when we get shipped again
Aug. 16	Arrive at Fortress Monroe, where we lay quiet till the 18th. A. Manser of Co. B was drowned here, by falling off.
Aug. 19	Arrive at Aqia [Aquia] Creek and take the Cars, for our old Camp at Fredericksburgh
Aug. 21	March again at 9 oCl P.M. Rains hard, march all night and the next day till 12 oCl Midnight when we stop for the night
Aug. 24	March again to Warrenton
Aug. 27	Left Warrenton again
Aug. 28	Arrived at Bull Run
Aug. 29	Fought all day, rested at night laying in Picket line, and fired at every moment through the night.
Aug. 30	Fought again, and being on the extreme left, and left uncovered by support we had to give way under a destructive fire and Bull Run No. 2 turns out bad for a while. The right under Sigel holds out. Co. B had 4 killed and 4 wounded. We fell back to Centreville. Went on picket and left behind by the Regt. till the [ ]
Sept. 1	We got back to Arlington Heights.
Sept. 6	Marched to Washington, via Long Bridge at Night. Passed through the City, and at 5oCl A.M. we halted.
Sept. 7	Marched all day and arrived at Mechanicsville at 9 oCl P.M.
Sept. 10	Arrived at Brookville, drew Clothing.
11 – 12	Passed through Richville and New Market.
Sept. 13	Marched all day
Sept. 14	Marched 14 miles and rested in the vicinity of Frederic City. Fought at Middleburgh[3] and Boonsboro the rebels got whipped (This was South Mountain).

---

3. Elsesser may have been referring to Middletown, Maryland, which is between Frederick and Boonsboro, rather than Middleburgh.

Sept. 15	Left Boonsboro and passed through Curtisville[4].
Sept. 16	Had a Skirmish, and in the evening had a hard Artillery Duel
Sept. 17	Fight again all day, and our Co. looses 2 killed and 10 wounded. Our 1st Lieut. Longbein was killed here. Also Privates Danner[5] and Shoemaker (A. Schumacher) Co. B and Co. G each capture a rebel Flag – This was the Battle of Antietam, and the Rebels were badly used up.
Sept. 18	The Rebels under flag of Truce carry off their wounded and bury the dead. But leave most behind.
Sept. 19	We march over the Battlefield to the River, where we laid till the 24. In these few fights our Regt. lost at South Mt.
	K
	W10
	33
	Brigade 132
	Div 393
	10 killed and 33 wounded – Brigade 132 killed, Div. 392 killed. At Antietam our Regt. 16 killed, 67 wounded – Brigade 174 killed, Div. 598 killed.[6]
23 – 24	Hard frost
Sept. 26	Marched all day from Camp and part of the night
Sept. 27	Marched again till night, when we got to Berlin, where we encamped till the [ ]
Sept. 30	When we crossed the Potomac again into Virginia

---

4. Elsesser may have been referring to Keedysville, Maryland, which is between Boonsboro and Sharpsburg.

5. Both Danner and Schumacher were killed at Antietam. Although Elsesser indicated Schumacher was in Company G, there was no soldier of that name on the Company G roster.

6. Elsesser's casualty numbers were divided into two columns, one with a K and one with an M. For South Mountain, he placed 132 brigade losses and 392 division losses in the K column. Those numbers are closer to total casualties rather than total killed: Ent gives the number of 3rd Brigade casualties (killed, wounded, and missing) as 131 and division casualties at 392. Ent, *Pennsylvania Reserves*, 141. For Antietam, Elsesser placed 174 brigade losses and 598 division losses in the K column. Those numbers are closer to total casualties rather than total killed: Ent gives the number of 3rd Brigade casualties (killed, wounded, and missing) as 175 and division casualties at 573. Ent, *Pennsylvania Reserves*, 141, 158.

Sept. 31	Mustered again by Col. Anderson
Nov. 1	Marched to, and passed Waterford marched all day and go to Harmony Church at dark, went on picket right away.
Nov. 3	Marched again
Nov. 4	Passed through Uniontown
Nov. 5	Passed through Leesburgh, Middleburgh and to Whiteplain[7], where we arrive at 1 oCl A.M. Here we had a cold night of it, no fuel to burn.
Nov. 6	Marched at 6 oCl A.M. to Warrenton, where we stopped at night (cold again)
Nov. 7	During the night snow fell several inches.
Nov. 10	Review, and Genl. McClellan bids the Army farewell, as Genl. Burnside takes command.
Nov. 12	Marched again 10 miles and laid over till the [ ]
Nov. 17	Marched to Fredricksburgh and stopped over night
Nov. 18	Marched to Aquia Creek, and laid till [ ]
Nov. 22	Marched 6 miles and Paid again late
Dec. 5	Great Snow.
Dec. 8	Left Camp, and marched to the river Rappahannock
Dec. 10	Midnight 12 oCl marched again to the river bank, where Pontoons were built across.
Dec. 11	Heavy Canonading on our part, but no reply by the rebels.
Dec. 12	We cross over, and after "feeling'" we rest for the night. "North Light" seen
Dec. 13	Artillery in it again, but no reply, untill our troops moved up to the heights when all at once the rebel guns were in operation. We pushed forward, and after hard fighting, we succeeded breaking through the rebel lines, but as our support failed to come up in time, the Pa. Res. Had to fall back with loss of 2300 men. 9th R. loosing 40 men, Brig. Genl. Jackson killed
Dec. 14	All quiet, save occasional shelling.

---

7. Elsesser may have been referring to the area now known as The Plains, Virginia.

Dec. 15	Quiet through the day, and at dark the Army moved back across the river again
Dec. 16	Camped in the woods (Whisky ration)
Dec. 18	On picket, and were posted in line of the Army
Dec. 24	½ of Co. B. on picket again. Commenced building Winter Quarters at Belle Plain.

1863

Jany. 20	Moved again to cross the river, but owning the incessant rains we had to give up and go back to Camp this was Burnsides Mud March
27 – 28	On picket again. Snow all day
Feby. 8	Marched to Potomac Bridge, where we were shipped on board Canal Boats
Feby. 9	At Alexandria, staid aboard the boat till the 10th when we marched through the City and camp at the Seminary. Marched to Minors Hill and took the Camp of 40 Mass. Rgt. in possession. Went on picket same day. Snow.
April 20	Moved to Washington, and were put into Carrol Hill Barracks, where we staid till
June 1	When we recrossed to Virginia to Upton Hill
June 17	Marched to Vienna.
June 24	Left Vienna and went back to Upton Hill
June 25	Left Upton for Vienna again
June 26	Marched to Leesburgh pike, passed Drainesville, camped at Broad Run
June 27	Crossed the Potomac at Edwards Ferry camped at the Monocasy [Monocacy]
June 28	Passed through Buckytown, camped at night
June 29	Passed by Frederic City and Mount Pleasant. Waded the Monocasy [Monocacy] barefoot at night
June 30	Passed through Liberty, Jonesville, Unionbridge, Middleville, and Uniontown.
July 1	Passed by Babylon Mills, Fritzelburg [Frizzelburg], Kurtzburg and Loustown and arrived at Pa. line at 5 oCl P.M. Marched at night passed

	Hanover and West Sherryton and went into Camp at 2 oCl A.M.
July 2	Marched 16 miles till noon. And in the Evening we took our position in line of Battle on the extreme left. Our first Brigade goes in on a charge and drive the rebels to the Wall.
July 3	We fortify by making Stone Walls and the Reserves are intrusted to Round top mountain
July 5	Marched till 12 oCl night
July 6	Marched again.
July 7	Got into Maryland again, passed by Emmetsburgh and Riegerstown (camped at night)
July 9	Passed South Mountain
July 10	Marched all day
July 11	Marched in Close Column.
July 12	Marched in Close Column [ ]
July 13	We build Rifle Pits, and throw up Works
July 14	We moved forward again, but as we get to Williamsport, we find the Bird Flown, great many prisoners are brought in. We camp in the afternoon
July 15	We march again a distance of 25 miles and pass South Mountain again.
July 16	We pass by Burkittsville and Petersville and encamp near Berlin.
July 17	It rained, and we crossed the Potomac again, and camped at Lovettsville.
18 – 19	Marched again
July 20	Marched to Union into Camp, near Goose creek.
July 21	We have rest
July 22	Fr. Rectortown. in Camp
July 23	Marched through Manassas Gap, and reached the Enemy in the Evening.
July 24	Lost sight of the rebels, we skirmish through the woods for miles but find no Rebels.
July 25	Marched again toward Warrenton, passed Orleans and rested till afternoon. Marched again and rested.
July 27	Came into the neighborhood of the Rappahannock.

July 28	Moved Camp again 1 mile to the rear for want of Water. Went on Picket till
July 29	When we were relieved, more rain.
July 31	Had inspection
Aug. 1	Moved Camp again
Aug. 3	Marched and moved Camp, broke up Camp the same day again and marched again till 2 oCl A.M. when we rested on Franklin Farm
Aug. 6	Thanksgiving day. Attended meeting.
Aug. 7	Signed Payrolls.
Aug. 8	Marched again to Rap. Station
Aug. 9	Got paid of $26.00
Aug. 10	We had Drill. Weather warm
Aug. 11	Moved camp again
Aug. 17	Marching Order. Dress parade and –
Aug. 19	The Regiments while at Dress parade were ordered to fall in, and after packing up and marching a few hundred yds, we went back to Camp.
Aug. 21	On Picket
Aug. 23	On Picket
Aug. 28	Grand Sword presentation.
Aug. 29	Execution of 5 Union Soldiers by Death. To Wit. Chas. Walter. Emil Lay [Lai]. Jno. Ranasse [Gion Reanese]. G [George] Kuhn Jno. [Gion] Folany. All are of the 118 Pa. Vol.
Aug. 30	Fair Weather Inspection
Sept. 1–10	Fair and nothing new.
Sept. 14	On Picket
Sept. 15	Sign Payrolls, Marching Orders
Sept. 16	March again, crossed the river, and passed Brandy Station,
Sept. 17	Got to Culpeper and got paid off
Sept. 18	Rain
Sept. 19	Inspection
Sept 20–21	Cold and drill
Sept. 28	Review by Genl. Meade
Sept. 29	Review and Inspection by Brigade.

Sept. 30	Picket. We lost one man killed by Guerillas, and we killed one of them.
Oct. 1–3	Rain
Oct. 9	Review by Brigade and Division
Oct. 10	Marching Orders We march at 2 oCl A.M. to the Rapidan to support the 6 Corps went back to Camp, put up our tents and left in the morning again.
Oct. 11	The whole Army falls back, and our Corps are rear guard, we march back cross the Rappahannock, into our old Camp.
Oct. 12	We march again, cross the river, drive the rebels before us, and go as far as Brandy Station, laid there till 12 oCl night, fall back again across the river, to our old Camp.
Oct. 13	We march to Catlet Station.
Oct. 14	We still march, to Kettle Run, here we rested, made Coffee &c. As we rested the rebels opened a Battery on us, Killing 18 of our men. The 2nd Corps being within our supporting distance, pitched in, flogged then complete, took 400 prisoners, took the Battery of 6 guns and drove them away. We fell back to Manassas, but went back again to support the 2nd Corps. We crossed Bull run in the night, and camped near Centreville
Oct. 15	Marched to Fairfax.
Oct. 16	On picket, was on picket two hours in a hard rain, when we got orders to move again, the mud was knee deep. Marched at night near Centreville
Oct. 18	Marched again back to Fairfax then back to Centreville again, and crossed Bull run to the Battlefield where we camped the night
Oct. 20	At 1 oCl A.M. we moved again along the Warrenton pike, and passed through Mechanicsville.
Oct. 21	We rested.
Oct. 22	" " " "
Oct. 23	Moved our Camp. Rain
Oct. 24	Rain. March Orders. And at dark we leave camp, move to Auburn, where we lay all night on piles of Stones.
Oct. 25	We move Camp again.

Oct 26 – 29	Rest
Oct. 30	Move to 3 Mile Station
Oct. 31	Mustered and Rain.
Nov. 1	Rest and frost
Nov. 2	Review by Genl. Crawford.
Nov. 7	Marched to Rap. Station took position in line of Battle, toward dark we pushed forward, but did not get into the fire.
Nov. 8	We marched to Kelly ford. Crossed to river, and went on picket. Took possession of Rebel Shanties.
Nov. 9	Co. B. guarded rebel House.
Nov. 10	Altered the picket line.
Nov. 14	Signed Payroll.
Nov. 15	Got paid. Marching Orders. Sub. and gave $1.00 for Widow Epple[8] and Riemenschneider[9]
Nov. 17 – 18	Brig. Drill. fair Weather.
Nov. 19	Rain and mud
Nov. 22	Inspection
Nov. 23	March Order
Nov. 24	5 oCl am we move to cross the Rapidan but it rains so hard that we are obliged to return to Camp.
Nov. 26	We march again, and cross the Rapidan at Culpeper Ford
Nov. 27	We have a Skirmish. We lay in line as Skirmishers, when the rebels open a Battery on us, doing no damage however, only a slight tap on the leg which I get.
Nov. 28	We fall back rain all day hard
Nov. 29	Pass by Roberts Tavern and took our place in front.
Nov. 30	2 oCl A.M. we move without knapsacks to the right wing to storm the rebel rifle pits. Bitter cold we enter a piece of woods, are not allowed to make fire. One of the 6th Regt. freezes to death. Same night we fall back to Camp.

---

8. Sergeant Florian Epple had been reported as missing in action at Charles City Cross Roads (Glendale) on July 30, 1862.
9. Private Conrad Riemenschneider was killed in action at Second Manassas.

Dec. 1	We relieve the first Corps, and at dark we fall back also.
Dec. 2	3 oCl A.M. we cross the Rapidan and get 2 hours rest. We march till night and camp.
Dec. 3	Next morning we march again, and cross the Rappahannock while the other Corps go into their old Quarters.
Dec. 4	Move to Bristow Station
Dec. 5	To Manassas Junction. Same Ev. back to Warrenton Junction and back toward morning.
Dec. 6	We build Winter quarters.
Dec. 7	On R.R. picket
Dec. 8	releived
Dec. 26	March again back to Bull run, several of our men Killed on the railroad. We relieve the Bucktails.
Dec. 27	We have to build Winter quarters again. Here we guard the Rail Road.
Dec. 28	Great many of our men reinlist, from our Co. B no less than 8 men enlist again.

1864

Jany. 1	We have a good roast Beef in our Mess. Cold weather, but still no snow.
Jany. 2 – 3	Cold and stormy
Jany. 4	Today Snow falls rapidly, commencing at 9 oCl A.M. Co. B. goes on picket, we are short of rations, not having had any for 3 days. Draw rations in the evening.
Jany. 5	Relieved off picket. Snow and rain. We hunt rabbit today
Jany. 6	On Guard. More snow, we go out on a hunt and bring home Partriges.
Jany. 7	Snow and rain. Freezing
Jany. 8	Wash day.
Jany. 9	Furloughs granted to veterans Eiffler, Kimpel, Solomon, Weber, Werner and Reinehr of Co. B for 35 day[10]. They leave Camp for the

---

10. All of these men had initially enlisted later than May 1861, when the company was formed; all transferred in early May 1864 to the 190th Regiment, Pennsylvania Volunteers. It would not be unreasonable to conclude that the furloughs may have been a recompense for their reenlisting.

	Cars at 2 oCl P.M. This is the coldest day and night of the season. Orders issued to prohibit gaming, also picket day as well as night.
Jany. 10	General mending day, but no Thread. Weather fine and cold.
Jany. 11	Weather fine. Rec. Letter from home of Jany 7
Jany. 12	Weather fine. On fatigue at Brig. H Quar. Sent Letter home.
Jany. 13	Weather fine and warm snow melting. ~~Receive Letter from H. Boertzler~~.
Jany. 14	N. Koleman [Kohlman] leaves on 35 days furlough. Weather fine, and warm. Social Tete-a-Tete at our Quarters. Capt. F. Lieut. B[11] and Capt. W [Winans] of Co. H. present.
Jany. 15	On Picket duty. I get an overcoat from Reg. for a pr. of pants. Weather quite warm.
Jany. 16	Relieved from picket day by Co. A. We get our dress Coats from Alexandria. Maj. Barnes home on furlough, Capt. Ballentine comdg. Rgt.
Jany. 17	Sunday. Inspection of Quarters. report good.
Jany. 18	Genl. Inspection countermanded by reason of hard rain which set in during the night.
Jany. 19	On Guard. Today we have severe storm, the wind blowing hard and very cold. The Reserve Picket quarters are getting fixed up, so as to make it tenantable during the heavy rain. The trains were not running, probably on acct. of some damage done to the R. R.
Jany. 20	F. Schoal detached to Brig. Commissary as Guard
Jany. 21	Weather fine and fair. Officers to report at Brig. Headqs. in relation to the mustering out. Receive a letter from H. Boertzler.
Jany. 22	Commences to snow. Send letter to Boertzler.
Jany. 23	Made purchases at Brig. Comssy. [ ] on Fatigue. The 5th Rgt. goes to Alexandria, and 5 of our Cos. [companies] supply their place. Workman is detailed and leaves our mess. I make buckwheat cakes for supper.

---

11. This may be a reference to Charles Becker, who was promoted from sergeant to second lieutenant in August 1862 and to first lieutenant in April 1863.

Jany. 24	On Guard.
Jany. 25	Relieved off Guard.
Jany. 26	Nothing new.
Jany. 27	On Picket. Maj. Barnes returns from furlough.
Jany. 28	Relieved off Picket. Today we fell all the trees in and around the camp, and commence to dig rifle pits.
Jany. 29	Some Guerillas make their appearance near our Camp, Cos. B. and K. ordered out. They scout but return without having seen anything. Get Letter from home with Thread.
Jany. 30	Send Letter home. On Guard. Guerilla brought into Camp.
Jany. 31	Relieved off Guard. Cold rain. Co. B. goes on picket. Get Paper from Boertzler. on Fatigue.
Feby. 1	On Picket
Feby. 2	Relieved off Picket. Wash day and cleaning Quarters. We draw 6 days pork.
Feby. 3	On Fatigue and Train Guard. Go out to Bull Run for logs. Return safe. Genl. Crawford visits Camp. Today quite a storm prevails.
Feby. 4	Purchase at Brig. Commissary. Get some Tobacco and Segars [cigars] from home per [ ] Gift. Weather fine.
Feby. 5	Nothing important save that Maj. B. gets relieved of his command[12], and the Lt. Col. of the 1st Regt. takes command.
Feby. 6	On Picket. Heavy Artillery firing heard all day in the direction of the Rapidan.
Feby. 7	Relieved from Picket. Get Letter and Thread from home. The Letters of the 3rd inst.
Feby. 8 – 9	Nothing new. Inspection of Camp and Quarters. On Fatigue.
Feby. 10	Cold. On Train Guard to Bristow. Send Letter and signal flag home.
Feby. 11	Nothing New
Feby. 12	Two of the 10th Regt. captured by Guerilla and a sergeant of Co. K. Killed.

---

12. This is likely a reference to Captain James Ballentine, who served as a brevet major and commanded the 9th Regiment briefly in 1864.

Feby. 13	On Picket.
Feby. 14	Releived off Picket. Wash day. great storm all day.
Feby. 15	Wash day. Maj. Larimer of the 5th Rgt. Killed by Guerillas, our Calvary on persuit, but supposed to be fruitless.
Feby. 16	On fatigue at Brig. Commissary
Feby. 17	Nothing important. Very cold/
Feby. 18	Veterans Reinehr, Kimpel, Solomon, Eiffler, and Werner get back to Regt.[13]
Feby. 19	On Guard. Capt. F. Tent burns down.
Feby. 20	Draw 5 rations, we improve our Bread depository by sinking a Box.
Feby. 21	On picket. "Lincoln" visits the front
Feby. 22	Releived off picket. Get Letter from Boertzler.
Feby. 23	Sent Letter to Boertzler, also a profile. Mustering out rolls are brought to us. Today we begin to make rifle pits. Capt. Ballentine takes a squad out scouting. Get Letter from home and one from Wm. Howenstein. Veteran N. Kohlman arrive at Camp from furlough. Warm cloudy at night
Feby. 24	Sent Letter to Howenstein mentioned the pipe in it. part of the Regt. goes to Bull Run to fix up graves, and bring in the remains of some of our fallen ones.
Feby. 25	On Guard. We have regular Guard mounting. another detachment of six men of our Regt. are made to Brig. HQrs.
Feby. 26	Releived off Guard. Today we have severe Storm, the wind blowing furiously, and the grass all around the neighborhood on fire. I write a brief history of Co. B. for Genl. Crawford.
Feby. 27	On Fatigue. today we tear down the Quarters of Co. I and K and clean the Camp in general. Lieut. B. comes back to Co. again.
Feby. 28	Rec. marching Orders at 4 oCl A.M. to take the R. R. for the front. we pack up and are ready and move to R. R. and after lying there a short time, we march back to Camp.

---

13. Of the seven veterans whom Elsesser names as departing on furloughs, he only reports six as having returned. He did not comment on the return of John Weber, whom Bates reports as having deserted, date unknown.

Feby. 29	On picket. Paymaster on hand and pays $26. Mustering day. Toward Evg. it rains cold and snows, and continues all night. Cold and wet. F. Schoal returns to Regt.
March 1	Rain and hail
March 2	Nothing important
March 3	On Guard
March 4	Releived off guard
March 6	Nothing new
March 7	Send Letter with $3 home for Children and give Lieut. $15 for Wife
March 8	On picket. Lieut. B. goes home on furlough.
March 9	Releived off Picket. Get Letter from C. Gshwend
March 10	Wash day. Today it rains all day. I make out application and furlough for Schoal.
March 11	On Guard at Camp. Get Letter from Howenstein it rains hard all day. 2 of Co. K get captured by the guerillas. Jackson and Caldwell.
March 12	Releived from Guard. Send Letter with 30 cts. to F.C. Bowen Box 220 Boston for Microscope.[14] Send Letter home with 20 cts. for Post. Stamps and two Photo. of Meade and Ord
March 13–14	Nothing new. Snow
March 15	Get Letter from home. money all right. same day Send Letter home advise wife to Exchange for 55 pr. ct.
March 16	On Picket
March 17	Releived from Picket. Genl. Inspection at 2 oCl P.M.
March 18	On Guard. As we expected a Calvary raid we strengthen the line of picket and Guard. Orders rec. at midnight to be ready for march at daybreak.
March 19	Regiment fall in and stack arms, we are kept in duty 24 hours longer. Get Microscope from Bowen. Boston
March 20	Releived off Guard. today we post Cav. Pickets and Inf. pickets on the opposite of the R.Road. Regt. under arms from 7 oCl am. Get Letter

---

14. F. C. Bowen advertised a microscope for sale that would magnify "small objects 500 times." One such ad appeared in the February 27 and March 4, 1864, issues of *Harper's Weekly*, shortly before Elsesser placed his order.

	from little Mary. Send Letter to little Mary. Capt. F. moves his Quarters to the one usually occupied by Major B. Lieut. B. returns to furlough. cold and windy.
March 21	On Wood Guard for Brig. Commissary. Today it is very cold and windy. At night it commences to snow and continues all night.
March 22	Snow deep and cold
March 23	Nothing new
March 24	On Picket. Get Letter from home.
March 25	Relieved off picket. Snow disappearing fast. send Letter home.
March 26	On picket
March 27	Easter Sunday. Relieved from picket.
March 28	Wrote Letter to Gschwend with [drawing of skull] Photograph. On picket. Got Pocket handkerchief from home.
March 29	Relieved off picket. Col. Snodgrass comes back. It rains all afternoon and night. Great many troops pass to the front, among them is the 3d Div. 6 Corps. and some heavy Artillery, great storm during the night.
March 30	On picket. Snow all day and high wind.
April 1	On Fatigue. today we had a bright morning, the sun being out early, but after noon it commenced to rain, and continued all day. Troops are still going home on a 35 day furlough.
April 2	Rain and snow, all day. Outposts taken in through the day. Genl. mending day. Orders for Co. B. to be Reserve Guard for tomorrow.
April 3	Co. B. on Reserve Guard.
April 4	Relieved off Guard. Today it rains all day again. Send Letter home, for some [ ].
April 5	On Picket. Rain all day and night.
April 6	Relieved from Picket. this morning it clears off.
April 7	On Out Post. Weather cloudy but no rain. clears up toward evening. Moderate
April 8	Relieved off Out Post by Co. C. Weather fair with prospect of continued fine weather.
April 9	On Guard "Camp" Today it rains again, having commenced during the night. We draw clothing, rains all night hard.

April 10	Releived off C. Guard. During last night, the creeks and runs has swollen to such extent that many of the R. R. bridges were swept away, among them the Bull Run bridge, causing a stoppage of Trains and Mail. Today the weather has been fair, but still there are indications of more rain. We have it rumored, that Orders have been issued that all surplus Baggage be sent to the rear, but no credit seems to be given to the report. Today Sunday is turned to Washing day. Orders have been issued for all Sutlers to leave the Army. What next?
April 11	On R. R. Guard.
April 12	On R. R. Guard. (rape) committed by [ ] of Co. E upon a helpless Girl, arrested and put under arrest.
April 13	Releived. Today was confronted by the Girl, and those who were with her at the time, He is identified.
April 14	Today he is sent away heavily ironed. We have Dress Parade at [ ] oCl P.M..
April 15	On Camp Guard. Last night our Guard fired upon three supposed Guerillas, but unfortunately did not "drop" them. Weather fair and warm, but still an indication for a change of wet. Paymaster on hand, pays off $26. Two of the 10th Rgt. and one of the 13th cavy Killed last night by Guerillas. It commenced to rain in the Evening.
April 16	Releived off Guard. Got Letter from home. Sent Letter home with a ring, two photographs and an order for $20 on Recpt. after raining all night it brightens up this morning, we have general inspection at 10 oCl A.M., and we also pack all surplus clothing. I pack my Overcoat and Dress Coat to send to Gvrmt. Warehouse in Alexandria.
April 18	On fatigue. Exceeding fine weather. Sent Letter home with 3 photographs and 10 cts.
April 19	On Camp Guard. Fine weather and cool. The ravish is brought down to Camp, and placed in charge of our Guard, to be tried tomorrow.
April 20	Releived off Guard. Orders read in Dress Parade to have 4 Rolls Calls each day, and drill morning and afternoon. The Ravish Trial over, the prisoner taken back to Provost Guard. Weather fine in the forepart of the day, but cloudy toward night.

April 21	Nothing new
April 22	On picket. Fair weather. today I kill a large black snake, measuring 5 ft. 7 ½ inch.
April 24	Sunday. Inspection at 10 oCl A.M. Weather fair but turns cloudy towards night. Old [ ] Tent inspected and [ ]
April 25	On Guard at Bristow. Get marching orders with 3 day rations in haversack. This Evg. we subscribed a Petition for our Discharge it is to be sent to the U. S. Senate. Weather fair and warm. It is reported that we will be releived by the 9th Corps.
April 26	Genl. Meades Order concerning the expirate term of Regt. read at Dress parade, on which occation a new Flag is exhibited, and Maj. B. makes a speech in favor of the old one.
April 27	Today a passing Train on the R. Road takes fire, and two cars loadened with hay burn up. No Letter yet from home, we also have a Dress parade again. Day fair, but cloudy at Evg.
April 28	Sent Letter home with gold [ ] Evg. the 9th Corps under Burnside [page torn] among them a colored [page torn] [T]he order for the 5th Regt. to join us was today countermanded.
April 29	We are releived by "[N s]" at 8 oCl A.M. and march to Warrenton Junction Va.[15] where we arrive at 7 oCl P.M. Got Letter from home.
April 30	March again at day break and march till 5 oCl P.M.. Men in low spirits. Order came into Camp, to the affect that we will get discharged on the 15. but it does not create satisfaction.
May 1	Inspection at oCl A.M. We camp near Culpeper. Tonight it rains.
May 2	Weather fair
May 3	Send Letter home. Get orders to go home.
May 4	March at 3 oCl A.M. to Brandy Station. Take the R. R for Alexandria, arrive at Alexandria at 7 oCl P.M. Take supper at Soldiers Rest. Take the Cars for Washington, arrive at Washington at 12 oCl at night,

---

15. This may be a reference to General Edward Ferrero's 4th Division, consisting entirely of Black troops, in Burnside's IX Corps.

lay at Soldiers Rest till next morning at 9 oCl when we again take the Cars and arrive at Baltimore at 1 oCl. Take [ ] and march to Station. Take the Cars again arrive at Pittsburgh and put in at the U. S. Barracks in Second Street next day. Go home night at 10 oCl P.M. Mustered out Pittsburgh on the 12th 1864.

BIBLIOGRAPHY
BOOKS AND ARTICLES

Acken, J. Gregory, ed. *Inside the Army of the Potomac: The Civil War Experience of Captain Francis Adams Donaldson*. Stackpole Book, 1998.

Allardice, Bruce. *Confederate Colonels: A Biographical Register*. University of Missouri Press, 2008.

Andrew, Rod, Jr. *Wade Hampton: Confederate Warrior to Southern Redeemer*. University of North Carolina Press, 2008.

Barrett, Faith. *To Fight Aloud is Very Brave: American Poetry and the Civil War*. University of Massachusetts Press, 2012.

Bates, Samuel P. *History of the Pennsylvania Volunteers, 1861-1865*. Vol. 1. Harrisburg, PA: Singerly, State Printer, 1869.

Bearss, Edwin C. *Fields of Honor: Pivotal Battles of the Civil War*. National Geographic, 2006.

Bennett, William W. *The Great Revival*. Philadelphia, PA: Claxton, Remsen & Haffelfinger, 1877.

Bigelow, John, Jr. *The Campaign of Chancellorsville*. Yale University Press, 1910.

Blackman, E. V. *Miami and Dade County, Florida: Its Settlement, Progress and Achievement*. Victor Rainbolt, 1921.

[Boykin, Samuel]. *History of The Baptist Denomination in Georgia: With Biographical Compendium and Portrait Gallery of Baptist Ministers and Other Georgia Baptists*. Atlanta, GA: J. P. Harrison, 1881.

Bradwell, G. "Spotsylvania, May 12, 13, 1864," *Confederate Veteran* 28 (March 1920): 102-103.

Brinsfield, John Wesley, Jr. *The Spirit Divided: Memoirs of Civil War Chaplains: The Confederacy*. Mercer University Press, 2006.

Broadwater, Robert B. *Civil War Special Forces: The Elite and Distinct Fighting Units of the Union and Confederate Armies*. Praeger, 2014.

Brock, R. A., ed., *Southern Historical Society Papers*. Vol. 15, *Paroles of the Army of Northern Virginia*. Richmond, VA: Southern Historical Society, 1887.

Bryan, T. Conn, ed. "Letters of Two Confederate Officers: William Thomas Conn and Charles Augustus Conn." *Georgia Historical Quarterly* 46 (1962): 169-189.

Burnes, Stanley B. "Civil War Disease and Wound Infection." PBS Learning Media Background Essay, accessed July 10, 2020, https://mpt.pbslearningmedial.org.

Burton, Brian K. *Extraordinary Circumstances: The Seven Days Battles*. Indiana University Press, 2001.

------*The Peninsula & Seven Days: A Battlefield Guide*. 2007. University of Nebraska Press, 2007.

Busey, John W. and Travis W. Busey. *Confederate Casualties at Gettysburg: A Comprehensive Record*. McFarland, 2016.

Butler, John Campbell. *Historical Record of Macon and Central Georgia*. Macon, GA: J. W. Burke, 1879.

Caldwell, J. F. J. *The History of a Brigade of South Carolinians*. Philadelphia, PA: King & Baird, 1866.

Carmichael, Peter S. *Lee's Young Artillerist: William R. J. Pegram*. University of Virginia, 1995.

-------"We Respect a *Good* Soldier, No Matter What Flag He Fought Under: The 15th New Jersey Remembers Spotsylvania." In Gary W. Gallagher, ed., *The Spotsylvania Campaign*. University of North Carolina Press, 1998.

[Carrigan, Joseph G.] *Cheat Mountain; or Unwritten Chapter of the Late War, by a member of the Bar*. Fayetteville, TN: Albert B. Tavel, 1885.

Christ, Elwood. *"Over a Wide, Hot... Crimson Plain": The Struggle for the Bliss Farm at Gettysburg, July 2nd and 3rd, 1863*. Savas Beatie, 2022.

Citron, Joel D. *Confederate Prisoners at Fort Delaware: The Legend of Mistreatment Reexamined*. McFarland, 2018.

Cloyd, Benjamin G. *Haunted by Atrocity: Civil War Prisons in American Memory*. Louisiana State Press, 2010.

Cohen, Stan. *The Civil War in West Virginia: A Pictorial History*. Quarrier Press, 1999.

Cole, Gary C. *Three Hundred and Sixty Six Days at Fort Delaware*. Trafford, 2017.

Cometti Elizabeth, ed. "Excerpts from Swann's 'Prison Life at Fort Delaware," West Virginia Department of Arts, Culture, and History, *West Virginia History* 2 (January 1941): 120-141 and (April 1941): 217-230, http://www.wvculture.org/history/journal_wvh/wvh2-1.html.

Commager, Henry Steele. *The Blue and the Gray*. Bobbs-Merrill, 1950.

Connery, William S. *Civil War: Northern Virginia 1861*. History Press, 2011.

Cox, Richard P. *Civil War Maryland: Stories from the Old Line State*. History Press, 2008.

Crenshaw, Doug. *The Battle of Glendale: R. E. Lee's Lost Opportunity*. History Press, 2017.

------*Richmond Shall Not Be Given Up, The Seven Days' Battles, June 25-July 1, 1862*. Savas Beatie, 2017.

Cropley, Thomas G. "Dermatology and Skin Disease in the American Civil War," *Dermatology Nursing* 1 (February 2008): 29-33.

Culbertson Charles. *The Staunton, Virginia Anthology*. Clarion Publishing, 2013.

Cunningham, H. H. *Doctors in Gray: The Confederate Military Service*. Louisiana State University Press, 1986.

Cunningham, L. D. *A History of Florida Baptist's Sunday School: Facts, Stories, Legends and Dreams*. n.p. 2005.

Cushing, Thomas, ed. *A Genealogical and Biographical History of Allegheny County, Pennsylvania*. Reprint, Genealogical Publishing, 1975.

Davis, James A. *Music Along the Rapidan: Civil War Soldiers, Music, and Community during Winter Quarters, Virginia*. University of Nebraska Press, 2014.

Davis, William C. *Lincoln's Men: How President Lincoln Became Father to an Army and a Nation*. Free Press, 1999.

Dew, Charles. *Ironmaker to the Confederacy: Joseph R. Anderson and the Tredegar Iron Works*. Yale University Press, 1966.

Donnelly, Caitlin. "Looking Back: The Civil War Adventures of Birmingham's John Bigelow." *Birmingham-Bloomfield Eagle*, May 12, 2018. https://www.candgnews.com/news/looking-back-the-civil-war-adventures-of-birminghams-john-bigelow-107038.

Dowdey, Clifford. *Lee*. Stan Clark Military Books, 1991.

------*Lee's Last Campaign: The Story of Lee and his Men against Grant – 1864*. Skyhorse, 2011.

------*The Seven Days: The Emergence of Robert E. Lee*. Fairfax House, 1964.

Dowdey, Clifford and Louis H. Manarin, ed. *The Wartime Papers of R. E. Lee*. Bramhall House, 1961.

Dyer, Frederick H. *A Compendium of the War of the Rebellion*. Dyer Publishing, 1908.

Early, Jubal A. *Memoirs: Autobiographical Sketch and Narrative of the War Between the States*. Konecky & Konecky, 1994.

Eicher, David J. *The Longest Night: A Military History of the Civil War*. Simon & Schuster, 2001.

Ent, Uzal W. *The Pennsylvania Reserves in the Civil War: A Comprehensive History*. McFarland, 2012.

Faust, Drew Gilpin. "Christian Soldiers: The Meaning of Revivalism in the Confederate Army." *Journal of Southern History* 53, no. 1 (Feb. 1987): 63-90.

-------*This Republic of Suffering: Death and the American Civil War*. Vintage, 2008.

Fetzer, Dale and Bruce Mowday. *Unlikely Allies: Fort Delaware's Prison Community in the Civil War*. Stackpole Books, 2000.

Folsom, James M. *Heroes and Martyrs of Georgia: Georgia's Record in the Revolution of 1861*. Macon, GA: Burke, Boykin, 1864.

Foote, Shelby. *The Civil War: A Narrative*. Vol. 3. *Red River to Appomattox*. Random House, 1974.

Fox, John J., III. *Red Clay to Richmond: Trail of the 35th Georgia Infantry Regiment, C.S.A.*, Angle Valley Press, 2006.

Frassanito, William A. *Grant and Lee: The Virginia Campaigns, 1864-1865.* Charles Scribner's Sons, 1983.

Freeman, Douglas Southall. *Lee: An Abridgement in one volume by Richard Harwell of the four-volume R. E. Lee.* Simon & Schuster, 1991.

------*R. E. Lee: A Biography.* 4 vols. Charles Scribner's Sons, 1934.

------*Lee's Lieutenants: A Study in Command.* 3 vols. Scribner, 1970.

Gallaher, Gary W., ed. *The Spotsylvania Campaign.* University of North Carolina Press, 1998.

Gerard, Philip. "Deserters and Outliers," *Our State,* Jan. 29, 2014. https://www.ourstate.com/deserters-outliers/

Gilchrist, Michael R. "Disease & Infection in the American Civil War," *The American Biology Teacher* 60 no. 4 (1998), 258-262.

Gillespie, James M. *Andersonvilles of the North: The Myths and Realities of Northern Treatment of Civil War Confederate Prisoners.* University of North Texas Press, 2008.

Gillum, Jamie. *History of the Sixteenth Tennessee Volunteer Infantry Regiment in the American Civil War, Vol. 1, We Were Spoiling for a Fight, April 1861-August 1862.* Spring Hill, TN: CreateSpace Independent Publishing Platform, 2011.

Glatthaar, Joseph T. *General Lee's Army: From Victory to Collapse.* Free Press, 2008.

Gourley, Bruce T. *Diverging Loyalties: Baptists in Middle Georgia During the Civil War.* Mercer University Press, 2011.

Gottfried, Bradley M. *Brigades of Gettysburg: The Union and Confederate Brigades at the Battle of Gettysburg.* Skyhorse, 2012.

------"Fisher's Brigade at Gettysburg: The Big Round Top Controversy." *Gettysburg Magazine* 19 (1998): 84-93.

------*Lee Invades the North: A Comparison of the Antietam and Gettysburg Campaigns.* Turning Point Publications, 2022.

------*The Maps of Antietam.* Savas Beatie, 2020.

-------*The Maps of Gettysburg.* Savas Beatie, 2007.

------*The Maps of the Wilderness.* Savas Beatie, 2016.

------*The Maps of Spotsylvania through Cold Harbor.* Savas Beatie, 2023.

Gray, Michael P. *The Business of Captivity: Elmira and Its Civil War Prison.* Kent State University Press, 2001.

Grubbs, Lillie Martin. *History of Worth County, Georgia, for the First Eighty Years, 1854-1934.* J. W. Burke, 1934.

Hall, Mary T. "The Civil War Diaries of Private George Washington Hall, 14th Georgia Infantry." *Fort Delaware Notes* 69 (February 1919): 15-21.

-------"George Washington Hall – a.k.a. "Uncle Hall" – Florida Baptists' First Sunday School Evangelist to Children." *Journal of Florida Baptist Heritage* 24 (2022): 58-68.

-------"'Taking the cars' at Staunton: The Civil War Experiences of George Washington Hall." *Augusta Historical Bulletin* 57 (2021):43-58.

Hamilton, J. G. de Roulac. "The Prison Experiences of Randolph Shotwell: II. Fort Delaware." *North Carolina Historical Review* 2, no. 3 (July 1925): 332-350.

Handy, Isaac W. K. *United States Bonds or Duress by Federal Authority: A Journal of Current Events During an Imprisonment of Fifteen Months, at Fort Delaware.* Baltimore: Turnbull Brothers, 1874.

Hardy, Michael C. *General Lee's Immortals: The Battles and Campaigns of the Branch-Lane Brigade in the Army of Northern Virginia, 1861-1865.* Savas Beatie, 2018.

Harman, Troy D. "The Great Revival of 1863: The Effects upon Lee's Army of Northern Virginia." *The American Civil War in 1863: Programs of the Eighth Annual Gettysburg National Military Park Seminar.* National Park Service, 2001. https://npshistory.com/series/symposia/gettysburg_seminars/8/essay5/pdf

Harrison, Noel G. "Belle Plain and 'The Punch Bowl' in 1864: A Research Report from Virginia." *Military Images* 22, no. 1 (July-August 2000): 20-29.

Hartwig, D. Scott. "'Never Have I Seen Such a Charge: Pender's Light Division at Gettysburg, July 1." *High Water Mark: The Army of Northern Virginia in the Gettysburg Campaign: Programs of the Seventh Annual Gettysburg Seminar.* National Park Service, 1999. http://npshistory.com/series/symposia/gettysburg_seminars/7/essay3.pdf

Haynes, Draughton Stith. *Field Diary of a Confederate Soldier.* The Ashantilly Press, 1963.

Henderson, Lillian. *Roster of the Confederate Soldiers of Georgia, 1861-1865.* Vol. 2. Longino & Porter, 1959.

Hepburn, Donald S. and E. Earl Joiner. *Favored Florida: A History of Florida Baptists.* Vol. 1, *1784-1939.* Florida Baptist Convention, 2013.

Hess, Earl J. *Field Armies and Fortifications in the Civil War: The Eastern Campaigns, 1861-1864.* University of North Carolina Press, 2005.

------*Pickett's Charge: The Last Attack at Gettysburg.* University of North Carolina Press, 2001.

------*The Rifle Musket in Civil War Combat: Reality and Myth.* University Press of Kansas, 2008.

------*Trench Warfare under Grant & Lee: Field Fortifications in the Overland Campaign.* University of North Carolina Press, 2007.

Hesseltine, William Best. *Civil War Prisons: A Study in War Psychology.* Frederick Ungar, 1930.

Hessler, James A. and Wayne E. Motts. *Pickett's Charge at Gettysburg: A Guide to the Most Famous Attack in American History.* Savas Beatie, 2015.

Hewitt, Lawrence Lee, ed., Thomas E. Schott, and Marc Kunis. *To Succeed or Perish: The Diaries of Sergeant Edmund Trent Eggleston, 1st Mississippi Light Artillery Regiment, CSA.* University of Tennessee Press, 2015.

Holland, Lynwood M. "Georgia Military Institute: The West Point of Georgia: 1851-1854," *The Georgia Historical Quarterly* 13, no. 3 (September 1959): 225-247.

Howard, McHenry. *Recollections of a Maryland Confederate Soldier and Staff Officer under Johnston, Jackson and Lee.* Williams & Wilkins, 1914.

Irvine W. T. "Old 35th Georgia," *Atlanta Sunny South*, May 2, 1891.

Jones, J. Wm. *Christ in the Camp: Religion in Lee's Army*. Richmond, VA: B. F. Johnson, 1887.

------*Army of Northern Virginia Memorial Volume*. Richmond: J. W. Randolph & English, 1880.

Johnson, Robert Underwood and C. C. Buel, ed. *Battles and Leaders of the Civil War: Being for the Most Part Contributions by Union and Confederate Officers*. 4 vols. Reprint. Thomas Yoseloff, 1956.

Keegan, John. *The American Civil War: A Military History*. New York: Alfred A. Knopf, 2009.

-----*Fields of Battles: The Wars for North America*. Alfred A Knopf, 1996.

Konstam, Angus. *Seven Days Battles 1862: Lee's Defense of Richmond*. Praeger, 2004.

Korda, Michael. *Clouds of Glory: The Life and Legend of Robert E. Lee*. Harper, 2014.

Krakow, Kenneth. *Georgia Place-Names: Their History and Origins*. Winship Press, 1975.

Krick, Robert K. "An Insurmountable Barrier between the Army and Ruin: The Confederate Experience at Spotsylvania's Bloody Angle." In Gary W. Gallagher, ed., *The Spotsylvania Campaign*. University of North Carolina Press, 1998.

-------*Civil War Weather in Virginia*. University of Alabama Press, 2007.

------*Lee's Colonels: A Biographical Register of the Field Officers of the Army of Northern Virginia*, 5th ed. B Broadfoot Publishing, 2009.

------*Stonewall Jackson at Cedar Mountain*. University of North Carolina Press, 1990.

Kurtz, Wilbur G., Jr., "The First Regiment of Georgia Volunteers in the Mexican War," *Georgia Historical Quarterly* 27, no. 2 (December 1943): 301-323.

Lee, Laura M. and Brendan Mackie. *Fort Delaware*. Charleston, SC: 2010.

Lesser, W. Hunter. *The First Campaign: A Guide to the Civil War in the Mountains of West Virginia, 1861*. Quarrier Press, 2011.

-------*Rebels at the Gate: Lee and McClellan on the Front Line of a Nation Divided*. Sourcebooks, 2004.

Levin, Kevin M. "'They Met Their Fate without a Sigh': An Analysis of Confederate Military Executions." In *Upon the Field of Battle: Essays on the Military History of America's Civil War*, edited by Andrew S. Bledsoe and Andrew F. Lang. Louisiana State University Press, 2018.

Longacre, Edward G. *Gentleman and Soldier: A Biography of Wade Hampton*. Rutledge Hill Press, 2003.

Longstreet, James. *From Manassas to Appomattox*. Konecky & Konecky, 1992.

Lonn, Ella. *Desertion during the Civil War*. University of Nebraska Press, 1998.

Lowe, Jeffrey C. and Sam Hodges, ed. *Letters to Amanda: The Civil War Letters of Marion Hill Fitzpatrick, Army of Northern Virginia*. Mercer University Press, 1998.

Mackowski, Chris. *Strike Them A Blow: Battle Along the North Anna River, May 21-16, 1864*. Savas Beatie, 2015.

------"The Turning Point of the War: The Wilderness, not Gettysburg." *Emerging Civil War* (blog) July 4, 2013. Accessed July 25, 2020. https://emergingcivilwar.com/2013/07/04/the-turning-point-of-the-war-the-wilderness-not-gettysburg/

Mackowski, Chris and Kristopher D. White. *A Season of Slaughter: The Battle of Spotsylvania Court House, May 8-21, 1864*. Savas Beatie, 2013.

------*The Furious Struggle: Chancellorsville and the High Tide of the Confederacy, May 1-4, 1863*. Savas Beatie, 2014.

Matter, William D. *If It Takes All Summer: The Battle of Spotsylvania*. University of North Carolina Press, 1988.

McArthur, Judith N. and Orville Vernon Burton. *A Gentleman and an Officer: A Military and Social History of James B. Griffin's Civil War*. Oxford University Press, 1996.

McCarthy, Molly. "Dear Diary." *New York Times Opinionator Blog*, Aug. 15, 2013. https://opinionator.blogs.nytimes.com/2013/08/15/dear-diary/?_r=0

McGuire, Samuel B. "Desertion." *The Civil War in Georgia: A New Georgia Encyclopedia Companion*. University of Georgia Press, 2011.

McPherson, James M. *The Atlas of the Civil War*. Skyhorse, 2022.

------*Battle Cry of Freedom*. Oxford University Press, 1988.

------*Crossroads of Freedom: Antietam*. Oxford University Press, 2002.

McWhiney, Grady and Perry D. Jamieson. *Attack and Die: Civil War Military Tactics and the Southern Heritage*. University of Alabama Press, 1982.

Meier, Kathryn Shively. "The Man Who Has Nothing to Lose." In *The Blue, the Gray, and the Green*, edited by Brian Allen Drake. University of Georgia Press, 2015.

------*Nature's Civil War: Common Soldiers and the Environment in 1862 Virginia*. University of North Carolina Press, 2013.

Miller, William J. *Mapping for Stonewall: The Civil War Service of Jed Hotchkiss*. Ellott & Clark, 1993.

Mills, George H. 1902. *History of the Sixteenth North Carolina Regiment in the Civil War*. Rutherfordton, NC: n.p., 1902.

Moon, William H. "Prison Life at Fort Delaware." *Confederate Veteran* 15 (May 1907): 212-214.

Moore, George Ellis. *A Banner in the Hills: West Virginia's Statehood*. Appleton-Century-Crofts, 1963.

Moore, Robert H. II. *Gibraltar of the Shenandoah: Civil War Sites and Stories of Staunton, Waynesboro, and August County, Virginia*. Donning, 2004.

Morrison, James L., Jr., ed., *The Memoirs of Henry Heth*. Greenwood Press, 1974.

Murray, Williamson and Wayne Wei-Siang Hsieh. *A Savage War: A Military History of the Civil War*. Princeton University Press, 2016.

National Park Service. "Guards Death Rate." Accessed Aug. 7, 2020. https://www.nps.gov/ande/learn/historyculture/guardsdeathrate.htm

Newell, Clayton R. *Lee vs. McClellan: The First Campaign*. Regnery, 2016.

Nichols, G. W. *A Soldier's Story of His Regiment (61st Georgia) and Incidentally of the Lawton-Gordon-Evans Brigade Army Northern Virginia*. Printed by author, 1898.

Noe, Kenneth W. *The Howling Storm: Weather, Climate, and the American Civil War*. Louisiana State University Press, 2020.

Noll, Arthur Howard, ed., *Doctor Quintard, Chaplain CSA*. Sewanee, TN: University Press, 1905.

O'Neal, Maston. *Prologue*. Printed by author, 1985.

O'Reilly, Francis (Frank) A. "Busted up and Gone to Hell": The Assault of the Pennsylvania Reserves at Fredericksburg." In *Blood on the Rappahannock: The Battle of Fredericksburg*, edited by Theodore P. Savas and David A. Woodbury, *Civil War Regiments: A Journal of the American Civil War*, Vol. 4, No. 4 (1995), 1-27.

------"Chancellorsville: The Generals' Battle." *Blue & Gray* 29 no. 4 (2012).

------"Chancellorsville: The Soldiers' Battle." *Blue & Gray* 29 no. 5 (2013).

------*The Fredericksburg Campaign: Winter War on the Rappahannock*, Louisiana Paperback ed. Louisiana State University Press, 2006.

Orrison, Robert and Dan Welch. *The Last Road North: A Guide to the Gettysburg Campaign, 1863*. Savas Beatie, 2016.

Osborne, Charles C. *Jubal: The Life and Times of General Jubal A. Early, CSA, Defender of the Lost Cause.* Louisiana State University Press, 1992.

Patterson, Gerard A. *From Blue to Gray: The Life of Confederate General Cadmus M. Wilcox*. Stackpole, 2001.

Perry, Adam H. "Reconsidering the Wilderness's Role in Battle, 4-6 May 1864," *Journal of Military History* 82 (April 2018): 413-438.

Petriello, David R. *Bacteria and Bayonets: The Impact of Disease in American Military History*. Casemate, 2016.

Phifer, Evan. "Reminiscences of an Exiled Marylander." *Military Images* 35 no. 4 (Autumn 2017): 68-70.

Pickenpaugh, Roger. *Captives in Gray: The Civil War Prisons of the Union*. University of Alabama Press, 2009.

Pippin, K. A. "Jewelry Making at Fort Delaware During the War Between the States," *Fort Delaware Notes* 40 (February 1990): 2-4.

Pocahontas County Historical Society, Inc. *History of Pocahontas County West Virginia 1981: Birthplace of Rivers*. Taylor, 1982.

Powell, William H. *The Fifth Army Corps (Army of the Potomac): A Record of Operations during the Civil War in the United States of America, 1861-1865*. New York: Putnam's Sons, 1896.

Pratt, Edwin A., *The Rise of Rail Power in War and Conquest, 1833-1914*. Lippincott, 1916.

Quincy, Samuel M. *History of the Second Massachusetts Regiment of Infantry: A Prisoner's Diary*. Boston: George H. Ellis, 1882.

Quint, Ryan T. "Ambrose Burnside, the Ninth Army Corps, and the Battle of Spotsylvania Court House," *The Gettysburg College Journal of the Civil War Era*: Vol. 5, Article 7 (2015).

Rable, George C. *God's Almost Chosen Peoples: A Religious History of the American Civil War*. University of North Carolina Press, 2010.

Rafuse, Ethan S. *Antietam, South Mountain & Harpers Ferry: A Battlefield Guide*. University of Nebraska Press, 2008.

Rasmussen, Chris and Jim Owston. "History of The Ninth Pennsylvania Reserve Corps." http://www.9thpareserves.org/Library11.htm. Accessed August 4, 2020.

Reardon, Carole and Tom Vossler. *A Field Guide to Gettysburg*, 2nd ed. University of North Carolina Press, 2017.

Pickett's Charge in History and Memory. University of North Carolina Press, 1997.

Reimer, Terry. "Smallpox and Vaccination in the Civil War," National Museum of Civil War Medicine. November 9, 2004. https://www.civilwarmed.org/surgeons-call/small_pox/.

Rhea, Gordon C. *Carrying the Flag: The Story of Private Charles Whilden, the Confederacy's Most Unlikely Hero*. Basic Books, 2004.

------- *The Battles for Spotsylvania Court House and the Road to Yellow Tavern, May 7-12, 1864*. Louisiana State University Press, 1997.

------ *The Battle of the Wilderness: May 5-6, 1864*. Louisiana State University Press, 1994.

------ Foreword to *Lee's Army During the Overland Campaign: A Numerical Study* by Alfred C. Young III. Louisiana State University Press, 2013.

Robertson, Jr. James I. *General A. P. Hill: The Story of a Confederate Warrior*. Random House, 1987.

------ *The Untold Civil War: Exploring the Human Side of the Civil War*. National Geographic, 2001.

------ "The Scourge of Elmira." In *Civil War Prisons*, edited by William B. Hesseltine. Kent State University Press, 1992.

Rogers, William Warren. "The Confederate Nation Reflected: Names of Georgia's Civil War Companies," *The Georgia Historical Quarterly* 93, No. 1 (Spring 2009): 77-85.

Rosenburg, R. B., ed. *For the Sake of My Country: The Diary of Col. W. W. Ward, 9th Tennessee Cavalry, Morgan's Brigade, C.S.A*. Southern Heritage, 1992.

Rollins, Richard. "The Second Wave of Pickett's Charge." *Gettysburg Magazine* 18 (1988): 96-113.

Royall, William L. *Some Reminiscences*. Neale Publishing Co., 1909.

Rumburg, H. Rondel. *George Boardman Taylor: Chaplain – Pastor – Missionary*. Appomattox, VA: SBSS, 2019.

Runge, William H. ed. *Four Years in the Confederate Artillery: The Diary of Private Henry Robinson Berkeley*. Virginia Historical Society, 1991.

Sartin, Jeffrey S. "Infectious Diseases during the Civil War: The Triumph of the 'Third Army,'" *Clinical Infectious Diseases* 16, no. 4 (1993), 580-584.

Savage, John. *The Life of John H. Savage.* Nashville, TN: 1903.

Scott, Carole E. "The Butts County Boys' War: The Stories of Benjamin Lewis McGough and John Oliver Andrews." Accessed July 19, 2020. https://sites.rootsweb.com/~cescott.butts.html.

Scott, Joseph C. "The Infernal Balloon: Union Aeronautics During the American Civil War," *Army History*, No. 93 (Fall 2014): 6-27.

Sears, Stephen W. *Chancellorsville.* Houghton Mifflin, 1996.

------ *Gettysburg.* Houghton Mifflin, 2004.

------ *Landscape Turned Red.* Houghton Mifflin, 1983.

------ *To the Gates of Richmond: The Peninsula Campaign.* Tichnor & Fields, 1992.

Shadburn, Don L., ed. *Crimson and Sabres: A Confederate Record of Forsyth County, Georgia.* McNaughton & Gunn, 1997.

Shattuck, Gardiner H., Jr. *A Shield and Hiding Place: The Religious Life of the Civil War Armies.* Mercer University Press, 1987.

Sheehan-Dean, A. "Desertion (Confederate) during the Civil War." *Encyclopedia Virginia.* http://www.EncyclopediaVirginia.org/Desertion_Confederate_during_the_Civil_War.

Simmons, R. Hugh. "A Confederate Prisoner's Experience in the New Barracks." *Fort Delaware Notes* LII (2002): 1-5.

------ "Parole & Exchange." *Fort Delaware Notes* LI (2001): 5-7.

------ "Prisoner of War Delivery Places on the James River in Virginia." *Fort Delaware Notes* LV (2005): 8-14.

Small, Abner R. *History of the Sixteenth Maine Regiment in the War of the Rebellion, 1861-1865.* Portland, ME: B. Thurston, 1886.

Smedlund, William S. *Camp Fires of Georgia's Troops: 1861-1865.* Kennesaw Mountain Press, 1994.

Smith, Gustavus Woodson. *The Battle of Seven Pines.* C. G. Crawford, 1891.

Smith, Dale C. "The Rise and Fall of Typhomalarial Fever: I. Origins." *Journal of the History of Medicine and Allied Sciences* (April 1982): 182-220.

Sneden, Robert Knox. *Eye of the Storm.* Free Press, 2000.

Snell, Mark A. *West Virginia and the Civil War: Mountaineers are Always Free.* History Press, 2011.

Sommers, Richard J. Foreword to *The Pennsylvania Reserves in the Civil War: A Comprehensive History*, by Uzal W. Ent. McFarland, 2014.

Southern Historical Association. *Memoirs of Georgia: Containing Historical Accounts of the State's Civil, Military, Industrial and Professional Interests, and Personal Sketches of Many of Its People.* Atlanta, GA: Southern Historical Association, 1895.

Spruill, Matt III and Matt Spruill IV. *Echoes of Thunder: A Guide to the Seven Days Battles.* University of Tennessee Press, 2006.

------*Summer Lightning: A Guide to the Second Battle of Manassas*. University of Tennessee Press, 2013.
Stackpole Books, ed. *Gettysburg: The Story of the Battle With Maps*. Stackpole Books, 2013.
Steere, Edward. *The Wilderness Campaign*. Bonanza Books, 1960.
Steiner, Paul E. *Disease in the Civil War*. Charles C. Thomas, 1968.
Stinson, Dwight E., Jr., "Eltham's Landing – the End Run that Failed," *Civil War Times Illustrated* 1 (No. 10 February 1963): 38-41.
Symonds, Craig L. *A Battlefield Atlas of the Civil War*. Nautical and Aviation Publishing, 1985.
Sypher, J. R. *History of the Pennsylvania Reserve Corps: a Complete Record of the Organization; And of the Different Companies, Regiments And Brigades; Containing Descriptions of Expeditions, Marches, Skirmishes, And Battles; Together With Biographical Sketches of Officers And Personal Records of Each Man During His Term of Service*. Lancaster, PA: E. Barr, 1864.
Tate, Thomas K. *General Edwin Vose Sumner, USA: A Civil War Biography*. McFarland, 2013.
Taylor, Walter H. *General Lee: His Campaigns in Virginia, 1861-1865*. University of Nebraska Press, 1994.
Temple, Brian. *The Union Prison at Fort Delaware: A Perfect Hell on Earth*. McFarland, 2003.
Tebeau, Charlton W. *The University of Miami: A Golden Anniversary History, 1926-1976*. University of Miami Press, 1976.
Thayer, Bill, ed. *George W. Cullum's Biographical Register of the Officers and Graduates of the United States Military Academy at West Point, New York, since its establishment in 1802*. http://penelope.uchicago.edu/Thayer/E/Gazetteer/Places/America/United_States/Army/USMA/Cullums_Register/home.html.
Thomas, William G. *The Iron Way: Railroads, the Civil War, and the Making of Modern America*. Yale University Press, 2011.
Thompson, Robert N. "William Averell's Cavalry Raid on the Virginia & Tennessee Railroad," *America's Civil War* (November 2000). https://www.historynet.com/william-averells-cavalry-raid-on-the-virginia-tennessee-railroad.htm.
Tibbets, J. J. "The Battle of Spotsylvania C. H. May 12, 1864." *Confederate Reminiscences and Letters*, IX. Atlanta: Georgia Division, United Daughters of the Confederacy, 2008.
Tolles, Zonira Hunter. *Bonnie Melrose: The Early History of Melrose, Florida*. Storter Printing, 1982.
Torrance, Eli. "The Pennsylvania Reserves." In Military Order of the Loyal Legion of the United States, Minnesota, *Glimpses of the Nation's Struggle*, vol. 3. New York: Merrill, 1893.
------*Pickett's Charge: A New Look at Gettysburg's Final Attack*. Skyhorse Publishing, 2018.

U.S. Army Center of Military History, *Wilderness-Spotsylvania Staff Ride Briefing Book*. https://history.army.mil/staffRides/_docs/staffRide_Wilderness.pdf

U.S. Sanitary Commission. *Narrative of Privations and Sufferings of United States Officers and Soldiers while Prisoners of War in the Hands of the Rebel Authorities*. Philadelphia: King & Baird, 1864.

United States War Department. *The War of the Rebellion: A Compilation of the Official Records of the Union and Confederate Armies*. Washington, DC: U.S. Government Printing Office, 1880-1901.

Vignola, Victor. *Contrasts in Commant: The Battle of Fair Oaks, May 31-June 1, 1862*. Savas Beatie, 2023.

Walker, Joe. *Rebel Pulpit: The Civil War Prison Diary of Lt. James Vance Walker, Company G – Third Tennessee Confederate Infantry*. Printed by author, 2014.

Warner, Ezra J. *Generals in Gray: Lives of the Confederate Commanders*. Louisiana State University Press, 1959.

Waters, Zack C. and James C. Edmonds. *A Small but Spartan Band: The Florida Brigade in Lee's Army of Northern Virginia*. University of Alabama Press, 2010.

Welch, Spencer Glasgow. *A Confederate Surgeon's Letters to His Wife*. Neal Publishing, 1911.

Weitz, Mark A. *A Higher Duty: Desertion among Georgia Troops during the Civil War*. University of Nebraska Press, 2000.

Wert, Jeffry D. *The Heart of Hell: The Soldiers' Struggle for Spotsylvania's Bloody Angle*. University of North Carolina Press, 2022.

Wheelan, Joseph. *Bloody Spring: Forty Days that Sealed the Confederacy's Fate*. Da Capo, 2014.

Wilcox, Cadmus M. "Lee and Grant in the Wilderness." In *The Annals of the War Written by Leading Participants North and South*, edited by Alexander K. McClure, 485-501. Philadelphia: Philadelphia Times Publishing, 1879.

Wiley, Bell Irvin. *The Life of Johnny Reb: The Common Soldier of the Confederacy*. Louisiana State University Press, 2008.

Wilkeson, Frank. *Recollections of a Private Soldier in the Army of the Potomac*. New York: G. P. Putnam's Sons, 1886.

Wills, Brian Steel. *Inglorious Passages: Noncombat Deaths in the American Civil War*. University of Kansas Press, 2017.

Wilson, W. Emerson. *Fort Delaware in the Civil War*. Delaware City, DE: Fort Delaware Society, n.d.

Wittenberg, Eric J., J. David Petruzzi, and Michael F. Nugent. *One Continuous Fight: The Retreat from Gettysburg and the Pursuit of Lee's Army of Northern Virginia, July 4-14*. Savas Beatie, 2013.

Young, Alfred C. III. *Lee's Army During the Overland Campaign: A Numerical Study*. Louisiana State University, 2013.

Zeller, Bob. *The Blue and Gray in Black and White: A History of Civil War Photography*. Praeger, 2005.

Zinn, Jack. *R. E. Lee's Cheat Mountain Campaign*. McClain Printing Company, 1974.

MANUSCRIPTS AND CORRESPONDENCE

Champion, David. "Memoirs," United Daughters of the Confederacy, Richmond, Va.
Patterson, Josiah B. "The Incomplete Correspondence of Lt. Josiah B. Patterson and the 14th Georgia Volunteer Infantry – An Outline," annotated by Carroll Ruffin Patterson, Atlanta Historical Society, Atlanta, GA.
Waddell, Joseph A. *Augusta County: Diary of Joseph Addison Waddell (1855-1865)*. https://valley.lib.virginia.edu/papers/AD1500

NEWSPAPERS

Albany [Georgia] *Patriot*
Americus [Georgia] *Weekly Recorder*
Central Georgian [Sandersville, GA]
Confederate Union [Milledgeville, GA]
Daily Exchange [Baltimore, MD]
Daily Morning News [Savannah, GA]
Fayetteville [Tennessee] *Observer*
Florida Baptist Weekly
Jackson Progress-Argus [Jackson, GA]
Macon [Georgia] *Telegraph*
Miami Herald
Miami News
Nashville Union
New York Times
Pittsburgh Gazette
Pittsburgh Post
Pittsburgh Press
Philadelphia Inquirer
Richmond Dispatch
Savannah Republican
Southern Confederacy [Atlanta, GA]
Southern Federal Union [Milledgeville, GA]
Southern Recorder [Milledgeville, GA]
The Sunny South [Atlanta, GA]
Washington National Tribune [Washington, DC]
Weekly Constitutionalist [Augusta, GA]

POEMS AND SONG LYRICS ATTRIBUTION

Fagan, W. L., arranger. *Southern War Songs – Camp-Fire, Patriotic & Sentimental*. New York: M. T. Richardson, 1889.

Lee, J. Edward and Ron Chepesiuk, ed. *South Carolina in the Civil War: The Confederate Experience in Letters and Diaries*. Jefferson, NC: McFarland, 2000.

No. 3 Southern Flag Song Book. "The Volunteers" attributed to "An Old Soldier." Vicksburg: H. C. Clarke, 1863.

"Root Yank or die!" Sheet Music, Library of Congress. Accessed August 5, 2020. https://www.loc.gov/item/amss.cw201550/

Southern Literary Messenger. "Editor's Table: 'My Soldier.'" *Southern Literary Messenger* 34 no. 4 (April 1862): 271-272. https://quod.lib.umich.edu/m/moajrnl/acf2679.0034.004/277:10

Wrighton, William Thomas; Francis Weiland; and Robert M. Gaw. "Dearest Spot of Earth to Me Is Home" (1857). Historic Sheet Music Collection 51. https://digitalcommons.conncoll.edu/sheetmusic/51

MISCELLANEOUS

American Battlefield Trust. Transcript: Krick, Robert E. L. "Malvern Hill: Then & Now, Interview with Robert E. L. Krick." January 10, 2021. https://www.battlefields.org/learn/articles/malvern-hill-then-now

Harrower, Annie L. "Architectural Description of Building Called Belmont," WPA Historical Inventory Project. Richmond: Virginia Conservation Commission, 1938. http://image.lva.virginia.gov/VHI/html/18/0457.html

McMillan, John Martin. "'Impracticable, Inhospitable, and Dismal Country': An Examination of the Environmental Impact on Civil War Military Operations in West Virginia." Master's Thesis, Marshall University, 2018. https://mds.marshall.edu/cgi/viewcontent.cgi?article=2151&context=etd

O'Reilly, Francis (Frank) A., *Battle of Chancellorsville Map Set*. Fort Washington, PA: Eastern National, 1998.

-------*Battle of Spotsylvania Map Set*. Fort Washington, PA: Eastern National, 2000.

Petty, Adam H. "Virginia's Wilderness: Investigating the Landscape of War." Doctorate Dissertation, University of Alabama, 2018, available through ProQuest.

ACKNOWLEDGMENTS

In 2015 my sister Hope Perry used the camera feature on her cell phone at the Library of Congress to photograph the cover and over 200 pages of the *Diary of George W. Hall, 14th Georgia Volunteers, Confederate States of America, 1861-1865*. Although the diary had long been the stuff of family legend, it was Hope who made it possible for her siblings to read it for themselves. A spiral-bound book of Hope's photographs became my working document for this book.

The list of individuals and organizations who have supported me in this project is quite lengthy. I apologize if I have inadvertently omitted someone.

Library and archival resources: the staff of the St. Mary's College of Maryland Library (especially Kat Ryner, Pamela Mann, Melissa Johnson, and Brenda Rodgers); the staff of the Leonardtown Branch of the St. Mary's County (Md.) Library (I spent many an hour in the study rooms); Jill Kloberdanz of the Blackshear Library, Americus, Georgia; Zach Hottel of the Shenandoah County Library, Edinburg, Virginia; and multiple members of the staff of the State of Florida Archives, Tallahassee, FL.

At the battlefields: National Park Service Rangers Frank O'Reilly (including the best two-hour history lesson I've ever had, his extremely insightful comments on several draft chapters, and a foreword that leaves me humble), Maureen Lavelle, and Nathan Varnold of the Fredericksburg-Spotsylvania-Wilderness-Chancellorsville regional battlefield centers; Jennifer Hopkins of the Andersonville National Historic Site (and a descendent of a soldier in Hall's Company G); and National Park Service rangers and volunteers at Gettysburg, Richmond, Antietam, and Manassas.

Historical societies: Local and state historical societies are the unsung heroes of projects such as mine. I owe such a debt of gratitude to Marcia Young-Whitacre of the Worth County Historical Society; R. Hugh Simmons and Martha Bennett of the Fort Delaware Society; Arlene Vouse and Debbie Jay of the Wakulla County (FL) Historical Society; Leah Lefkowitz of the Atlanta History Center; Becky Howard of the Nelson County (VA) Historical Society; Nancy Sorrells and Bill Miller of the Augusta County (VA) Historical Society; Penny Baumgardner and Donald Hepburn of the Florida Baptist Historical Society; David Cuff and Kim Brace of Historic Prince William; James P. Marshall, Jr. of the Eatonton-Putnam County (GA) Historical Society; Matthew Guillen of the Virginia Museum of History and Culture; Richard L. Armstrong of the Bath Co. (VA) Historical Society; and Caitlin Donnelly, of the Birmingham, MI, Museum. I would also like to acknowledge the critically important work of the American Battlefield Trust, the largest battlefield preservation group in the United States, and its commitment to educating the general public about the Civil War. Thanks to their untiring efforts in battlefield preservation, we can walk on battlegrounds where Hall and Elsesser trod.

Historians who shared their research and writing expertise: Bradley Gottfried, Ph.D. (thanks for the trek up Big Round Top to help me place the 9th Pennsylvania Reserves at Gettysburg); John J. Fox III for his exceptional research on Thomas's Brigade; M. Jane Johansson, Ph.D.; Bruce Allardice; Charles F. Bryan, Jr., Ph.D.; and W. Hunter Lesser.

My writing mentors: David Ulbrich, Ph.D., and Edward Kohn, Ph.D. of Norwich University; and John Kuehn, Ph.D., U.S. Army Command and Staff College. My thanks also to Keith Bohannon, Ph.D., University of West Georgia, whose familiarity with the diary and his belief in its value was so encouraging in the early days of this project.

St. Mary's College of Maryland alums and colleagues who provided encouragement and feedback on my manuscript: Captain Andrew J. Wilhelm, U.S. Army (Class of 2016); Alyssa Thompson (Class of 2018); Kara Feidelseit (Class of 2019); Caitlyn Sarudy (Class of 2020); Morgan Sorrell, Luke Miller, and Elisia Lewis (Class of 2025). Kara performed a Herculean job as the initial proofreader. The students in my Fall 2024 SMCM course on the Civil War provided me fresh insights into the war. I also thank my friends and colleagues at St. Mary's College of Maryland who kindly continued to ask "how's the book going" as the years rolled by. These include Lucy Myers, Joanne Goldwater, Adrienne Dozier, and my colleagues in the History and Political Science

Departments. Thank you, Professor Emerita Linda Jones Hall, Ph.D., for the delightful and productive working lunches on the process of book publication.

For maps and illustrations: Cartographer Hal Jesperson (especially for his boundless patience and advice) and Doug Crenshaw, who kindly permitted me to use maps from two of his books.

Road trip companions: Some of my favorite days working on this book were spent on research road trips. Brian Mullen, thanks for the excursion to Jacob Elsesser's hillside gravesite in Etna, Pennsylvania. Cousin Mary Jeanette Howle, Ph.D., thank you for your encyclopedic knowledge of Hall family Florida history, the voluminous material on Leta, and the excursion to Rachel and Leta's gravesites in Melrose, Florida. Marcia Young-Whitacre, thank you for the tour of Worth County and for helping me obtain copies of the courthouse display photographs. Michael Hall, thanks for the day trips around Richmond and Seven Days battlefields – your knowledge of Civil War artillery and munitions never fails to astound me. To my Navy shipmate and good friend CAPT Carol Cooper (U.S. Navy, Ret.), thank you for your hospitality and for accompanying me to the multiple museums, courthouses, and a church cemetery in Tallahassee, Crawfordville, Sopchoppy, and Bristol, Florida. I also thank my Civil War Institute cohort (Molly Hutchins, Melissa Schuster, Jeff Magill, and Bob Harrell) for their kind encouragement at Gettysburg, and Lucia and Chris Durbin for their publishing expertise.

My cheering squad of southern Maryland neighbors: Robin and Barry Mock and Carissa and Peter Bruno.

I will also forever be indebted to COL Adele Higgins (U.S. Army, Ret.) who so kindly agreed to proofread my manuscript, even after learning it was over 150,000 words long. You have earned your jewels for that, Adele. Any errors that remain are entirely of my own doing.

I owe a special thanks to Mel Truman, descendent of Private Jacob Elsesser, who gave unselfishly of his time to answer questions about his family and who provided me with photographs and his transcription of Elsesser's *Diary of Company B*.

Most authors reserve their greatest thanks to their families. As do I. For a multitude of reasons, this book would not have been possible without the support of CJ and Alexis; my siblings and their spouses Robert E. and Nancy Hall; Hope Perry; Michael G. and Desiree Hall; Annie Hall Simms; and my Florida second cousins Mary Jeanette Howle and David and Faye McGregor.

My parents, Colonel Robert E. Hall, a career U.S. Army artilleryman, and my mother, Maude W. "Theresa" Hall, are no longer alive. How I wish I could have shared this experience – and the final product – with them. To them I credit my love of reading, my mulish perseverance, and my intellectual curiosity. I hope I've written a book they would have enjoyed reading.

AUTHOR'S BIOGRAPHY

(Photo St. Mary's College of Maryland)

Mary Hall was born at Fort Belvoir, Virginia. Her father, George Washington Hall's grandson, was a career Army officer whose combat service included duty as executive officer of an anti-aircraft battalion which received the Distinguished Unit Citation for its contributions to the Allied amphibious landings at Biak, New Guinea, in 1944. Her mother was a homemaker, a title which doesn't come close to capturing the devotion and sacrifice of a woman married to a career soldier and who raised seven children, five of whom served in the military.

Hall received her B.A. in history from Columbus College (now Columbus State University). She was commissioned in the U.S. Navy JAG Corps while she was a student at the University of Georgia School of Law, where she earned her J.D. at the age of 22. While on active duty, she earned an LL.M. in Military Law from the Judge Advocate General's School of the Army while simultaneously finishing the U.S. Naval War College's Non-Resident Command and Staff Program. Hall, the first female judge advocate to serve on long-term assignment to a U.S. Navy ship, considers her time on USS *Proteus* (AS-19) as the best tour of her career. While on board USS *Proteus*, she qualified as a Surface Warfare Officer.

Hall retired from the U.S. Navy in the rank of Commander in 1996. She continued to practice military law until closing her practice in 2012 to devote her time to teaching and writing. Hall is an adjunct professor at St. Mary's College of Maryland, where she has taught political science courses since 2005. After earning an M.A. in Military History from Norwich University in 2015, she added military history courses to her teaching portfolio at SMCM. She and her family reside in southern Maryland, along with a menagerie of rescue Dalmatians, senior horses, and barn cats who prefer napping to mousing.

INDEX

A

Abbeville, South Carolina 359
Abbott, Armstead 237
Adams Express 362, 390, 404, 406
Adams, Salathiel 64, 96
Adler, George 406, 407
Alabama units
   3rd Alabama Infantry Regiment 60
   5th Alabama Battalion 285
   10th Alabama Infantry Regiment 234, 235
Albany, Georgia 5, 8, 353, 359
Albright, Charles 158
Alexandria and Orange Railroad 230
Alexandria, Virginia 304, 378, 391, 461, 466, 472, 477, 478
Allegheny County, Pennsylvania 364, 421
Allegheny Mountains 136, 138, 265
Americus, Georgia xii, 415
Amissville, Virginia 244
Anderson, Joseph R. 55, 69, 71, 72, 74, 75, 77, 79, 84
Anderson, Richard H. 239, 289, 301
Anderson, Robert 363, 370, 371, 372, 465
Anderson, Samuel R. 17, 18
Anderson's Brigade 73, 75, 76, 77, 81
Andersonville Prison, Georgia 314, 316, 422
Andrews, John A. 201
Antietam, battle of 107, 109, 117, 137, 372, 375, 464
   casualties 107, 375, 464

Dunker Church 372
Miller's Cornfield 372, 374
Aquia Creek, Virginia 370, 463, 465
Archer's Brigade 155, 377
Arkansas units
   3rd Arkansas Infantry Regiment 18
Arlington Heights, Virginia 371, 463
Army of Northern Virginia 111, 114, 165, 200, 225, 226, 229, 260, 261, 270, 286
   casualty reports 81
   day of fasting, humiliation, and prayer 224
   desertion 226
   Lee as commanding general 54
   religious conversions 114, 225
   reorganization after Chancellorsville 188
   reorganization after Seven Pines 69
   retreat after Gettysburg 204
   revivals 114, 224, 261
   Seven Days battles 72
   troop strength prior to battle of Gettysburg 190
Army of the Northwest 9, 13, 14, 24
Army of the Potomac 228, 285, 370, 375
   Burnside as commander 152
   corps at Wilderness 282
   Dranesville, battle of 365
   grand divisions at Fredericksburg 375
   Grant as general-in-chief 382
   Harrison's Landing, Virginia 370

   Hooker as commander 152
   illness during Peninsula Campaign 80
   Lee's retreat after Gettysburg 204
   living conditions at Harrison's Landing, Virginia 370
   McClellan as commander 104
   Meade as commander 203, 282, 363, 378
   Peninsula Campaign xi
   strength prior to Gettysburg 190
artillery 401, 412
   Antietam, battle of 374, 464
   artillery seized at Frayser's Farm 87
   bombardment of Harper's Ferry, Virginia (WV) 107
   Bristoe Station, battle of 229
   Chancellorsville, battle of 155, 157
   Confederate artillery at Antietam 117
   Dranesville, battle of 364, 460
   firing shell on the Peninsula 410
   Frayser's Farm, battle of 77, 369
   Fredericksburg, battle of 465
   Fredericksburg, Virginia 398
   Gettysburg, battle of 199, 202, 209, 210, 211, 217, 218
   grapeshot 45, 54, 57, 76, 85, 87, 209, 218, 302
   guarding artillery 29, 30, 39, 44, 48
   Harrison's Landing, Virginia 370

impact at Fair Oaks 56
Jackson's flank march at Chancellorsville 155
lack of Confederate artillery at Fair Oaks 52, 53
loss of tactical value at Chancellorsville 152, 153
Malvern Hill, battle of 80, 87, 88
movement to Virginia Peninsula 408
Shepherdstown, battle of 107, 117
siege artillery at Yorktown 38
Spotsylvania, battle of 291, 292, 293, 294, 296, 297
Union batteries at Fair Oaks 53, 54, 57, 59
Union batteries at Gaines's Mill 75
Unit batteries at Gaines's Mill 75
Wilderness, battle of the 282, 285, 289
artillery units
  1st Pennsylvania Light Artillery 363
  Cooper's Battery B, 1st Pennsylvania Light Artillery 369
  Easton's Battery A, 1st Pennsylvania Light Artillery 398, 405
  Pegram's Artillery Battalion 190
  Poague's Artillery Battalion 289
  Randol's Battery, 1st U.S. Artillery 369
Ashland, Virginia 36, 37, 42, 450
Atlanta, Georgia 5, 6, 8, 281, 329, 341, 415, 485
Augusta, Georgia 104, 127, 260, 271, 276
Averell, William 230, 231, 268

B

Bacon Race Church, Prince William County 29
Baker, Elbert 55, 58, 67, 96, 108, 110, 140
Baker, Nathan 67, 81, 96
Ballentine, James W. 472, 474
balloons 38
  Potomac River 33

Virginia Peninsula 38, 46, 411, 412, 413
Baltimore Crossroads, Virginia 39
Baltimore, Maryland 54, 133, 135, 190, 204, 307, 334, 335, 364, 460, 479
Baltimore & Ohio Railroad 11, 123, 137, 207, 216, 258, 405
Bandi, John 393, 405, 408
Banks, Nathaniel P. 105, 404, 405
Barnes, Charles 472
Barnett, Georgia 359
Barnetts Ford, Virginia 251
Barrett, Edward B. 114, 151, 176, 416, 480
Barrett, Faith 432
Bass, James 22, 64
Bass, Malcolm J. 65
Baty, William A. 68, 96
Becker, Charles 362, 367, 370, 386, 399, 472
Belle Plain, Virginia 120, 304, 318, 365, 378, 466
Belmont House, Nelson County, Virginia 125, 452
Bentley, Read M. 260, 261, 275, 293
Berlin, Virginia 464, 467
Berry, Hiram 157
Berry's Division 157
Berryville, Virginia 108, 207, 215
Big Springs, Virginia (WV) 20
Bland, W. H. 358
Bliss Farm
  Gettysburg, battle of 191, 193, 194, 195, 198
blockade vessels off Hampton Roads 47
Blue Ridge Mountains 104, 121, 122, 127, 136, 138, 161, 206, 207, 208, 212, 222, 269
Boeing, Richard 385
Boertzler, John H. 389, 472, 473, 474
Boonsboro, Maryland 463
Bostick, Nathaniel B. 67
Bostick, Thaddeus M. 64, 81, 96
Bozeman, John R. 21, 67
Bozeman, Luke C. 67, 96
Bragg, Braxton 228, 241, 251, 281
Branchville, South Carolina 276
Brandy Station, Virginia 382, 468, 469, 478
Bray, Harmon 64, 99
Brecht, Lewis 388, 407, 410
Breitlauch, John C. 408

Brett, Samuel J. 65
Bristoe Station, battle of 223, 228, 229, 381
Bristoe Station, Virginia 244, 471, 473, 478
Brockenbrough, John 195, 205
Brockenbrough's Brigade 195, 198, 199, 200, 205, 377
Brock Road, Spotsylvania County, Virginia 282, 291, 292
Brock Road, Wilderness, battle of the 282, 283, 284, 289, 290
Brookville, Virginia 463
Brown, Joseph 6, 160, 251
Brown, Pearson D. 22, 65
Brumby, Arnoldus V. 6, 7, 9, 18, 21, 25, 30
Brunn, Jacob 403
Buckeystown, Maryland 466
Buffalo Gap, Virginia 230, 231
Bullock Road, Chancellorsville, Virginia 156, 157, 297
Bull Run Creek, Manassas 396, 463, 469, 471, 474
Bunker Hill, Virginia 108, 123, 139, 205, 212, 220
Bunyan, John 113, 148, 150, 316, 339
Burkhart, Baxter 389
Burnside, Ambrose 135, 294, 318, 466, 478
  assumes command of AOP 465
  Mud March 378, 466
  Overland Campaign 282
  replaced as commander, AOP 152
  Second Manassas, battle of 116, 132
  senior to Meade in Overland Campaign 282
  Spotsylvania, battle of 292, 293, 294, 296, 297, 303
  strategy at Fredericksburg 109
  strategy for AOP 375
Butler, Benjamin 63, 64

C

Calhoun, Joseph 65
Calhoun, Nathan T. 65, 96
Calhoun, Thomas O. 65, 96, 110, 161
Camp Bartow (Fredericksburg, Virginia) 7, 36
Camp Bartow (Pocahontas County, Virginia (WV)) 17

Camp Curtin, Pennsylvania 364, 460
Camp Gregg, Virginia 108, 151, 166, 172, 446, 447, 449
Camp Jackson, Virginia 460
Camp Lee, Virginia 352, 358
Camp Misery, Virginia 391, 461
Camp Ord, Virginia 461
Camp Pickens, Virginia 25, 365, 394, 461
Camp Vason, Georgia 5
Camp Wilkins, Pennsylvania 364, 397, 460
Camp Wright, Pennsylvania 364, 394, 460
Carlisle, Pennsylvania 190
Carr, James B. 157, 158
Carroll, Samuel S. 158
Cashtown, Pennsylvania 189
Catharine Furnace 154, 155
Catharine Furnace, Spotsylvania County, Virginia 154
Catlett's Station, Virginia 245, 365, 395, 405, 461, 469
cavalry 220, 222, 240, 248, 399, 400, 401, 405, 406
   Averell 230, 268
   Cedar Mountain 105
   Dranesville, battle of 364
   escort to Belle Plain 304, 317, 318
   Hampton 395
   Pennsylvania Reserves 363
   retreat after Gettysburg 205, 212, 219
   retreat from Gettysburg 204
   Rosser 257, 266, 267, 268
   Stuart 241
   Union movement to Peninsula 408
   Wilderness, battle of the 299
   Williamsburg 44
Cedar Mountain, battle of xiii, 104, 115, 135, 199, 233
Celestial City 148, 174
Centerville, Virginia 244, 394, 461, 463, 469
Chamberlain, Joshua 379, 380
Chambersburg, Pennsylvania 190, 207, 217
Chambersburg Pike, Gettysburg 190
Champion, Daniel 65, 96, 107, 117
Champion, David xvii, 32, 67, 97, 108, 140, 286

Memoirs xvii, 20, 23, 107, 201, 293, 295
Chancellorsville, battle of xiii, 114, 151, 158, 159, 165, 199, 228, 303, 378
   aftermath 159
   bloodiest morning of the war 157
   casualties 159, 164, 165, 213, 226
   Hooker's strategy 152
   Hooker wounded 158
   impact on war strategy 188
   Jackson's flank march 154, 155
   reorganization of Jackson's Corps 188
Chancellorsville, battle of casualties 158
Chancellorsville, Virginia 153, 207, 282, 453
chaplains 11, 112, 114, 176, 188, 234, 235, 278, 416
   9th Pa Res 384, 389, 400
   10th Alabama 234
   14th Georgia 114
   at Staunton 112
   divine services 152
   duties 112, 113
   McGowan's Brigade 246
   Thomas's Brigade 113, 151, 166, 171, 173, 175, 177, 179, 180, 186, 221, 247
   western Virginia 10
Charleston Harbor, battle of 171
Charleston, South Carolina 143, 149, 171, 332
Charlotte, North Carolina 276, 359
Charlottesville, Virginia 25, 28, 115, 125, 230, 252
Cheat Mountain
   summit fort 13, 17
Cheat Mountain, battle of 16, 26
   Confederate brigade assignments 17
   failure of Lee's strategy 19
   Lee appoints Rust to lead assault 18
   Lee's strategy 17, 18
   Rust's failure to give signal to attack 19
   summit fort 17
   weather conditions 19
Chesapeake Bay 43, 47, 304
Chestnut, Jacob 65
Chickahominy River 82, 84, 85, 88

9th Pennsylvania Reserves encampment 410
   advance of the 14th Georgia 57
   Anderson's position 73
   crossing on Grapevine Bridge 52
   Hill attacks at Beaver Dam Creek 73
   Johnston's strategy 51
   location of Hampton's Brigade at Fair Oaks 50
   march to Frayser's Farm 91
   McClellan divides corps 50
   picket duty 61
   Porter's location 72
   retreat to Richmond 45
   V Corps abandons north of river 367
Chimborazo Hospital, Richmond, Virginia 81, 82, 159
Christian Index's *History of the Baptist Denomination of Georgia* 416
Cincinnati, Ohio 133, 135
Clark's Mountain, Virginia 228, 230, 282
clothing 27, 402
   ANV lack of 139
   burned 27
   CSA pay allowance 27
   CSA troops nearly naked after Gettysburg 205
   donated by citizens 1, 23
   insufficient at Fort Delaware 351
   issued to Company B, 9th Pa Res 397, 403, 462
   obtained from enemy 75, 116, 164, 267, 462
   removed from corpses 27
   requisition for Company B, 9th Pa Res 396
   seized from enemy xi
Cold Harbor, battle of 329
Collier, Charles 65
colporteurs 112
Columbia, South Carolina 276
Company B, 9th Pennsylvania Reserve Regiment xi, xiv, xviii, 361, 362, 363, 371, 377, 380, 381, 382, 390, 397, 403, 424
   Antietam, battle of 374
   formation 363
   Frayser's Farm 367
   Frayser's Farm, casualties 370

Gaines's Mill, battle of 367
history 362
initial assignments 364
living conditions at Harrison Landing, Virginia 370
march to Gaines's Mill 366
Mechanicsville, battle of 366
muster out 382
officers 363, 364
reenlistments in 1864 471
Second Manassas, battle of 463
Second Manassas, casualties at 371
shoes issued 397
South Mountain, battle of 372
Company G, 14th Georgia Infantry Regiment xii, xiii, xvii, xx, 5, 6, 15, 24, 27, 32, 40, 55, 81, 107, 110, 159, 201, 213, 227, 230, 252, 257, 261, 491
casualties at Fredericksburg 109, 161
casualties at Seven Pines 56, 58
company officers 2, 3, 4, 6, 20, 21, 32, 56, 65, 108, 159
county support 24
enlistment bounty 32
illness in western Virginia 22
initial recruits 5
Mechanicsville, battle of 73
movement to Fredericksburg 35
Second Manassas, battle of 106
strength 31, 32, 110
Yancey Independents xii, xiv, 1, 2, 3, 4, 5, 6, 22, 24
Concord, Florida 414
Contrabands 396, 401, 405
Cooper, James B. 369
Corinth Baptist Church, Hosford, Florida 414
Corps, Confederate
First Corps 188, 228, 282, 288, 289, 300
Second Corps 188, 248, 282, 293
Third Corps 188, 189, 204, 239, 282, 283, 289, 294, 295
Corps, Federal
I Corps 372, 375, 471
II Corps 52, 228, 282, 283, 284, 293, 469
III Corps 156, 228
IX Corps 282, 292, 293, 295, 297, 318, 478
V Corps xi, 72, 73, 74, 228, 282, 283, 367, 378, 379

VI Corps 282, 284, 469, 476
XI Corps 155
Crawford, Samuel 378, 379, 470, 473, 474
CSS Arkansas 99
CSS Virginia 400
Culpeper Court House, Virginia 28, 107, 120, 121, 136, 167, 206, 207, 223, 232, 233, 243, 247, 248, 468, 478
proximity to Cedar Mountain 104
Culpeper Ford, Virginia 470
Curtin, Andrew 363, 375, 385, 407
Custer's Brigade 205

D

Daily Pocket Remembrancer for 1862 xx
disappearance xv, 426
Elsesser's use xi, xiii, xvii, 362, 366
Hall's use xi, xiv, xvi, xvii, 75, 156, 234
obtained by Hall 90, 366
Thayer manuscript xvi, 156, 424
Danner, Matthias 464
Danville, Virginia 358
Davis Ford, Prince William County, Virginia 29, 30, 32, 35, 40
Davis, Jefferson 9, 14, 18, 86, 224, 228, 259, 265, 278
Davis's brigade 198
Dawson, Samuel 67
Deariso, James 58, 65, 97
Deariso, Michael W. 68, 97
Deariso, Thomas J. 68, 97
Delaware River 307
desertion 225, 227, 240, 241, 258
Dethlefs, Mathias F. 387
Diary of Company B xviii, 362, 364, 409, 426
disease 11
bronchitis 110, 111, 123
Chickahominy Fever 83
deaths 81
diarrhea 81, 83, 315
disease-bearing insects 83
dysentery 81, 83, 315
erysipelas 111, 123, 142, 143
fever 11
inflamation 146
lung disease 144
measles 10, 11, 14, 22

mumps 10, 11
new recruits 15
officers 83
Peninsula Campaign 81
pneumonia 10, 81, 108, 111, 123, 144, 315
scurvy 315
smallpox 104, 110, 111, 112, 123, 315, 385, 452
typhoid fever 10, 14, 22, 82, 315
western Virginia 24
whooping cough 335
Dispatch Station, Virginia 462
Dix-Hill Cartel 306, 308
Dixie, Georgia 261, 272
Dixie (pen name) 25
Dixie (song) 435
Dixon, Romulus 228
Doles's Brigade 199
Donelson, Daniel S. 16, 17, 18, 23, 24
Donelson's Brigade 18
Dranesville, battle of 364, 365, 384, 460
Dranesville, Virginia 364, 466

E

Eady, Edward 65, 97
Eady, James E. 67
Early, Jubal 153, 225, 255, 257, 289, 292, 293, 294, 334, 343
Gettysburg 194
Moorefield expedition 257, 258
pursuit of Averell 230, 231
Edenburg, Virginia 254, 263
Edray, Virginia (WV) 15, 19, 20, 27
Eiffler, George 471, 474
Eliam Baptist Church, Melrose, Florida 415
Elk Mountain 27
Elk Mountain, Virginia (WV) 15, 20, 27
Elkwater 13, 17, 18, 19
Ellerson's Mill 75, 365
Ellsworth, Ephraim 393
Elmira, New York 304, 316
Elsesser, Jacob L. xi, xviii, 74, 75, 77, 297, 360, 361, 362, 364, 365, 369, 371, 372, 374, 377, 380, 381, 382, 387, 389, 409, 421, 422, 423, 424, 425, 426, 431
Army pay 386, 394, 406, 460, 461, 468, 475, 477
assistance to other veterans 422
birth and early childhood xiii, 360

bootmaker 360, 361
children 361
cholera outbreak in Etna 361
clothing 390, 399, 477
clothing accounts 398, 399, 405, 406
death 422
diaries 362
Diary of Company B xviii, 362
Dranesville, battle of 364
enlistment 361
expiration of enlistment xiv
illness 396, 408, 409, 412, 413
military service documents xv
name in Daily Pocket Remembrancer xi
naturalization 361
occupation as bootmaker 360
officer in G.A.R. 421
photograph taken 387
picket duty 390
proclamation from G.A.R. Post 38 422
service as magistrate xiv, 361, 362, 421, 422
shoes 363
stripes for pants 407
studied law xiv, 360
tapped on leg at Mine Run 470
tours Alexandria, Virginia 393
vaccination 385
veteran's pension 422
wife 361
wife and children 423
writes history of Company B 474
Elsesser, Mary Salome Hieber 361, 399, 407, 423
Eltham's Landing, battle of 39, 40, 450
casualties 39
Emmitsburg, Maryland 190, 467
environmental factors xx
Peninsula Campaign 83
Western Virginia Campaign 10, 11
Epple, Florian 384, 470
Etna, Pennsylvania xiii, 360, 386, 391, 421, 425
Evans, Clement A. 289
Ewell, Richard S. 188, 204, 248, 282, 283, 284, 286
executions 225, 227, 241, 380, 381
Exum, Benjamin E. T. 65

F

Fairfax Court House 116, 394, 461, 469
Fairfield, Pennsylvania 204
Falling Waters, battle of 205
Falling Waters, Maryland 204
Falls Church, Virginia 461
Falmouth, Virginia 365, 370, 398, 400, 402, 406, 407, 461
Fielder, James M. 158, 159, 165
field fortifications
   abatis 19, 74, 286
   breastworks 29, 76, 85, 86, 157, 158, 159, 164, 250, 289, 292, 294, 295, 296, 300, 301
   rifle pits 29, 41, 74, 75, 366, 467, 470, 473, 474
   trenches 13, 17, 19, 57, 60, 73, 106
   types 292
Fisher's Brigade 380
Fisher's Hill, Virginia 255, 343
Flint Hill, Virginia 136, 207, 222
Florida units
   1st Florida Reserve Infantry Regiment 260
   2nd Florida Infantry Regiment 60, 260
   5th Florida Infantry Regiment 261, 280, 298
Floyd, John Buchanan 13, 23, 24
Folsom, James M. xvii
Folsom, Robert W. xviii, 21, 30, 72, 74, 105, 160, 227, 291
   Cedar Mountain, battle of 105
   Chancellorsville, battle of 159
   death xviii, 291, 300
   formal promotion to colonel 108
   Mechanicsville, battle of 74
   nickname 105
   promotion to lieutenant colonel 21
   Wilderness, battle of the 286
   wounded at Wilderness 290
food 319
   diminished rations 221
   half-rations 22, 45
   obtained from enemy xi, 60, 75, 159, 164, 258, 267, 462
   plentiful in Shenandoah Valley 254
   prices 394, 405, 408, 410, 412

   prices in Fredericksburg 399, 407
   prices in Richmond 90
   sea horse 410
Ford, Garry G. 68, 92, 97
Ford, James H. 64, 96, 108
Ford, John 413
Ford, John J. 65, 97
Ford, Robert G. 65, 97, 101
Ford, William J. 68, 97
Fort Delaware, Delaware xiii, 113, 305, 332
   articles made by prisoners 323, 324
   blankets 311, 346
   clothing issue to prisoners 351
   construction and location 307
   death rate 316
   debate over adequacy of rations 313
   disease and illness 315, 335
   divisions 309, 337
   enlisted prisoner barracks 309, 321
   enlisted prisoner barracks life 309, 311, 315, 346
   enlisted prisoner rations 313, 321
   escapes 332, 333, 336
   food availability 312, 313, 346
   food privileges for senior officers 312, 313
   food rations 312
   fresh water issues 311, 321, 335
   July 4 gun salute 333
   location 321
   newspaper perception of life as POW 314
   political prisoners 308
   prisoner correspondence restrictions 330
   prisoner deaths 315
   prisoner housing 309
   prisoner transfers 342, 343, 357, 358
   prison population 308, 327, 342
   privileges for senior officers 309, 312
   rats as food 313
   structure 307
   suitability as POW camp 307, 315
   sutlers 312, 314, 351
   waste disposal 311

Fort Donelson, battle of 388
Fort Mulligan, West Virginia 225, 257, 258
Fort Pulaski, Georgia 342
Fortress Monroe, Virginia 33, 36, 37, 320, 370, 463
Fourteenth (14th) Georgia Infantry Regiment xii, 9, 11, 81, 104, 158, 201, 223, 227, 228, 230, 231, 255, 257, 258, 282, 285, 295, 297, 327, 365
   15th New Jersey monument 294
   absent from Antietam, battle of 107
   aftermath of failed attack on Cheat Mountain 19
   after Seven Days 82
   after Spotsylvania 326
   Army of the Northwest 13
   assigned to Anderson's Brigade 55, 69
   assignment in western Virginia 23, 24
   at Davis Ford 29, 30, 32
   battles in Hall's absence 104
   brigade assignment after Seven Pines 69
   brigade assignment for Cheat Mountain Campaign 17
   campaigns xii
   casualties 81
   casualties at Chancellorsville 158
   casualties at Fredericksburg 109
   casualties at Seven Pines 55, 58
   casualties at Spotsylvania 297
   casualties at the Wilderness 290
   Cedar Mountain, battle of 105
   Chancellorsville, battle of 156, 157, 162
   Chantilly, battle of 106
   chaplains 114
   Cheat Mountain, battle of 18, 19
   Davis Ford 30
   deaths in western Virginia 11
   duties at Manassas 25, 28
   Eltham's Landing, battle of 39, 44, 48
   Frayser's Farm, battle of 77, 79, 369
   Fredericksburg, battle of 109
   Gaines's Mill, battle of 76
   Gettysburg, battle of 200
   Harper's Ferry, Virginia (WV) 107
   hunger on retreat to Richmond 39, 45
   illness in western Virginia 15, 22, 23
   initial movement to Virginia 8
   Jackson's flank march at Chancellorsville 155
   joins Jackson at Gordonsville 103
   living conditions in western Virginia 10, 11, 14
   Malvern Hill, battle of 80, 370
   Manassas, Virginia xii
   march to Gettysburg 189
   march to Huntersville 25
   Mechanicsville, battle of xi, 73, 74, 75, 365
   missing regimental records xviii
   movement on the Huttonsville-Huntersville Turnpike 20
   movement to Fredericksburg 35
   movement to Gordonsville 102
   movement to northern Virginia 25
   movement to Virginia Peninsula 36, 37, 42, 43
   movement to western Virginia 9, 25
   new battle flag 160
   New Jersey monument 294
   orders to northern Virginia 24, 25
   Peninsula Campaign xii
   poor drill 36
   pursuit to Gaines's Mill 75
   regimental officers 6, 11, 21, 30, 55, 72, 108, 290, 291
   regimental strength 23
   Second Manassas, battle of 106, 371
   Seven Pines, battle of 50, 53, 56
   skirmishing at Gettysburg 194
   sources xvii, xviii, 23
   Spotsylvania, battle of 294, 318
   strength 22, 23
   strength at Gettysburg 190
   strength at Halfway House 38
   strength in northern Virginia 31
   strength in western Virginia 22
   troop movement to Gordonsville 115
   Western Virginia Campaign xii
   Wilderness, battle of the 286, 288
Fowler, Levi T. 55, 65, 97
Fowler, Nathan J. 65, 97
Franklin, William B. 39
Frayser's Farm, battle of xiii, 69, 72, 76, 79, 81, 365, 367, 451, 462
   9th Pennsylvania Reserves 367
   casualties 79
Frederick, Maryland 107, 116, 204, 378, 463, 466
Fredericksburg, battle of xiii, 104, 108, 142, 151, 375, 378, 465
   casualties 110, 363, 377
   Marye's Heights 109
   Prospect Hill 377
   Slaughter Pen 109
Fredericksburg Road, Spotsylvania Court House 292
Fredericksburg, Virginia 42, 109, 113, 142, 160, 164, 165, 167, 213, 250, 298, 300, 304, 317, 318, 397, 398, 401, 405, 450, 463
   Camp Gregg 160
   Hall departure for Virginia Peninsula 42
   Johnston's move south 33, 35, 36
   movement to Camp Gregg 108
   prelude to Chancellorsville 153, 178
   prelude to march to Pennsylvania 188, 189, 206
   Union occupation 398
Front Royal, Virginia 107, 121, 136, 161, 207, 222, 243, 262
Frostown Gap, Maryland 372
Fuchse, Frederick 408
Fuhren, Henry 362, 364, 389, 400, 401, 402, 405, 406, 408, 472, 474
Fulton, Robert H. 2, 65, 96, 108, 167, 233
   elected captain of Company G 159
furloughs 225, 260, 271, 273, 426, 473, 476
   Company B 471, 472, 474, 475
   Company G 167, 213, 264, 269
   following POW exchange 358
   Lee's policy 236, 259
   policy 258
furloughs Company B 476

G

Gaines's Mill, battle of xi, xiii, 75, 365, 398, 410, 451, 462
   casualties 76
Gaugh, Benjamin 65, 81, 97

Gaugh, John H. 65
Georgia
  political elections 242
Georgia Central Railroad 276
Georgia units
  9th Georgia Infantry Regiment 159
  10th Georgia Infantry Battalion 249
  13th Georgia Infantry Regiment 295, 302
  19th Georgia Infantry Regiment 41, 54, 57
  23rd Georgia Infantry Regiment 155
  25th Georgia Infantry Regiment 71
  35th Georgia Infantry Regiment 69, 71, 74, 180, 200, 202, 229, 231, 240, 241, 257, 288, 295
  45th Georgia Infantry Regiment 69, 74, 79, 114, 194, 231
  49th Georgia Infantry Regiment 69, 74, 82, 86, 113, 179, 180, 181, 184, 186, 200, 231, 257, 262, 266
Germon, Joseph B. 65
Gettysburg, battle of xiii, xiv, xvii, 190, 199, 200, 204, 205, 206, 217, 224, 225, 226, 228, 233, 289, 306, 323, 380
  9th Pennsylvania Reserve Regiment arrives 467
  artillery duel on July 3 196, 202
  Big Round Top debate 379
  Lee's retreat after Gettysburg 203
  Long Lane 189, 191, 194, 199
  Pickett-Pettigrew-Trimble charge 76, 195, 198, 199
  prisoners 308
  Round Tops 379, 380, 467
  skirmishing 210, 218
Gettysburg Campaign 379, 467
Gettysburg National Military Park 190, 202, 383
Gettysburg, Pennsylvania 190, 203
Getty's division 284
Gibbon, John 109
Giddens, Asa 4, 6, 20, 64
Gilham, William 20, 21
Gillis, Norman G. 55, 66, 97, 110, 161, 316
Gillis, William Daniel 68, 97

Gilmore, Harry 334
Gleaton, Dudley C. 65
Goodman, James I. 55, 56, 57, 58, 64
Gordon, John xxi, 281, 289, 294, 295
  Spotsylvania, battle of 293, 294
  Wilderness, battle of the 284
Gordon's (Evans) Brigade 302
Gordonsville, Virginia 28, 103, 104, 107, 115, 120, 124, 125, 130, 230, 252, 277, 282, 451, 452
Grant, Ulysses S. xiii, 281, 382
  appointment as general-in-chief 281
  Overland Campaign 282
  strategy to defeat Confederacy 281
Grapevine Bridge 52
Green, Bartley C. 65, 97
Greenbrier River 14, 26, 27, 28
Greencastle, Pennsylvania 204
Greenwich, Virginia 244
Gregg, Maxcy 106
Griffin, James B. 29, 33, 55
Griffin, Simon 295
Gschwend, Charles 387, 388, 391, 393, 400, 401, 404, 405, 406, 411, 412
guard duty 118, 140
  drill 119
guerillas 381, 395, 400, 409, 469, 473, 474, 475, 477
Guinea Station, Virginia 113, 151, 160, 167
gunboats 44, 80, 88, 89, 99, 135, 143, 370
Gunter, William J. 22, 66

H

Hagerstown, Maryland 116, 189, 190, 204, 207, 216
  retreat to Virginia 204, 205, 212, 219, 220
Hagerstown Pike, Antietam 372
Halfway House, Virginia 38
Hall, Amanda M. E. Mobley xiii, 260, 261, 275, 300, 414, 418, 419, 420, 425
Hall, Burwell A. J. 414
Halleck, Henry 80
Hall, George Washington 110, 418
  Army pay 27, 41, 61, 140, 247, 257, 265
  attends local church 186, 254
  baptism 151, 174

barefooted at Fort Delaware 351, 353, 354
birth xii, 129
captured at Spotsylvania xiii, 297, 302, 317, 318
childhood xii
clothing 27, 36, 41, 62, 108
clothing allowance pay 140, 257, 265
clothing at Fort Delaware 351, 353, 354
clothing, lack of 139
clothing supply in Staunton 252
Confederate veteran pension 420
correspondence received 108, 127, 139, 141, 178, 239, 242, 249, 265, 298, 300, 343
correspondence sent 93, 100, 127, 131, 140, 147, 167, 175, 213, 214, 235, 236, 240, 242, 246, 251, 269, 276, 277, 278, 298, 329, 345, 346
daily log xvii, 36
Daily Pocket Remembrancer xiv
death 420
DeLand promissory note 419
departs Fort Delaware 352, 358
disappearance of diaries 426
enlistment xiv, 1, 7
faith as a prisoner of war 316
food rations at Fort Delaware 312
Frayser's Farm, battle of 85, 91
furlough to Florida (1864) xii, xiii, 255, 258, 261, 270, 277
Gaines's Mill, battle of 85, 90
home to Florida (1865) 353
hospitalization 108, 110, 125, 414
hunger 205, 313, 339
illness during war 15, 18, 20, 26, 27, 83, 89, 92, 93, 141, 229, 334, 335
joy in attending prayer meetings 234, 236, 238
leave of indulgence 352
Malvern Hill, battle of 87, 91
Mechanicsville, battle of 84
ministerial work in Miami 420
ministry as Baptist preacher xiv
oath of allegiance to Confederacy 7
ordination to ministry 414
parole 351, 356
photo taken on furlough 276

picket duty 19, 27, 39, 61, 63, 181, 214, 236
pocket notebook xiv, xv, xvi, 36, 75, 82
police duty in Richmond 100, 451
post-release furlough xiii, 420
preaching after war 415
religious conversion 111
return home, March 1865 358, 359
selling meals for stamps 314, 338, 341
Seven Pines, battle of 56
sharpshooter duty 39, 45
shoes, lack of xiii, 108, 136, 139
Sunday reflections 170, 171, 173, 176, 186
Sunday Schools in Florida 417
supplication to God 143, 147, 148
transport to Belle Plain 304
transport to Fort Delaware 305, 319, 320
typhoid fever 20, 27
vaccination 111
visits Richmond 49
weather log xvii, xx
wounded at Chancellorsville 159, 165
Hall, John E. xii, 415
Hall, Lyman xii
Hall, Minnie Viola 415
Hall, Robert E. 414, 415
Hall, Willis W. xv, 415, 419, 424, 426
Hamilton, David 67
Hamilton's Crossing, Virginia 108, 109, 188, 206, 375
Hamilton, William B. 65, 97
Hampton Roads, Virginia 33, 38
Hampton's Brigade 25, 29, 36, 38, 39, 46, 50, 52, 53, 54, 60
Hampton's Legion 29, 41, 53, 54, 55, 56, 57, 395
Hampton, Wade 25, 29, 30, 33, 36, 38, 39, 55, 59
    wounded at Seven Pines 55
Hancock, Jackson M. 67
Hancock, Winfield S. 67, 282, 283, 284, 285, 288, 289, 290, 293
Handy, Isaac 308, 313
Hanover Court House, Virginia 410
Hanover, Pennsylvania 467
Harden, John Fletcher 22, 65
Hardtmeyer, Francis (Frank) 363

Harper's Ferry, Virginia (WV) 107, 371
    capture of xiii, 104, 107, 116
Harrisburg, Pennsylvania 190, 217, 364, 460
Harrisonburg, Virginia 231, 253, 256, 257, 263, 264, 265, 268, 269
Harrison's Landing, Virginia 72, 79, 80, 370
Harris, Thomas M. 181, 184, 187, 245
Harris, William A. 2, 3, 10, 20, 22, 64
    company commander 2, 4, 5, 64
    lawyer and elected official 2
    leg injury 6, 20
    promotion to regimental officer 4, 32
    resigned from regiment 108, 159
    service in Mexican-American War 2
    sick furlough 20
Harris, William M. 68, 97
Hartwood, Virginia 461
Hayes, John D. 68, 97, 252
Henderson, Manassah 65
Heroes and Martyrs of Georgia xvii, 202
Heth, Henry 184, 239, 285, 286, 289
    Chancellorsville, battle of 158
    division review 184
    Gettysburg, battle of 190, 195, 202
    retreat to Virginia 205
    Wilderness, battle of the 284, 286, 288
Heth's Division 205, 283, 284, 286
Hieber, Daniel 361, 389
Hieber, John D. 389
Hill, Ambrose Powell xi, 69, 73, 75, 76, 77, 79, 81, 85, 105, 107, 109, 133, 158, 184, 188, 189, 190, 223, 229, 239, 286, 367, 369, 381
Hill, Daniel Harvey 80
Hill, Haskell H. 66, 97
Hill, Lott W. 64, 96, 110, 161
Hill's Division 81, 116, 155, 156
History of the Baptist Denomination in Georgia with Biographical Compendium and Portrait Gallery xii, 416
Hobby, James 65, 96, 110, 161
Hobby, James N. 65
Hobby, Jesse 68, 105
Hobby, William 67
Hoell, Andrew 403
Hoke's Brigade 377

Holiday, Edward G. 66
Holly, Edwin N. xii
Holly, Rachel xii, 7, 94, 100, 101, 127, 131, 275, 426
Holmes Rifles 2, 3
Holoman, Daniel T. W. 66
Hood, John B. 39
Hood's Brigade 372
Hooker, Joseph 152, 153, 154, 155, 158, 162, 189, 190, 282, 375
Horn, Michael J. 67
hospitals 15, 112, 393
    Belmont House 104, 126
    death rate 329
    smallpox death rate 111
    smallpox tents at Staunton 111
    Staunton, Virginia 108, 110, 111, 113, 142, 452
Howard, McHenry 309, 313, 324
Howard, Oliver O. 155
Howenstein, George W. 389, 390, 391, 405, 407, 474, 475
Huger, Benjamin 77
Huntersville, Virginia (WV) 9, 10, 11, 14, 17, 18, 20, 21, 23, 24, 26, 27, 28
    14th Georgia departs for northern Virginia 25
    description of town 10, 11, 14
    move to new camp 14
    strategic value 11, 12
Huttonsville-Huntersville Turnpike 11, 13, 15, 17, 18, 19, 20, 23, 231
Huttonsville, Virginia (WV) 13, 18
Hyman, John J. 113, 114, 179, 180, 186, 217, 221, 233, 235, 242, 278, 416
hymns 152
    Afflictions, Though They May Seem Severe 185
    Amazing Grace 170
    A Minister's Farewell 182
    Holy Bible, Book Divine 144
    The Gospel Invitation 183

I

Indiana units
    14th Indiana Infantry Regiment 13
Isabella, Georgia 2, 5, 8, 64, 94, 212, 220

J

Jackson, Conrad Feger 363, 366, 375, 384, 397

death 377
health at Second Manassas 371
promotion to brigadier
 general 370
regimental commander 363
Jackson, Thomas J. 72, 75, 77, 84,
 105, 113, 121, 122, 132, 133, 154,
 158, 162, 188, 330, 371, 375, 462
James River 33, 37, 72, 76, 79,
 80, 86, 88, 89, 91, 93, 99, 102,
 281, 289, 306, 352, 463
Jenkins, Micah 369
Jenkins, Royal R. 249, 251
Jerkins, John T. 66, 97
Jeter, Jeremiah J. 68, 97
Johnson, Bradley 334
Johnson, Edward 293
Johnson, Thomas 66
Johnston, David D. 66, 97
Johnston, Joseph E. 29, 32, 33, 36,
 38, 50
 movement to Fredericksburg 32
 movement to Virginia
  Peninsula 36
 wounded at Seven Pines 54
Johnston, William A. 4, 21, 32,
 64, 81, 96
Jones, Isaac 68, 97, 105, 115
Jones, Julius M. 66, 96, 97, 108
Jordan, Sylvanus Q. 64, 81, 92, 96
Junkin, George 330

K

Kanawha Valley, Virginia (WV)
 13, 23
Kauffley, Martin 410
Kearny, Philip 106
Keegan, John 72
Kelly Ford, Virginia 470
Kelly's Ford, battle of 167
Kerce, Albert B. 66, 97
Kerce, Barney 68, 97
Kerce, James M. 68, 82, 97
Kerce, James O. 66, 68, 97, 110, 161
Kettle Run, Virginia 469
Kimple, Christian 410, 471
Kingsville, South Carolina 271, 276
Kohlman, Nicholas 472

L

Land, William L. 66, 97, 159,
 165, 213
Lane, James 109, 194, 205
 Spotsylvania, battle of 294
Lane's Brigade 188, 195, 240

executions 227, 228
Fredericksburg, battle of 109
Gettysburg, battle of 190,
 194, 195, 198
Spotsylvania, battle of 295
Wilderness, battle of the
 284, 288
Lane, William 68
Larrimer, James Harvey 474
Lee, Robert E.
 appoints Thomas to replace
  Anderson 84
 assumes command of Army of
  Northern Virginia 54
 atonement for sin 224
 Bristoe Campaign 228
 casualties from Gettysburg 223
 defending Fredericksburg 109
 desertions 226
 division review 184
 furlough restrictions 258
 Gaines's Mill 75, 76
 Glendale, battle of 369
 Glendale, strategy 77
 Maryland campaign 106, 371
 Mechanicsville, battle of 74
 orders artillery removed at
  Spotsylvania 293
 orders Averell pursuit 230
 Overland Campaign after
  Spotsylvania 326
 relationship with Loring 14
 reorganization after Jackson's
  death 188
 retreat after Antietam 107
 retreat after Gettysburg 203,
  204, 380
 saves Richmond 80
 Seven Days battles 72
 splits forces before
  Chancellorsville 153, 154
 splits forces in Maryland 107
 Spotsylvania, battle of 291,
  292, 293
 strategic goals 188
 strategy after Second
  Manassas 106
 strategy at Chancellorsville 162
 strategy at Cheat Mountain 17
 strategy at Gettysburg 195
 strategy at Glendale 77
 strategy in central Virginia 104
 strategy in central Virginia
  (1862) 104

strategy, Seven Days battles
 76, 79
strategy to invade
 Pennsylvania 378
troop strength in western
 Virginia 11
troop strength, spring 1863 153
western Virginia 9, 14, 15, 24
Wilderness, battle of the 282,
 284, 286, 288, 289
Leesburg Pike, Leesburg,
 Virginia 364
Leesburg, Virginia 116, 121, 123,
 133, 465
Leitersburg, Maryland 204
Lester, Richard P. 21, 291, 295
Liberty Church, Caroline County,
 Virginia 186
Liberty County, Florida xiii, 260,
 261, 275
Library of Congress xv, xvi, 426
Lincoln, Abraham 7, 22, 107, 364
 1860 election xiv
 1864 election 347
 Presidential pass-in-review
  364, 404
 reason for Hall's enlistment
  1, 7, 36
 Revere court-martial 157
 status of POWs 306
 suspension of habeas corpus 308
 visits troops 474
 wartime commander-in-chief
  80, 104, 109, 205
Longbein, John 375, 389, 464
Longstreet, James 75, 153, 188,
 204, 228, 281
 comments on Hill at Gaines's
  Mill 76
 division review 184
 Frayser's Farm, battle of 77,
  367, 369
 Gettysburg, battle of 210
 Manassas, Second, battle of 371
 Seven Pines, battle of 52
 Wilderness, battle of the 282,
  286, 288, 289, 300
Longstreet's Division 85, 133
Loring, William W. 11, 13, 14, 15,
 17, 18, 19, 23, 24
Lost River Valley, Virginia
 (WV) 257
Louisiana units
 3rd Louisiana Infantry
  Battalion 69, 74, 77, 79

7th Louisiana Infantry
Regiment 411
Lovettsville, Virginia 467
Lovingston, Virginia 103, 125, 452
Lowe, Thaddeus S. C. 38, 411
Lowrance's Brigade 195, 198
Lunsford, James C. 27, 66, 97
Lynchburg, Virginia 6, 8, 11, 23, 25, 81, 115, 230

M

Macon, Georgia 225, 359
Mahone's Division 292
Maine units
   20th Maine Infantry
     Regiment 379
Malvern Hill, battle of xvi, 79, 80, 88, 370, 451, 462
Manassas, First, battle of 6, 8, 25, 28, 100, 105
Manassas Gap Railroad 25
Manassas Junction, Virginia 25, 29, 31, 105, 244, 365, 394, 461, 471
Manassas, Second, battle of xiii, 104, 105, 106, 131, 132, 133, 135, 199, 285, 286, 371, 375, 463
Manassas, Virginia 28, 40, 245, 371, 391, 394, 469
Manser, Adolph 463
Marlin's Bottom, Virginia (Marlinton, WV) 14, 20, 23, 24
Martinsburg, Virginia (WV) 107, 116, 120, 122, 123, 137, 138, 139, 205, 212, 220
Massachusetts units
   9th Massachusetts Infantry
     Regiment 367
   40th Massachusetts Infantry
     Regiment 466
Massey, Abel C. 66, 98
Massey, George W. 66, 97
Massey, Robert B. 66, 98, 159, 165, 316
Massey, Silas M. 66, 98
McCall, George A. 74, 363, 364, 365, 403, 460
   Presidential pass-in-review 404
   taken prisoner 79, 369, 370
   withdrawal to Gaines's Mill 366
McCall's Division 77, 364, 367, 369
McCalmont, John S. 364
McClellan, George B. 36, 38, 95, 104, 105, 135, 370, 392, 404, 405, 406, 407, 435, 443

1864 election 347
abandons potential siege of Richmond 74
construction of Fort Delaware 307
divides corps at Chickahominy River 51, 72
evacuation to Harrison's Landing 75, 76, 79, 80
failure of Peninsula Campaign 104, 134
march towards Richmond 407
movement to northern Virginia 104
movement to Virginia Peninsula 36, 37
movement towards Richmond 38, 39, 40, 50
orders Pennsylvania Reserves to Dranesville 364
Peninsula Campaign xi, 54, 72, 134, 327
Presidential pass-in-review 364
Rappahannock strategy 32
replaced by Burnside 109, 465
request for more troops 80
Second Manassas, battle of 116, 132
strategy for Peninsula Campaign 33
withdrawal from Peninsula 80
Yorktown 38
McCullohs, William 202
McDowell, Irvin 392, 405, 461
   Presidential pass-in-review 404
McElhannon, Richard 55, 58
McGowan's Brigade 246, 284, 287, 288
McGregor, Mary Ida Hall 414, 424
McGruder, John 38
McNair, John A. 260
McNair, John G. 260, 273
McRaney, Daniel J. 68, 98
McRaney, George W. 66, 81, 98, 110, 161
McRaney, John 98
McRaney, Manning 22
Meade, George 204, 206, 228, 230, 283, 294, 369, 378, 382, 468, 475
   Antietam, battle of 372, 375
   appointed commander, AOP 190
   assumes command of PA Reserve division 375

Bristoe Station 228
Bristoe Station Campaign 228, 229
commander of Pennsylvania Reserve Division 363
division casualties at Fredericksburg 377
Fredericksburg, battle of 375, 377
Gettysburg, battle of 203
Gettysburg, pursuit after 203
grand sword presentation 380
Lee's retreat from Gettysburg 205
losses at Gettysburg 223
Mine Run Campaign 298, 381
ordered PA Reserves to Little Round Top at Gettysburg 379
Overland Campaign 282
promotion to commander of AOP 363, 378
V Corps commander 378
Wilderness, battle of the 284
Meade's Brigade 369
Meadows, William T. 66, 98, 316
Mechanicsville, battle of xi, xiii, 72, 364, 365, 462
   casualties 74
Mechanicsville, Virginia 329, 462
Melrose, Florida 415, 417, 418, 424, 426
Mexican-American War 2, 13, 18, 71, 81, 223, 363
Michigan units
   6th Michigan Cavalry 205
Middleburg, Virginia 465
Middletown, Virginia 204, 262
Milford Station, Virginia 42, 450
Millboro, Virginia 9, 25, 28, 231
Milledgeville, Georgia 359
Millen, Georgia 276
Mine Run Campaign 223, 230, 250, 298, 381
Missionary Baptist 175, 176
Missionary Baptist Church 151, 173
Mississippi Rifles 22, 35
Mississippi units
   42nd Mississippi Infantry
     Regiment 236
Mobile, Alabama 281
Mobley, Robert S. 261, 273, 280, 293
Monocacy River 466
Monterey Pass, Pennsylvania 204

Monterey, Virginia 9, 14, 21, 24
Monticello, Florida 260, 272
Moore, Alexander W. 114, 176, 234, 240
Moorefield, West Virginia 225, 257, 258, 267, 268
Moore, Thomas C. xviii, 11, 23, 53, 105, 109, 159
Morgan, John Hunt 101
Mounger, John C. 159
Mounger, Terrell T. 3, 40, 96, 159, 164
    company commander 32
    death 159
    elected company commander 32
    elected to 1st Lieutenant 20
    profession before war 2
    relation to Robert Shine 32
    service prior to joining Company G 32
Mount Crawford, Virginia 253, 263, 264
Mount Elon Baptist Church, Sopchoppy, Florida 260, 273, 414, 418
Mount Jackson, Virginia 25, 254, 258, 263, 265, 268, 269
Mount Sidney, Virginia 253, 264

N

Newbury Court House, South Carolina 359
New Jersey units
    15th New Jersey Infantry Regiment 294
New Kent Church Road 38
New Kent Court House, Virginia 37, 39, 43, 45, 450
New Market, Virginia 231, 253, 254, 256, 258, 263, 265, 269
newspapers
    Christian Banner (Fredericksburg, Virginia) 408
    Frank Leslie Illustrated Newspaper 387
    misidentifies 14th Georgia 7
    report of 11th Georgia movement 6
    Richmond Dispatch 55
    Richmond newspapers 82, 432
New Verdiersville, Virginia 283
New York units
    11th New York Volunteer Infantry Regiment 393
    13th New York Infantry Regiment 400
    14th New York Infantry Regiment 403
    38th New York Infantry Regiment 396
    70th New York Infantry Regiment 403
    72nd New York Infantry Regiment 158
Nichols, George Washington 202, 358
Nichols, Madison C. 68, 98
Ninth (9th) Pennsylvania Reserve Regiment xi, xiv, 361, 363, 364, 365, 369, 370, 371, 372, 375, 377, 378, 380, 381, 383
    Antietam, battle of 372, 374, 375
    casualties 370
    composition 363
    executions 381
    expiration of obligated service 382
    Frayser's Farm, battle of 77, 369
    Fredericksburg, battle of 375, 465
    Gaines's Mill, battle of 366, 367
    Gettysburg, battle of 379
    Gettysburg casualties 380
    Mechanicsville, battle of xi, 74, 366
    movement over Chickahominy 367
    mustered into federal service 364
    mustered out 382, 479
    personnel 385, 389
    petition for discharge 478
    regimental officers 363, 371, 372
    South Mountain, battle of 372
    total casualties 382
    winter quarters 381
North Carolina units 233, 240
    16th North Carolina Infantry Regiment 17, 25, 35, 41, 54, 57
    20th North Carolina Infantry Regiment 232
    24th North Carolina Infantry Regiment 226
    33rd North Carolina Infantry Regiment 227
    37th North Carolina Infantry Regiment 226
    38th North Carolina Infantry Regiment 198
    desertion 226
Norwood, William xviii

O

Occoquan River 25, 29, 30, 32, 33, 40, 41
Ochlockonee River 275
Ohio units
    8th Ohio Infantry Regiment 189, 195, 196, 197, 198, 199, 200, 201, 203
O'Mooney, J.C. 67
Orange & Alexandria Railroad 25, 84, 115, 229, 245
Orange Court House 28, 103, 115, 161, 162, 230, 233, 250, 252, 258, 277
    campsite 234, 250
    departure for Shenandoah Valley 252
    encampment 282
    Hall rejoins regiment 261
    march towards Wilderness 298
    Perry's Brigade 278
    proximity to Cedar Mountain 104
    work detail 252
Orange Plank Road 284, 288, 297, 298, 299, 303
    Chancellorsville 153, 162
    Mine Run Campaign 230, 250
    overnight position at Wilderness 287
    overnight position at Wilderness, battle of the 286, 288
    Wilderness, battle of the 282, 283, 284, 285, 286
Orange Turnpike 153, 155, 156, 157, 282, 283
Ord, Edward 362, 364, 365, 390, 396, 399, 401, 402, 405, 461, 475
    Presidential pass-in-review 404
Orkney Springs, Virginia 257
Overland Campaign xiii, 295, 297, 326
    casualties 327, 329

P

Pastre, Phillip 403
Patterson, Josiah B. xvii, 21, 22, 23, 31, 32, 37, 75, 82
    conditions on the Peninsula 40
    death at Spotsylvania 297
    illness due to living conditions 82

on Arnoldus Brumby 21
on Felix Price 21, 31
Pea Patch Island, Delaware 305, 307, 308, 311, 333, 351
Pender's Division 188, 190, 204, 205
Pender, William Dorsey 158, 188, 190, 194, 195, 204, 205, 226
Peninsula Campaign xvii, 37, 82, 83
  casualties 37
  environmental factors 82, 83, 370
  McClellan's strategy 33
Pennsylvania Reserves Division 380
  Antietam 375
  command 372, 375
Pennsylvania Reserve Volunteer Corps 363
Pennsylvania units
  1st Pennsylvania Light Artillery 369, 398, 405
  1st Pennsylvania Reserve Regiment 369, 473
  2nd Pennsylvania Reserve Regiment 365, 408
  3rd Pennsylvania Reserve Regiment 461
  4th Pennsylvania Cavalry Regiment 407
  5th Pennsylvania Reserve Regiment 472, 474
  6th Pennsylvania Reserve Regiment 397, 398, 399, 402, 408, 470
  8th Pennsylvania Reserve Regiment 386, 398, 412
  10th Pennsylvania Reserve Regiment 380, 397, 398, 408, 411, 473
  11th Pennsylvania Infantry Regiment 379
  12th Pennsylvania Reserve Regiment 366, 389, 403, 408, 413, 462
  13th Pennsylvania Reserve Regiment 382, 395, 400, 471
  13th Pennsylvania Reserve Regiment 395
  62nd Pennsylvania Infantry Regiment 366, 410
  63rd Pennsylvania Infantry Regiment 413
  88th Pennsylvania Infantry Regiment 400

118th Pennsylvania Infantry Regiment 380, 468
139th Pennsylvania Infantry 389
190th Pennsylvania Volunteers 382
Peoples, Henry 405, 407
Perrin's Brigade 188, 194
Perry's Brigade 260, 261, 273, 278, 279, 280, 293
Petersburg, Virginia 260, 276, 289, 326
Petersburg, West Virginia 225, 257, 261, 266, 271
Pettigrew, James 195, 205
Pettigrew's Division 198
Philadelphia, Pennsylvania xiii, 321, 360
Pierce, John T. 96
Pilgrim's Progress 113, 147, 148, 316, 339
poems
  Dearest Spot of Earth to Me is Home 440
  Far Away in the Deep Blue Sea 434
  Flag of Virginia, The 436
  My Soldier 441
  Stars and Bars, The 438
  To One Brave Young Spirit 437
  When the War is Over 447
Point Lookout, Maryland 304, 316, 334
pontoons
  bridge at Falling Waters 204, 205, 212, 220
  bridge at Fredericksburg 109, 304, 318, 465
  bridge over Shenandoah River 222
Pope, John 104, 105, 106, 135, 370
  Second Manassas, battle of 116, 132, 371
Porter, Fitz John xi, 72, 73, 74, 75, 76, 107
Posey, James 68, 98
Posey, Littleton B. 68, 98, 110, 161
Posey, William W. 66, 98
Posey's Brigade 194
Potomac River 121, 203, 207, 364, 460, 464, 466, 467
  Belle Plain 304, 318
  Davis Ford 386
  Early's Moorefield expedition 267

end of Lee's Maryland Campaign 122, 137
Hall en route to Fort Delaware 319
joins Shenandoah River 121
Lee's Maryland Campaign 116, 117
Lee's Pennsylvania campaign 189, 207, 215, 216
Lee's retreat after Gettysburg 204, 205, 212, 219, 220, 380
Shepherdstown, Virginia 107, 117
transport to Alexandria 466
Potts, Valentine E. 68, 98
Price, Felix 6, 21, 31, 32, 35, 55, 105
  allegation of being drunk 31
  arrest 6, 21
  court-martial 6, 21
  elected to colonel 30, 31
  loss of respect 31
  not cited as regimental commander during Seven Days battles 72
  reprimanded in orders 21
  resigned from regiment 108
  Seven Pines, battle of 55
prisoners of war 339, 426
  comparison of treatment 314
  disposition 306, 307
  holding area at Punch Bowl 304
Punch Bowl, Belle Plain 304, 318
Putnam County, Florida 415
Pyatt, James B. 384, 389, 400

Q

Quiett, Henry C. 66, 98, 159, 165
Quincy, Florida 260, 261, 272, 275, 353, 359

R

railroads 103, 120, 353
  9th Pa Res troop movement 364, 382, 460, 463, 478, 479
  14th Georgia troop movements 5, 6, 28, 37
  bridge construction 403
  Contraband working party 405
  damage 472
  deaths 471
  destruction 116, 123, 229, 231, 245, 258, 395
  forms of utilization 8
  furloughs 472

guard duty 399, 471
Hall furlough to Florida
    (1864) 260
Hall return from Florida
    (1864) 261
Hall return from hospital
    (1863) 160
Hall return to Florida
    (1865) xiii
hay cargo fire 478
logistics 134, 381
riding in box cars 9
strategic importance 11, 50
tactical use 106, 206, 228, 289, 375
train stoppage 477
uses during war 8
railroad station
    Rappahannock Station, Virginia 470
    Three Mile Station (Casanova), Virginia 470
rail station
    Ashland, Virginia 37, 450
    Dixie, Georgia 260
    Fair Oaks, Virginia 52, 54
    Gordonsville, Virginia 84, 103
    Lovingston, Virginia 130
    Milford Station, Virginia 36, 37
    Millboro, Virginia 9, 12
    Rappahannock Station, Virginia 468
    Salem, Virginia 230
    Staunton, Virginia 9, 25, 110, 113, 151, 160, 167, 230, 231, 252, 253, 271
    Tunstall Station, Virginia 462
    Warrenton, Virginia 395
Ramsay, Whiteford 6, 21
Ramseur, Dodson 294
Ramseur's Brigade 199
Rapidan River 115, 136, 289, 470
    bridge burned 120
    Lee's Pennsylvania Campaign 207
    Union crossing at the Wilderness 282
Rappahannock County, Virginia 136
Rappahannock River 157
    Fredericksburg, Virginia 42, 465
    Hall's baptism 151, 174
    Johnston's movement to Fredericksburg 32
    Kelly's Ford 167
    route to Belle Plain 304, 318

Rawl, Fred 403
Read, Thomas 391
Rectortown, Virginia 467
Red Oak Baptist Church, Worth County, Georgia 414
Reinehr, Andrew 471, 474
religion
    baptism 188, 236, 239, 242
    Confederate day of fasting, humiliation, and prayer 224, 225, 236, 251, 278
    conversion in ANV 225
    conversions 112
    Hall preaching after war 415
    prayer meetings at Fort Delaware 316, 326
    prayer meetings in camp 152
    preaching 112, 232, 235, 264, 265, 280, 298
    preaching after war 415
    preaching at Fort Delaware 326
    revivals 224
    sermons 145, 152, 173, 223, 237, 239, 280, 402
    sermons after war 415
    sermons at local church 186
    sermons by brigade chaplains 168, 173, 175, 176, 177, 184, 187, 233, 247
religious books 113, 149
Revere, Joseph W. 157, 158
revivals 114, 224, 225, 236, 261, 326
    Rappahannock 114
Reynolds, John 363, 370, 372, 375, 378
Richmond and York River Railroad 39, 40
Richmond, Fredericksburg and Potomac Railroad 36, 109, 151, 160
Richmond, Virginia 39
    collapse of Peninsula Campaign 134
    Confederate defenses 36, 38, 39, 50, 69
    Elsesser's view of church towers 412
    food prices 90, 410
    Georgia Soldiers Wayside Home 277
    Grant's Overland Campaign strategy 281
    Hall tours city 100
    James River prisoner exchange 306

McClellan fails to capture 80
McClellan forgoes seige 74
prisoner exchange 352, 358
rail hub 260, 271, 358
strategic importance 11, 33, 39, 40
Union troops distance from city 88
wounded at Seven Pines 59
Ridley, W. Jonathan 68, 98
Riemenschneider, Conrad 470
Robinson River, Virginia 248
Rockbridge Alum Springs, Virginia 15
Rodes, Robert 194, 294, 372
Rodes's Division 293
Rodgers, Asa C. 66
Rodgers Martin J. 66
Rosser, Thomas L. 257, 258, 268
Ross, John L. 68, 98, 120
Rouse, John W. 66
Rust, Albert 17, 18, 19

S

Salem, Virginia 230, 231
Salisbury, North Carolina 358
Sandrock, Charles A. xv, 423
Savannah, Albany & Gulf Railroad 260, 271, 272, 275
Savannah, Georgia 10, 149, 260, 261, 271, 275
Scales's Brigade 188, 195, 228, 289, 292, 293, 294, 295
Schoal, Frederick 472, 475
Schoepf, Albin 309, 351
Schumacher, A. 464
Sedgwick, John 52, 282
Sende, Andrew V. 382, 397, 400, 402, 403, 404, 405, 406
Seven Days battles 69, 72, 79, 81, 82, 134, 365, 369
    casualties 72, 81
Seven Pines, battle of xii, 52, 451
    casualties 59
    Confederate errors 52
    Hall's narrative of battle 58
    Johnston's strategy 51
    marshy conditions 57
Seymour's Brigade 77, 369
Seymour, Truman 74, 77, 369, 402, 403, 406, 461
Sharpsburg, Maryland 107, 205
sharpshooters 39, 74, 75, 284, 380, 450
Sharp, William 318
shelter 40, 62, 247, 375, 405

housing for sick soldiers 11
no shelter in snow 42
no tents or shelter 48, 62, 254, 255, 258, 262, 270, 461
shanties for winter 229
Sibley tents 392
tents abandoned 35
tents blown away 389, 461
tents burned 27, 474
tents destroyed 41
tents obtained from enemy 59, 159, 166
tents rotting from rain 14
Shenandoah River 107, 121, 123, 136, 161, 205, 207, 221, 255, 262
Shenandoah Valley, Virginia xiii, 11, 25, 72, 230, 231, 255, 258, 268, 281, 343
Shepherdstown, Virginia (WV) 104, 107, 117, 122, 137, 215
Shield's Division 404
Shine, Robert F. 32, 40, 55, 56, 58, 64, 108
Shiver, Anthony 68, 98
Shiver, Green 66
Shiver, Henry 68, 98
Shiver, Jackson J. 55
Shiver, James 68, 98
Shiver, Jehue 98
Shiver, John J. 58, 66, 98
Shiver, Manning 98
Shiver, William J. 66
shoes 204, 211, 255, 265, 385, 393
    issued by Union 363, 398, 399, 400, 402, 404, 407
    issued to Company B, 9th Pa Res 397
    lack of 27, 108, 110, 139, 248
    lack of shoes after Gettysburg 205, 212
    Lee's correspondence 108, 265
    obtained from enemy xi
    price in Richmond 90
Sickles, Daniel E. 156
Simmons, Marion F. 67
Simpson, Alexander 67
Simpson, James 67
Simpson, Marion F. 98
Simpson, Morris F. 67
Smith, Alex. 385
Smith, Gustavus W. 36, 38, 50, 53
Smith, John C. 66, 98
Snodgrass, James McKinney 371, 396, 476
Soldiers Wayside Home, Savannah, Georgia 260, 271, 275

Solomon, Frederick 471, 474
Sommers, Richard J. 363
songs 445
    After Battle - A War Song 439
    Dixie 409, 432, 435
    Soldiers Farewell 448
    Soldiers Song (2) 442
    Soldiers Song, The 433
    Star-Spangled Banner 409
    Yankee Stampede 443
Sopchoppy, Florida 260, 414, 418
Sothen, Emil von 362, 363, 365, 366, 392, 393, 399, 400, 404, 462
South Carolina units 188
    5th South Carolina Infantry Regiment 60
    6th South Carolina Infantry Regiment 60
    Jenkins's Brigade 369
South Mountain 204, 371, 467
South Mountain, battle of 371, 463
    casualties 464
Sperryville, Virginia 107, 121, 136
Spotsylvania, battle of xii, xiii, xiv, xx, 174, 291, 297, 318, 326, 351, 382
    Mule Shoe fighting of May 12 293
Spotsylvania Court House, Virginia 291, 300, 301, 338
Spring, George W. 55, 58, 66, 98, 110, 161
Spring, Joseph L. 66, 98, 110, 161
SS Buena Vista 408
SS Columbia 408
SS Forrest City 462
SS Georgia 408, 409
SS Jno. Brooks 408
stagecoaches 260, 261, 272, 275, 359
Staunton-Parkersburg Turnpike 11, 13, 17, 18
    strategic value 11
Staunton, Virginia 9, 14, 21, 24, 28, 112, 123, 230, 231, 252, 256, 263, 269, 452
Stephens, Rienza 66
Steuart, George H. 293, 309
Stewart, Thomas H. 270, 278
Stone's Brigade 284
Strasburg, Virginia 25, 254, 255, 262, 343
Stuart, James E. B. 157, 167, 241, 364, 365
Sumner, Edwin V. 50, 52
Sumner, Joseph L. 67, 96, 110, 161

T

Tabor, Andrew J. 67, 98, 316
Tabor, Napoleon B. 68, 98, 110, 161
Taliaferro, Addison 120
Taliaferro's Brigade 105
Talladega County, Alabama xii
Tallahassee, Florida 260, 261, 272
Taylor, George B. 112, 113, 416
Taylor, James B. 113
Taylor Springs, Virginia 257, 258, 264
Tenleytown, Washington, D.C. 364, 460
Tennessee units 17
    9th Tennessee Cavalry Regiment 309
    16th Tennessee Infantry Regiment 17
    41st Tennessee Infantry Regiment 388
Texas units
    1st Texas Infantry Regiment 372, 374
Thayer, Clarence Putnam xv, 423, 424
Thayer manuscript xv, xvi, 68
    editing protocols xix
Thayer, Mary Leta McGregor xiii, xv, 424
    birth and childhood 424
    correspondence with Bell Wiley 426
    death 426
    requests for Elsesser's war records 425
The Saint's Everlasting Rest 113, 143
Thomas, Edward L. xvii, 71, 72, 74, 84, 195, 223
Thomas's Brigade 82, 151, 188, 229, 230, 231, 284, 285, 288, 297
    Chancellorsville, battle of 157, 158
    Chantilly, battle of 106
    desertions 227
    flank march at Chancellorsville 154, 155
    Fredericksburg, battle of 109
    Gettysburg, battle of 189, 190, 194, 195, 196
    Harper's Ferry, Virginia (WV), capture of 107, 116, 371
    history xviii
    Moorefield expedition 257
    movement to Spotsylvania 292
    Pennsylvania campaign 189
    poorly clad and ragged 230

prelude to Chancellorsville 153
pursuit of Averell 230, 231
retreat after Gettysburg 204
Second Manassas, battle of 106, 371
Shenandoah Valley 231, 255
Shepherdstown, battle of 107
Spotsylvania, battle of 292, 294
utilization in Pickett-Pettigrew-Trimble charge 199
Wilderness, battle of the 284, 286, 288, 289
Thompson, Calvin 68, 99
Thompson, Daniel 68, 99
Thompson, Elihu 68, 98
Tipton, Thomas 66, 67, 98
tobacco 389, 399, 407, 412, 473
Trimble, Isaac 195, 198, 200
Tygart Valley River 13

U

Ulrick, Charles 384
Uniontown, Virginia 465
University of Georgia xv, 426
Upton, Emory 292
Upton Hill, Virginia 466

V

Valley Mountain, Virginia (WV) 15, 17, 19, 20, 27
Valley Turnpike 121, 253, 269
Vermont units
   2nd Vermont Infantry 215
Vickery, Eli 67, 98, 110, 161
Vicksburg, battle of 99, 224, 388
   prisoner exchange 306
   prisoners 308
Vicksburg, Mississippi 149
Vienna, Virginia 466
Vincent's Brigade 380
Virginia and Tennessee Railroad 230
Virginia Central Railroad 84, 102, 115, 230, 252, 277
Virginia units
   21st Virginia Infantry Regiment 20
Von Schendel, Emil 384

W

Waddell, Joseph 110, 230
Wadsworth, James S. 285
Wakulla County, Florida 260, 261, 273, 275
Walbruch, Henry 385
Walker, William W. 67, 98
Ward, William W. 309
Warden, John 388
Warden, William 388
Warm Springs, Virginia 12, 15, 20, 22
Warren, Gouverneur K. 282, 379
Warren, Lewis W. 67, 98
Warrenton, Virginia 109, 228, 229, 244, 245, 395, 463, 465, 467, 469, 471, 478
war rumors 143, 146
   European intervention in war 141
Washington, D.C. 133, 135, 364, 460, 463
Washington, George
   Farewell Address 389
   route to Yorktown 37, 43
Washington, Georgia 359
Washington, Virginia 136
Waterford, Virginia 465
Waynesboro, Pennsylvania 204
Waynesboro, Virginia 204, 212, 216, 219, 252
weather
   impact on warfighting xx
Weber, John 471
Weed's Brigade 380
Weeks, Robert 4, 20, 22, 64, 67
Weeks, Romulus 55, 58, 81, 99
Welch, Glasgow 227, 228
Weldon, North Carolina 260, 271
Wells, Rev. 239, 240
Werner, George 471, 474
Western Virginia Campaign 13, 22
   command structure 14
   condition of Union troops 17
   CSA command structure 14
   deaths 4
   hospitals 15, 22
   illness 14, 17, 24, 26
   logistical issues 14
   medical care 11
   number of hospitalizations 15
   weather conditions 14, 17, 20, 27
Westfall, Thomas G. 55, 58, 64, 96
West Point (U.S. Military Academy) xii, 6, 39, 223, 363, 490
West Point, Virginia 409, 450
Wheelus, Thomas L. 55, 58, 67, 99, 120
White House Landing, Virginia 40, 50, 72, 365, 409, 462
Whiting, William H. 33, 36
Wilcox, Cadmus 239, 261, 282, 284, 286, 294
   appointed new division commander 223
   Frayser's Farm, battle of 369
   Gettysburg, battle of 202
   Spotsylvania, battle of 292, 293, 294, 296
   Wilderness, battle of the 285, 286, 287, 288
Wilcox's Brigade
   Frayser's Farm, battle of 369
Wilcox's Division 229, 261, 283, 286, 294
Wilderness, battle of the xiii, 120, 225, 282, 286, 289, 290, 297, 327, 382
   Folsom's death xviii
   casualties 290
   Chewning's Farm 289
   fighting on May 5 283
   fighting on May 6 286
Wilderness, Virginia 153, 230, 282
Wiley, Bell 1, 426
Wiley, Edward J. 67, 99, 159
Williams, Berrian A. 67, 99
Williamsburg, battle of 38, 44
Williamsburg, Virginia 38, 39, 44, 52, 91, 403, 450
Williamsport, Maryland 116, 203, 204, 212, 220, 467
Wilmington, North Carolina 260, 271, 307
Winans, Jacob S. 472
Winchester, Virginia 107, 108, 121, 122, 123, 136, 137, 139, 207, 220, 221, 253, 255, 257, 262, 264, 267, 269, 404, 405, 452
Wingate, Green B. 110, 161
Wise, Henry 13
Woodstock, Virginia 254, 263
Workman, John P. 407, 472
Worth County, Georgia xii, 1, 2, 5, 8, 24, 32, 131, 220, 249, 414
   contributions to Company G 23
   history 2
   recruiting 32, 64
   volunteers xii, 1, 2
Worth Guards 3
Wright's Brigade 236

Y

Yancey, William Lowndes 4
York River 47
Yorktown, Virginia 36, 37, 38, 39, 43, 44, 47, 399, 409, 411, 432, 450

www.ingramcontent.com/pod-product-compliance
Lightning Source LLC
Chambersburg PA
CBHW081426070526
44586CB00020B/2506